SERMONS BY WILLIAM GADSBY
1773–1844

with a short biography
by
B. A. Ramsbottom

Gospel Standard Trust Publications
7 Brackendale Grove
Harpenden, Herts AL5 3EL
England

Gospel Standard Trust Publications
7 Brackendale Grove
Harpenden
Herts AL5 3EL

This edition published 1991

ISBN 0 903556 91 X

Printed and bound in Great Britain by
Biddles Ltd, Guildford and King's Lynn

WILLIAM GADSBY
1773–1844

Apart from those who attend chapels where "Gadsby's Hymnbook" is used, the name of William Gadsby is comparatively little known. Yet in his day the popularity of William Gadsby as a preacher was immense. In fact, in the religious census of 1829, a number of Baptist congregations registered as "Gadsbyites" or "Gadsby Baptists" whilst we find a leading figure in the Baptist Union (Charles Williams), when giving an example of a strong Calvinist, as opposed to John Wesley as a strong Arminian, selecting the name of William Gadsby.

1. His Life

Born at Attleborough, near Nuneaton, on January 3rd, 1773 (or thereabouts—the exact date is uncertain), the ninth child of a poor roadman, William Gadsby spent his boyhood running almost wild about the village, barefoot and ragged. After receiving the bare essentials of education, at the age of thirteen he was apprenticed to a ribbon weaver, and ran to great lengths in sin. Already he was a leader among his friends, entertaining them for hours to their great amusement and delight.

But about the age of seventeen, the Lord began to work in his heart. He strikingly describes this:

"When the set time came, He arrested me, broke my heart, and brought me to stand before His throne as a guilty criminal, brought me to sign my own death warrant. I gave God leave to damn me if He would. I had nothing to offer, and I could do nothing to save myself."

He now began to attend the Independent chapel at nearby Bedworth, and almost wore out his only pair of shoes by his constant visits there!

After a few months of sore spiritual distress, the Lord greatly blessed his soul with gospel liberty. Speaking of this in later years, he said:

"I was then solemnly and blessedly led to believe in God's free mercy and pardon; and could look up and say, 'He loved *me*, and gave Himself, for *me*.' O what sweetness and solemnity and blessedness there was in my poor heart! I sang night and day the wonders of His love."

Before long, William Gadsby was brought into contact with the Baptists of Coventry, eight miles away, and began to walk over each Lord's day, never being late for the seven o'clock morning prayer meeting! On December 29th, 1793, shortly before his twenty-first birthday, he was baptized at the chapel in Cow Lane, the minister remarking (almost prophetically) on that occasion that he "could see something in the young man, although so illiterate and uncouth, that seemed blessedly to prove that he would sometime or other be made useful to God's dear family".

Circumstances necessitating his moving to Hinckley, about five miles from his home, he joined the Baptist church there, at that time meeting in a barn in Hogg Lane. He commenced stocking weaving and soon afterwards married. After a time, the solemn weight of the ministry was laid on him. But preach? Gadsby was determined he never would—till the Lord settled the matter by powerfully applying 1 Corinthians 1. 27-29 to his heart.

It was on Whit Sunday, 1798, at the age of twenty-five, that William Gadsby preached his first sermon in an upper room at Bedworth. Though many were astonished that such a rough-looking and clownish young man should attempt to preach, the more discerning marked the powerful effect of the Word, and also the exemplary life of the preacher.

The barn in Hogg Lane now became the scene of many of his labours. Years later he wrote of his Hinckley days:

"I preached to a number of poor people in an old barn and truly we had many precious visits from the Lord, which made the old barn a consecrated place to our souls, notwithstanding the thatch was off in so many places of the roof that we could see the sky through the numerous holes, so that when it rained the people had to remove from one part to another during preaching to prevent getting wet through; and what was worse, we were too poor to get it repaired."

Yet much blessing attended Gadsby's preaching so that eventually a chapel was built for him, and another at Desford, his practice being to preach at both chapels each Lord's day. But it was at Manchester that the greater part of his life was to be spent.

"There was as much prospect of the mountain of Gibraltar coming to Manchester as I!" exclaimed William Gadsby not long before his death. Yet how remarkable the unfoldings of providence in bringing him there! Really, he invited himself. Hearing that the people at Back Lane Chapel (as it was then known) were without a minister, and being anxious to raise funds for the building of the new chapel, he wrote saying that he had business in Manchester, and would willingly preach three or four Sabbaths. His business was to beg for money.

How much could be written concerning his first remarkable visit to Manchester! The people were divided between those who agreed with Andrew Fuller's duty-faith writings and those who opposed them. Gadsby made a great stir among the Fullerites, and the

longer he stayed, the more people came to hear him. The Word
entered many hearts. One godly member was so impressed by the
power attending Gadsby's announcing the opening hymn ("Awake,
my soul, in joyful lays") that he was persuaded this was to be their
pastor. At his first appearance many were astonished; he was at
that time very thin, and dressed in a coarse brown coat, drab
trousers, and wearing a coloured neckerchief—in fact, "Not a bit of
black except inside me," as he said. But the doctrines he preached
had a gracious effect, and the hearts of many of the people were
united to him. It was on this occasion that the well-known John
Warburton, then a poor weaver, came with his heart full of
prejudice but, feeling so blessed in his soul, went home with his
"very soul knit to him as closely as Jonathan's was to David." Soon
the good old veterans were saying, "This is the man for us; let us
arise and anoint him," and they began to cry mightily to God to
make a way.

It was during this first visit to Lancashire that one who heard
him, said: "Before he had spoken ten minutes, I saw more beauty
and glory in Christ than I had ever seen before. My cup of joy
overflowed. I saw that this glorious Christ and His finished
salvation were mine."

The outcome of all these events was that, after much opposition
had been overthrown, William Gadsby, at the age of thirty-two, left
Hinckley to become the pastor at Back Lane Chapel, Manchester
(now Rochdale Road). His farewell sermon was preached at Hinckley
on September 29th, 1805, from the text; "The grace of our Lord
Jesus Christ be with you all. Amen."

He remained as pastor at Manchester till his death over 38 years
later.

2. His Writings

During his early years at Manchester, the *Gospel Magazine* began
to review favourably Gadsby's first productions for the press, mainly
controversial works on the gospel (not the law) as the believer's rule
of conduct. William Gadsby has been much condemned on this
point, many failing to understand his position. Briefly, this was
that "the gospel contains the sum and substance of all the laws
which God ever promulgated," and so is *a much higher standard*,
the glory of the gospel excelling the glory of the law. He also wrote
against Arminianism and Sandemanianism, published some of his
sermons, and also a catechism.

In 1814 appeared his Selection of Hymns, designed as a
hymnbook "free from Arminianism and sound in the faith." No
doubt it is through his hymnbook that Gadsby has had the greatest
influence on succeeding generations. Many of the hymns he wrote

himself, some admittedly mediocre, but others of excellent quality. It seems sad that while modern evangelical hymnbooks contain hymns by Roman Catholics and Unitarians, few of William Gadsby's beautiful Christ-exalting hymns appear.

On the other hand, increasing numbers in the U.S.A. are showing interest in "Gadsby's Hymnbook".

Then in 1835, Gadsby and his energetic son, John, a Manchester printer, "launched into the wide ocean" the *Gospel Standard*, a monthly magazine seeking to "comfort, instruct, and edify the flock of Christ." (John Gadsby later wrote that this was at a time when "Dr. Owen's works were lying dormant; Bishop Hall's were known to few; and even Newton's seemed almost forgotten.") The *Gospel Standard* still continues on its original foundation.

3. His Public Work

In one aspect of his life, Gadsby differed from almost all other well-known ministers—the active part he took in public affairs. For this he has been severely criticised by some. But, right or wrong, it is certain he exerted a wonderful influence in the city of Manchester. His sympathy for all who were oppressed was so deep that many a good cause gained his interest and active support.

When a severe famine prevailed in Ireland (many having to live on sea weed), Gadsby advertised a special service at which £40 (a large sum in those days!) was collected. When he heard of a poor soldier unjustly sentenced to a severe flogging, he again had a collection, and bought the man off. Whilst in London he made what efforts he could to arouse sympathy for the Lancashire poor—the papers suggesting that other ministers should do likewise. When all denominations united in efforts to obtain a new cemetery in Manchester, William Gadsby took the lead.

Frequently he would appear on a public platform on such issues as the repeal of the cruel Corn Laws, which kept bread so dear; temperance (believing that strong drink had ruined thousands); the grievances of Dissenters; the distress of the handloom weavers; whilst his pointed criticism of the ill behaviour of King George IV toward Queen Caroline caused the Government to send the deputy constable of Manchester to hear him and observe his views. (What minister of truth would so arouse the Government's interest today?) Invariably when there was to be a collection for any good cause, Mr. Gadsby was appointed to make the appeal—his special ability in this direction causing people not only to put in all they had with them, but sometimes a note also, promising more! And be it remembered that there were sometimes as many as 8,000 to hear him at such public meetings.

4. His Character

But it was William Gadsby's *life* which especially made a deep impression on the general public. Stigmatized as an Antinomian (because of his belief that the law is not the believer's rule of conduct), despised, opposed, treated with contempt by Church and Dissenting ministers alike, he lived to see his enemies, in great measure, at peace with him. And the secret was the God-glorifying life he lived. He came to be respected and honoured as a man by those who hated the truths he preached.

After his death, in *A Tribute of High Esteem and Love*, J. C. Philpot (not given to flattery!) issued the challenge: "Who ever found a visible blemish in him?" In his funeral sermon, John Kershaw declared, "He was all practice himself; and a more practical Christian has rarely been known." (He also testified. "I never heard practical godliness so preached up by any man.") But it was a Wesleyan Methodist who bore perhaps the sweetest testimony to his character—and Gadsby severely denounced the Arminianism of the Wesleyans! While travelling by coach, happening to overhear two men speak against Gadsby, she ventured to interrupt, observing, "I lived near Mr. Gadsby for some time and *I believe him to be one of the holiest men in Manchester*," adding, "I am one of those whose sentiments he preaches against."

His tender spirit, his love for children, his kindness and humility were ever apparent. Especially was he renowned for his liberality to the poor—of whatever creed. It was a poor Irish woman who said, on hearing of his death, "He once kept me from starving when my own priest would not give me a farthing." It is estimated that towards half of his regular income he gave away.

When in his old age he broke his leg, the Manchester papers said, "Any cessation of the activity of such a man is a public calamity." Dr. Halley, Principal of New College, London, wrote of him: "No minister in Manchester lived a more moral life, or presented to his hearers a more beautiful example of Christian discipline and self-control." Dr. Robert Newton, at various times President of the Methodist Conference, said he was one of the Lord's "most useful and valuable ministering servants, and besought the Lord to raise up many more such men." And on the day of his funeral, thousands lined the streets of Manchester to show their respect.

But how different William Gadsby's own opinion of himself! "Less than nothing, and vanity!" he would often say. It is very typical of Gadsby's religion, and that of his friends, that when John Kershaw preached his funeral sermon before towards two thousand people, the text was: "Less than the least of all" (Ephesians 3.8)!

5. His Death

If William Gadsby honoured the Lord in his life, the Lord honoured him in his triumphant death. He was able to preach on his last Sabbath on earth, thus fulfilling a desire not to be laid aside for long. One present made a note in his Bible opposite the text (Isa. 43.2: "When thou passest through the waters, I will be with thee"): "Mr. Gadsby preached this sermon with very great fervour, but with very great difficulty of breathing, especially in the evening, when it took him four minutes to ascend the pulpit, having to stop upon every step. But the Lord was very gracious to him in supporting his mind, although suffering in body. He was got home with much difficulty." The trouble was inflammation of the lungs, and he died the following Saturday.

Just before the end, when it was felt his voice was gone, he most solemnly and affectionately prayed for the church and his family. Shortly afterwards he said, "There is nothing too hard for Christ; He is the mighty God—from everlasting to everlasting. He *was* precious: He *is* precious." Then raising his left hand, for his right was cold and motionless, he exclaimed, "Victory! victory! victory!" Then after a short sleep, he testified that he was on the Rock.

"Is He precious to you?" asked his friend and fellow-member, John Ashworth, who was constantly with him.

"Yes," he firmly replied. "King, Immanuel, Redeemer, all glorious!"

"You will soon have done here."

"I shall be with Him, shouting Victory! victory! victory!" raising his hand, "for ever."

Shortly afterwards he said, "Free grace! free grace! free grace!" and fell asleep in Jesus. It was Saturday, 27th January, 1844.

In his desk, when he died was found a slip of paper on which he had written his own epitaph. "Let this be put on my stone," it read. And surely nothing could be more fitting:

> "Here rests the body of a sinner base,
> Who had no hope but in electing grace;
> The love, blood, life, and righteousness of God
> Was his sweet theme, and this he spread abroad."

GADSBY THE PREACHER

It was as a *preacher* that William Gadsby made such a marked impression during his lifetime. Wherever he preached, there were crowded congregations, whether in his own chapel at Manchester, or during his annual visits to London—where sometimes as the people were coming out at the end of one service, they found others queueing to make sure of a place at the next. How difficult it is for us to gain any real impression of the atmosphere that must have prevailed among such crowded congregations in those days of spiritual prosperity! It would appear that at this time many Baptists were weakening in doctrine, whilst others, though doctrinally correct, had become exceedingly formal. Typical of the effect his preaching had on those who had been starved under such preaching is the following testimony of an aged saint: "I must say he is the best preacher I ever heard in my life. I was never so blessed in my soul under any minister before. He does not preach a new gospel; *it is the old gospel blessedly calculated to meet the cases of the Lord's tried family.*"

Dr. Halley wrote thus of Gadsby's preaching in *A History of Nonconformity in Lancashire*:

"A man of plain sense, he sought to be nothing more than a plain preacher of Christ's plain gospel. He had not a particle of affectation. He spoke thoroughly good English; perhaps more like the English of William Huntington (some say of William Cobbett), than of any other speaker of his time. Scripture he knew well, and quoted it with verbal accuracy and often with great effect . . . He had no learning, but he had no small share of mother wit and native humour. A little learning would probably have spoiled him. Illiterate as he was, he sometimes attracted men of culture and learning (I could mention remarkable instances), who heard him with great pleasure. His thoughts were natural, closely connected, logically arranged, and lucidly expressed. Quietly earnest, never impassioned, never vehement, but always arresting attention, he is said to have presented, in manner as well as in doctrine, a remarkable contrast to the popular Methodist preachers of his early days.

"His voice was wonderful, and he knew well how to manage it. I heard him once in the old Free Trade Hall of Manchester (holding 8,000 persons), that huge building, ill-constructed for public speaking. When other speakers had made strange efforts to be heard, sometimes in vain, he seemed to me, sitting near him, to be speaking in a pleasant, conversational tone; but the voice of the old man rolled like an equable wave of sound across the great hall and filled the ear of every auditor."

What was the general drift of William Gadsby's preaching? He would solemnly open up the depths of the fall and the aboundings of sin, often touching on things another dare not even mention. Often under the leading of the Holy Spirit his remarks were so pointed (one new hearer thought he must be a fortune-teller!) that they brought the hearer under deep conviction. On one occasion, hearing him speak of infidelity, two men who had just attended an atheistic meeting fainted away, and on more than one occasion, people who had acted dishonestly had to confess it when the service ended, and seek to put things right. (The little tract, "*Lord, help me,*" 50,000 of which were printed by the Book Mission in 1883, deals with one of these incidents.)

Then he would set forth what he delighted to call "the riches of matchless grace", dwelling on the glories of Christ, His fulness, His eternal union with His church, His finished work, His suitability in His offices, and often exclaiming, "Honours crown His head for ever!" The points commonly known as Calvinism he strongly insisted on, while solemnly warning his hearers, and sweetly emphasising the invitations of the gospel. It was said, "His heart went, as it were, direct into the hearts of the Lord's people."

There were, undoubtedly at times, coarse expressions and eccentricities—though many false reports were spread by his enemies—but the solemnity and weight with which he spoke, especially of the sufferings of Christ, soon outweighed this.

The outstanding feature of his preaching seems to have been the power with which the Holy Spirit attended it. Magazines of the last century abound with testimonies from those who heard Gadsby preach. One hearer said, "There was a power attended his ministry that I hardly ever felt under the ministry of any other man." Another stated that those who had never heard him could have "little idea of the living energy, life and power in the preacher." Another said, "I was only conscious of the dew, unction, and divine power that attended his words." And another. "The gracious words that fell from his lips were to me like ointment poured forth and more precious than fine gold." John Warburton the younger, minister at Southill, Beds., wrote:

> "I can almost fancy I see him in the pulpit, his face shining as the effect of the love of God, and in a powerful voice directing sin-burdened souls, ready to perish, to the God-Man, mighty to save. O! how grandly and profoundly would he explore that mine of glorious truth, bringing up from its depth golden wedge after golden wedge of doctrinal and experimental truth."

Indeed, one aged saint wrote:

> "Ah! if you had but heard that voice of his, rolling like peals of thunder, and seen those eyes of his, like balls of fire piercing

through the congregation, you would never have forgotten it while you lived."

This last was the testimony of one who, as a young man, went to mock, but was cut down in deep conviction as Mr. Gadsby solemnly announced his opening hymn, "Alas! and did my Saviour bleed?"

Perhaps the most striking outward instance of divine power attending his words was when he was baptizing in the open air at Little Harwood, near Blackburn, in November, 1819. A great crowd of several thousands had gathered to make a mockery of the service, and the scene was one of merriment and confusion. William Gadsby walked to a little eminence and "in a voice which thrilled through the vast concourse, said, 'In the name of the Lord God Almighty, I command silence.'" The effect was marvellous. Those present said his voice went like an electric shock through the whole multitude and all was quiet till the service was ended.

And there was a *lasting* effect of his preaching; it was not mere momentary impressions. During his early years at Manchester, there were constant additions to the church, each one having first had to give a satisfactory account of their conversion. John Warburton and John Kershaw were both blessed under Gadsby's preaching at this time, and baptized by him.

Because William Gadsby opposed the teachings of Andrew Fuller and insisted that *the gospel invitations are only to the poor, needy, hungry and thirsty,* he has been stigmatised as a "hyper-Calvinist," with dark suggestions that those who hold such views are unconcerned about the unconverted. Gadsby's own life adequately answers this criticism. In his labours he was untiring, preaching at home four times each week, and usually three times elsewhere, going many miles by foot, often over wild moors; and then besides his annual London visit, preaching in various parts of the country. J. H. Philpot writes in *The Seceders*: "His energy, his bodily vigour and his zeal in spreading the gospel seem almost super-human," whilst his preaching was blessed to the conversion of many, and indeed, to the commencement of forty new places of worship. Even Dr. Halley (no friend of Gadsby's beliefs) had to admit:

"In the manufacturing districts of Lancashire, Baptist ministers holding moderate views of the disputed articles, although they have been men of acknowledged ability and piety, have done little for the working classes, compared with their extreme Calvinistic brethren. . . . It may be said that more moderate and correct expounders of Christian truth would have done it (this work) better; to which I must add, provided they could have done it at all."

         *   *   *

In sending forth these sermons, we realise that they can only bear the same resemblance to the sermons originally preached that a skeleton does to a living body. However, we pray that the gracious, soul-establishing truths will be made a comfort and blessing to the Lord's people today. How this would have rejoiced William Gadsby's heart!

B. A. Ramsbottom
November 1991

PART OF THE ORIGINAL PREFACE

The apostle Paul was evidently not what the world would call an orator; for the people said his speech was contemptible; but O how weighty are his epistles! It was somewhat otherwise with my father. His preaching was more effective than his writings. "His voice," as Dr. Halley, the Principal of the Congregational College, London, said of him, "was wonderful." He heard him, on one occasion (about 8,000 persons being present), and he says, "The voice of the old man, though seeming to speak in a pleasant, conversational tone, rolled like an equable wave of sound, and filled every ear."

But it was not merely his voice. The sermons were from his heart, what he had himself tasted, handled and felt of the good word of life. In *reading* them, very little idea can be formed of the power attending the *preaching* of them. His heart went, as it were, direct into the hearts of the Lord's people. I now and then meet with some good old friends who testify to the truth of this, they having many times heard him.

As dear John Newton said of Whitefield, "Many may say the same things; but they cannot say them in the same way. If I were asked who is the second-best minister I ever heard, I could not say; but if I were asked who was the best, I should say Whitefield." And as another good man said: "Whatever these sermons were, some of those few spirits which you found in hearing will be missing in the reading of them. It is as easy to paint fire with the heat, as with pen and ink to commit that to paper which occurs in preaching."

His prayers, too, were singularly his own—from his very heart; unlike those of any other man I ever heard, and I have heard many. I must mention also, he never quoted verses of hymns in his prayers. Far be it from me to say it is wrong to do so, as some good men do. I merely state the fact.

Though dead, he yet speaketh; and may the Lord bless his printed speeches [sermons?] to the hearts of His people for generations to come.

John Gadsby
October 1884

Immortal honours rest on Jesus' head;
My God, my Portion, and my Living Bread;
In him I live, upon him cast my care;
He saves from death, destruction, and despair.

He is my Refuge in each deep distress;
The Lord my strength & glorious righteousness;
Through floods and flames he leads me safely on,
And daily makes his sovereign goodness known.

My every need he richly will supply;
Nor will his mercy ever let me die;
In him there dwells a treasure all divine,
And matchless grace has made that treasure mine.

O that my soul could love and praise him more,
His beauties trace, his majesty adore;
Live near his heart, upon his bosom lean;
Obey his voice, and all his will esteem.

William Gadsby

SERMONS

BY

MR. WILLIAM GADSBY,

OF MANCHESTER.

THE GREAT THINGS GOD HAS DONE FOR HIS PEOPLE.

Preached on Tuesday Evening, Sept. 13th, 1838, *in Jewry Street Chapel, London, on Behalf of the Aged Pilgrims' Friend Society.*

"The Lord hath done great things for us, whereof we are glad."
Ps cxxvi 3.

THERE are three things in the great mysteries of salvation that many professors of religion seem almost alarmed at. One is that God really saves sinners. If a minister of Jesus Christ is led to describe a sinner half as he really is, for to the bottom of him he never can, he shocks their delicate minds, and they are almost paralysed, and call it the high road of licentiousness to suppose that God saves such naughty sinners as those; whilst a poor soul under the quickening, enlightening, teaching energy of God the Spirit, fears that his case is desperate, and if God sends a minister of truth, who hits upon such a desperate case, and points it out as one that the Lord has in hand, the poor creature is astonished, and wonders where he has been; for he never heard that. Another branch of truth that men seem almost alarmed at, is the method that God takes in saving those sinners. If we come to trace salvation to its spring-head, God's electing love—"O! This is horrifying. We must not talk about election in these polite days. If we believe in it, we must put other words for it, and say, 'The Lord's people,' and 'The Lord's family,' and 'The pious;' but never talk about 'election;'" and thus the doctrine of God's discriminating, electing love is discarded. And then another branch of divine truth, that men seem alarmed at, is the power of God the Spirit in making this salvation known to the conscience, and bringing it with divine power and majesty to the heart and maintaining it there as the poor sinner sojourns in this wilderness. Some people are alarmed at all the

three, and some only at the last; some of them will chatter about
election till their tongues almost cleave to the roof of their mouth;
but if you insist upon vital godliness, the power of God the Holy
Ghost in the conscience producing a corresponding conduct, they
will call you an enthusiastic legalist. And thus divine things are
set at nought on one hand or the other. But God will vindicate
his own honour, and "make bare his arm," and bring his loved ones
at some period or other to adopt the language of our text: "The
Lord hath done great things for us, whereof we are glad."

No doubt the psalmist had in view, in the first instance, God
delivering Israel out of a dreadful national captivity; and here we
are told of them that they were "like them that dreamed," and they
began in wonder to "laugh" in the sweet enjoyment of God's dealings with them. But Israel of old being a typical nation and God's
spiritual family being amongst that nation, the Lord has something
more in view than this; he has in view a spiritual captivity, that
his people are delivered from; and when delivered from it, and
brought feelingly and experimentally to know it, then they sing,
"The Lord hath done great things for us, whereof we are glad."

Now from this passage, as far as God shall assist me, I shall consider,

I. Who the *us* are, who have any right to adopt the language
of our text, and say, "The Lord hath done great things for *us*."

II. Point out some few of the *great things* that God has done for
them.

III. Endeavour to notice that whenever God makes manifest
these "great things," or a measure of them, in their hearts, it is sure
to make them *glad*. "The Lord hath done great things for us, whereof we are glad."

I. Now what persons are these? Who are the *us?* They are
God's spiritual Zion—that family he has predestinated to eternal
life, "predestinated to the adoption of children," "predestinated to
be conformed to the image of his Son," and brought, by his spiritual
power and grace, to know their own ruined condition and the mercy
of God in Christ Jesus towards them—who have felt themselves in
captivity and felt themselves brought out of it. Some people tell
us that there is no cause now-a-days for a sinner to have "the
letter" brought into the conscience, no cause for a law-work, and
that many go to heaven who never had a law-work in their hearts.
But that is a heaven that was invented in Italy; it is not God's
heaven, it is a kind of purgatorial heaven. For God has solemnly
declared that "the law was given that every mouth might be stopped
and all the world become guilty before God." And if God's law
does not stop *your* mouth, is not brought to your conscience, does
not destroy all your false projects, and bring you in guilty and condemned at the feet of the Lord—if you never feel that, I believe you

will be damned, as sure as God is in heaven. Let your profession be what it may, let you be as tall as you may in a profession of religion, you will never enter into God's blessed place above, if you have never been brought to know your ruined condition below. Why, you might as well talk about a man praising a physician, as one who had cured him of a disease, when he never had an illness in his life; you might as well talk about a man speaking of a skilful surgeon, who had set his bones, when he never had a broken bone since he drew breath. "The whole need not a physician, but they that are sick." I do not mean that all God's people are led into the same depth in this. Here the Lord works as a sovereign; but the law *must* stop their mouths, the law must bring them in guilty, the law must make them feel that they are in bondage, that they are "under tutors and governors," and under such tuition that they are bound by the ties of the law either to fulfil it or be damned by it, and that they cannot fulfil it, and that therefore they can feel no ground of hope upon law principles.

Now when the Lord the Spirit brings a poor soul to this, he finds himself in dreadful captivity. I cannot exactly say how it is in London; but I know in our way we have a great many who begin in election, and go on with election, and never get one step either below or above high-seasoned election; and if you ask them what they know about "the plague of their own hearts," or what they know about "the sentence of death," "O! They do not meddle with such low things as that; they live upon high ground." Ah! And the devil will never disturb you there. If God does not, you will find that such an arrogant presumptuous profession is nothing more nor less than the devil's chariot to carry men to hell in delusion; and, if God does not upset them and bring them to know their ruined condition, they will never enter into the mysteries of God's blessed kingdom, that kingdom that stands in God's own power. But now, when a poor sinner feels the bondage of the law and feels "the sentence of death," he finds himself in a captivity, from which he cannot deliver his own soul. He feels himself without might and without power, and feels the truth of what God says, that he is "not sufficient of himself" so much as "to think" a good thought, or to pray; as says the apostle, "We know not what to pray for as we ought." I often think, why what fools the disciples and apostles were to the great men of our time; for they have found out how to pray for themselves and to make prayers for other folks for a thousand years to come; but the disciples asked the Lord to teach them how to pray, and the apostle was brought to confess that he was "not sufficient of himself" and did not know even how to pray "as he ought." And so God's people will be brought to this, when the Lord brings them to know their spiritual bondage and captivity. And then, when he brings peace to the conscience and pardon to the eart, and sets the soul at liberty, then they are the people that can say, "The Lord hath done great things for us, whereof we are glad."

II. But having thus gone over this description, let us look now at some of the *great things* that God has done for us.

And we must take into the account each glorious Person in the one undivided Jehovah,—God the Father, God the Son, and God the Holy Ghost. For in the "great things," that the eternal Trinity has done for the church of God, each distinct Person has a solemn part, a part that redounds to the glory of all and the blessedness of them that are brought to trust in God. God the Father, God the Son, and God the Holy Ghost, as one blessed Triune Jehovah, hath entered into a solemn covenant before all worlds to bring an infinite number of mortals to immortal glory. In this solemn contract, this covenant of grace, the eternal Trinity took a survey of all their sins, and all their weaknesses, and all their misgivings, and all their backslidings, and all their temptations, and all their besetments, and all their slips, and all their falls, and all their tumblings, that this body would have from the beginning to the end of time; and in this immortal covenant God made provision to meet it all, and so to meet it as to be glorified in saving them all from all the horrors and consequences of sin. Now is that not a "great thing?" Why, if we make a provision, as we think, for our children, and make it over to them, one gets proud and profligate, sets up to be a gentleman, and soon destroys the provision; and the others do the same thing in some other way; so that by and by the mistaken provision we made for them has been a kind of means of leading them into deeper ruin than they would have been in if they had been obliged to work for every penny they have. But our God made no mistake of that nature. One "great thing" he did in his council and covenant was to make the provision sure—"the sure mercies of David;" certain mercies, "ordered in all things." Why, he saw all thy temptations, before ever thou didst. When he gave thee to Christ, he saw all thy besetments, all thy bewilderments, all thy hard-heartedness, all thy darkness, all thy coldness, all thy barrenness; and in the eternal purpose of his grace, he made such a provision for thee that it is not possible for Satan himself to drive thy poor bewildered soul into any place where God's provision will not reach thee and be sufficiently powerful to bring thee out. Is not this a "great thing," a matchless thing? It was this that made David so sweetly and solemnly sing, "Although my house be not so with God, yet he hath made with me an everlasting covenant, ordered in all things and sure." David's house "not so with God!" Not *how?* Why, if you read the context, he is speaking about a "morning without clouds," without anything that seems gloomy, when the sun arises upon it, and about the "tender grass springing out of the earth by clear shining after the rain;" and he says, "My house is not so." Poor creature! He felt clouds and darkness, and often sharp biting frosts that seemed to nip the tender herb. There seemed no sweet going forth of faith, of love, of prayer, of thanksgiving; there seemed a bewilderment in the conscience. But, says he, this is my salvation and all my desire—new covenant blessings stand sure, "ordered in *all things* (not in one thing only) and sure." This is the strength of divine grace, when God is pleased to give it to a poor sinner to realize such immortal blessings; and this is one of the "great things" that God the Eternal Trinity in Unity has done for his people.

But we must come to retail it out a little. I am a kind of retail preacher; as a friend of ours, who lived in a country place, used to say, " I like to hear our friend, when he retails it out. Sometimes our parson wholesales it, and we poor folks cannot go to a wholesale shop; it suits me to have it retailed out, for those are the shops we poor folks can go to." And so the people of God are continually brought into such a state that they want to have it retailed out in little parcels, as we may say, that God may be glorified and themselves made glad through his grace.

1. Then if we endeavour to look a little at this blessed covenant, we first of all notice that "herein is love; not that we loved God, but that he loved us, and gave his Son, and chose us in his Son;" so that in the purpose and councils of God, God fixed Christ and the church in his eternal heart together, the church in Christ and Christ in the church, and God in Christ and Christ in God. And thus the church was made the special charge and care of God the Son before the world was; and, I speak with reverence, God the Father looked to Christ to bring them all to heaven. "Thine they were and thou gavest them me." And "all that the Father giveth me shall"—shall what? Have a chance of coming? No, not so. Have an offer of mercy? No, not so. Have conditions proposed to them—easy terms? No, nor so either. Well, then, how is it? " All that the Father giveth me *shall come* to me." Unbelief says they shall not, and pride says they shall not, and the devil says they shall not, and their hearts say they will not, for they love sin, and after it they will go; but God has taken his stand and Christ has taken his stand upon eternal fixtures, and God and Christ have said, " They *shall* come." Yes, poor souls! And when he comes with invincible power to the heart, he will make them glad to come as poverty-stricken sinners, and be glad to be made partakers of the riches of his Son; and "him that cometh," says Christ, " I will in no wise cast out." This is the reason why the apostle so sweetly sums up: " Blessed be the God and Father of our Lord Jesus Christ, who hath blessed us with all spiritual blessings in heavenly places,"—where? " In Christ." When God created man, he created him holy, in his own image; and it appears he put

man in the care of this holiness and this image; he gave the key into his own hands, and man unlocked the door of his heart and let the devil in and all that was holy out, and God will never trust to man again while the world stands. No; he has secured all spiritual blessings "in Christ," and given him the key of the house; and he opens and no man shuts, and shuts and no man opens. "It pleases the Father that ALL fulness " should be there; and therefore there is nothing but emptiness anywhere else. And he is said to be "full of grace and truth;" and "of his fulness we receive, and grace for grace." So then the Father, in his great part in this solemn economy of salvation, gave his Son to be the Head and Representative of the church, the grand repository of heaven; and God locked up his honour, his truth, his grace, and "all spiritual blessings" in the heart of Christ, and Christ pledged his honour to save all securely, and to magnify all the honours of God in making this mystery known by the power of his Spirit to the hearts and consciences of his people. And this is a "great thing," that God has done for them.

2. But it will not do to enlarge, and therefore we will proceed to notice what Christ has done for them. There is a great deal said about Jesus Christ in our day. "What a merciful Christ he was," they say, "to come and die for sinners!" But some people tell us that such is the nature of his death, that after all it may be the means of damning us deeper than we should have been damned if he never had died. Why, what an awful thing that is to say! I recollect a minister saying to me some years ago, "You do not love sinners as you ought to do, or else you would preach to them universal offers and universal proffers." "Indeed," said I. "Let me ask you one thing. Will any sinner that ever gets to heaven be saved by your universal offers and universal proffers?" "No," he said, for he was a sort of a Calvinist, "they will not." "Well, what will become of the rest?" "Ah!" said he; "they will have a deeper damnation, because they rejected the offers of mercy." "So that is the method you take," said I, "to show you love sinners; as if they could not be damned deep enough, but you will damn them the deeper by your universal offers, when you admit that they cannot be saved the more for your preaching to them? What an awful way that is! It is not according to the riches of God's grace that he has ordained in the salvation of the church."

Now the Lord Jesus Christ, in his rich mercy, undertook to stand accountable and responsible, as the Surety of the family of God, and to have all laid upon him that was chargeable to them ; and he bore it, and will communicate to them all that can flow from his blood and love, that can crown God's brow and honour his name; and thus he stood the glorious Head and Representative of the church of the Most High, to the honour of God and the blessedness of all them that are brought by rich grace to believe. But he must be something in his own person beside essential Godhead; for essential Godhead could not accomplish this. The law demanded blood for blood; essential Godhead could not bleed. "Eye for eye, and tooth for tooth;" essential Godhead could not do that. Essential Godhead could not shed blood, could not die; yet "without shedding of blood there is no remission of sin." And yet such is the measure of the "great things," that the Lord Jesus Christ has done for his people, that it is emphatically called "his dying," and his blood the blood of God. "Yes," say you, "but I do not believe it was the blood of God." Well I *do* in my very soul believe it; not that Godhead could bleed, but that the Person who did bleed was God and man, and therefore the Godhead in union with the manhood made the one Person Immanuel, and it was his blood. If you want a simple argument upon the subject, suppose, when I go home to night, some person was to stab me, and I was to be bleeding in the street, you would say, "Why, yonder lies Gadsby bleeding." Now my *soul* could not bleed, you know, and that is what makes the person, is it not? But then you take me as a man, and cry, "He is bleeding;" all that can suffer and bleed is suffering and bleeding. And as it respects Immanuel, the God-man Mediator, all that could suffer and bleed and agonize and die in him did suffer, bleed, agonize, and die; and the Godhead gave immortal validity to the atonement, so that it is emphatically called the blood of God: "God purchased the church with *his own blood*."

The Lord Jesus Christ, then, the Second Person in the glorious Trinity, in order to accomplish this "great thing" that he was going to do, took up a life to be able to die, took our nature into union with his personal Godhead, and became really man, truly and verily man as well as truly and verily God, that he might be able to wade through all the miseries that sin and the devil had heaped round his elect, and to go after them, and bear their sins in his own body and soul on the tree, that they might be set for ever free. And thus his sacred Majesty stooped to bear their weakness and infirmities, and to take their sins upon him. Hence it is said he was "made sin for us." Why, that is a strange saying, for he was "holy, harmless, undefiled, and separate from sinners," and "guile was not found in his mouth." "Made sin?" Aye, he was made murder, and made adultery, and made fornication, and made theft, and made treason. "Shocking!" say you. "How can that be, if he was holy, harmless, undefiled, and separate from sinners?" Because he was made so by solemn contract and solemn transfer. The murder, the adultery, the fornication, and the abominations of David, and Solomon, and Peter, and all God's elect were transferred and placed to his account, and he

acknowledged the debt.   " Sacrifice and offering thou wouldst not,"
said he; these things would not do,—were not sufficient.   "Then
said I, Lo I come to do "—what sacrifices could not do—" to do thy
will, O God."   And Paul tells us roundly that " we are sanctified
through the offering of the body of Jesus Christ, once for all."   And
this was a " great thing " that Jesus Christ came to die.   Look at
him as the Babe of Bethlehem; look at him as a traveller without
house or home; look at him hunted by Satan forty days and forty
nights in the wilderness under all the iron tyranny that devils could
inflict upon him, when he had too much work to do, too much solemn
engagement with all the powers of hell to have a moment's time
either to eat, drink, or sleep for those forty days and forty nights;
and this was all in espousing the cause of the church, in doing a
great work for his people.   He fought their battle manfully, he vanquished all their foes; but at length his blessed Majesty was brought
to be in a solemn agony, and he said, " My soul is exceeding sorrowful, even unto death."   Good John Berridge has a solemn view
upon this subject:

> " How his eyes astonished are !
> Sure they witness huge despair !
> On his face what sadness dwells !
> Sure he feels a thousand hells ! "

Aye he did—a million hells.   Poor child of God !   All the hell thy
sins have merited was poured into his soul, and all the hell that all
the millions of the elect of God ever merited was poured into his
holy soul.   And had he not been God as well as man, humanity
could not have sustained the load and rolled it over.   But immortal
Godhead supported humanity under the weight of wrath; his holy
soul endured it, and he died "the Just for the unjust to bring us to
God," and so to accomplish a salvation, rich and free, as extensive
as the necessities of his people, as deep as their miseries can possibly be.   Has he not done "great things" for us?

And all to give them *a chance* of being saved,—according to
some people.   I do not know that I hate any thing more in my soul
than to hear that.   It makes Jesus Christ so little, that he should
do so much, and after all only get us a *chance* of being saved.
Why, if a man is set up in business, you see how often it happens
that he fails in it; and if man cannot manage the paltry things of
time and sense without being insolvent, what will he do with eternal
realities?   And if you come a little closer, when God "made man
upright" and he had no sinful nature, what did he do with his
innocency?   Why, he lost it all.   And yet poor presumptuous man
has the vanity to think you and I could manage the chance of being
saved.   What an insult it is to the Lord Jesus Christ, to fix the
eternal honour of God upon chance, and *that* chance to be managed by a poor sinful creature who is tumbling into half a dozen

holes every hour of his life. No, no. Thanks be to God for immortal *realities* and *certainties*. What is said concerning what Christ has done? He has "put away sin by the sacrifice of himself;" he has "finished transgression and made an end of sin;" he has "redeemed us from all iniquity;" he has "redeemed us from the curse of the law,"—from destruction and from the power of the devil; he has "obtained eternal redemption for us;" he has "redeemed us to God." To the honour of the Eternal Trinity, it is said, not that the redeemed shall have a chance, but that the redeemed *shall* "come to Zion with songs, and everlasting joy *shall* be upon their heads, and sorrow and sighing *shall* flee away." The Lord Jesus Christ has done this "great" work, and he is gone to heaven, shouting "Victory;" for "God is gone up with a shout; the Lord with the sound of a trumpet." He rose from the grave as a demonstrative proof that sin was destroyed, law satisfied, God honoured, his people eternally and everlastingly saved. And the immortal honours of God unite in their salvation; and therefore he ever lives at the right hand of the Father to make intercession.

And in order that there might be this great work and this great wonder carried on manifestively, Christ is manifested as the Shepherd to gather his sheep in and to feed them when they are in; as the Captain, to fight their battles for them; and as the High Priest to plead their cause, bear them upon his shoulders and present them before God with the plate of "Holiness to the Lord" as they stand complete in him and he is their Surety ever to represent them before God; as it is said, "He is entered into heaven now to appear in the presence of God for us" in his Surety capacity. He is a Prophet, to teach and instruct us, as well as our Priest, to atone for and to bless us; and he is a Husband, to sympathise with us, and (as it is written so it stands firm) as a Husband he "gave himself" for his wife, "that he might sanctify and cleanse her with the washing of water by the word, and that he might present her to himself a glorious church, not having spot, or wrinkle, or any such thing;" and he is the Rearward, to bring up the rear. I have often thought good John Bunyan made a little mistake when he said there was no armour for the back, because then the enemy would soon get behind and shoot between our shoulders; but, while our Jesus has provided weapons for us to meet the enemy with, he is the Rearward to look after the scouting foe; and he watches over the church night and day, and waters her every moment; and he solemnly declares that he will be "her God and her guide even unto death." What "great things" these are!

3. But God the Holy Ghost is also engaged in this solemn work of doing "great things." There are two things that God the Spirit keeps his eye upon—the enrolment of God, and the sinner enrolled there. And at the time specified in God's enrol-

ment, when that sinner shall be taken and made willing, the Spirit comes with his power and does it. If it is a Zaccheus in the tree, he must come down. If it is a Peter, busy among his nets and his fish, he must come. If it is a Philippian gaoler, lulling his conscience to sleep because he has been giving the apostles a good hearty drubbing, for he thought he had plague enough without being plagued with such fanatics, and he would make them remember coming there, and so he "made their feet fast in the stocks,"—but at midnight the time is come, God puts the cry into his heart, the Holy Ghost makes no mistake, he must cry, "What must I do to be saved?" If it is a Magdalene, who has been a kind of devil's showbox carrying through the streets to delude you, she must come. O! Blessed be God. The Spirit of God laid hold of her heart, and brought her to weep at the feet of Jesus and cry for mercy. And so if it is the dying thief and he is upon the cross, he must come.

And now let us come a little nearer; where were you, and where was I, and what were we doing? Perhaps there is some poor sinner in this assembly to-night who has come here on purpose to have some little ridicule when he gets away, and is pleasing himself with the idea of having a little fun with some of his wicked companions. O! If this is the day of God's power, may the Holy Ghost send an almighty message to your presumptuous heart! Where are you? WHERE ARE YOU?* May God the Spirit pursue you, and bring you to know your ruined condition and perishing state before a heart-searching God! If it is the Lord's time, he will; for the hour cometh and now is, when the dead shall hear the voice of the Son of God, and they that hear shall live." The Holy Spirit keeps his eye both upon God's secret enrolment and the sinner enrolled there, and he never loses sight of him; no, not even if he is going to Damascus with letters to persecute the church. When the set time is come, down he must fall. O that the Lord would quicken some of your dead souls, bring you this night to feel what cursed wretches you are in the sight of God, and make you cry to him as perishing sinners; and then eventually you will know some of the "great things" that God has done for you.

Well, when the Holy Ghost has quickened the dead soul to feel, and enlightened the dark soul to see, then the poor creature sets about amendments. He finds, in some measure, that he is in an awful state, and he begins to try to amend it. He shakes off perhaps his companions in drink, he will begin to be dutiful to his master, and he will set about pleasing God and doing something to

---

* We have heard the dear man thus exclaim, with a voice so powerful and rolling it has run through our very bones and made the walls of the chapel to ring again.

make amends for the bad things he has done before. But, strange to tell! Everything that he does God the Spirit discovers to be empty, and vain, and wretched; discovers it to be evil, discovers it to be sin; and all the man's doings, and all his sayings, and all his attempts to help his own soul only make him so much the worse in his state and in his own feelings before a heart-searching God. And then the poor creature thinks he has missed it here and he has missed it there; he will try again, and may do better the next time; but he misses it again. "Well," says some poor soul, "that is the way I have been going on from month to month, and I have always missed it yet, but I hope to manage better soon." I tell you, you will never be right till you have lost that hope. "Lost that hope! What! Must I lose that hope? Why, man, you will drive one mad! What! Must that go—that hope of being able to manage it better?" Yes, that it must. That must go, and you must sink with it; and when that is gone—when all hope is gone, not only that you have not saved yourself, but that you never can, then Christ is preached by the Holy Spirit in the conscience, and the soul is brought to know something of "the hope of Israel," instead of the hope of flesh and blood. And this is a "great thing" that the Lord does for the poor sinner, to strip him of false hope and false confidence and all that would lead him astray, that he may lead him, as a perishing sinner, to the Lord Jesus Christ and magnify the riches of God's grace in his soul.

"Well," says some poor creature, "I think I have been a lost helpless thing in my own feelings for many a month, and yet I do not enjoy God's salvation." I should question whether you are brought to this. Now is there not a little bit of something, a little secret lurking something at the bottom, that still gives you some hope that a favourable moment will come when you shall manage it a little better? Now just ask your conscience, whether it is not so. ("Yes," say you, "it is.") That must go. I know you will cling to it as long as ever you can. I know you will. It is like a man giving up his life, it is like a man giving up every thing, to give up this; but the Holy Ghost will make you give it up at last, or else you are none of his.

And when he has done this, will he leave you to destruction? "Why," say you, "really I am afraid he will; for I have been tempted many times to put an end to my existence. Once, the Lord knows, I had the instrument in my hand, and I think if he had not taken care of me, I should have done it." Well, he *will* take care of you; though he his hunting you out of all props, and all self, and all false comfort, he will administer true comfort. I have often thought of one occurrence that took place, connected with my own ministry, some years ago. A poor woman in very great distress thought she could go on no longer, and she would know the worst of it; and so she appointed a time in her own mind when she would drown herself; and when the time came she went to the river; but just as she was going to plunge in, it occurred to her, "Why, if I drown myself now, the folks at home will not know where I am, and they will hunt everywhere to find me, and they will waste so much time in looking after me that I shall add to my other sins that of bringing my family to poverty. I will go back and bring my little girl with me another day, and then she can tell them where I am." And so the Lord overruled it for that time. Well, she went again accordingly, and took the child with her, and was just going to plunge in, when she thought, "Why my poor little girl will be so frightened that she will jump in, and I shall drown her too. I will go back, and take some other method of doing it." Well, after this she came to the place where I preached, and God set her soul at liberty, and she was brought to know the blessings of salvation. O! How carefully the Holy Spirit looks after the flock of the Lord! How carefully he guards them, when they have neither power nor intention to guard themselves! So great is his love, so great his compassion, so great his care, that he does these "great things" for them, and eventually they "are glad."

Well, then, this is one of the "great things" he does in the end—he reveals pardon; but it is one thing for people to talk about believing in Christ and having pardon, and it is another thing for them to believe and for them really to have pardon. The Holy Ghost comes and brings into the soul the pardoning love of Christ, removes bondage, gives a sweet quiet in the conscience, and gives the happy song, "In the Lord have I righteousness and strength;" "In the Lord have I mercy; in the Lord I am free." Well, by-and-by the poor creature is brought to think, "Now it will be comfortable all the days of my life." But I tell you, if you live long, the Lord will teach you more of Christ. If any one was to ask you what is intended by Christ in all his offices, in all his relations, in his oath and promises, in all his fulness, you would be ready to say, "O! I do not understand all those divisions and subdivisions. I believe he has pardoned my soul, I believe he has loved me, I feel that I love him, and that is enough for me." O no. You must know more than that; and therefore you shall be brought into straits and difficulties which shall make the offices and relations, the oath and promise and fulness, of Jesus Christ, just suited to your condition. You shall see that what is said about Christ is not like titles of honour given to our noblemen—mere puffs of empty air—but that every thing which is said about Christ is essential, real, suited to the honour of God. God will bring his people more or less, to the solemn feeling of necessity—of knowing that they need such a Christ; and then the blessed Spirit makes him manifest to the conscience as "a very present help in time of need." He reveals Christ in the conscience, and goes on from the first moment of his quickening energy, and carries us through this vale of tears, and lands us in ineffable bliss, redeemed through the Lord Jesus Christ, decorated in his righteousness, robed with his salvation, dignified with his honour, and having the dignity of God's glory stamped upon our character, in which we shall shine for ever and ever, to the praise and glory of God's grace. The Lord does these "great things" for sinners—poor, ruined, helpless sinners. "The Lord has done great things for us, whereof we are glad."

And now let me ask you, Do you know anything of this yourself? I will tell you one "great thing" that the Spirit of the Lord will do for a poor sinner who knows anything of these things in reality. There will be times and seasons when you really cannot pray. I do not mean when you cannot say your prayers. God the Spirit will bring you to know that saying prayers and praying are very different things. Your mouth will be so completely stopped sometimes, that, when you are praying, conscience, enlightened and quickened by the Holy Ghost, will say, "You do not feel *that*," and, "You do not feel *that*. What a hypocrite you are! You are speaking things to God, and you do not feel them." So that you are completely shut up and confounded, and feel as if you could say nothing but this sentence, "Lord, I am vile!" and you do not feel *that*, and you so confess before the Lord. Now the Lord sometimes brings a poor sinner to this very point, and the poor creature thinks he can never pray again; but he does pray again. If he lives in the country, he goes moping about the fields, and if he lives in the city, he goes about his work, and sometimes he is looking for some instrument that he wants for his employer, and perhaps he has it in his hand all the time, and he is so bewildered and confused that he feels fit for nothing. Satan tells him he his going mad, and he looks in the glass to see whether he is looking wild; and he thinks there is not another mortal so wretched as himself. Well; when this is the case, and all things seem so gloomy, the Holy Spirit comes, and comes as a Spirit of prayer, humbles him, and puts a cry into his mouth, till he really feels a *majesty* in prayer, and a *power* in prayer; and anon he is drawn forth into *energy* in prayer, and he can feel that God is owned of him, and he is owned of God, and he says, "I will not let thee go, except thou bless me." O! What a delightful thing it is, when God the Spirit puts such a word into the mouth of the poor worm of the dust! This is one of the "great things" that he does at times; and THEN "the kingdom of heaven suffers violence" indeed. There is THEN a solemn might and violence in prayer to storm Satan's strongholds, and a great blessing comes through the power and energy of the Holy Ghost. But none but the Spirit of the Lord can produce this in the heart of a sinner; and when a sinner is brought here, he knows something eventually of God "having done great things for him."

But I must conclude; my strength tells me that I must.

III. When the Lord makes this manifest in us, it is sure to make us GLAD. Then we can say, joyfully, sweetly, and blessedly, "The Lord is my rock and my fortress, and my deliverer, my God my strength, in whom I will trust, my buckler, and the horn of my salvation and my high tower"—my ALL. What gladness in the heart when Jesus is thus revealed, and when our souls can sweetly and blessedly triumph in him! "He hath done great things for us whereof we are glad."

May the Lord the Spirit lead you and me to know more of the Gospel of Christ, and to show especial concern for the poor and needy, for his mercy's sake. Amen.

GOD'S PEOPLE LED BY HIM IN HIS PATHS.

Preached on Tuesday Evening, May 21st, 1839, in Gower Street Chapel, London.

"Hold up my goings in thy paths, that my footsteps slip not."
PS. XVII. 5.

ONE difference betwixt the presumptuous professor and a child of God, blessed with a tender conscience, is this : the presumptuous professor seems anxious to know how far he may go without being particularly criminal, what steps it is possible for him to take in pleasure or in vice without bringing himself in as false and vile; but the child of God, with a tender conscience, is constantly praying, " Hold up my goings in thy paths." *He* is not wanting to know, "Can I do such a thing that is pleasing to flesh and blood, and yet not be criminal?" But he wants to be preserved tenderly walking in the fear of God, and giving proof that there is a solemn vitality in the religion of the cross of Christ. I do not mean that he will never be tempted to some evil thing; but that is not his home, that is not his element, that is not his joy.

There are people in the world who, if they speak of the workings of their inbred corruption, speak of them rather as a virtue than a vice, as if they were to be nursed and cherished and delighted in; but God's people, when in their right minds, have to speak of them with abhorrence, to detest them, to loathe them. And there are professors in the world who, if you give a description of a part of the workings of the human heart (for you can only give a part; give as much as you will, you will never get to the bottom); and if you point out the preciousness of Christ to such sinners, those call you corruption-preachers. They know nothing about the matter; they are like Jonathan's lad, they are not in the secret. If ever God, in the riches of his grace, had taught them the plague of their own heart, the exceeding sinfulness of sin, and the preciousness of Christ as suited to such sinners, they would have a better opinion of such preaching. Such men will talk very soundly upon the letter of doctrines, and go swimmingly on; but they have never had any loggers tied to their heels; they never had their sore laid open; they have never been brought into God's hospital. And till God brings them there, they will know nothing about the preciousness of a cure. They cannot understand what the Lord spiritually means when he says, "The whole need not a physician, but they that are sick."

We read this portion as a text last Tuesday evening, and promised, first, to make a few remarks upon God's *paths;* secondly, to speak a little of God's people's *goings* in those paths; thirdly, their liability to *slip* in those paths; and lastly the nature and necessity of this *prayer,* "Hold up my goings in thy paths, that my footsteps slip not."

I. Now as to God's *paths* we noticed :

1. That solemn path that is laid down in God's own infinite mind —the counsel and purpose of his grace, by the which and according to which he moves in all the bearings of the great economy of salvation.

2. Next we consider that glorious path, the Person, blood, and obedience of Christ, by which the eternal God comes down to sinners, in which he leads sinners to him, and in which God and sinners meet—the Lord Jesus Christ, in his blessed love, blood, and obedience.

3. Now we come next to a path that is not very pleasant to any, and much set at nought by many,—the path of tribulation.

"But," say you, "is that one of the Lord's paths?" God has said that it is "through much tribulation ye shall enter the kingdom." And there is one solemn portion of God's Word that has been at times very blessèd to my own soul, and that is, "Tribulation worketh patience." It does so in two ways. It finds patience something to do. Men talk about being very patient, who have nothing to try their patience. They know nothing about whether they have any patience, for they have had nothing to put it to the test. But let God, either by his permission or in the dispensations of his providence, suffer or bring his people into this path of tribulation, and that tries their patience and finds patience something to do. And then eventually it produces patience, as they are brought by the Holy Spirit to know something of the power of God overruling their crosses and trials, to the glory of his name and the blessedness of their own souls. And this tribulation is one of the Lord's paths. "By these things men live."

But what are we to understand by *tribulations?* I might take up the whole evening with this, and yet say but little about it. However, I will just notice that, as it respects troubles, God's people have all things in common with other men; such as poverty, disappointments, worldly difficulties, worldly trials; but then each real spiritual believer in the Lord Jesus Christ has conflicts peculiar to himself, and which the world knows nothing of. As Hart very beautifully observes in one of his hymns,—they all have to suffer "martyrdom within." God sends tribulation into their souls, dries up almost every spark of light, every drop of love, every particle of life that God communicates to their souls; and through an infinite variety of chequered scenes they are brought to such an internal conflict as to be "at their wit's end" almost, and wonder where the scene will end; and they are ready to conclude that God has given them up and will have no more to do with them, and that these things are come as evidences that they are not his children. I was going to say I do not believe God takes such pains with any but his children; he lets others nurse up themselves in their delusions and go comfortably on; but he sends tribulation to his children which seems to dry them up, and to bring them from all false confidences, false comforts, false evidences, and false joys, and appears, at times, as if he was burning all up. But he only burns up the hay and the stubble; for whatever you may think of yourselves, if you have known much of the working of nature, I am certain you have been building up, at times, some tolerably high heaps of hay and stubble, and you have looked at them and thought they looked so very pretty, and you have said, "Aye, we are going to get on a little now." But God sent a storm, or sent a fire, and set it alight and burnt it up, and you were "saved, but so as by fire." Thus you have known something feelingly and spiritually of the path of tribulation. There is no such thing as a child of God missing it; for the Lord says, we "*must* enter into his kingdom through much tribulation." Yet what pains have we taken to make a better road, what pains to smooth the path, what pains to lay a fine carpet all the way, that we may go to heaven without any difficulties or trials! But God has determined that his people shall have conflicts within and such conflicts that nothing short of the Lord himself can support them in and deliver them out of; and thus they must walk through the path of tribulation.

4. Another path of the Lord is the path of walking into the various branches of God's revealed truth in the glorious doctrines and promises of the Gospel.

If you are a child of God, and have been brought to know something experimentally of the power of divine truth on your conscience and at the same time have a tolerable acquaintance with the doctrines of truth (such as the doctrine of God's eternal election, the inseparable union betwixt Christ and the church, the glorious pardon of sin through the atonement, the free justification of the sinner by the righteousness of Christ imputed, the fulness of Christ to supply all our needs, the final perseverance of the saints, and the ultimate glory of all God's people); and if you never really got at them through the path of tribulation, they will make you giddy and you will walk very unsteady, and by and by all your stock will appear to fail you, and you will have to get at every particle of these divine mysteries through hot fires and deep waters, and then you will find they are solemnly sweet and solemnly precious to your soul, and you will be led to glorify God even for crosses. It was so with myself at any rate; and every one has a right to talk of the road he has gone. I recollect I believed the doctrine of election naturally, as far as nature goes. I had not been taught it, but I used to reason with myself, when a youth, that as to supposing God did not know who will be saved and who lost, why we might as well say he is no God at all. And I think so still; at least he cannot be the God of heaven, who "sees the end from the beginning." Why, precious soul, if he is a God that does not know that, you might as well worship that pillar. But the child of God may get a knowledge of these things in the judgment, and by and by be brought into such a fierce conflict that all will tend to weigh him down, rather than give him any support or consolation. But when he is brought by the Spirit of God to walk in these things, to enter into these truths, what a blessed immortal mine opens to him, what solemn lettings down there are! He can take a survey of the purposes of God in the settlements of heaven, in the gifts of Christ, in the blessed work of the Spirit, in the building up of his people in fear and love, propping up their souls in storms, and at last leading them triumphantly to glory. A solemnly sweet matter it is, when God the Spirit leads us with vital faith to walk in this path. John speaks very highly of the elect lady's children, who "walked in the truth." But mind, it is consecrated ground; it is not to walk with levity, with lightness, with indifference. He must be no light frothy professor, that is "carried about with every wind of doctrine." He will feel a solemn weight in his soul, in his sense of the importance of these doctrines.

5. Lastly, the Lord leads his children also in the path of his precepts.

I know some people say, when you start that, "O! It is legal; I have nothing to do with precepts." Why, they are in the Word of God, and if the preceptive part of the law of Jesus, as King of Zion and Head of the church, is too trifling for your notice, surely you cannot be much attached to the Lord of the house. His blessed Majesty says, "If ye love me, keep my commandments;" and therefore it is an awful look-out, when professors can slight them.

Now we can only mention here a few of the things which God enjoins upon his children. That they " love one another." Then they must not be proud, consequential, above the poor broken-hearted child of God. If we say we love the Lord and love not his poor mourning child, we deceive ourselves; for he is a member of Christ, a limb of Christ, a part of Christ. He says so himself. You and I should remember every one of these is a limb of our blessed Christ and a part of ourselves, for it is one blessed body, and there can be no separation betwixt Christ and his mystical members.

Then another branch of Christ's precepts is "not to forsake the assembling of ourselves together." It becomes the child of God to meet with God's dear family, to hear and for prayer; and their united prayer, under the inditing of God the Holy Ghost, is more powerful than a million armies of men.

Another branch of the Lord's precepts is to "contend earnestly for the faith once delivered to the saints," and not to consider any branch of divine truth of little moment, but to remember God has connected his honour with it. It is not that we are to be quarrelling; but we are to maintain divine truth in the meekness and love of Christ.

Another branch of the precepts is this (it comes very close, God help us to walk in it): "Endeavour to keep the unity of the Spirit in the bond of peace." What is the "bond of peace?" Why, love and blood. In the bond of the love and blood of the God-man Mediator, may we be concerned to show ourselves one blessed family, born from above and bound for the world of ineffable glory, where "God shall be all in all." And if there were time, I could go over the preceptive parts of divine truth enjoined upon the members of Christ, according to the office they fill in the world, the church, or the family, as masters or servants, husbands or wives, parents or children. In your station, be concerned to know the will of Jesus concerning you, and to walk in obedience to it under the divine anointing of his Spirit.

II. We pass on to notice next *the "goings"* of God's people in his paths.

Now one of the first paths that we move in, with peace and joy, is that path which God moves in to come to us and draw us to him. Ah! How sweet and precious it is, when the Holy Ghost draws the sinner from self to Christ, and leads him, by faith and in feeling, to walk in the Redeemer as the Lord his righteousness and strength! God the Spirit draws his feet up to heaven, to walk in the " fountain opened for sin and for uncleanness." He is plunged in that immortal flood, loses his guilt from his conscience, and feels a solemn enjoyment of interest in the Lord the Lamb, more prizeable than a thousand worlds. Well then, he looks and finds his own emptiness; and God the Spirit draws him by faith to walk by faith in the fulness of Christ, who is "full of grace and truth."

Perhaps there is some poor soul here to-night, just upon the threshold of this road, and yet he cannot take a step in it. I have often seen a poor sinner standing at the borders of the fulness and glory of Christ as suited to him, and he has looked, and, as we commonly say, he has longed. It is like a poor famished creature looking through a window and seeing a table richly and wonderfully loaded with the bounties of providence, but he dare not hope to be the partaker of a crumb; and there he stands, thinking and quaking. Perhaps here is some soul in this state to-night. Some people tell you, "O! You must venture in." Ah! It is pretty talking; but doing is another thing. Perhaps now he is sure there is every thing his soul needs; but he thinks there is certainly nothing *for him*. But by and by the dear Lord comes, and, by the sweet power and blessed energy of his Spirit, he draws the soul in to walk into the glorious mysteries of the love of Christ; he lets down a sense of the fulness of Christ into his heart, and says, "Eat, O friend, and drink, yea, drink abundantly, O beloved; and let your heart delight itself in fatness." And as his blessed Majesty thus speaks, he gives an enlarged heart to receive, and thus fills it from his own heart; and thus brings the soul, by faith and in feeling, to walk in the Lord Jesus Christ. Do not you recollect what the Lord says by the mouth of the apostle: "As ye have received Christ Jesus the Lord, so walk ye in him?" He would not have said so, if he had not known that his people are very prone to forget that. Why, sometimes they walk round and round Christ, and look and look, and yet, poor souls! they cannot walk one step into him, so as to bring the power of his blood and fulness into their hearts. But when the blessed Spirit leads them to walk in, then they have holy liberty. And sweet work it is, when Christ and the soul sit together, and there is an immortal union and communion at the banquet, which the world knows nothing of.

And so, again, when a poor soul feels a load of guilt; how is he to get rid of it?" "O!" say some people, "Begin to do your duty; and when you have done a little duty, then you are to take the comfort of the Bible." I believe it is the devil's trap, to insult the Spirit of God and to deceive sinners. "Why," say you, "you would not encourage them *not* to do their duty?" Nay, that is another thing. It becomes them to walk in the precepts of God and practice all what are called duties; but that will not do for a ground of comfort and happiness. If ever we feel guilt, and if God the Spirit does not apply the atonement and bring us to walk into the efficacy of the blood of the God-man Mediator, and we get rid of guilt without it, it is the devil deceiving our souls and we have wrapped up ourselves in some sad delusion. Nothing but that can bring solid peace to the conscience and clear our sky of clouds. That is what makes matters straight with God, and he crowns our faith with divine apprehensions, and faith crowns him with all the glory. And thus there is a solemn coming and going betwixt the soul and the Lord, when God the Spirit is pleased to lead us by faith to walk in this way. But we shall find we only walk there as "necessity is laid upon us" and God the Spirit draws us. We may talk about the fitness of things, as if it were a matter that we could get at because it was a fit matter. It is no such thing. It is as God the Spirit draws us, and leads us, and guides us, and fills our souls with his heavenly dew and his divine love ; and then we are brought to walk in this path, which God himself has laid down.

Well ; by and by we get into the path of tribulation ; and we must walk there. The first branch of my walk in the path of tribulation I cannot forget. After I had had the bondage of guilt for a few months and the Lord had delivered me, I went cheerfully on for a few more months, and thought I should be happy all the days of my life. But at length I was brought into such gloom, such darkness, such wretchedness, such rising up of sin, such teeming or oozing up of filth, pollution, misery, unwholesomeness, that I really could not compare myself to any thing better than a walking devil, and imagined that I was enough to breed the plague upon earth and that I carried a pestilence about with me. I dreaded, at the time, meeting any one that I thought a child of God, for I was afraid the moment I met him he would find out what a monstrous hypocrite I was ; and as I knew every one that lived in the village where I then was and they knew me, I thought if one of them found out what I was and came to tell the people, I must run away and leave the country, for they would point at me and jeer me and hoot me,— I was such a wretched monster. "Aye," some will say, "you are joking, man ; you never thought you were such a vagabond as that." Yes, indeed I did ; and I think I am not much better now ; for when I look at the corruption that there is within, I feel that nothing but Christ's blood can give me rest, and nothing but his Almighty power can bring me safe along. However, by and by, God, in the dispensations of his providence, made this a path to lead me into the mysteries of his kingdom. I believe there is more in that text than many of his people think of : "Through much tribulation we must enter the kingdom." We do not merely enter the kingdom of heaven through much tribulation, but we really enter feelingly and spiritually into the kingdom of his manifested grace in the soul through tribulation ; and as we are brought to have tribulation upon tribulation, the Lord appears, and blesses our souls with the unction of this truth, and we begin to walk blessedly into it.

I will just tell you how it was with me. When in this state, I made up my mind to keep out of the company of all God's people. But on one occasion a poor woman, who is now gone to glory, saw me come and called me by my name, and said, "Are you going to Coventry?" which was about eighteen miles from where I lived. I said, "Yes, I am." "O! Stop a moment then," said she; "for my John is going there." Now I had rather it had been a bear; for I am pretty swift of foot and I might have outrun a bear; but I knew this John was a child of God. "Now," thought I, "I shall be found out, and I shall be just like Cain, going about with a brand upon me. I must take care that John does not talk to me about religion. I will talk to him about trade and politics all the way to Coventry. I will take care we have nothing about religion." And so, when he came up, I began about those things; but he cut the matter short, and took me up at once: "I want to know why you go to the meeting-house?" "Ah!" I thought. "This is cutting me up at once. Do not ask me," said I. "But I must know," he said. "I really cannot tell you." "Well, what do you think of yourself?" said he. "What are your feelings?" "I dare not tell you," said I. "Do not ask me, for really I dare not." "Nay," said he; "but let me have a little of it;" and so he began pumping and supping (I think he had a tolerably good sup of me), and he got one little bit and then another, till at last he began to smile. And then I thought, "Ah! He has found it out, and he is laughing at my calamity, and mocking while my fear is coming." But at length he said, "Now who do you think taught you this? Nature never taught it." And he began to point out the Word of God as suited to such a condition, and showed how it was the state that God led all his people into, from time to time. God sweetly brought it to my heart, set my soul at liberty, and the Bible became a new Bible to me. It seemed to unfold mysteries that I never knew before. And thus my poor soul was led to walk in the truth of God while I was walking in this path of tribulation. And then I began to talk about the blessed enjoyment given me of God's revealed truth, and the people called me an Antinomian. Why, they might as well have called me a Pagan; for I did not know what an Antinomian was. But I never since have got off this ground, and I trust I never shall, of having Christ all and self nothing. And I believe through this path, however trying it may be to us, God teaches his people, by the teaching of the Holy Spirit, a tolerable measure of divine truth. We learn through our own fickleness the necessity of God's immutability; we learn through our own weakness the necessity of God's strength; we learn (for the blessed Spirit teaches us) through our own emptiness the necessity of the fulness of Christ; through our own foolishness the necessity of the wisdom of Christ; through our own unholiness the necessity of the holiness of Christ; and through the channel of our own degradation the necessity of the glory of Christ. God the Spirit leads us into this blessed channel of divine truth, through the path of tribulation. And thus the Lord glorifies himself in the hearts and consciences of his people, and glorifies truth in them too; and so leads them sweetly and blessedly to know that God's kingdom stands in God's power and does not consist in the observation of men. And thus we "walk in the truth."

Now when God the Spirit has brought the poor child of God sweetly and solemnly thus to walk in his paths, what a solemn mystery is unfolded, when God comes to make known his own path of eternal purpose and counsel, by which the Lord walks in all his dispensations! Have you ever felt it? Have you ever seen it by faith? Has God the Spirit drawn you to walk, by faith and in feeling, in this path,—to trace (notwithstanding all your uncertainty, unsteadiness, fickleness, wanderings, foolishness, vanity, and wretchedness, which have burdened and oppressed you) the stability, and firmness, and glory of God's eternal counsel? Has he brought you, in heart and soul, to walk out of your own fickleness into God's eternal fixtures, and find there a settledness, more blessed than a thousand worlds? If God the Spirit thus leads us, we then, in some blessed measure, walk in God's paths, and know what it is to hold converse with the Father, and with the Son, and with the blessed Spirit.

I am sure, when this is the case, it will be no task to walk in the path of obedience. To "run in the way of God's commandments" will be no burden then; no, not even if the Lord brings us so into the path of obedience as to expose us to the scorn and derision of men. We then know something of the blessedness which Moses felt, when by faith he esteemed even "the reproach of Christ greater riches than the treasures of Egypt." What an idea! Why, if the *reproach* of Christ was greater riches than the treasures of Egypt, what is the *glory?* What is the *blessedness?* Come, come. Let us sum up with some of God's gems. It is an honour put upon the Lord's people to suffer for the Lord's sake, and the Lord crowns it with his own promises; and so we are led sweetly to walk in that path, we find a solemn pleasure in yielding obedience to the Lord, and showing forth the Lord's praises as taught of him.

Now do you know anything of this? It is very easy to talk about this thing being the best, and that thing being the best. There is a great deal of talk among men about a variety of things of an external nature; but the kingdom of God has an immortal mystery in it. It stands in God's power, God's truth, God's justice, God's holiness, God's pity, God's compassion, all in divine harmony; and the mystery of godliness is for God to let out his heart as a covenant God into our hearts, and to bring our hearts into his heart, and thus lead us sweetly and spiritually into the glorious mysteries of his kingdom. May the Lord the Spirit lead you and me to walk in his paths, and to be moving on; for he tells us we are to "grow up into Christ in all things," and not to grow up in pride and self-conceit in our own ability and our own knowledge and our own way. The most blessed and spiritual walking that we can enjoy in the world is when God the Spirit leads us to sicken at all self-pretensions and to walk out of self into the Lamb of God, and stand before God sweetly and solemnly in the mysteries of the cross; and so to glorify him with our bodies and souls, which are his.

III. But we observe, in the next place, there is a possibility of our footsteps *slipping*. "Hold up my goings in thy paths, that my footsteps slip not."

There is one blessed thing, we shall never depart entirely out of his paths. The Lord will invariably so order it that his people shall move on in some way or other. But we know there is a possibility of slipping. We may temporarily slip as to the doctrines of the Gospel. How was it with the Galatians? Paul says, "Ye did run well; what hath hindered you?" Ah! Their feet had slipped. And if you mind, he calls the men who had been the means of leading them to slip, *wizards*, because it must be a wizard or a witch which had "bewitched them." That is the name he gives to the Judaizing teachers, the men who had seduced them from the truth. And I will tell you how they did it. If they happened to be a little bewildered in their mind, up comes one of the religious wizards (and God knows there are plenty of them in our day), and says, "I fear you have been turning Antinomian, I fear your minds have been entangled with some notions about particular feelings and particular points of doctrine. "Now mind," says he, "the religion of Christ is a holy religion, and what you have to do, is to mind to be holy, and to walk holily. I wish to preach Christ," he says; "but then you must have your own holiness as well. That must be maintained, and the law must be your standing rule, and you must yield obedience to it, or you cannot be saved." Well, this seems very right; and sometimes the poor creature begins to say, " Why, Sir, I really felt so; but when the glorious Gospel of Christ came with power to my heart, I found it had every thing in it of precept and life and power, and it seemed to fit my soul well." "O!" answers he; "that is Antinomianism." Thus they try to get the old veil over the poor creature's eyes; and if they succeed in that, he gets bewildered, and cannot tell what he is about. Now you mind what the apostle says about that: "Stand fast in the liberty wherewith Christ has made you free, and be not entangled again with the yoke of bondage." Why, if there is this "entanglement," who in the name of conscience, can walk straight? With a veil over his eyes, or an entanglement upon his heart, he is sure to make some slip, and be brought into such a state of mind as to cry out, as my text does, "Hold up my goings in thy paths," for he finds himself slipping a great deal from "the simplicity that is in Christ," and this brings bondage and entanglement into his conscience.

Well; there is a possibility of this slipping in precept; and that is an awful thing. Solomon slipped; and perhaps some here have solemnly slipped, though it has been hid from the world. If Tell-tale Truth were to write your slips on parchment upon your foreheads, where would you put your heads? But Tell-tale Truth will come to your conscience some day or other, if you are a child of God, read you your own souls, and make you feel your awful state, however you may cover it for awhile from the world. And I am sure, if you have a tender conscience and feel the natural proneness that there is to slip into practical sin, as well as to wander from the simplicity of the Gospel, you will send up this prayer, day after day.

IV. And that will lead us just to say a word as to the nature and necessity of this prayer: "Hold up my goings in thy paths, that my footsteps slip not."

For my part I can say I really dare not trust myself. Sometimes when I enter a little into the world and have not felt suspicious of myself nor been enabled to commit myself to God's care, I have been brought to stand amazed, and say, "Lord! What a presumptuous arrogant monster I am! What a wonder it is that thou hast not let me slip!" I solemnly declare that I wonder, at times, that God has not let my feet slip into some awful labyrinth which would have disgraced my character; it is a wonder of wonders, that by the grace of God I stand. O the wonders of the love of God! Perhaps some high-towering professor here says, "O! I feel no danger!" Why, you do not know your sore, poor creature; you never had your heart laid open; and the worst wish I have for you is that God would lay it open and make you feel and see what you are. I should not like you to stay there long, for it would drive you mad if there were nothing else. But when a poor soul has laid open to his view what an awful sinner he is and he feels how prone he is to slip, then he comes with all his heart to this prayer: "Hold up my goings in thy paths, that my footsteps slip not."

Now is this your prayer? Perhaps there is some professor in this assembly who makes a glaring show and is thought very highly of, yet is living in practical guilt in a scandalous way every day of his life, only it is concealed. Perhaps he has a plan now, before he reaches home, to practice some unhallowed crime. "Be sure your sin will find you out." May the Lord have mercy upon you, strip you of your presumption and bring you to know something of your lost condition, that you may be led, as a perishing sinner, to the Lord Jesus Christ. Whilst you can live in the practice and delight of these things, you do not know what it is to use this prayer; you do not come with it daily to the Lord, as a pauper and a pensioner. If you feel now and then a few qualms of conscience, you want to drown them and get rid of them; you want to have a little more elbow-room for the practice of the unhallowed feelings of your hearts. This is the work of the flesh; and may God the Spirit cut up your false hopes, and bring you to cry vehemently before him, "Hold up my goings in thy paths, that my footsteps slip not." And as you are led to pray, you will find, at times, the necessity of being in an agony, as it were, with the Lord. It will not be a mere tale; it will not be a mere formal prayer; there will be such plans laid to catch your feet, such suggestions and temptations of Satan, the world, and yourself, that it will really be an agonizing crying, "Lord, hold me up." You will feel as if you were that moment sinking and wanting present aid and present power; and it will be a vehement crying to the Lord, "Hold up my goings in thy paths, that my footsteps slip not." For the children of God will certainly wish to live as witnesses for God, to crown the brow of the Lord, and to prove that God's truth produces holiness in the conscience and leads a man to walk in the life and power of the truth of God. May the Lord bless you and me with a vital concern for his honour, and lead us to walk in his paths, spiritually and blessedly, for his own name's sake. Amen.

THE SCRIPTURE RULE FOR TRYING THE SPIRITS THAT ARE IN THE WORLD.

Preached on Sunday Evening, May 31st, 1840, in Gower Street Chapel, London.

"Beloved, believe not every spirit, but try the spirits whether they are of God; because many false prophets are gone out into the world. Hereby know ye the Spirit of God: Every spirit that confesseth that Jesus Christ is come in the flesh is of God: And every spirit that confesseth not that Jesus Christ is come in the flesh is not of God; and this is that spirit of antichrist, whereof ye have heard that it should come; and even now already is it in the world."—1 JNO. IV. 1-4.

It has always been the case, ever since God sent prophets, that the devil has endeavoured to imitate him and send prophets too; and the Lord told Moses to give the people this advice, that if a prophet rose up, or a dreamer of dreams, and prophesied things that came true, yet they were not to believe him except he brought forth in his prophecy the real truth of God. It seems good in the sight of God that, for wise purposes, there should be false prophets and false teachers, for the trial of his people's faith, for putting them upon the important work of measuring and weighing up the spirits of men, and "trying the spirits whether they be of God." In one place the Lord tells us that heresies must abound, "that they which are approved may be made manifest." This seems, in some measure, rather trying to flesh and blood; but it is God's method, and it becomes the saints of the Most High to be concerned to look to the Lord for wisdom to direct them in a matter of such moment and importance.

Some one, perhaps, is ready to say, "O! I can 'try the spirits' of men in a moment; I can measure them to a nicety." Well; what rule do you go by? "My own experience." Indeed; and have you tried *that* by the standard of God's Spirit and God's truth? If you have not, perhaps your experience is delusive; for God tells us, he will send some "strong delusions, that they may believe a lie." So that you should be concerned to bring your experience to the standard of God's unerring Book; and if it is not according to that, depend upon it you will deceive your soul, if you make a stand upon it or attempt to try the spirits of men by it.

"But," say you, "do you suppose that all Christian experience is according to the Word of God? Do not you believe that the Holy Ghost sometimes works in the heart of a child of God without the Word?" Yes, I do; but never contrary to it. He always brings about things exactly according to the Word of God, and never contrary to it.

Perhaps there may be some one in this assembly who may say, "O! But I believe he never works except through the Word and by the hearing of the Word." What a pretty sweep you make then! You send all infants to hell at once, for they are all born in sin and shapen in iniquity; and unless they are renewed in the spirit of their minds and blessed with an interest in the Lord Jesus Christ, they cannot go to heaven any more than adults. They never could go on the ground of their innocence; they are not innocent, they are guilty. Therefore you sink all infants to hell. Now so far as I am from believing that, I believe rather that infants, dying in their infancy, are amongst the number of God's elect, and that God works a divine change in them without the hearing of the Word. And we might just glance at one sentence which gives us a little encouragement on this ground. When Mary was pregnant with the Messiah, and Elizabeth her cousin, pregnant with John the Baptist (and God tells us he was sanctified "from the womb"), Mary went to see her cousin; and as soon as she stepped into the house, Elizabeth said, "Blessed art thou among women, and blessed is the fruit of thy womb; for lo! as soon as the voice of thy salutation sounded in mine ears, the babe leaped in my womb for joy." How, in the name of a good conscience, did little John in his mother's womb know anything about it, if God the Spirit had not revealed it to him? It could not be from any natural circumstance; and yet she says, "The babe within me leaped for joy." And I believe millions of babes have "leaped for joy in their mother's womb," and leaped out of their mother's womb into heaven, by the blessed power and energy of God the Holy Ghost, who can work without the Word. But, you see, it was not contrary to it; for it was the salutation of Mary, pregnant with the Messiah, and John was led to leap for joy at the Messiah being there. And so, as the Lord the Spirit makes manifest the truth, whether in infants or in adults, it is according to the Word of God. Therefore you must bring your experience to the standard of God's Word; and when you have a "Thus saith the Lord" for what you do, a "Thus saith the Lord" for what you feel, a "Thus saith the Lord" for what you experience, a "Thus saith the Lord" to comfort you, it is a nail that all hell shall never extract out of your conscience. It is "a nail fastened in a sure place." A "Thus saith the Lord" is worth a million of "Thus saith this man, or the other man." It is a blessed thing in the conscience, when God the Spirit brings a "Thus saith the Lord" there. I hear of many people talking of being very heavenly and very blessed in practising what they call righteous acts, and I believe it has all been a delusion of the devil; their practice has been all the while exactly contrary to God's Word, and therefore I am sure God the Spirit was never there. But when our experience and God's Word agree,— the testimony of God in the conscience and the testimony of God in his Word, then we are fit to come forth to measure the spirits of men, to "try the spirits of men whether they be of God."

I shall pass on, then, to notice the rule which is laid down in our text, by which we are to "try the spirits" of men. "Every spirit that confesseth that Jesus Christ is come in the flesh is of God; and every spirit that confesseth not that Jesus Christ is come in the flesh is not of God." And this "spirit of antichrist," John tells us, was already in the world in *his* day. In *our* day there is a great stir about the progress of Popery, and some men seem trembling alive lest Popery should reign; but I believe thousands of those who are making the greatest stir about it are feeding the soul of Popery from week to week, with all the doctrines they preach, however much they may fight against the shell, and against the body; for that "without the soul would be dead." The life and soul and blood and pulse and energy of Popery and antichrist is couched in what the Lord has in view here: "Every spirit that confesseth not that Jesus Christ is come in the flesh is not of God," but of antichrist.

"But," say you, "every body almost 'confesses that Jesus Christ is come in the flesh.'" Now that is the matter we have to look to a little. May God direct us!

Every body almost in this nation talks about a "Christ that is come in the flesh;" but the Lord of the house assures us that there shall arise false Christs, and shall deceive many. (Matt. v. 24.) And Paul said in his day there were many who "preached another Jesus;" which is not God's Christ, and, therefore, it is antichrist.

Our business, then, shall be, as God shall assist (and may God in very deed assist us), to point out God's Christ, that has "come in the flesh."

I. Now what is the Christ of God? In what capacity did he stand, as having "come in the flesh,"—as *the elect Head of an elect body?*

"O! Come," say you; "you begin high at once; you are beginning with election, and we do not believe that." Why, then you have the very spirit of antichrist. If you deny that, if God the Spirit has not convinced you of that, no matter what you profess to be, the life and soul of your religion feeds Popery; yours is the spirit of antichrist.

II. That he has come to *accomplish a manifested work for the elect.*

III. That he came to work out *a complete righteousness for them.*

IV. That he is their *witness, life, and light.*

I. If we come to examine the Word of God upon this subject, we find the Lord says he "chose a people in Christ before the foundation of the world," and that Christ, as the Head of this people, was "set up from everlasting," and "his delights were with the sons of men" when the heavens were prepared and the foundations of the earth appointed. And when his blessed Majesty "came in the flesh," in what capacity did he come? God tells us, in Isa. xl.: "His reward is with him, and his work before him." What is "his reward?" Why, his church, his elect, the people chosen in him. And he brought them "with him." Before he came in the flesh all the elect were in union to him by the divine appointment of the Father; and when he came, he represented them, in his life and sufferings and death and resurrection. Hence it is said, they "are crucified with Christ," that they "suffer with him," that they "are risen with him," and (if that is not enough) that they "sit together in heavenly places with him." God's Christ never took a step in the flesh without the whole elect in his heart. This is the Christ that is "come in the flesh," for the accomplishment of salvation.

Now the greatest part of the professing world—it does not matter what they call themselves, Independents, Baptists, Church people, Methodists, Moravians, or Quakers,—fifty out of every fifty-one, deny this. And therefore theirs is antichrist; it is not God's Christ. However pleasing it may be to flesh and blood, if they deny this foundation and fundamental truth, if they deny Christ and one mystical body in union with him, and his coming into the world to represent them and to accomplish a work for their eternal salvation, they deny God's Christ, and they set up a Christ of their own, which is antichrist. We therefore solemnly charge it upon the people of God, if you hear men denying this fundamental truth, whatever they may say about piety and holiness and charity and benevolence, and mortifications and alms deeds and prayers and tears and watchings, and all that they can heap up besides, in your heart weigh them up, and say, It is antichrist. For God's Christ and his people are one; one, never to be separated, and never to be made two. (1 Cor. xii. 12; Rom. xii. 5; Eph. v. 29, 30.)

II. But then we observe that another branch of this rule is, that the Christ of God, who is "come in the flesh," is not only come to represent his people who are in union to him, but he is come *to accomplish a complete salvation for them.* Not come to make it possible for them to save themselves; not come to open a way whereby, through their exertions, they may secure their own salvation. A Christ of that nature is one of the devil's inventing. It is antichrist. It is not the Christ of God. No, no. The Christ of God is come "to put away sin," "to finish transgression and to make an end of sin, and to bring in everlasting righteousness," to "redeem from all iniquity," and to "redeem unto God." So we find, when the Holy Ghost is speaking upon the subject, he says, "Husbands, love your wives, as Christ also loved the church, and gave himself for it." Do you not see, beloved, how it is? Has God made you to feel it? If this little word *it* gets into your conscience, it is a blessed thing, if God the Spirit puts it there. He gave himself for *it.* Not "gave himself" indefinitely "for all sin of all men,"—the doctrine of the day, to accomplish a great salvation, and make it possible for those who please to save themselves; that is antichrist; I do not care who preaches it, nor who believes it; it is not the Christ of God. No, no. God's Christ has finished transgression, and made a complete atonement for sin; such an atonement that, as the Holy Ghost solemnly declares, "the redeemed of the Lord *shall* come to Zion with songs and everlasting joy upon their heads, and sorrow and sighing *shall* flee away." Now the Christ that you believe in and have felt in your soul, is it a Christ of this nature? Or is it a Christ that you say gives all men a chance of being saved, has done the best he can to save them, has made it possible for them to accomplish the conditions of salvation and so to save themselves? That is antichrist; as the living God is in heaven, that is not his Christ. God's Christ has so completed the work that all the perfections of the Eternal Jehovah harmonize in it, to the complete salvation of God's people. Hence it is said that "Israel shall be saved in the Lord;" not have a chance of being saved. A chance of being saved? Why, bless you, when I hear men talk about a chance of being saved, I am led to reflect— Then the declarative glory of the Eternal Trinity hangs upon a chance; the honour of God the Father hangs upon chance; the honour and effect of the work of God the Son hangs upon chance; the honour of God the Spirit, in his quickening, enlightening, sanctifying power, hangs upon chance! And that chance, too, to be accomplished by man—a poor, dying, crawling reptile!—the eternal Trinity having to wait in heaven to see if perchance we will let him work! Talk of Christ! It is antichrist. It is an insulting of God's

Christ; a despising of the Christ God has revealed in his Word and makes known in the hearts and consciences of his people.

If we believe that God's Christ "is come in the flesh," then, we believe that he has come as the Head and Representive of his people, and that he has completed their salvation and entirely finished the work. Yea, bless his holy name, we are brought to believe and feel in our souls that he has accomplished such a work that it can neither be mended nor marred. The manifestation of it may go through a variety of changes, and we through a variety of changes under it; but the work is as firm as the throne of God, and it shall stand for ever. "His work is perfect; a God of truth, and without iniquity, just and right is he." The Christ of God that has "come in the flesh" is one that has accomplished this blessed, this God-glorifying work. Any other Christ is not the Christ of God, but it is antichrist, another Jesus, one of those "false Christs" that the Lord said should arise, and should deceive many; and so, God knows, there are many who are deceived.

III. But, then, we observe further, the Lord Christ that is "come in the flesh" is that blessed Christ that has wrought out a *complete right-eousness* for the justification of his people; not only atoned for their sins, but wrought out a righteousness, to present them just and perfect and righteous in his blessed and pure obedience.

I know some people say, "O yes; we have a righteousness *through* Christ; he has accomplished such a work that if we are faithful and add our faithfulness to his work, we shall obtain righteousness and holiness too; but not without." Why, then, the Christ that has done that is not God's Christ; it is antichrist. The Christ of God that has "come in the flesh," is emphatically called "The Lord our righteousness;" and God tells us plainly that it is not *through*, but "*in* the Lord," that "all the seed of Israel shall be justified." And this is the reason why an inspired Paul was anxiously concerned "to be found in Christ, not having his own righteousness." "Not having your own righteousness," Paul? Why, you were a very zealous man, a pious man, a suffering man, a man led to undergo a great deal for Christ, in shipwrecks, and prisons, and stripes, and perils, and after all cannot you wear your own righteousness? No, says Paul; do not let me have that on! Well, but what righteousness could Paul wish to appear in then? "Not having mine own righteousness, which is of the law, but that which is through the faith of Christ, the righteousness which is of God by faith." And here it is, that the poor child of God is brought, in solemn silence sometimes and in solemn awe, to bow before God, when "clothed and in his right mind," and to see that he is "complete in Christ;" complete in him, who is "Head over all principalities and powers," "God blessed for ever."

I know, antichrist mocks at the idea of looking for imputed

righteousness, or depending upon imputed righteousness.   Imputed righteousness, some say, is imputed nonsense.   Now, so charitable am I, that I believe that a man who lives and dies declaring the imputed righteousness of Christ to be nonsense, dies to be damned, as sure as God is in heaven.   I do not care who he is, nor what he is; the spirit by which he is guided is antichrist.   It is not "the Spirit of God;" for God's Christ is Christ "our righteousness"—"the end of the law for righteousness to every one that believeth."   Of God's Christ it is said, that "in him we have redemption through his blood, the forgiveness of sins," and that we are "justified freely through the redemption that is in him."   And when the Lord the Spirit brings this solemn mystery into the conscience of a poor, burdened, dejected, drooping sinner, O what glory teems into his heart!   To be led in faith and feeling to see that he stands before God in the spotless, pure, perfect obedience of Christ; his righteousness justifying him so fully and completely that God himself, by the apostle, challenges all creation to "lay any thing to his charge," this is Christ! Hence, says the apostle, "There is no condemnation to them that are in Christ Jesus;" not to them that talk about, nor to them that bring forth a false Christ, but to them that are really in God's Christ. Why, that poor soul is so wrapped up in God's Christ that in the sight of God it is Christ that is seen, and the man is seen in Christ; and therefore he is just and righteous and complete.   This is the Christ that is "come in the flesh,"—Christ "our righteousness;" and we in his righteousness are brought to stand "complete in him."

"But then," say some of you, "we must have holiness.   Talk what you will about being righteous in Christ, we must have personal holiness.   Except we have personal holiness, and are made pure and sanctified, what will the righteousness of Christ do for us?   It will not save us."   Well, where will you look for personal holiness?   In your Christ, which is a Christ that has done something for you, and leaves you to complete the work, by your penitence and mortification and alms-deeds and wonders that you are to manufacture?   Is that what you mean by personal holiness?   If it is, I hope you will keep it to yourselves.   I hope God will not suffer me to be plagued with it; I have plague enough without it.   But if, by personal holiness, you mean being made a partaker of the divine nature, by the quickening, enlightening power and divine communications of God the Holy Ghost, having Christ formed in the soul the hope of glory, being saved by the washing of regeneration and renewing of the Holy Ghost, all centering in and proceeding from Christ, then you have a holiness that will stand the test of God's Word: "For Christ is made of God unto us wisdom and righteousness and sanctification and redemption." And when his blessed Majesty is being spoken of under the Old Testament dispensation, this is his language: "I am like a green fir-tree; from me is thy fruit found."   What is the holiness of a child

of God, then—his real personal holiness? It is couched in this one
blessed thing, in all the manifested bearings of it—*Christ in you.*

Here perhaps I stagger some who are noted for their high views
of election, predestination, and eternal union. "O!" say they, "I
have nothing to do with a Christ in me; I want a Christ without
me." Why, then, you have not God's Christ; you are just on a
level with the other, and your Christ is antichrist. The Lord's
blessed Christ that has "come in the flesh," is by the blessed Spirit
of God as truly communicated to the hearts of his people, and especially conceived in their hearts "the hope of glory," as ever he
was corporally conceived in the womb of Mary. If you have not a
Christ that is formed in your hearts by the invincible energy of God
the Holy Ghost, you are not fit to "try the spirits" of men; you
have no sort of rule by which you are capable of trying them.

IV. But some poor soul is led to say, "Well; but what gives a
proof that Christ is formed in my soul, the hope of glory?" Why,
Christ is *life.* "I am the resurrection and the life; he that believeth
in me, though he were dead, yet shall he live." And Christ is *light.*
"I am the light of the world," that lighteth every (spiritual) man
that cometh into the (spiritual) world. Life and light go together;
and when God the Spirit communicates this blessed Christ to the
conscience, he communicates life, and the sinner begins to feel; and
he communicates light, and the sinner begins to see. And what
does he feel and see? His own emptiness, darkness, blindness, weakness; his own lost condition; and he is brought in real experience
before God to be sick of himself, sick of his prayers and his tears and
his repentance and his faith, if he professed to have any; he sickens
at his vice, and sickens at his piety. A stranger is come into the
temple; and he has overturned "the tables of money changers" in the
heart, to make room for himself. This is God's Christ, that is "come
in the flesh." All these principles, whether of open profaneness or
professed piety, go to ruin. There must be room to realize God's
Christ as a perfect salvation; and that will never be till we are brought
to self-loathing and self-detesting before a heart-searching God. There
will be a hard struggle for it too; especially if we have got a little
piety. If you are openly profane, when God the Spirit is pleased to
reveal the communicable nature of Christ to you, it will not be such
a hard struggle to part with open profaneness; but to part with piety
and religious duties and church-going and chapel-going and sacrament-
going and reading the "Whole Duty of Man," and all those pious
things—O bless me, it is just like driving a man mad. He imagines
he had been a little remiss in some of these things; but then he will
not be so again; he will be more diligent and more cautious. But
no; God's Christ cuts the man up, root and branch, and leaves him
no more help in himself than the damned in hell; and he feels himself as truly cut down as a wretch can be, before a heart-searching God.

Now have you come to this? If not, you do not know God's Christ, which is "come in the flesh." You may talk a great deal about it, but you have not got into the mystery of it. And all your knowledge, till it begins here, is like the fine oil of antichrist; it is only deceiving you, and wrapping you up in a false odour. You have only got a Christ of your own; and it is antichrist. *God's* Christ roots up, and brings the poor sinner, not in judgment merely, but in feeling, to say before God, "There is no help in me;" to feel that he can neither will nor do, and to justify that declaration: "It is not of him that willeth nor of him that runneth, but of God that showeth mercy." He is brought in his very feelings before a heart-searching God to justify God in condemning him; and he gives God leave (as far as a creature can do) to enter into judgment with him; for he says, "Lord, I deserve it, and there is no help in me."

Well, now, have you been brought there? "No," say you, "and I hope I never shall be." I believe you will be damned, if you never are. I do indeed. I solemnly believe that all your religion is nothing but the religion of antichrist, if God has not brought you there; you have never known the Christ of God, the blessed Christ that the Lord has provided for the salvation of his people.

"But, then," say you, "if this be the case, what do you make of such a text as, 'Blessed are the pure in heart, for they shall see God?' Where do you find any purity in such a statement as this?" The very life and soul of it. It is the pure life and communicable nature of Christ which God the Spirit forms in thy soul that is acting in thy soul, and letting thee feel and see what a dark and black wretch thou art in thyself. You never felt it, and never believed it, till God granted you divine life and light; and just in proportion as Christ is spread abroad in the rays of his life and glory in your hearts, do you discover your own wretchedness and darkness and blindness and weakness and deformity; nor can anything short of a perfect Saviour, brought home to your conscience by the glorious power of God the Holy Ghost, ever satisfy you; but when he is realized, felt, and enjoyed by vital faith, you feel that in him you are blessed indeed.

"Well really," say you; "if I could believe that, I think I should have a little hope; for I am there; but I have been thinking that I have nothing to do with Christ and Christ has nothing to do with me, because I should always be very humble and patient and meek and holy." Why, if, in self and of self, you were very humble and patient and meek and holy, you would not need a Christ, you know. "It has pleased the Father that *in Him* should all fulness dwell." If we could bring it forth of ourselves he might keep his fulness to himself, for we should never trouble him about it. No; and we never do till he brings it to us, and makes us heartily glad to disgorge all our fancied religion. And O what a poor creature the soul looks when God the Spirit brings him low; and there he lies, without any righteousness of his own, as dark and as wretched a creature as he well can be!

"Why," say you, "you surely would not call that any part of holiness?" It is just the very beginning and soul of it. It is God the Spirit that is making a stir in thy foul nature, beginning to purge it, and to make thee sicken under it, and under a feeling sense of it say, "Lord! I abhor myself."

"Ah!" say some of you, "That is preaching corruption." "I never preach corruption," says one; "I preach Christ." O! But if you do not preach a Christ that is fitted to a sinner in all his vileness and corruption and pollution, your Christ is not worth my spectacles. It is not God's Christ; it is antichrist. The Christ that is "come in the flesh," is a Christ just suited to such a poor lost and wretched sinner, in all his wretchedness and loathsomeness. Hence, when we come to examine the Book of God, and are led feelingly and spiritually to trace it, what does it say? "He giveth power to the faint, and to them that have no might he increaseth strength." *Now* what do you do with all your "might" and all your power? And again, "Not of works, lest any man should boast." "O!" say you; "that is what I believe; it is 'not of works,' and therefore I believe in a Christ without me." And you are capable of doing that, are you? "Yes," say you. Why, then, you are capable of a great work, and you may make the best of it; for it is not God's Christ nor faith in God's Christ. You may rest assured it is presumption, and you will find it so when you come to be tried up in the grand court of God. But when the poor sinner comes to be cut up and brought down, and in his feelings is worse than a dog, then God the Spirit leads him to see what he has to hope in; and that is—God's Christ. Therefore do not be alarmed, sinner, at finding all your little stock go. I dare say, you are afraid of being insolvent, and so you have tried to set up a fresh stock, and charged your hands from handling, and your eyes from seeing, and your ears from hearing, and have been determined to bring something to God at last; and yet it is always going, and going, and going. "Ah!" say you; "now that is just it." And God grant it may go, and you may never be able to pick it up again; for it is a spurning of God's Christ. But when God the Spirit is pleased to form this Christ in the heart, "the hope of glory" and the glory of hope, then you will cling to him, twine round him, hang upon him, and with a solemn consecrated conscience say, "None but Jesus, none but Jesus, for such a sinner as I."

Now, then, when this is the case, this blessed Christ that is "come in the flesh" lives in you and you in him. You breathe in his life; you walk in his light; you stretch forth your hands in his strength; you find a divine shining in your conscience. "In his light you see light." It comes with such divine penetration that it appears to ransack the whole soul, and all things appear in very deed to be different from what they were before.   Then you know something of what it is to be brought out of the kingdom of darkness into the kingdom of God's dear Son; and that is a solemn translation.

Remember, then, poor child of God, that this blessed Christ that is "come in the flesh," is come to be thy deliverance; he is come to be thy sanctification; he is come to be thy life and thy light; he is come to be thy strength and thy succour and thy support; he is come to be thy hiding-place from every storm and from every tempest; he is come to stand betwixt holy Justice and thee, and to present thee to God complete in himself; to strip thee of all idols, and to bring thee bare, naked, empty, vile, polluted, foolish, ignorant, and condemned, to the foot of the cross. Is God's Christ thus manifested in you? Have you had a little of this sweetness in your conscience? O what solemn moments they have been! For you have been led then to say, "Bless the Lord, O my soul, and all that is within me, bless his holy name; who forgiveth all thine iniquities, who healeth all thy diseases, who redeemeth thy life from destruction, who crowneth thee with loving-kindness and tender mercies!" In this blessed Christ is all law can require, justice demand, God give, or a sinner need. He gives thee a title to heaven and a meetness for it, and will convey thee safely to it, and crown thee when thou art there.   It is Christ "all and in all." You want no other. If ever God the Spirit reveals this, you will say, "It is enough."

This is the Christ that is "come in the flesh;" and you are to "try the spirits" of men by this rule. If they preach any thing, easy or hard, save the Lamb and his blood, lay any other foundation, proclaim any other deliverer, set forth any thing, however pious or good it may appear in itself, to present the sinner before God but this Christ, and the Spirit of the Lord manifesting this Christ in the conscience, it is antichrist. Reject it, abhor it; it is the soul of Popery. Creature merit, creature works, and creature worthiness in matters of salvation,—this is the life and soul and spirit of Popery. The life and soul and spirit of Christianity is—God in Christ, and Christ in us, and we in him; God and Christ and conscience brought together through the blood and obedience of Immanuel, by the invincible power of God the Spirit. This is what promotes the declarative honour of Christ, and supports the poor soul that is led by the Spirit into the life of God.

Now I shall conclude with a hint or two upon what has been said.

I charge you in the name of the living God, mind what you hear —mind who you hear. If a man comes and preaches a Christ *without* you, that is never formed *in* you and that you have never been brought from necessity to submit to, whose life and power you have never felt; and if the preacher endeavours to direct your attention from a feeling religion, and bolster you up with what he calls a Christ *without* you, and never unctuously preaches a Christ *in* you, the hope of glory, having him formed in your hearts as such, constraining you to cling to, hang upon, and live in him; whatever kind of tale he may tell you, reject him as you would reject the devil. It is not God's Christ; it is antichrist, and he would wrap you up in delusions, and cry, "Peace, peace," when God had not spoken peace. You may have your ears pleased, and your judgment fed; but your conscience is starved, and your soul is deceived. There is a solemn vitality in Christ in the heart. Without it, all our religion will dry up; but if we are brought to feel the necessity of hanging entirely upon Christ, to cling to him, with nothing but Christ to rest upon before God, and there find rest to our souls, then storms and tempests and hurricanes may come, but our anchorage is sure, and the cable shall never break; for it is a three-fold cord —the love of God the Father, God the Son, and God the Holy Ghost. Remember how God tells us, that there shall be false Christs and false teachers, "bringing in damnable heresies;" you must expect they will come to try you, and it becomes you to try them. Try them by their confession of "the coming of Christ in the flesh." Ask your conscience now what hope you had till God the Spirit gave you hope in Christ—what life and light you had till the Holy Ghost communicated life and light from Christ your living Head—what hope and love you have that does not come from Christ as revealed and shed abroad by God the Holy Ghost; and if men want to take you to something that is not this, abhor it with your whole soul as the spirit of Popery and antichrist.

As I said before, I consider there is very little else in our day but the spirit of Popery. I look among the Baptists (though I am a Baptist), they are going after it in shoals. There was a circular letter published last year, signed by the ministers of thirty-five Baptist churches in the midland counties of England; and what did they circulate? Why that the atonement is universal, and that every man has it in his power (wherever the Bible comes) to do that that is required to save his soul. I solemnly believe that not one man living, who can with his heart sign or sanction such a statement, has a particle of the life of God in his soul. They are all dead to God as sure as the devil is. It is antichrist; and whether Baptists or Church people or Independents or Methodists, I solemnly believe they are all going to hell, if God's grace does not save them; they are "in the gall of bitterness and the bond of iniquity." It is creature merit. But we know that his blessed Majesty said, "It is finished."

Holy Ghost! Repeat that word—"It is finished," in our hearts. Then we shall know something of God's Christ that is "come in the flesh," and that he has come into our hearts, as a proof of it, and led us to know something of his preciousness. May the Lord the Spirit blessedly apply his own Word, for Christ's sake.

THE SACRIFICE OF THANKSGIVING.

Preached on Lord's Day Morning, Nov. 1st, 1840, in Manchester.

"I will offer to thee the sacrifice of thanksgiving."—Ps. cxvi. 17.

UNDER the Jewish dispensation, God had appointed a variety of offerings and sacrifices for the Jews, under certain circumstances, to be attended to; and if you turn to Leviticus vii. you will find that the offering of the sacrifice of thanksgiving was to be accompanied with unleavened bread, mingled with oil, with wafers anointed with oil, and with cakes fried in oil. Now in reality, beloved, there is no sacrifice of thanksgiving without this oil; and it is not necessary merely that the wafers should be anointed with oil, but that the fat of the offering should be mingled with oil. The figure imports the essential necessity of the Divine anointings of God the Spirit in the conscience, and the same anointings being made manifest in our external worship. Alas, brethren! If you or I examine the various branches of our external worship and professions of thanksgiving, where do we find the oil? There may be the tongue, there may be the judgment and the bodily exercise; but where is the oil? If there be no oil in our worship, whether betwixt God and the conscience, whether in our families in private or in the public assembly of God's saints, if there be no oil, there really is no true thanksgiving. And yet our God tells us that "he that offereth praise glorifieth him, and to him that ordereth his conversation aright he will show the salvation of God."

If I may be allowed this morning just to give a word of advice before I enter more particularly upon the subject, it will be that you would endeavour to cry to the Lord for oil, that both you and I may feel the solemn unction, the Divine anointings of God, all in all. I do not know anything that has tried me more for the last two days than that I should be suffered to come before you for the first time after this affliction* without oil. O Lord, forbid it! Whatever thou withholdest, graciously grant us the Divine oil and anointing of the Holy Spirit, that we may be led feelingly into the truth of the gospel of God, and feel its sweetness and unction in the heart.

I shall not attempt to give you many divisions, but just drop a hint or two:

I. That we have all *cause for thankfulness*, whether we are thankful or not.

II. That *God's people have more cause to be thankful* than the holy angels in heaven; for God has done more for them than he ever did or ever will do for the holy angels.

III. I shall give you a *short statement* of some little that God has lately *done for me*, to sanctify my affliction.

* This was the first sermon Mr. Gadsby preached after he broke his leg, on Sept. 14th, 1840.

I. Is there a poor sinner in this assembly who has not *cause for thankfulness?* Young men and young women, if you are kept in the path of morality and virtue, O what cause for thankfulness you have! Your nature is no more pure in itself than the youth that is dying with rottenness, and, to all appearance, likely to be damned. It is the Lord that preserves you. May the Lord make you feel it, and teach you to be thankful for it. And if he has kept you hitherto, may he lead you to be cautious, and humbly to seek his aid, to keep you in time to come. Alas! There are some present who tremble, whose consciences tell them they are guilty, and who are ready to say, "Then what cause have I to be thankful?" Why, that God does not cut you off in the midst of your transgressions, and say to you, "Young man, young woman, you have violated your conscience, and set yourself against your common understanding, to sin against me, and I will honour my justice in damning you for ever." He has spared you. And has he spared you, and you have nought to say? God forbid that it may be to fill up the measure of your wickedness! O come, blessed Spirit, with thy divine power, and bring the oil of life into their dead souls, if it be thy sovereign pleasure. Make them thankful that thou hast not given them their deserts; and may they be concerned to cry to thee for favour and preservation in time to come.

Young friends, harden not yourselves in sin. Be assured that the period will come when your sins will find you out. Then you must stand before God naked, exactly as you are, without disguise or covering.

But we have cause to be thankful for the common necessaries of life. Few of you, if any, are in that extravagant want and distress that numbers of your fellow-creatures are. And remember that numbers of those who are in the most agonising distress, want, and calamity are as good as you. No thanks, then, are due to you. Thanks are due to a kind, preventive God; to God's mercy that is over all his works. Perhaps some of you, in the stiffness of your hearts, and it is a stiff heart we have, will say, "I am more prudent, more economical, more industrious and cautious than many I see in extravagant distress." This may be true; but, instead of this pampering you up with pride, it calls for thankfulness. Who has made you prudent? Who keeps you prudent? The Lord. Sin has rendered us all mad, and there is not a prudent man in the world if God do not make him prudent; not one, if we were left to the workings of our corrupt hearts. There are no bounds to our folly but what God fixes; and, therefore, we have great and constant cause to be thankful for all the common necessaries of life. And we never shall enjoy a particle of the blessedness of becoming pensioners upon God till God makes us feel that, and feel it under need of a little oil. No. Then shall we bless him for all we enjoy more

than the damned in hell; for it is God's mercy that we have anything more, or are any way better, than they.

II. But *God's people*, called by Divine grace, made partakers of
the Divine nature, have great cause to be thankful *above all the rest;*
yea, above the angels in heaven. I do not know, but perhaps some
of you may think this rather extravagant; but I have been brought,
through the grace of God, to feel that I would not thank God to
make me an angel. I envy them not. If there are different races
and orders of angels in heaven, I do not envy,—when in such a
solemn frame of mind, with the oil of rejoicing in my heart, I do
not envy the highest rank of those adored beings. They are not sinners; but, as Hart very solemnly said,

> "If sinless innocence be theirs,
> Redemption all is ours."

O the riches of the love of God! The redemption of the soul by the
blood of the God-man-Mediator is all ours; and the angels cannot
even sip it. It is out of the reach of their pure lips and holy hearts;
but the Lord, in the riches of his grace, bestows that especial favour,
with all the blessings connected with it, upon the objects of his
precious choice, of his love, his own love.

Have you, my friends, been brought, as poor sinners, poor broken-
down sinners, to believe in the Lord Jesus Christ? Have we been
brought to cast our cares upon Christ, to feel a little measure of his
love and blood? O how amazing, then, how wonderfully amazing
the feeling, when sometimes we have been drawn up by the power
of God the Spirit to behold the glory of the workings of a faith
entering into the bosom and the love of the God-man, and saying,
" My Lord and my God!" How amazing! Reason is confounded;
even Unbelief is obliged to skulk away for a moment; but it is such
a devil it will soon come again; but it is obliged for a moment to
skulk away, while the soul has solemn, sweet, and blessed intercourse
with God in Christ Jesus. To speak of a millionth part of the
blessings that God's people have secured to them, which are causes
for thankfulness, we never can. Just let us drop a hint or two,
if we can, upon the suggestion, and then leave it.

First. Before God made the world, before a creature existed, his
loving heart wrapped the people of his choice in himself, and, by
an eternal, immutable, unalterable decree, fixed the eternal glory
of millions of millions that should live with him at last. And when
his blessed Spirit brings you and me to feel, by a vital faith, that
we are of that blessed number, does it not call for thankfulness?
" Why," say you, " do you think you can prove such a statement
as that from the Word of God?" Really, if I could not, I would as
soon have, not only another leg broken, but my neck broken into the
bargain, if that would put me out of existence entirely,—if I did not
believe such a truth as that. "Why," say you, "what comfort can

there be in that?" I will tell you. It is a cord of infinite strength, that ties the blessedness of believers so firmly to God's honour that God's honour and their degradation must, blessed be God, go together. If they sink into degradation, the Lord's honour must sink too. The Lord has coupled the church of the living God and his own honour; and the pages of the written Word have connected it with his own honour and glory, and "his glory he will not give to another." Now this blessed truth, therefore, is what the apostle triumphed in when he said, "Blessed be the God and Father of our Lord Jesus Christ, who hath blessed us with all spiritual blessings in heavenly places in Christ Jesus, before the foundation of the world." Again: "Who hath saved us and called us with a holy calling; not according to our works, but according to his own purpose and grace, which was given us in Christ Jesus, before the world began." O Lord, of thy mercy and grace to us, give our poor, lumpish souls a dead lift, and lead us solemnly and sweetly, by grace, into the mysteries of thy love, to taste the glory of God, as secured to us in Christ; and may we find a rest in our souls that the world can neither give nor take away. Well, now, connect with this that the Lord has given his Son to be a propitiation for us. Believers, if you can forget your poverty, and come to your stock,—I do not mean the stock you are keeping of your good deeds, for that is not a bit better than lumber and rags; it is only fuel for the fire, and I should like to see it all in flames; and yet I am such a fool that I often get another stock of lumber ready for God to burn up. Lord, what fools we are! What a wonderful thing it is, after the working of God in our souls, that we should be such fools as to gather such lumber together, which brings to us so much pain and anxiety. But what I mean is that stock of treasure laid up in Christ. There is immortal life; there is immortal holiness; there s immortal grace; out of the reach of sin; out of the reach of death, or hell, or Satan. All the vomitings up of the filth of our guilty nature cannot drown it. No, blessed be God, it cannot. I have proved that; and the sea of love and blood secured in the obedience of Christ is a crown of consolation for the church of God in the mids of their trouble. And surely it calls for gratitude and thankfulness

"But," say you, "I am such a fool; such a poor, weak, helpless, worthless sinner." If you were not, I would not give you my spectacles for your religion. That a poor, weak, worthless sinner cannot be saved is the devil's invention to deceive souls, and wrap them up in strong delusions; to insult Christ, and to dishonour the revelation that God has made of his Son. But the poor, the needy, the loathsome, and the lost are just fit for Christ, and Christ is just fitted for them; and God fits them together; and there is not a better fit in being. And when the blessed Spirit does put Christ in us and us in Christ, fits us together with the bonds of love, and anoints us with oil, O what a sacrifice of thanksgiving there is then! All the powers of the soul have been drawn sweetly and solemnly into exercise, and we are able feelingly to say, "Bless the Lord, O my soul, and all that is within me, bless his holy name; who forgiveth all thine iniquities, who healeth all thy diseases, and who crowneth thy life with loving-kindness and tender mercies."

Secondly. In this blessed gift of Christ there is strength for the weak; but there would be no need for it if there were no weak folks to be found. Here is wisdom for fools; but if all the fools were out of the world, what must the Lord do with his wisdom? Here is holiness for the unholy; for he "is made of God unto us sanctification." But if all men were holy, then he might keep his holiness to himself, for we should not want it. Here is fulness for the empty; but if there were no hungry souls, of what use would be Christ's fulness? God shall "supply all your need, according to his riches in glory by Christ Jesus." Poor, burdened, dejected, cast-down, broken-hearted, worn-out sinner, as God is God, it is all thine. God help thee to believe it, and to receive it under the Divine unction and anointing of the Holy Spirit; that thou mayest then have mingled with the cake of the offering the holy oil, and offer thanksgiving to God in spirit and in truth; that so you may know the blessedness of vital religion, and worship the Lord in the beauty of holiness.

III. But I must leave this part of my subject, and just take up a few minutes in relating a little of the dealings of the Lord with myself. And the first thing I must do, shameful as it may appear, must be to criminate myself before you all. I had made up my mind for more than a month before this providence took place, that I would spend a few days at Buxton, in what we call a holiday. I had proved, it is true, that the bathing and the air of Buxton had done my poor old hobbling carcase a deal of good, and, therefore, I expected it would again; but, at all events, I determined to try it. And, therefore, I made up my mind that whoever might write, and however urgent they might be for me to go and preach, I would go nowhere that week; I would have a pleasure and a holiday; and no one nor any set of people should dissuade me from it. So that I was quite as fixed as man could be. You know well that the day before, which was the Lord's day, I was at Oldham. A friend was to go with me to Buxton, and I left it with him to engage our places in a coach that left at two o'clock on the Monday, as I should get home in time to get a few things ready, and call at his house for him, or meet him at the coach office. So I came; and really I cannot see at this moment any real reason why I came off but to break my leg. It appeared that so God had ordered it. I know some people have said my leg was not broken; but I do not think them worth powder and shot; and all I shall say is, if their jaw-bone were broken as much as my leg, they would say a little less; and here I leave them. But I came home, and I found that my friend had sent word that there was no room in the coach. So I posted away my servant-girl instantly to tell him that there was another coach which went a little afterwards. When she was gone, I said, "If that is full, I will take it for granted that God does not mean me to go." I went up stairs, stripped off my coat, put another on, and went into the garden, and there saw a friend who had been doing a little job for me. I asked him what it would be. I came into the house for the money, and paid him, and then went into the garden; and, to cut the matter short, my leg slipped under me and caught against a side-flag; my whole body fell upon it, and I heard it break just like a stick. I had never sat down in the house. It appears evident that the design of the Lord was that I should come home for that very purpose, to break my leg. And the Lord and I had evidently agreed in this one thing, that I should have a holiday; only we were not agreed as to the place where and the means how. I meant a holiday at Buxton, like a gentleman; and God meant at home, with a broken leg. There was the difference between the Lord and me; but, at the same time, so kind has the Lord been that I have blessed him for his choice since then, and felt satisfied that it was infinitely preferable to mine, and I could not murmur or grumble against the dispensation of God.

The first thing that struck my mind and that I said to myself, as soon as I fell, and found that I could not move, was this, "God would have done right if he had broken your neck." "O, then," say you, "you must be a wicked creature." Yes, the Lord knows I am; but I am a sinner saved by grace. Devils tremble, the Lord is honoured, Christ is glorified, and my soul is filled with joy. "But why should you imagine that it would have served you right if the Lord had broken your neck?" Well, I will tell you. I began to reflect in a moment that my intended journey to Buxton was a job of my own, and I never asked leave of God. I had never consulted him in prayer, or at least very little upon the subject; and, therefore, the Lord was determined to let me know that he loved me too well to let my pride carry me anywhere without the guidance of the Lord. And O what a mercy it is when God brings us to feel our own wickedness, when we have sought him in prayer, and when he leads us to feel, at the same time, his tender compassion towards us. Well, his blessed Majesty was graciously pleased to bring the sweet text to my mind, after I was laid in my bed: "The mercy of the Lord is from everlasting to everlasting;" and I never saw and never felt more glory in the mercy of the Lord in my life. His mercy, in the solemn opening of his love in a covenant of grace, in the Divine operations of the Holy Spirit, was opened in such a glorious way to my soul that I felt a sweet, a solemn giving up of self and a bathing in the flood of the love and blood of the God-man Mediator, Christ Jesus. No waters, no air of Buxton, could be like those glorious, those heavenly waters, those Divine breezes, when God's Spirit filled me with love and joy unspeakable, under a feeling sense of the mercy, the atonement, and the everlasting love of our covenant God.

By and by my mind began a little to decline, and I began to tremble and wonder where it would end. At length my whole attention appeared to be interested in Heb. xii. 11: "Now no chastening for the present seemeth joyous, but grievous; nevertheless, afterward it yieldeth the peaceable fruit of righteousness unto them who are exercised thereby." The text dwelt in my mind, especially the words, "Nevertheless, afterward it yieldeth the peaceable fruit of righteousness." "Why," said I, "there are tens of thousands who are chastened in various ways. Their property goes, their strength goes; they are brought into a great variety of trials; and yet no fruits of righteousness arise." But then it arrested my mind, "It is God's people that are intended in the verse." "Well, true," said I; "but I cannot help hoping that I am a child of God; yet I have been afflicted myself in a variety of ways, and it has yielded no peaceable fruits of righteousness in me." I began at home, and recollected a number of instances in which I had been afflicted, in body and circumstances, and I could not recollect any peaceable fruits of righteousness arising therefrom. And I remembered that others of God's people besides me had been just the same, and have come out of affliction just as they went in. If anything has been yielded, it has been some rebellion of heart against God; but no "peaceful fruits of righteousness." Yet the text says, without any equivocation, that the affliction is afterward to yield the peaceable fruits of righteousness. How is it, Lord? Must it be solemn, sweet joy, or are they impostors that are afflicted, and no peaceable fruits of righteousness are afterwards yielded to them? I prayed and cried, and prayed and cried again, that God, in his mercy, would open the passage to my soul, and lead me into it. I searched other branches of Scripture to see if I could find the key; and I found some that staggered me almost as much as that: "Blessed is the man whom thou chastenest." "Well," said I, "this seems as positive as the other. How is it?" At length I believe the Lord solemnly broke into my poor heart, let me a little into the mystery of the text, and let me feel that a deal of the marrow of it is couched in the last two words, "exercised thereby." "Lord, I see it now!" We may have affliction, and no discipline; we may have affliction, and yet never be exercised thereby. We may be like a boy taking a little firelock and putting on a soldier's garments; but by and by he strips it off again, and is just where he was. He has never been drilled; he has never been exercised; and, therefore, he is just where he was. And so it is with those who are

afflicted. I was led to see for myself that sometimes the Lord
suffers afflictions of a variety of natures to come upon us, and we
wear them just as a person may wear a soldier's garments; yet we
are not drilled or exercised. We learn no discipline from them; and,
therefore, they leave us hard, careless, cold, and mad-brained, just
as they found us. Here is no exercise. Then I was led a little
further, and a solemn feeling I had at this time. There is no real
fruit of righteousness without spiritual exercise, and there is no spiritual exercise unless God be the Exerciser. You may make what
you will of it; but I was led to the feeling that God is condescending to be the Commander-in-Chief, to command afflictions, and to
govern them, and rule them, and exercise his people thereby. And I
could like to bring him down to a drilling-sergeant, to drill us again
and again, until we are made into good and obedient soldiers,
marching uprightly, and that when his blessed Majesty called upon
us, and our own corrupt nature resisted, he paid no attention to our
groanings under it, but went on to hunt us out of self to himself.
When this is the case, there is the peaceable fruit of righteousness;
and without that exercise, the Lord himself working in it, with it,
and by it, there really will be no real fruits of righteousness produced. But when that is the case, it does away with self-confidence and self-hope, opens the mysteries of the cross of Christ, and
brings our souls to a solemn, sweet, and blessed deep feeling of the
Lord our God, the fruits of the love and blood of Christ springing
up in the soul, and we adore God for the affliction.

I speak that I know, and set forth a little of the love and truth
of God to a poor, perishing sinner, like myself.

Well, after a sweet and solemn enjoyment of this truth, my comfortable feelings appeared to go. One thing or another that I had
to cross me, that I cannot state, worked upon my very nature, and
I began to kick and to rebel again. O, brethren! If God were not
to exercise us, we should kick ourselves into hell after all. What
a mercy it is that he has commanded; is it not? What a mercy
that he does not leave our poor nature to itself. In this fit of rebellion and kicking against the dispensation of God, the Lord was
pleased to bring this text with power to my mind: "It is hard for
thee to kick against the pricks." I felt it; I fell under it; and
with solemn freedom I said, "Ah, Lord, it is hard to kick against
the pricks, *especially with a broken leg!*" There was I. Prior to
that, I was kicking against the Lord, and he made it evident that I
was kicking against the goads; but his blessed Majesty was graciously pleased to bring a heavenly calm and serenity into my soul,
and I was led once again into the sweet and blessed enjoyment of
the mysteries of the cross of Christ.

"Ah," say you, "I would not be such a fool as to be moved about
like that." But you never were tried. Do not talk about it. Let

a man be brought to feel it, and then he will know that he can only enjoy this as the Spirit is given to him; not a bit more. It comes from the Lord, and the Lord must have the glory.

Well, after that, I came into such a dead, cold frame of mind that I said to myself, "I hope none of the folks will come to see me;" and every time I heard the bell, I was glad it was a beggar, and none of you coming to try me and probe me; for I felt such a poor wretch that I could say nothing but what would be to my own dishonour and your distress.

But to sum it all up in a few words. After all these changes, I live a monument of the mercy of God; and now solemnly declare that I have been brought to adore God for the dispensation. I believe the Lord has prevented something or other that I should have done, I cannot say what; but perhaps I should have been getting into some more lumber, and the Lord has prevented me, and brought me to some sweet and solemn enjoyment of the mysteries of the love of God, to lead me to salvation, and to taste of the grace, the free grace of God. Every principle that would make it conditional in man, I hate as I do the devil; because God, in the riches of his grace, has brought me so solemnly to feel that it is all a rich, precious teeming out of the love of God.

May the Lord bless you and me with the oil of joy, that we may be thankful to God for his mercies towards us unto this day.

THE SENTENCE OF DEATH IN OURSELVES.

Preached on Sunday Evening, May 9th, 1841, in Gower Street Chapel.

" But we had the sentence of death in ourselves, that we should not trust in ourselves, but in God which raiseth the dead."—2 Cor. i. 9.

In the fourth verse the apostle says, " Who comforteth us in all our tribulation, that we may be able to comfort them which are in any trouble, by the comfort wherewith we ourselves are comforted of God." Now I have been there in some solemn measure in my conscience; and sometimes I have been there not very pleasingly, and sometimes more pleasingly. My flesh and blood, at times, have murmured to think I must go deeply into certain conflicts, certain tribulations, certain distresses, certain miseries, both within and without, to be an instrument in God's hand of leading some hobbling soul in the same hobbling hole; and I have been ready to say to the Lord, "Lord, I think I have enough to do with my own troubles, without being plagued with other people's;" and thus insult the Lord, instead of taking it kindly in him that he should make me the instrument of comforting his family. But at times, when the Lord has been pleased to appear in a sweet and blessed way, I really have been enabled to give God leave to put me where he will, and do what he will with me, so that it may but be the means of leading his poor, tried people in *their* temptations, and thus comforting "them which are in any trouble, by the comfort wherewith we ourselves are comforted of God."

"For as the sufferings of Christ abound in us, so our consolation also aboundeth by Christ." Now did you ever enter into the spirit of that text, that it is "through much tribulation we must enter the kingdom?" It does not appear to me that it really means only people going *to heaven* through tribulation; but I believe in my conscience we never get spiritually, feelingly, blessedly, and God-glorifyingly into *any branch* of God's blessed kingdom, but through tribulation. The mysteries of the Gospel of God are suited to the various conflicts and trials of his people; and when God is about to reveal any special blessing, any special, manifested mercy to his children, there is always some conflict or other connected with it. I have proved it in my own experience, that it has either been to prepare the mind for some trouble, support it in some trouble, deliver it out of some trouble, or in some way or other there has been trouble connected with it; and I really would not give a "Thank you" for any man's religion, if it is not connected with trouble. And yet my fleshly heart will sometimes tell God that I want no more trouble. But then he will not believe me, nor act upon it. God, in the riches of his grace, sees to it that we shall have conflicts, internal and external; and the more we slip, the deeper those conflicts shall be. And then God sends consolations,—consolations greater than the miseries; and we are brought to feel the blessedness of the salvation of God, in the rich openings of it, as suited to our condition; and he is glorified therein. I believe an untried minister may preach his people up to a condition of presumptuous confidence; but their consciences will be as dry as these candlesticks. If there be no conflict, if there be no trial, there will be no dew there. There must be trials and perplexities; and it is in them that mercy rejoices over judgment, and the soul is brought to enter spiritually into God's glory, and to know that the comforts and consolations of the gospel are suited to the condition of the church in their various trials; and God is glorified thereby.

"And whether we be afflicted, it is for your consolation and salvation." What! Must the apostles be afflicted for the consolation and salvation of the church? I felt a little of this in my last affliction; and I thought, "Lord, I am suffering; but why should I murmur and grumble? Perhaps thou hast some wise end in this." And I believe he had; and I was brought to see that it was the design and will and purpose of God to bring me into such places, both in body and mind, as to make a way for God to open the mysteries of his love and grace to me, that I might carry a little of the tidings of the goodness and love of God to poor, hobbling sinners. When I am in a right mind, there are none in the world I feel so much agreement with as poor, hobbling sinners. As for those who can help themselves, I have nothing to do with them, and do not want to have; but when I find those who can do nothing, who are altogether dependent upon the Lord, I feel a blessed union of soul with them.

"Which is effectual in the enduring of the same sufferings which we also suffer." I know how you go on (at least how my people go on, and I believe you are all alike). Sometimes you are ready to think the minister gets rather dry, and then you secretly pray, perhaps, that God will bring him into trouble. You never dream that perhaps *you* are dry, and that God must bring *you* into trouble. No, no; none of that. It is the poor minister who is to have all the trouble and you must have all the profit. But God overrules you; and he brings the minister into trouble and brings you into trouble; and his trouble and your trouble and his consolation and your consolation bring you into a blessed oneness; and so you are led to glorify God's method of opening his love and mercy and consolation to your souls.

"And our hope of you is steadfast; knowing that as ye are partakers of the sufferings, so shall ye also be of the consolation." Why, it is so, brethren. We feel a sweetness sometimes in the matter before God, that these poor, tried, troubled, and helpless creatures will by and by come away with the sweet, unctuous enjoyment of the consolations of the Gospel of God, and that we and they shall meet together to crown the brow of God in the world to come, and to show forth his praise for ever and for ever. And therefore we have this "hope," and a "steadfast" one too.

"For we would not, brethren, have you ignorant of our trouble, which came to us in Asia, that we were pressed out of measure, above strength, insomuch that we despaired even of life." Now even in a bodily sense they were "pressed out of measure, above strength;" aye, and in a mental sense too, in a soul sense. There are times and seasons when the child of God, when the minister of Christ, is so "pressed out of measure" in the conflict of his mind that he has no more manifest strength to support himself than he has to hold up the world; and he is obliged to sink; and he wants strength to *sink*. It really appears sometimes to me that he can neither walk nor stand still, nor sit still; he seems as if hung upon nothing. And how it is that he does not sink into black despair, he sometimes stands amazed before God. And thus he is in a variety of ways "pressed out of measure."

But eventually the matter appears, agreeably to God's Word, to the consolation of his people. And the apostle tells us in the next verse how it is: "We had the sentence of death in ourselves, that we should not trust in ourselves, but in God which raiseth the dead."

Now let us just endeavour,

I. To look at this *sentence of death in ourselves.*

II. *The design* God has in view in it; which is, to cure us of self-trust: "That we should not trust in ourselves."

III. Well, then, is he to leave us in black dispair? No; but eventually to bring us to *trust "in God* which raiseth the dead."

I. I would just notice that sometimes when God begins a work of grace in the heart of a poor sinner, and especially if that sinner is young, he brings the *sentence of death* upon all the poor creature's earthly pursuits, earthly joys, and earthly prospects. There may be a young man, or a young woman, just springing up into life, so as to begin to look about them for greater prospects; and the principal concern for a while is to see how they shall manage to make their fortune in the world, how they shall manage to go on with what the world calls great respectability; and just as they are laying their plans, God sends the sentence of death into their souls and slaughters all their prospects and plans. They had imagined that they had a little foresight and a little wisdom, and perhaps looked upon some others with a degree of astonishment that they should be such fools and not manage things better; they themselves have laid their plans with a good understanding, and no doubt but they shall be prosperous. God mows them all down. God slaughters the wretch, makes him into a fool, a mere fool; and he feels before God that he has not wisdom to direct his steps for a single moment. And now he is confounded and wonders where this will end. And it is thus, while things are just springing up into pleasing appearances, whatever state he may be in, that when God quickens his dead soul he sends the sentence of death into his conscience upon all his creature enjoyments. If the man is living in carnal pleasure and prospering, as he thinks, in the pursuit of it, the sentence of death comes into it,—mars it all, spoils all. Terror, misery, despair hunt him out of all his creature enjoyments and all his fleshly pursuits. Sometimes he thinks he will struggle against this; he will drown it in some vain amusements of the world. Perhaps he takes himself to the play-house, to some merry company, to some amusement, with a view to drown this perplexity and confusion of mind that he feels. And God goes there too. "Why," say you, "you do not think that God goes to the playhouse?" Aye, many a time, and to dancing-houses too, when he has a poor sinner there that he is determined to bring under the sentence of death. He goes to mar the creature's comfort. While the man goes to drown his guilty fears, God goes to send a fresh spring, to make them rise higher. And the poor creature concludes that all his happiness and all his enjoyment are gone for ever, and that there is nothing but misery for him. In whatever station of life he is, the sentence of death is passed upon it all.

And if he has been a person brought up in what they call religion; if he has had religious instruction and his judgment is pretty well stored with religious knowledge, so that he can talk about election, predestination, redemption, final perseverance, and all the leading truths of the gospel, and is ready to think that, owing to the judgment that he has, though there must be some little change, it need not be very conspicuous, because he knows so much already and has got so far on in knowledge;—if ever God begins a work of grace in that poor sinner's heart, he will make him into a mere fool. All his knowledge will give way; the sentence of death will come upon him; and he will find, instead of his knowledge being of any real service when God sends his quickening Spirit and gives him divine life, it only seems to puzzle him, to confuse him. And perhaps there is some poor soul here this night who wishes he had never known a word about truth till God had been pleased to quicken him; for he is ready to conclude that all he has is what he knew before, and that he has no real vitality; he wishes he had never had a particle of knowledge about it. And thus comes the sentence of death upon all his knowledge and all his understanding of religious things; as it is said, "That we should not trust in ourselves, but in God which raiseth the dead."

But by and by, whatever our state may be when the Lord takes us in hand and quickens us by his Spirit, and brings a sentence of death upon all our worldly prospects and enjoyments, anon he gives us a little feeling after mercy, a little breathing after pardon and manifested salvation; and then most likely a legal feeling begins to induce us to rest in this feeling after mercy and this breathing after salvation, to take satisfaction there, so as not to be looking for any more. Now if you are endeavouring to walk there, as sure as there is a living God, the sentence of death will come upon that. This is a trusting in your breathings and pantings rather than any real thirsting for that which cannot die,—the life of God; and, therefore, the sentence of death shall come upon it; and you will be brought perhaps by and by to such a state that you cannot breathe after mercy, you cannot pant for mercy, you cannot feel a thirsting for God; and you wonder what is the matter now. All seems to go wrong now. You did have a little hope some short time ago, when you could have a little breathing and feeling and panting after God; but that is gone, that is sunk; and you feel as if you had no feeling. If you have any feeling at all, it is to feel that you have no feeling, that you are a kind of dead weight, and that you sink under it, and cannot revive your soul. And thus you have the sentence of death in yourself, that you should not trust in yourself, but in God that raiseth the dead.

Now, however, the Lord, in the riches of his grace and mercy, is pleased to come with his reviving power, and put it into your heart to be vehement with God in prayer; for whatever you may think, there is such a thing as being mighty in prayer. It is not the idea of doing your duty, a duty religion, being "pious." Merely doing your duty is a mere fleshly religion altogether. There is a solemn vitality in the mysteries of the cross of Christ; and the poor soul is brought to be vehement and agonizing with God, sometimes in a state of desperation, and is ready to cry out as in agony, "O Lord, undertake for me; for I am ruined. O Lord, if it be possible, save me; for I am undone." And he feels what he says, and says what he feels; he is brought from real necessity to be violent in praying about his soul to God, and knows something of the kingdom of heaven suffering violence; though he cannot at present feelingly say that "the violent take it by force."

Now almost beyond doubt the enemy will be ready to say, "Ah! Now, as you have been so vehement, so powerful in your prayers, you may expect a blessing. You have now, as it were, tired the Lord; he is sure to come *now.*" Do you not see how artful, how detestably artful the enemy is, to blunt the edge of prayer and to bring you to some creature trust, instead of looking to the Lord for all you have and all you are that is above nature? As sure as ever you get *there,* this vehemence will go. You will find you cannot pray mightily or vehemently. And then you become so wretched that at length you are obliged to say, "Lord, what am I? I can neither pray nor let it alone, neither believe nor disbelieve, neither hope nor do anything that is worthy of a sinner who needs help. All I can really say of myself is that I am a mass, a dead mass, of stinking pollution. That is all I am and all I have in self and of self." Well, the sentence of death has come upon all your self-trust,—your religious self as well as your profane self; and this is making way for God's blessed salvation, in a way according to the mysteries of his everlasting love.

But anon the Lord is pleased, perhaps, to reveal pardon. I recollect the time when God was pleased to reveal pardon in my poor soul at first. O what sweetness and solemnity and blessedness there was in my poor heart! I sang night and day the wonders of his love; and I never dreamed but I should go singing all the way to heaven. I never expected to hang my harp upon the willows, or even to find it out of tune. But, alas! alas! The harp *was* afterwards out of tune; and it wanted God to string it; I could not put it in tune. It is when the Lord the Spirit comes that he teaches the soul how to sing the wonders of his love. I could see afterwards how my poor soul had been led on. I had had a zeal for God, but it was grounded in self; and I had felt God's free love come to my soul as a matter of free favour, but there was self at bottom thinking, " I will keep this, and cultivate it, and bring it more and more to maturity, till I grow up into such spiritual enjoyment that there will not be one in the neighbourhood who shall excel me." And I really was sincere; but then this was the sincerity of self; for if it had not been self-sincerity, it would not have put in this *I* —the great *I*—what *I* will be and what *I* will do. Whenever it comes to this, poor child of God, whenever you begin to swell with your great *I*, what *I* will do and what *I* will not do, depend upon it, death is at the door; there will be something that will bring the sentence of death upon all your comfortable feelings and enjoyments.

I could tell you how it brought me to lose my sweet enjoyment, or rather to have it removed. I have thought very blessedly sometimes of that sentence of the Lord by the apostle John: " I have somewhat against thee, because thou has left thy first love." He does not say lost it, but left it. No, thanks be to God, it is not lost; it is secured in our blessed Christ; but we go from it in our feelings. The fact is, I was amazingly zealous. I was a youth between 17 and 18 years of age, and very moderate in my living; and I looked upon anyone that conducted himself with any degree of immoderation (or what they called moderation) as proving that they had not vital godliness. Two old men I cut off entirely; one for going to sleep in prayer, and the other because he told me that he should not wonder if I became intoxicated that week; it was in the fair-time. "For," said he, "you seem so lifted up with your power to keep from it; and the only thing in your favour is that you do not like it;" for I did not like liquors then. I looked at the poor old man as an old hypocrite. "What! *I* get intoxicated, when God has been so gracious as to stop me in my mad career, and give me pardon, and a sweet, conscious enjoyment of it!" I could not believe it; and I could not believe he had the life of God in his heart; because he could think it possible. And so I went singing on. But before the week was out, there was poor I, intoxicated! Ah! How dreadful I became in my feelings! I must tell you that I did not take anything you would think was drinking to excess; for I had only had one three-halfpenny worth of stuff. But there, all my comfort was gone and enjoyment gone. Then I thought, one night, I would put out my light and go upon my knees by my bedside, and never cease praying all that night until God pardoned me. You see there was a little *I* still. So on my knees I went with a determination to pray all night. Some time in the morning I awoke, and found I had been asleep on my knees; and so there was poor *I*, who had cut off one poor old man for going to sleep in prayer and another for saying he should not wonder if I got intoxicated, actually getting intoxicated, and going to sleep in prayer myself into the bargain. *There* was the sentence of death upon all my joy and all my comfort; and for several months after that, I walked in the very depth of agony and distress, such as I

could never describe; so much so that if any child of God came into
my company who knew the preciousness of Christ, I believed they
would see it directly we began to converse, and go and tell all the
people in the village (for I knew everybody, and they knew me), and
that I should go wandering about like Cain with a mark upon me; and
so I kept out of their company.   And then the enemy of souls would
come in : "Where is your peace with God *now?*   Where is your power
in prayer *now?*   Where is your meekness, your humility, and your
tenderness of conscience *now?*   Where is your hope in the Lord *now?*
Where is your trust in the God of Israel *now?*   And where are *you?*"
"Ah! Lord," I was obliged to say, "I do not know where I am, nor
what I am, nor what the end will be."   The sentence of death was
passed upon the whole.   And, perhaps, here is some poor soul who
really has had the sentence of death upon all he has had and all he has
enjoyed, upon all he has done and all he thought he was capable of
doing.   "Well," say you, "that is just my case."   Then if you have
passed through this path and had your hopes of a religious nature (as
far as they have been formed in flesh) all cut off, and the sentence of
death has come upon you and mowed you down and rooted you up,
and made you feel as dry as the bones in Ezekiel's vision, I believe he
will come in his own blessed time, and that the sentence of death is
bound upon you that you may not trust in yourself, but be brought
feelingly and spiritually to trust in the living God.

But even after the Lord has delivered you, self works up in a variety
of ways : "Now I will be more watchful; I will be more cautious and
tender; I will not be so rash.   I will keep my eyes open, and my ears
open, and my heart open to the truth, and I will walk more circum-
spectly and steadily, that I may not again bring the sentence of death
upon my joys and my peace, and that I may not again get into this
trouble."   Well; for a little time, perhaps, you maintain it; perhaps
not a week.   You begin to be incautious; you get into company, perhaps, and a light and trifling spirit comes over you, and you let out a
few light and trifling words; and those words come like daggers to
your heart and strike you to death.   The sentence of death is upon
you again.   And thus you go on, from time to time; and the sentence
comes upon all your hopes and expectations that spring from self in
any bearings of it whatever.

But by and by you get to what you think a sweeter frame of mind
than this.   You have some sweet peace and heavenly joy, some blessed
intercourse with the Father and the Son and the Holy Spirit, some
divine springings up of love and of patience.   Then God puts you into
circumstances to try your patience; and you take it patiently too,
meekly and resignedly, as it becomes you.   You also give some demonstrative proof that the fear of God awes you and draws you, that
you really do act more as becomes a child of God, and that there is
more tenderness of conscience maintained.   And now, if you are not

led by the Spirit of God to beware, you will begin to trust in this tenderness of conscience and patience and meekness of yours.

Really, brethren, I hardly know how to decide the matter; for I feel it very difficult to maintain a distinction in my own conscience, betwixt being satisfied without feeling and making feeling my trust. I believe an unfeeling religion is the devil's own religion, and is not the religion of the Son of God; and yet to put trust in the feelings rather than in the God whence they come, is insulting the Spring-head, insulting the Fountain. But we are as prone, in some of our sweet feelings, to put a little trust and confidence in our feelings as we are to breathe. And then the Lord takes these feelings away, and we have none to trust. Then the enemy tells us it has all been a delusion, all a deception, and we have no real, vital godliness; for if we had and these feelings had been real, we should have remained in them. Perhaps I am speaking in the ears of some who "know they are not going to be such crazy fools as that; they have more sense." Let me tell you God's people's religion is not a common-sense religion; they cannot move on by a common sense religion. They find it has the sentence of death in it, and they sink under it, because there is no ground of rest in it. And so, perhaps, they go to the Lord, and say, "Lord, how is it? I really wish to love thee and to live in thy fear; I desire to honour thee. I want to have my mind stayed upon thy precious, manifested mercy. I should not like to degrade the religion that I profess, nor to bring reproof upon thy Name; and, dear Lord, thou knowest I cannot be happy without having some sweet moments of intercourse with thee. How is it, then, that I should be so barren and cold, so hard and wandering, and that all my comforts and sweet feelings seem to go, and I am left to be in such a cold and indifferent frame?" Have you never been there? If you have not, I know who has; and the Lord has come with such a passage as this: "Trust in the Lord, and do good; so shalt thou dwell in the land, and verily thou shalt be fed." Or, "They that trust in the Lord shall be as Mount Zion, which cannot be moved." "Blessed is the man that trusteth in the Lord." "Cursed be the man that trusteth in man and maketh flesh his arm." Why, this staggers us. "Lord," we say, "what is it to trust in thee? I should like to trust in thee; I want to trust in thee; tell me what it is. Did I not trust in thee, Lord, when I enjoyed thy presence and felt the power of thy love; when my soul was satisfied with the love and blood of the dear Redeemer, and I poured out my soul to him? Tell me, Lord, what it is to trust in thee, and enable me to do it; for I want to trust in thee." And then, perhaps, such a portion as our text will come: "We have the sentence of death in ourselves, that we should not trust in ourselves, but in God which raiseth the dead;" and God begins to explain the mystery,—that though all those sweet frames, sweet feelings, sweet manifestations of mercy were his work, our trusting in them was the work of self; and the Lord will cut off this arm of self, and let us have no self of ours to bring before him, and thus make us know that our rest is in the Lord, as the God of salvation, and our boast in his confidence and not our own. And so "we have the sentence of death in ourselves, that we should not trust in ourselves."

II. But we shall pass on to notice *the design*,—that this is to cut us off from all our self-trust.

"Why, then," say you, "does it not make us miserable?" Miserable! Why, suppose you were a skilful surgeon, and went to see a patient, and the patient's complaint was of that nature that it led him to deceptive views, and that he needed some painful operation to cure him. The operation would not be pleasant; but there is a needs-be for it. There are deceptive views,—I had almost said a state of derangement; and they need some very painful operations sometimes to cure them. And so, blessed be our God, he knows what poor, deranged creatures we are, and what false views we have, and what false movements we make; and, as Hart says in one of his hymns, we   "Make e'en grace a snare."
We turn to a wrong use the revelation God makes of his love, and, instead of trusting in the Lord, put our trust in our own management of what the Lord has done in us. And indeed I do not wonder at this being the case with some of God's people; for the ministers tell them they must do it,—they must cultivate faith, and cultivate love, and cultivate hope, and cultivate confidence. When I hear men talk in this way, it sounds to me as though a farmer were to take a piece of barren ground in hand, and when he had brought his plough and his manure and harrow upon it, and begun to knock about and spread his manure, and so cultivate the land, some one were to get up and say to the land, "You must cultivate the plough; you must cultivate the harrow; you must cultivate the manure." Why, would you not think the man crazy? It is the plough and the manure and the harrow that are to cultivate the land. And so it is our God that by the communication of his love to the conscience by the power of the Spirit is to cultivate our barren souls; and he will make, he says, the desert to rejoice and blossom as the rose. It is the Lord's grace that is to cultivate us. And when we begin to cultivate, instead of submitting to God's cultivation, why, then the sentence of death must come upon it, "that we should not trust in ourselves, but in God that raiseth the dead."

I do not know whether you have felt it or not; but I solemnly have felt, in hundreds of instances, that I need this sentence of death to keep me from self-trust,—as a minister and in every stage that I have passed through in life. Sometimes I have been prone to think, "Now I have so many passages of Scripture turned down that have been very sweet to me when I have been reading them. I have them ready to preach from; I can turn to one of them when I choose, and go with my text and subject made ready, in order that the people may be benefited." And when I have gone, there has been the sentence of death upon me; not a passage that would fit me, not a passage that I could fit. All my cultivation would not bring one passage into my conscience, nor my conscience into one passage. I have been as deathly and cold and unable to lay hold of a single passage of God's Word to come before the people with as I was the first moment that I was brought to speak in his Name; and sometimes I have been ready to think that I never did speak anything, and never shall be able. And I have to go, groaning and sighing and panting and crying; and what is worse than that, at times I really cannot groan, nor sigh, nor pant, nor cry. "O," say you, "you must be a queer creature indeed." Indeed I am; and that is just *what* I am; so that I can neither trust myself for praying, nor trust myself for preaching, nor trust myself for hoping, nor trust myself for confidence. I often tell the Lord to keep and to be with me; "for, Lord, thou knowest that I am neither fit to be trusted with myself, nor trusted in company, nor trusted anywhere; and I can put no confidence in myself in any sense whatever."

Now, has the Lord brought you there? If he has, you have been necessarily weaned from self-trust. And yet you will get at it again. This cursed pride of ours, do what we may, will be making us in a measure pass by the Lord, and not trust in him. And all the cuttings up you have, all the harrowings of your feelings, all the death of your enjoyment and your comfort and your imaginary power to keep your peace and your happiness,—if you are a child of God, the Lord sees it all necessary to wean you from the cursed pride of trusting in yourselves, that there may be nothing but a sinner saved by the grace of God, and that Jesus may be glorified in the manifestation of his grace in saving your soul. And so we have the sentence of death in self, that we may not trust in self.

I tell you, brethren, do not you venture to trust yourselves anywhere, unless you can, in some small measure, find that you have been led to put your trust in God. Now I have known men be very inquisitive concerning other people's practices, and be led to conclude they were not altogether walking very becomingly, and they have watched them cautiously that they might be able, as they thought, to give them seasonable rebuke and reproof; but they never dreamed that all the time in watching them they might create the same working in themselves, till it actually came, and they were in the very same snare, and felt that God had to give *them* a reproof; and thus cured them of self-trusting. And I would advise you, in the Name of the Lord, do not trust your eyes, do not trust your ears, do not trust yourselves, without the Lord being your Guide; for really we are not fit to be trusted for a moment. And so the

Lord will bring us to have the sentence of death in ourselves, "that we should not trust in ourselves."

III. Now, lastly, the great design is to bring us to *trust "in God that raiseth* the dead." This is a blessed expression: "God that raiseth the dead." He raised Christ from the dead; he raiseth us from our death in sin. He raised the dry bones in Ezekiel's vision; and if you and I have had the sentence of death in ourselves, we have been there. We know how it was with those bones, when they were all distorted, and no bone seemed in its proper place, and there was neither flesh nor sinews; and when flesh and sinews came, and the judgment appeared to get hold of some truth, still there seemed to be no life and no motion, till the Spirit of God sent life. Therefore we know a little of what he can do in raising the dead.

"That we should not trust in ourselves, but in God." Trust him for what? Trust him for pardon, manifested pardon, again and again. "But," say you, "we do not want fresh pardon; for God pardons all at once." But we want fresh manifestations of it. Suppose I were a farmer, and had my rick-yard full of stacks of corn, and my granary full, and my fields full of cattle, so that I had as much food as would last my family two or three years, could I sit down and say, "Now I want no bread-making and no cooking? I have plenty in the yard, and the granary, and the fields, and that is enough for me." I should cut a poor figure with all my plenty; I should die, you know. The Lord has told us that there is fulness in Jesus Christ; but that is nothing for the poor soul, unless it has a little of the manifestation of it and enjoyment of it. If a hungry man, who has been working in the field for six or seven hours, comes in to sit down to a meal, and his master says, "Ah, well! You have done your work well; sit down. There is plenty of food in the barn and in the cupboard to last you for years; so be content." "Yes," says the man, "but I want to taste a little of it; knowing it is there is not enough." And God's people want to be feeling, and tasting, and handling of the Word of life. They do not want merely the judgment-knowledge of it,—that there is enough; they want the feeling enjoyment of it,—to have it brought into their consciences. They ask God for fresh communications of pardon, fresh lettings down of peace into the conscience, fresh revelations of the glory of Christ and of their interest in him. And they are led to trust in the Lord for it. Trust in the Lord, says God, and thou shalt be established. "They that trust in the Lord shall be as mount Zion." And thus the Lord puts us off from all self-trust, in order to bring us to a solemn and sweet trust in Christ for the blessed openings of this to the mind; that so we may be led to eat the flesh and drink the blood of the Lord Jesus Christ; without which we have no life in us. He does not say, "You must believe there is enough in me;" but there must be an eating and drinking, a spiritually entering into the vitality of it, by the power of that vitality entering into you. And I tell you, in the Name of the living God, that if God never gives you an entering into the vitality of this truth, as God lives you will be damned,—if the Lord the Spirit never gives you a vital experience of Divine truth in the conscience. If you are his people, he will bring you from all self-trust to trust in him for the vital manifestation of the mysteries of his cross to your soul; that you may know blessedly and vitally what it is to have the Lord for your strength and your succour and support.

"We have the sentence of death in ourselves, that we should not trust in ourselves, but in God," to keep us in time of temptation. This was the case with David. Not when he was on the house-top. No, no, poor soul; but when he was brought to his right mind, he was brought feelingly and spiritually to say, "Hold thou me up, and I shall be safe." "Keep back thy servant from presumptuous sins." Why, David! Could you not hold yourself up, so famous a man as you, so much of the presence of God as you have enjoyed? And "presumptuous sins!" Is there any danger of a man of God like you, who have had such manifestations of Divine favour, getting into presumptuous sins? Aye, there was; and God convinced him of it by strange methods, till he was brought of necessity to know that his trust was in the Lord; and so he says, "Hold me up, and keep me back, Lord." And so with poor Moses. When he had to lead Israel, he said, "If thy presence go not with us, carry us not up hence." He felt himself incapable of managing either himself or the people.

Our trust, therefore, is in God, for strength to keep us in the hour of temptation, to keep us from the workings of in-bred corruption, the snares of the devil, and the allurements of the world; to keep us from all those bewitching things that are suited to flesh and blood. And we have to trust in the Lord for the opening of his promises and the mysteries of his love, in bringing again the sweet sense of the love of Christ, the blood of Christ, and the power of Christ into the heart, and leading us into it; so that there may be a sweet coming of Christ into us and a going out of self into Christ. May you be enabled to trust in Christ, then, poor soul, if you want real comfort and real support.

"But," says some poor soul, "how dare I venture to trust in the Lord when I have such a dead heart and conscience?" Do you not see, poor soul, it is "God that raiseth the dead?" He raises us again out of those deathly frames and feelings that we have to go through. And there is no saying what the Lord cannot do, poor creature. He can come into the deepest depth of thy death and wretchedness, and lift thee out of it all, and lift thee into himself.

May God bless you and me with a feeling sense of solemn confidence in him. Amen, and amen.

THE SOUL'S DEATH UNTO SIN.

Preached on Tuesday Evening, May 25th, 1841, in Gower Street Chapel, London.

"For he that is dead is freed from sin."—ROM. VI. 7.

IN the chapter preceding this, the apostle has been led by the Divine Author of the Word to take a view of the two Adams and their two seeds; that Adam the first, by his awful sin and apostacy, brought death and condemnation upon all his offspring, so that in him, in his very first act of transgression, they "all sinned and came short of the glory of God," and thus, "by one man's offence death reigned by one;" but that Adam the Second, "the Lord from Heaven," represented an elect seed, and had them all in his loins, chosen by the Father and locked up safe in him. Though that seed fell with the rest in Adam the first, in Adam the Second they were preserved from the awful damnation that their sin had merited, and, by his obedience and the invincible power of the Spirit, all are brought to newness of life and to justification of life, and so are made the rich partakers of the mysteries of the gospel of God; and concerning them it is said, that "where sin abounded, grace did much more abound." I recollect preaching, I think three times, in an Arminian chapel; and the last time, one of the leaders of the place said, "I should like you to preach from that text: 'Where sin abounded, grace did much more abound.'" "Well," I said, "if the Lord should lead me to speak from it, I must necessarily upset your creed;" and I believe the Lord did lead me to speak from it; and I endeavoured to prove that their creed must go to wreck, according to that truth, if laid down fairly. "Where sin abounded, grace did much more abound." If that is universal, what an awful lie it is! Because grace has not kept pace with the sins of the damned in hell; they are under the dominion of sin now, and will be for ever, and, therefore, grace has not "much" more abounded than sin" there. Consequently, that text must be limited to the spiritual seed of Christ. "Where sin abounded" in them, and it awfully abounded too, "grace has much more abounded;" for grace has not only put away their sin, and so kept pace with sin, to undermine it in all its bearings, but grace has brought them into a more blessed state in their union to Christ, than they had in Adam the first. Immortal honours to the Lord! He raised them to higher heights of glory than that from which they fell. "Where sin abounded" in the elect of God, "grace does much more abound." It undermines, it upsets, it overturns, it takes the advantage of it to put a crown of glory upon the saved sinner which he could never have worn, had he lived as holy as God made Adam for ever. And thus we shall have to sing for ever, "Grace, grace, unto it." May the Lord the Spirit grant that you and I may feel something of the aboundings of this grace.

Now if there should be any free-willers here to-night, and I dare
say there are in some corner or another, who have come for some
purpose or other, they are ready to say, "O! Then it does not matter;
we may take our swing in sin; we may live in sin; we may take the
whole pleasure of the heart in sin; for if grace 'much more abounds,'
and takes advantage of sin to show more of its aboundings, the more
sin the more grace." Why, the devil has not so much impudence
as you, whatever you may think of your piety. For you never find,
with all that the enemy of souls said to Christ, when he tabernacled
here below, though he knew him and knew the work he was come
to accomplish, that he ever charged him so insolently as that. And
indeed I do believe in my heart and soul that Arminianism produces
an impudence that outstrips anything that Satan could do, in arraign-
ing God at its bar and professing to judge the Almighty; and it en-
courages licentiousness thereby.

But what says the Lord the Spirit? "What shall we say, then?
Shall we continue in sin that grace may abound?" Is that the real
nature of the doctrine of God's superabounding grace, to bring us to
"continue in sin?" Will it induce us to live a life of licentiousness?
"God forbid." I can tell you this, if God never brings you feelingly
and spiritually to hate sin and love holiness, irrespective of the fear
of hell and the terrors of the damned, you will never go to heaven.
If you only profess to hate sin and love holiness because you are
afraid you shall go to hell if you do not, you are out of the secret to
this present, and do not know the vitality of God's religion. For
wherever the religion of Christ is revealed in the conscience by the
power of the blessed Spirit, that man would hate sin, if there were
no hell; and because he feels it as a plague in him, that is the very
reason why he is so wretched in his feelings. That which he hates,
he feels a something in him that loves; and it is his conflict. It is
not so much the fear of hell as it is the nature, the horrible, filthy,
unhallowed, ungodly nature of sin; and he would hate it if there
were no such thing as a place called hell, and no wrath to come.

So said the apostle: "What, then! Shall we continue in sin that
grace may abound? God forbid. How shall we that are dead to
sin, live any longer therein?" Now this staggers a child of God
sometimes. He says, "Well, then, I cannot be of that number that
are 'dead to sin,' if it is not possible for them to 'live any longer
therein;' for I find myself plagued and tortured with it every day."
I can tell thee this, poor soul, it is one thing for sin to live in thee,
and another thing for thee to live in sin. When you were dead to
God, and were alive to sin, sin was your home, your element, your
delight, your pleasure; you were never happy but when committing
it. Now that you are made alive to God, you still find sin lives in
you, like a horrible, artful, detestable thing, which is plundering you,
torturing you, robbing you; and you have often prayed that the arro-

gant thief might be turned out of the house. But there he is, and I believe he will be there till God pulls the house down. But, then, at the same time, it is not you that live in that, it is not your ele-ment, it is not your home, it is not your pleasure; it is that that lives in you, and so is your plague and torment whilst here below; and, therefore, you may say with the apostle, "How shall we that are dead to sin live any longer therein?"

"Know ye not, that so many of us as were baptized into Jesus Christ were baptized into his death? Therefore we are buried with him by baptism into death; that like as Christ was raised up from the dead. by the glory of the Father, even so we should also walk in newness of life." Now there is a solemn, a God-glorifying, soul-humbling im-mersion into the death of the Son of God, by the power of the Holy Ghost; thus truly and really being buried with Christ spiritually in spiritual baptism, solemnly immersed in him by the energy of God the Holy Ghost; and if this is spiritual baptism, water baptism, you know, must be something like a burying, or else the figure has lost its de-sign. There must be a burial there, to set forth in a figure what God in substance has revealed to the conscience. And being brought by the Spirit of God to have this spiritual immersion, there is a spiritual resurrection in the conscience to "newness of life" in the Lord Jesus Christ; and we are brought spiritually to be "planted together in the likeness of his resurrection."

"Knowing this, that our old man is crucified with him, that the body of sin might be destroyed, that henceforth we should not serve sin." "Our old man crucified?" Yes. Sin was crucified with Christ, first when his Majesty personally hung upon the cross; and it is cru-cified with him when his cross is spiritually revealed in the con-science. But observe, crucifixion was a lingering death; and so it is in the heart and conscience of God's people. They find that, though "the old man is crucified," still it lifts up its hateful head, and often brings them into bondage.

Then come the words read as a text: "He that is dead, is freed from sin."

I. I shall notice this *death*. II. This *freedom*.

I. First, this *death*.

Now it has various branches in it. And I was going to say, as in nature so in grace. Now and then we hear of a person who appears healthy and strong in nature, dying suddenly; but that is not the general method of God. The greatest part of us have a lingering death,—some lingering affliction to bring on death. "But," say you, "do you think there are any sudden deaths in a spiritual sense?" Well, I do. I think the poor thief was not long in dying; for one of the evangelists tells us that both the thieves railed upon Christ while he hung upon the cross, and yet by and by we find one of them "dead" in the sense of our text, and saying, "Lord remember me when thou comest into thy kingdom." And many a poor child of God has lived without God and without hope till his dying moments, and then God has appeared and made known the mystery of his cross, to let it be seen what grace can do. And sometimes I have thought, and I still think, and more than think, I *believe*, that the methods God takes in the dispensations of grace are such that he will put it out of the power of the devil to be able to say that there is any circumstance whatever that is a match for grace. If the whole church of God were to be taken to heaven, like the dying thief and some others, as soon as God is pleased to quicken their dead souls, the enemy might have it to say, "Ah! The Lord knows very well that if they were to live long, I should get them after all; I should upset their confidence and bring them back into my power; therefore he is obliged to take them to heaven." Now the Lord says, "No, Satan. They shall go through a variety of toils and troubles and distresses; and as it was in the case of Job, so shall it be with numbers of my people. The devil shall have fair play to do all the devil can do, and yet I will save them and let the power of my omnipotent grace be known." But then, again, Satan might say, the Lord is obliged to take such lingering steps, or he could not accomplish the work. "No," says the Lord. "You shall not have that to say. I will let you know that my grace is such that it can 'cut the work short in righteousness;' and there shall be no case or circumstance out of the reach of the power and efficacy of my grace." Thus grace shall "reign through righteousness unto eternal life," and the whole church shall be brought to triumph in the mysteries of his love.

But now for this *death*. One of the first branches of it, in a general way, for I do not mean to insist upon every one being exactly alike, is a solemn cut to the world. Perhaps here may be some in this assembly, young men or young women, who were just springing up into life, gayety, and pleasure; and, ere they were aware, something has come into the conscience, given a desperate cut to all their worldly pleasure, and made them as dead to it almost as if they were already really dead; and they can take no pleasure in the world. And they think it very hard: "What! A young man, a young woman, like me, just ready to have a little pleasure, to have all my prospects dashed away in a moment?" It looks very desperate, does it not? But I can tell you, poor soul, you will have to bless God for it, some day or another. The Lord's design is to be the death of the world in thy heart, and to let thee know that all thou canst have of pleasure in the world, or all that it flattered thee with, brings nothing but delusion. Thy soul sinks and finds that everything is dismal. And perhaps you will try to struggle against it. Many a poor child of God has struggled against it, taken a little pleasure again, and for a little while conquered these gloomy feel-

ings. And if they have companions or relatives, especially if they
are well off in this world, and these see them getting so gloomy,
what methods will not be taken to put a stop to it! They will have
about twice as many parties at their house as they used to have, and
get them to go to all the amusements they can muster up, in order
to bring them to be charmed with the world. They might as well
try to charm them with the horrors of hell; for even if the poor soul
is left for a while to find a kind of fleshly charm in these fleshly
things, when God brings it in secret silence before him, it is *death*—
death—to their minds, and they are ready to wish they had never
been born.

This is one method God takes with his people. And now is there
any person here who is just giving up the ghost, as it were, with
the world? And have you, in order to keep a little liveliness in your
souls, tried a little activity, a little pleasure and amusement? Perhaps you say, "I have." Then I will tell you, poor creature, what
you have done; you have done all you can to damn your own soul:
and, if God had let you, you would have done it. And in reality, I
believe, there is not a sinner that would ever go to heaven, if God
would let him go to hell; no, not one. But God is determined to
bring death in the conscience, and bring the poor soul in dead to the
world and to its charms; and so to come before the Lord as a poor
guilty sinner, wanting to know what to " do to be saved."

But we observe, further. The poor creature, beginning to find
that he has no pleasure in the world, begins to try in earnest to have
some pleasure in pleasing God, in obeying the Lord; and if he
knows the letter of the law, he will do his best to keep it to the letter.
How he watches to love God with all his heart! How he watches
to keep his eyes from covetous desires and his heart from covetous
workings! And how he watches to keep the mind chaste, and to do
that which is right before God! Sometimes the poor creature is
ready to go to the Lord, and say, "Lord, if thou wilt but pardon what
is past, if ever I do the like again, if ever I get into such company,
into such practices and take such methods again, Lord, I will not
find fault with thee if thou art pleased to damn me; for I shall know
then that indeed it is righteous in thee, and I deserve it." And he
thinks, when he has made such a solemn engagement as this, that
he never dare sin again. But a thousand to one, he will do the very
thing, or something worse. "Why," say you, "do you think he
will?" I am beyond thinking; I *know* he will. He will do that, or
something worse, as sure as he breathes; and all his legal vows and
legal promises will prove rotten, and not able to support him a single moment; not able to prop up his mind. And when they are taken
from under him, he is brought then to be dead to the law. How so?
The " sentence of death" comes upon all his power to keep the law
of God; and he feels, in his very soul, that if God's law is " holy and

just and good," he must inevitably perish; and he is brought to be as dead to any hope of salvation from the law, or by his works according to the law, as a corpse can possibly be. And you will never know much of your ruined condition till God has slaughtered you, and made you as dead as a sinner at the borders of hell, entirely dead, to have no help or hope in yourself of obeying the Lord in his law, or bringing anything like peace or salvation to you by it.

Perhaps the poor soul, when brought to this point, may be under the painful situation of listening to legalizing preachers; and they will tell him he must repent and believe and love God and do his duty and be decidedly pious, and then God will love him. And very often they will stretch forth their hands, and apparently their heart, wonderfully, and say, "Come *now*, repent *now*, believe *now*; *now* is the time; if you do not embrace this opportunity, perhaps you will never have another; *now* is the time; it is now or never." And the poor creature, raised up with a kind of zeal to imagine that he will try to do his best, is struck dead again; and if he is to be damned that moment, he can neither repent, nor believe, nor do anything that they set him to do. He finds his heart hard as a flint and his mind in such a confused way that he can neither repent nor believe, nor have tenderness of conscience, nor love of God. And thus he becomes dead to all help or hope in self, grounded upon these legal efforts and these legal exhortations. And perhaps there may be some poor soul in this assembly to-night who is there; who has been trying for many a long month again and again, making fresh vows and promises and doubling his diligence in order to do something pleasing to God; and you feel in your very soul that the more you try the further you are off. I congratulate you. I thank God you cannot get on; and I pray that God will never let you get on, but that every step you take you may be more and more dead, till you are stiffly dead, and without ability in your feelings to lift up a finger or do anything towards helping your own soul. And if ever the Lord the Spirit brings you to *that* death, by and by he will reveal spiritual life, and lead you to know the blessedness of that truth: "I am the resurrection and the life; he that believeth in me, though he were dead, yet shall he live."

But we pass on to notice, that in God's own time such a poor soul is brought to be "dead to the law by the body of Christ." I admire the method that God the Spirit has taken to state these things. "I through the law am dead to the law," says the apostle; that is, through the law he is dead to all hope or help in or from the law; it kills him; it leaves him no ground of expectation. But by and by he comes to this point: "Know ye not, brethren (for I speak to them that know the law), how that the law hath dominion over a man as long as he liveth? For the woman which hath a husband is bound by the law to her husband so long as he liveth; but if the husband be dead, she is loosed from the law of her husband. Wherefore, my brethren, ye also are become dead to the law by the body of Christ." Now this is another death, another solemn stroke of death. To be " dead to the law through the law," and to be " dead to the law through the body of Christ," are two things. "Why," say you, "what is it, then, to be dead to the law by the body of Christ?" When the poor soul has been killed out and out, again and again in his own feelings, to all hope and expectation in self or the law, by and by Christ is revealed to him "the hope of glory." By "the body of Christ" we are to understand the whole body of the finished work of the Son of God; it is what Christ calls " eating his flesh and drinking his blood;" it is taking him, a whole Christ, by divine faith, through the teaching of the Holy Spirit; and thus, when the whole body of the work of the Lord Jesus Christ is blessedly and sweetly revealed to the conscience by the Spirit of the living God, the man becomes dead to the law.   How? Dead to law curses, dead to law claims; it is no longer a yoke of bondage, while he enjoys this; it is no longer a killing letter to him, while he enjoys this; no longer is the sentence of condemnation felt, while he enjoys this. The blessed "body of Christ," his atonement, his finished work, and the blessings connected with it, revealed to his conscience, bring a free pardon,—a pardon of all sin, past, present and to come, a free justification, and he is justified freely by the grace of God, through the redemption that is in Christ Jesus the Lord. Yes, it comes, and brings a constraining energy with it; and instead of the man sinking in gloom and dismay, he finds that the law can no longer keep him from crying to the Lord, hoping in the Lord, trusting in the Lord, resting in the Lord, holding solemn and sweet and blessed intercourse with the Lord.   He feels his heart at freedom with the Lord, and the Lord at freedom with him. Christ is graciously pleased, by the power of his Spirit, to make manifest that blessed truth, "If the Son shall make you free, ye shall be free indeed." Bondage is gone, guilt has taken wings and fled away; the soul is drawn forth in a blessed enjoyment of the Lord, and he sings the wonders of redeeming grace and triumphs in it. And I tell thee, poor soul, when the Lord the Spirit brings thee here in thy conscience, wraps thee up manifestively in Christ, and brings Christ and his atoning blood into thy heart, there is not a sentence in God's law that can bring death to thy conscience; not a sentence in God's law that can make a claim at thy hands. Thou art brought to deliver up in the court of God a receipt in full, signed and sealed by the blood of the God-man Mediator; and thus thou hast enlargement of heart.   And while thou art dead to law curses and law claims, thou art alive to grace blessings and grace unfoldings, and thus art brought to have a sweet and solemn blessedness in Christ as "the Lord thy righteousness and strength." And he that is thus "dead," " is freed from sin."

It is the soul thus "dead" that the Lord had in view when he influenced the apostle to say, "Who shall lay anything to the charge of God's elect?" Some people say, "Ah! It means those who have got the second blessing, those who are perfect in the flesh, who have no sin about them." You cannot find any of them. You may find some impudent arrogant hypocrites, as hard as the devil can make them, who talk about it; but you never find a soul that is really in that case. But you find the apostle, and the Lord by the apostle, does not lay that down as any ground upon which he sends this challenge: "Who shall lay anything to the charge of God's elect?" He says, "It is God that *justifieth*. Who is he that condemneth? It is Christ *that died.*" The death of Christ is revealed in the conscience by the Spirit of God; faith realizes it and triumphs in it, and thus becomes dead to the power of any one to lay any charge against it in the court of God. Here law is magnified, justice satisfied, devils defeated, sin destroyed, death swallowed up in victory, and the world overcome; and God brings this justification, this entire and blessed atonement, to the conscience. But then it is added, "Yea, rather, that is risen again; who is even at the right hand of God, who also maketh intercession for us." God help thee, poor soul, to read this and feel it! God the Spirit reveal it to some poor trembling conscience this night, and give him faith to realize it,—that the justifying act of God, through the finished work of Christ and the glorious resurrection of the Son of God, his ascension and intercession, all plead before the throne of God the poor soul's eternal acquittal, and defy either devils or men to bring him in guilty. O the blessedness of such a death as this in the conscience, when the Lord the Spirit reveals it there! Thus we "become dead to the law by the body of Christ."

But we pass on to another branch of this death. While the poor child of God enjoys this, he goes singing away. These are very cheerful moments, very pleasant enjoyments. "Well, but," say you, "if he once enjoys it, he always enjoys it; does not he?" No; not unless God is about to take him home directly, as he did the dying thief. Grace must be tried. God will try every step of his work, and he will try this. If the poor soul lives long, it will be tried. You may hear some people talk about being always "on the mount," and being in the blessed enjoyment of this always; and they will say, "Why, now, do not you enjoy it? You talk about it, and say you wish you could get at it; it is free; why do you not fully enjoy it?" And thus they stagger many a poor, tried child of God; but still the poor soul cannot get at a constant, unshaken joy. No; and I do not believe God will ever let his children thus "get at it," if they live long in this world. There must be a trial of faith, and a passing into the various branches of the kingdom of God through tribulation; and we only know the sweetness and blessedness of it as we obtain it through tribulation.

Well. After we have had our sweet moments, our sweet enjoyments, we must, all of us, have another stroke of death. And what is that? The Lord tells us a little about it in the prophecy of Hosea: " I will allure her, and bring her into the wilderness." That is another step. When God has allured her by the charms of his love, the manifestations of his mercy, then she must go into the wilderness, and see what wilderness work is, where beasts of prey appear, and where darkness and storms are. And what then? Why, after she has tried the trackless desert for a while, is ready to give up, and to look upon all hope as gone, the Lord says, "And I will speak comfortably unto her, and I will give her her vineyards from thence, and the valley of Achor for a door of hope." You know what the valley of Achor was, I suppose. It was so called from Achan being stoned there, when he had stolen the Babylonish garment and the wedge of gold, and had troubled Israel. And so the poor child of God sometimes is carried away, so as to steal a Babylonish garment, when he has been brought into enjoyment, and imagines that he can now dress himself and adorn himself and be very beautiful. Come, come, poor soul, thou wilt be brought to a trial just now. God will cast the lot upon thee, and thou wilt be brought to acknowledge the Babylonish garment and wedge of gold led thee to swerve in some degree from the simplicity of the gospel. But even then in the valley of Achor there shall be "a door of hope." God will open some "door of hope" in the midst of thy distresses. But whilst thou art there, and hast no "door of hope," what a death it is to all thy sweet feelings and views, and to all thy imaginary power. Why, you will become so dead in your feelings that the enemy of souls will tell you that all was a delusion, that all was a deception, and that Satan wrought it all and accomplished it all. And very often his infernal majesty will talk to you, and say, "Where is your tenderness of conscience? Where is your spirit of prayer? Where is your praise? Where is your adoration of God now? What a bewildered fool you look like!" Ah! How bewildered you do feel and look like a fool, when you find you are in a desert, and feel in your heart that you are as dead as Ezekiel's bones were, and you cannot raise any joy or peace or hope in your conscience! And yet you hear men say you can and you ought to do it. But instead of that propping up your hope, it sets you raging and sinks you deeper and deeper in dismay; and all hope seems gone. You really cannot feel the lifting up of your heart any way; you are so dead, and left a lifeless lump in your feelings. But God brings forth "a vineyard of red wine" manifestively into your conscience, and "gives you your vineyards from thence." He opens the mysteries of his blood and love more than he did before, and now you see it is so manifestively of grace that you have not a word of self to plead; and "he that is" thus "dead, is freed from sin."

Now do you know anything of this death? Has God ever killed

you? If it is the will of God, I wish he may kill you. I do not mind your being affronted at me, if God is pleased to kill you. You may grumble and murmur against me as long as you will, if God will but kill you to self and self hope, lead you to know that you must be slaughtered to it all, have your soul bathed in the blood and love of Immanuel, and find your rest in him. And when you are brought to this death, you will be led to see that you cannot enjoy one particle of the mysteries of the gospel but as God brings it to your conscience, and to feel that you as much need the revelation of the truth to your conscience by the Holy Ghost as you need a Christ to atone for your sin, and that you can no more bring the life and power of God to your conscience than you could die for your sins and atone for your sins. And then you find that God is to have all the glory from first to last. This will be the death-blow to your Arminianism, and the sooner it is dead and buried the better. May God Almighty, in his rich mercy, produce a solemn death and burial in some of your consciences, and revive his love and life and power, that you may know the blessedness of a free-grace gospel, a free-grace salvation in your souls; and then you will know the blessedness of being "dead." "He that is dead, is freed from sin."

II. Now we pass on to this *freedom*. And I must be brief.

First, negatively. It is not a freedom from the inbeing of sin. As I have hinted, though the man does not live in sin, sin lives in him; and the Holy Ghost leads us to say, "If we say that we have no sin, we deceive ourselves and the truth is not in us;" and if the truth is not in us, there must be something else in us; therefore we must be filled with lies and errors and confusion. You will find that if you are dead to sin, sin is not dead to you. There it is; it works in your members and brings you into bondage. And it is a sweet thing when we can come to the apostle's conclusion (I do not mean presumptuously and arrogantly, I know what it is both ways), when we can say, "It is no more I that do it, but sin that is in me." You cannot always get there; and you will try, poor soul, sometimes arrogantly and presumptuously to get there; I know you will, especially if you have a judgment well stored with the doctrines of the gospel. You will think, "Why should I be so much tossed about with the workings of corrupt nature? It is not I; it is sin in me;" and you will think for a moment that sin is but a little thing, and you will begin to trifle with sin. Now, whenever you begin to trifle with sin, you may know it is the devil's work; it is the life of hell in your poor soul; it will bring hell into the conscience, depend upon it. You may stiffen your conscience as much as you will; but if you are a child of God, it will bring hell into your conscience, as sure as God is God. A child of God, then, is dead to sin; but still the workings of it are there. Dead sin does not plague him; but it is sin alive in him that tortures him.

Further.˙ He is not dead to the possibility of falling into practical sin. David was a man of God, and he sinned practically. Solomon was a man of God, and he sinned practically. Peter was a man of God, and he sinned practically. And if there are any of you who are men of God or women of God, and have been so for half a dozen years, and have felt proof of it, and given proof of it, and have never sinned practically, GET UP, AND LET US LOOK AT YOU!* Show your faces; and let it be seen what a wonderful phenomenon you are. But, alas! alas! If you have proper feelings, you hang down your heads; and there is not a soul that can lift it up upon that ground. You know that you have' brought bondage into your minds, with some unhallowed thing or other, though it may not have been what has been noticed by others. So you are not "dead" in this sense.

Well, then, in what sense are they "dead" and "freed from sin?" If they are brought by the blessed Spirit of the living God into the things we have been looking at, they are dead, first, to the damning power of sin.

> "If sin be pardon'd, I'm secure;
> Death has no sting beside;
> The law gives sin its damning power,
> But Christ my Ransom died." ·

Sin, though that horrible thing which has ruined the whole creation, and brought death and devastation, is destroyed by the body of Christ. He "condemned sin in the flesh;" and when his blessed condemnation of sin is revealed in the conscience, it brings life and pardon and peace, and the soul becomes dead to the damning power of sin.

Further. They are dead to the reigning power of sin. "Sin shall not have dominion over you, for ye are not under the law, but under grace." Now our preachers in general say that if we are not under the law, then we are at liberty to sin. I wonder whether they would have courage to get their pen and scratch out that passage. Scratch it out, and say it ought not to be in the Bible, if you insist upon it that not to be under the law is the high road to sin. God says it is just the reverse. While we are under the law, and it comes with its commanding and condemning authority, it stirs up sin; but when we are brought to be "dead to the law by the body of Christ," grace makes the heart tender, brings us to have holy freedom with God, and delivers us from the reigning power of sin, for sin shall not reign. True enough, now and then it will kick up a riot; but rioting is not reigning. It is a monstrous enemy, and sometimes kicks up such a riot in the conscience of the poor child of God that he is ready to think that it does reign, and that he must be under the dominion of it; but eventually he will find that its reigning power is gone. And sometimes you will find, when Moses

---

* No one who never heard Mr. Gadsby preach can form any idea of the powerful and impressive way in which he would utter that sentence.

comes, if I may so speak, and reads the Riot Act when sin is terrifying your conscience, it almost terrifies you to death, and you think you shall be taken up at last as a traitor, for you cannot quell it; nor can all the Riot Acts in the world. But when the great High Priest of our profession comes, and reads love, blood, pardon, peace, and reconciliation in your heart, the very rioting is subdued; and you feel yourself "dead to the law by the body of Christ," and so are led to glorify him.

Further. They are dead to the love of sin. But here wants a little distinction made betwixt that in the child of God which is alive to God, and the working of sin still; for sin is still there,—"the body of sin," the image of Satan, and it sometimes works so powerfully that really the child of God is afraid he does love sin, for there is something about him that loves it. "What!" say you. "Do you think that a child of God, really called by grace, has anything about him that loves sin?" I am beyond thinking; I know it; and it plagues and tortures his poor mind sometimes till he hardly knows where to look. But when God opens to him a little of Solomon's prayer, he gets into it! "What prayer and supplication soever be made by any man, or by all thy people Israel, which shall know every man the plague of his own heart, then hear thou in heaven." There are some people that do not appear to know the meaning of it; they do not feel any heart-plague within them. Well, then, they are not interested in that prayer. But other people feel the plague of it. Yet they have something about them that loves it, and that makes the plague so much the more torturing to the mind; but then there is something about them that does not love it. Do not you find in secret something thirsting after Jesus, crying to Jesus, loving Jesus? And now and then it appears to be heaved up, as if it were under an intolerable mountain; and its breathings are, "O Lord, I hate vain thoughts." Is it not so? Now, this very principle that "hates vain thoughts" is the life of God, that has been the death of your sin, and the death of your soul to all creature-help. Here is a death, therefore, a real death in the spiritual mind, to all the pleasures and enjoyments and love of sin.

But, to conclude. It shall be a complete death at last to the inbeing of sin, and sin in all its bearings. Poor child of God! A few more struggles, a little more conflict, and thou shalt sing victory over thy pride and lust and bad tempers. There shall be a complete death below, and thou shalt be raised above into the enjoyment of it all, and eternally sing, "Victory through the blood of the Lamb." And then thou shalt enter fully into the ineffable glory of him who has been the death of deaths, the death of sin; and the life of lifes, the life of God in thy soul.

May God bless you and me with the sweet enjoyment of this immortal truth, for his mercy's sake. Amen.

THE TRUE JOSEPH.

Preached on Wednesday evening, May 26th, 1841, in Regent Street Chapel, City Road, London.

"And of Joseph he said, Blessed of the Lord be his land, for the precious things of heaven, for the dew, and for the deep that coucheth beneath."—DEUT. xxxiii. 13.

THE word of God does not appear to contain a more solemnly pleasing history, as a history, than that of Joseph. And I have no doubt that every particle of it has a divine mystery in it, whether we can get into that mystery or not. But I have proved, in thousands of instances, that I can only get spiritually into any branch of the mystery of God as that gets into me. And when the glorious mysteries of the gospel of God's grace, under the divine operations and teachings of the Holy Ghost, get into my conscience, my poor conscience slides into those mysteries as sweetly and as easily as if it were oiled; and indeed *it is* so; and then I find the blessedness of entering into the solemn realities of the gospel of God's grace.

I shall endeavour to make a few remarks upon the passage read as a text, in the following order :

I. Considering Joseph as *typical of Christ.*

II. His land as typical of the *inheritance* of Christ.

III. The *blessing* pronounced upon this land, his portion, his people. "The precious things of heaven, and the dew and the deep that coucheth beneath."

And if the Lord the Spirit should grant me a little dew, and you a little dew, we shall find it blessedly sweet and solemn to enter into a little of the glory of God, couched in the passage.

I. Joseph *typical of Christ.* Joseph, you know, was ordained of God to be the saviour of Israel; and God had given him intimations of that by dreams. And no doubt poor Joseph's mind would sometimes be lifted up with the prospect of what was couched in his dreams. He little thought what God's high road to it was. Now God's high road to Joseph's exaltation was a vastly deep one; and indeed it seemed to be such a one that none but the Lord could have accomplished it, in the way that he did, to the bringing about of his own purpose. I know, characters who find fault with the decrees of God get hold of a variety of things to mock the Lord. I recollect one once saying to a friend of mine, "Why, you had better say that God decreed Jonah's going to Tarshish, instead of going direct to Nineveh." "Why," said my friend, "so he did; for no one but Jonah ever went to Nineveh on that road before or since, and none but God could have made such a road." And really it could be no other being who could make such a wonderful way as God did in bringing Jonah to Nineveh, in spite of all the workings of his corrupt heart. And so poor Joseph had a variety of trials and workings of his corrupt nature to go through, to get to the place and state appointed for him by the Lord.

But now, as far as this may look to Christ, we find that poor Joseph was hated, abhorred, sold, and in reality in heart murdered, by the very characters he was destined to save. When he went on his father's business, to see his brethren, they combined together, and said, "Behold, this dreamer cometh; come, and let us slay him, and we shall see what will become of his dreams." God ordered it otherwise; he was not to be slain; but their enmity was the same, and they were as truly his murderers in the sight of God's law as though they had actually slain him. And do not we see what a solemn beauty there is in this, as connected with Christ? Who murdered Christ? Who hated Christ? Who slaughtered Christ? The very characters that he came to save. I have often felt a little solemnity in that portion of God's word, "We esteemed him not," "We hid as it were our faces from him." Beloved, you and I may look at the conduct of Jews and Gentiles as being the actual instrument which put him to death, but it was your sins and mine that slaughtered him. It was the sin of the church of God that tore his heart and horrified his soul. "The Lord laid upon him our iniquities;" and, bless his solemn Majesty, "with his stripes we are healed." I never was brought to have a proper view of the hateful nature of sin till the Lord brought me to feel that I had been the means of bathing the Son of God in his own blood by my abominable crimes, that I was really his murderer, and that he bore my guilt and was slaughtered with my vile transgressions; and yet his blessed Majesty was determined to love.

But notwithstanding Joseph's brethren hated him, sold him, and in their hearts slaughtered him, and no doubt thought they had got rid of him and his dreams too, this was the very high' road for the accomplishment of God's purpose that he should be their Saviour. And if the Lord Jesus Christ had not been hated, abhorred, sold, crucified, and slaughtered, where would our salvation have been? The cross of the Lord Jesus Christ was God's high road for saving sinners. And when the Lord the Spirit brought the apostle Paul to enter sweetly and blessedly into this subject, he considered all things but dung "for the excellency of the knowledge of Christ Jesus his Lord;" and he says, "God forbid that I should glory save in the cross of our Lord Jesus Christ." Why, into what a degraded state think ·you, must the learned man's mind be brought? Paul was a wise man, a learned man; and yet he had given up all his connections, all his literature, and all his knowledge, to make his boast of a crucified Christ. Why, it would be as degrading in the eyes of the Greeks as it would be in our eyes if he were to say, "God forbid that I should glory save in the gallows or in the gibbet;" for you know this was the contemptible idea of a crucifixion. And yet, notwithstanding it appeared so degrading, it was the life, glory, and spring of the apostle's emulation; he was "determined to know nothing, save Jesus Christ and him crucified." Now the blessed Lord accomplished the salvation of the church through this very channel; and though he was put to cruel mockings and scorn and shame, yet this was the method by which he accomplished salvation and brought life and immortality to light.

We cannot enter upon all the particulars which might be named concerning Joseph; but there is one that I have often thought of, as typical of a false church. When Joseph was sold into the hands of Potiphar, Potiphar's wife professed great attachment to him, a great liking for him, and laid herself in his way in order to manifest her great liking and attachment," but when his purity, under the teaching of God, forbade the connection, she became his betrayer,—brought false accusations against him, and was the means of putting him in prison. And this is just the spirit of free-will at the present moment. O! How prettily she will talk about Christ! What a bustle and stir she will make about her love to Christ! But if Christ will not commit fornication with her, and let it be, "Christ doing *his* part and she doing *her* part," she will turn accuser, and call him a tyrant, and worse than a devil, and a cruel monster. If he acts purely, and will keep his bosom sacred and his heart sacred, communicating blessings only to his spouse and setting at nought all the poor empty parade of free will, then she turns his enemy, sets him at nought, scorns and betrays him, and despises him in his own Person, in his ministers, and in all the members of his mystical body. I have often thought of one portion of God's word: "Yea, and all that will live godly in Christ Jesus shall suffer persecution." Mind how that text reads. It does not say, "All that will live a godly life." Men may live what they call a godly life, and be very "pious," what the world calls "decidedly pious," have a very pretty name into the bargain, and all things go on very nicely and meet with no persecution; but if any man is brought, by the power of discriminating grace, to trace all his godliness up to Christ, to "live godly in Christ," to have no foundation or spring for godliness except what centres in Christ, comes from Christ, and leads to Christ, "he shall suffer persecution." They will act as Potiphar's wife did; they will turn accusers; they will belie the truth, charge him with everything that is ungodly and licentious, and set at nought the sacred name of Christ in the hearts of his people, in the ministry of the word, and in the power of his grace, and say, "These men do evil that good may come." And thus they demonstrate the same unhallowed spirit that Potiphar's wife demonstrated concerning Joseph. But it comes to nothing, brethren. Our Jesus will keep his bosom sacred; he never will let the harlot of free-will lodge there. No, no. Honours crown his brow, he opens his ear and his bosom to empty, weak, polluted, lost sinners; and as you have been singing to-night,

> " Sinners can say, and only they,
> How precious is a Saviour."

And he will have all the glory. He brings them by the power of his love to the blessed enjoyment of himself; and he will have all the glory:

Now we find by and bye, when Joseph is put in prison, that God makes known a wonderful dispensation of his providence, in order to bring him to enlargement; and that very dispensation is the very means that finds him in prison ready for the enlargement. Why, bless you, if Joseph had stopped in Potiphar's house, and been a great man, and all that might have been expected of one that was pure and virtuous, there would have been no visiting Potiphar's two servants in the prison and explaining their dreams, and so being brought into the presence of Pharaoh when Pharaoh had a dream. But this is God's way. And indeed nobody else can work as our God does in the dispensations of his providence and grace. He is a wonder-working God to this present moment. And we may see, in this dispensation of the Lord to Joseph, a little of the dispensations of God to his people in every age of the world. He "makes darkness light, crooked things straight, and rough places plain." Some people like to talk about these things, but they never like to be in darkness, nor in the crooked things, nor in the rough places; and they will try to make you believe as if there were none; but how, then, can the Lord make them light, and make them straight and plain? There must be such things, or how could the Lord do this? But I have often thought of a dream I had some few years ago. I was in trouble of mind, and I dreamed in the night that I was in a smithy (as we call it), that is, a smith's shop; and round it there were a number of very crooked wires; so I took a hammer, and got some of them upon the anvil in order to straighten them; and I dreamed that the more I hammered them, the more crooked they got; and so I laid down my hammer, and said, "I believe I must die with all the things crooked about me." I awoke, and, behold, it was a dream. And bless you, I have been at the anvil many a time; and I believe, yes, I am sure, that all my hammering only makes things the more crooked; but when I lay down my hammer and come as a pauper to the Lord, God can make crooked things straight, rough places plain, magnify the riches of his grace, and give me a little of this blessedness,—to know that he does all things well, and that "these things will he do and not forsake us."

But we find that through this channel Joseph was brought to the high estate of glory of being next to the king on his throne. And so the blessed Jesus, in his mediatorial capacity, passed through all the dark agonies and trials and distresses that his solemn Majesty

had to wade through,—through the enmity of men, the wrath of
devils, and at length the fierce anger of incensed Justice; and he had
to die, "the just for the unjust." But that very channel was the
appointment of God, to lead him forth to exaltation above all principalities and powers, in his mediatorial capacity, to be exalted at
God's right hand, there to appear, the God-man Mediator, as the
glorious Head of the church for ever and for ever. And let me tell
thee, poor child of God, there is a solemn ground of consolation
in this to thy poor tried soul. When thou comest to an exalted
Christ, and art led in faith and feeling to trace a little of the blessed
exaltation of Christ, thou comest to a Christ who has waded through
all the afflictions and troubles thou canst ever have. "In all your
afflictions he was afflicted." Yes, bless his name, he was "tempted
in all points like as we are;" only, "without sin."

Now perhaps you may have some particular trial and conflict
connected with some particular temptation, and you sometimes wish
you had a bosom friend that you could dare to unburden your heart
to; but you are afraid; you are afraid of trusting the best friend you
have under heaven. Sometimes you have a little conversation, and
you do your best to pump it out of them whether they know anything about such things; but somehow or other you cannot get it
out that they know anything you are labouring under; therefore
you conclude your case is singular and that they know nothing
about it; and you dare not tell, for fear they should throw it at you
and do you an injury. Now I can tell you this, the case is so bad
that God's people have most of them something they really dare not
tell one another. They try to pump it out of another, but they dare
not tell it all out; they keep a portion to themselves. But now
you may go to our Joseph, and tell him all your heart, unbosom
your soul. He knows your trials, he knows your temptations, he
knows your afflictions; and he was "tempted in all points" for that
very end, that "he might be a merciful and faithful High Priest,"
"able to succour them that are tempted," knowing how to succour
thee,—that he might not only have all power as Almighty God, but
that he might have a smypathetic feeling and sympathetic power;
his heart going to thy heart, and thy heart being opened to receive
his heart; so that there might be a solemn dropping of his love and
grace to thy case and circumstances, that thou mightest find him a
very present help in trouble, and thus be made to glorify him. The
most solemn and blessed opportunities the Lord, in the riches of
his grace, has ever favoured me with have been when he has led me
spiritually and feelingly to Gethsemane, and when, under the teaching of the Lord, I could feel my heart drop into the heart of a
tempted, agonizing, slaughtered Lord, and raised through that channel
to the glorious exaltation of Jesus, having vanquished all foes
and "brought life and immortality to light." When we are brought

there, there is a blessedness in the gospel that the world knows nothing of; and this we have in our spiritual Joseph.

I shall pass over many things, and just come to one ; and that is, what brought Joseph and his brethren together,—manifestively together. Famine. Had there been no famine, and no preservation of food in Egypt against the famine, Joseph's brethren would not have been there. But there was a famine over all the land, and God had raised up Joseph to provide for the famine, to get provision ready in Egypt for the supply of a famishing world, and he was lord of all the stores, to give out to the necessitous and the distressed. And so, among the rest, the famine gets to Canaan, and Jacob sends ten of his sons to Egypt to buy corn. Benjamin (poor lad!) must not go. No, no. Benjamin must stay at home. And when the brethren arrived there, Joseph knew them; but mind, they did not know him. Now what method did he take to bring about a knowledge of himself to them ? Why, he spoke roughly to them, and asked them if they were not spies; he took care to be very inquisitive, too, about their family; for he wanted to know whether their old father was alive. But he did not want them to know that he knew their father, or knew them ; and therefore he spoke to them through an interpreter, as if he did not know their language. And by and by he begins to treat them as prisoners; and then they conversed together (not supposing Joseph knew their language), and they get directly to the guilt of selling their brother. They begin to say, "Ah! It has all come upon us now; the Lord has made our sin find us out." Joseph heard them and understood them; and though it was not his time to discover himself, his bowels yearned; he turned aside and wept, and dropped a few sympathetic tears over his trembling and penitent brethren. And is it not the case with our spiritual Joseph? Many a poor sinner goes to him and confesses his sins; yet he dare not and cannot believe that the Lord Jesus Christ is his brother; but still he is obliged to open his heart. He is ready to think that Christ seems rather like an awful and solemn king, who is determined to bring him to ruin and not to show mercy. But I can tell thee, poor child of God, thy Jesus often turns aside to weep while he seems to frown upon thee. And he will make the matter clear by and bye, and make known to thee the solemn mysteries of his kingdom.

Well; Joseph sent them home, only keeping one a prisoner to secure their coming again, and with their money in their sacks; for he was not going to have their money. No, no; he was exalted for another purpose. And, poor child of God, the Lord Jesus Christ will have none of thy money. His blessed salvation is "without money and without price;" and though he mysteriously loads thy sack sometimes with a little degree of hope, he always returns thy money in the sack.

But anon they are in complete want again; and their father requests they will go down and buy corn again, take their money with them, fresh money to buy with, and the best of Canaan into the bargain. The old man is determined to produce something that will bring them favour in the sight of the lord of the country. And so they go. But with great reluctance the old man parts with Benjamin. Says he, "Joseph is not, and Simeon is not, and ye will take Benjamin away; all these things are against me." Ah, my brethren! How many of our Josephs and Simeons have we thought were gone, and our little Benjamins going; and what groaning and moaning and sighing we have been making over them, thinking that these things were all against us and the Lord dealing hardly with us; whereas, the issue proved that it was the high road to the greatest blessings God ever made known to sinners! So it fell out in this case. When they get down into Egypt, Joseph commands them all to be brought into his house and to dine with him; and they take all this as "against them." "O!" say they; "the lord of the country is about now to take us for spies and treat us cruelly." And they begin to make their confession about their money, and how it came in their sacks they declare they cannot tell. "O!" says the steward of the house; "make yourselves easy; I had your money;" and they are all ordered to sit down, Benjamin amongst them, and Simeon is brought out. They have a meal, and a greater share is given to Benjamin than to the rest; they cannot make it out; they do not understand it; they are all in confusion; there is a mystery in their mind.

Passing over many things, we observe that at length Joseph is about to make himself known. Now here is a secret coming out,— the Egyptians must all leave; the secret must be directly and immediately and *exclusively* betwixt Joseph and his brethren. He says, "Cause every man to go out from me;" and they all went out but Joseph and his brethren. O! How the poor creatures would look one at one another, and say, "Why, all the Egyptians are dismissed; what is he going to do now?" But just as they are full of surprise, he stands up, and says, "I am Joseph your brother, whom ye sold into Egypt." They never were so paralyzed in their lives before. It was like a paralytic stroke that went through their whole frames and their whole souls, to find that this lord of Egypt was Joseph their brother, and that he charged upon them the crime of selling him. No doubt they sank in their feelings every moment a thousand fathoms. But he soon cheers them. He says, "Now, therefore, be not grieved nor angry with yourselves that ye sold me hither; for God did send me before you to preserve life. For these two years hath the famine been in the land; and yet there are five years, in the which there shall neither be earing nor harvest. And God sent me before you to preserve you a posterity in the earth, and to save your lives by a great deliverance. And, behold, your eyes see, and the eyes of my brother Benjamin, that it is my mouth that speaketh unto you." O! What a change was this to their feelings and in their minds! And how wonderful the change is, when, by the power of the Spirit, the sense of our guilt upon the conscience has made us feel our iniquity and acknowledge it, when we have been sinking in confusion and disorder, expecting nothing but the sentence of death, and he has come with the sentence of life: "*I am Jesus, your* Brother; I came to save!" Have you felt it, poor soul? Has there not been a majesty and a glory brought into your conscience that you can never describe, when Christ, by the power of the Spirit, has come into your conscience, and has said, "I am Jesus, your Brother, your Saviour, and I am exalted to save you from all famine, all plague, and all pestilence, and to bring you eventually to the immortal enjoyment of myself and to glory?" And thus we find how Joseph wonderfully fits the nature of our blessed Christ, in the glorious methods of his love that he takes with his people.

A great number of things might be mentioned here; but if I proceed on this ground, I cannot get to any other. And, therefore, I shall leave this part, and come, as typical of Christ, to Joseph's *land.* "And of Joseph he said, Blessed of the Lord be his land."

II. No doubt a fertile part of the land of promise was given to the seed of Joseph; but what I have in view is the *land* of our precious Christ. "What! Has Christ any land?" "The Lord's portionis his people; Jacob is the lot of his inheritance." The land of promise, you know, was divided among the tribes by lot,—lotted out; each one had his part allotted; and our Jesus has also his lot. Here is a world lying in iniquity, and here is a "lot" of antichristian professors, and a "lot" of profane swearers; a "lot" of characters that live and die in sin; and our Lord has also *his* "lot;" and this lot is "his people." So we find the Lord says by the prophet Isaiah, "This people have I formed for myself." Why, God formed *all* people; but here is a people he formed "for himself." "They shall show forth my praise." He does not say: "They shall have a chance." When I hear men talk about having a chance of being saved, it really offends my nostrils; I hate it in my very soul. Blessed be God, we stand upon better ground than this chance work: "They shall " —not "have a chance" merely—but "*they shall* show forth my praise;" and where God comes into the conscience, it does bring the vilest sinner to show forth the praises of God. Why, are you not shocked at hearing about a chance of being saved? As though God the Father had left his honour to chance, and God the Son had left the efficacy of his love and blood to chance, and God the Spirit had left his operations to chance! So that the Father may love and elect, the Son may love and redeem, and the Spirit may love and quicken, and yet, by chance, if the creature does not do his part, the whole work may be null and void; and the whole glory of God, according

to this, rests upon chance! Why, can you worship in your soul a
God who has no better ground for his declarative glory and the
blessedness of his people than chance, and that chance dependent for
the accomplishment of it upon such poor creatures as you and I,
who are not steady for five minutes together in the day from January
to December? No; blessed be God for a better salvation than that,—
a salvation which stands upon God's *wills* and *shalls*, and which will
save his people from all the power of sin and Satan. And thus,
blessed be God, he has a portion, or inheritance, in a people that he
has "formed for himself."

"Why, then," says some poor soul, "if this is the case, if God has
a people of his own, a people formed for himself and that shall show
forth his praise, I am such a poor shortsighted creature, and so set
upon going after my own folly and sin, that the Lord will never have
me; he will have better characters than I am." But do you just look
at what the Lord says of these characters: "He found him in a desert
land, a waste howling wilderness;" "The beasts of the field shall
honour me, the dragons and the owls; because I give waters in the
wilderness and rivers in the desert, to give drink to my people, my
chosen;" and he makes "the wilderness into the garden of the Lord."
Why, our blessed Joseph takes in hand such that nobody could
manage but himself; and when a poor sinner is brought, in real sense
and feeling, to find himself in such an unmanageable state that all
the world cannot manage him and he cannot change himself, then
the Lord picks him up, brings him into a manageable state, and gives
the poor soul to know, in his own heart's experience, that "the Lord's
portion is his people." It is not any worthiness of ours that induces
him to take us in hand; it is his love, his grace, his mercy; and he
delights to manifest them to the needy and the poor. If you will
only look through the volume of inspiration, you find the greatest
part of the promises are to the poor, the weak, the helpless, the ready
to perish; yea, those who have no might nor power. And thus our
God brings to himself immortal renown; for he builds his house of
such materials as nobody else could square, and makes it a glorious
house too—a house that shall bring him eternal praise. And so he has
his portion—his inheritance—his "lot."

III. Now we come, in the last place, to the *blessing*. "Blessed
of the Lord be his land, for the precious things of heaven." That is
one part of the blessings, secured to God's spiritual family. And
what are they? The apostle gives us a little hint of them in one
place: "Blessed be the God and Father of our Lord Jesus Christ,
who hath blessed us with all spiritual blessings in heavenly places
in Christ, according as he hath chosen us in him before the foundation of the world." These are "the precious things of heaven." What
are they? There is pardon, reconciliation, peace, righteousness, holiness, prayer, praise, brokenness of spirit, tenderness of conscience,

humility, godly simplicity, love, peace, joy; in a word, a title to heaven, a meetness for it, a safe convoy there, and the glory of God when we get there; and all locked up in the heart of the Son of God, who himself has the key, and can open and none shall shut, and can shut and none shall open. These are "the precious things of heaven," —the immortal blessings which God has secured in the Person of Christ for his blood-bought family. It is on this ground we are told that he gave us grace in Christ before the world was: "Who hath saved us, and called us with a holy calling; not according to our works, but according to his own purpose and grace, which was given us in Christ Jesus before the world began." And thus, when the Lord is speaking of our spiritual Joseph, he says he is "full of grace and truth." What is he to do with them? He did not want grace for himself in his own Person in glory. "Of his fulness have all *we* received, and grace for grace." So that this fulness of grace and fulness of truth, which are locked up in the heart of Christ, are put there for the purpose of God giving them to beggars, to paupers, to poor ruined sinners. And mind, poor tortured soul, he does not give thee his blessings reluctantly. He lets his people know that "it is more blessed to give than to receive," and that he really considers himself honoured in poor beggars possessing these blessings at his hand—this grace and this glory at his hand. It crowns his brow, and heightens manifestively his glory in their consciences, and they are brought to crown him Lord of all. Thus his gracious Majesty has all fulness in him, for "it hath pleased the Father that in him should all fulness dwell." Well, then, if "all fulness" is there, there can be nothing but emptiness anywhere else. And consequently, poor burdened soul, it is thy privilege and mine, under the blessed teachings of God the Spirit, to come to our spiritual Joseph in our famishing condition. Are we not brought to feel a famine from day to day? There is "corn in Egypt,"—in the heart of our blessed Christ. There is abundance; the "fulness" is there. And, honours crown his brow, we shall have to say as poor old Jacob did, when his sons came back and brought the wonderful tidings, though he could not believe it till he saw the provisions and the waggons come to fetch him and all the family: "It is enough. Joseph my son is yet alive. I will go and see him before I die." Poor soul, you may have your frames and feelings sometimes dead enough, and your enjoyment sometimes dead enough; but *Joseph lives!* Bless his holy name, "he is yet alive." God help you and me, in faith and feeling, to visit him, and to go in our famishing condition to our spiritual Joseph, that we may enter blessedly into the mysteries of his love and the fulness that in him dwells, and know the truth of that text: "I am like a green fir tree; from me is thy fruit found."

If I have any free-willers here to-night, I know what you are saying now. "Why, the Lord says we are to 'work out our own salvation.' What do you think of that?" I will tell you what I tell my people sometimes,—that Arminians always carry a pair of religious scissors about them; and when they get hold of part of a passage which tells for them they cut it in two, take that part and throw the other away, and so make nothing but confusion in the Word. Now the passage reads, "Work out your own salvation with fear and trembling; for it is God which worketh in you both to will and to do of his good pleasure." And when "God works in us," it is very blessed to work it out; but there is no working it out till God works it in, and works in us to do, and then it flows out freely in prayer and praise and thanksgiving and adoration; and we bless God for the manifestations of his love and mercy, and glory in the fulness of grace that is in the Lord Jesus Christ.

Another branch of these blessings is "the dew." But my strength tells me I must conclude with only a hint or two. By "the dew" I understand spiritually the divine penetrating, softening, reviving dew of the blessed Spirit of God, when it descends "like small rain" upon our poor parched consciences. And have you never been brought to find that when faith seemed as if it were low, and love low, and prayer and praise low, and that when you looked (if I may so speak) at the vegetation of your soul, you were ready to say, like David, "My strength is dried up like a potsherd, and my tongue cleaveth to my jaws" (Ps. xxii. 15)? And when there seems to be no putting forth of one single spiritual plant or blade, then if the Holy Spirit comes with the divine dew of heaven, with his immortal droppings of love and power and unction, supplies the conscience and bedews the soul, O what a springing up there is! Faith begins to revive, and hope begins to revive, and love begins to revive, and prayer begins to break forth, and praise begins to take place in the conscience, and you feel a sweet springing up of the blessed grace of the Spirit of the Lord in your heart, under the bedewing power of God the Holy Ghost.

Now "the dew" is one part of these blessings; and God has promised it to his people, and secured it in the Lord Jesus Christ. Hence we find, in connection with our text, that the Lord tells us "his doctrine shall drop as the rain, and his speech shall distil as the dew." Dew, you know, penetrates very deep and very powerfully, though it seems to come very softly; and so it is with the child of God. When the Holy Ghost comes with his secret and yet majestic and divine operations, he penetrates to the bottom of the heart; he penetrates to the root of every spiritual blessing in the soul, and makes it all spring up to the glory of God and the blessedness of our own mind. And thus the Lord has secured, in the Person of Christ, "the dew" as well as other blessings, to be bestowed upon the church of the living God.

"'And for the deep that coucheth beneath." What are we to understand by this "deep?" The Lord in one place says that he has cast all his people's sins "into the depths of the sea." What "sea" is that? Sin is of a very inflammable nature—of a burning nature. I believe, humanly speaking, that were it possible to cast our sins into the main ocean, into what is called the sea naturally, and could they there operate with all their inflammatory burning power, they would make the sea boil over and drown the world, instead of being themselves drowned in it. And yet here is a sea which drowns sin; and God has cast his people's sins into those depths. What is it, then? Why, that sea which was figured forth in the temple of the living God; which is neither more nor less than the blood and love of the God-man Mediator. God has cast his people's sins into this sea, and there they are drowned. And this is "the deep," the great deep, the solemn abyss of love and blood, "that coucheth beneath." All our monstrous and damnable sins, and all the implacable enmity of the heart against the living God—this deep "coucheth beneath" it all, and rises up with springs of mercy and love and joy to every poor sin-tortured and burdened soul.

O that the Spirit of the living God may lead you and me, in spirit and in truth, to know something of the blessings of the Lord revealed in these words; for his mercy's sake!

THE PECULIAR PEOPLE.

Preached on Thursday Evening, May 13th, 1841, at Edward Street Chapel, Dorset Square, London.

"A peculiar people."—1 PET. II, 9.

THE whole verse reads thus: "But ye are a chosen generation, a royal priesthood, a holy nation, a peculiar people; that ye should show forth the praises of him who hath called you out of darkness into his marvellous light."

There is one little word contained in this verse which includes in it everything that is worthy of our desire. And with this little word, together with its connection, sealed in our consciences, all the devils in hell will never be able to destroy our interest in heavenly things. "Why," you will say then, "what can this word be?" It is "*ye.*" "But ye are a chosen generation." O this little dear *ye!* If God, in his infinite mercy, applies it to your consciences, with the rich blessings connected with it, it is one of the most valuable gifts that God can possibly bestow on sinners.

"Ye are a chosen generation, ye are a royal priesthood, ye are a holy nation, ye are a peculiar people." Now turn for a moment and examine individually whether such a sentence belongs to you or not;

or are you satisfied with a mere knowledge in your judgment of this truth, namely, that there *is* a chosen generation, that there *is* a royal priesthood, a holy nation, that there *is* a peculiar people? Devil's know this as well as you do; but it does them no good, for they rather take advantage of this knowledge to work more of their devilism and show more enmity to God. But when the poor sinner, under the Divine teachings of God the Spirit, is brought feelingly and experimentally to enter into this "*ye*,"—this direct "*ye*," O what indescribable blessings then follow! May the Lord the Spirit, by the wonders of his grace, make bare his arm and bring some poor dejected rooted-up sinner this night to experience the truth of it in his own bosom, and then he will enter a little sweetly into the mystery of the sentence we have just read as a text: "A peculiar people."

I. From this sentence we shall endeavour, by Divine assistance, to notice that there is *a peculiar people;* that God, in the riches of his grace, has set them in a particular and special way *apart for himself.*

II. That they are *loved with a peculiar love.*

III. That they are brought by the Spirit into *very peculiar circumstances.*

IV. That they have a *peculiar standing before God.*

V. That they find *the flesh lusting against the Spirit, and the Spirit against the flesh.*

I. The Lord has set this peculiar people *apart for himself,* in a particular and special way. Yea, he has so set them apart for himself as to bid defiance to all the roarings and dreadful powers of hell, and all the bubblings and workings-up of sin and pollution both within and without, to separate this people from God's bosom and God's heart. His solemn Majesty has said, when speaking of them, "This people have I formed for myself." Now God formed all people, they are all the workmanship of God; but there are a few characters set especially apart as a little lot, whom God has ordained to glorify; and to them he says, "This people have I formed for myself, and they shall show forth my praise." "O yes," says free-will; "they shall have a chance to do it, if they will." But God says they *shall;* unbelief says you shan't; carnal reason says you can't; and inbred corruption says you won't." But when God says "you *shall,*" and when he speaks the Divine "shall," it comes with an invincible energy to the conscience, and that blessed truth is made manifest, that "he raises up the poor out of the dust, and lifteth up the beggar from the dunghill." God could not possibly do this unless the men were first in the dust and on the dunghill. Now what is this dunghill? Why it is the horrible depravity and the cursed corruption of our filthy nature. And what is the dust? It is the working up and manifestation of the loathsome particles of the guilt and filth of this dunghill. And when God suffers Satan to stir up this dunghill in the conscience of a poor sinner, he finds the dust so overpowering that the poor soul thinks he shall really be suffocated with it and never expects to breathe again. Yet, all the while God has set these humble souls apart for himself; and he will raise them from the dust, and off the dunghill, and will set them among princes, even the princes of his people; and will make them inherit the throne of glory.

Now if you will look at this, in connection with the text just named, "*This* people have I formed for myself," you will find there is nothing very amiable said about them. If God compares them to animal nature, he calls them "beasts of the field," and "dragons and owls." Who besides God would have said so, "These beasts, these dragons, and these owls shall honour me?" No one else would. They would have fixed upon something more amiable. But this is God's method. When God compares his people to inanimate nature, he calls them a wilderness and a desert; but this desert and this wilderness are to become "the garden of the Lord;" and these beasts, dragons, and owls are to be brought forth manifestively to be a people to praise the Lord; and God says "*They* shall glorify me." Now I should not wonder but that there are some persons here who would not be called such creatures as these on any account. You think you do good. How dutiful and "pious" you have always been. Perhaps you have been brought up in piety, and have received a pious education, and hope to continue pious, and do all the pleasure of God. Now I tell you what, if God does not burn up your natural religion, if he does not root up your creature piety, and make you know that you are vile and filthy, you will never know the blessedness of God's blessed salvation. You can only know it in the way that his gracious Majesty pleases you should know it; and his way is to show you the horrible state of your own corrupt nature and the oozings up of that fountain of sin that is within you; and when you feel your own wretchedness and utter incapacity, you are by necessity obliged to place your whole dependence on the Lord. You will then trace something of the matchless wonders of God, who has chosen you as one of his special people, who are formed for himself. "They shall show forth his praise," and you will then know a little what it is to be "a peculiar people."

The doctrine of God's discriminating grace is not fashionable among a certain body of professors; but it is nevertheless true. According to their views, Jehovah himself is the only being in existence who is not allowed to make a choice. To talk of God's making a choice, and setting apart a people for himself,—they say he is an unjust God and the fault of damnation is his; he is not a holy and just God in that case. According to them God is unjust because he chooses; yet you find these very characters vindicate their own right to make a choice, in almost every instance. They think they have a right to choose a companion for life; to choose their own food; to choose or reject God; and yet Jehovah has no right to make a choice. He is the only being without that right. Consequently they sink God lower than the lowest beggar in existence, they make him lower in their estimation than the poorest sinner under the heavens. But when they have used all their arguments and spent all their pride and enmity against God's right to make a choice, he still chooses as he sits on his unshaken throne; and, in his electing, immortal, and everlasting love, chooses a people for himself; a people that shall glorify him and be his portion for ever. "The Lord's portion is his people, and Jacob is the lot of his inheritance." God did not find Jacob full of "pious" cultivation with which some persons wish to recommend themselves to God: but he found him in a desert land, where no one but the Lord would have looked for him. No one else would ever expect to find God's gems and jewels and the crown of his rejoicing in a desert land! O what a mercy it is that the Lord comes to seek and to save his own. If it had not been his work, they would never have been found. No one else would ever look for them there. They would never expect to find them in that low situation in which sin has plunged them. But God knows where to look, and he finds them in a desert land and a howling wilderness. And after he has found them, what does he with them? He leads them forth and instructs them in his glorious dispensations; he teaches them fresh lessons as long as they shall live; and, amidst all the bewildering and dangerous parts of their journey, he keeps them as "the apple of his eye." O what a text that is! The apple of the eye is considered to be the most tender part of the human body. And what is the apple of God's eye? It is his own glory! And where is that secured? In the Person of the Son of God. There the glory of God is secured. So that the Lord keeps those whom he has consecrated and set apart for himself, to be a peculiar people, as sacred and secure as his own glory, in the Person of the God-man Mediator; for he keeps them "as the apple of his eye." What a blessing it is to be among the number of this peculiar people.

II. But I notice further, that this people are *loved with a peculiar love*. When God created the heavens and the earth, and all things visible and invisible, he saw that it was all very good. After this, some of the angels, and the whole of man, fell from their original purity; but such is the special and peculiar love fixed on this people, whom God has formed for himself, that they have never fallen from God's love. I know there is a kind of doctrine abroad, which is this—that Christ has purchased the love of God. "Why," some will say, "do you not believe it?" No; not a tittle of it. But does not the Scripture say something about it? No. I find Scripture language is quite contrary to this. It says, "God so loved the world that he gave his only-begotten Son," not the Son purchased. And again: "Herein is love, not that we loved God, but that he loved us; and has given his Son to be a propitiation for our sins." So that it was the love of the eternal Jehovah alone which was the spring-head and fountain cause of Christ in his mediatorial capacity as our Surety; dying the just for the unjust. And therefore peculiar, special, unmoved, and unalterable is the love with which God has loved his own, before the foundation of the world. Is not this peculiar love? Now, if you or I know anything about our own selves, we know the love which we possess in nature is not very special or peculiar. Let us bring the matter home to our consciences. I do not mean you who have a seared conscience; but you who have a tender conscience. Just bring the matter home to yourself. How often have you insulted the love of God, the kindness of God, the blessings which God bestows on you naturally? You eat and drink, and sometimes feel as if you could almost declare vengeance against the Lord, for not letting you have more, for not increasing your stock. Now, have you not, at times, felt something like this? And is it not a wonder that such insulting and ungrateful conduct has not caused the Lord to swear in his wrath that you should not enter into his rest? And how often have you been led to experience greater mercies than eating and drinking! Some of you have enjoyed a little intimation of an interest in this love; have felt a little melting down of your hard hearts, a little of the joys of salvation; a little of going out in faith towards Christ; a little bringing home of the blessings of Christ to the conscience, by the influence of the Holy Spirit; and have felt, in some measure, that you have fed on the bread of God. You then thought that surely you could never insult the Lord again, or be so hardhearted as you have been. But in a little time the world gets hold of you, sin gets hold of you, and you become as hard-hearted, as dead, as cold, as frozen as before. The enemy of souls has tempted you, and you join in the temptation, abuse the constant kindness of God, and exhibit all the evils of your sinful corrupt nature against manifest mercies. It is no use your hiding the secret. Some of you well know this is too often the case. Yet such is the love of God, notwithstanding all this rebellion, that it continues as strong and unshaken as ever. Then is not this peculiar love? Are you able to describe its peculiarity? No. It is love which wraps up the sinner in God's own heart. It is love which, in spite of all within and all without, is determined to bring the poor, vile, helpless wretch to the immortal enjoyment of God, in a world of ineffable felicity. Was ever love like this? They are loved, then, with a peculiar love.

How manifest will this love appear if we look at its openings, its various forms, and watch its operations, in the condescension and matchless work, as exhibited in the Person of the dear Redeemer. What was it that brought the Son of God to take our nature into union with his Godhead? What induced him to be despised and dishonoured, to be without a home, to travel through the desert, to be the butt and enmity of both devils and men, to be spit upon, scorned, despised, and set at nought? What induced him to suffer the malice and

rage of the powers of hell? What induced him to pick up the miseries, the filth, the wretchedness, the loathsomeness, the horrible scum
of our hateful nature,—to bear it in his own body and to suffer the
vengeance due to a lost world; while, at the same time, the characters
for whom he did all this hated him, abhorred him, set him at nought,
scorned his counsels, and despised his love? What induced him to
do all this? Love, everlasting love, unparalleled love. It lay deeper
than our miseries, was higher than our rebellion, was more extensive
than the wanderings of our hearts. From everlasting to everlasting,
this special, this peculiar love is always the same; nor can all the
overwhelming waters of the dreadful deluges of sin ever quench this
immortal flame, which is put forth by God the Father. It shall for
ever burn with undiminished lustre, in the Person of the Lord Jesus
Christ. Here is love which can never, never be fully entered into
whilst we are in this vale of tears. But the people of God are thus
loved with this peculiar love.

When the great apostle of the Gentiles was brought, by the special
power of God's grace, to know something of this for himself, this is
one part of his song: "He loved me, and gave himself for me." Now
Christ died for the sins of the elect, and it is only those who have
grace given them to realize and enjoy this love who can truly sing
this glorious song. But some will say he loved all men, and gave
himself for all men. If that be true, the damned in hell might rise up
and say, "He loved me, and gave himself for me, and yet we are
damned!" Does not such a thought as this horrify the soul, after
having been brought to see the wonders of the love of Christ? But
this love was never fixed upon devils and damned spirits. It was
locked up in the heart of God the Father, and God the Son, and was
made manifest through the atonement of God's dear Son; and the
blessed Spirit, as the Great Teacher, comes down from heaven, for
the special purpose of teaching rebels this love,—to lead poor vile
wretches to know something of the nature of this great, this amazing,
this peculiar love. Well, then, herein is love; not that we loved God,
but that he loved us! Does this love suit you? Perhaps you do not
believe you want so much of it, but think you can manage a little for
yourselves. Well; the Lord knows, after fifty years' experience, I
have been brought to have all my creature doings rooted up, and
burnt before my eyes; and I have stood and looked on, like a ruined
fool. I have nothing to stand on in self but emptiness before God;
and what is not empty is worse, for it is guilt and confusion. I would
not stand upon anything short of Christ for ten thousand worlds;
now that all my guilty pretences are made manifest by the love of
Christ, brought into my conscience by the blessed power of the Holy
Spirit. It sets my soul solemnly going out after God, and brings me
to wonder at and adore the riches of God's peculiar love, to such a
poor, vile, and wretched sinner.

The love which God manifests towards his people is also peculiar in another respect; that is, no other creatures can realize the blessedness of this love. Angels cannot enter into the glories of this love; for Christ never took on himself the nature of angels, but took on him the seed of Abraham, and died the just for the unjust, to bring us unto God; and this *us* must and shall be brought to God. It does not matter where the sinner is. When the appointed time is come to make this love manifest, wherever the poor sinner happens to be, he seeks him out, and finds him. If it is the Zaccheus in the tree, down he must come. If it is the Philippian jailor, putting the apostles' feet in the stocks, he finds him out. If it is a Magdalene with seven devils, she is made to go to the feet of the Lord, with brokenness of heart and contrition of soul.

Some of you in this assembly, I dare say, recollect how strange a thing it was when the Holy Ghost sought out you. I know how strange it was with me. When young, I gave myself up to profane swearing and hardness of heart, though often horrified in my conscience, for I used solemnly to declare I would never think about religion, except I was forced. Is it not a wonder that God stooped to make known and manifest his love to such a vile wretch? The natural conscience will terrify a man to distraction, but will never bring him to feel that all his sins have been against a holy, just, and good God; that he stands guilty at the bar of God; and that all the faults of our hearts, the whole loathsome evil workings of our minds, have been high treason against a holy God. Few, perhaps, have felt more heart-rending, in the workings of the natural conscience, than I have. I was in that terrible state for years ; and when alone, I expected hell to open and let me in; and I thought the devil was ready to drag me to hell. I verily believe that this was all nature. But when God the Spirit came and manifested sin in my conscience, and opened a little of the mystery of iniquity, I then found that all my nature and practice had been nothing less than one constant heaving up of rebellion against a holy, just, and good God. And there I was, with all my sin and guilt torturing my mind; feeling myself as an accountable being to a holy God, whose mercy I had abused, whose goodness I had despised. If the blessed Spirit had not loved me with a peculiar love, he would never have taken so much pains with so hard-hearted and vile a youth as I was. No. He would have said, "Let him alone; let him seal his own damnation and reap the wages due to his sin." But O the mercy, the special mercy and love of our covenant God! When the set time came, he arrested me, broke my heart, and brought me to stand and bow before his throne as a guilty criminal; brought me to sign my own death warrant. I felt that God had a right to damn me. I had nothing to offer, and I could do nothing to save myself. I felt that God would be perfectly just, in cutting me off and sending me to hell. But O! God's peculiar love, that was shed abroad in my heart by his blessed Spirit; which brought me to feel the love and blood of Christ, led me to trace something of the wondrous work of his wonder-working grace. Then, how my hard heart was melted! I was brought to his footstool, with all humility, simplicity, and godly sincerity; filled with gratitude and love for God's unspeakable mercies, in opening these great mysteries to my poor soul. I was then solemnly and blessedly led to believe in God's free mercy and pardon, and could look up and say, "He loved me and gave himself for me." Oh! These little words, this "me," this "ye," this "I," may we all know the preciousness of them; and may the Lord the Spirit bring our hearts to enjoy the blessings they convey. We shall then know something of those glorious blessings of God's pardoning mercy and love which cannot be described and which belong to his peculiar people.

III. This peculiar people are the special choice of God,—they are loved with this peculiar love; and are brought by the blessed Spirit into *very peculiar circumstances*. God works as a sovereign, in his manifestations of mercy to them. Though his gracious Majesty varies in the methods he takes with his people, he brings them all, in a discriminating way, to know and abhor their own vileness, and to know and feel something of the blessedness of his rich love and grace. It may be there are some sinners here, not like such a wretch as I was,— profane and openly wicked; but who think themselves very "pious," and are very holy in their own estimation. They go to church or chapel, read "pious" books; when they go to bed at night say their prayers, and then think themselves quite safe. If they should happen to go to sleep before they have said their prayers, they will get up again, if sufficiently roused to say them; then they think they have made all straight between God and conscience; and if they sometimes do that which conscience tells them is not quite right, they make some kind of confession to God; but it is more of promise than confession. Now the blessed Spirit will, perhaps, take a step and discover to them the hypocrisy of their religion, the vainness of their prayers; and bring them to feel that all they had been building on is nothing but hypocrisy before God. The sinner determines with himself to be more sincere and to try to make up the breach. He begins to mortify the deeds of the body, shuts himself up from all society, that he may increase in the divine life; eats little, drinks little, and tries to be more sincere in his professions of "piety;" so that, by and by, he may be able to appear before God with a little hope of glory. The blessed Spirit suffers him to go on a little, and he begins to think he has conquered his sin, or nearly so; and with a little more exertion, a little more of his own help, he shall conquer it altogether; and he shall then have something to bring before God. But there comes another touch of pain in the conscience. The blessed Spirit gives him another cut in the heart, and discovers to him more iniquity, more of the evil of his own nature. He feels a fresh oozing up of sin in the conscience, which brings his mind to a state of despair. Now his fleshly religion is gone far away; and he is ready to conclude there never was such a wretch as he under the sun. He is left completely bare, and all his fancied good works are rooted up.

"Well," say you, "I have felt something like this. I know my case is very bad; but I hope to be better." I hope you never will in yourself, of yourself, and by yourself. "Why," say you, "you will almost drive me crazy; if I never do better, what can I do?" Do nothing, but sigh, groan, and cry for the pardoning mercy of the Lord, and wait till God takes you in hand; and when the Holy Ghost touches your conscience, giving light, life, and love, communicating the grace and power of Christ, bringing the light of God's glorious countenance to shine upon your conscience, you will then know how vain is every attempt of yours to make up the breach; for the blessed Spirit comes and roots up all hope grounded on self, and you will only know yourself as a poor, ruined, lost, sinner. This is a peculiar fact, is it not? Many professors are the reverse of all this; they offer up thanksgiving for the good they accomplish. Many young ladies and gentlemen think what "pious" acts, what mighty wonders they are doing; but when God the Spirit comes into the conscience, he sets fire to all this, roots up all this; and all this heap of "pious" wonder becomes a heap of impious lumber. All supports then are gone, and the poor soul stands before God as a guilty, perishing sinner, deserving of nothing but wrath and indignation from a justly-offended God. I tell you what, poor soul, if God has really brought you to have these feelings in your heart, you are one of his peculiar people; for he does not take such pains with any one else. You are one of God's own. He takes these pains with his elect, but the rest are blinded and cannot see, and feel, their own detestable state before a holy God. The blessed Spirit will bring the elect help, in his own time. He will bring peculiar mercies to the heart, and all shall go on according to the blessed appointment of the Lord. The Redeemer says, when the Holy Spirit comes "he shall glorify me." Now, some of you want to glorify yourselves; but when the Spirit comes, you will only want to glorify Christ; for, says he, "He shall take of the things of mine and show them unto you." God does this to the sinner because he loves him, and delights in him; so he points out his vileness, pollution, and wretchedness; he throws all in confusion; and then his blessed Majesty comes with peculiar love, and brings home Christ to the conscience; fills the mind with the love of Christ, the holiness of Christ, the fulness of Christ, the compassion of Christ; gives peculiar faith to believe all this, receive all this; not merely as a religious fact, but to receive it with vital faith, feeling a real entering into it, and the unctuous power of it in the conscience. The shell of religion is broken and God brings you to the kernel. You stand before God purified by the blood of Christ, which has cleansed away all your sins. What peculiar blessings these are for God to bestow upon such wretched monsters as we are in ourselves. But this is God's method, and there is nothing under heaven like it.

Now sin is not what some people think it is, a mere empty thing. Some persons talk of sin as if it were a thing of little moment; but when a man is brought to know its bitterness,—to feel that it is a horrible evil against a holy and righteous God, the man then feels that it is a soul-damning and God-dishonouring evil, and he abhors himself for this vileness and wretchedness, because he is the subject of it. He feels he is ruined and lost for anything he can do; but it is then the blessed Spirit comes and manifests his mercy; reveals Christ; brings salvation which is more deep than the miseries; glorifies Christ; reveals him to the conscience; and gives him vital faith in the mysteries of his love and glory. Now do you not see the necessity of all this? "Yes," say you, "I do; but there is one thing I cannot make out. I really cannot make out myself, for I find such contrary workings within." I don't wonder at it. Such peculiar people cannot be made out; none but God can make them out. Paul could not make it out; he found one thing contrary to another. But I was going to say, methinks I see some poor creature going to say, "I have sometimes felt a kind of rejoicing in my heart, that there was really such a blessed salvation, and which just suits the condition of perishing sinners, just suited to man; yet I dare not say it is mine, dare not say it is particularly my own; yet I have felt it in my soul, a kind of rejoicing that it was such a salvation." Have you been there? "Yes," says some poor soul, "I have." Then you have this faith working in you, and which shows you the suitableness of this salvation; but there wants another lift in your conscience to set all matters right, to show you the willingness and determination of God to make known this salvation to you. You can say sometimes in your feelings, "Lord, I feel and see there is enough; if thou wilt, thou canst make me clean; but, I am afraid after all, thou wilt not." Some people will say, "Never mind; simply believe, and then you are all right." This is the devil's high road to destruction, to make men satisfied without feeling a life-giving power, a vital godliness in their conscience. Rest assured of this, if you have the peculiar life which the apostle enjoyed, if you have the Spirit of God in your hearts, you will never be satisfied, short of a feeling sense of interest in the Lord Jesus Christ. You will want to feel what Paul felt when he said, "He loved *me*, and gave himself for *me*." Is not that what you want? Anything, short of this blessedness, and you are left unsatisfied; you are thirsting, panting, groaning after it in your souls. This, poor sinner, is what I want, this is what I thirst for; and if you are one of God's peculiar people, his Holy Spirit will bring you to have it. This blessed love of God will bring you to know this his method; will seek you out, and show you the life, power, glory, holiness, blessedness, of the Three-One God. The Lord the Spirit will make all this manifest to your souls, and you shall feel and see a measure of the glorious suitableness and preciousness of God's salvation.

But some poor child of God is ready to say. "If I could once realize this, that he loved *me*, and gave himself for *me;* if I could once enter into this, I would never doubt again, never murmur again; I would bear anything the Lord pleased to lay on me; and I would tell him so too." Well, poor soul, you had better not tell the Lord too much. He may try you. I will tell you how it has been with me. I was led to tell the Lord that if his blessed Majesty would guide me through present troubles, would give me a lift by the way, would give me some precious gleams of glory, fresh manifestations of my interest in him, I would give his blessed Majesty leave to do what he pleased with me. But I have had so many lessons on things of this nature that, when I am on my knees, I leave off this address to the Lord,—to give him leave; for I soon began to tremble. I soon saw something coming to try me, that I would try to get off the bargain. But no. God keeps to it; he will let you know that what you said to him he will abide by. He will bring you into some peculiar trial and conflict to try your faith, to try his people's sincerity; just to see how they can manage it. Not that *he* wants information; but for *our* spiritual information, and for the glory of Christ who saves to the uttermost. Thus be brings his peculiar people on their way, and to have no might of their own, from time to time.

I recollect about forty years ago, a particular friend of mine was very wretched in his conscience, and seemed so peevish and fretful, so rebellious against God, that my heart was grieved for him. I knew something of it for myself; yet I thought at that time I could bear it better than he. I went to the throne of grace, and prayed to God that he would be pleased to take some of my friend's trouble and lay it on me. I said I thought I could bear it, if God would let him have less; but I have had plenty of my own since. The Lord brought me to know what a poor fool I was. I had no more power to bear up under trouble than my weak brother. Perhaps some of you have been there. Perhaps some poor child of God is there now. Very well; make the best of it while you have it; but know this, the blessed Spirit does not play with his people. He brings them real trials of faith. They must be tried by fire; for God himself declares that every man's work shall be tried by fire. However, this peculiar people shall come out of the fire, kept alive by the life-giving power of the Holy Ghost, in the midst of the fiercest flames, and themselves saved, though their lumber shall be burnt up, yet "so as by fire;" in the midst of the fire they shall glorify God. This peculiar people shall be brought through all their troubles by the blessed Spirit; for he takes peculiar methods with them. He will lead them forth in spiritual life; he will lead them to God, and to know something of the preciousness of the Lord Jesus Christ. When a child of God is first brought to know Christ, if the blessed Spirit gives him faith to realize him as a Saviour, the poor sinner thinks he has got all, and he says, "This is my God; I have waited for him. How richly I am laden now!" And he thinks he shall always go on cheerfully.

Now, I tell you what the Lord will do. It was the case with me when I enjoyed a sweet sense of pardon of sin and reconciliation with God in my soul. I felt, in some measure, the power of the love and blood of the Lord Jesus Christ; but I knew vast little of the glorious offices and characters of the Lord Jesus Christ by vital faith and feeling. Men are prone to look upon them as mere ornaments or titles of honour; but in the Lord's time I was brought to feel and see that they were blessed branches of the glorious riches of God's grace suited to my case. His offices are not mere titles like our nobility, who are called by various titles of honour, which are nothing but baubles; this is not the case with the Lord Jesus Christ. There is not a name he sustains; not an office he fills; not a character he bears; not a relationship in which he stands; but what he fully supports. On him devolve the promises. The blood, the obedience, the righteousness, the wisdom, the strength, all he is, and all he has done, is just suited to a sinner, just what a sinner needs, and God designed. And his "peculiar people" are brought to see the necessity of his offices; they feel that they cannot do without them. The riches of God's grace are manifested to their consciences; they are brought to experience and to handle and feel the Word of life; and to know that there is a glorious reality in all the mysterious openings of the love of God in the gift of his Son and the blessedness of free salvation. But none but God's peculiar people enter into these things, and they can only enter into these things, as these things enter into them. I have found by experience that when my judgment went into these things and my heart has not felt them, they have rather made me giddy; they have brought me into some giddy step or another. My brethren, brain religion will not do; and I sometimes tell my people that brain religion breeds a brain fever; but God brings us down a step, and so we are brought to a proper feeling before a heart-searching God. Don't you be satisfied with the knowledge of truth in the judgment. If any one wants to persuade you so, hold such a one as a vagabond, as a man who wants to deceive you. "The kingdom of God is within you." It stands in God's power, and must be maintained in the soul by the power of God. Don't you suffer yourself, if you can help it, to be satisfied with mere judgmental knowledge; but be resolved to have the vital power of it. If you have to go through ten thousand hells, and wade deep in them a thousand times, never mind; the blessed Spirit will bring you through, and eventually enable you to bless God for his manifold mercies, in making known to you the offices of Christ, and the fulness of Christ; he will bring you in your consciences near to him, and cause you to pour out your souls and glorify him as the covenant God of his peculiar people.

Now, people who are thus taught and led, are God's special and peculiar people.

IV. But we now observe further, that this peculiar people have *a peculiar standing before God.* They do not stand before God on the ground of their own obedience, on the ground of their own holiness. Paul tells us that "being justified by faith, we have peace with God, through our Lord Jesus Christ, and herein we stand." "What? Stand in this grace justified by faith?" say you. No; not justified by faith, only experimentally, but justified by the personal obedience of the dear Redeemer. Yes, in the sight of God this is our exclusive justification to acquit us. But, in the court of conscience, we have faith given to receive that obedience into our hearts, and that faith brings pardon into the conscience. We have not peace with God, we cannot have peace with God in our souls, till the blessed Spirit reveals to us that God is the Author of our peace and perfect righteousness; and then we are brought to feel that we really stand before God in the spotless obedience of the blessed Redeemer. Thus God's peculiar people will have his blessed revelation brought unctuously to their feelings; and they are made to stand in Christ, to love Christ, to press on Christ, to have Christ's righteousness applied to their conscience; they are found "not having their own righteousness, which is of the law, but that righteousness which is of God, by faith." When the child of God is brought to these feelings, the great enemy of souls will ask him, in all the malice of his infernal nature, "What! You righteous,—a poor, polluted wretch like you? Look at your prayers; look at your vain thoughts; remember how you wander in hearing; look at your practices; how can such a wretch as you stand holy and spotless before a heart-searching God? Can you venture? No, no. You would stand condemned. Can you challenge, 'Who shall lay anything to your charge?'" Now, if God the Spirit does not give the soul, at that time, a peculiar faith, a putting forth of faith, faith in its various branches, with peculiar power to realize Christ, the poor soul will stagger to and fro like a drunken man, and he will think he has been deceived. But, if the blessed Spirit puts faith in exercise, upon Christ's finished work, in Christ, as having brought grace and glory in his Mediatorial capacity, then the poor soul can stand before God in Christ; and is enabled to say, "I know I am a poor sinner; I know I have a thousand short comings; but God's rich grace has supplied all my necessities by his Divine power, and has made me to stand in Christ. Is there any lack there, is there any want there? No. There I will live or die, on the ground of God's rich grace, made manifest to me. I am in Christ, and Christ is in me. This is my standing, this is the glory and boast of my heart." When the Lord the Spirit brings us to this point, by vital experience, there is a peculiar solidity felt in the conscience, which enables the sinner to rest entirely on the Lord; and if he has to press through ten thousand troubles, the Lord will bring him through them all, by the manifestations of his peculiar love and grace and mercy. The Lord will bless with peculiar blessings his peculiar people, who are the favourites of God.

V. But I might notice further, that this peculiar people, when engaged in this peculiar work, find that "*the flesh lusteth against the Spirit and the Spirit against the flesh*," and these are contrary the one to the other. And I believe, in my heart and soul, that what the Holy Ghost calls the flesh is not our body, but that principle of sin that is in us, and which we feel to work in a variety of ways, in our various members and powers of the mind; so that, when Paul takes a survey of it, he says, "It is no more I that do it, but sin that dwelleth in me." That is the flesh, that is the old man of sin, in its spring fountain, and oozing up in the old man; but mind, it is his dead body, and it is too bad ever to be mended; it will never be mended; there will be always this work oozing up in the minds of God's people, more or less, to their dying moment, waging war. But, then, there is the blessed image of God, the new man. This new creature stands in the glorious image of Christ, in the light of Christ, in the life of Christ, in the power of Christ, in the truth of Christ, in the love of Christ, in the various branches of the Divine members; and this wars against the flesh in every vessel of mercy. While the children of God are in this wilderness, there will ever be this war carried on,—whether grace shall reign, or whether grace shall not reign. Should the Riot Act of Moses be read in the conscience, the riot is made worse. But when Christ comes with the power of the Holy Ghost, grace is made manifest. The Holy Ghost comes and lifts us into Christ, in his love, blood, and obedience. The grace of God sweeps all before it, and brings in signal victories by the blood of the Lamb, makes the poor sinner to sing victoriously that he has overcome by the blood of the Son of God; and this shall be his immortal song, and the testimony of God's peculiar people, for ever and ever.

While you are feelingly in the sweet enjoyment of Christ, all appears well; but in all wars there is a bone of contention. Now, what is the bone of contention in the real Christian's warfare? This I believe to be the great bone of contention—whether Christ or the creature shall have praise. The old man will exalt the creature in some shape or other; he does not care about the purposes of the Creator. But the new man, the man formed in God's image, has made up his mind that, "the strong man shall not glory in his strength, neither the wise man in his wisdom; but he that glories shall glory in the Lord." *No flesh* shall be the object of glory, but the good man shall glory in God alone. Now, this is the bone of contention; consequently, while the creature stands opposed to Christ, warfare lies in the bosom. But, then, Jesus assures us that grace shall reign triumphant; and by and by the child of God shall have deliverance and shall enter into the presence of God, in the holiness of Christ, at the great resurrection morn. There will then be a peculiar rising. First the saints shall rise, with bodies like the glorious body of the Son of God, and they shall appear with him in glory. They will then fully enter into the mystery of that truth, "I in them and thou in me."

Do you know anything of these things? Has God ever cut up your false hopes? Has he ever upset your creature religion? Has he ever brought you to feel the plague of your own hearts? Has God ever pulled down what you have built up? Has the blessed Spirit revealed Christ to your souls, the hope of glory, and brought you to rest in him alone? If he has, bless God for his peculiar mercies. And may the Lord bless us all with the sweet enjoyment of his peculiar love, for his mercy's sake. Amen.

THE BENEDICTION.

Preached on Tuesday Evening, June 1st, 1841, in Gower Street Chapel, London, on taking leave at the Close of his Annual Visit.

"The grace of the Lord Jesus Christ, and the love of God, and the communion of the Holy Ghost, be with you all. Amen."—2 COR. XIII. 14.

If God is graciously pleased to grant you and me the sweet unction of the blessings contained in the passage read as a text, we possess the rarest blessings it is in the power of God to bestow upon creatures. Angels do not enter into the glorious mystery of some part of it; and therefore we have a song to sing more divinely glorious than that of the angels in heaven.

Some people tell us that it should not be read as a prayer of the apostle that this *might be* the case, but as a declaration that *it is* the case. But I am wonderfully mistaken if the heart of God's people, at one time or another, would not give that statement the lie. For though these things are secured in the Person of Christ, can you, can I,—dare we, *always* say that we possess in our souls the sweet, melting, cheering grace of Christ and the communion of the Holy Ghost? Communion springs from union, and there must be both a giving and a realizing; and do you and I always feel a solemn coming in and a blessed going out of communion with the Holy Ghost? Alas! If we search our hearts, we shall often find that there is a different sort of communion, which staggers and confounds us, and often makes us wonder what sort of outrageous animals we are; for we really cannot make it out; at least *I* really cannot make out what sort of a crea-

ture I am, because of the worthlessness and wretchedness that I feel.
And yet, to the honour of the Lord I would speak it, there are moments when there is a solemn coming in, by the power of the Spirit,
and a solemn going out to the Lord, by the same; and then I want
no mortal living to tell me that "the communion of the Holy Ghost"
is "with me." Now the apostle does not merely say, "This is secured in Christ," but, "be with you." It is a personal and a sweet
and a blessed matter. And the real child of God, quickened and made
alive by divine grace, wants the immortal blessings couched in our
text to have a residence, a dwelling, a sweet springing up and a Divine flowing in his own heart; and then he knows something of what
it is, for "the grace of the Lord Jesus Christ, and the love of God,
and the communion of the Holy Ghost" to be "with him."

I shall just make a remark or two upon the passage as it lies before me; and I shall speak, as far as God shall enable me, as standing on the verge of eternity; for perhaps you and I shall never see
one another again in the flesh; but if we meet *here*,—that is, in
"the grace of the Lord Jesus Christ," if we meet in "the love of
God," if we meet in the solemn "communion of the Holy Ghost,"
and if, through the divine teachings and operations of the Spirit,
"the grace of Christ" is in us, "the love of God" is in us, "the
communion of the Holy Ghost" is in us,—if we could be a million
miles distant, we should stand before God on the same ground. Yes,
brethren, if God takes some of us to heaven, and leaves others to
grovel a little longer here below, we still stand before God, whether
in heaven or on earth, upon the same solemn ground. And the event
shall prove that we shall at last meet together in the mystery of everlasting, immutable love, to "dwell for ever with the Lord."

Perhaps some of you will say, "The text does not lie exactly in
proper order; it should begin with 'the love of God,' and then 'the
grace of Christ' appears richly and blessedly to spring from that."
But I believe it lies in that order in which God teaches his people.
Whatever view we may have of the love of God in the spring-head of
grace or mercy, what is it that God reveals to the conscience which
first springs up in our hearts and leads us to know something of the
mystery of it! Did you ever know anything spiritually of the love
of God till you felt a little of the grace of Christ? Is it not by being
brought by the sweet teachings of the Spirit to have a little of the
meltings and divine operations of the grace of Christ that we are led
solemnly into the love of God? And so, through the channel of the
grace of Christ, we "enter into rest;" and God is glorified in opening the mysteries of his everlasting love to our souls.

You may ask, "Who are they that are intended in the text?"
Why, God's heaven-born family. And mind one thing; as far as it
stands in Christ, the whole elect are interested in it, whether they
are born of God or not; but as far as it stands in the manifestation

of it in our consciences, none are interested in it till God quickens their dead souls and brings them to a spiritual acquaintance with it. And it is the latter the apostle has in view,—that we may have a sweet, a blessed acquaintance with the mysteries of the gospel in our own hearts.

I. We will first, then, drop a hint or two upon *the grace of our Lord Jesus Christ*.

II. The *love of God*.

III. The *communion of the Holy Ghost*.

I. The *grace of our Lord Jesus Christ*.

And really what a cluster of divine blessings there is in this single expression! We may talk of the grace of a king, a fellow-creature; but here is the character set before us that is the wonder of heaven, —the Lord Jesus Christ, Lord of heaven and earth, God over all; in the glorious character of the Saviour, who saves his people, with the immortal openings of God's love, in confirming them manifestively in his saving office by the divine unction without measure,—the Christ, the Saviour, the anointed Saviour, who has grace to bestow upon rebels. And it is grace, the solemn grace of this glorious Person, the Lord Jesus Christ, which the apostle prays might be with the church.

And what is couched in this grace? Though I attempt to tell you, I shall tell you vast little about it; for we must die to know much about it; and every little God is graciously pleased to teach us only teaches us that we know very ltttle; and the more we have, the more we know that we know but very little, and that we must enter into a state of immortal glory, really and truly to know much of the grace of the Lord Jesus Christ.

There is one portion of Scripture upon this subject: "Ye know the grace of our Lord Jesus Christ, that though he was rich, for your sakes he became poor." Now that text has set me fast many a time. How set me fast? I never yet have been able to get into the glory of the riches of Christ—fully and blessedly so; and I never yet have been able to get into the glory of the poverty of Christ Jesus, the riches and the poverty meeting together. A little measure of it in the conscience brings the soul to such divine humility that we are lost in holy amazement. So "rich," that he is "the brightness of the Father's glory and the express image of his Person;" so "rich," that he has treasured up in himself all the immortal mystery that ever God did and ever God will reveal to the millions of his elect. It is all locked in his heart, treasured up in him; the fulness is there,— "full of grace and truth." And so "poor," that he had not where to lay his head; so "poor," that he could call no where his home; so "poor," that he met with worse treatment than foxes: "Foxes have holes and the birds of the air have nests;" so "poor," that he had to wade through all the trials and distresses and temptations and miseries that devils and men and (perhaps I shall stagger you) sin,

damnable sin, could lay upon him; and this, too, accompanied with
the wrath of insulted Justice, the terrors of God; and so "poor," that
when overwhelmed in this misery, he had not a soul of the human
race to sympathize with him.　His disciples who were nearest him
went to sleep; Judas betrayed him; a band of vagabonds met him to
take him and torture him; he was cruelly mocked and scourged, and
everything that was awful was poured upon him.　And yet this very
Person, who so emptied himself as to submit to this scorn and contempt, was the God of all worlds,—the Maker and Supporter of all
worlds.　The pillars of hell tremble at his bidding; devils acknowledge his might; and yet he so emptied himself in the solemn displays of his grace to his people as to be the sport,—the mark for the
arrows and darts of devils, men, and sin.　And this, poor tortured,
poor tempted soul, to come down to thee; to come into thy case and
circumstances; to be a sympathizing Friend with thee.　Talk of an
exalted Christ!　It is very blessed to get in feeling to an exalted
Christ through the poverty of Christ.　To get to him through the
channel of a bleeding, tortured, slaughtered, tempted, abused, scorned, despised, humbled Christ,—under the teaching of God the Spirit,
to get to an exalted Christ, through this immortal channel of Divine
grace, brings the soul into a state of solemn exaltation and deep
humiliation at the same time.

Now here is a little measure of "the grace of the Lord Jesus
Christ."　"For your sakes he became poor."　You and I have no
cause to look with any degree of indignity upon the power of Satan
and men who abused him.　Neither devils nor men could have
touched him, had he not put himself under the solemn gracious con-
straint of lying under their power in this sense, to come down to your
case and circumstances, and so to sympathize with you.

Now some poor soul is ready to say, "Would ever Christ stoop so
low, bear such indignity for such a vile wretch as I?"　He did it
for none but vile wretches.　If there is not a vile wretch in this congregation, he did not do it for a soul of you.　He never took this
upon himself, he never thus "became poor," for any but vile wretches.
And, therefore, those who imagine they are not vile, nor base, nor
wretched,—let them take their own heaven.　God knows I never
wish to be with them in it; they are welcome to it, with all the
exaltation they can boast of in it.　My glory is, under the blessed
teachings of the Spirit of the Lord, to have a heaven that comes to
me through the channel of a once slaughtered, agonizing, poverty-
stricken Christ, who is exalted now at the right hand of the Father,
to bring the characters for whom he was then smitten to the blessed
enjoyment of himself.　And may this grace be with you,—"the grace
of the Lord Jesus Christ."　"For *your* sakes he became poor," ye
self-loathing, pulled-to-pieces sinners.　There is not a set of men
or women in the world that I love to have intercourse with but such

as these. A whole-hearted, pretty, nice-stepping, neat-spoken, sinner in matters of eternity! I would as soon have to do with a bubble upon the water as with him. In matters of civil society, I desire to be as courteous as I can to all my fellow-sinners; but the characters I feel love to are poor, wretched, pulled-to-pieces sinners, groaning under the sense of their misery. And these are the very characters the Son of God was made poor for. And why? That they, "through his poverty, might be made rich." Through his humbling himself, they are exalted; through his becoming "a worm and no man," they are brought richly and blessedly to the enjoyment of the adoption of sons; through his weakness (for he was "crucified through weakness") they are made "strong in the Lord and in the power of his might;" through his poverty, they are made "rich in faith" and manifestively "heirs of the kingdom" of God. And thus, through the *homelessness* of the Lord Jesus Christ, through his having no home, they are made to possess the blessedness of having "an inheritance incorruptible and undefiled and that fadeth not away." We have to travel, brethren, to our home and our exalted state through the solemn steps of a suffering God in our nature,—a tried Jesus in our nature; bearing our offences and dying "the Just for the unjust, to bring us unto God." "The grace of the Lord Jesus Christ be with you."

But, then, we observe, further, "the grace of the Lord Jesus Christ" couches in it what the Holy Spirit says of him: "Full of grace and truth." Do you want the grace of prayer? It is in Christ. If that is "with you," you find the same Spirit that breathed out to God at Gethsemane breathe out in your souls. "But," say you, "I am in darkness, and sometimes I am afraid I shall die in darkness." Aye, so am I too; the Lord knows I am. I do not know that death ever appears to me more terrific than when I feel a fear that I shall die in darkness; I do not want such a death as that. But I can tell you what the Lord has brought me to know a little of, and to feel a little satisfaction in, and that is, that if God should see good that I should die in darkness, I am but level with the Lord Jesus Christ. He was in darkness, and cried out in darkness, "My God, my God, why hast thou forsaken me?" Why, bless you, poor souls, we have solemn company when we have such company as this, have we not? Even in our dark moments, when we are able, in some measure, to feel that we are in such company, we trace a little of "the grace of the Lord Jesus Christ," that he put himself so low as to be a pillow in death to his poor people, if they were dark there, that they might find rest in him eventually, and be led to glorify him. "The grace of the Lord Jesus Christ be with you."

If you want faith, there is a fulness in him. And if you want patience, there it is. And I do not know sometimes whether that is not what I stand in need of more than anything else. I feel it every day. I have had afflictions, torturing afflictions, close afflictions, for more than twenty years, and one upon the heels of another, tearing my poor flesh and blood, till sometimes I think there is not a mortal under the heavens that stands more in need of patience; and I am ready to think that God gives me none at all,—I feel so dissatisfied with the Lord's dealings. "And," say you, "do you let folks see it?" Too much, at times, I assure you; and I am very much ashamed that ever I show it, or feel it. But so it is; and I feel in my very soul the necessity of the patience of the Lord Jesus Christ. O! How patient he was in his afflictions! If they reviled, he "reviled not again;" if they scorned, he scorned not again; he bore the insults of men with patience and submission. O brethren! May the patience of Christ be in your hearts and mine. Lord the Spirit! Pour the patience of Christ into our hearts, and detain it there, that we may be "patient in tribulation," and that patience May "have its perfect work." And if, under the sweet teachings of the blessed Spirit, we are brought there, we know something about "the grace of the Lord Jesus Christ."

We want sometimes a little strength, to support us under troubles and afflictions. And I dare say here is some poor child of God who has thought before now that he had got a tolerable share of strength. I remember the time when I felt very grieved for a brother, one that I believed to be a child of God, because he seemed so very impatient in trouble; and I prayed the Lord to take some of his troubles off from him, and give me some of them; I thought I could bear them better than he. But it is a long time since I have prayed for any of other people's troubles, I can assure you; I soon gave up that business. God taught me how weak I was, and how much I needed the strength of Christ. But then, in "the grace of the Lord Jesus Christ," there is the strength of God,—"Christ, the power of God." If we have "the grace of the Lord Jesus Christ" with us and in us manifestively, we have the spirit of prayer and the spirit of praise, the spirit of love, the spirit of patience, the spirit of meekness, the spirit of humility, the spirit of strength, the spirit of brotherly kindness, the spirit of godly simplicity, the spirit of holy adoration, the spirit of deadness to the world, the spirit of union to one another in and through the blessed Redeemer. We have, in reality, the sweet unfoldings of the mystery of a Three-One God, in the heart and love and blood of Christ, to be with us and in us.

Now do you know anything of this? Could I wish you better than pray with the apostle, if I should never see you again, "The grace of the Lord Jesus Christ be with you?" Brethren, God help you to pray for me, that it may be with me; and me for you, that it may be with you; that we may this night have our consciences loaded with the grace, the matchless grace, of the Lord Jesus Christ, and that it may have an abiding place in our hearts, that so we may trace our interest in him, and live to the praise of his Name, who has done such mighty wonders for us. "The grace of the Lord Jesus Christ be with you."

II. "And the *love of God*." Now, if I know anything of "the love of God," and I believe I do, I know that I was brought to a sweet enjoyment of that love through "the grace of the Lord Jesus Christ." And there is one thing I can say,—that though the child of God may and frequently does doubt his interest in Christ, yet there are doubts, fears, suspicions, bondage, and distress, which do not amount to the point of questioning his interest in the love of God. "O," say you; "if I believed I was interested in the love of God, I should have no doubts nor fears nor suspicions." You do not know what you are talking about, and you had better hold your tongue till you do. If ever God brings you feelingly and spiritually to know your interest in "the grace of the Lord Jesus Christ and the love of God," and you have to come through sharp conflicts, you will have fears and doubts and miseries, and yet at the same time, if it were put close to your conscience, you could not, at all times, call in question your interest in Christ. I do not mean to say that you may not *say* you do, because you do not always speak the truth, you know. We sometimes keep back a little of the truth, in order to get a little pity from our brethren. "But," say you, "I wish you would describe a few of the doubts and fears and suspicions we can have and yet know our interest in the love of God; what can they be?" I will tell you what it has been with me, and what, if I live long, I am afraid it will be again. I have feared, for one thing, that one day or another I shall be left to tumble some horrible thing out which makes me groan within,—that it will not keep its place even within, but that it will come out, and that after all I shall bring my own character, the church over which God has made me overseer, and the cause of God with which I am connected, into contempt and disgrace. "O! You have no cause to fear that," say you. "Why, God has kept you these fifty years, and he is sure to keep you to the end." But what feeds, at times, my fear is, he *has* suffered some of the most eminent of his family to dishonour themselves and the cause of truth; and why not me? He suffered David to do it; he suffered Solomon to do it; he suffered Peter to do it; and why not me? O! How my soul trembles, at times, lest it should be sounded through half the empire: "That Gadsby has become a public disgrace and nuisance in his character, and has dishonoured the cause of God!" And yet, while I feel, at times, dreadful fears of this nature, I dare not call in question my interest in the Lord; but believe that if I were suffered to do that, his blessed Majesty would restore me. But then I would rather die, I would rather die to-night, than do it. O! It is torturing to the mind; and yet the enemy of my soul and my fleshly feelings and unbelief get sometimes such hold of me that if you would give me the world I cannot help fearing that I shall live to be a spectacle of contempt, and that it will be said of me, "Is *this* the man that made the earth to tremble?" O! My soul has trembled before God under such feelings! And therefore I need "the grace of the Lord Jesus Christ and the love of God," not only to be secured in Christ, but to be "with me;" to support me, to keep me, to prop up my soul, to awe my mind, and to preserve me from the damnable snares which my corrupt nature and a tempting devil would lead me into, if God's grace did not keep me. And that has been a blessed text to me sometimes: "My grace is sufficient for thee, and my strength is made perfect in weakness."

Now I might name other things; but perhaps this will be a key sufficient to unlock a variety of things to your souls, where you may have great fears, great faintings, great distress, and yet not doubt your interest in the Lord Jesus Christ. So that if you have the blessedness of having an interest in Christ, that will not quit you of all fear and all distress. And I should say it was presumption, if it did; because we are such poor wretches that we stand upon very, very fickle ground, as far as self goes, and are just safe as God keeps us and no further. And so the church are brought to know the truth of that declaration, that there is an inheritance, incorruptable and undefiled, "reserved in heaven for them that are *kept*." Do you know any thing of this "keeping?" Keep *yourself!* Well, I am glad you have not to keep *me*; for if I had no better keeping than *your* keeping and *my own* keeping, I should be a very devil outwardly, and that soon. But as I am led solemnly, by the blessed teaching of God the Spirit, to trace the keeping of the Lord, and in that channel to trace the love, the immortal love of God, and that love in some blessed measure "shed abroad in my heart by the power of the Holy Ghost," I find it a blessed fountain of mercy, a spring-head more prizeable than a thousand worlds.

God tells us, in one place, that "the love of God is shed abroad in the heart." Now the love of God,—Father, Son, and Spirit, is one immutable, eternal, unalterable love, fixed upon his people and kept upon his people. It never was taken from them; it never will be taken from them. "Having loved his own which were in the world, he loves them to the end." But, then, here is another branch of the blessed manifestation of this,—to have that love "with us," "shed abroad in our hearts;" to have it there to sweep away guilty fear, and to bring us to that blessed feeling and the sweet enjoyment of that "perfect love which casteth out fear," slavish fear. Now says the apostle, "the love of God be with you;" that blessed love, that leads us to love God, leads us to love his Word, leads us to love the Person of the Father and the Person of the Son and the Person of the Holy Ghost,—leads us to love the church of God as our brethren, as our nearest companions; that love which makes sin look ugly and hateful and awful, and makes us abhor it; and that love which clasps Christ in the conscience, wraps him up in the heart, and brings to bathe in him, and to find him "a fountain opened" to our soul, that so we may know the blessedness of this truth, "He loved *me* and gave himself for *me*." "The grace of the Lord Jesus Christ and the love of God be with you."

Why, then, brethren, if I never see you again, my prayer is, that this grace and this love may be with *you*. O what riches it will be! What honour it will be! What glory it will be! There is nothing under heaven like it; and there is nothing *in* heaven above it, only a greater measure of it; and thus, when we get out of this vale of tears, we shall only be complete in him, and swallowed up in this grace and in this love. "The grace of the Lord Jesus Christ and the love of God be with you."

III. But we pass on, further, to notice "the *communion of the Holy Ghost*."

We have already hinted that communion springs from union; if there be no real union, there can be no sweet communion. Now the church of the living God, and every member of the mystical body of Christ, are all united to Christ, bone of his bone, body of his body, flesh of his flesh; and when his blessed Majesty is speaking of it, he says, "The head cannot say to the foot, I have no need of thee." Is there a "foot" here now? Perhaps there is some poor member of the mystical body of Christ, that finds himself but a "foot," and can seldom be half a minute out of the dirt in his own feelings; for if he gets out of it one moment he gets into it the next; and so he goes hobbling on, and can never get higher than a "foot," and is ready to conclude the Lord will never have any thing to do with him because he is on such low ground. Come, poor soul, thy Christ cannot do without thee. I was going to say, and I *will* say,—He would not be a complete Christ mystical in heaven without thee. No. He cannot part with a "foot;" he cannot part with a joint. And every part of this mystical body is to be supplied; and the supplying is couched in the communion. Now here is the union which makes the mystical body united together as one body. So that though you be only a joint, you are still part of the body; and if you be any part, you belong to the body. If you be but a hair, you belong to the body. I do not mean a wig, as I have more than once said, which free-will and Arminianism can dress and trim up very prettily; I mean the hair of the head, which grows in the body; and not one hair shall perish. No. In this sense "the very hairs of the head are all numbered," and our blessed Jesus will not part with a joint, will not part with a foot, will not part with a hair, will not part with a single member of his mystical body. They are one church, one body; he is one Head and they are one body; and, blessed be his holy name, he loves them as he loves himself. Now having this union, the Spirit of the living God meets the church of the living God upon this ground,—for he is to "glorify Christ" and "take of the things of Christ and show them unto us;" and, therefore, the apostle says, "The communion of the Holy Ghost be with you."

What is this "communion?" He communicates life, and you feel; then his blessed Majesty draws forth that life into exercise, and you communicate, if I may so speak, or pour it back again from whence it came,—pour it out in feeling, pour it out in confession, pour it out in supplication, and sometimes pour it out in thanksgiving. He communicates the Spirit of prayer; for "the Spirit helps our infirmities; for we know not what we should pray for as we ought; but the Spirit itself maketh intercession for us with groanings which cannot be uttered." Why, then, there is "communion" carried on. We receive this from him; and, under his divine teaching, we pour it out back again in sighs and groans and moans and pantings and breathings after mercy, in "thirsting for God, the living God," and in pouring out our souls unto him for the mercies we need.

He communicates faith; for he is the "Author and Finisher" of it. This faith is "the substance of things hoped for" in the conscience; and the same blessed Spirit enables faith to go out of the believer, as it were, in solemn acts, upon the truth of God, the Persons of God, the love of God, the cross of the Lamb, the mysteries of redemption, the fulness that is in Christ; and, as the Spirit shows to faith and hangs out to faith these blessings, faith brings them into the conscience and settles them in the heart. I have sometimes thought that faith is like a busy bee amongst the flowers in such weather as this; it goes and sucks virtue from every flower and brings it back,—comes loaded into the conscience and drops honey into the heart; and then that same faith enables us to pour it out into the Lord. (Song iv. 11.) And this is "the communion of the Holy Ghost." The Holy Ghost leads faith into the promises, into the doctrines, into the glorious mysteries of the love of God, in the grand openings of it; and faith brings it into the conscience, brings virtue and honey out of it, and the soul realizes it, and gives it back to the Lord to be in his keeping. For really, if the Spirit of the living God were to give us ever such a stock of faith or prayer or love or any other grace, and to say, "Now I leave you to manage it; you have a stock, and I will give up my operations and my teachings and you must manage it," I believe you would lose every particle of it within four and twenty hours; and if God never brought you to feel that you are a fool in religion, you know nothing of the power of vital godliness. But if he *has* brought you to feel that, do not you see how much you need the constant communion of the blessed Spirit? You need him to be constantly dropping blessings, drawing forth the grace he communicates, constantly enlivening, constantly teaching, constantly showing you Jesus, constantly cherishing you with the mysteries of the love of God and the great solemn realities of his blessed revelation; and thus to have "the communion of the Holy Ghost." And as he is graciously pleased thus to lead you, how sweet it is (is it not?) to go back again with this, and to cast it into the hands and keeping of a faithful God! We know something then of what David meant when he said, "I pour out my soul unto the Lord;" as if he had unsouled himself,—given the Lord his soul to keep, and had no care (if I may so speak) about the keeping of his own soul. And so the church is led to say, under the teachings of the Lord the Spirit, "Or ever I was aware, my soul made me like the chariots of Amminadib;" and by these communications the Lord Jesus Christ says to his church, "Thou hast ravished my heart;" or, as some read it, "Thou hast unhearted me." The Spirit communicates Christ so blessedly to the conscience that he leaves Christ, if I may so speak, no heart of his own, drops the heart of Christ into the church, and leaves the church no heart of their own, but gives it to Christ. Thus the church and Christ give their hearts to one another; and they are thus knit together and united together by the blessed Spirit of God, to carry on this immortal communion,—"the communion of the Holy Ghost."

Now do not you find sometimes in your souls a little of this work carried on in secret silence betwixt God and your conscience? Have you never been secluded from society,—when no eye saw you but God's, and have you never felt in reality for a few moments that the Spirit was really letting God down into your hearts and that the same blessed Spirit was really drawing your heart up into God, and effecting such union and communion that your very soul was led to say, "This is my Beloved and my Friend?" Well, here is "the communion of the Holy Ghost." And as we are brought, in the life and power of Jesus, to know something of this blessed communion, we shall feel a oneness with each other and with the Lord which none but God can maintain.

Thus I have dropped a hint or two upon the passage. And now, brethren, all that I can say is, Farewell. Perhaps—but I will not make use of that word, I leave it to God—I might say, *finally* farewell. I leave that with God; he knows better than I. But I feel myself so unfit to travel; such a poor, old, broken, moping creature that I seem as if I had lost all spring of action, as it respects my body, and am ready to think my travelling days are ended. Be it as it may, I cannot, if I were sure I should meet you again a hundred times, leave you with any better blessing than praying in my very soul that "the grace of the Lord Jesus Christ and the love of God and the communion of the Holy Ghost may be with you."

May the Lord God of Israel bless your souls with this; and may it be our happiness to enjoy the life and power of vital godliness in our hearts.

THE CHURCH COMMENDED TO THE WORD OF GOD'S GRACE.

Preached on Tuesday Evening, May 31st, 1842, in Gower Street Chapel, London, on taking leave at the Close of his Annual Visit.

"And now, brethren, I commend you to God, and to the word of his grace, which is able to build you up, and to give you an inheritance among all them which are sanctified."—ACTS xx. 32.

THE characters here addressed, are the brotherhood; and the apostle "commends them to God"—commits them to the care and safe keeping of God the Father, God the Son, and God the Holy Ghost. The Lord has brought me to this point a great number of years ago, that if you take away the Trinity, or one Person in his Personal Godhead out of the Trinity, I really have no hope of salvation. If the doctrine of Three Distinct Persons in One Undivided Jehovah be not a truth, I believe I shall as surely be damned as the devil is damned. I have no hope, separate from that solemn doctrine. If not interested in the Father's election, and the blessings he has treasured up in his Son, which are called "all spiritual blessings," there is not what will supply my needs. If not interested in the atonement and righteousness of the God-man Mediator, I have no hope of pardon, nor of standing just before God; the blood of a mere man, however good a man he might be, will never touch the core of my infernal disease; nor can the righteousness of a mere man ever justify a wretch like me, and present me before God spotless and pure. An external knowledge of these truths, as revealed in the Word, may fill the judgment and furnish ground for speculation and conversation; but I feel before God that I must have a divine application of them to my conscience by the invincible energy of God the Spirit, or they are of no real use to me. And thus I prove that without an interest in the distinct Personality and the Personal engagements of a Three-One God, and without an interest in this Three-One God in union in my salvation, I really have no salvation at all. I must sink, and sink for ever. Then into the hands of this One Triune God, I wish to be enabled, in the fear of God, to commend you. "And now, brethren, I commend you to God, and to the word of his grace, which is able to build you up, and to give you an inheritance among all them which are sanctified."

But what we are about to notice to-night is: *

I. In the first place, the *brotherhood being "commended to the word of God's grace."*

II. Which is *able to build you up.*

---

* This Sermon is the *third* which was preached from this text, the preceding parts being spoken from on Lord's day, May 29th, so that this is the *conclusion* only of the subject. The previous ones do not appear to have been reported. This was the last Mr. G. ever preached in Gower Street.

I. The *brotherhood being commended to the word of God's grace.*

Now to me it appears that the Bible, whether law or gospel, is published by the Lord, in the strictest sense, for the use of his own elect; and I believe, if God had not had an elect people, there would never have been the Bible in the world. I ground it upon such portions of the Bible as these: "Whatsoever things were written aforetime, were written for *our* learning;" and again, "All Scripture is given by inspiration of God, and is profitable for doctrine, for reproof, for correction, for instruction in righteousness, that *the man of God* may be perfect, thoroughly furnished unto all good works." And so we find that this truth, in all the bearings of it, belongs to the man of God.

"Then," say you, "of what utility can the law be to the man of God?" It comes, in the hands of the Spirit, to cut up his false hopes, blast his legal prospects, tumble down the old fabric and lay it in ruins, and let them lie as a heap of lumber, as filthy as the devil can make it. For the law discovers sin and guilt; and what sin is, —"all manner of concupiscence." And so we find that when the Lord is speaking upon this subject he tells us: "From his right hand went a fiery law for his saints." Some people tell us that this law is the saints' rule of life; but then they try to quench the fire before they make it a rule of life; they say it is not "a fiery law," as a rule of life to them. But God says it is "a fiery law for his saints." And so it must be, to burn up the lumber and to bring them to ashes, as it were, before God; and then his blessed Majesty brings forth "the word of his grace," to be a blessing to them in every situation of life.

I consider, then, by "the word of his grace," unto which I wish in the fear of God to commend you, we are to understand his blessed gospel, in all the bearings of it. For I do not know a particle of the gospel which is not a word of grace. "Why," say you, "then you will not find a precept in it, or a command; that cannot be grace." Yes, it is. The command which exhorts God's people to love God and to love one another is a gracious command; the very precept which enjoins upon them obedience is a gracious precept; and the very rebuke which rebukes them for their disobedience is a gracious rebuke, to stop them from straying and to be the means of bringing them nearer home. And, therefore, every particle of the gospel of God, in all its bearings, is a gracious dispensation.

But, a few thoughts upon this "word of God's grace." You will find that the Holy Ghost tells us that this "word of grace" is the word of the oath. God hath solemnly issued it into the world,—aye, and into the consciences of his people, under the solemn sanction of his own oath. "Wherein God, willing more abundantly to show unto the heirs of promise the immutability of his counsel, confirmed it by an oath." What a strange, mysterious thing is this! Here is a company of poor sinners, to whom God has made promises,—"ex-

ceeding great and precious promises," and such is the unbelief of
their hearts, they do not believe the promises of God. "Why, then,"
says God, "will you believe my oath? If you cannot believe my
word, I will give you my oath." And because there was no greater,
he took an oath upon his own holiness, his own justice, his own
truth,—"he sware by himself, in which it was impossible for God
to lie, that we might have strong consolation, who have fled for refuge to lay hold upon the hope set before us." Now, they must be
houseless wretches who "flee for a refuge;" and for those houseless,
homeless wretches, who are brought from necessity to flee to Christ
for refuge, God hath sworn by an oath that he will be their God,
and that he will never leave them nor forsake them. Is not this a
matchless display of unparalleled grace? And may it not well be
called "the word of God's grace?"

But such sinners are we,—at least I must say for myself, that I
am such a polluted, unbelieving wretch that there are moments when
I appear unable either to believe God's word or oath; and I am
much mistaken if it be not the case with some of you. I can believe
the doctrine as the doctrine of God, as the truth of God; but then
vital religion consists in being at home in these truths, and these
truths being at home in my heart,—being enabled to say with David,
"I have hid thy word in my heart," and knowing the blessedness
of that truth, "Sanctify the Lord God in your hearts." "Why,
how can that be? We cannot make the Lord God holy." No; but,
under the divine energy of God the Spirit, there is a solemn feelingly and spiritually setting apart God and his gospel in the heart,
the heart being solemnly set apart of God, and faith realizing the
glorious mysteries of the gospel of God's grace; and when the blessed
Spirit brings the conscience there, we know something of the vital
realities of the mysteries of God's kingdom.

Now this "word of God's grace," under the solemn promise and
oath of God, proclaims, carries in it, and reveals to the conscience
of his people, by the power of the Spirit, a free pardon of all their
sins. That must be grace, must it not,—a pardon of all their sins,
past, present, and to come? And there are solemn moments, when
this "word of grace" comes with such sweet, divine, glorious power
that the soul feels that God has "cast all its sins into the depth of
the sea"—"blotted them out as a cloud, and as a thick cloud;" and
hat when they are sought for they shall not be found.

I "commend you," poor, broken-hearted, rooted-up sinners, to
this "word of God's grace;" and may God commend it to your
hearts, that you may feel the blessedness of the pardon which proceeds from the Father, through the blood of the Son, and is sealed
upon the heart by the energy of the Holy Ghost,—that you may
know what it is, indeed and in truth, to realize the pardon of your
sins and to triumph in the Lord Jesus Christ.

Perhaps there is some sinner here who says he once enjoyed that, and yet now can trifle with every particle of vital godliness. "O!" says he, "I have enjoyed pardon; God told me I was pardoned, I believed it, and I believe it now; and what do I care about enjoying pardon *now*, or enjoying the presence of God *now?* I do not care about that. I know I am pardoned, and I shall go to heaven." And what do you want to go to heaven for? I cannot make out what such reptiles want to go to heaven for. If the presence of God, if the joy of the Lord is of such little moment, that while they are passing through such a desert as this and need so many props, they are careless about it, what do they want to go to heaven for? It is presumption; and if ever a child of God is left to tread such unconsecrated, presumptuous ground, I tell you, as God is God, by and bye you will be in some awful labyrinth. It is awful, awful trifling with God, awfully inviting sin and Satan to unite with you to insult God and trample upon the blood of Christ. May God have mercy upon you, and preserve you from such awful presumption, before it leads you into open disgrace. For unless the Lord stops you, *it will*. And perhaps in this company there may be some who are already there. You can drink, take your glass, and chatter about religion; sing joyfully, make yourself merry, and wantonly go into forbidden paths; commit fornication and adultery, and still be happy. Horror seize your souls, before God sends you to hell for your horrible blasphemy! It is awfully insulting God, and sporting with eternal truth. I hope the Lord will awe my mind and yours, brethren, against such dreadful presumption.

But "I commend you to the word of God's grace," in the rich, sweet display of his pardoning mercy. I know what that will do in some measure for a sinner in his conscience; it will humble him, it will melt him, it will shame him for his sins, and shame him out of his sins. He will know what the Lord means when he says, "Thou shalt remember and be confounded, and never open thy mouth any more, because of thy shame, when I am pacified toward thee for all that thou hast done." Have you ever rejoiced with shame? Triumphed with shame? Been ashamed and confounded because of your vile nature and practice, and yet triumphed in the mysteries of the cross of Christ, and God's pardoning mercy in it? If you have, you have known a little of the blessedness of God's free pardon. I commend you to that blessed "word of grace."

But further. "I commend you to the word of grace" which brings justification to the ungodly. "To him that worketh not, but believeth on him that justifieth the ungodly." This seems a strange mystery, does it not? "Justify the ungodly." How in the world can a just and holy God holily "justify the ungodly?" Why, you know, in civil society we should think it a horrid crime for a judge to justify the ungodly; and yet our God proclaims this upon the

housetop, and in the conscience of a sinner, that he "justifies the ungodly," and justifies him without works. How? Has he justified
his sin—connived at that? No; to show his holy, righteous indignation against sin, he has punished it to the uttermost in the Person
of his Son, and laid upon him that which mere man could never have
borne. But he was the God-man; as Hart says,

> "With strength enough, but none to spare."

He passed by his people, gathered all their sins together, their
sins of omission and commission, against light and against knowledge,
in principle and in practice; and placed them all to the account of
his Son. He drew his divine sword, and demanded full satisfaction;
and if an iota had been left unatoned for, justice must have damned
the whole elect. But the blessed Redeemer fully cancelled every
demand; he bore the penal wrath, atoned for all sin, and "put it
away by the sacrifice of himself." And he wrought out a righteousness which he did not want for his own use; he wrought out one to
give away,—to *give to them who had none*. And God takes this
righteousness, *claps it upon the ungodly*, and says, "Thou art just in
this righteousness." And thus "he justifies the ungodly" in the
perfect obedience of his Son. It is on this ground, therefore, that
the Holy Ghost says, when speaking of Christ, "He was made sin
for us who knew no sin, that we might be made the righteousness
of God in him." And there is such a glory in this righteousness,
in this "word of God's grace," that even an inspired Paul, when he
had been "caught up into the third heaven," and "whether in the
body or out of the body he could not tell," when he heard unspeakable language of immortal glory,—after that ravishing visit, his soul
was bent upon this,—"to be found in Christ, not having his own
righteousness, which was of the law, but that which is through the
faith of Christ, the righteousness which is of God by faith." This is
such a glorious righteousness, so immortally excellent that, as good
Berridge says, with that you may shame an angel; for there is not
an angel in heaven which has one half so good, or half so glorious
as this. For the angels in heaven appear in a creature holiness, and
a creature righteousness, in which they were created; but here is
the holiness, here is the righteousness of God in our nature, placed
to our account; and when God the Spirit reveals it to the conscience
and clothes us manifestively therein, we are brought in solemn pleasure to rejoice in the gospel of God's grace. "I commend you to
God, and to the word of his grace." "Put on the Lord Jesus Christ."
Poor child of God, try to wear him in your approaches to God, in
your reading his Word, in your attendance upon hearing, in your
entering into his house, in your entering upon the ordinances of his
house, in the approaches of death, in the very arms of death. Having
the Lord Jesus Christ, by faith and in feeling, under the unction of
God the Spirit, will make the arms of death a pleasant couch, and

there you will sweetly fall and go to sleep in Jesus. "I commend you to the word of his grace;" and may this "word of grace" enrich you in your souls, and may you find a blessedness in it, living and dying.

"I commend you to the word of" the promise of his grace. Troubles, trials, temptations, and difficulties you *must* have in this world. God tells us that they that "are not in trouble as other men, neither are plagued like other men," are the ungodly; and I would rather believe what God says than what all the parsons in the world say, put them all together. *He* says, these are the ungodly. But as for God's people, they are "plagued all the day long, and chastened every morning." Their plague is a daily plague. Solomon knew something of it when he dedicated the temple, and said, "What prayer and supplication soever be made by thy people, which shall know every man the plague of his own heart, hear thou in heaven thy dwelling-place;" for he never expected any really and truly to turn there who did not know something of the plague of their own hearts, and I am sure nobody knows that if it does not plague them, if they do not find it a plague. But in all your troubles, the promises of God in Christ Jesus are "in him Yea, and in him Amen." What a sweet word of grace is that: "Fear thou not, for I am with thee; be not dismayed, for I am thy God!" "But," says unbelief, "Lord, there is a deep 'water of affliction' there, and I dare not attempt to go in." When thou passest through the waters, I will be with thee." "But there is a hot fire, Lord; it is already kindled, and it seems to burn furiously, and I am expecting it to be more furious still." "When thou walkest through the fire, thou shalt not be burned, neither shall the flame kindle upon thee." In your troubles, your trials, temptations, scorching fires and chilling waters, I commend you to this "word of God's grace." May God support your minds, lead you sweetly and blessedly into its contents, and let you know the truth of his declaration that he is "a very present help in trouble," and will never leave you nor forsake you.

"But," says one child of God, "my enemies are numerous; they are both crafty and powerful, and come like a flood; and as to myself, I feel myself nothing but vanity. I have no more strength than a feather, and a flood would sweep me away in a moment; I have no power, no life, no help." I can tell you this, poor child of God, the less help you have in self the better, and the longer you cling to it the worse plight you are in. *I* have proved this. The sooner we are brought to give it up, and have no power, no help, no might, so much the better. Hear what the Lord says: "When the enemy cometh in like a flood, the Spirit of the Lord shall lift up a standard against him." Not the web of your own sincerity and your own goodness; that is not to be Standard-bearer; the Spirit of God is to be Standard-bearer. And the Standard that he lifts up is the cross of

Christ,—the blessed Redeemer in his blood and righteousness, and that is a Standard against all the floods of hell. Now, what a precious "word of grace" that is to a poor child of God! "I commend you to God and to the word of his grace."

You will perceive, we might go on as long as God would give us time and strength; but my strength tells me I must endeavour to come towards a conclusion.

Are you in a wilderness world, as witnesses for God? Be concerned to bear a faithful testimony. Let truth be a matter of moment and importance with you. Do not trifle with it, do not sport with it, neither in promise, doctrine, precept, ordinance, or any branch of it. It is God's truth, and "the word of God's grace." A blessing runs through the whole. Remember it is God's truth, and we are to be witnesses for God, not to consult our own ease, our own pleasure, our own profit; but the honour of God, the glory of God, and the salvation of immortal souls.

"I commend you" to the revelation that God has made of his love, his grace, his kingly authority, his priestly authority, and all he is and has, as revealed to his church, to regulate your consciences, to regulate your conduct, and all your deportment in the world. Are you husbands? Love your wives; do not be brutes to them. Some people act as if they thought a wife was to be nothing in the world but a slave at their feet, and they were to be "my lord." Are there any here of this description? May God mow you down, lay you level as poor sinners, and let you know that "he that loveth his wife loveth himself," and "no man ever yet hated his own flesh." Are you wives? Be obedient to your own husbands, as unto the Lord. Are you parents? Love and cherish your children and bring them up, as far as you are able, in the admonition and fear of God. Do not sport with truth and say, " O! Because I believe in election I will let my sons or my daughters go where they will; if they are elected, they will be saved." That is hell's use of God's truth; it is sporting with the honour of God, and bidding defiance to the glory of his name. Be concerned to set a good example before your children, to act as in the fear of God, under the teachings of his grace. Are you children? Love your parents, and obey them in the Lord; but not if they want you to disobey the Lord. Are you ministers? Perhaps there may be some here. Give demonstrative proof that it is the honour and glory of God and the welfare of souls which lie upon your hearts; that you are concerned to be faithful witnesses for God, and not to keep back or conceal any branch of his divine will. Are you hearers or members of a church? Do not be the means of leading a minister astray, do not be the means of clapping a cordial to your own minds, when you can go astray yourselves. God help you to act in the fear of the Lord, in the love of the Lord, with God's eye sensibly upon you, and God's fear in you! Whatever station you fill, in the world, the family, or the church, you will find in "the word of God's grace" something to suit your circumstances, to suit your case and condition. And to this word, this blessed word, in union with the God of the word, I commend you. "I commend you to God, and to the word of his grace."

But we come—

II. Lastly, to consider, but for a few moments, what the apostle says of this word: "*Which is able to build you up.*"

God's law, as the effect of our sin, has laid us in ruins; brought down the whole fabric, and made it all appear a heap of filthy ruin, a mass of dirt and devilism; the whole of us, in nature or of nature. And yet it is the intention of God to take that sinner and have his mind, his soul, transformed into the image of God, and God to dwell there; and it is the intention of God to take the body of that sinner and make it the temple of the Holy Ghost, and eventually to change and "fashion it like unto the glorious body of his Son;" and soul and body shall be like the soul and body of Christ. But who can raise such a building as this, think you, out of such a heap of lumber? When the Lord has slaughtered us and laid us low, and we find in self and of self nothing but ashes and lumber and filth, who can raise such an edifice? The Lord, and the word of his grace; plucking the brand out of the fire, creating the man anew in Christ Jesus, and eventually conforming him, both in body and soul, to the image of his Son. That is "able to build us up," and to erect a building, as God says, "for a habitation of God, through the Spirit;" to build it together in Jesus, in union to him, and every part of the building to be under the special care and divine management of God and the word of his grace. "Upon this Rock," says Christ, "will I build my church, and the gates of hell shall not prevail against it." Is it possible, then, to commend you to better hands than those which can accomplish such mighty wonders for such detestable sinners? Why, this will be the wonder of heaven, and in measure the confusion of hell,—that God has raised out of such ruins a glorious edifice, which he calls "the house of his glory;" thus honouring the whole church, as one immortal mansion for his eternal residence, where the eternal Trinity will dwell for ever and ever. He is "able to build you up." And he is "able to build you up," for edifying in faith, and hope, and love, and joy, and peace, and stability, and tenderness of conscience, and a regard to God and truth here. The Lord is able to do it; and "the word of his grace" in his hands can accomplish it.

But he is able "to give you an inheritance among all them which are sanctified." There is such a mystery in the gospel of God's grace that it has sweetly constrained me many a time to stand in awe of God and filled me with wonder and amazement. When God is speaking of his people, he says, "The Lord's portion is his people;

Jacob is the lot of his inheritance." And a pretty inheritance he has, has not he? None but God would ever have fixed upon such an inheritance as that, I am sure,—such a portion as that. But it was "the Lord's doing." "He found him in a desert land, and in the waste howling wilderness; he led him about, he instructed him, he kept him as the apple of his eye." And then, in the riches of his grace, he brings him to say feelingly, "The Lord is my portion," "The Lord is the portion of mine inheritance." So that God has so managed it as to make himself his people's portion and them his portion. And really, to tell you the truth, neither God nor they will be fully manifested in Jehovah's declarative glory till portion gets to portion and they enjoy each other; for God has said, that they who are gone to heaven before us cannot be perfect without us, and the Lord Jesus Christ himself is gone to heaven, "from henceforth expecting," awaiting at the throne of glory, "until his enemies be made his footstool," and the whole church are brought together to be glorified in him and with him.

Now "I commend you to God, who is able to give you" this inheritance, and to give you a sweet manifestation of it in this world,—a hint of it in the court of your conscience.

May the Lord bless you with it; for it is an inheritance possessed by none but God's "sanctified" ones; and they are truly sanctified. We might notice (but really my strength will not allow me to proceed) that they are sanctified by the Father, by the Son, and by the blessed Spirit; and when they are brought home, so gloriously sanctified that angels wait upon them, and go forth, as it were, with a solemn blessing: "The Lamb's wife is coming and made ready for her husband." Indeed the holy angels think it an honour to wait upon us while here; and what will it be when we arise in the ineffable glory of the Lord the Lamb, to fully possess that inheritance which God has provided for us?

Into the hands of this God, and to the word of his grace, I commend you. Lord! Take us all into thy care, for the Redeemer's sake.

THE ACCEPTABLE YEAR, AND DAY OF VENGEANCE.

Preached at the old Surrey Tabernacle, Borough Road, London, Wednesday Evening, June 1st, 1842.

"To proclaim the acceptable year of the Lord, and the day of vengeance of our God."—ISA. LXI. 2.

OUR text contains one part of the ministry of the Lord Jesus Christ; and as a solemnly glorious minister of the New Testament, *he* was anointed by the Lord for the important work. And the two things mentioned in our text his Majesty proclaims in the Word, and in the conscience of all that he takes to heaven. A man, whose notions are all he has of religion, a mere judgmental knowledge of it, can be satisfied with the proclamation made in the letter of the Word; but I believe that any man, and every man, who can feel satisfied with that, is a stranger to God. God brings his people to feel that their disease is deep. He lays it upon their hearts; and they must have a proclamation that reaches the disease and comes *to* the heart. The Gospel of God must come to them, "not in word, but in power, and in the Holy Ghost, and in much assurance." And when the blessed Redeemer, by the power of his Spirit, "proclaims the acceptable year of the Lord and the day of vengeance of our God" in the conscience of a poor sinner, if the sinner is sunk as low as sin can sink him, it lifts him up, and brings him to have a peace which the world knows nothing of; a peace and joy in believing. And thus he knows experimentally that there is a solemn reality in God's truth and in God's kingdom, and that God's kingdom "stands not in word, but in power."

It is now fifty years since God first made a proclamation of this in my conscience. I have had many other visits since then; but I really cannot go on without fresh visits to the present moment. I have heard that there are men, very high in a profession of religion, who say they do not care if they never enjoy the presence of God again upon earth; they know they shall go to heaven. But, as I said last night at Gower Street, I cannot make out what such men want to go to heaven for. They might almost as well go elsewhere as to heaven, if they are not to have the sweet and blessed presence of the Lord. If the presence of the Lord here in this vale of tears is of such little moment that they do not care whether or not they have it again, I believe in my heart they are strangers to God and vital religion. For wherever the Lord, in the riches of his grace, reveals this blessed truth under his divine anointings, and grants the sinner an unctuous feeling of his presence, he wants it again—and again—and again—and will be thirsting for it till his dying moments. "To proclaim the acceptable year of the Lord, and the day of vengeance of our God." I shall endeavour, as God shall assist, to make a few remarks upon these two things:

I. "The *day of vengeance* of our God and the *acceptable year* of the Lord."

II. The *proclamation* of them by the blessed Lord of life and glory.

I. Now we read in the Word of God of some solemn displays of God's vengeance and wrath; and yet our text speaks as if there were but one "day of vengeance." Why, was it not "the day of vengeance" when he destroyed Sodom and Gomorrah? Was it not "the day of vengeance" when he swallowed up Korah, Dathan, and

Abiram, and all their company, and when they went down into the
pit alive? Was it not a "day of vengeance" when he hurled Satan
and his adherents from their high-towering thrones, and sank them
into "blackness of darkness?" Was it not a "day of vengeance"
when he drowned the Egyptians in the Red Sea? And are not the
damned in hell, devils and damned spirits, feeling "the day of vengeance" now? And yet, put it all together, it were as nothing compared to "the day of vengeance" in our text. Therefore the Holy
Ghost fixes upon this important subject as "*the* day of vengeance"
that outstretches all the rest.

And what was it? The "day," when Divine Justice unsheathed
its sword, and the wrath of that incensed Justice was poured with
all its inflexible fury upon the God-man Mediator; when all the sins
of the church,—heart sins, lip sins, sins however circumstanced,
were gathered together, and put upon the Surety, and when the
whole of the wrath due to the millions of God's elect was poured
into the heart of their covenant Head,—the Lord Jesus Christ. That
was "*the* day of vengeance" with a witness. Here Justice exacted
its utmost mite, and made no abatement; and his solemn Majesty
paid the debt to the full.

Sin may appear a trifling matter to you or me; we may be sufficiently hardened to laugh at it, to trifle with it; but it did not trifle
with the Son of God. It broke his heart, it tortured his soul, and
harrowed up his mind; and with all the majesty and glory of his
infinite Godhead, he had but strength enough to bear up under the
tremendous wrath that he had to endure for his people. This was
"the day of vengeance," and here the wrath of God was poured out
to the uttermost.

Neither did Divine Justice look upon sin as a trifling matter. If
God the Father loved the people with an everlasting love (and he
did), if he fixed his heart upon them in eternity, if he considered
them his jewels, the crown of his glory, and yet this people could
not possess the bliss he provided for them till Justice was satisfied
in the Surety and sin was punished there, sin was no trifling thing
in the eyes of God. The wrath of God poured upon devils and
damned spirits is for their various transgressions; but here is the
holy, the harmless, the innocent Lamb of God, the glory of heaven,
and he for whom all things were created, he for whose pleasure all
was made, standing as Surety for sinners; and though he was the
Father's infinite delight, the people whose cause he had espoused
must be set free, and the wrath of God must be poured upon him,
as the Surety, and poured there to the uttermost. Thus Jehovah
demonstrated his holy, his righteous indignation against sin; and it
was "the day of vengeance."

To know what sin is, we must not go to some few trifling things
that we suffer here in consequence of sin. Nay, if we could pos-

sibly sink into the regions of the damned, and hear their yellings, behold their tortures, and return back, we should come far short of knowing the evil of sin. It is at Gethsemane, it is at Golgotha, where the God that supported all worlds, in union with our nature and that nature in union with its Godhead, bled and was tortured, agonizing with indescribable misery as the effect of sin,—it is here we see what an evil sin is. Can you trifle with sin? Can you sport with it? Can you speak of it as a light matter? Is there a hardened wretch here who can do it? Conscience! Where art thou? Good God! Arouse them to feel what an awful thing sin is, and let their hearts tremble before thee on account of their various transgressions, and lead them to Golgotha, lead them to Gethsemane, and let them have a feeling of the fellowship of the sufferings of the Lord Jesus Christ, and then they will know a little of the solemnity of our text,—" the day of vengeance;" for there it was executed with all its awful terrors and its tremendous power.

And now, before I proceed, I ask you, Have you a hope, a spiritual hope, that Christ suffered for *you?* that he weltered in blood for *you?* that "he was wounded for *your* transgressions, bruised for *your* iniquities," that "the chastisement of *your* peace was upon him?" And do you feel, now and then, a sweetness in this truth, that "with his stripes you are healed?" Can you profess to cherish this hope, and yet trifle with that which tore his heart, which tortured his soul, which brought vengeance upon him as your Surety? Can you play with it? Is it a trifling matter with you? If it is, your hope is a horrible delusion, and you know nothing at all of the life and power of vital godliness in your soul. For wherever the Spirit of the living God brings a sinner to have good hope, through the precious atonement of Christ, the glorious and solemn sufferings of Christ, he knows what it is to be a little in that spot: "They shall look upon Me whom they have pierced, and they shall mourn for him as one mourneth for his only son, and shall be in bitterness for him as one that is in bitterness for his first-born." And when we have been for a season mourning over ourselves, because of the light and life and love of God, made manifest by blood, we shall have a solemn mourning for the Lord of life, that he should suffer vengeance for such reptiles as we are, for such brutes as we are; and so we shall know something of being humble at his feet, whilst we bless God for the mysteries of his cross.

Now, do you know anything of this in your own souls? Has God ever presented it to your conscience? Has he brought you to feel something of the solemn sufferings of a once-slaughtered Christ, and to feel that it was your sins that were the daggers that pierced his heart,—your sins that pressed blood through every-pore? Sometimes, when I have been led to feel the horrible oozings up and workings of a corrupt nature, and I should be worse than a vaga-

bond if I said I never did, and when God the Spirit has then led
me in faith and feeling to Gethsemane, dropped a little of the
atoning blood of Christ into my conscience, and brought me to feel
a sweetness in the efficacy of his blood, with contrition of soul I
have been brought to bow before him, and say, "Lord, it is such a
salvation that I wonder thou wouldst bestow it upon such a wretch;
I wonder that such mercy should be given to such a brute." But
so it is; and God is exalted, self abased, and Christ reigns, and the
conscience triumphs in the efficacy of his precious blood, and adores
God for such a blessed method of pouring out his wrath upon his
Son, that we might be free.

Sinner! Trembling, broken-hearted sinner!

> "Sinner! THOU hast done the deed;
> THOU hast made the Saviour bleed.
> Justice drew its sword on me;
> Pierced my heart to pass by thee."

God help thee to feel it, and to glorify God for such amazing grace,
such matchless grace, manifested to sinners.

But we pass on to make a few remarks upon "the acceptable
year of the Lord." This solemn "day of vengeance" was at the
same time an "acceptable year."

Here was the glorious body and substance of the jubilee; and
the holy prophet appears to have this in view. Through the finished
work of Christ, the blessed obedience and righteousness of Christ,
the real spirit of the jubilee is proclaimed and made manifest, both
in the Word of God and in the conscience of the sinner. "The
acceptable year of the Lord." A word or two upon this point, as
connected with the jubilee.

In that solemn year, when the proclamation went throughout all
the land of Israel, all the Hebrews had their debts discharged, their
legal servitude put an end to, their mortgaged inheritances restored.
A proclamation was made of plenty without labour. No farmer, no
person that kept a vineyard, was to sow or reap for himself; but
the fruits of the earth were free for every Hebrew to pluck and partake of. And this was "the acceptable year of the Lord" amongst
the Jews. So through the Person, blood, and obedience of Christ,
every spiritual Hebrew has his debts discharged; for "he is not a
Jew," saith the Lord, "which is one outwardly; neither is that circumcision which is outward in the flesh; but he is a Jew which is
one inwardly, and circumcision is that of the heart, in the spirit, and
not in the letter." Now, has God cut off all your legal hopes, cut off
all your legal expectations? Some one may say, "He has; and yet
I am not happy." Perhaps, if you examine closely, he has not quite
cut them off. Say you, "I have no hope in anything that I have
ever done." But have not you a little hope at the bottom that there
will come some favourable juncture when you shall be able to manage

a little better than you do now? "Why," say you, "if I had not that, I should despair." Then the sooner you despair the better, poor soul. You are not entirely a self-despairing sinner whilst you can have any hope of mending the matter in time to come; but when you are brought to be entirely hopeless, both now and for time to come, as it relates to anything you can do to help yourself, here is "the acceptable year of the Lord." Christ has paid the debt fully; cleared it, discharged it, without leaving an iota undone. He has "put away sin by the sacrifice of himself;" made an end of it, and finished it.

> " Justice, when the Surety died,
> Acquitted the believer;"

and here it is, poor soul, that it is an "acceptable year" of the Lord. Justice is satisfied. And when God brings it with power to thy conscience, it will be an "acceptable year" to *thee;* for thou wilt be satisfied, and say with the apostle, " God forbid that I should glory, save in the cross of the Lord Jesus Christ."

If a Hebrew had sold himself or hired himself in service, "the acceptable year of the Lord" proclaimed his liberty. No master could keep him, if he wished to go. And so, if God has given you a heart really, truly, feelingly, to be at liberty (ponder over it, and ask whether he has), though you have " sold yourself for nought," you are " redeemed without money." Though you have become the slave of sin and Satan, and are under bondage and fetters, if the Spirit of God has made you willing to be saved in God's own way, here is "the acceptable year of the Lord." Legal servitude must be given up. When this is proclaimed in the conscience, conscience must rejoice in liberty, and in that liberty that is accomplished by the Son; and "if the Son shall make you free, ye shall be free indeed." " Well," say you, "I feel as if I were willing, and yet I am not quite set at rest." Perhaps not quite willing. There is some little lurking, knavish thief or other, in some corner of thy heart, that wants to cling to self, wants to cling to something of thine own. Thou art not yet an entire bankrupt, willing to be saved in God's own way, by the precious blood of the Lamb and " the acceptable year of the Lord." If God brings thee *there*, Christ has discharged the debt, the Son has made thee free, and thou art "free indeed."

But further. Is it the case that you have lost all that you had, —forfeited every morsel that you ever possessed in Adam the first? Yes, you have. And some people tell us that Christ came to restore that. So he did; but that is not all he did. He brings a better life than ever old Adam had to lose; and that is a mercy for God's people. He comes to give us life, and to give it "more abundantly," and to give a glorious life in himself. Thine inheritance that thou hast mortgaged or sold, by thy sin in Adam the first, was at best but a glorious earthly inheritance; but the Lord the Redeemer has se-

cured for thee, not only a glimpse of an inheritance here, but one
that is "incorruptible, undefiled, and that fadeth not away, reserved
in heaven for them that are kept by the power of God." Do you
feel you need "keeping by the power of God?" *I* do; and I solemnly declare to-night that, old as I am, I never felt myself more
liable to stumble, nor ever felt a greater need for God to keep me,
than I do now. I feel in my very soul that if God does not keep
me, I shall bring disgrace upon his name. I know it, and feel that
that would be the case. But then, that blessed God who has made
manifest this "acceptable year," has engaged to "keep the feet of
his saints," and to watch over their path, night and day. And then
there is an inheritance, secured by the love and blood of the Lord
Jesus Christ; and he is gone, poor child of God, through the channel
of his own obedience, to take possession of it himself. And there
is one text that has confounded me scores of times. Christ says,
"I go to prepare a place for you." To "prepare a place!" That
is very strange. Is not heaven already prepared? It would appear
as if created heaven was not glory enough for God's people; and I
do believe it is not. I do not believe created heaven is what God
considers sufficient glory for his people; and therefore Christ, as their
Mediator, as their Head and Representative, has "gone to prepare a
place for them." How? To bespangle heaven with his blood and
righteousness, and to exhibit to view the glory of his own work,
and to bring his saints into the blessedness of the glory of that work,
that they may glory in that only. Through his blood and righteousness he has ascended up on high to bring this to pass! And this is
"the acceptable year of the Lord."

We noticed that in the jubilee everything was to be free. And we
should vastly well relish a jubilee of that sort at Manchester, I assure you. What work there would be with thousands of poor, famishing creatures! They would soon make clearance of the fields, if it
were, "Pluck and eat." But, however it may be in nature, it is plain
enough in grace. We have the promises; all the blessings of the
oath, of the love and blood of a precious Redeemer; all the blessings
of the fulness of his heart; all are freely given, "without money
and without price." Not an iota of creature merit to obtain it. The
poorer the wretch, the more welcome he is.

    "Come needy, come guilty, come loathsome, come bare;
        You can't come too filthy; come *just as you are*."

God, in the riches of his grace, keeps jubilee all the year round,—
open house and open field for famishing sinners. May God bless
us with hearts to enter into the field of the mystery of God's grace,
and pluck and eat, by Divine faith in the love and blood of the Lord
Jesus Christ; and then we shall know that it is the "acceptable year
of the Lord."

But it is "the acceptable year of the Lord," inasmuch as it is acceptable *to* the Lord. "In an accepted time I have heard thee; in a day of salvation have I succoured thee." This is "the accepted time." Divine justice, poor sinner, has accepted the Person of Christ as thy surety, the work and obedience of Christ actively as thy righteousness, and the sufferings and death of Christ as the atonement for thy sin. It is passed current in the account of God and filed up in heaven; and God says, "I am well pleased for his righteousness' sake." He will magnify the law, and make it honourable. Thus it is "the acceptable year of the Lord." There is nothing, therefore, that the blessed Redeemer contains, or that he has done, as the Head of the church, but what is received in heaven with the Divine approbation of God; and as a demonstration of it, it is said, "God is gone up with a shout, the Lord with the sound of a trumpet." God and angels, and glorified spirits which were gone before, have all shouted him home; and when God gives you and me faith in the mystery of it, we help them to shout too. He is "gone up on high," as a demonstrative proof that he is accepted of the Father; and he is seated at the right hand of the Father, there to live and make intercession for his people. It is "the acceptable year of the Lord;" and I am sure it will be acceptable to you, if Jesus, in the riches of his grace, manifests it in your consciences.

Perhaps there may be in this assembly some who think they do not need such a salvation as this. You say, "Christ has done a great deal; he has done his part, and I must do my part; and, notwithstanding all that Christ has done, if I do not do my part too, I cannot be saved." There is a deal of talk in our day about Popery being likely to be established; and I know no men in the world who are more likely to establish it than these "*do part*" men, for their sentiment is the very life and soul of Popery. What is Popery? What is Antichrist? Creature-merit. If you could destroy creature-merit, man's doing his part, in all its bearings, and creature-merit could entirely be put out of existence, the devil himself could not make a Pope. There could be no such thing in existence. But creature-merit is the blood, and sinews, and pulse, and life of Popery; and, therefore, where men go on with the strange idea that, notwithstanding all that Christ has done, they must do their part too, or they cannot be saved, they are bidding Popery "God speed," and doing their part to establish it. They find fault all the while with some of their external things, such as their dolls, and a few mummeries of that nature; but the poison is in the soul of Popery, and the soul of Popery is creature-merit. And in fact, what can we find flourishing in our day but creature-merit, in some form or other? You will find some men, who would be vastly strenuous against creature-merit in the shape of free-will; and yet they have got it in another shape. They say, "O! You may always believe. Why *don't* you believe? *Simply believe,* and be happy." Why, that is creature-merit; it is the old leaven; it is another name, but it is creature-merit. But God's people are brought to feel that they can no more *believe* themselves into the mysteries of Christ than they can work themselves into the mysteries of Christ by labour; that it must be the Lord himself who must "work in them to will and to do of his good pleasure," and that faith is his entire gift. And so they glorify God for the mysteries of his cross, and are brought to know something of the freedom there is in the finished work of the Lord Jesus Christ, and the blessings connected with it.

II. But we pass on to the *proclamation:* " To *proclaim* the acceptable year of the Lord, and the day of vengeance of our God."

Now our blessed Christ proclaims this truth in the written Word. Hear his blessed Majesty proclaim it: "Ho, every one that thirsteth, come ye to the waters; and he that hath no money, come ye, buy and eat; yea, come, buy wine and milk, without money and without price. Incline your ear and come unto me; hear, and your soul shall live." Now, some say that proclamation is made to sinners dead in sin; and, as a proof of it, they say that it runs, "Hear, and your soul *shall* live." But it would be very strange for a corpse to be invited to come to the queen's palace in order to be banqueted. It would want something to move it; and if it was dead how could it "come?" The fact is, they are living souls who are here spoken of; but they are famishing, they are starving, they are wanting food; and when God the Spirit brings them to Christ, then they live, and live well too; for they have the fatted calf, the paschal Lamb, and the mysteries of the cross revealed to the conscience. Therefore, says the Lord, " Come unto me; hear, and your soul shall live." So again: " Come unto me, all ye that labour and are heavy laden, and I will give you rest. Take my yoke upon you and learn of me; for my yoke is easy and my burden is light." Just as if the blessed Redeemer had looked upon a poor burdened, dejected sinner, and said, " I see, poor creature, you are yoked down by Moses; you have got the burden of the law, and you have got the burden of a guilty conscience; there you are with your yoke on, and you cannot get ease, you cannot get rest. Now come to me; my yoke is easy." Why, what is his yoke? Everlasting glory: and O! How easy that fits the neck of a poor sinner, when God puts it manifestively on! And what is his burden? The divine fulness of the glory of God, treasured up in Christ; and O! How solemnly glorious is that, when the conscience receives it under the divine teaching of the Holy Spirit! Then we shall find a rest and a contentment the world knows nothing of.

Then, the Lord Jesus Christ, being anointed, proclaimed this day. He proclaimed this jubilee, and he proclaimed his own sufferings. O! How solemnly he by his Spirit proclaims it in the 53rd chapter

of the prophecies of Isaiah, where he is spoken of as "led as a lamb
to the slaughter, and as a sheep before her shearers is dumb, so
opening not his mouth!" And how solemnly he proclaims it when
he speaks in his Word and says, "Is it nothing to you, all ye that
pass by?" And, poor wretch, *is it* nothing to you? Can you hear
of the sufferings of Christ, the agonies of the Son of God, and be
unmoved? Can you hear of them and have no feeling? Perhaps
some poor living souls say with the poet,

> "The rocks can rend, the earth can shake,
> The seas can roar, the mountains quake ;
> Of feeling all things show some sign,
> But this unfeeling heart of mine."

Well, then, if the proclamation made in the Word again and again
cannot move the heart, cannot soften the heart, cannot melt the heart,
cannot bring the heart into obedience, and cannot lead to the sweet
enjoyment of it, is there nothing that can? Has sin brought us into
such a state of ruin, such a state of disease, unhallowed ungodly
disease, that there is nothing that can move the sinner, nothing that
can bring him to feel something of "the day of vengeance," nothing
that can bring him to realize "the acceptable year" and the blessings that it contains? Yes, brethren, there is. When God, by his
blessed Spirit, proclaims it in the conscience, brings it with power
to the heart, leads the soul feelingly into that blessed text, "Thou,
Lord, hast wrought all our works in us ;" when he makes manifest
that precious truth, "I will bring the blind, and the lame," and the
burdened, and the dejected, and "they shall come and sing in the
height of Zion, and shall flow together to the goodness of the Lord,
for wheat, and for wine, and for oil, and for the young of the flock
and of the herd, and their soul shall be as a watered garden ;" when
he makes the proclamation with divine power into the soul, and leads
the soul solemnly and sweetly into the mysteries of the cross, then
he raises the hope and expectation of his people, and they are
brought, in some blessed measure, to know that the proclamation
of "the acceptable year of the Lord" is made to them.

Now do you know anything of this? Has God ever brought you
to feel it? Say you, "I do not like you to talk about a feeling religion." And I would not thank you for any that is not; and so
there is just that difference between you and me. AN UNFEEL-
ING RELIGION IS THE DEVIL'S RELIGION. It is not the
religion of Christ; for God brings his people to know what it is to
"handle and taste and feel of the Word of life." He brings them
to know what it is to have the Word sealed in their hearts, and
hidden there. And, therefore, do not you deceive your soul. If you
die without a feeling religion, as God is God, you will be damned.
I am sure you will. And whatever trials, difficulties, or distresses
you may have, a sweet feeling religion, revealed to the conscience

by the power of the Spirit of Christ, will support your soul under your troubles, prop up your mind, and bring you sweetly to rejoice in the mysteries of the cross of the Lamb; and then you will bless God for the wonders of his grace.

I leave the few hints that have been dropped in the hands of the Lord.

[The poor thief on the cross, short as was his spiritual life, had a feeling religion. Hence he said to his fellow-thief, "We suffer justly; for we receive the due reward of our deeds." (Lu. xxiv. 40–43.)]

THE LORD'S PEOPLE HIDDEN.

Preached at Bedworth, on Wednesday Evening, Aug. 24th, 1842.

ISA. XXVI. 20.

I AM about to read a portion of God's Word, which I thought I could find very easily. Indeed, I thought it was in the 40th chapter of the prophecies of Isaiah; but I cannot find it; so I must leave you to find it when you get home. I feel entirely unable to preach. If the Lord is not pleased to make me a little better, I shall be very short. The passage of Scripture I thought to read runs thus: "Come, my people, enter thou into thy chambers, and shut thy doors about thee; hide thyself, as it were, for a little moment, until the indignation be overpast."

Through the kind providence of God, I have enjoyed better health since I was here last than I have done for some years. But to-day a bad cold has laid hold of me, and quite upset my mortal frame. Should it be the will of God that it should end in my death, O how blessed to look forward, under the sweet influences of God the Spirit, to this hiding-place: "Come, my people, enter thou into thy chambers, and shut thy doors about thee; hide thyself, as it were, for a little moment, until the indignation be overpast!"

We may notice from these words:

I. The Lord has a *special people* dedicated to himself; and that people shall show forth his praise.

II. These people are *hid from the indignation of the Lord.*

I. We notice, 1st, that the one undivided Jehovah has a special property in these people. The Father says they are *his* portion. The Son says this is *his* spouse; he loved and redeemed her, "that he might present to himself a glorious church, not having spot or wrinkle." And the blessed Spirit has separated them from the world; he lays a sovereign claim to them, constantly keeping his eye on the sovereign purpose of God. Wherever they are, when God's time is come to call them by grace, the Holy Ghost will quicken the dead soul, communicate divine life, and bring them to a saving acquaintance with Christ. All things were made for Christ and his church.

Hence it is said, "For all things are yours, whether Paul, or Apollos, or Cephas, or the world, or life, or death, or things present, or things to come; all are yours; and ye are Christ's, and Christ is God's." Nothing shall alter the security of the people of God. The blessed Three-One-God lays a claim to this people, by ways and means suited to his own purpose of grace. Hence the Father, when speaking of them, says, "They shall be willing in the day of my power." "I will bring the blind by a way that they knew not; I will lead them in paths that they have not known."

Proud man gets schemes and plans for himself; but God opposes all his schemes, and solemnly declares he will bring down the loftiness and greatness of man, "and the Lord alone ahall be exalted in that day." What proud, pompous work it is for poor dying worms to puff up their minds with the empty vanity,—that if God do his part, they will do theirs! Why, I am an old man, nearly 70 years of age, and I have no more hope of being saved on such ground as that than I have of pulling the Almighty from his throne. I have tried *doing my part* many times; it has invariably undone me, and brought me feelingly and sensibly to ruin. This the Lord is determined to do,—to bring down the loftiness of man, and the greatness of man, that the Lord alone may be exalted in that day. You have no scriptural proof of being one of God's people if you do not know something of this,—of God cutting up all your vows, all your promises, all your prayers, all your repentance, and all your holiness, laying you low, and making you, in your own feelings, as wretched as the devil. If the Lord never brings you, in a measure, here, you will never go to heaven, with all your prettiness. You may foster up your mind with your self-prettiness and your own strength ; but our God " giveth power to the faint, and to them that have no might he increaseth strength." Besides, it is written, " The lame take the prey."

Thus God the Father, in his discriminating power, has a distinct, separate people from the rest of mankind, and has solemnly said, " These people have I formed for myself; they shall show forth my praise." When this truth comes with power to the conscience, how cutting it is! It brings the poor sinner, in his feelings before God, to lie on a level with Manasseh, Magdalene, or with bloody, persecuting Saul; cuts up all his fine ideas and makes him ashamed of himself; so that he is obliged to cry, "God be merciful to me, a sinner!" "But," say you, "you do not suppose they are the people of God that are thus crying?" Yes; this is the solemn method that God takes to distinguish them from the self-righteous world. All their loftiness is brought down and they are bowed before God.

This people is the property of Christ; for he espoused their cause before all worlds. He has betrothed them to himself: "He hath betrothed them to himself for ever, in righteousness, and in judgment,

and in lovingkindness, and in mercies, and in faithfulness." He has
also entered into such an engagement, that when he viewed the elect
of God in their sins and blood, his heart was fixed upon them; he
engaged to redeem them, to wash them from all their filthiness, and
to present them before God unblameable in love.   Hence Paul says,
"Husbands, love your wives, even as Christ also loved the church,
and gave himself for it, that he might sanctify and cleanse it with
the washing of water by the word, that he might present it to himself a glorious church, not having spot, or wrinkle, or any such thing;
but that it should be holy, and without blemish."   But who besides
the Son of God would have engaged to accomplish this work for such
sinners?   He saw the end from the beginning; he saw their hard-
heartedness, their impenitence, their blindness, and their determination to insult their Lord.   Had the Lord allowed them to go on
in their own way, not a soul would have been saved, but all would
have gone to the bottomless pit.   Not one of them would have left
their idols, but after them they would have gone.   Therefore, the
Lord Jesus Christ engaged to espouse their cause, to satisfy the
claims of Justice, to honour the Father, to redeem them from all iniquity, and to make them, by the power of his Spirit, a holy people,
zealous of good works.

Has there any power come to your conscience to separate you
from the world, and to separate you from yourself?   It appears far
easier to be separated from the world than to be separated from self.
"What!" say you; "separated from pious self! holy self! patient,
meek self!   Must these have no place in the matter?"   No.   You
must, by the power of God, be separated from all, be enabled to
give up all, and be brought to feel your awfully guilty state before
God.

The blessed Spirit makes manifest his sovereign claim to the Lord's
people, by thus quickening their dead souls, enlightening their dark
understandings, and cutting them off from all creature holiness.   It
is very painful work.   Sometimes the Lord's people, when first
brought to know something of their ruined condition, have many
pleasing ideas about them and think they can do well.   But I can
tell you that you will find the contrary to be the case, if you belong
to God.   "O, you are an Antinomian," say some, "and want us to
live a life of licentiousness; we can do many things for God."   No.
God's Spirit teaches his people to deny ungodliness, yet brings them
feelingly to know that if they were damned this moment, they cannot put a finger to the work; they cannot help themselves; but
"the Lord giveth power to the faint, and to them that have no might
he increaseth strength."

Has the Lord brought you here? Perhaps some poor soul says,
"But I cannot conceive this to be a proof that I am one of the Lord's
people; for I am told that if I am one of the Lord's chosen ones, I

should be very zealous in doing my part, by helping the blessed Spirit in saving my soul." Well; have you tried to do anything? "Yes," say you, "I have." What have you done? What have your doings produced? Have they not brought guilt, confusion, and bondage? Have you not been obliged in the end to say, "Lord, save me, or I perish?" "Yes," say you, "I have." Bless the Lord for it. It is the Spirit's testimony that he does not design you to be your own eternal ruin; therefore he stops you from all self hope, and will eventually reveal Christ in you the hope of glory, and make you sensibly feel that salvation is of the Lord.

My dear brethren, if you are the people of God manifestively, you know something of this; if the Lord has called you by his grace, and made manifest that you are one of his people, he has brought you to feel something of what we have been talking about,—to bow at his footstool, to be willing to be nothing so that you may be one of his, and constrained feelingly to cry to God to make bare his arm to save your soul with an everlasting salvation. Do I hear some poor soul say, "That is where I am, really and feelingly?" Are you? Then you are one of the Lord's people. "Really," say you, "I cannot believe it, I am so dark, in bondage through the fear of death, and so gloomy." He "will bring the blind by a way that they knew not; he will lead them in paths that they have not known; he will make darkness light before them, and crooked things straight." These things he does unto them, and will not forsake them. Though heaven and earth are made for the honour of his blessed Majesty, nothing is so dear to the Father, so dear to the Son, so dear to the Spirit, and nothing occupies the mind of God so much (if I may be allowed so to speak) as this people. This people "shall be saved in the Lord with an everlasting salvation." Blessed people! They know the joyful sound.

Now, before we proceed, have you ever been rooted up in your feelings? Have you ever been brought to stand before God, loathsome and guilty in your own feelings, and being in such a state that you could not possibly help yourselves? By and by, he speaks to you as he speaks to his people in this prophecy, where his blessed Majesty says, "Thy tacklings are loosed; they could not well strengthen their mast, they could not spread the sail. Then is the prey of a great spoil divided." Who ran away with it? These poor mariners, who were all in confusion and disorder, could neither spread the sail, nor put the tacklings in order, nor strengthen the mast. Thus the Lord brings them to know they are his people, and shall show forth his praise. "This people have I formed for myself, they shall show forth my praise."

"Come, my people, enter thou into thy chambers, and shut thy doors about thee; hide thyself, as it were, for a little moment, until the indignation be overpast." What is this indignation? The Lord going forth, cutting up and cutting down the pride of man. He has made up his mind, as it were, that no flesh shall glory in his presence. All who expect to go to heaven singing the wonders they have done for God will be deceived, if they die in that state. The Lord brings all his people to know that there is neither might, power, nor help in themselves. The indignation of the Lord must be endured. The revelation of God's wrath against sin is contained in his law. What a deal of pains are taken by men to keep the law! How often they say, "Lord, have mercy upon us, and incline our hearts to keep this law!" If ever the Lord leads you to feel his indignation, he makes you feel that, do what you will, the law curses you. All your own obedience, vows, and promises will only bring upon you the curse of God in a broken law. The voice of the law is, "Cursed is every one that continueth not in all things that are written in the book of the law, to do them;" "He who offendeth in one point is guilty of all." Now, sinner, where are you? There is not a soul here but what, on law grounds, is justly and righteously condemned. Rather than God could repeal his law, says one, he would sooner damn the whole world. "For we have all sinned and come short of the glory of God."

When the Lord reveals his law, in its spirituality and purity, to the conscience of a sinner, it is the day of God's indignation. The law condemns the sinner, and he feels obliged to acknowledge the condemnation. This is where the Lord brings most of his people, even after they are called by divine grace, viz., into severe trials, crosses, and difficulties of mind. I remember that when the Lord was first pleased to reveal his love to my poor soul, I was very happy, and thought I should be so all the days of my life; I expected no other. But, by and by, sin revived and I died. The Lord revealed a measure of his indignation in my conscience, as a wretched backslider against his solemn Majesty, and as one who had broken his law. Have you felt this? Perhaps some of you may say, "Sometimes I do wrong; and when such is the case, I begin to think about it, simply believe that God loves me, do my duty, and all is set right again." If you can live in *that* religion, and you die in it, you are living to be damned, and you will find it so at the great day of God. The Lord will reveal his indignation against all your righteousness, and you will be brought to know, sooner or later, that you are as an unclean thing, and all your righteousnesses are as filthy rags. When this is the case, you will find that, unless you have a better religion than nature can produce, you will sink into hopeless despair.

Do you know anything of this? Have you ever had your *pious* vows and promises, even your Amen promises, though made when you called God to witness them, broken to pieces? And have you ever been cut up, root and branch, and been without help and without hope? "No," say you, "and I hope I never shall." You might as well say you hope you shall not go to heaven. If the Lord means to take you to heaven, he will root up all these; for his solemn indignation will be against all your righteousness, and you will know the truth of that declaration, "We are all as an unclean thing, and all our righteousnesses are as filthy rags." When this day of indignation comes on, the poor sinner trembles before God, and wonders where the scene will end. Say some, "I think I know a little of that; I know what it is to be plagued with unbelief, and groan by reason of a tempting devil and the hidings of God's countenance; to feel also the naughtiness of my nature, and the plague of my heart, and sometimes to feel as if I had nothing but my plague to cry about, nothing but my plague to bring." "But then," say you, "surely you would not suppose there was any hope for such a sinner as that!" Yes, there is. God says to such a poor soul, "Come, my people, enter into thy chambers, and shut thy doors about thee." What! This poor sinner,—this loathsome sinner?

"A sinner is a sacred thing,
The Holy Ghost hath made him so."

If thou art brought to feel thou art such a sinner as the Lord says thou art, and brought to confess that feeling and to groan under it, thou art a vessel of mercy. God will save thee in the Lord with an everlasting salvation. "Come, my people, enter thou into thy chambers, and shut thy doors about thee."

II. We come now to notice these *chambers* and what is meant by shutting the doors. The Lord tells us in one place, "He is a refuge and strength, a very present help in trouble." One cries out, "Thou art my refuge; therefore will I hope in thee." These chambers were typified under the law by that solemn ordinance that the Lord instituted for Israel in Egypt, when he told them to take a lamb, and slaughter it, according to their families; and to shut the door on them, sprinkling the blood of the lamb on the door-posts. So when the destroying angel came to destroy the first-born in Egypt, they were hid, shut up. The blood shut the door, and the wrath revealed by the Lord could not enter there. So the people of Israel slaughtered the lamb, by appointment of God; they stood with their loins girt about them; and it was eaten with bitter herbs. Now, mind you, it was roasted; all was eaten; none was thrown away. Well, what does this show? That the Lamb of God was roasted in God's wrath, with all the damnable propensities of his people. O the matchless wonders of his discriminating grace! He was made sin, *really* made sin; not in his nature, for he was holy, harmless, undefiled, separate from sinners; but he was made sin in covenant contract, as the Head and Representative of his people. Poor tempted child of God, poor believer, thy blindness, thy hardness, thy pride, thy lust, thy unbelief, and the plague of thy heart, were all imputed to Christ; he bore the blame, and put away sin by the sacrifice of himself. When we are brought in faith feelingly to realize the atonement, to enter into the atonement, and rely on it, the door of atoning blood is shut about us; and there is not a devil in hell or man on earth can bring us in guilty. Thus, we say, "There is, therefore, now no condemnation to them which are in Christ Jesus, who walk not after the flesh but after the Spirit; for the law of the Spirit of life in Christ Jesus has made me free from the law of sin and death; for what the law could not do, in that it was weak through the flesh, God sending his own Son in the like-ness of sinful flesh, and for sin, condemned sin in the flesh, that the righteousness of the law might be fulfilled in us, who walk not after the flesh, but after the Spirit." "Yes," says some poor child of God; "but I fear my walking is after the flesh; for I feel such dead-ness, darkness, and wretchedness that I dare not trust my prayers, my tears, my vows, my promises, nor my duties; none of these dare I venture to trust." I don't think this is walking after the flesh. Let us hear what the Lord says. When Solomon dedicated the temple, being the representative of Israel, he said, "What prayer and supplication soever be made by any man, or by all thy people Israel, which shall know every man the plague of his own heart, and spread forth his hands toward this house, then hear thou in heaven thy dwelling place, and forgive." The Lord knew none would turn to him till they knew the plague of their own hearts. When they know this, they seek the Lord; and he, in the riches of his grace, saves them in himself with an everlasting salvation. Thus, beloved, they are hid, hid with Christ in God.

Our Lord, when speaking of those chambers, gives us to under-stand that it is here where his people are hid: "One thing have I desired of the Lord, and that will I seek after; that I might dwell in the house of the Lord all the days of my life, to behold the beauty of the Lord and inquire in his temple;" "For in the time of trouble he shall hide me in his pavilion, in the secret of his tabernacle shall he hide me." Now, where is God's pavilion, the secret of his taber-nacle? The heart of Christ. There God secludes himself, there he meets his people, there his blessed Majesty stands in the heart of Christ, and says to his poor mourning, broken-hearted people, "Come, my people, enter thou into thy chambers; hide thyself in the blessed atonement, the blood and righteousness of the Lord Jesus Christ." And here it is the Lord's people are savingly hid. It is an indescribable mercy that their hiding-place can never be broken down.

Some people tell us we may be in Christ to-day, and fall away to-morrow and go to hell after all. I don't envy them. Go on, make the best way; but as sure as God is God, if you go on that ground, at the end you will be cursed, and sink into black despair. The Lord brings all his children to know they have no hiding-place but

Jesus, and they are brought feelingly to say, "Thou art my hiding-place." The Lord God says he is a very present help in trouble; "therefore will we not fear, though the earth be removed and the mountains be carried into the midst of the sea." Christ is this refuge, this hiding place. The Lord God Almighty secures his church in the midst of all the storms that may come upon them, and brings them safe through to glory, to be with him when time shall be no more.

"Come, my people, enter thou into thy chambers, and shut thy doors about thee." But, say some, how does the poor sinner enter this chamber? By the door of hope, the door of faith. He that believeth shall never be confounded, shall never be put to shame, and shall never be forgotten. Poor sinner, thy Jesus has entered heaven on this ground himself. The Shepherd has entered by the door into the sheepfold. And when he comes by the power of his Spirit, he draws thee into the atonement, into the sweet enjoyment of the mysteries of his love. He says, "All that the Father giveth me shall come to me." Some people say they will not, unless they are made. But the Lord says they shall. But then, say you, how is it they do not? "No man can come to me, except the Father, who hath sent me, draw him." Do you feel the need of the Lord to draw you into the blessed efficacy of the blood of the Redeemer, the atonement of Christ? When you feel your need of the Lord to open the door and draw you in, he will do so. Whoever climbs up any other way is a thief and a robber. The Lord hide me in his great burning day! There is hope, poor child of God; for in Scripture there is a door called "the door of hope." We will just see where the Lord opens this door: "I will give her the valley of Achor for a door of hope; she shall sing there as in the days of her youth." Do you know what the valley of Achor was? It was the valley where Israel was when Achan stole the golden wedge and the Babylonish garment. When they had just passed over Jordan, their enemies pursued them; they seemed as if they must be defeated; the Lord sent his indignation against them; and they fell before their enemies. The Lord then commanded that they should cast lots, that they might see who had done this wicked thing, and the lot fell on Achan, who had stolen the Babylonish garment and the golden wedge; and God brought solemn trouble on the family of Achan, and he was destroyed. How kind the Lord is; for after this he tells the children of Israel that he will give them the valley of Achor for a door of hope! Is there a poor sinner here who knows something of this, who has had his idols taken away, and felt that the Lord has tumbled all his imagined holiness and "piety" about his ears, and stripped him of his golden-wedge idol? If so, the Lord is about trying you with fire, bringing you into the furnace. How burnt up you are in your feelings! Go bow before the Lord as a guilty sinner; for his gracious Majesty gives this as a door of hope, to enter into the mysteries of his love; so the valley of Achor proves a door of hope. "Come, my people." Art thou in Achor, found out, stripped of God? Art thou upset? Remember, he is stripping and bringing thee to a door of hope in the valley of Achor, where thou shalt sing as in the days of old. He will give vineyards—what! In this desert? Yes, he will give vineyards for such guilty sinners; they shall go into the mysteries of his love.

There is the door of faith. When the Lord is pleased to draw forth faith in exercise, however great the storm may be, he shuts this door; that is, faith in Christ encloses them, hope in Jesus encloses them, and the soul is ready to say, "Why art thou cast down, O my soul, and why art thou disquieted within me? Hope thou in God, for I shall yet praise him." Come, poor soul, are you in the valley of Achor? Has all your fruitfulness been burnt up? Has God sent you out here? He opens a door of hope. The Lord the Spirit brings the poor soul to hope in the mercy of Christ, and, feeling this hope as an anchor, sure and stedfast, enters within the vail.

"Come, my people, enter thou into thy chambers, and shut thy doors about thee." The Lord is pleased to shut them up in love. Christ sheds abroad his love in the heart of a poor sinner; love embraces him; God is felt and enjoyed; the mysteries of redeeming love enter into the soul; the man is feelingly and solemnly hid with Christ in God; and when Christ, who is his life, shall appear, then shall he also appear with him in glory. "Come, my people, enter thou into thy chambers, and shut thy doors about thee; hide thyself, as it were, for a little moment" in the atoning blood and obedience of the Lord Jesus Christ. The Lord will rest in his love. If any of you, my friends, feel yourselves to be poor wretched sinners, I would say to such,

"The poorer the wretch, the welcomer here."

What a blessed salvation it is that our God has appointed for poor, lost, ruined man! May the Lord bless you with a feeling sense of your interest in it. And may he bless these few broken hints to your consciences, lift you into Christ and his salvation, and enable both you and me to live to his glory.

[The copy of the preceding sermon was sent to Mr. Gadsby by the friend who took it down in shorthand. Mr. G., however, said it was not worth publishing, as he remembered how confused he was while preaching, in addition to great affliction of body. It is now, however, sent forth, and we trust will be made useful.—"G.S.," 1844.]

THE CHURCH REMEMBERED IN HER LOW ESTATE.

Preached in Zoar Chapel, Great Alie St., London, on behalf of the Aged Pilgrims' Friend Society, on Thursday Evening, May 25th, 1843.

"Who remembered us in our low estate; for his mercy endureth for ever."
Ps. cxxxvi. 23.

JEHOVAH, as the God of nature, chose the seed of Abraham, by Sarah his wife, as a special people distinct from all other nations of the world. He remembered Abraham, and made a covenant with him; he chose him, and separated him from his idolatrous people, and brought him into a strange land. And when in after days his posterity were sunk and degraded, and had become slaves in the drudgery of brick-making, the Egyptians having made their tasks heavy, they groaned and sighed unto God, and were brought into a very low state indeed; but God remembered them, and the covenant which he had made; and when the time was fully come that they should be delivered, he said, "I have surely seen the affliction of my people which are in Egypt, and have heard their cry by reason of their taskmakers, for I know their sorrows, and I am come down to deliver them out of the hand of the Egyptians." Poor creatures! They thought God had neither heard nor observed them; but "his mercy endureth for ever;" and therefore he came, in his own time, for their help and salvation.

Now it appears that Moses, who was honoured as the chosen instrument in God's hand of delivering the people out of Egypt, had such a faith and confidence on this point that God had designed and purposed him for the work that he set about it forty years before God's time came. He was so very zealous that he ran upon the errand and imagined that the people would run with him too and that he should very soon deliver them out of the hands of their Egyptian taskmasters. Instead of which, God sent him to College for forty years in his own experience; and the little learning he had obtained in his head in Egypt was of no use to him in this College. He was not taught here the study and use of different languages; but he was taught the plague of his own heart, and the glory and majesty of God! But when the time was indeed come that God would really deliver his people, through him as his servant, instead of running before he was sent, as before, he was now full of excuses, and tried to get away from it, saying, "Lord, send I pray thee by the hand of him whom thou wilt send, but do not send me, for I am not eloquent." There was not a word spoken about the want of eloquence when he wanted to run before God had sent him; but when God's time had arrived for him to do the work, it made a wonderful difference in his feelings. He must now go and be the instrument in delivering God's people, and he now feels the solemnity and importance of it. But still, notwithstanding, the bondage and misery of the people are increasing; they are sunk exceedingly low, even almost to desperation, and are nearly without hope; yet God remembered them, and brought them through their oppressions and sorrows, because "his mercy endureth for ever."

Now this people were a typical nation; they were types of God's spiritual people, his elect, his chosen family; and his dealings towards them in the wilderness are typical of the wonderful deliverances which he works in and for his spiritual people. And as such, I shall now endeavour, as God shall graciously be pleased to enable me, to make a few remarks from the words before us, as applicable to God's elect family, of whom it is said, he "remembered us in our low estate; for his mercy endureth for ever."

We might take up considerable length of time in pointing out the persons intended by the word "us;" but we will omit it in this part of the subject, as, if the Lord will, we shall meet with it in another branch of the discourse; and, therefore, we will notice,

I. The *low estate*.

II. God *remembering them* in this low estate.

III. The *reason assigned:* "For his mercy endureth for ever."

I. The *low estate*. Now this low estate may be considered in three bearings: 1. The estate into which God's elect are plunged by the Fall in their Adam relation, as they stand before God; 2. This solemn estate, this low condition, this awfully low estate, as it is made manifest in their consciences, and as they are brought to feel it; 3. Then, if they live long after God has been pleased to manifest his remembering mercy to their consciences, they will have to feel a third low estate, which is a Babylonish captivity, a going from Jerusalem down towards Jericho, and a falling among thieves, where they will be stripped, and wounded, and left half dead, and where they would be quite dead, only God takes care of their life, which is hid in Christ; and while they are in this state, they will find they are no more capable of helping themselves, or extricating their souls from it, than they are of pulling down the skies, or creating a world; but God, in the riches of his grace and mercy, remembers them in this low estate, because "his mercy endureth for ever."

1. Then let us notice the Adam Fall. We all stand guilty before God there, as law-breakers. Every particle of God's law is directly against us. And if God is holy, just, righteous, and good, he must, upon the ground of his holy, just, righteous, and good law, condemn us as traitors and rebels; for "we have all sinned, and come short of the glory of God." Sin has ruined every particle of the image of God in which he originally created the conscience; it has laid us low, and sunk us down so low that the devil himself has as much holiness as any unregenerate man under sin; and God solemnly de-

clares in his Word, that "whatsoever the law says, it saith to them that are under the law, that every mouth may be stopped, and all the world become guilty before God;" not only to bring us in guilty, but to keep us guilty before him. Now every sinner is cursed by the law of God, if it be but for an evil thought; and if you could prove that you had never committed a criminal act, yet the principle of sin which is in you, and the thoughts which proceed from it, are sufficient to damn your soul for ever! So low is your estate, so awfully low, that if hell were opened to your eyes, and you could see the bottomless pit; if you could even behold the flames issuing out of it, and smell the sulphur and the brimstone, and hear the groans of the damned, you are sunk so low, and gone so far away, and indeed are in such an awful condition, that you have not the least power to help yourselves. But there are some men who tell us that man has it in his power to regenerate his own soul, to repent, to believe, and to save himself. But I do not scruple to say that every minister who says so is a minister of the devil, be he whom he will. He has not his message from God; he never knew either the mystery of the law or the mystery of the gospel, nor has he ever had his conscience enlightened by the blessed Spirit. But now, in this low estate we all lay, for there is no difference; and the apostle asks this question under the teachings of God, "What, then? Are we better than they?" Are we, the disciples and followers of Jesus, better than the ungodly? Am I, Paul; or is John, or Peter, or Timothy, or James, or any of us, or all of us, better than they, whose damnation is just? He says, "No, in nowise; for we have before proved, both Jews and Gentiles, that we are all under sin." Sin, therefore, has levelled the whole of the human race. It has laid them low and brought them into an awfully low condition. And what renders the case so totally desperate, as it respects the creature, is, that what the Lord says, speaking by the prophet Jeremiah, we find to be the truth, that "the wound is incurable;" neither men nor angels can cure it. O what a low estate this is to be in! But, perhaps, there may be some in this assembly to-night who are ready to say, "We go to church, and have the commandments repeated every Sunday, and at the end of each we say, 'Lord, have mercy upon us, and incline our hearts to keep this law!'" But the Word of God says, "He that offends in one point, is guilty of all!" The law once broken is broken for ever, and there can be no longer any keeping of it; consequently, if God be true, there is no help in us, nor can there be any possibility of sinful man keeping God's holy law. Has the Lord ever made any of you to feel it so? Has he ever mowed you down in your hearts, and brought you to feel yourselves really ruined, lost, and undone? Some poor creature may say, "I really have but little expectation of keeping the law; but still I think if I could keep it, and do something to please God, I might have some hope;" which is as much as to say if you could save yourself, then the Lord Jesus Christ need not come to help you! Why, bless you, if you are made low in your feelings, and brought to see what a poor ruined, wretched sinner you are, and your heart is directed by the blessed Spirit to say, "Lord, have mercy upon me, and manifest thy pardoning love and the precious atoning blood of the Son of God to my soul," there would be hope indeed for such a one as you are; but in vain attempts to keep the law there is no hope; for that cuts all down to despair and leaves us without any hope whatever. O what a very low estate every man by nature is in! But there are some professors here, who may be living very cheerfully in this low estate. You can sing and rejoice, go along merrily, and follow your vain amusements; and others of you may perform your religious duties, as you call them, trying to bring God in debtor to you; and you have a kind of satisfaction that all is well and right, when in reality you are living in an awful state of delusion, have never been delivered from Satan's service, are sleeping on the borders of destruction, and will at last sink to hell, if grace prevent not. But, if it be the sovereign pleasure of God, may this be the time for him to circumcise your heart, and cause you to feel the state you are in, that you may have to rejoice in his mercy, and say, "Who remembered us in our estate; for his mercy endureth for ever."

But, secondly, when God makes manifest this truth in the conscience, O what a low estate the poor creature gets into then! Now I remember, when a youth, I was not without solemn and awful twangs of conscience, expecting hell would open her mouth and let me in; and yet I do not believe that God's Spirit had quickened my soul at that time; and though I was terribly alarmed about wrath, hell, and condemnation, I could commit sin, and take pleasure therein, in order to get rid of and to stifle my miserable feelings; and many a time I have endeavoured to sing my misery away and insult God with my hardness of heart, while at the same time the terrors of hell were in my conscience. And I often wonder now that God should have put up with my impudence, with such an incarnate devil, but it was because "his mercy endureth for ever." But when the Lord was graciously pleased to quicken my soul, being then just turned seventeen years of age, and show me something of what sin was, I really feared it then, and a turn in my mind took place of a very different kind. I was brought to feel now that my sins were against a holy, just, and good God; that I had not merely to be alarmed for the consequences and punishment due to sin, but that I had to stand before the bar of infinite purity, and give an account of my awful practices, which made my soul solemnly to tremble at the Word of God, and before the glory of his majesty! It is one thing to be alarmed at sin through the fear of going to hell, and quite another sensibly to feel it as against a holy, just, and good God, and that the soul is accountable to him for it. And while I remained in this state, all the efforts I used to extricate myself only seemed to make my case worse; for every step I took appeared as though the Lord had designed to open a fresh wound in my conscience, and only to let me experience more deeply the abominable and loathsome disease of sin. And O what a low estate is this for a poor sinner to be in, without a single ray of satisfactory hope of ever receiving the blessings of salvation!

But some will say, "Then you should pray, repent, and believe, and attend to religious duties, and then you would get peace and comfort." But, alas! I found I had no power of my own either to pray, repent, or believe. I have long since come to a point about what some people call "the duty of all men to believe," and I say it is a doctrine of devils and calculated to harass and sink the child of God into feelings of hopeless despair. I found myself helpless, and utterly unable to practice duty-faith, and felt that I should as certainly sink to hell with duty-faith as with duty-works. And when at any time you are told to "believe," and it is your "duty to believe," and that "Jesus Christ died for sinners, and as all mankind are sinners, so they may all believe in him, be saved, and become completely happy, if they like;" I say, all such statements are a lie, and such happiness is nothing but the devil's happiness, and he communicates it on purpose to delude the souls of millions; all which a person may have without possessing one spark of real gospel grace. But when the gospel of God comes home to the heart, it comes "not in word only, but also in power, and in much assurance." Do not, then, deceive yourselves with the deceits and delusions of men, and cunning craftiness whereby they lie in wait to deceive. But the point is, have you been brought in guilty, and made to feel and groan over your low estate, without any power to help or raise yourself up from this destitute condition, and unable to pray yourself out of it? Have you ever appeared to be sunk and lost in nature's ruin, both God and conscience seeming to be against you, and that all the prayer you have consists of nothing but sighs and groans on account of what you feel? If you have been here, it is a blessed token, though you may not know it at the time, that the Holy Ghost is fulfilling his covenant engagement, in making intercession in your heart with groanings that cannot be uttered.

But, thirdly, after God makes manifest his remembering mercy and the riches of his pardoning grace, and gives a little faith in Christ, bringing sweet hope and peace in the conscience, we go on happily for a while, and think that all troubles are ended. I remember how it was with me. My soul seemed so sweetly wrapped up in God's pardoning mercy, and I thought he had so blessed me for evermore that I should always possess this peace and joy, and never know sorrow again. Poor wretch! So foolish was I, I began to throw my religion about every body's ears, and tell it unto every one. But before long, it all appeared to leave me, and I sank in ruin and misery; and when in this solemn low estate of wretchedness, my religion seemed to be nearly at an end. I knew what it was to go from Jerusalem, the vision of peace, and go down to Jericho, the world, and to feel stripped, wounded, and robbed. I was soon stripped of all my sweet enjoyments of the Lord's salvation, robbed of peace in my conscience; my joy all fled, every limb of the spiritual man was wounded, and instead of delight and joy in my soul, I was filled with sadness and mourning. O what a low estate is this for the soul to be in,—when all enjoyments are gone, all peace and happiness gone, no access to the Lord, and no smile from his sacred presence! Why, my case now appeared to me to be more desperate than when I lay under the sentence of death at the first instance. "Nay," say some; "I cannot believe that." Well, I tell you how it was with me while I was in that condition. In the first distress of my soul, I knew nothing of the joy of the light of the Lord's countenance. I knew nothing of sweet intercourse with Father, Son, and Spirit. I knew nothing of unbosoming my soul to God, and of God unbosoming his eternal love and grace to me. But when brought into this backsliding state, I found my soul to sink deeper into distress, and to come into a much lower estate. There are some who say there can be no backsliding; but every child of God knows that it is a lie! I say, when they are brought into this backsliding state, there is no joy from this vision of peace, until it is revealed again through the precious blood of the Lamb. But O what a low estate is this to be in! We look backward at our past experience, but cannot see the Lord there, and the enemy says it was all a delusion; we go forward to God's promises, but we cannot cast anchor there, and dare not say that it belongs to us; we go to the left hand, where God works, for and in his people, but it does not seem to be there, nor can we get any rest or peace for our souls; and we look on the right hand, at the finished work of the Son of God, and though it appears very glorious, yet we cannot get joy or comfort there either; so that of ourselves we cannot find it, and are ready to say, "O that I knew where I might find him, that I might come even to his seat, and order my cause before him." But while in this condition, we are in a low estate; death, darkness, gloominess, and sorrow are our chief companions. If we attempt to be cheerful, we cannot, and if we attempt to be happy, we cannot; but at last the Lord will appear for the relief of the soul. "He raiseth the poor out of the dust, he lifteth the beggar from the dunghill, to set them among princes, and to make them to inherit the throne of glory." But while we are on this low ground, we feel it to be a low place, and a dreadfully low place indeed it is! But "he remembereth us in our low estate; for his mercy endureth for ever."

II. But we pass on to God's *remembrance of them* in their low estate. First, he remembered the elect of God in one blessed body, when he considered them ruined in the fall, and lost in Adam the first, lost in his transgressions and our own too; and he remembered them so in his own love as to enter into a covenant for them, in his distinct Persons and distinct Personalities, to save them from perdition; and Jesus covenanted to come into their law-place and circumstances, to deliver them from the horrible pit, to accomplish salvation for them, and to open a way whereby all the claims of law and justice should be satisfied, all the perfections and attributes of God honoured, and a glorious redemption opened up for them in the blessed Redeemer, in the Person of God's dear Son. The Lord Jesus Christ also remembered them in his own blessed time, when he took into union with his Godhead their nature, and stood in their law-place and stead; when he died for poor ruined guilty sinners, for poor broken-hearted sinners; and when he stood up for them between insulted justice and their insulting souls; and took their precious cause, and all the cares connected with it, into his own hand. O what a remembrance was this! "He was made sin for us, who knew no sin;" and that we might have a complete salvation, he makes us "the righteousness of God in him." What a wonder of wonders! For if he had merely put away sin, if he had only been the destruction of sin, taken our offences away, and left it there, what an astonishing display of loving-kindness and mercy would that have been! But he has not only put away sin by the sacrifice of himself, and been the destruction of it, but, O for a tongue to speak it forth! He hath given his life a ransom for sinners to bring them to God; he hath fulfilled all the requirements of law and justice for them; he hath arrayed them in the majesty and glory of his righteousness, and they stand complete in him. And thus he demonstrates how blessedly he remembers us. He "remembers us in our low estate; for his mercy endureth for ever." I do not wonder at the psalmist being led by the blessed Spirit of God to rejoice in language like this: "Blessed are the people that know the joyful sound; they shall walk, O Lord, in the light of thy countenance; in thy name shall they rejoice all the day, and in thy righteousness shall they be exalted." Here we see how he remembers us, and we discover that it flows from the loving heart of God from eternity. O the matchless and astonishing mercy of the Lord! "Who hath remembered us in our low estate; for his mercy endureth for ever!"

Again. His glorious Majesty, the eternal Trinity in Unity, hath so remembered us as to lock us up for ever in the heart of Christ, and to make everything everlastingly secure in him, that so he should raise up his elect to holiness, to happiness, to God, and to eternal glory; that they should be enabled to meet every trial and temptation they are called to contend with in the wilderness, as well as

finally to overcome all their enemies, and that they should be more
than conquerors through him that hath loved them; that all their
necessities and wants should be supplied out of his fulness; that
nothing should do them any real hurt; that this is secured in the
heart of Jesus; that all the blessings they receive flow to them from
him, which are called the "sure mercies of David," and secured in
the Lord the Redeemer, who is David's Lord and David's Son.
Thus "he remembered us in our low estate; for his mercy endureth
for ever."

Again.   When the Lord is speaking unto his children by his servant Isaiah, he says, " Come unto me; hear, and your soul shall live."
But who is it that he is speaking to?   Such as are in want of mercy,
and are full of wants and necessities.   It is not to the decent Pharisee, nor to those who always have faith at their command, who can
come with a price in their hand, and can pray and get promises when
they please; it is not for those who feel themselves rich and increased in goods, and know not that they are miserable, and poor,
and blind, and naked; but it is for those who are without money and
without price; who are humbled before God, and are in need of
his mercy; it is to them he says, "Come unto me; hear, and your
soul shall live."   Some say, in these words the prophet is addressing dead sinners.   But can the dead do any work?   Can they arise
and perform living acts?   No indeed.   Then they must belong to
the people of God, those whom the Holy Ghost has quickened, who
are poor, sensible, needy sinners, drawn by his power to the dear
Redeemer, to all those who have spiritual faith given to them, and
who are led to Christ for life and salvation; these shall hear the
voice of mercy, and their souls shall live, and live well too; for they
shall eat of the Bread of God, and they shall be satisfied as with
marrow and fatness.   Thus he will feed the soul and cause it to rejoice; and "he will make an everlasting covenant with them, even
the sure mercies of David;" for "he hath remembered them in their
low estate; for his mercy endureth for ever."

"Well, but," some may say, "how does the Lord remember us
when we are sensibly in this low estate?"   What Christ has accomplished as our Head, by the appointment of God the Father, the
Spirit reveals to us as our necessities may require.   The Trinity in
Unity remembers the church of God; for each glorious Person has
a solemn part to perform in the great work of salvation; and, therefore, David could sing and rejoice, saying, "God is my salvation; I
will trust, and not be afraid;" for a covenant God, Father, Son, and
Spirit, is my salvation.   And when the poor child of God is brought
manifestively into this low estate, feelingly to have his hope cut off,
and he wants to experience afresh the forgiveness of his sins, through
another application of the blood of Jesus to his conscience, and to
know that justice is satisfied on his account; I say, all the while he

is thus a stranger to peace, feeling his props cut away, the blessed Spirit remembers him in this low estate by giving him grace to cry out for mercy, and by inspiring groans, sighs, and bitter cries in his heart for the revelation of God's mercy to his soul. Perhaps some are ready to say, "It cannot be that the Lord will remember such a wretch as I!" But if the Lord had not remembered you, and had thoughts of mercy towards you, there would be none of these feelings in your heart; the Lord the Spirit would not have indited these things in your conscience; but it is evident that he remembers his people by thus communicating to them in a time of need a little help, by giving them a little peace, a little prop to raise up their sinking spirits, and giving power to feel a little pure breathing towards Zion. And really, when the poor heart feels a little breathing to the Lord, a little relief, and a little fresh communication of his mercy, well he remembers the hand that gives it to him; and this little peace in the Lord Jesus Christ will keep the soul from sinking; it will prop up the mind, and cause it to say, "Who can tell but that the Lord will have mercy upon me?" Thus he remembers his people by keeping them poor in spirit. In all the backwardness they feel in going to a throne of grace, all the perplexities they are the subjects of, Satan's fiery darts and suggestions, with the fear of giving up their hope, and throwing up all for lost; yea, in the midst of all he remembers them still; he keeps them in the hollow of his hand, and all hell cannot drag them out! Why, bless you, the Lord is always with his people; and in this way he makes it manifest that he remembers them in their low estate. Many times they would give up again and again, if he did not hold them up.

But perhaps some poor soul present is saying, "Well, I do not know what to make of myself! I get nothing to satisfy my mind. I cannot be happy in myself, either with my religion or without it, and I cannot tell what the issue of it will be. Many times I think I must give it up altogether!" Why do you not give it up then? "O," says the soul, "I do not know." Then I will tell you. Because it is the Lord's work; for had it been your own, you would have given it up long ago; but as it is the Lord's work, he remembers you in your low estate, and you are now brought to feel your wretchedness and misery, and to cry out to the Lord for help and deliverance. He remembers you so as to keep you to this point; and because the life of God is in you, the breath of life is going back to the fountain of life from whence it proceeded, and mercy is now springing up in your conscience.

But the Lord remembers the soul more especially when his blessed Majesty reveals directly to the conscience of the poor soul the glorious Person and precious blood and obedience of the Lord Jesus Christ. And I believe when the child of God is favoured with real spiritual faith to apprehend and lay hold of Jesus as his dear Saviour, and is privileged to see the dignity of his Person, and feel an interest in his great salvation, he will have a much greater degree of consolation. But some of the Lord's people would give worlds to be able to say that Christ loved them, and had eternally saved them; but though they dare not use such language, yet they cannot give up the point. They will still be seeking to the Lord to have these things made clear to them. Here it is seen that he remembers them by keeping them to the point, anxiously pleading with the Lord, in the name of Jesus Christ, that he would reveal to them that he has shed his precious blood for them; and, in the Lord's own blessed time, he will give such a faith in the atonement of Jesus, so apply it to the conscience and speak it home to the heart with such power, saying, "I am thy salvation," as shall give peace to the soul and make it full of joy. Christ and the conscience now are in sweet peace together. Christ appears to the heart just suited to its wants, and the sinner feels Christ to be all that he desires; and here the two have but one heart, while the soul is thus under the divine unction of the Holy Spirit. O what a time of remembrance is this, when the Lord brings the soul thus sweetly to enjoy these feelings, and to say with the apostle, "He loved *me*, and gave himself for *me!*" And when the riches of his mercy are so manifested to his heart, he proves it to be a solemn and a glorious remembrance, and he rejoices in the sweetness of the truth that "he remembered us in our low estate; for his mercy endureth for ever."

But we must pass on and notice further, that in our low estate of backsliding he also remembers us. Now, have you ever been there? I know there are some persons who say that all the doubts and fears, and exercises of mind the children of God are the subjects of, they can do very well without them. Well, one thing I can say most certainly, that I do not envy them either their feelings or their state; and I tell such professors that there is no case of which I should be more jealous than of theirs. Depend upon it, God will make the consciences of his people tender. And when the dear child of God falls into a state of backsliding, and the world gets hold of him, while family troubles increase upon him, he sinks into such a low estate that every little trouble is too much for him, and everything he meets with fills him with dismay. He has no sweet enjoyment of the Lord's presence, but is harassed and buffeted by a tempting devil, and perhaps temporal things are going back with him also; in addition to which he feels a nature which serves him worse tricks than the devil himself. "Nay," some are ready to say, "you do not mean to say, worse tricks than the devil?" Yes, I do; for our vile nature will do things which the devil cannot do. Therefore, the poor soul is so tossed about in his feelings in this backsliding state that he knows not what to do. But the Lord remembers him still, even when he dare not say that he remembers the Lord. How does he then remember him? By giving him now and then a solemn check, a pull-back, a rebuke; and when the poor wandering affections are about entering into forbidden paths, there will be something come powerful to the conscience, and say, "Whither art thou bound? Will the pursuit of it carry rest to thy soul?" And the wanderer will be constrained to cry out, "Lord, keep back thy servant from presumptuous sins." By and by there will again be a fresh seeking and panting in the mind after carnal objects, but the blessed Spirit will convince of sin, and bring back the heart with such a cry as this, "Lord, help me!" For the poor soul feels now that he wants his mighty and saving help to raise him up from this low estate, or he might sink to rise no more! But now, all these checks, rebukes, and pull-backs; all these sighs, groans, and cries, arise from God's remembering mercy, and are an evidence that the Lord remembers him with the favour that he bears to his chosen. Therefore, in his own blessed time, he will remember him by manifesting the tenderness of his heart, and the sympathy of his soul towards him; and he says to the poor backslider, "Is Ephraim my dear son? Is he a pleasant child? For since I spake against him, I do earnestly remember him still. Therefore my bowels are troubled for him. I will surely have mercy upon him, saith the Lord." What heart-work is this, when the Lord comes thus, and reveals his grace! O how it melts the heart, softens the stubborn feelings, and brings the soul to say, "There is no God like unto my God! There is none can be compared unto him! He is so full of pity, of compassion, and of long-suffering! And who hath remembered me in my low estate, because 'his mercy endureth for ever!'"

I well remember once being in a state of backsliding, and brought into great want in my feelings; and while reading Ezek. xvi., everything seemed to tell me that I was the very person there described; that I was the guilty, vile creature there set forth; and though I had never been suffered to commit carnal fornication (nor does the passage mean that), yet I found that I had committed spiritual fornication, and I sank many fathoms low in my mind, and saw the desperate wickedness of my nature in a way which I had never done before. And O! When the Lord comes in thus powerfully, what a change is wrought in the mind! How it quiets the soul when he says, "That thou mayest remember, and be confounded, and never open thy mouth any more because of thy shame, when I am pacified towards thee." And when God thus speaks, grace breaks in upon the soul, and matchless mercy overwhelms the mind! O what a holy joy I found at this time! There was a sweet serenity in my heart, a confounding of all my reasoning powers, and I was brought to wonder at God's overwhelming grace and mercy toward me. And in thus revealing himself to my soul, I felt it to be a solemn remembrance indeed! And I tell you what, poor child of God, there is nothing so solemn, or so blessed, as for the Lord to shame you out of sin by pouring in of his mercy, and melting down the soul under a sense of his goodness!

III. But to conclude. The *reason assigned* for God's remembrance is, because "his mercy endureth for ever!" O what a prop this is! May the Lord set it up, and make it more powerful in the sinner's conscience! Mercy endures! Well, if mercy follows us, surely we shall need this mercy through all the wilderness, and we shall never be without a feeling sense of our need of mercy! But O the matchless grace! God's "mercy endureth for ever!" What, then? Does God keep mercy for thousands? Yes, he does; for "mercy is built up for ever!" He hath everlastingly locked up an abundance of mercy in the heart of Christ, and hath opened up in him a fountain of mercy for poor broken-hearted sinners, because "his mercy endureth for ever!"

May the Lord the Spirit make manifest in our souls the abundance of this mercy, and his name shall have the praise. Amen.

THE WRESTLINGS OF NAPHTALI.

Preached in Zoar Chapel, Great Alie Street, London, on Sunday Morning, May 28th, 1843.

"And of Naphtali, he said, O Naphtali, satisfied with favour, and full with the blessing of the Lord."—DEUT. xxxiii. 23.

IT is a blessed time with the soul, when it can really feel, and sweetly enter into the enjoyment of the language you have just been singing:

"While Jesus shows his heart is mine,
And whispers I am his!"

But I believe the Lord never bestows such solemn favours either to be sported or trifled with; and when the favour comes to our souls in this way, it is either to prepare us *for* trouble, to prop us up *in* trouble, or to deliver us *out of* trouble. It is now more than fifty years since God first spake this to my heart; and from that time to the present moment I have always found, more or less, that any spiritual visit to my soul, any soul-overcoming visit, has been attended with one of these three things: If I have not been in any particular trouble at the time, one has been very near; or it has been given when in the midst of trouble, to prevent me from sinking under it; or it has come as a deliverance out of trouble; so that, when God does favour the soul with such blessed visits, it is for a solemn purpose, and never either to be sported or trifled with.

That is a precious portion of the Word of God recorded by the prophet Zechariah; but I know that poor fallen sinful man does not like it, or he is very different to me, for God knows my heart and flesh do not. You will say, " What is it?" Why, to be brought into the fire, and to be led through the fire. For though I have been a thousand times in the fire, and brought out of it again, yet I do not like it now a whit more than I did fifty years ago. My flesh shrinks away and tries to escape from it as much as ever. But the Lord says to the prophet, "I will bring the third part through the fire; I will refine them as silver is refined, and try them as gold is tried." And what will they do then? That which they did not do before: " They shall call on my name, and I will hear them, saith the Lord." When they were not in the fire, they went back in their affections into the world, they pursued after the things of the world, and their backsliding hearts were wandering after every forbidden object, so that they had not much time to call upon the Lord; but when they get into the fire, and begin to feel the heat of it, when they are brought into trouble, then they will cry out, and call upon the name of the Lord. But will he not refuse to listen to them then? No! He says, " I will hear them." O how full of grace and mercy he is! How different to the actings of our minds! He gently reproves us for our wanderings; and it is as though he said to us, " You now come to me because of your necessitous circumstances, but you would have done without me if you could; there are no thanks due to you; you would not have come, if it had not been for this." God knows we can never do without him, he knows that well; and therefore he brings us into these necessitous circumstances that we should find that we cannot do without him. But when he puts us intothe fire and into the furnace, and we feel it to get hotter and hotter, then, saith the Lord, they will be glad to come unto me, and to call upon my name. And what do you think he will say to them? O the wonders of his matchless mercy! He says, " I will say, It is my people; and they shall say, The Lord is my God!" Now it is under such solemn and special circumstances as these that Christ appears so gloriously blessed to the poor sinner, when the Lord the Spirit is pleased thus to manifest him under trials and conflicts.

But the portion of Scripture I now design to read, and from which I shall make a few remarks, you will find recorded in Deut. xxxiii. 23: " And of Naphtali he said, O Naphtali, satisfied with favour, and full with the blessing of the Lord."

Moses was now about taking a farewell of the world and of the people of God. He had led them through the wilderness for forty years, and yet he found them still to be the same stiffnecked and gainsaying people they had ever been. And as it was with typical Israel then, so it is with spiritual Israel now. They are more than a match for the management of Moses. He never did, he never *can* manage them. He gave them many thundering lectures as they passed through the desert, and brought the people into a multitude of legal forms, concerning which they said, " All that the Lord hath commanded us we will do!" But they never did a jot or tittle of them; for they failed in all the legal forms which they promised to perform. And just so it is with the poor child of God now. While he is immediately under the terror of the law of works, O what vows and promises he makes! But he never performs one of them. But now, when Moses was going to give up the charge, and was about committing the people into better hands, even into the hands of Jesus himself, he says, "Yea, he loved the people." What a wonderful thing that he should love such a reptile race as his children are! "Yea, he loved the people. All his saints are in thy hand; and they sat down at thy feet; every one shall receive of thy words." It is as though Moses had said, "I have been trying to teach them for forty years, and they are now just as dull and absent as ever; but I will deliver them up altogether into the hands of Jesus; they shall become his scholars and sit at his feet; they shall be taught of him and receive of his words." And I have thought before now that Paul had this circumstance in view when, in writing to the Galatians, he said, "The law was our schoolmaster unto Christ;" but when we are brought to Christ, and made partakers of Christ, we are no longer then under that schoolmaster, but receive at the hands of the blessed Redeemer, by the power of the Spirit, solemn, sweet, and spiritual instruction. Moses then pronounces a variety of blessings on the different tribes of Israel, according to the design of God; and the portion we have read this morning as a text are the words which are spoken concerning Naphtali; and as I believe it is not to be confined to its mere literal meaning, but is to be taken in a spiritual sense also, I design, with the Lord's help, to look at it in that sense at the present time. We shall, therefore,

I. Make a few remarks upon the *person* spoken of, Naphtali.

II. Show that these Naphtalis, in God's own time, are *satisfied with favour*.

III. Prove how they are full with the blessing of the Lord. "O Naphtali, satisfied with favour, and *full with the blessing of the Lord*."

I. The term "*Naphtali*" signifies one that struggles, or wrestles, or is a great fighter; and I consider it is applicable to three characters: 1. To the Son of God himself, as our blessed Immanuel; 2. To the whole church of God, and to every individual member of that church while here below. And, 3. To every man whom God calls, qualifies, and sends into the ministry. Now all these are found to be wrestlers, strugglers, and fighters unto a better country, and in the end they are "satisfied with favour, and full with the blessing of the Lord!"

The foundation-stone, then, in this solemn building is our blessed Immanuel. There is no building without him, no standing without him; and all God's people find that whatever wrestling, struggling, or fighting they may have, if God did not bring them to feel that their standing was upon Christ, they would be sure to sink; but when they are brought, by faith, to find that they are fixed upon this immovable Rock, and to know that their standing is alone upon Christ, by the blessed revelation of the Spirit to their souls, why all the fury of hell is unable to move them, and Satan's rage is no more than the shaking of rushes against them. And while God thus maintains his power in the consciences of those who, by precious faith, are building alone upon the Son of God, they will find that all their enemies will give way, and flee from them, and Christ alone be exalted.

But, first, we said that the term "Naphtali" was applicable to Christ himself. Now, in his mediatorial capacity, Christ was made in all points like unto his brethren; he was made low and little. I have often been struck with an expression of Hart's, in one of his hymns; I do not know that I can quote it correctly; but the substance of it is:

"We speak of his greatness and power,
But who his weakness knows?"

And one solemn branch of the mystery of God is, to have a faith's view of the feebleness, weakness, meanness, and littleness of the Son of God! For if we could only view his majesty and glory as God, it would be terrific to the poor, weak, struggling sinner; but when, under the teachings of the blessed Spirit, we can view our mighty Captain struggling, buffeted, tempted, tried, burdened, cast down, and low as "a worm, and no man," as he calls himself; I say, when we can see him thus low, wrestling, struggling, and cast down; and yet, at the same time, to view him as the mighty God, and the upholder of all things; to behold devils alarmed at his look, obliged to obey his nod, and ask his permission where they may go; I say, what blessedness have such views afforded me many a time, to see him come down thus into such low circumstances, even into our low estate; so that, poor child of God, he not only knows thee by his infinite power and knowledge, but sympathetically he knows thy state, for he has been there before thee, yet without sin! Look, then, at this blessed Redeemer, in his low estate, made in all points like as we are, yet without sin; for no sooner was he made known as the Babe of Bethlehem born, but his strugglings and wrestlings came on; and as he grew up to youth and years of maturity, they increased upon him. And I could wish that God's ministers, when they immerse in the name of the Father, Son, and Spirit, would keep this more in view, as there is no other emblem that sets forth so strikingly the amazing strugglings and overwhelmings of the Son of God as baptism! When Jesus was baptized, the Eternal Three appeared solemnly to sanction it; and I really do not know any ordinance that God instituted, either under the Old or in the New Testament, that was so manifestly honoured with the Persons in

God. While the Person of the Son was being solemnly immersed in our nature, the Person of the Father spoke from heaven, saying, "This is my beloved Son, in whom I am well-pleased!" And the Person of the Spirit descended from heaven like a dove, and rested upon him; so that the blessed Trinity, in his Divine Persons, appeared to crown this sacred act, to show that the majesty and glory of God were figured forth to us in the blessedness of this ordinance for all time to come. But no sooner had the Holy Ghost descended upon him, and the Father had given this glorious testimony concerning him, than we are told that he was driven by the Spirit into the wilderness to be tempted of the devil. "Driven!" say you? Aye, he was; but it is his humanity that trembles and struggles; nevertheless, he must go. Do not wonder at it, brethren. He was now going to wrestle against all the malice, rage, spite, and venom which the devil ever has hurled out against his church, or ever will. It was all thrown upon him, and he bore it all; or you and I must have sunk under the weight of it, to rise no more! I know some poor child of God is ready to say, "I cannot believe that Christ was ever tempted as I am." Well, then, if he were not, for certain you could never get through your temptations. If Christ had not been tempted like unto his brethren, how could he succour and support them under temptation? But, having passed through the same conflicts, he can sympathize with his suffering people and enter into all their sorrows and trials. "O," says one, "it is impossible that Christ could have been tempted like unto me. He was not a sinner; but I am a poor, polluted, vile, and guilty sinner. He was 'holy, harmless, undefiled, and separate from sinners.'" But stop; though this is the case, yet I will prove to you that his temptations were more painful than yours. Let me only ask you a question or two. Was there not a time when you did those things that would be horrifying to you to do now? Could you not, some of you, blaspheme, curse, and swear, and even call upon God, with awful oaths, invoking his solemn judgments upon your person, and run into all manner of obscenity and uncleanness? And yet, the mere temptation or suggestion from the enemy of souls to do any of these things now, or to gratify the vile passions of your carnal nature, is horrifying to you! How came all this to pass? From whence this change in your feelings? "O," say you, "I can hardly tell." I will tell you then. God, in the riches of his mercy, hath communicated unto you a measure of his grace; he hath imparted unto you a new nature, a principle of divine life; and the actings of that life cause you to sigh and groan under the temptation of these horrible things; and this measure of God's communicable nature, this principle of holiness, is that which produces in your conscience so much distress at things which are so contrary to God and holiness and so horrifying to your mind. Well now, if these things are so with you, in a little measure, what must temptation have been to the Son of God, who was altogether holy, both in his essential Godhead and in his perfect manhood? If the infernal foe could hurl such blasphemies at the head of Christ, what may not you and I expect from him in the force of his temptations? Yet Jesus bore the whole of his fury and malice; he struggled and wrestled against him and all his subtle temptations; but he fought to conquer; he overcame the prince of darkness; he bruised his head; and, blessed be his name! he vanquished him for his tried and tempted people. But we are told that Christ was in the wilderness for forty days and forty nights, without eating or drinking, and all that time tempted of the devil. Who can number the amount or extent of his temptations during the whole of that time of his sufferings? But the two or three which are left on record are quite sufficient to show the nature of them and serve to prove that it was not possible for any temptation to be worse. He was poor. He said, "The foxes have holes, and the birds of the air have nests, but the Son of man hath not where to lay his head;" and yet it appears that the devil showed Christ the kingdoms of the world, and the glory of it, and promised to give it all to him, if he would only fall down and worship him! The devil had the impudence to tempt Christ to worship him, when he could appeal to the Father, and say, "All mine are thine and thine are mine!" I say, could anything be worse than this, for Christ to be tempted in our nature to worship the implacable foe of God and his church; and for no better purpose than worldly gain? And if he came thus, with his "ifs" and "buts" to the Son of God, do you think he will let us go free? As Hart says,

> "That impious *if*, he thus
> At God incarnate threw,
> No wonder if he cast at us,
> And make us feel it too!"

But he is a blessed and a true Friend. "He is a Brother born for adversity, and he sticketh closer than a brother." Well; for forty days he struggled with his and our enemies; he met them in the field, and struggled with all the temptations and fiery darts that Satan ever has hurled in the consciences of God's elect, or ever will be able to do. And though Christ had to sigh and groan, while fighting the battle, yet he gained the victory. He rose triumphant over sin, death, and hell. He overcame all our foes, and the church is blessed and saved in him with an everlasting salvation.

But if we leave him for a moment or two, or rather pass on from this spot of his temptation in the wilderness, and follow him to his travail in the Garden of Gethsemane, we shall there see how he had to struggle with, and to wrestle against the coldness, indifference, worldliness, and hard-heartedness of his own people. O how cold and indifferent we are at times! How full of base unbelief and carnal reason! He said, on one occasion, to his disciples, "How is it that ye have no faith?" Why, the people of God sometimes are not able to move a step, faith is so low with them. Gracious dispensations seem nothing at all to them, they are so cold and lifeless; and sometimes they can look upon a suffering Christ with a degree of indifference which would surprise an infidel, if an infidel were capable of unders'anding it. But, blessed be the dear Redeemer, he struggled with all this; he put up with the hard speeches, and felt for the infirmities of his people, and nothing prevented him from manifesting his mercy towards the objects of his love.

But O! What a solemn scene was that which took place in the Garden of Gethsemane! Whom do we now see on the ground, weltering in his blood? What was it caused that solemn conflict, that heart-rending struggle? Child of God, poor trembling sinner, it was thy sins, thy lusts; aye, thy internal lusts; all thy wanderings in heart and affections; all the sin that thy nature containeth, which thou knowest to be sin, and which thou knowest not to be sin, but which is all *here* (the preacher putting his hand upon his heart); for there is not a sin in hell which does not exist in thy nature. All the sin that has ever been committed and shown forth by those in the bottomless pit is in the nature of every child of God. Well, then, all the ponderous weight, all the awfulness of thy sin, united with the malignity, enmity, spite, and rage of hell, accompanied with the wrath of God and the curses of a broken law,—all met together upon Christ at Gethsemane. He must now do battle with them all single-handed, receiving no help or aid from man; no, not even from his disciples! I often wonder at those who talk about being such wonderful helpers of God, why they did not aid and help him when he looked for some help; when his disciples fell asleep; when such sleep and heaviness came upon them as they had never felt before; and when even Peter, who only a few hours before had boasted that he would die for him and that, though all men forsook him, *he* would never deny him, had, along with the rest, all fallen asleep, and forgotten their suffering Lord and Master! But O! These sleepy, selfish feelings, how they pierced the heart of the Son of God and caused him to groan in the Garden of Gethsemane! All the accumulation of sorrows met together upon him here. He "looked, and there was none to help," and "wondered that there was none to uphold; therefore his own arm brought salvation, and his fury it upheld him!" Poor believer! *Thy salvation is the single-arm salvation of Immanuel,* God with us! Thy works, good or bad, have no hand in procuring it; it is accomplished wholly by the Lord for such a poor sinking, feeble, tempest-tossed, devil-driven sinner as thou art! O what a mercy it is sometimes to be brought to feel that this single-handed salvation, accomplished by God the Son, is wrought out for such a poor helpless worm as I am! Blessed be his name, he hath finished the work alone; he hath brought life and immortality to light; he has fulfilled the requirements of law, satisfied the demands of justice, and honoured all the perfections of God!

But, behold our struggling Naphtali triumphing in the solemn scene, while wrestling against the rage of hell, the wrath of God, and the terrors of a broken law! In the midst of his agony, an angel is sent from heaven to minister unto him, to afford a little help and consolation, but not to help him in the amazing work of salvation. He only came to strengthen him in his dolorous sufferings; for angels witnessed the pressure which he was enduring on account of sin. They saw his awful conflicts, beheld the blood falling to the ground and saw it smeared with it; and all this, poor trembling sinner, for such wretches as you and I! Does it not appear too much for belief? Some talk about believing just as they like, and can always believe when they please. Why, bless you, it is too much for *our* belief. But when the Lord the Spirit really gives faith in this blessed mystery, and we can get spiritually into the Garden of Gethsemane, feel a little of the flowings in our heart of the love of this blessed struggling Hero, this mighty Captain of our salvation, and trace his glorious work in our souls, why then we can with confidence say, "The Lord hath done great things for us, whereof we are glad!" And we can solemnly declare and show forth the mysteries of his love.

Well, then, Christ is our spiritual Naphtali, the great struggler, wrestler, and burden-bearer of sin. All that law and justice required was charged upon him. There is not one iota of the law's curse but was laid upon him; not an iota of sin and death but was laid upon him; and he bore it away; yea, sins which we have never known, nor ever been conscious of, were all laid upon him; for "the Lord hath laid upon him the iniquity of us all." I do not know how it is with you; but I have forgotten mine many a time; and if it had been left for me to lay my sins upon Christ, I should not have remembered a thousandth part of them, and, therefore, must have sunk under them for ever. But infinite wisdom gathered them all together and laid them all on Christ, and he hath sunk them into everlasting oblivion. But O! What an amazing burden he must have had to wrestle and struggle with! When my sins are so great and enough to sink a world to hell, what must have been the ponderous weight of all the millions of the sins of God's elect laid upon him, which ever have been committed or shall be till the end of time; when all the lust, anger, vain glory, ungodly pursuits; all our fleshly devilism, which is enwoven in our nature, or has ever been suffered to come out of the secret corners and inmost recesses of a desperately wicked heart; when all this accumulation of guilt was gathered together and laid upon the head of Christ; when justice demanded and received full satisfaction for the infinite debt, and would not let him go till the last mite was paid; I say, what an intolerable burden it must have been! But, glory to God in the highest! Our Immortal Struggler, our Divine Wrestler, our Blessed Naphtali, overcame sin, death, and hell, and all the power of the foe. He triumphed gloriously, and hath brought life and immortality to light.

And now, after he had accomplished his bloody sweat in the Garden, he arose to awake his disciples; and he awoke them to some purpose now. He awoke them before; but they went to sleep again. I do not know any place where the cankerworm of fleshly doings is to be seen more than in' the Garden of Gethsemane. You that are so fond of your mighty works, your exploits, and of showing what you will do for God, just observe what now is about to take place. I say, Jesus arose up, awakes his disciples, and calls them forth; and now Peter began to brisk up a little, to see what great work he should do for him; and seeing the soldiers coming, he rubbed his eyes, drew his sword, and cut off the ear of the high priest's servant. And what good did this do? None at all. It only gave his Master a job, for he had to put it on again; all that it did was to give him another job. Jesus told him to put up his sword; for, he said, "All they that take the sword shall perish by the sword." And this is just what our legality does, with the use of carnal weapons; but the Lord says, "the weapons of our warfare are not carnal, but mighty, through God, to the pulling down of strong holds." We are not to fight with carnal weapons. In ages past, our Christian nation, as it is called, fought with carnal weapons, and burned their fellow-creatures to make them Christians. They might as well suppose that burning in hell would make the devil an angel of light as to suppose that burning and torturing men could make them Christians. It must be the life and power of God alone to accomplish this. But we are fast hastening on to a time when, if I am not greatly mistaken, something of the kind will take place again; for there has not been such a dark foreboding time over the church, since you and I were born, as there is at the present time. Now I am quite easy about who may be offended or pleased at what I am going to say; but I tell you, if that infernal Bill, which is now agitating the country, should pass into a law, it will be food for Popery, and it will not be very long before you will have to seal the testimony of God with your blood. I believe this in my soul; and I say, it becomes the church of God zealously to oppose this infernal Bill, and to let it be publicly known that our hearts are alive for the interests of Zion. But if after all our efforts it should pass into a law, why then we must leave the issue with God; but it becomes us to act with boldness, and to use with diligence the means which are given to us to frustrate it; and if you are anxious for the welfare of yourselves and posterity, you cannot be indifferent or unconcerned about it. Why, I cannot suppose that any one but the devil himself could have put it into the heart of any man to frame such a God-dishonouring Bill! Therefore, let us stand in awe while we are in this solemn position, which is likely to bring the church into so much trouble and distress! (The Bill referred to was the Romanist Emancipation Bill.)

But to come back to the point. After the blessed Redeemer had left the Garden of Gethsemane, they bring him to the judgment-seat. See how low he is, and how they degrade him! They use him worse than a wretched match-carrier, or a vagabond stroller, who is brought before the Lord Mayor, or City officer! He is treated with insult and contempt, and mocked and derided as the Son of God! What would the newspapers say, if a poor vagabond stroller were brought before the Lord Mayor, and one of the officers of the court should pluck the hair from his cheek, another spit in his face, and a third smite him with the palm of his hand; and yet that the Lord Mayor sat quiet and easy all the time, and took no notice of it? Would not all the newspapers in the country be up in arms against such an outrage? Certainly they would; yet this was the treatment which the Son of God, the Lord of life and glory, met with! And why did he suffer these indignities to be heaped upon him? Because he was enduring the curse due to the sins of his beloved people. Therefore he allowed every insult that men and devils could invent or inflict to come upon him. But he rose above it all, and accomplished the glorious salvation which he had designed! Peter, the great co-worker Peter, who a little before was boasting what great things he would do, and who had just cut off the ear of the servant of the high priest, now begins to show his infirmity, by cursing and swearing that he knew him not! And this was another thrust in the heart of the Son of God; for Peter's cursing and swearing went to the heart of Jesus! Was he not, then, a wrestler, a struggling and a fighting Naphtali? Yes, indeed; and it is a mercy for you and me that he was! And did he not take a sword, and stab Peter for stabbing him? Yes, he did; but his sword was the rebuke of love, a silent manifestation of his mercy and compassion. He "turned, and looked upon Peter;" but it was a look of love. O how it stabbed him to the heart, and made him go out, and weep bitterly! O the wonderful mercy of a covenant God to such sinners as we are! Who is there that pities like him? Who is so full of loving-kindness and tender mercy? May it be our happiness to feel more of the flowings of his loving heart to us in the time of trouble, when we are called to endure something of the sorrows and conflicts which he passed through. "O Naphtali, satisfied with favour, and full with the blessing of the Lord."

But the dreadful work is yet to come! After he had come from the Garden of Gethsemane (a place most dear to the sinner), had been mocked at the judgment-seat, and sentence given against him, then they proceed to scourge him, and to make deep furrows in his back. They strip him naked and hurl him prostrate on the ground! Bless you, if it were possible for the vilest person in England to be used so cruelly, the whole nation would be up in arms against it! He had to bear his cross; and it was not till he had fainted under it that they allowed one to bear it for him; and at length, when they had spent the fury of their infernal malice, they nailed him to the cross and suspended him between heaven and earth, as the vilest of men! And what had he done to merit such treatment? He had healed the sick, raised the dead, caused the dumb to speak, and opened the eyes of the blind; and this was the return he met with for it! But none of these things could alter his purpose of love. He struggled and wrestled through the whole of it. He fought it manfully out, and accomplished such a mighty work that none but himself could have effected, and which shall fill all heaven with endless praise!

I have often thought of the saying of an old countryman now dead, a simple-hearted man of God, and which is now brought fresh to my mind. About thirty years ago I had been baptizing in a place called Boroughbridge, and it made no little bustle in the neighbourhood to see what they called "dipping." An old friend, who was known in that place by the name of Richard, but who was generally called "Dickey," was asked by an old countryman, "Who are these dippers? Do you know anything about them? What are they?" "O!" replied Dickey; "the Head of them was the finest man that ever lived! He healed the sick, clothed the naked, opened the eyes of the blind, and caused the dumb to speak; he fed the poor, and the people flocked to him from every quarter; yet he never turned one away that came to him in the time of need, and all without charging one farthing for it. And, what do you think? They nailed him, at last, to a piece of wood!" The person said, "Why, what wicked folks they must have been!" And just so are we. We should have committed the same sin, if left to ourselves and brought into the same circumstances and condition. But our spiritual Naphtali struggled under, overcame, and rose triumphantly, the mighty Hero over all!

But now, he is brought to the cross, and his humanity begins to tremble! The clouds gather thick darkness, and the sun puts on mourning! The rocks rend and the earth quakes! Some of the sleeping dead are so alarmed that they come out of their graves to see what God was doing upon earth, and to witness the solemn scene! But, I say, while our immortal Hero was thus struggling against the enemies of his church, he shook the pillars of the earth, and made them to tremble! The sun refused to shine while it beheld the solemn effects of sin! But man, more careless than the devil—monster man! could view the awful scene, and yet be unfeeling and unconcerned! Aye, so it was. But did this cause the dear Redeemer to give up the point? No; he undertook our cause and was determined to go through with it! And at length, the struggling Hero, in his last conflict, gave a death-blow to sin, and a death-blow to the king of terrors; and in the last words which he uttered on the cross, when he said, "It is finished!" he for ever gave a death-blow to the prince of darkness, leading captivity captive, spoiling principalities and powers, and making a show of them openly, triumphing over them in it! Poor sinking heart! Poor tried believer! If this is revealed to thy conscience, and thou art brought into a faith's apprehension of it, it will give thee a sweet resting on the finished work of Christ! I would say, "Holy Ghost, impart more powerfully to our souls an enjoyment of the finished work of Christ, that we may feel that he is gone to the right hand of the Father, exalted above all principalities and powers, to reign as our immortal Hero for ever and ever!" "O Naphtali, satisfied with favour, and full with the blessing of the Lord."

Now from this part of the subject, let us just notice one or two things. Can you, poor sinner, look over a subject of such a solemn nature, be indifferent and unconcerned about it, and not desirous of knowing whether you are interested in the strugglings of this mighty Hero, who made heaven and earth to tremble, and who will shortly "come in flaming fire taking vengeance on them that know not God?" Careless sinner! What will then become of thee, when the heavens and the earth shall pass away, the elements melt with fervent heat, and the sky become like a useless scroll of parchment; when the devil and the damned shall be brought to receive their sentences, to hear their final doom pronounced, and the church be raised up to indescribable glory and happiness, in body and soul for ever and ever with their Lord! Careless sinner, I say again, what will then become of thee? No father to pray for you then! No mother's sympathy for you then! All the scorn and contempt, all the ridicule and derision which you have showed to your parents, will pierce your heart then. You will have the terrors of a guilty conscience, and sink into the blackness of hopeless despair for ever! But may the Lord have mercy upon you, even our blessed Hero, who struggled and overcame all his foes! O Lamb of God! Struggle in the heart of some poor careless sinner, and bring him to God; show him that his sin is put away, that it has been laid upon One who was mighty to struggle, and who has gained the conquest and triumph, that so he may be brought to glory in thee alone as his blessed Redeemer.

Poor struggling child of God, who art tried with sin, troubled with Satan's suggestions, and tempest-tossed in thy mind, see what a sympathizing Saviour thou hast; and may you never forget that he knows all your wilderness trials, that he knows the path you are now walking in; and though you may have lost the sight of him, and are ready to say with Job, "O that I knew where I might find him,

that I might come even to his. mercy-seat!'" his eye of compassion
is fixed on thee, and he will appear for thy deliverance. Well, poor
soul, I had very nearly said, Keep where thou art; do not go away
from this spot; thou shalt be brought to see. greater things in thy pilgrimage; keep on sighing, groaning, and waiting at his footstool; he
knows when to come to you. What a mercy, he will come in his
own blessed time, and bring all thy conflicts to a peaceful end, on the
ground of his own strugglings and wrestlings. He will come, and
bring it to thy heart, and thou shalt rise up in immortal glory, and
be brought at last to triumph in him as thy covenant God. O may
the Lord then direct your mind to look more unto him, to rest on his
finished salvation, and to wait on him till he appears for your deliverance.

But again. Is there a child of God here who is tempted to backslide from the simplicity which is in Christ, who is tempted to sin,
and to think lightly of sin? God carry you to Gethsemane! See
what our murderous crimes did to Immanuel there! Now, what
would you think of a child, who knew the person who murdered his
father, and yet could hug and cherish the wretch to his bosom?
Would you not say to such an unnatural child, "James, John, Sarah,
or Susan, you could have no feeling for your father, to cherish the
monster who put him to death!" And when you and I attempt to
sin, and to think lightly of sin, we cherish in our bosom the monster
that put to death the Son of God! Shall we then trifle with that
which brought our Jesus to an ignominious and a solemn death?
Shall we cherish such a monster as this? The Lord forbid! O! May
he give us grace and strength to struggle against it, through the precious blood of the Lamb! May we be enabled to fight manfully the
"good fight of faith, laying hold of eternal life;" and thus may we
be strengthened, through our mighty Hero, to wage war with all our
foes, and to overcome them in the power of his might. "O Naphtali, satisfied with favour, and full with the blessing of the Lord."

But I shall leave the subject till the evening. May God give you
and me a solemn faith's view of the triumphs of Christ, and speak it
powerfully to our hearts, for his name and mercy's sake. Amen.

EVENING SERMON.

We proposed this morning to take up this portion of God's Word
in three spiritual things.

    I. To give a short *description* of "Naphtali."

    II. To notice the *favour* he is satisfied with; and

    III. To show that he is *full with the blessing of the Lord.*

The first head we proposed to consider in three senses: 1. That
it had respect to the Person of the Lord Jesus; 2. To that of every
individual member in his mystical body; and, 3. To all his own God-
called, and God-sent ministers.

The meaning of the word "Naphtali" we said signifies one that is a wrestler, struggler, or fighter; and we noticed at large, how fully it was applicable to the Lord Jesus Christ, from the cradle to the cross. And indeed, if you take Jesus away from any part of truth, nothing but emptiness remains; take away Jesus, and there will be nothing but an eternal bankruptcy for poor sinners; take away Christ, and all the holiness in the world will not save a sinner. There is not now, never was, neither ever can be, since the fall of man, holiness enough, separate from Christ, to save a single sinner! If any of you had it all, and had not Christ, it would profit you nothing; you would be damned without him; for there is no salvation in any other way; nor is there any other Name given under heaven among men whereby you can be saved but the Name of the Lord Jesus Christ! But if we are blessed with a living faith in Christ, we have it all; as Hart saith:

> " Some this some that good virtue teach,
> To rectify the soul;
> But we first after Jesus reach,
> And richly grasp the whole."

For when a soul is brought to feel where the holiness of God's glory lies, that sinner is made a partaker of Christ, and then he blessedly and spiritually enters into the mysteries of Christ. But without going over the ground which we noticed in the morning, we will notice,

2. That the term "Naphtali" is applicable to the church of God, and to every individual member of his mystical body; they all become fighters, strugglers, and wrestlers. When God is graciously pleased to quicken a dead soul, and communicate divine life to it, from that moment he commences wrestling and fighting; and whether the sinner is left to struggle in self, so as to feel the horrors of the damned, or if he does not sink quite so low as another, yet this one thing is certain, that every quickened soul must be brought to feel that he is lost, helpless, and ruined, and desperately ruined too; and that there is no more ground for hope in self than there is for Beelzebub! All his self-hope and self-confidence must give up the ghost. And what does the sinner, under the feeling sense of all his self-hope and confidence being cut off wrestle under and struggle for? He wrestles under darkness, deathliness, confusion of mind, guilt, and wretchedness; and he struggles for pardon, peace, reconciliation, liberty, and joy; he struggles hard to find the ground upon which a sinner like him can have peace and access to God, and wherein God can be just and yet appear gracious to him! The matter is not with him a trifling thing now. Eternity lies open before him; and to him eternity is of that solemn moment and importance that everything else is of no weight compared to it. He wants now to feel pardon through the blood of the Lamb, to enter into an enjoyment of reconciliation with God, to have spiritual power and life communicated to him, to feel

divine truth sealed on his conscience, and to be enabled to say, "He loved me, and gave himself for me!" But a number of things will rise up to damp these feelings, and, if possible, to drown them, and he will have to struggle against them. If a youth, whether male or female, all will be opposed by their flesh and the world; and a tempting devil will set on such a one, and say, "Why, you are going to unman yourself, you are going to give up all pleasure, you are going to set aside every thing which youth embraces, and you are going to become a fool, to be the laughing-stock of your companions, to be considered a mere dunce and a novice; you have plenty of time before you, and there are many pleasing things and pretty prospects await you. Do not throw yourself thus away in your young days, to become gloomy and inactive, teazing and perplexing your mind about religion." And I tell you, such is the power of Satan's temptations, the allurements of the world, and the deceitfulness of sin, that these things would damn their souls, if God did not prevent it by his grace; for so bent is the heart upon pursuing the world and the things of it that the carnal mind will rush on in pleasure, or something which it calls pleasure, that it will not stop till it has hurried the soul into black despair! And when these temptations come thus upon it, after the first awakenings, they will act as a check, or a damper, and will appear for a time to extinguish every thing therein; but he who imparted the spark of divine life will draw forth that life in wrestlings, sighings, and cryings after God, the living God, and all hell cannot extinguish it! Why? Because the life of God is in the heart, and the Lord the Spirit still keeps it there, causing the poor soul to struggle after God!

Now, do you know anything of this? Let me speak for a moment or two to you, young people. Do I hear one say, "Why, Sir, if I were to tell you a secret or two, you would be alarmed!" The poor soul may be ready to say, "God knows I went to a playhouse, in order to get rid of my misery!" Well, and how did you feel while you were there? "O," say you, "for a time I tried to be amused; but, alas! alas! All my amusements turned into misery, and I became in a worse state of mind than I was before." Another, perhaps, would say, "I went along with my companions, and we set up a dancing party, and I thought I could dance my convictions away; but it was all in vain!" But how came that to pass, think ye? Because God went there with you? "Ah," says one, "you will not say God goes to the playhouse and to a dancing party?" Yes, but I will. When any of his church are there, God will go there too; and he will keep the poor soul still, and cause it to struggle, to fight, and to wrestle after the living God. He will never suffer him to give up the point; but his glorious Majesty will show forth the riches of his grace by bringing him to himself. I know a little of what I am talking about. I remember how my fleshly mind tried to get rid of religion.

I was a mere fool, and so full of frolic that I was the provider of sport for all my companions. I was the life of their society, and they seemed as though they could not live without me. I recollect once, when between sixteen and seventeen years of age, I left a shop of work; but three of my companions came to me and said unless I came back they should leave the place too; they would not work without me; and as they came with a full determination to have me again, it so filled my fleshly mind with delight that I went back. But in that very shop God met with me; and O the wonders of grace! All their strugglings and wrestlings were of no avail then. They could not quench what God had put into my soul. All that they laid before me was not able to keep me from struggling hard after God, and fighting and wrestling for God. And under these things the sinner cannot help struggling, when God thus puts in life, and when the Lord is pleased thus to manifest his grace.

Now sometimes the soul may be brought to such a point as not to be able to make use of one sentence that seems to fit his case, when sin, Satan, death, destruction, and carnal reason are all up in arms against him, and when he feels just as though he was struggling and gasping for his last breath, and with a deep sigh says, "Lord, help me!" But the Spirit will come at such a time, draw forth power and life, and bless the poor sinner with faith to look to the Lamb of God. And O what a blessed look it is, when this is the case!

Well; the child of God will have an abundance of wrestling and fighting all the way. But I like that sentence of Hart's,

"Prayer's a weapon for the feeble;
Weakest souls can wield it best."

And the prayer of the man who has the greatest wrestlings and strugglings and feels himself the weakest, can storm heaven the most. God hears the sighs, groans, wrestlings, and pantings of such a soul, and in his own time he will come down to deliver him. And thus he will be brought to know and enter into some enjoyment of the mysteries of grace. I recollect somewhere of a story, concerning a poor creature being possessed with the devil; and at that time people had an idea that if they could get together a number of ministers to pray, the devil would go away. So the ministers assembled, and began to pray over the man who was possessed; but in the company there was a poor old woman, who got behind a screen to watch their proceedings; and after they had been praying some time, as the tale goes, the devil says, "Turn out that old woman, or else I must come out!" So you see, if that be true, the poor old woman had more power to cast him out than all the parsons who had assembled together for that purpose; and when that was done, he came forth, and the victory was obtained. Well; be that as it may, it is so with the child of God. When he is brought into circumstances of sorrow and distress, he supplicates the throne of God, and struggles, fights, and wrestles.

under the power of sin and Satan, and he is brought to cry in his heart to the Lord; and the Lord will appear for his help and deliver him; for "is there anything too hard for the Lord?"

And, brethren, do you and I, at any time, ever fear about the things that belong to Zion? God help us to be wrestlers with him! O that God would pour out upon us a wrestling spirit, and make us more earnest with him at the throne of grace! The Lord says, "Call upon me in the day of trouble; I will deliver thee, and thou shalt glorify me." And he also says, "Whatsoever ye shall ask the Father in my name, I will do it." Yet how many times do we make mention of the name of the Lord, and pray to him for special things, and they are not done. "How is that?" say you. Because we do not feel it; for when a poor, weak, worthless, sighing, mourning worm, from necessity pleads entirely in the name of the Son of God, it is impossible but that he must, sooner or later, prevail. When he thus wrestles in the name of Jesus, our conquering Hero, God will hear and appear for his relief. But time will not allow me to enlarge any more upon this part of the subject; and, therefore, I shall proceed to notice,

3. That the term is applicable also to all God-qualified, God-sent ministers. I believe that all the literature and learning that was ever taught at the college or academy never did nor ever will make a man spiritual. And when men imagine they are qualified for the ministry by attending such institutions, they are sporting with God, and set at nought, as far as they can, the power of the Holy Ghost. When God designs to make a man a minister, no matter what a fool he may be, he knows how to manage him. I am sure of this; and I can bear witness to it for one. When the Lord first put into my heart a spiritual concern about preaching the gospel, a greater fool never had existence! I had been brought up in a country place, where my speech was so broad that I could only say *maun* for man, and *caun* for can; and my appearance and manners were all of a piece; and as it respected literature, or learning, I could not read a single chapter in the Bible. All were full of what I called hard words, from beginning to end; and what with my want of learning, and want of language, and my great ignorance, it appeared altogether the highest pitch of presumption for a fool like me to attempt to preach at all; yet I could not get rid of the feeling. I dare say some of you think I am only a fool now. But I got into such a state of mind that I could not rest in my bed; and many a time I have gone into the cellar, with only my night-clothes on, in order to take cold, and get my death; but I could not die for the life of me! Still I have gone again and again, in the most dejected state; yet I could not die, nor in reality take cold; and really at last I got into such a state of misery that I did not know what to do. Till at length, in the midst of my wrestling, struggling, and sighing to God, to know the worst of my case, and beseeching his Majesty to take the thought of preaching away

from such a fool, since he knew what I was, he was pleased to apply this blessed text to me in such a way as to set me for ever at rest on this point: "But God hath chosen the foolish things of the world to confound the wise; and God hath chosen the weak things of the world to confound the things which are mighty; and base things of the world, and things which are despised hath God chosen; yea, and things which are not, to bring to nought things that are, that no flesh should glory in his presence." And it came to me with such power that it set my tongue moving, and my heart was so lightened that I said, "Ah, Lord, if this is the way of thy working, thou never hadst a better opportunity, for thou hast never given it to such a fool before!" And so I had solemn access to his blessed Majesty, and felt liberty and joy in my soul; and the very next Lord's day I was sent for to preach; and from that moment to the present, with the exception of the time I lay in bed for six weeks with a broken leg, there have not half-a-dozen days elapsed without my being once or more engaged in the work. God has never left me, and I have proved the truth in my own experience of this declaration which he gave me. But if anything ever troubled me in my life it was the thought of preaching! And I would say to any that may be exercised about preaching, Do not try to select your sermons out of books, nor think to take sermons down in shorthand to smother your brains, and fill them with other men's matter. But may you wrestle, struggle, and pray unto the Lord for the manifestation of his mind and will, that he may deal with you in his grace and mercy, that you may know his design, and find prayer a weapon for you; that you may be filled with his Spirit, when all human inventions fail. I believe that that man who gets his sermons from books and other men's preaching is never sent of God; for God empties all whom he sends. He takes every thing away from them and then fills their poor earthen vessels with his rich treasure, and enables them to come forth in the name and strength of the mighty God of Jacob! And you may be sure of this, if God designs a man for the work, he will bring him forth as a light in his blessed hand, and all the men in the world will not be able to put it out!

II. But we pass on to the second thing proposed—the *favour* with which he is satisfied. "O Naphtali, satisfied with favour." Now what favour was Jesus Christ, our spiritual Naphtali, satisfied with? Why, as man, he desired life; and in Psalm xxi. it is said, "He asked life of thee, and thou gavest it him; even length of days for ever and ever." All earth and all hell were enraged against him to take away his life; but he was rich in the favour of a covenant God. As the Head, he was in union with his people as his members, and they are secured to him in eternal length of days; their souls shall live in him for ever. And, blessed be his name, he lives now for them, and is satisfied with this favour as the immortal Head of his Church!

Another blessed favour which his solemn Majesty is satisfied with is, "He shall see his seed, he shall see of the travail of his soul, and shall be satisfied!" He shall have every sinner for whose cause and in whose name he stood for ever with him. Not a hoof of his family shall be left behind; not a soul shall perish who has been committed to his care, and on whose account he wrestled, struggled, and conquered. Some men tell us, "there are surely those in hell for whom Christ died!" What a mercy for them God does not stop their blaspheming mouths! Why, it is daring and open blasphemy! What would they have? That Jesus Christ loved them so well as to struggle, wrestle, and die for them; but that neither God the Father, nor the Spirit, would call them by grace; so that, in this sense, the Deity would appear divided! Here is the Son, in his mediatorial capacity, suffering all the horrors of hell to redeem them; and yet the Holy Ghost sits silently by, and will not so much as stretch forth his arm, or draw it out for their help and salvation! What awful blasphemy is this! But no. The eternal Trinity in Unity chose them unto eternal life, and, therefore, he hath saved them with an everlasting salvation; and so the Lord Jesus Christ shall "see of the travail of his soul, and shall be satisfied." Every soul that was given to him in eternity shall surely come to him in time, according to what his gracious Majesty has said, "Thine they were, and thou gavest them me;" and "All that the Father giveth me shall come unto me; and him that cometh to me I will in no wise cast out." And again, he says, "Neither pray I for these alone, but for them also which shall believe on me through their word." And thus the Lord Jesus Christ is satisfied in having the reward of his work; in having a whole host of sinners saved by grace, as the effect of his eternal love and precious blood, to be with him for ever, to behold his glory; as he says, "I pray not for the world, but for them which thou hast given me;" and, "Father, I will that they also whom thou hast given me be with me where I am, that they may behold my glory." And thus he struggled to have the whole of the purchase of his precious blood with him, to sing the praises of his love throughout a blessed eternity! "O Naphtali, satisfied with favour, and full with the blessing of the Lord."

But again. Now that he is raised to the right hand of the Father, where "he ever liveth to make intercession" for his beloved people, he is looking forward to that solemn moment when the whole church of God shall be raised up to glory, and when all his enemies shall be for ever trampled under foot; for mind, it is said, "After he had offered one sacrifice for sins, he for ever sat down at the right hand of God, from henceforth expecting till his enemies be made his footstool." And O! How will he be "satisfied with favour," when his ransomed are brought into the possession of that glory to which they were predestinated! As he says, "That they all may be one, as

THE WRESTLINGS OF NAPHTALI.

thou, Father, art in me, and I in thee, that they also may be one in us;'' and, ''The glory which thou gavest me I have given them; that they may be one, even as we are one; I in them, and thou in me, that they may be made perfect in one; and that the world may know that thou hast sent me, and hast loved them as thou hast loved me.'' ''O Naphtali, satisfied with favour!''

But O what solemn satisfaction did he feel when he received the immortal approbation of Heaven, when all the perfections of God were glorified; when he had honoured the law, and satisfied the claims of divine justice, and when it was said, ''Lift up your heads, O ye gates; even lift them up, ye everlasting doors; and the King of Glory shall come in!'' When he had finished the work which the Father gave him to do, he went home to glory. He ascended up to God, and he led captivity captive, dragging the devil and all hell at his heels, trampling them under his feet; and he enters into heaven with majesty. As it is written, ''God is gone up with a shout, even the Lord with the sound of a trumpet!'' O how solemnly satisfied is the Lord Jesus Christ with his finished work! And now, in his mediatorial capacity, he is exalted far above all principalities and powers, and sits upon a throne of glory, with garments dipped in blood, pleading the cause of his people, and sending down the Spirit to rest on *this* sinner, and on *that* sinner, as the effect of his amazing love. But O! How satisfied will he be with the final accomplishment of his work, when the whole church shall be brought to glory at last, to celebrate the praises of his love for ever!

Well, in the next place, how is the poor sinner satisfied, who is wrestling, struggling, and crying out under a feeling sense of his sinfulness, and who is panting after a manifestation of pardon from the Lord! What will satisfy him in this state? I can tell you what could not satisfy me. When I was wrestling with legal workings, a friend thought to satisfy me by putting into my hands ''The Whole Duty of Man;'' and when I opened it, I thought what a nice book it was; but it never gave me satisfaction, for when I tried to keep up to its requirements it was too fast for me, it ran me out of breath; and there I lay, a poor crawling reptile, without any relief from the ''Whole Duty of Man!'' I did not then understand God's method of salvation, nor did I know the necessity of knowing Christ crucified.

But our God gives his church degrees of satisfaction. To some he just gives a little hope, and a little faith, and reveals Christ in such a way as to prop up hope, and bring the soul to say, ''Well, who can tell, but after all the Lord will have mercy upon me?'' Now there is some degree of satisfaction in that; but especially so when it is accompanied with freedom and liberty, and the mysteries of salvation are opened up in view, and when the poor sinner, who has long been shut up in bondage and fetters, has his hope now stayed upon Christ—why it produces such a wonderful change in his mind that he knows not how to make it out; yet there is a considerable feeling of satisfaction even in this!

But there is another degree of satisfaction which the soul experiences; and that is, when it is brought spiritually to believe in Christ as a sure Saviour, and to see that there is an all-sufficiency in him, that he is able to save, and willing to save to the uttermost; and when a little hope and a little faith are given, so that he feels a degree of longing satisfaction; and though not fully satisfied, there is something realized in the conscience which he would not give up for ten thousand worlds. Then in a little while the Lord will be pleased to speak with power to him, "Believe on the Lord Jesus Christ, and thou shalt be saved." But, perhaps, in the first instance, he will say, "Ah, Lord, I cannot believe this is for me! I believe that Jesus is the Christ! I believe there is no other method of salvation! I believe that Christ is able to save! But, somehow or other, I feel such darkness, such deathliness, that I cannot believe that he has saved me!" But the Lord comes in his own blessed time, with power to his soul, and says, "This people have I formed for myself, they shall show forth my praise." And when the Holy Ghost gives him a hope that he is amongst that people, and speaks home to the conscience such a sentence as this: "It is finished!" he cries out, in holy faith, "Lord, it is enough! I want no more!" He is blessedly satisfied with the love and blood of the dear Redeemer, and sings his matchless grace to sinners,—to such a reptile as he is. O what a divine satisfaction there is in Jesus! And the poor soul who is thus led is satisfied with God's salvation, and sings the wonders of his grace and mercy. "O Naphtali, satisfied with favour!"

And let me tell you, poor child of God, it is all of free favour; "not of works, lest any man should boast." All of it, from first to last, is from the free grace of God. You and I can no more merit any of this favour than the devil himself can: and, depend upon it, you do not know the plague of the heart, or what sin is, till God makes you to feel it; and when he reveals it to the conscience, you will then see what a rich and free favour his sovereign grace is.

Again. If we look at it as applicable to God's ministers, O how satisfied are they with favour when God gives them his word and causes them with it to separate the precious from the vile; and when he blesses them to feel that their preaching is from the Lord. But I know and am obliged to confess that I often have to come to preach without feeling his presence; and my proud heart kicks against it; yet the Lord is full of grace to such poor wretches, and he brings us to see that "the counsel of the Lord shall stand, and he will do all his pleasure." Here, therefore, we rest. It is God's counsel: and when his gracious Majesty in some measure opens up the mysteries of his salvation to us, O how it satisfies the soul then! "O Naphtali, satisfied with favour!"

What a wonderful favour it is for such poor sinners as we are to be employed by the Lord as his messengers and his ambassadors! What a bustle there would be in this nation, if the Queen were to send for some poor beggar, who was dying on a dunghill, to enrich him, make him a nobleman, and send him abroad as an ambassador! All the newspapers in the land would not want anything else to write about for a month! And yet this is the way our God acts! "He raiseth up the poor out of the dust, and lifteth the beggar out of the dunghill, that he may set him with princes, even with the princes of his people." The Lord enriches him with matter from above. He will be with him, and make him a blessing to his people; he will enable him to separate the precious from the vile; and his word is sure to accomplish his gracious purposes. The Lord's servants come forth in these senses, and they are representatives of God's truth, and stand forth as his messengers to speak forth the messages of his love. And while we are thus enabled to see our standing, and feel the kindness of our God in bestowing such favours upon us, when there is such an infinite disparity between him and us, O how we stand astonished at his grace! "O Naphtali, satisfied with favour!"

III. Lastly, they are *full with the blessing of the Lord*. The failure of my strength and the departure of your time tell me to come toward a conclusion; and, therefore, I must be very short on this head.

But, first, let us view it in Christ. O what a fulness there is in him! All spiritual blessings in heavenly places are treasured up in him. He is full of grace, full of mercy, and full of truth! Do you want help? He is full of it! Do you want peace? He is full of it! Do you want reconciliation? He is full of it! Do you want holiness? He is full of it! He has an inexhaustible fund, an overflowing fulness of grace to bestow on poor sensible sinners. As it is written: "Out of his fulness have all we received, and grace for grace." Bless you, if any poor empty vessels want filling, here is an overflowing fulness to satisfy all their needs. There would be no use for it otherwise. He does not want it for himself; the fulness is not for his own personal use. As God, he is infinitely holy, and as man, he is perfectly pure; and in his complex character, he has an everlasting fulness to give out to the necessities of his people. He has a fulness of life, a fulness of holiness, a fulness of power, a fulness of wisdom, and a fulness of bliss and blessedness, and all treasured up in his glorious Person, to satisfy the wants of his poor and needy family, who have no might nor wisdom of their own. He has it to bestow on such poor wretched, ruined sinners as they are, that they may be "full with the blessing of the Lord!" Blessed be his name, he delights in mercy, and he has a fulness of covenant mercy to bestow upon his people! He is full "with the blessing of the Lord!"

But when may it be said of the poor child of God that he is "full with the blessing of the Lord?" There are times in the experience of the soul when the Lord satisfies it with favour and when it is "full of the Holy Ghost;" but you that are spiritual will too frequently feel it to be otherwise. And I will tell you how you will find it. You will want to be "full with the blessing of the Lord," and you will try to pray; but you will feel so empty and barren as to be able only to utter a few lifeless words, and honest conscience will be accusing you all the time. Then the devil will take an advantage of it, and begin to tempt and harass you, and will suggest that you are only acting the hypocrite; and if in this state, you should be among a few friends, and called to engage in prayer with them, you will be so full of confusion, and so ashamed of what you feel, that you will say, "If ever I get out of this place I will never get into it again;" and if in secret, and you want to pour out your heart in prayer to God, you will be obliged to get off your knees, for your heart at such times will feel so cold, so indifferent, that you will have but little power to call upon God. But the life of God in your soul will not allow you to give it up. You will be praying, wrestling, and struggling against it. And by and by, the poor soul, in the midst of his distress, will be brought to feel the truth of that declaration, "I will pour upon them a spirit of grace and of supplication;" and when God appears for the soul in this way, and works out a blessed deliverance, the poor sinner enters spiritually into that text, "I will honour them that honour me." Now the Father honours Christ, and Christ honours the sinner, and the sinner is led to honour the love and blood of the Lord Jesus Christ; and thus heaven is begun below in the peace of his soul, in the sweet foretastes of that bliss and blessedness which God has provided above for his people; and they are "full with the blessing of the Lord!"

And so again, with the Lord's ministers, whatever satisfaction, at times, they may have from feeling the presence of the Lord with them, yet they will never be fully satisfied until they, with the whole mystical body, awake up in the likeness of the Lord Jesus, and get to glory! What a wonderful fulness of "the blessing of the Lord," will that be, when every corruption will be for ever removed, and when the glorified soul shall inhabit a body fashioned like unto that of the Lord Jesus Christ, when the Eternal Three-One Jehovah shall be filling us with his own declarative glory, and when we shall be rising up into the enjoyment of his love, to live with him for ever and ever! "O Naphtali, satisfied with favour, and full with the blessing of the Lord!" O that the Lord would give us now to know and enter more into these truths in our hearts by precious faith!

And now to conclude. We are all passing into eternity; some of us are just ready to step in; none of us know how soon; and the youngest cannot say they shall live to see to-morrow. Then where is your hope placed? What are your pursuits? Where do you look for satisfaction? What is the ground of your hope? O Lord, if it is thy sovereign pleasure, open some poor sinners' hearts, and bring them to cry to thee for mercy!

And now, the Lord grant that these solemn truths may be accompanied with the blessing of the Spirit of the living God; for his name and mercy's sake. Amen.

THE TONGUE SPEAKING OF RIGHTEOUS-NESS.

Preached in Zoar Chapel, Great Alie Street, London, on Thursday Evening, June 1st, 1843.

"And my tongue shall speak of thy righteousness and of thy praise all the day long."—Ps. xxxv. 28.

PERHAPS some child of God may say, "Well; a text like this cuts me up, root and branch; for I consider it the language of a child of God, and I cannot, I dare not, say that my tongue speaks of God's righteousness and praise all the day long!" But, then, poor benighted soul, you should recollect it is not always day with God's people; there is night as well as day; and when night comes on, darkness appears, and the beasts of prey begin to show themselves. Unbelief, carnal reason, and unhallowed feelings rise up, thick and foul; and when in this state, we see very little in the soul to talk about God's righteousness, or of his praise; and if we say anything at all, it appears nothing but a little moving of self-pity; we want to be pitied, and for others to think our case a pitiable one; and if we meet with any of our brethren and tell our case to them and they do not pity us, we think them very hard and very unkind towards us. But as soon as the Sun of Righteousness arises and shines on our souls; as soon as day breaks and we are brought sweetly and spiritually to see light in God's light and to enter unctuously into the mysteries of his grace, we then know a little what it is for the mouth of the dumb to speak, and the tongue of the stammerer to be unloosed and to speak plainly, so that, while it is day in our souls, we are blessedly employed in speaking forth God's righteousness and praise. "My tongue shall speak of thy righteousness and of thy praise all the day long."

But, on this portion of God's Word, I shall, as the Lord may direct,

I. Drop a hint or two upon the *nature* of God's righteousness.

II. Give a short *description of the tongue* speaking of this righteousness; and then,

III. Notice what it is to *praise* God, and how the tongue is *employed* in speaking of it.

But of the righteousness of God, what can I say, or where shall I begin? We will look at it in three bearings. First, that righteousness which God, in the riches of his grace, imputes unto and puts upon his people, and wherein he justifies them fully and freely. Secondly, the solemn (and solemn they are) righteous acts of God in executing his judgments upon his foes and his people's foes. And thirdly, the solemn acts of God in communicating special mercies unto his people, in supplying their needs, and in defending them in the midst of all the trials and difficulties they have to encounter. And I consider each of these things is couched in God's righteousness.

I. Then what is the *nature* of the righteousness of God, which is "unto and upon all them that believe," and upon (and may God apply the truth to our souls to-night) the heart of every poor, sensibly-ruined, lost, and ungodly sinner? And here I would say to such a poor creature, that he is as naturally destitute of holiness in and of himself as hell itself; but here the soul is fully and freely justified from all its enemies that come up against it, on the great account of God's righteousness. It is upon this solemn ground that God says, "There is, therefore, now no condemnation to them which are in Christ Jesus!" Now you and I, at least I know for myself it is so, are naturally prone to bring a righteousness of our own. We want some pretty work of our own to recommend us to God; but when we have done all that we can do, what does it produce? A clothing of filthy rags, put upon an unclean thing! Poor polluted wretches, we want to come before God as an unclean thing covered with these filthy rags, and for God to be pleased with us on this account; but he will not! What does he do? Why, he sets fire to it, and burns it all up; and you will find sometimes when you want to appear before the Lord in some decent work of your own, Satan will be at your right hand to oppose you, as he did Joshua, when he was clothed in filthy rags. He will do with you as he did with him; he shook his filthy rags in his conscience, and said, "You appear before God? You plead with God? You have hope in God? What, such a filthy wretch as you are? For shame! Stop your mouth; never open your lips again, such a vile, loathesome, detestable creature as you are!" And thus the poor sinner before the Lord is ready to conclude there is no hope left; till God, in the riches of his grace, is pleased to come forth and show him that he is clothed in his righteousness; and when he applies it to the conscience, gives us unctuously to know that we have on the Lord's righteousness, are arrayed in the Lord's strength, and that it is the Lord himself that justifies us; I say, when the Spirit of the living God reveals this to the heart, it sets the tongue going to talk of God's righteousness and to show forth his praise. And though all the devils in the world may be in the way, it could not prevent him; for when the heart is under the blessed unction and anointing of the

Holy Spirit, feeling the glory of Christ's righteousness, which is "unto and upon all them that believe," it is sure to cause the tongue to speak forth the amazing wonders of God's matchless grace!

Perhaps some high-gifted professor may say, "For my part, I never for a moment forget it, but I always sing of the righteousness of Christ; I want no other. Here I stay and rest, and can speak of this, let what will take place. As for sin and filthy rags which you are talking about, I can get above all that!" I had like to have said then you can get above the devil, for the devil is obliged to sink under sin; and I believe in my heart some professors have more impudence than the devil himself. But when God winds up the business, and they come to stand before him, they will find their false confidence to be not only a delusion, but a strong delusion; that they have been left to believe a lie, and will discover that their refuge was a "refuge of lies," and no shelter at all for them. But the soul whom God is teaching and whom he clothes in this righteousness is brought really to feel what a lost and ruined sinner he is, what a weak and guilty sinner he is, what a vile, loathsome, and polluted sinner he is, and to say, "Do you think there ever was such a sinner as I?" Some say I never preach to sinners; but, bless you, I find none else but sinners to preach to! If I should meet with a man who was not a sinner, I should have nothing for him; there is not a particle that would suit him in my ministry. A sinner, really and truly in his feelings, such as God saith he is, is a sacred thing. He is solemnly set apart for the Lord and by the Lord. He is a sacred sinner, as I call him; and such a one shall speak forth the matchless righteousness and glory of God in blessing his soul. Such a sinner as this finds God's righteousness suited to his state and condition; and when God is pleased to make known Jesus Christ as his Representative, as having stood in his law-place and stead, between an insulted God and him; and how he has engaged to be responsible for all his sinful practices and transgressions, and to work out a righteousness in every sense suited to the requirements of the law, the claims of justice, to honour and glorify the perfections of God, and to impute that righteousness to him for his entire justification before the Lord, he cannot but speak of his righteousness and praise, and rejoice that he is "justified freely by his grace, through the redemption that is in Christ Jesus."

Now if the law gets hold of your conscience, and God's Spirit should at the same time reveal this righteousness, it will answer all law claims that come against you. Suppose we look at it for a moment or two. The law saith, "Thou shalt love the Lord thy God with all thine heart, and with all thy soul, and with all thy might." Well, now, I tell you what—if you cannot bring a righteousness to God adequate to this, your soul is ready to sink into black despair. And where will you find it? We have some who attempt to moderate it; and

they say, if we are sincere in our desires, God will accept of our
sincerity, and so Christ is put in the back ground in their mode of
obedience. But this will not do. We must have a righteousness,
not only in which you and I cannot find a flaw, but in which *God*
cannot find a flaw. And if we ourselves see nothing but sin in our
own, and find fault with the very best that we can do and say all
our righteousnesses are but filthy rags, how heart-breaking must we
feel to present such a one before infinite purity and perfection!
We must have a righteousness in which Jehovah himself cannot find
a flaw, a righteousness which Jehovah cannot mend, a righteousness
which neither sin nor Satan can mar; and unless we have on a
righteousness of this nature, we can never enter into the blessedness
of the world to come.

Where, then, are we to find it? Eternal praises to the matchless
mercy of a covenant God, we have it in the blessed Person, glorious
work, and spotless obedience of the Lord Jesus Christ! And, therefore, as it was essential for him to fulfil all righteousness for his people, he loved the Lord his God with all his heart, with all his mind,
and with all his strength. He began at the beginning, and went
through holily, righteously, and steadily every step of the law of
God; and all in justice and righteousness. He fulfilled every iota
of it, and gave it immortal glory and honour. The law could only
require the perfect obedience of a perfect man, but he gave it the
perfect obedience of the God-man, and stamped for ever a holy dignity and majesty on it, in order to manifest that this glorious righteousness is suited to every sinner's case, to all their needs, and to
honour and glorify all the perfections of God; and thus he has "for
ever perfected them that were sanctified,"—all those who were set
apart for himself. They are perfected for ever in his own blessed
obedience and spotless righteousness; and this righteousness which
God gives shall endure for ever. As for you who have a righteousness of your own, you never can feel your need of Christ's righteousness; and if any one should insult you by speaking of it, you are
wrapped up so snugly in your own pretty works that it would be an
insult to your dignity to have his. The same as it would be an insult to the queen for you to make a basket of bulrushes, and present it to her as something very valuable; she would not receive it
at your hands. So it is with you, when we speak of this blessed
righteousness. You do not know your need of it, and it is an insult
to your pride to mention it. But for the poor creature who feels
himself to be a loathsome, vile, and ruined sinner, and is brought experimentally to feel what he is before a heart-searching God, and that
every iota of the law is against him—for God to give this righteousness to him, to put it upon him and communicate the power of it to
his soul, why it will raise and exalt him to such a blessed enjoyment
of God's righteousness that his tongue will sing aloud and speak

forth praise to the honour and glory of his blessed name; and he will say, "My soul shall be joyful in my God; I will glory in the God of my salvation; for he hath covered me with the robe of righteousness; he hath adorned me with the garments of salvation." And thus his tongue shall speak of God's righteousness and of his praise all the day long.

Now, let me ask, does this righteousness suit you? For observe, when it is realized in the conscience by faith, through the Spirit's teaching, the sinner will not bring forth his goodness or worthiness to make a kind of exchange with God; for he enters now into what the Holy Ghost saith, "Now to him that worketh not, but believeth on him that justifieth"—Who? The pious? No! The holy? No! The good? No! Who then? "The ungodly!" What an ungodly world? Yes, those who are brought to feel in their consciences that they are vile and ungodly, and that they must be lost for ever without a better righteousness than their own! "To him that worketh not, but believeth on him that justifieth the ungodly, his faith is counted to him for righteousness." Such a poor soul as this hath worked till he could work no longer; he hath worked till he has worked himself into wretchedness; he hath worked till he has worked himself into despair; he hath worked till he has worked himself into self-desperation. Nothing now is left for him to bring to God. His soul is out of heart of any more working and he is obliged to lie where he is, without anything of his own to present before the Lord, and to come as a poor, ruined, wretched, and undone sinner! And God imputes this righteousness to such a soul as this; he puts it on all those who are led to believe in Jesus by a living faith. This righteousness is imputed to them; and so they stand complete before the Lord. As it is written: "Ye are complete in him." And this blessed righteousness makes the sinner just before him.

I will tell you how I found it. Until God was pleased to reveal it to my conscience I never could find peace; and until you have a measure of it brought into your heart, you can never have solemn confidence before God; for on every occasion Satan will be sure to be too much for you. He will tell you you are blind, and cannot see; he will tell you you are lame and cannot walk; he will tell you you are dumb and cannot speak; he will tell you you are hardhearted and that you cannot pray; that you have left off watching, that the world has got hold of you, and that you are trying to get hold of the world; he will tell you if you love the world you have not the love of the Father; and thus he will cause you to faint, and you will have nothing to say on your own behalf. But if the Lord bless you with a faith's view of the mediatorial work of Jesus, with the active and passive obedience of Jesus, and show you that all his infinite purity and perfect obedience to the law of God is *yours*, that he has honoured the perfections of God for *you*, and blesses your conscience with an apprehension of it, then you can say to Satan, "I acknowledge that all thy accusations are true, Satan. I am ashamed of myself, and confess that I am nothing but a vile, crawling, sinful worm; but then, believing and resting on Jesus, the righteousness of God is unto and upon all them that believe." So that now he is ready to submit to this description of his state,—that he is as an unclean thing, and that all his "righteousnesses are but as filthy rags;" and he is led to ask himself the question, if his righteousness and the best of his works are but filthy rags, what indeed must his sins be? What must his guilty acts be, when the best that he can do are nothing but filthy rags? Thus he sees that his best and his worst are all as an unclean thing; and then this, through the matchless mercy and grace of God, brings him feelingly and solemnly to enter into and rest upon the perfect obedience of Christ. And when his faith, through the Spirit's blessed teaching, is thus stayed upon the Lord, he can present the spotless obedience and perfect righteousness of Jesus, as his acquittance before God and the ground of his future bliss and joy. Satan cannot come in here; none of his enemies can approach him here; there is no coming short, no deficiency here. There is nothing wanting in the perfect obedience of Christ; and the sinner that is hurled out of every other refuge, from necessity creeps into this. Here he stands complete before the Lord, "accepted in the Beloved;" and the Lord declares that he is beautiful through the comeliness which he hath put upon him. O how the soul then rejoices in this salvation, in this glorious righteousness, which justifies the ungodly! "My tongue shall speak of thy righteousness and of thy praise all the day long."

Now, perhaps, there may be some here who have but little light, I mean spiritual light; and have never known the necessity of the imputation of this righteousness in a doctrinal way. I speak this from some past feelings. I recollect the period when I rejoiced in Christ, and was enabled to sing of the wonders of his salvation; but I knew nothing about imputed righteousness, as to the doctrine of it. A familiar friend at that time, on one occasion, said, "Why, William, we are justified freely by another, through the righteousness of Christ imputed to us." I said to myself, what does she mean? Is it a new doctrine? But to ask her I could not, for I was afraid; so I said, "Good night," and went home burdened in my conscience to know what this could be which was to be my justification; and as I did not know what it was, I thought after all I may be deceived, and be lost at last! It was such a weight on my soul that I was led diligently to seek after a knowledge of this righteousness of God, the imputed righteousness of Christ. And after some searching of the Word, and crying to the Lord, I began to think, "Surely it must be the perfect obedience of Christ." But, then, there was this word "imputed," which I could not make out;

for I knew no more about it than an infant, I was such a dextrous scholar; and I said, "What can this word 'imputed' mean, which must, according to her account, be our justification before God; for without it the sinner must sink into hell." I was so puzzled for some time with this word "imputed," that I sent to a neighbour to borrow a dictionary to make out the meaning of the word; but when I got it, somehow or other, it did not help me, for I was such a poor bewildered fool that it seemed to plunge me deeper in confusion; till at last the Lord was pleased to bring home with power this portion of Scripture, with some others: "He was made sin for us, who knew no sin, that we might be made the righteousness of God in him!" I said, "O! I should not wonder if this is the meaning of the word 'imputed!' Christ taking our sins, and giving us his righteousness!" And by and by the Lord led me on, step by step, until at last he showed me that it was a divine transfer,—a taking away of my guiltiness and a putting upon me the obedience of Christ, so that I might stand complete before the Lord without sin! Aye, I had believed this truth before in the spirit of it; but I did not know that this was the meaning of "imputed righteousness;" and I believe many have the spirit and glory of it in their souls who cannot understand it in the letter, so as to explain it; while hundreds have it correct in the letter and can contend for it who have never received it in the spirit, who are nothing more than mere speculatists in religion. But when God reveals it in the conscience, and they are brought to understand it through the Spirit's teaching, they have it both in the spirit and in the letter; and then the poor soul will come from necessity and build upon Christ, rest upon Christ, and trust in Christ alone. And I believe further, that nothing will bring glory to God but a divine resting and trusting in Christ. Take away Christ, and you must sink for ever. Without Christ, how can you face law, or how can you face justice? But with Christ, you can make a solemn stand. If the Lord the Spirit has brought you to feel this, if he has assured you of this, poor trembling sinner, this righteousness is thine; and thou shalt, in the Lord's own blessed time, enter fully into the mystery of it, and speak forth the riches of God's glorious grace. "My tongue shall speak of thy righteousness and of thy praise all the day long."

But we observe further. David, in this psalm, is speaking of the ungodly and of his enemies, and of the head they had made against him, and of God's judgments being executed upon them. Now if there should be an enemy here to-night, who is taking pleasure in persecuting the church of God, and in defaming the character of God's people, and who is laying plans and schemes to bring them into wretchedness and ruin, by spreading some trap to catch their feet, I tell thee, in the name of the Lord, according to what is revealed in this psalm, that into the very snare, into the very trap, which thou hast laid for them shall thy own feet fall. God, to vindicate the honour of his people, will execute righteously and justly against thee all that thou hast plotted against Christ and his church. For mind, all thy rage and wrath, directed against the church of God, or against any individual believer, is considered as against Christ; for he says, "In all their affliction he was afflicted," and, "He that toucheth you, toucheth the apple of his eye;" so that whosoever persecutes the church of God, persecutes Christ. Hence says the Lord the Redeemer to Saul, "Saul, why persecutest thou me?" We may suppose that Paul might have said, "I am not persecuting thee, Lord; it is only a few fanatics, some poor bewildered creatures, who are disturbers of the neighbourhood. I only want to scatter these troublers, to make Jerusalem quiet, and to get rid of these fanatics." But the Lord says, "Why persecutest thou *me?*" and when he replies, "Who art thou, Lord?" he says, "I am Jesus, whom thou persecutest. It is hard for thee to kick against the pricks." Sinner, self-righteous sinner, God-dishonouring and believer-despising sinner, who art laying plans and schemes to bring the church of God into disrepute, and doing what thou canst to injure the Lord's people, beware, for a holy God is wetting his sword for retribution, and by and by he will come forth and not spare. He will mow thee down, cut thee up, and lay thee low; and the righteousness of God shall be seen in executing his vengeance, and in sending thee to hell for thy persecutions against his people! Thus, the church of God, under the teachings of the blessed Spirit, shall be brought in solemnity to speak of his mighty acts. Now this was the case with the church of old. They sang of God's judgments in executing his vengeance on their enemies, in overthrowing "Pharaoh and his host in the Red Sea, for his mercy endureth for ever;" and in destroying "famous kings, for his mercy endureth for ever." "What!" say some. "Was it mercy in God to drown the Egyptians, and mercy in God to destroy these famous kings?" It was all in solemn and righteous judgment. And when God's righteous judgments are executed in the destruction of the ungodly, it is always in mercy to his own people. This was the cause of raising them to hope, and showing them that the Lord was their defence; and here they traced his everlasting mercy to them, in bringing these judgments upon the ungodly and upon their foes. And thus they sang of his righteousness in his solemn acts of judgment. "My tongue shall speak of thy righteousness, and of thy praise all the day long."

I will tell you one thing I have proved, and it is well for the church of God that it is so. You and I may have met with some other foes, who have been laying plans and schemes against us, and digging pits to engulf us; who have been working secretly, and at other times more openly, to do us some injury; but God's eye is fixed upon them, and it is written, "Vengeance is mine, and I will repay it, saith the Lord!" But in the book of Isaiah, it is said, "He that believeth shall not make haste." Now, perhaps, for a moment or two we believe God will accomplish his word; but, if we are called to wait long, and there appears a delay in the accomplishment of God's word, we become hasty, and think him so long that we set on to do it ourselves; but for one stroke that we lay upon our enemies, we inflict a dozen upon ourselves. And a blessed mercy it is, for here we see that the Lord will execute his righteous judgments upon our enemies, appear for the defence of his people, and cause us to speak forth the honours of his name. "My tongue shall speak of thy righteousness and of thy praise all the day long."

But we observe further. Another branch of this righteousness is, a revelation of the righteous acts of God's grace to such poor sinners as we are. I do not know what you may feel at what I am now going to say, but there is such a solemn disparity between God and ourselves that the soul is brought to wonder how God can be righteous without sending it to hell! This is the difference between the poor child of God, and a self-righteous free-willer. A self-righteous free-willer thinks that God cannot be just without giving him a chance of being saved; and the poor child of God wants to know how he can be just without damning him! Now, have you ever been here? I remember the time when this text was applied with great power to my soul: "A just God and a Saviour;" and, "If we confess our sins, he is faithful and just to forgive us our sins, and to cleanse us from all unrighteousness." Have you entered into a feeling sense of this? I recollect an old friend of ours, in dying moments, said to the brethren, "God has been pleased to bless that text to my soul in a wonderful way! O what an amazing thing that he should be faithful and just, not merely in forgiving sins, but in forgiving *me!* I wonder he is not faithful and just to damn me!" And the poor child of God knows what it is, before a heart-searching God, to feel so convinced of his sin and sinfulness as to know that God would be faithful and just to damn him, if he were to enter into judgment with him; but, being brought sweetly and spiritually to see that he is pleased not to impute sin unto him, that he delights in his mercy, that he has forgiven him all his sins and transgressions, is pleased to seal home pardon in his conscience, and bring him to feel reconciliation through the blood of the Lamb, the poor soul is brought to speak forth his honour and praise for his righteous acts, in thus bringing salvation to him; so that he honours his justice, as well as his mercy. And here he sees that the work is complete. And when God confirms these things in the conscience, by the teachings of the blessed Spirit, then the soul sings of God's righteousness and of his praise all the day long.

Now have you never been brought into very great straits, either in your soul, family, or circumstances, not able to see any way of escape, and that all your contrivances to extricate yourselves have served only to plunge you into greater difficulties? And have you not found that so long as you could contrive any way of deliverance or make any plan of your own, you never came to the Lord or entirely depended upon him; but when all your plans and schemes have failed and come to ruin, being nothing but useless lumber, and you were brought from necessity to come and spread out your case before the Lord, and lay low in the dust at his blessed feet, sink or swim, that then he has risen up for your help, and graciously smiled upon you? How then you were enabled to speak of his mercies and, with the church of old, to "rehearse the righteous acts of the Lord," show forth his praise, and say, in the language of the text, "My tongue shall speak of thy righteousness and of thy praise all the day long."

II. But we pass on to give a *description of the tongue* that will really, truly, and spiritually speak of God's righteousness. It is not the tongue of man by nature, for he never speaks of it spiritually. It is true, he may speak of it in the letter, but he can never understand it in the spirit, until he is made a partaker of it. God tells us in his Word, "The natural man receiveth not the things of the Spirit of God, for they are foolishness unto him; neither can he know them, because they are spiritually discerned." I tell you what I have often wondered at,—that professors in our day have not petitioned the legislature to alter the Bible, that they might take out some passages t omake it fit to their creed. "Well," say some, "a natural man may repent and believe, if he will; he has it in his power." But God says he cannot, for it is "foolishness unto him." God says "he cannot know them, for they are spiritually discerned." Now, who tells the truth,—God, or these accomplished fools? Why, God tells the truth; and his people are brought to know that no man can believe spiritually till he is quickened by the Holy Ghost, and made a new creature in Christ. Well, then, all the natural ability, natural strength, and natural wisdom of man must give up the ghost. So that the man who is brought to wait patiently till the mercy of the Lord brings a little hope, a little life, and a little deliverance and peace into his conscience, will bless and praise God for his righteous acts of mercy towards him, in bringing him peace, strength, and prosperity. And here God reconciles the mind to his sovereign pleasure, in a way of providence, to see that his dispensations are right; so that whatever he may have to suffer from the unrighteousness of men, and whatever he may be called to pass through or endure from friends or enemies, he is brought to see that it is all right and under the sovereign control of the Lord; and when he thus appears and manifests his love to our hearts, we are satisfied with all his ways and dealings towards us; we sing of his righteous acts and talk of his praise; and then, O what peace these flowings of mercy bring into the soul!

I have known many of God's wonderful dealings in a way of providence towards me, and I could tell you of several of them, if I had time. But I will relate one in particular, and a striking one too. When my family were young, we had a large school-bill came in, and where the money was to come from to pay it, neither wife nor myself could possibly tell; and she gave me a few pillow pills to know how the money was to be had. "O!" said I, "we shall have it in good time; the Lord will appear for us!" "Ah, there it is," she said. "You have all the faith, and I have all the tugging, sighing, and mourning;" while, in point of fact, I had not much more faith than she had; but it was no use for me to cherish her unbelief. You husbands, do not nurse up the unbelief of your wives, when they discover it, for that will make it double unbelief; and you wives, whose husbands are cast down, do as Manoah's wife did, cheer them up, and say, "If the Lord had meant to have destroyed us, he would not have shown us the things which he has!" And whatever trouble you may be in, never try to deliver yourselves in any unlawful way, but may you be led to be earnest at the throne of grace in prayer, that he would not lead you into temptation, but that he would keep you waiting at his throne of grace until he appears for you in your distresses. I make these remarks, because some poor child of God may be tempted to do that for his own profit, to save himself from ruin, which carnal reason may suggest, but which can never meet with the Lord's sanction; therefore follow no one to do evil; it will bring disgrace upon the cause of truth, and wound your own soul. And ever recollect that God knows all about you; his eye is fixed upon you and watching for your good; his ear is open to all your cries; he knows all your necessities, and in his own good time he will come and make good every promise that he has made concerning you.

But to return to the deliverance which God wrought for me. The following morning a young man called upon me, and brought me a twenty-pound-note.* I was so amazed that I hardly knew what to say, for such a thing had never entered into my heart; but he said, "Do you not recollect what you said last night, how God knew all the wants and distresses of his people, and would be sure to appear for them, and deliver them out of their troubles? It is the Lord that has sent you the money!" So that I was constrained to bless and praise his name, and my tongue was enabled to speak of his righteousness all the day long. And O! How wonderful our God appears in these acts of mercy! What a kind God he is in his providence. He will not allow anything really to hurt us. His arm is stretched out for the defence of his church. He will uphold and protect them from the spite and malice of their foes and execute vengeance upon their enemies. He will rain down blessings upon them, preserve them on every hand, make them victorious over every trial; and bring them to

* See note in Sermon on Heb. x. 36, farther on.

praise and adore him for revealing a precious Christ and his salvation to them, in unfolding the riches of his grace, in bringing them to feel his everlasting love, the preciousness of his blood and obedience, and the glories of his righteousness. And thus their tongues will be constrained to speak of it all the day long.

But what is the tongue that speaks of this righteousness spiritually? It is the tongue that David speaks of, where he says, "My tongue is the pen of a ready writer. I will speak of the things which I have made, touching the King." Now mind, what was David's tongue like? It was like "the pen of a ready writer." But who is that ready writer? It is God the Holy Ghost! He is the great Writer of God's law in the heart, and the great Writer of God's salvation. David's tongue then was the pen; but it was a very dry pen in itself; it made no impression, though used by a dextrous penman. But when the divine Spirit makes use of the pen, that is, the tongue, and dips it in the love and blood of Christ, then the words that are written will be full of sweetness to the church, and words that come with power, being full of grace and truth, when they are thus sent by the Holy Ghost to feed and comfort his people. Now when the poor sinner's tongue is moved by the blessed Spirit and he feels a divine unction resting upon him, he wants both his heart and tongue to go together; for "with the heart man believeth unto righteousness, and with the tongue confession is made unto salvation;" and when that is the case, the heart and the tongue will both go forth in speaking of the righteousness of God. "My tongue shall speak of thy righteousness and of thy praise all the day long."

Now do you know what it is to have the tongue thus solemnly moved, at times, under the teachings of the blessed Spirit, to speak of God's righteousness? If you do, you are sure to speak forth God's praise and give him all the glory. You will speak of the praises due unto his name; you will speak of the honours of Jesus, of his glorious characters, of his preciousness, of his suitability, and of his fulness. And as the Lord the Spirit leads and guides you, you will make mention of it in your dying moments, and then speak forth the matchless mercy of his amazing grace.

May the Lord, therefore, give you and me, while here, to speak more and more of the matchless wonders of his grace! Amen.

THE MYSTERY OF CHRIST.

Preached in Zoar Chapel, Great Alie Street, London, on Sunday Morning, June 4th, 1843.

"Continue in prayer, and watch in the same with thanksgiving; withal praying also for us, that God would open unto us a door of utterance, to speak the mystery of Christ."—COL. IV. 2, 3.

To be employed by the Lord, to be fitted and qualified by him, to speak forth the "mystery of Christ," is the most solemn work that ever God set a creature to be employed in! Angels have been God's ministers to execute his judgments upon ungodly men and ungodly nations. They have been commanded to cut down thousands, and send them to black despair as an effect of their sin; and they have been employed to protect and defend the church of God. But it does not appear to me that angels can ever make good ministers of Jesus Christ. "Come," say you, "you are getting on high ground with a witness, to make it appear that a poor crawling worm like you is employed in that for which an angel is not qualified." I really believe it, and therefore I speak what I believe. The most an angel could do in preaching the gospel would be to preach it in the letter and to others; and not in the spirit, nor to themselves. Now just see a short illustration made of their employment in this business, and the circumstances at the birth of Christ. Angels had left their seats above, to come down and contemplate the amazing scene. They looked on with solemn and holy awe; and while they wondered and gazed, and gazed and wondered, at length one broke silence, and said, "Unto *you* is born this day in the city of David a Saviour, which is Christ the Lord." It was good tidings of news to man! It was "unto *you*," and not unto *us*. Angels could only hold forth and declare unto those who were immediately interested in it. But when the prophet of God, Isaiah, was led to speak on the solemn subject, he comes much nearer home, and says, "Unto *us* a child is born, unto *us* a Son is given!" Now there is a great difference between *you* and *us*—the one is at a distance, and the other is close at home. And so we find that the Lord's ministers of old spake of the things which they had known, tasted, handled, and felt, and their eyes had looked upon; and therefore the apostle said, "That which we have seen and heard declare we unto you, that ye also may have fellowship with us!"

Now the gospel of Jesus Christ is the mystery of God; and was designed of God to be fitted for poor, perishing, guilty sinners. It was intended only to suit poor, needy, ruined, guilty, wretched creatures, as we are; because, if it were not for poor sinners, it would not belong to us. Why, bless your poor hearts, it was never designed for any one else! And if you search the Word of God throughout, you will find it is only adapted for poor, needy, crawling worms; for the halt, the lame, the blind, the burdened, the dejected, and such as are ready to perish. As for those who can get light and power when they please, who can manufacture a religion for themselves, get access to God, feel happiness and light, and do not sigh and pant after Christ and entirely depend upon him to do every thing for their souls, they do not want such a remedy as this. But when God lays the axe to the root of the tree, and cuts down self-importance; when he lays it prostrate in the dust, and they are brought to feel they are without God, it makes a wonderful difference. And

if God should give any of you a solemn cut or stab, you will feel yourselves as dead as possible, without any help of your own; and when
thus brought to ruin, you will lay low as a perishing sinner at the
feet of Christ, till he is revealed in your heart as the hope of glory.
And when his blessed Majesty is thus made known as your salvation,
O how you will triumph in the glorious "mystery of Christ!"

I candidly declare to you I hardly know where to begin; but I think
I shall commence at the latter end first; and, my brother, that is the
way I have been going on all the days of my life, according to the
views of man; for I have been moving in a way which is altogether
contrary to what men call right reason, right judgment, and right
movements.

I. I shall, therefore, make a few remarks upon *the mystery of Christ*,
that Foundation Stone, that great subject, and that fundamental
point.   If you take away that, all else that remains would be nothing but wretchedness, barrenness, and ruin!

II. Notice the *characters* whom the apostle addresses; and look a
little into the nature of the address, that they are said to "pray," to
"watch," and to be "thankful," and "withal praying also for us."

But what *us* is this? It is *us*, who are called in our public capacity
to deal out the "mystery of Christ." And what are they to pray
for? That we should be great men, talented men, highly respected
men, opulent and rich men? O no! But they are to pray for open
doors, that God would "open to us a door of utterance to speak the
mystery of Christ." All things short of this sank in the apostle's
mind into insignificance. Hence we find, in another place, the same
apostle, inspired by God to preach the gospel of his grace, calls all
things short of "the mystery of Christ," nothing but dung and dross.
He might have used a prettier expression than "dung." But no.
God had so sickened him of all his free-will powers and qualifica-
tions of nature, and had so sharpened his conscience for Christ and
sweetened it with the love of Christ, that every thing that came in the
way of Christ, every thing that opposed self to Christ, he rejected as
a horrible nuisance, too filthy to touch with his fingers; and, therefore, he accounted it all but dross and dung for the excellence of the
knowledge of Jesus Christ. Now has the Lord the Spirit brought
you and me to an experimental feeling of this point? If so, he has
really done more for us than he has done for the holy angels that
are in heaven; for there is not an angel in heaven that now surrounds
the throne that can sing this song. They can sing of electing love,
and of preserving love; but they cannot sing of redeeming blood to
save their souls. There was no redeeming blood to save or quicken
them. No; this blessing is peculiar to poor sinners; it is only for
those who are interested in Christ and can say, "In whom we have
redemption through his blood, the forgiveness of sins, according to
the riches of his grace." No angel knoweth the sweetness of the

song of the poor sinner who is saved by sovereign grace: "Unto him that hath loved us, and washed us from our sins in his blood, and hath made us kings and priests." Look at the exaltation to which they are raised! Who were they? Poor, wretched, ruined sinners, whom God picks off the dunghill, and takes out of the dust, whom he raises to princely dignity, and causes to inherit the throne of glory. Why, bless you, some of those who are brought by the Spirit of the living God to experience a little measure of this in their consciences were some of the worst creatures that ever were brought into existence; but it is all to the praise of God's glory, and they will say, "Not unto us, not unto us, O Lord, but unto thy name give glory!" The blood of Jesus can cleanse the vilest sinner that ever existed; as the apostle saith, "Such were some of you; but ye are washed, but ye are cleansed, but ye are justified." Why, this is a wonder of wonders! It is the greatest wonder that the devil ever met with. It has staggered Beelzebub himself, and it has proved the greatest of all wonders in every age of the world. When this blessed atonement is applied to the conscience of the poor sinner, if he is the weakest fool or idiot, it does not matter, the devil, with all his infernal cunning, can never fool Christ out of his soul, "for his soul is hid with Christ in God," and not a hoof nor hair of the elect body shall ever be lost or missing. And when God's Spirit leads the soul into this truth, and he is blessed with vital experience to feel the power of it, it causes him to triumph in the riches of God's matchless grace!

I. But, first, let us speak a little of *the mystery of Christ!* Now where shall we begin with this solemn subject? I honestly tell you, before the Lord, that I feel a degree of solemn trembling in my mind lest I should make an awful bungling job of such a mighty subject as this; for I am such a fool; but I will endeavour, as far as the Lord shall be pleased to help me, to speak of it, and as he shall lead me to see and feel the glory of it.

"The mystery of Christ." We will begin, then, first of all, in the eternal settlements of the Three-One God, before a creature was made. In the mind of Jehovah, Christ was set up from everlasting. Now he could not be set up as God. To talk of a set-up God appears to me contrary to the nature of God; but he was set up in the mind and purpose of Jehovah. The Eternal Trinity, with one glance, surveyed all circumstances that ever took place; and in this mystery of God, in the immutable mind, Christ, in the Person of the Son, was appointed to be the Mediator betwixt God and man, and in that middle capacity to be heir of all things and head over all things to his body the church; yea, to be so really devoted for their benefit that a company of poor crawling reptiles, under the teachings of the blessed Spirit, should crawl out of self and creep into Christ; that so the Lord might justify them in his mantle, fully and freely from every law-charge for ever and ever. Now here is a wonderful mystery hid

in God. But this was not declared till after the fall, and then it began a little to be made known.   This mystery was hid in God, of Jew
and Gentile being taken into union in Christ's mystic body. When, in
his immutable love, all new covenant blessings were secured in the
Person of Christ, then this divine mystery was hid with God in his
own bosom. And I often think, with some degree of solemn pleasure,
of what is said concerning Christ. He is emphatically called the
"Word of God."   "In the beginning was the Word, and the Word
was with God, and the Word was God."   And he sits in heaven, with
a garment dipped in blood; and his name is called the "Word of God."
Now I do not know a single passage where the Father or the Spirit
is called "the Word."   The solemn term is applied exclusively to
the Son; he is "the Word;" and as through our words we make
known the thoughts and purposes of our hearts, so through and by
Christ, God makes known and reveals the mystery that is hidden in
his heart towards us.   All the hidden things of God are in him; and
when Christ came forth from the Father, he made known the hidden things which were in God from before the world was.   Here the
mystery begins, and has its origin, in the settled mind and purpose
of God, in the councils of eternity.

But we observe further.   When this mystery began to be made
known a little, it was revealed in types and shadows, and in figurative expressions.   No sooner had God created man, given him a law,
favoured him with blessings, and created him in his own image, as
the God of nature, than man sinned.   Perhaps some of you may think
that the favour of God depends upon the cultivation of grace, in your
doing your part. But how comes it to pass that you, a poor, wretched sinner, should think you could manage it better than holy Adam
did?   Adam had no sin in his nature to grapple with; he was all
holy in the image of God; yet notwithstanding that, he lost it all.
He has really done his part; for he has let the devil in and God out,
and has brought his posterity to ruin.   But even now, fallen men
think they can do something to please God; they think they can do
something to save their souls, that they can do a part of it.   But
the Lord knows, I am an old man now, more than seventy years of
age, and I speak it in the presence of God and you; and I say, if my
salvation depended upon anything that I have done, or expect to do,
I am sure to be damned.   I have not a particle of hope on that ground.
No. I have no hope but in this glorious "mystery of Christ," in
which all blessings were secured and settled, according to the purpose of the Three-One God before the world began!

I consider, then, that when God first began to make known this
"mystery of Christ," he revealed it unto his servant Adam, in his
fallen state, when he said unto him, "Adam, where art thou?"   I
believe Adam was the first Arminian, and the first which I call a Low
Arminian; for an Arminian professes to have power to do a some-

thing, and yet does it not; and if this is not Arminianism, I do not know what is. Now Adam had this first in his fallen nature. What did Adam say, when the Lord asked him, "Hast thou eaten of the tree whereof I commanded thee that thou shouldst not eat?" He said, "The woman whom thou gavest to be with me, she gave me of the tree, and I did eat." Just as though he meant to say, if it had not been for the woman which God had given unto him, he should not have eaten of it. He wanted to lay the blame upon God for giving him a wife, and also to throw it upon her. But what does the woman say to God? "O," she says, "the serpent beguiled me, and I did eat." She was ready to lay the blame anywhere else but on herself. What a council of mischief there was between them both! And what did they do, when they felt their misery? They sewed fig-leaves together, and made themselves aprons, as if to hide their shame, and to cover it over by a little of their own doings, so that God should not see it. Man is ever ready to charge his sin upon God; and when sin is opened up and discovered to him, he is ever ready to take some method of his own to cover it.

But now God began to make known a little of this mystery. How does he do it? In the first promise which was made to our fallen parents, wherein God says to the serpent, "I will put enmity between thee and the woman, and between thy seed and her seed; it shall bruise thy head, and thou shalt bruise his heel." And God knows he has done it many a time. Satan has bruised the heel of Christ, till the heel of Christ in the members of his mystical body have been so hurt as often to get out of their centre, so that they have not been able to creep one step towards the Christ of God; yet his gracious Majesty has healed the wound; he has felt the effects of his bruise, but the Seed of the woman has bruised the serpent's head. Now after their fall God gave skins to cover them, as an emblem of the covering which the slaughtered Lamb wrought out by his active and passive obedience, and imputed to his people to hide their sins from view. And from this moment, the "mystery of Christ" began to appear; and so it was gradually developed and opened up by the direction of God in the appointment of sacrifices, wherein these declarations of mercy acted as restraints and pull-backs upon the spiritual worshipper, when the flesh would stir and draw away the heart from the Lord; and it went on, from time to time, to be further revealed, until the great point of this mystery came to be made known, and was near at hand. And when was that? When the Person of the Son was taken directly and immediately into union with a personal body, the nature of his people; for in that nature he gave a demonstrative proof that the whole of the elect were in his heart, in union to him, and were never separated from him. He became incarnate as Immanuel, God with us; and the Holy Ghost tells us it is a great mystery, "great is the mystery of godliness, God was manifest in the flesh, seen of angels;" but he was not preached unto them; he was only preached unto the world. Well; here this mystery was opened up,—"God with us!" Here was God in our nature, love in our nature, power in our nature, wisdom in our nature, infinity in our nature, omniscience in our nature, omnipotence in our nature, omnipresence in our nature, holiness in our nature, justice in our nature, and the fulness of God, the Godhead bodily, concentered in our nature; for "in him dwelleth all the fulness of the Godhead bodily." And Christ, the incarnate Word; Christ, the Head of his church; Christ, in all his travels below, travelled as God with us and in us, as God with you and me! Our covenant God was never separate from Christ, and never will be. All the solemn steps and movements which God takes, in manifesting his mercy, pity, love, and compassion, in apportioning strength unto our day, are all in Christ. God is in Christ; and in the revelation of this solemn "mystery of Christ," all the glorious realities of his gospel grace are made known to the objects of his love. And this is one of the branches of this mystery of which we have to speak, of a covenant God in Christ Jesus!

Now have you ever felt that a God out of Christ must necessarily be a consuming fire? Have you ever felt such a solemn disparity between you and God that you have really not been able, at times, to speak unto his blessed Majesty? Has it ever entered into your conscience that no man can come unto the Father but through Christ? Perhaps there are some here who can, with a light and trifling manner, repeat the Lord's Prayer four or five times a day, and say, " Our Father, which art in heaven;" and yet have never felt in their souls, and known solemnly what it is to call God Father in the Person of Christ. Then I say all that you are now doing is nothing but insulting his blessed Majesty; it is mocking him. You have no Scripture authority for it; and if ever God convince you of your sin, by laying it on the conscience, he will make you to tremble for it. I remember, when under the first teachings of God, how I was torn to pieces with feelings of horror on account of this; and I no more dare say "Our Father," than I could leap into a burning fiery flame. I knew that I had sinned against a pure and holy God; and I could not see how there was the least probability of a holy God being the Father of such an ungodly sinner as I was; and I never experienced a measure of the blessedness of this mystery, "God with us," until by the spirit of adoption I was enabled to call him Father. As for you who can call him Father with unhallowed lips, and mock God with a form of words, your worship is nothing but a solemn insult to him; and he will say unto you one day or the other, "Who hath required this at your hand?" He will not be mocked with impunity. "Whatsoever a man soweth, that shall he also reap; for he that soweth to the flesh, shall of the flesh reap corruption; but he that soweth to the Spirit shall of the Spirit reap life everlasting." O, sinner!

Remember, you may trifle with yourself, and with your fellow-creatures; but God will not be trifled with with impunity. Sooner or later, he will come and reckon with you. And you who can preach about God's everlasting love and his electing grace, and live anything but according to the doctrines of Jesus Christ, he will be sure to bring you to a reckoning at last. But now, God be thanked, there is no other way of knowing this but through the revelation of this mystery by the blessed Spirit; for, from my heart I can say, if there were any other way, alas! I am sure I should make some mistake; and therefore I praise his blessed name that this is the only way in which the mystery of God in Christ Jesus, "God with us," can be opened up.

But again. This "mystery of Christ" was figured forth under the law. The mercy-seat was typical of this; for there God said, "I will meet with thee, and commune with thee." Now, poor sinner, if ever you have been brought here, and know what it is to have a little faith and a little hope; if you have been made to sigh, groan, and pant in your feelings after Jesus, and you have met a covenant God in Christ, O what a happy welcome have you found, and how you have blessed and praised his holy name for seeing where his glory and his majesty were shining, that it was all in the Person of Christ, that Christ was "the brightness of his glory, and the express image of his Person." And the soul who thus meets a covenant God in Christ Jesus meets him in his declarative glory; and there is nothing here but joy and peace to his poor sinking spirit; and in the opening up of this, O what a wonderful mystery it is!

But another branch of the "mystery of Christ" is, that the whole church of God, Jew and Gentile, bond and free, rich and poor, all that ever have been and ever will be, they all stand in inseparable union to the Lord Jesus Christ as their Head; they all have their being, and are one in and with him, and were never separated from him. I have said many times, and I say it again, that that was a wonderful figure of this mystery which was revealed to Peter. You know he was much devoted to the Jews; and the Lord wrought a kind of miracle to show unto him the mystery of the calling in of the Gentiles. He put Peter into a trance. Peter saw the heavens opened, and a certain vessel let down near him, as it were a sheet knit at the four corners, wherein were all manner of four-footed beasts of the earth, and wild beasts, and creeping things, and unclean fowls of the air; and there came a voice, which said unto him, "Arise, Peter, kill and eat." Now Peter never before had eaten such a meal, and he said, "Lord, I cannot; they are all unclean; and I have never eaten anything that is common or unclean." But the Lord replied to him, "What God hath cleansed, that call not thou common." Now mind, they were not cleansed in themselves; and if any of you are clean, it is not surely in yourselves, but you were cleansed in

God's secret mind, in union to the Lord Jesus Christ, from eternity. I believe that all his people were eternally in him; and when he came from heaven, all his elect were in him. Jesus is God's bread for them. He is the food of their souls; they were never separate from him, but were all set apart in him, chosen in him, accepted in him, and blessed in him. And mind, this vessel was let down from heaven and taken up again three times; the Lord here showing the divine approbation of the Eternal Trinity, the Three-One God, who were in union to these creeping things and flying things; and that in this solemn mystery they were all shut up; for the vessel was taken up again to heaven, to show that it was all settled and completed in the purpose of God from eternity. Here was set forth the "mystery of Christ" in his union to the church, and their union to him. And when he came on the grand errand of salvation, all the church came with him. He never lost one of them; and, therefore, he says, "All that the Father giveth me shall come to me, and him that cometh, I will in no wise cast out." Unbelief says, "They shall not come;" and carnal reason says, "They shall not come;" and the devil says, "I will take care to hinder them; I will devise some means to stop them from coming;" but they belong to Christ, and at the appointed time they shall come, and neither sin nor Satan can stop them. So that here God's mysterious love is set forth in Christ being crucified for them; here they are brought to know something of God's everlasting mercy revealed to them!

But again. When God is speaking, at another time, of this "mystery of Christ," and of the inseparable union that subsists between the members and the Head of Christ's mystical body, he says, "The head cannot say to the feet, I have no need of thee." Now, you know the Head of the body is Christ; and the feet are always a part of the body, but they are continually hobbling into some puddle. And so, some of God's people are poor hobbling creatures; for they do not know all their lives how they have been hobbling on; they have been in such dirty holes, or they have so staggered in faith, that they hardly know where they are or what they are. But this divine "mystery of Christ," of the Head and the members as one with him, and that he cannot do without them, is calculated to rejoice their poor sinking hearts. Blessed be his name, the whole church is complete in him; and he cannot present it to the Father as a glorious church until every hoof is presented with him before God as a perfect church. The "mystery of Christ" will be gloriously unfolded when the whole church is brought into a sweet manifestation of oneness with Christ; and that is a precious declaration, when praying to the Father for his church, he says, "I pray for them; I pray not for the world, but for them which thou hast given me out of it; for all mine are thine, and thine are mine, and I am glorified in them." And what does he there pray for? That they may be made one, manifested as one in union to him, and manifested as one in union to the Father through him. "As thou, Father, art in me; I in them, and thou in me, that they may be made perfect in one." But we are lost somehow or other in this solemn mystery of the glories of Christ,—that such as we should be made one in glorious union to him as the Head of the church, and that at last we should shine in immortal oneness as the members of his mystical body, in union to him the Head, and so to triumph in him for evermore. May we, therefore, take encouragement. It is for all those who are poor, sensibly lost sinners, for all who are poor helpless worms, for all who are poor crawling worms, and who are without help. And thus, "the battle is not to the strong, nor the race to the swift;" but "he giveth power to the faint, and to them that have no might he increaseth strength." Blessed be his name, it is for the poor burdened, convinced sinner, who is without help, who cannot do any work of his own, and who is made to struggle and pant after the mercy of God in Christ Jesus. And I tell you, poor soul, the Lord Jesus Christ came to pick up such as you are; he came to pick up these nothings in self; and thus he is glorified in opening up the mysteries of his salvation. And here the child of God will be brought to feel that there is a union and oneness subsisting between him and Christ; and that in this mystery every one is in his proper place, are all fixed according to divine appointment, and that all the millions of Christ's redeemed shall be presented to the Three-One God in perfect union to God incarnate. Thus God will be glorified, and the church for evermore sing the wonders of his love. And this is one branch of the "mystery of Christ!"

But I observe further. Another branch of this "mystery of Christ" is, what it has been done for; and why this people have been taken into union with him. Some persons tell us he has brought all mankind into a salvable state, and put salvation upon very easy conditions; and the better to gild the lie, they say, "that by God's aid and help we may do it all." Now, if this were not a lie, I should be ruined; for if my salvation depended upon this, I should be entirely lost. And if you are among this class of persons, you had better send me about my business; for I am sure such a poor helpless creature as I am, without any might or power, you will not find of any use whatever; but that blessed portion of God's Word just suits me: "Who hath saved us, and called us, with a holy calling, not according to our works, but according to his own purpose and grace, given us in Christ Jesus before the world began." Now some people wish to make a distinction here, and say, "We are not saved for works, but in accordance to works." Then God is not true. Now which are we to believe? God, or man? God says, it is "not according to our works." What is it according to, then? It is "according to his own purpose and grace, which was given us in Christ Jesus before

the world began." This is the firm and unshaken basis; planned, settled, and arranged by God himself from before the foundation of the
world; and so our blessed Christ has for his people "finished transgression and made an end of sin." And is not that better than setting you and me about it to finish it? For what could such poor
polluted creatures as we do, if he were to set us about it? Why, I
will tell you what has proceeded from all that ever I have done; it
has driven me farther away than I was before. I never did anything
but what served to increase my confusion and misery. And Paul
was of the same mind; for, he says, "I was alive without the law
once;" and while he was under the law, in his carnal mind, he never
could enter into the spirituality of it. And I believe many a child
of God has felt this in its spirituality, who have not known it in the
letter of the word. But the apostle says, "I was alive without the
law once; but when the commandment came, sin revived, and I died."
He then felt that he should be damned with all his perfect obedience
to the law. And what became of Paul's holiness, what became of
his piety, and what became of his doing all the commandments of
God in order to get to heaven? Why, his fancied righteousness fled
away; sin revived, and he died to all hope of being saved in this way;
and had there been no other channel opened up, he must have sunk
for ever into eternal despair! Here he was delivered from all thoughts
of saving himself; he felt that he had no more power to do it than he
had to pull down the skies; and thus his legal hopes gave up the ghost
and vanished away. And those who have been taught this truth
will bless God that they have no part to do in their own salvation.
But, perhaps, some will say, "I do believe there is something for
man to do in it, and is it not written so in the Word of God? I will find
a portion to prove it; and I wonder that you have never read it before."
What is it, then? "Does not the apostle Paul say, 'Work out your
own salvation with fear and trembling?' There now; what do you
think of that? Does not that cut off your creed?" No, not a branch
of it. You have read only a part of the text: "Work out your own
salvation with fear and trembling, for it is God which worketh in you
both to will and to do of his own good pleasure." And if you and I, by
the working of the Spirit in us, are working out what God is working
in; and God is working in what we are working out—why our working will be one of the sweetest things that we can do. But until
God works in us his grace, by the power of his Spirit, there will be
no ability in us to work it out. Suppose now, a farmer's man had
nothing but straw to thrash, he might work from morning to night,
and no corn would come out; or, set a person to pump at a well,
where the sucker is dry, why he might pump from day-break to midnight, and no water would run out. Just so it is with a poor empty,
barren, and unprofitable creature, without either grain or water;
he is utterly unable to work anything out, until God, by his blessed

Spirit, is graciously pleased to work it in, and thus enable him to do it to the praise and glory of his blessed name. But it is the great work of the Lord to accomplish this in the soul; and when you are brought to know something of this in your heart and conscience, by the invincible workings of the Holy Ghost, you will enter a little into the blessedness of this "mystery of Christ;" you will then perceive that it is a salvation wrought out by the Lord alone, that it is complete, that nothing can be added to or taken from it; that no creature-doings can come in here at all, but that the work is all of the Lord, from first to last. It is a salvation which shows that the objects of it can never perish; that Christ has made an end of sin for them, and brought in an everlasting righteousness in which they are accepted; that he has redeemed them from the curse of the law, satisfied the claims of justice, overcome the world, and delivered them "from death, and him that had the power of it, that is, the devil;" and that he has obtained eternal redemption for them; consequently they can never be lost in time. It shows also that they are redeemed to God, that they are saved from the lowest state of wretchedness and degradation, and brought to the highest state of dignity and glory, even to that of "sons of God," of being "heirs of God and joint-heirs with Christ." And it not only shows that they are redeemed from the world, the curse of the law, and inflexible justice, but also that they are redeemed from the plague of their own hearts; yea, from all plagues both from within and without; that they are redeemed to hold sweet intercourse and blessed communion with God the Father, God the Son, and God the Holy Ghost. And when they are brought to have fellowship with the solemn "mystery of Christ," in his suffering, death, burial, resurrection, ascension, and exaltation, they will be brought to see that it was for this purpose that his blessed Majesty became poor; for this that he groaned; for this that he led a life of suffering here; for this that he bled and died; and for this that he has now sat down at the right hand of God, having "finished the work" which the Father gave him to do. Here the soul is brought to see how the glorious Three-One God has accomplished this "mystery of Christ," which had its origin in his everlasting love from eternity, and has flowed under-ground, as it were, till the appointed time for it to spring up in the hearts of his redeemed people, and which will at length raise them up to the election likeness of the Lord the Lamb!

But my strength tells me to give up for the present; and, therefore, I shall leave the subject to the evening; when with the Lord's help I hope to enter a little further on it, and then take my leave of you for this year.

And now, may the Lord bless the few remarks that have been made to the profit of our souls; and his name shall have the praise!

☞ The Evening Sermon does not appear to have been reported. At any rate I have not a copy of it.—J. G.

DOING ALL THINGS IN THE NAME OF THE LORD JESUS.

Preached in East Street Chapel, Walworth, London, on Tuesday Evening, June 6th, 1843.

"And whatsoever ye do, in word or deed, do all in the name of the Lord Jesus." - COL. III. 17.

I. FROM this portion of God's word, I shall, with the Lord's help, endeavour to mark out the *characters* addressed.

II. Drop a hint or two upon the glorious *Person* set before us—"the Lord Jesus."

III. Speak of the *injunction enjoined upon them:* "Whatsoever ye do, in word or deed, do all in the name of the Lord Jesus."

I. In the *characters* here addressed are such as are mentioned in the first few verses of the chapter: "If ye then be risen with Christ, seek those things which are above." They are characters that are risen with Christ. Now there is a threefold sense in which some of God's people are risen with Christ.

1. They are all risen with him by virtue of union to him. He was crucified as the public Head of his body, the church, and he rose as their public Head. All God's elect had the sentence of death passed on them in the death of Christ, and were in this sense crucified with him; and his solemn Majesty never took a step, from the cradle to the cross, nay, to the crown, without every soul of his elect being in him; so that when he rose, they rose together with him. But how? By virtue of their inseparable union to him, they sat together with him, and were presented before God as engraven upon his heart. Hence we find the Holy Ghost saith, Christ has "entered into heaven itself, now to appear in the presence of God for us."

2. In the Lord's set time to favour them, his people rise together with Christ, by virtue of his resurrection, above the dominion, the love, and the power of sin and the world. When the Lord the Spirit quickens their dead souls, it is by life communicated from Christ; and one of the results of it is, a cutting them off from the world and the things of it, and bringing them into a blessed resurrection from its ways and pursuits. And when this takes place, they cannot be kept any longer in good humour with the world, nor with Satan either. They are raised from the love of it; so that the world and they are no longer in union. They have received a principle of life which makes them dead to it, and they cannot remain any longer in love with it. And if they should be in a false profession of religion, they will rise from that also; they will come out of it; and this resurrection from a false profession is manifested in them by a death to that profession; they will come away from it and rise above it. If they have been free-willers, all their legal props will give way and leave

them helpless and destitute; and if they have been high free-willers, the result will be just the same. For my part I see no difference between them; for when men say they can believe when they please, and be happy and comfortable when they please, what is it but free-will in another shape? The poor, tempest-tossed, harassed soul finds that he has no power to believe or comfort his own soul. Yea, those who have risen with Christ, and have been taught the truth as it is in him, know that if this doctrine put forth were true, there is not a soul of them but must be damned. They are brought to feel, every one of them, that they cannot stand upon it; so that, under the teachings of the blessed Spirit, they are raised above these false delusions. Whether they perish or not, they find they cannot live upon any free-will system. But when the Lord is graciously pleased to reveal his pardoning grace, seal it home on the conscience, and the soul is brought to experience the blessed effects of the love and blood of Christ, O how blessedly then it is raised to joy and peace and can see that every thing is secured in the dear Redeemer. It can then triumph above all its foes, for a moment or two, and magnify the riches of God's grace and mercy in thus bringing them into a blessed resurrection-state with Christ.

3. If they live much longer, almost to a certainty they will be brought to experience another resurrection. They will come into a state of mind just where Ezekiel was in his vision, when he was set down in the midst of the valley which was full of dry bones. These bones were very dry, and what seemed to him so vastly strange was, they were not only very dry, but there was not a single bone in its proper place; and even when they were partly clothed, and the Lord said to the prophet, "Can these dry bones live?" as much as Ezekiel knew of the Lord's wonderful dealings and the power of his arm, yet it so staggered him, that he said, "O Lord God, thou knowest!" And the people of God sometimes, in a backsliding state, get into such a dry, barren, lifeless, distracted state of mind, that they do not feel a single joint in its proper place, nor a single joint moving aright. They are as gloomy, dark, and lifeless as the dry bones scattered in the valley. But when the Lord commanded his servant to prophesy to the wind, and say, "Come from the four winds, O breath, and breathe upon these slain that they may live," and breath came into these dry bones, they lived, and stood up, an exceeding great army. So it is with the soul, when the Lord is graciously pleased to breathe into it fresh communications of life and power; why there is a blessed resurrection takes place immediately. Faith is brought into lively exercise, hope is brought into lively exercise, love is brought into lively exercise, joy is brought into lively exercise, peace is brought into lively exercise, prayer is brought into lively exercise, and thanksgiving to God is brought into lively exercise; and the poor soul rejoices that he has been separated from the world and raised

up to God, to sing the wonders of his love and to demonstrate that
God has made him a living monument of his truth; and all the life,
strength, and power communicated to him, with all the joy and peace
he experiences, he feels that it all comes from Christ; and then he
solemnly shouts, "Victory, through the blood of the Lamb!" So
that the people of God know what it is to be risen with Christ, in
some blessed measure, in this threefold point of view.

There may be some here who are at present in the first resurrection-state I have been describing, and may want to enter more fully
into an enjoyment of the blessedness and glory of it. But I tell you
one thing; if you are God's people, as long as you can experience
the work of grace in your souls, you are on rich ground, and cannot
but be happy and rejoicing; but when God removes these feelings
of comfort, and brings you into a dry, barren, and wintry condition,
which certainly will be the case, why, then you will shrink up like
a poor worm in a frosty night; you will sink so low in your feelings
as to conclude that there is no hope left, and be ready to give up all
for lost. But when this is the case, "let no man take thy crown;"
because you may not have all you can want or desire, do not conclude from thence that you have nothing at all. Let me only put
this case to you. Suppose any of you now were journeying to Manchester, and when you reached Birmingham you met with a companion who had seen several of the factories in Manchester, and he
were to tell you how wonderfully they worked, and what a curious
specimen of machinery he had viewed, would you conclude that you
were in London, and not on your road to Manchester, indeed more
than half way there, because you had not seen it yourself? Certainly not. So it is with the child of God, who is hobbling and
crawling on, amidst temptations and conflicts, and who is not on
the high mountains of delight. He is still on the high road, and the
Lord will bring him there in his own time. Therefore let such a
poor soul wait where he is, sighing and crying, till God is pleased
to raise him up on high; for "he who hath begun a good work in you
will perform it until the day of Jesus Christ." And every one who
is raised up to an enjoyment of God knows what it is to be risen
with Christ, in this blessed way, in his own appointed time. But some
may say, "I have been waiting so long for it!" Aye; but how long
did poor Abraham have to wait for the accomplishment of the promise? And when, like you and me, his patience was exhausted, and
there was no appearance of the fulfilment of the promise; and when
Sarah and he, with their free-will efforts, tried to accomplish God's
work, what did it do for them? Why, they brought a plague into
their house! And just so it is with us; for that is all we can do with
our free-will plans. We can never enter into the sweetness of the
promise until we find the plague in our own proceedings; and then
God saith, "Cast out the bond-woman and her son; for the son of

the bond-woman shall not be heir with the son of the free-woman."
How often do we set to work with our legal plans to accomplish
God's work, and not leave off till he really brings a fresh plague
into our consciences, and then we must remain there until God opens
up afresh the mysteries of his love and salvation to us. Therefore
wait, poor soul, on the Lord; wait at the footstool of his mercy; and
if you cannot speak, groan; and if you cannot groan, sigh; for
you that are walking in such a path as this shall not sigh or groan
long before the Lord will appear for you. May you not, then, be
discouraged, but abide where you are, at the feet of the dear Redeemer, and there lie helpless in self. He will be sure to come, and
arise up for the deliverance of the poor and needy, for "he giveth
power to the faint, and to them that have no might he increaseth
strength." "He filleth the poor with good things," while "the rich
he sends empty away."

II. But we pass on to notice the solemn and glorious *Person* set
before us,—"the Lord Jesus!" "His name shall be called *Jesus*."
For what? Because he shall do his part towards saving his people,
and they are to accomplish the rest? No, no; not so. What then?
"Because he shall save his people from their sins." Now, mind you,
if Jesus is to save thee from thy sins, thou art not to set on to save
thyself, and then come to him to approve of thy wonderful works.
The sinner who is brought by the Spirit to the Lord Jesus comes
with all his sins on him, and all his sins about him. He comes as
a wretched, vile, ruined, and guilty sinner. "O," say you, "I am
frightened at that!" You may well be so; I do not wonder at it;
for if God has opened your heart to your view and brought you to
feel what a sinner you really are, it is enough to make you frightened.

The man that can laugh at sin and make sport with sin does not
know either the feeling sense of it, the sight of it, or the stench of
it; for it is enough to suffocate a Samson, and the strongest man, except Christ, and to bring him prostrate to the ground, just as you
and I are. Well, poor pulled-up, rooted-up sinner, without help in
self, God help you to come to Christ; he saves from sin; and, bless
his precious name, he does not half save only. A half salvation
will not do for me, whether it will for you or not! I must have a
whole and complete salvation,—a salvation, not only from sin and
the consequences of it, but one which Satan cannot mar, or it will
not suit my case or come into my conscience. But the salvation of
the Lord does; it is a perfect work; it meets all the circumstances
and enters into all the wants and requirements of the soul. Jesus
has mediatorially put away sin by the sacrifice of himself. Hence
the law is satisfied, justice is honoured, death and the devil are vanquished, and the world is overcome. And when the blessed Spirit
comes into the conscience of the ruined sinner with his divine power,

and gives the poor soul a dead lift, he is brought then blessedly to enter into the salvation of Jesus, as just suited to his needy case and circumstances. He feels that he has saved him throughout, completely and entirely, and that "his name is Jesus," because he has saved him from all his sins!

Now there is one thing I would notice in being saved from sin; and this part of salvation which I have in view, I have sometimes illustrated by this simple figure. Suppose a vagabond should have robbed and plundered every one he came near, and at last should be taken up, be tried, cast, and condemned; and that after this the queen should pardon him, and he be sent out of prison; would not all the neighbours be alarmed at the man, at such a vile fellow being set free, and say, "It is a pity such a vagabond should be let loose on society?" The man's character is gone; and though the queen has pardoned him, yet no one would like to employ him or have any thing to do with him. But if the queen could really prove him to be innocent, and should take him openly and manifestly into her family, why the man would not then merely be pardoned, but there would be a dignity stamped upon him! An act of this kind would appear something like salvation, would it not? Now our Jesus saves in this way. He not only saves his people from sin, and the awful consequences of it, but he raises them up to dignity and glory. They are saved in the Lord with an everlasting salvation, and they have an everlasting robe of righteousness imputed to them, in which they are glorified for ever; for "he raiseth up the poor out of the dust, and lifteth the needy out of the dunghill, that he may set him among princes, even with the princes of his people." And thus he brings them into a blessed enjoyment of his immortal salvation. Jesus is not only the *Saviour* of his church, but he is made such a *glorious* Saviour to them that he is Jesus the anointed; a tender-hearted, a pitying and compassionate Friend; capable in the sympathy of his nature of coming into the sorrows, pains, trials, conflicts, and miseries of his people. As Jesus, he has had to wade through the deep waters; he has been to the bottom of them, and knows their depth. You and I do not. He has gone through hot fires, and he knows the fierceness of the flames; but, blessed be his name, he has made a way through the waters, and through the fires, and says, "When thou passest through the waters, I will be with thee; and through the rivers, they shall not overflow thee; when thou walkest through the fire, thou shalt not be burned; neither shall the flame kindle upon thee." And thus he has by his love and blood quenched the flames, and comes now blessedly and manifestively to the soul, by a new and living way which he hath consecrated by his precious blood, for thy salvation and God's glory; so that, as Jesus, he is suited to thy state and circumstances, poor disconsolate child of God, poor broken-hearted sinner, and thou shalt be brought to feel that everything thou canst want is treasured up in his fulness for every time of need.

But again.   He is not only Jesus, but he is the *Lord* Jesus.   I often think I am one of the greatest fools that God has ever let live, for sin and Satan so much to obscure the glories of Christ's Person from my view.   In my judgment I firmly believe that the Lord Jesus is the "Lord of lords, and the King of kings,"—that God's providence is in his hands, that all my cares and all my trials are under his appointment, that devils and men must obey his sovereign nod,—that "he speaks, and it is done; he commands, and it stands fast," and that his eternal Majesty, as God, is in inseparable union with his manhood in his glorious Person; and all this for my everlasting welfare.   And yet how troubled I am, at times, as though I had never known him.   And these precious truths are not only laid down in his blessed Word, but now and then let into the conscience of the poor sinking sinner, to prop him up, and to comfort his soul.   Therefore, "whatsoever ye do, in word or deed, do all in the name of the Lord Jesus."

III.   Now it is not my intention to weary your patience to-night. I shall, therefore, pass on, and notice what it is the Lord *enjoins on his people*, and what it is that honours his gracious Majesty!   "Whatsoever ye do, in word or deed, do all in the name of the Lord Jesus."

First, then.   Do we pray unto God?   Of what use are our words, sighs, or groans, at the footstool of mercy, at the throne of grace, unless they are "in the name of the Lord Jesus?"   Never utter a sentence in your own name, your own work, or your own words! Remember, poor soul, and God give you a feeling sense of it, Christ himself said, "Whatsoever ye shall ask the Father in my name, he will give it you."   But mind, it must not be a divided salvation, for him to do half and the other half left for you to do!   No; there must be an entire stripping of self.   All your self-hope, self-confidence, self-duty, and self-piety must be rooted up; for no sinner that is really taught his lost and ruined condition can ever fall back upon self for help, either in whole or in part; but he will be led to place all his hope and dependence on the Lord Jesus!   And the poor soul, who is brought here by the solemn teachings of the blessed Spirit, will feel that all his sighs, his groans, and his prayers must be in the name of Jesus only; and therefore he pleads the blessed name of the dear Redeemer alone.   Here his hope anchors, and his faith rests; and here he finds something precious and suitable to him beyond all power of description.   But some one may be ready to say, "Do you not think that we ought, when we pray to the Lord, at the same time to promise him that if he would do this or that for us, we would do so and so for him?"   I tell you, you had better leave that on the background.   Be assured of this, no bondage cry is ever a safe one; but let all thy pleas be alone in the solemn name, life, blood, obe-

dience, and righteousness of the Son of God. Hear what the Lord
says: "No man cometh unto the Father but by me;" and if you
think that the blessing of the Lord proceeds or comes from the Father
in any other way than in and through the name of Christ, you are
deceiving your own souls; for the Lord of life says, "I am the way,
the truth, and the life; no man cometh unto the Father but by me;"
but in this way both Jew and Gentile have access by one Spirit unto
the Father, in the blessed name of the Lord Jesus Christ! And so
precious and glorious is this name, that whenever the Father saves
the poor sinner, it is alone upon this ground; and when the blessed
Spirit enables the sinner thus to place all his hope and confidence in
Christ, it crowns the mind of God with delight; as the Lord tells us
in the end, "he will save; he will rejoice over thee with joy; he will
rest in his love; he will joy over thee with singing." It is the work
of the Spirit of truth thus to glorify Christ. "He shall glorify me,
for he shall receive of mine, and shall show it unto you." Therefore, in all your addresses to the throne of God, may you do it "all
in the name of the Lord Jesus."

If any of you are invited to breathe out your exercise of soul, or
any enjoyment you have experienced of his name; and you should
have some fluency of speech, or possess some talent or ability to
pray, whether in private or public, do not go to it, poor child of God,
in your own name, your own strength, your own might, nor in your
own power; do not come with your own talent, with your own vows
and promises, not even after enjoying the Lord's presence; but may
all your prayers, whether in public or private, be grounded alone
upon the merit and blood of the Lord Jesus Christ; and if the Lord
the Spirit enable you thus to pray, "in spirit and in truth," you shall
certainly find access to God, and he will make it manifest that he is
free with you by holding sweet communion with your soul. Do you
not recollect the circumstance of Moses making the ark, and the mercy-
seat, and the lid of it? And what did God say concerning it? "Here
will I meet with thee, and commune with thee from above the mercy-
seat!" Come, poor soul, take thy standing at the mercy-seat, through
the blood of the Lamb. What is so pleasing to the Lord as to see thee
there,—whilst the Spirit brings thee thus into contrition of soul, to
leave thyself at his blessed feet, without any support or creature-help
in self, and enables thee to give up thyself to his service, and raises
thy soul into a sweet and blessed enjoyment of the Lord Jesus Christ?
"Whatsoever ye do, in word or deed, do all in the name of the Lord
Jesus."

2. Do we preach? Aye, what a mercy would it be if there were
no preaching but "in the name of the Lord Jesus?" I should be
thankful if I never came in any other name; but I confess I do not
always preach solely and exclusively in the name of the Lord Jesus!
Self works; and we want to do it prettily and neatly; and I tell you

that that filthy vagabond, self, brings so much of his poison into the man's mind, even while he is in the pulpit, and he has such a feeling sense of his own loathsome condition whilst there sometimes, that he knows not what to do. And I say, if at any time the devil vamps him up to think that he has preached a good sermon, if he is one of God's ministers he will be sure to be brought down into a very low place. And if any of you, who are professed ministers of Jesus, are ever vamped up in your mind at any time to think that you have been preaching a good sermon, God will make you smart for your folly. He will certainly do it; for there is no preaching that is acceptable in his sight but what is "in the name of the Lord Jesus." But if you come in his glorious name, O how sweet will your message be! How comforting to the Lord's weary and heavy-laden family! Shrink back for ever, then, in your own inability and incapability of doing what you want to do. If you are led to come "in the name of the Lord Jesus," he will strengthen you for the work; he will not leave, nor let you sink in it; but if it is only a job of your own, he will; and the sooner the better. But some may be ready to say, "Do you feel so?" No, indeed! For sometimes I am as fretful and peevish as a mortal can be, when the Lord is pleased to strip me of everything and to leave me bare; but when he brings me to see in my preaching that nothing will stand the test but what is "in the name of the Lord Jesus," and when his power comes in the ministry of his word, and he makes it manifest that there is a "savour of his knowledge by us in every place," then we have a blessed evidence that the Lord is with us. There is one thing that will always prove who are God's ministers; and that is, when their ministry becomes a sweet savour of Christ, so that their testimony will be either a "savour of life unto life, or of death unto death." And thus, when they come in the name of Christ, that name which "is as ointment poured forth," it will leave a solemn measure of unction in the conscience of the child of God, and he will feel its sacred power; while at the same time it will offend the proud, presumptuous free-willer, and he will speak against it. You may be assured of this, that whether they are high or low free-willers, it matters very little which, directly you preach that all the feelings of faith, hope, love, and every other grace in the soul, depend upon the power being communicated thereto by the blessed Spirit, that very moment they will begin to speak against it. But do not be alarmed at it; rather rejoice at it; for there is no proof of your coming "in the name of the Lord Jesus" unless presumptuous professors are made uncomfortable under it. Therefore, when we stand up to preach his word, may our ministry be in his fear, "in the name of the Lord Jesus!"

3. If we have conversation one with another, let it be only "in the name of the Lord Jesus." I have often thought of an old friend

of ours, a countryman, a man richly taught, who had a very deep
experience in his own soul.   Some time since he began to tell a few
friends of the dealings of the Lord with him; and as he had had great
conflicts, and had obtained many victories, he had something to talk
about; but while he was relating his many troubles and deliverances,
the old man observed tears falling from their eyes, and he stopped
short in his history; and to use his familiar expression, he said, "I
will tell you no more, for your eyes are getting up!"   He found now
that something else was about being introduced beside "the name
of the Lord Jesus."   He felt accursed pride at work and springing
up in him; therefore he found it best readily to give it up.   And so,
when you and I begin to vamp up pride, and want to be gazed at,
by and by we shall have little or nothing left for us to say.   What
good is there in speaking in each other's name?   The Lord give us
a tender conscience, under the unction of his blessed Spirit, that our
conversation may be more profitable to one another, and that we may
do it more "in the name of the Lord Jesus!"

4. In all our religious acts also, let it be our concern to do it only
"in the name of the Lord Jesus!"   Do we read the Word of the Lord?
God help us always to have Jesus along with us!   Take Jesus out
of the Bible, take his precious Name away from the Bible, and it
would damn every soul of you!   There is not a soul could live, if
Jesus be taken away!   Why, the whole contents of the Bible without Christ would condemn those who have the most imaginary holiness, as being "all under sin."   Nay, more than that; if any of us
had all the fancied holiness of all the men in the world, apart from
Christ, the Bible would damn us without Christ!   But O! What
sacred consolations have we found in reading the Word of God in
the solemn assembly!   What profit have we received from its warnings and rebukes!   What blessed instruction and consolation have
our souls derived from it, while we have sensibly attended to it
"in the name of the Lord Jesus!"   O how solemn at such seasons
has the Word of God been to us, with its reproofs, rebukes, admonitions, and exhortations, under the teachings of the blessed Spirit!
Well; we are assured it is all solemn to the conscience while it thus
comes home with power to the soul "in the name of the Lord Jesus."
We may not have a Bible always before us in the letter; but we
shall be satisfied with its blessed contents in the heart, and thank
God that it is written, "All Scripture is given by inspiration of God,
and is profitable for doctrine, for reproof, for correction, for instruction in righteousness, that the man of God may be perfect, through-
ly furnished unto all good works."   And, therefore, may all our
reading and praying be consecrated by this, that it is all to be done
"in the name of the Lord Jesus!"

But now, let me ask you, in whose name have you come here to-
night?   Perhaps some of you present may say, "To tell you the

truth, we have come to hear a queer fellow, a strange man!" Well; and what satisfaction will there be in that? May God, if it be his sovereign pleasure, open your heart, and put ears into your soul to hear his word; and if he give you ears to hear the "name of the Lord Jesus," you will go away with very different feelings to those with which you came! O Lord, accomplish thine own work in the heart of some poor sinner! And if the Lord should perform this work in thy soul, poor careless sinner, thou wilt have to praise him for it to all eternity; but if not, it would be better for thee if thou hadst never been born. "Whatsoever ye do, in word or deed, do all in the name of the Lord Jesus!"

5. Well, now, if we attend to order, and come to the ordinances of God's house, we must do it "all in the name of the Lord Jesus." And before you practise anything as an ordinance of God, turn to the Bible for a "Thus saith the Lord!" to sanction it; for if you have only tradition for its authority, you might as well have any other branch of Popery, and follow it; for all tradition is founded upon this system of human invention. But if you have the name of the Lord with you, and practise it with a "Thus saith the Lord!" and the Spirit of the living God lead you to attend to the ordinances of God's house, "in the name of the Lord Jesus," you will find it sweet and solemn to your soul, and glorifying to God!

Now suppose, for instance, a child of God is about to be baptized. If he is not enabled to do it in "the name of the Lord Jesus," it will be but a poor legal task at the best; but let him be convinced of its spirituality, and feel in his soul the power of it, and be brought by the blessed Spirit to see that it is, as Peter speaks of it, a figure of the resurrection of the Son of God, and an emblem also of his own death and burial to sin, and of his resurrection unto newness of life; as well as a sweet type of the solemn resurrection of his body to be fashioned unto the likeness of the glorious body of the Lord Jesus Christ; I say, when the poor soul thus attends to this ordinance, in the real exercise of a living faith, "in the name of the Lord Jesus," it is a solemn act; but if his name be wanting, there is no unction or power accompanying it, and it is nothing but a poor legal piece of business after all!

6. And so, again, if we attend to the ordinance of the Lord's Supper, it should be "in the name of the Lord Jesus!" Do not come with any of your preparations! Aye, what a tugging and toiling is there in some poor souls to get into a state of preparation, and to make themselves better before they come to the table! What a tugging and striving to do it in their own name! Do you not hear what Paul saith? "Whosoever shall eat this bread and drink this cup of the Lord unworthily, shall be guilty of the body and blood of the Lord!" "Ah!" says the poor soul; "that is the very thing which makes me so anxious and concerned to get prepared." But mind,

it is said, "*Not discerning* the Lord's body!" There is your unworthiness, poor sinner, when it is not done "in the name of the
Lord Jesus!" Come, then, poor poverty-stricken, ruined beggar,
with nothing to recommend thee; come as thou art, with all thy
wretchedness and misery, in the name of Immanuel, "in the name
of the Lord Jesus." Mayest thou eat and drink the elements by precious faith; and find his gracious Majesty manifest his love and blood
to thee, that it may be thy meat and drink! "Whatsoever ye do,
in word or deed, do all in the name of the Lord Jesus."

7. But we observe further. If you do an act of kindness, do not
do it grudgingly, but do it "in the name of the Lord Jesus;" and
remember his words, "It is more blessed to give than to receive."
But I will tell you what I have seen, and very likely there are some
of these characters here to-night. Perhaps a kind friend has been
benevolent to them, or done them some service; and they will say,
"Well, I do not thank you; I thank the Lord; for it is the Lord that
hath done it!" I say it is not true; you do not thank the Lord; for if
you had received the act of kindness "in the name of the Lord Jesus,"
you would thank the instrument raised up for your help as well as
the Lord. What you say about thanking him is nothing but a piece
of presumption and manifests that your heart is not right with God;
for if it were, you would thank the Lord and the giver too; the
giver and his gift would be received from God's hand, with tenderness of conscience, "in the name of the Lord Jesus," and both go
sweetly and savingly together,—the one who is blessed with a spirit
to give, and the other who is favoured to receive the bounties of
providence from his hands. "Whatsoever ye do, in word or deed,
do all in the name of the Lord Jesus!"

8. But again. If ye exhort or admonish each other, see that ye
do it in love, "in the name of the Lord Jesus.' Let it be made
manifest that you are concerned for Christ to be all in all! Do not
act one toward another, and before men, in a way contrary to what
you profess; but give evident proof that there is a holy solemnity in
the religion of Christ, and that your conduct is regulated by "the
name of the Lord Jesus." Thus may the Spirit of the living God
draw out your souls, and enable you to act in a way as becometh
the Gospel of Christ, that so you may walk before God as those who
are made alive from the dead and called to show forth his praise.
"Whatsoever ye do, in word or deed, do all in the name of the Lord
Jesus."

And now to conclude. Perhaps in this assembly there are many
who have never thought of the necessity of this Name—never thought
they were such sinners as to need the Name of Christ! You may be
ready to say, "We go to church (though I never expect many church-
folks to hear me), every Lord's day, and say, 'Lord, have mercy
upon us, and incline our hearts to keep this law!'" Why, what a

poor toil is this! If you could begin from this moment and keep the law; were it possible for you to fulfil it in every iota, in every jot and tittle of it, and you had not a better religion than that, you would be damned; your old sins would send you to perdition. What is to become of your old sins? They have already condemned you; and as to your keeping the law for time to come, supposing it were possible, that cannot make amends for old sins. Therefore, poor sinner, you stand guilty, and are condemned; and I tell you that unless you have something better than this, you must be lost. You must have a righteousness in which God cannot find a flaw, or you cannot be saved! And where is this to be found? In the "name of the Lord Jesus" alone; in the precious blood and obedience of the dear Redeemer! And the soul that is brought here, by the Spirit of Christ, and stands before God raised up "in the name of the Lord Jesus," shall be led to walk worthily and be brought eternally to praise and glorify him for ever and ever.

May the Lord bless you and me with a more feeling sense of the preciousness of "the name of the Lord Jesus." Amen.

GOD OUR SALVATION.

Preached at Bedworth, on Wednesday Evening, June 14th, 1843.

The following discourse was the last preached in Warwickshire by the late Mr. Gadsby. It was delivered on Wednesday evening, June 14th, 1843, at the Baptist Chapel, Bedworth. The chapel was densely crowded. While preaching, Mr. G. seemed to be quite at home. After often hearing Mr. Gadsby for the space of 26 years, and having outlived him upwards of 30 years, yet the savour of his preaching is not erased; for there are times and seasons when the words and the sweetness attending his ministry come quite fresh to my mind. Well; he has gone, and is beyond the reach of all trouble, safely landed; and we who are now past the age of threescore and ten, but yet in the wilderness, can and do look back with a grateful heart to God for his great mercy that we are still spared to show forth his power to the rising race. The simple reading of the sermon will give but little idea of the burning energy, life, and power in the preacher during its delivery.*

"Say unto my soul, I am thy salvation."—Ps. xxxv. 3.

You and I stand on the verge of an eternal world, and unless God himself say to the soul, "I am thy salvation," we must eternally perish. The great body of professors of religion are quite satisfied in talking about or hearing of a salvation. They tell us what great salvation God has accomplished for us, if we will but close in with it, if we will but do our part; and other professors please themselves with talking about the discriminating doctrines of the gospel, and

---

* The above remarks were made by Mr. T. Player, many years a local minister residing in Coventry. He was the reporter who took down a number of Mr. G.'s sermons, as well as this one.

more or less ridicule the inward teachings and workings of God the Spirit in the soul, and the feelings of the poor sinner under them. But whenever the Lord the Spirit circumcises the heart of a sinner by the knife of the law, he lays his heart open, and lets the contents of the heart begin to ooze up with abominable filth, guilt, and horrors. Nothing will then do for the soul short of the Lord speaking, and saying to such a soul, "I am thy salvation."*

All the efforts of nature will leave a man to perish in his sins. There is not strength enough in an angel to save him. In fact, if all the angels in heaven were to unite to save one sinner, that sinner must be eternally lost if he had not a better salvation than they could give him. He must have a salvation which none but the Lord himself is, and none but he can make known. If you are never brought to see and feel the need of such a salvation, your religion is not worth a thank'ee.

I shall endeavour, as the Lord shall give me wisdom and grace, and strength of body and mind, to make a few remarks on the following particulars:

I. Show what makes this salvation *essentially necessary* and *particularly suitable* for the sinner.

II. What this salvation *couches in it.*

III. That *God himself*, in his Trinity of Persons, *is this salvation.*

IV. Show the *effect* of a sinner being made to feel *his need* of this salvation. The quickened sinner, made alive to God, will be putting up this petition, and never rest satisfied without an answer, "Say unto my soul, I am thy salvation." It will not do for him to be told all have a chance of being saved; it is all lumber to such a poor sinner. The man must have a salvation that leaves no chance of being lost. This alone will fit his troubled conscience; therefore his soul will from time to time vehemently cry, "O Lord, say unto my soul, I am thy salvation."

V. Show what is *the effect* of the Lord *revealing this salvation* to the conscience.

I must be brief. May the Lord the Spirit lead me to speak such things as his solemn Majesty designs to apply to your hearts.

I. Show what makes this salvation *essentially necessary* and *particularly suitable* for the sinner. What a blessing it will be if the Lord lays open some poor heart to-night! If he does, and lets you feel what your heart is, you will not be able to find a greater wretch than yourself in all the town. There may be *practically* worse; but you will feel, between God and your soul, the seeds of all iniquity

---

* This is what some superficial religionists call "corruption preaching." Mr. Gadsby was wont to say such professors were sinners assuredly; but they were *pretty* sinners, never having seen their own ugliness as in the sight of God; and not having been made to feel the malady, they knew little or nothing in reality of the remedy. Let the poor tried child of God judge how far he was right.

within you. If they have not come out in practice, there is no merit due to you; for had the Lord placed you in the same circumstances as some are, and left you to your own workings, they would have come out. So we have cause to be thankful to God that we are preserved from the outward enormities and evil practices of others. I am a living witness of it, and can say now to the honour of God that he kept me from one awful branch of open vice and immorality; for had he not, I should have gone on the same as others. I remember the time well. I resided not more than three miles from this place, when I was bent on ruin, determined what I would do, and laid my plan most successfully, as I thought, being determined to gratify my carnal heart by committing gross uncleanness in its various branches. But the Lord restrained me, and I was not so well pleased, I assure you, that I was frustrated, so wretched and guilty was I at that time. But when his solemn Majesty laid my heart open, what a scene presented itself to my view! What a horrible wretch I appeared in my own eyes, my own feelings, before a heart-searching God. The truth is that law and justice, holiness, and everything becoming the character of God, as a just and holy God, is against sin, and sin is against this holy God. "For we have all sinned and come short of the glory of God." Every perfection of his nature will unite to cut down the sinner in his conscience if he has quickened his soul, and eternally if not interested in this salvation.

We need a salvation that is as extensive as the requirements of God's holy law, as extensive as the demands of justice, as extensive as the sinner's awful depths of depravity; a salvation,—I speak it with reverence, that the Lord cannot mend nor Satan mar. A salvation short of this will not reach the core of your heart. We may cover the outside of the wound, but the core is untouched. As we have sinned against God, and as his holy law says, "Cursed is every one that continueth not in all things which are written in the book of the law to do them," and, "Whosoever shall keep the whole law, and yet offend in one point, is guilty of all," do not we need a great salvation?

Perhaps some of you may say, "I have never gone the lengths that some have; I have never committed adultery or fornication." Neither have I, practically; but I say, when the Lord laid my heart open, I found, what you will, if he lays yours open, there were within all the seeds of evil. The law of God looks at the intents and thoughts of the heart. It condemns for filthy thoughts, it condemns for evil principles. So extensive is the law, in its searching power, and the sentence that it passes, that it solemnly declares, "He that offends in one point is guilty of all." Have you never offended in any one point? Now, when your heart has been laid open to the eye of infinite Justice, and the strictest scrutiny of God's law, where must you look for help?

Rather than that the Almighty can save the sinner at the expense of his justice, or to the disparagement of his law, his very nature binds him to doom to eternal misery the whole world. Some persons try to mend the law, and what they call mollify it. They tell us we must do by it as the schoolboy does by his copy, come as near to it as we can; but God's law will have nothing to do with their copies. You may depend upon this, you must either bring a holiness and righteousness that the Lord cannot find fault with, or he is bound to send you to hell. If you cannot produce a holiness and righteousness that the Lord himself cannot find fault with, his very nature binds him to send you to eternal punishment. "The soul that sinneth, it shall die." As we have all awfully sinned, we need a salvation, and a great one, and such a one as no creature can produce.

If the Lord has taught you, and you take notice, you will see there are two tribes of professors in our day who appear quite different in their creed, but both unite in self. One party says, "We all need salvation, and all have it in our power to save our souls if we perform the conditions laid down;" and another party says, "There are no conditions. Salvation is full and free; without any conditions on our part. We have only simply to believe in Christ and the doctrines of the gospel, and we have no cause to be concerned about the misery and wretchedness of our corrupt nature, or about our sins, or to look for any special manifestations. We have simply to believe and receive the doctrines of grace and truth as in the Word, and we shall be happy." The truth is, the devil would rejoice in such happiness; for all you do will never disturb any of the powers of darkness. One party says, "Work;" the other, "Believe;" and both act from their selfish nature. But when the Lord brings his people experimentally to know they can neither work nor believe, they are brought to feel, before a heart-searching God, they have need of this great salvation.

"Say unto my soul, I am thy salvation." Justice must be satisfied, the law must be honoured, sin must be destroyed, Satan defeated, the world overcome, and God glorified, or the sinner cannot be saved. We pass on to notice,

II. What this salvation *couches in it*. There are two distinct branches in salvation. First, what it saves *from;* secondly, what it saves *to*.

Before I enter on this point, allow me to illustrate it thus. Suppose you knew one of the vilest of the vile in the town of Bedworth, one who had committed all manner of abomination till the whole town rang with it; he is taken up, sent to prison, tried, cast, and condemned; but, through some interest, the queen pardons him; he is set at liberty, and escapes the gallows; that would be in one sense salvation. But this is not half a salvation; because nobody would employ him. The whole neighbourhood thinks it a pity and a shame such a vile character should be let loose to be the terror of the place again. As nobody would like to see him, in all probability the poor creature must have recourse to his old practices of stealing, or he could not get bread. So this would not be half a salvation. But if the queen could prove, and did so, that he was one of the royal family, and was in her heart and affections, and sent her state carriage to fetch him from the prison to the palace; washed, clothed, adorned, and fed him; made it known he was to be in the palace as long as he lived, and commanded the nobles to honour him; and put such honour on him that he was arrayed in the royal robe, and the nobles proclaimed, "Thus shall it be done unto the man the queen delighteth to honour;" so not only lifts him from the dungeon and saves him from the gallows, but raises him to the highest honours, conferring upon him the greatest glory the nation can confer, this looks like a great salvation; so that the poor wretch would not be in the danger he was in before.* But the salvation of which I am about to speak, if the Lord will lead me on to declare it, you will see is infinitely more than even this. It takes a poor man from the dust, and a beggar from the dunghill. Depend upon it, "he raiseth up the poor out of the dust, and lifteth up the beggar from the dunghill, to set him among princes," the princes of God's people, and makes the man inherit the throne of glory. He takes him from the lowest state of degradation, and exalts him far beyond angels. The Lord does more for the sinner he saves than he has done for all the angels in heaven, put them all together. That sinner who is blessed with God's salvation in his heart has blessings vastly greater than the angels. They were predestinated to a holy state, and confirmed in it; but they were never redeemed. They know nothing about redemption for themselves. Here is a poor sinner, a beggar, a pauper, a lawbreaker, a God-dishonouring sinner, a hell-deserving sinner, redeemed, quickened, consecrated, and raised from his degrading state of guilt and filth, and raised to the highest state of declarative glory that the Lord can possibly raise a poor sinner to. What a salvation it is that accomplishes this! O! This is God's blessed salvation. It is a salvation that saves from *the guilt* of sin; the *damning power* of sin; the *curse* connected with it; the *reigning power* of it, the *love* of it, and at death the *inbeing* of it. It is a salvation completely from sin. What a salvation, then, this must be; for sin conquered all the world. O, this horrid monster, sin! We read of one great conqueror who conquered all the known world, yet never conquered the hearts and affections of the people; but sin has done this. There is not a man or woman under the sun who has not in some way given their hearts and affections to sin; embraced it and cleaved to it, so that they would be eternally lost before they would part with it, if

---

* This was a favourite figure of the preacher's. See preceding Sermon.

the Lord did not quicken their dead souls, and give them divine life. Such is the vileness of nature, the love of sin, that they would never part with it.

Well, this salvation of which I am about to speak is a complete salvation from that enemy who has conquered the whole universe and every human being. This is a complete salvation from that monster sin; so that where sin abounded, grace did much more abound. Hence the Lord Jesus Christ is said to have finished transgression, made an end of sin, and redeemed his people from all iniquity.

This salvation is not only a salvation from sin in all its bearings, but it is a salvation from the curse of the law. The law cannot curse the sinner that is saved, because he has become dead to the law by the body of Christ. What adds to the blessedness of this salvation is, that it is a salvation of manifestive union to the Son of God. Those who are killed to the law are married to Christ, and are manifestly one with Jesus; they are bone of his bone, body of his body, flesh of his flesh, and spirit of his spirit. Then what a glorious salvation that is which the Lord has accomplished for poor sinners.

I have often thought of what Paul says: "For when we were in the flesh, the motions of sin, which were by the law, did work in our members to bring forth fruit unto death." Have you not found it so? When in the flesh, working such abominable things, sometimes it has brought forth legal vows and promises; at other times working wrath and rebellion; so that in the end it brings forth fruit unto death. This is all that ever the law can do for a sinner. All its workings in a poor sinner's heart only make it fruitful unto death. But, being delivered from the law by the blessed body of the Lord Jesus Christ, we bring forth fruit unto God; we bring forth fruit unto holiness. Thus it is a salvation that raises a sinner from the most awful state of degradation and ruin to the blessed, solemn, glorious state of manifestive union to Christ; to oneness with him. They therefore bring forth fruit unto the praise and glory of his name.

This salvation is a salvation from death in all its bearings. "The wages of sin is death." This is a salvation from death. Say you, "Will not the Lord's people die? Shall we not all die?" I will tell you how it is. The Lord's people go to sleep; they sleep in Jesus. That is what the Holy Ghost declares: "They fall asleep in Jesus." Death to the child of God, who is saved by the grace of God, is no worse than a gentle nurse coming and rocking a peevish child to sleep. They are rocked asleep in the cradle of the love and blood of the Son of God. "They that sleep in Jesus will God bring with him." They shall be eventually raised from this sleep. It is a salvation *from* every appearance of death; a salvation *to* all the glorious appearances of divine life and love. This is the salvation the Lord accomplishes for his dear people. You know what the Lord says concerning this people with the rest of mankind, that they are all dead in trespasses and sins: "You hath he quickened, who were dead in trespasses and sins." Then, whether you know it or not, if the Lord has not quickened your soul, you are as dead to spirituality as a dead corpse in the grave; and it has as much power to come out of the grave and work as you have to quicken your own soul. This salvation is a salvation that brings quickening power, and makes the dead soul alive to God; brings the soul that was spiritually dead up into life in the Lord.

That soul that is made a partaker of this salvation is brought to cry, sigh, groan, pant, pray, and wrestle again and again, day by day, and will never rest till the Lord manifests to him Christ's salvation. There being living movements in all his ways, after the Lord makes him alive, he has living movements towards God. It is as that blessed portion of the Word of God says, "The Spirit maketh intercession for the saints according to the will of God." That poor soul in which the Lord has begun salvation,—at times he cannot talk; he cannot speak in prayer to the Lord. Perhaps some poor soul may be here to-night who is so bewildered, who is so confused, when he is on his knees he has not words to speak. "But," say you, "if he cannot speak, he should use the prayer book." You might as well count twenty. There is no prayer book that will touch your case, or come to the core of your disease. Now, mind what the Lord says. The Spirit helpeth the infirmities of the saints: "For we know not what we should pray for as we ought; but the Spirit itself maketh intercession for us with groanings that cannot be uttered." The Spirit maketh intercession according to the will of God. Is there a soul here groaning, sighing, and panting for the living God? There is the inditing of the Spirit of God in your soul. He has commenced his divine life, seating himself there; and you may rest assured of this, he will maintain the life he has commenced. This salvation brings peace to the conscience, and is a salvation from death to life. That poor soul is alive that is in such a state that he sighs and groans to God to have this salvation brought down to his conscience. Once there was a time when he had no desire to groan; he had set his eyes, his ears, and his heart on pleasure; when he took his fill of sin, saying, "What is it to anybody? We are to do as we like. Come, let us have another glass to drive and drink away sorrow." Many thousands drink away sorrow, till they drink themselves into the wrath of God in black despair. It is through the mercy of the Lord he does not leave you to say this.

When this salvation is made known and manifest, it leads the soul to plead with God; sometimes there is such a blessedness in it, the man feels such fellowship between God and his conscience, that he is led to follow the Lord from Bethlehem to the wilderness, from the wilderness to Gethsemane's garden, from the garden to the cross, from the cross to the grave, and from the grave to the right hand of

God, who has raised his people up together with Christ, and makes them sit together with Christ. Thus he raises the soul up to have holy converse with God. Thus he can plead with God as a man pleads with his friend. This is the nature of this salvation; it takes away his filth and gives him Christ's holiness. Christ is make to such a sinner sanctification. It takes away his unrighteousness, and gives him the righteousness of Christ. Christ is made of God unto him righteousness. He delivers him from all his foes, internal, infernal, and external. In the end, it raises him up to have intercourse with God in glory. He shall reign with him and Christ for ever and ever.

What a blessed salvation this is! Talk about doing our best, and the Lord will do his part, is all foolishness, mere lumber. When the Lord, in the riches of his grace, comes into the soul and raises the sinner up to God, and brings God and heaven down to the sinner, then God and heaven meet in the sinner's heart. Here is immortal glory not to be described by all the powers of men and angels.

"Say unto my soul, I am thy salvation." You sometimes talk about the glorious body of Christ. Did you ever give it a thought what is intended by the glorious body of Christ? See the Lord Jesus Christ travelling in the desert; we do not see his glory. I have often thought of one thing that eclipsed his glory, and an awful thing it was,—the sins of his people. They were all imputed to him and put upon him. If only yours and mine are so great, what must all the sins of God's people be? Do you wonder the people saw no beauty in him? It was no wonder when he was covered with such an awful garment as your sins and mine. There was one place where his solemn Majesty appeared in his glory. That was on the mount of transfiguration. Peter, and James, and John were with him, and said, "It is good to be here." Peter wanted to stop there for ever. Poor creature! He was for setting about building three tabernacles; but the Lord had better work for him to do.

This salvation our God has accomplished,—a salvation from death in all its bearings, and which shall issue in life in all its matchless glories. By this salvation he will raise the bodies of his people and fashion them like to the glorious body of Christ. Body and soul be together glorified with Christ.

III. *God himself*, in his Trinity of Persons, *is this salvation.*

It is said in Isa. xii., "Behold, God is my salvation. I will trust and not be afraid; for the Lord Jehovah is my strength and my song; he also is become my salvation." Our prayer is, "Say unto my soul, I am thy salvation." Had I strength and you patience, we might attempt to notice how the Three-One God, in all his glory, is our covenant God, is this salvation. However, as there is not time, a hint shall suffice. Let us hear what the Holy Ghost says upon the subject: "Who hath saved us, and called us with a holy calling, not according to our works, but according to his own purpose and

grace, which was given us in Christ Jesus before the world began."
You see he saves us before he calls us. How so? "By his eternal
purpose and grace, which was given us in Christ Jesus before the
world began." This is what God says about it. Therefore the
Holy Ghost, in another place, speaking on the subject, says, "Sanctified by God the Father;" that is, set apart by God the Father; and
where God the Father put them they are preserved in that state;
there Christ preserves them. "Preserved in Christ Jesus." God
the Father put them in Christ, and Christ never lost them. They
lost themselves in Adam the first, but were never lost in or by Christ.
They were secured where the Father put them; and where the Father
put them he preserved them; he preserved them in Christ Jesus,
and in God's own time they are called, quickened, and made alive
by God the Holy Ghost, who manifests this salvation. The Father
brought, predestinated, and gave them to Christ. Christ secured all
the new covenant blessings. In Christ their Head the Father has
secured all that shall make them holy and righteous: "The Lord
shall glorify the house of his glory." In speaking to the believer
the Lord says, "Thy God thy glory." What a blessed glory this
is, compared with our poor creature fleshly glory that we are sometimes so foolishly built upon, which is nothing but rags when we
have done; but when we are brought under the sweet and blessed
teaching of the Spirit, and can enter into the mystery of God being
our glory, we then know what this means: "Thy God thy glory"—
God glorifying the house of his glory. We are led in some blessed
measure to know something of this salvation proceeding from the
heart of a covenant God.

Now we may ask, what part has Christ in this salvation? Bless
his holy name, honours crown his brow for ever and ever! O my
soul, adore him! He stood in his people's law place, called their
sins his own, took their debt as his own, cancelled it by his blood,
groaned, and sweat, and bled, and died. "He died the just for the
unjust, to bring us to God." Can you think lightly of sin? Can
you call it a trifle, while it tore the heart of our dear Christ, and
horrified him? His soul was in an agony, so that he lay on the
earth, and cried out, "My soul is exceeding sorrowful, even unto
death." He drank into his holy soul the hell that his children must
have endured. Yea, he put out the flames of hell with his heart's
blood, that my soul might obtain eternal blessedness. Then adore
him, my soul, and bless his precious name! He obeyed the law in
all its jots and tittles; for God says, "Not one jot or tittle shall fail
till all be fulfilled."

You who imagine you can go to heaven by taking the law as your
rule of life, how will you do? You have not fulfilled even its *great*
commands, leaving alone its jots and tittles. When are they to be
fulfilled? They are all fulfilled by the Lawfulfiller; by the living

and dying of the God-man Mediator. Therefore, "he died for our offences, and rose again for our justification."

When the Lord the Spirit gives a poor sinner faith in his great work, this immortal work of the Lord Jesus Christ, he presents to God a perfect righteousness. Thus the apostle says, "Do we then make void the law, through faith? God forbid! Yea, we establish the law." Under the teaching of the blessed Spirit, we find the Lord Jesus magnified it, made it honourable, and brought in an ever-lasting righteousness. When the Lord the Spirit gives us faith to put on the Lord Jesus Christ, then we are swallowed up in Christ, and can appear before a heart-searching God without blame. Christ has completed, by his blessed obedience, dying, and rising, this sal-vation. He hath redeemed us from all iniquity. It is said, he hath redeemed us from destruction, redeemed us from death, redeemed us from the curse of the law and all iniquity. He hath put an end to sin, finished transgression, and by one offering he hath for ever perfected them who are sanctified, or set apart. Then, to close the business, he hath blessedly redeemed us from sin, redeemed us from our foes, redeemed us to God. This takes in the eternal world, and this redemption being eternal, it cannot be lost in time. Blessed be God for this salvation.

"Say unto my soul, I am thy salvation." Do you think the Lord Jesus Christ gave his life, his honour, and his blood for an uncer-tainty? Now, mind what he says: "The redeemed of the Lord shall come to Zion." It does not say they shall have a chance of coming, but, "The redeemed of the Lord *shall* come." Unbelief says they shall not, their carnal hearts and fleshly appetites say they cannot come at present; flesh wants a little more pleasure. But when the Lord's time comes, when "*Shall come*" gets hold of them, he con-quers them by his constraining power, and says they shall come. "The redeemed of the Lord *shall* come." When the Lord's "*Shall come*" gets hold of the conscience, it not only says, "They shall come," but assures the poor souls that "everlasting joy shall rest on their heads, and sorrow and sighing shall flee away." Thus our blessed Christ has accomplished this great salvation.

What hand hath the Spirit in this? Christ says, "He shall glorify me." The Lord Jesus Christ says to the Father, "And now, O Father, glorify thou me with the glory which I had with thee be-fore the world was." The Spirit takes his stand on Christ; Christ says, "He shall glorify me." How shall he do this? He takes of the things of Christ and shows them to the poor soul, those things revealed in the Bible. We are such poor blind creatures, we cannot see them till the Lord the Spirit reveals them to the conscience; but when he reveals them, we can see and feel them, and bless God for this rich salvation. As the Holy Ghost lays our hearts open, and the heart of the Lord Jesus being open, what a blessed thing when these two meet! Our heart loses nothing but sin, and the heart of Christ brings nothing but blood and love, which is sweetly brought into ours by the Spirit. So we see this is the way the Lord healeth us. Well may we say, "O say unto my soul, I am thy salvation." Thus the Spirit of the Lord commends the blessings of the gospel to the conscience, and brings us to feel a sweet measure of the love, life, and power of it in our hearts.

Do you know anything of this salvation? However, I must draw towards a conclusion, and

IV. Show the *effect* of a sinner being made to feel his *need* of this salvation. Every living soul made alive to God will be putting up this petition, and never rest satisfied without an answer: "Say unto my soul, I am thy salvation." If you can go on satisfied, and do not care what religion you have, saying you have many things pleasing to the flesh, many external duties, and much internal piety; or if, with your exalted notions of the doctrines of grace, you are satisfied with anything short of God himself speaking to your soul that he is your salvation, you are in the gall of bitterness and the bond of iniquity. I do not care what your religion is; let it be what it may, if you are satisfied without this, it is not the religion of the Son of God. Where the religion of the Son of God is, that soul wants the revelation of God's salvation. This will cause the soul to supplicate, "Say unto my soul, I am thy salvation." If the Lord does not at once manifest himself, the poor soul will not give up until the Lord does condescend to answer his prayer. He must have some sweet meltings down in his mind, some little liftings up with intimations of mercy, some droppings of his love, here and there a berry just to wet the mouth of the poor creature, and keep it from parching up, in order to keep it still sighing, groaning, and mourning. They cannot be satisfied, they cannot rest who have been quickened until they have the life and power of a salvation in their own hearts, by being able sweetly and feelingly to say, "God *is* my salvation." They must feel the Lord has graciously and blessedly given them that sweet and blessed power to feel in their souls that God is their salvation. "Cannot be satisfied?" say you. "Do you not think that persons who are decidedly pious, and do their duty, and never injure anybody, but love everybody, and do good to every-body; do you not think that they are right?" And perhaps some may say, "My minister says it is all enthusiasm to talk about this salvation being revealed to their conscience; all we have to do is simply to believe the Word, be decidedly pious, do our duty, and hope for the best." Now with all this, with all your decision, if this is all the religion you have, you will, so dying, be eternally lost, as sure as the Lord lives. You must have some better ground of a living power in your heart, and not rest short of God saying to your soul he is your salvation. Nothing short of this will do. You must be made to say, "As the hart panteth after the waterbrooks, so panteth my soul after God, the living God." If any here are resting on the delusive ground of their decided piety, there will be nothing but confusion, when the Lord, by a mighty earthquake, is pleased to come and shake you off your sandy foundations. If you have no better resting-place, you will sink into black despair. I do not mean to say there are none of God's children living but what have enjoyed this salvation. O no. But this they will do; they will sigh and cry, with heart breathings, moanings, and pantings, and will not be satisfied without it. They want the power of it in their own consciences. They want the Lord the Spirit to speak to their souls, so as that they can sweetly and blessedly say, "He loved me, and gave himself for me," vile *me*. Until this is the case they will not be satisfied.

Are you breathing and panting for this salvation, for this life, this power? If so, the Spirit of the Lord has brought you to it. Come, poor soul, go on. Give the Lord no rest until he make your soul a praise in the earth, until he bring his salvation and reveal it with power, and set your soul at rest from the bondage of despair, and bring you to enjoy solemn intercourse with the Three-One God.

V. What is the *effect* of the Lord *revealing* this salvation to the heart?

Some may say, "Would not a certainty of the revelation of this salvation make us negligent, and careless, and love sin?" Let us hear what the Lord says upon it. When he is speaking of the revelation of this, he says, "That thou mayest remember, and be confounded, and never open thy mouth any more, because of thy shame, when I am pacified towards thee, for all that thou hast done, saith the Lord God." When the Lord brings salvation to the heart, and causes the poor sinner to feel his love, the Lord fills him with a holy and blessed shame before God. He is ashamed, on account of his many sins, and he is ashamed that he has so base a heart; and he is lost in wonder at the wonderful love of God to him. The apostle says the grace of God teacheth us the denying of ungodliness, &c. And all you who are acquainted with it remember when you were in the gall of bitterness and the bond of iniquity. Has there not been a change wrought in you? Has not something taught you to deny ungodliness and worldly lusts, and to live soberly, righteously, and godly in this present evil world? This is what the grace of God leads us to. This grace brings humility, humility brings patience, and patience is to have a great deal of tribulation. I tell you how you will find it when the Lord reveals salvation to your heart, blessing you with the manifestation of it. You think you will never have any more sorrow, no more oozing up of sin, no more darkness, no more dismal feelings, no more conflicts within; and you sometimes act as if you wanted a sweet enjoyment of salvation, for the same purpose that a lady places a trinket upon her mantelpiece, to make a display of it. But that is not the purpose for which the Lord gives it to us. If he gives patience, it must be tried with tribulation; if he gives us faith, we shall have something for that faith to do; faith obtains the victory; but there can be no victory without a battle, and faith has many battles to fight,—battles with sin, battles with unbelief, battles with the world, battles with the man's own heart, battles with the devil in various ways. And when the Spirit gives us light, it is that we may see Christ as a Saviour, and long for his salvation.

When this salvation is revealed to the heart, it is proof against the devil and sin, pride, lust, and every abominable thing working in our vile nature. It overcomes every evil, to the honour of God and the glory of God. It shall show forth his glory. Sure I am it produces the most blessed effects; it sweetly calms the mind, produces peace, and purges the conscience from dead works. Is there a child of God in bondage, guilt, and pollution? Perhaps you will find him so peevish and wretched as not to converse with you; he cannot be pleasant with any one. And it is no wonder, seeing the numerous enemies he has to contend with. But when the Lord reveals this salvation to his conscience, it brings calmness, serenity, holiness, happiness. The man knows a little of this truth: "God, who commanded the light to shine out of darkness, hath shined into our hearts, to give the light of the knowledge of the glory of God in the face of Jesus Christ." This light, this knowledge of the glory of God, transforms the mind in some blessed measure. Then we walk in the light as he is in the light, the whole mind being under a gracious feeling and very blessed enjoyment of this salvation.

To conclude. What do you know of this salvation? The greater part of you are strangers to me; but you and I must meet God and be seen exactly as we are; and if we have not this salvation, what an awful meeting it will be! Nothing short of this can do. Any salvation that does not come to the core, and give us freedom from sin and death, will leave us to perish.

May the Lord lead you and me feelingly into the blessings of God's salvation, for his name and mercy's sake. Amen!

DOING THE WILL OF GOD, AND THE NEED OF PATIENCE.

Preached at Attleborough, Warwickshire, on Wednesday, June 15th, 1842.

"For ye have need of patience, that, after ye have done the will of God, ye might receive the promise."—HEB. x. 36.

As the Lord shall direct me, I shall endeavour,

I. To make a remark or two on *the promise*. There is one great object set before us—"the promise."

II. Endeavour to enter a little into the solemn business of "*doing the will of God.*"

III. Notice that we "*have need of patience,* that, after we have done the will of God, we might receive the promise."

I. *The promise.* What is this promise? It appears to my view to be couched in this text: "In hope of eternal life, which God, that cannot lie, promised before the world began." (Titus i. 2.) This, then, is the promise, "eternal life;" and every promise in Christ Jesus is Yea and Amen, and tends to the accomplishment of this one; yea, the whole are subservient to this one, to bring about, in God's time and way, this great special promise, "eternal life, which God, that cannot lie, promised before the world began." And herein the Lord secures, and will fully maintain and make manifest his own declarative glory.

When we speak of eternal life, we do not mean eternal existence only, because devils and damned spirits who are confined in the prison of hell have eternal existence. There must be something more couched in eternal life, agreeably to what the blessed Redeemer said, "I give unto them eternal life, and they shall never perish, neither shall any man pluck them out of my hands." (John x. 28.) "None shall pluck them out!" say you? "But they may pluck themselves out." My friends, if it were possible that Lucifer could feel shame, he would be ashamed of such a lie; because the Lord of life and glory says, "I give to them eternal life, and they shall never perish." Those men who assert the contrary, though they do not say in plain terms that the Lord Jesus has not spoken truth, yet they say it in reality. But notwithstanding all the exertions of men to deprive the Lord Jesus of one of his own dear children, his gracious Majesty has solemnly declared, "All that the Father giveth me shall come to me; and him that cometh to me I will in no wise cast out." (Jno. vi. 37.) "No," say you; "not if they prove obedient." That is not the text. The promise intimates nothing of the kind respecting obedience as the cause or reason why he will not cast them out. If they were all obedient at all times there would be no sense in the expression, "*in no wise;*" because the very words pre-suppose that they may be disobedient; yet for all that he will not cast them out.

I have sometimes thought that some children in youth were better hearers than many professors. I was once preaching in my own chapel, and made use of the following expression: "That disobedience did not alter the relationship; it merited the rod, and the Lord would be sure to visit with it; for he says, 'If my children forsake my law, and walk not in my judgments; if they break my statutes, and keep not my commandments; then will I visit their transgression with the rod, and their iniquity with stripes. Nevertheless, my loving-kindness will I not take from him, nor suffer my faithfulness to fail.'"

(Ps. lxxxix. 30–33.) To illustrate this, I said something of this sort:

Suppose you should send your boy to school, and tell him to be punctual in his attendance and to mind his books; but, instead of doing this, he plays truant and never goes near the school, what would you say? Why, you would get the rod and correct him. And suppose a neighbour were to come in and say, "Why are you correcting that boy?" you would say, "He has disobeyed me." If the person said, "Well; but in consequence of his disobedience, he is *not* your son; he was your son when he was obedient, but not now," would you not say, or be ready to think, the man was not sane,— that he had lost his senses? "Yea," you would reply; "he is my lad, and I will let him know it, and I will teach him to play truant;" so you would give him another stroke, as a proof that he *was* your son, being determined to maintain your authority as a father, which is for his own good; yet your affection and kindness were still the same towards him, notwithstanding all that he had done. So it is with our God. Now one of my grandsons, only six or seven years of age, had been hearing me; and when the service was over and he was at home, he burst into tears, and said, "My grandfather had no occasion to expose me before all the people. If I did play truant, I don't mean to do it again." Thus, you see, he was in that sense a feeling hearer, which is more than many are who profess to know the gospel of our Lord Jesus Christ. But to return to our subject.

"Eternal life." This life we have in his Son: "For ye are dead, and your life is hid with Christ in God. When Christ, who is our life, shall appear, then shall ye also appear with him in glory." (Col. iii. 3, 4.) Matchless, unparalleled grace, that vile sinners like us should be raised to dwell with the Lord Jesus in glory; yea, and be made like him, and dwell with him for ever! For the blessed Redeemer has said, "Because I live, ye shall live also;" "I am the resurrection and the life; he that believeth in me, though he were dead, yet shall he live; and whosoever liveth and believeth in me shall never die." This eternal life is secured in the life of Christ, in the Person of the dear Redeemer. This is what God promised. All the promises that are in Christ Jesus tend to the accomplishment of this one. Some persons say that all the promises in the Bible are Yea and Amen in Christ. Not so. There are many promises in the Bible which are conditional, and were given to the Jews as a nation. If they obeyed the Lord, and walked according to his commands, they were to have divers blessings; if, on the contrary, they disobeyed his commands, the curses pronounced against them for their disobedience were to come upon them. These are not the promises that are "Yea and Amen;" neither are the law promises, "Do this, and live." This is a conditional promise. "Leave undone, and die." "But," say you, "does not the text say *all the*

promises are Yea and Amen in Christ Jesus?" It does not say so.
"Then," say you, "what does it say?" It says, "For all the promises of God in him are Yea, and in him Amen, unto the glory of
God by us." That is, those promises which God has made in Christ,
as Head of his church; all that are in him as Head of the church
are in him Yea, and in him Amen; there is God's solemn Amen to
them; they will be honoured with the divine manifestations of Jehovah, when the world is in a blaze.

When the promise was made to Christ, as Head, it was also made
to the members of his mystical body, that they may stand firm when
time shall be no more. "My mercy will I keep for him for evermore, and my covenant shall stand fast with him. His seed also
will I make to endure for ever, and his throne as the days of heaven."
(Ps. lxxxix. 28, 29.) And again: "Yet it pleased the Lord to bruise
him; he hath put him to grief; when thou shall make his soul an
offering for sin, he shall see his seed, he shall prolong his days, and
the pleasure of the Lord shall prosper in his hand." (Isa. liii. 10.)
In order to make manifest the blessedness of the promise, God condescends to seal it with an oath: "Wherein God, willing more abundantly to show unto the heirs of promise the immutability of his
counsel, confirmed it by an oath; that by two immutable things, in
which it was impossible for God to lie, we might have strong consolation, who have fled for refuge to lay hold upon the hope set
before us." (Heb. vi. 17, 18.) The immutable promise and immutable oath, taken on his own Nature, that we might have strong consolation! What a condescending God is ours! He blessed us in
Christ before the world was. As it is written: "Blessed be the God
and Father of our Lord Jesus Christ, who hath blessed us with all
spiritual blessings in heavenly places in Christ; according as he hath
chosen us in him before the foundation of the world, that we should
be holy and without blame before him in love." (Eph. i. 3, 4.) Yet,
such fools are we, that, at times, we cannot believe God's word. Our
unbelief makes us stagger at the promise of God, and we are ready
to conclude that it is not possible that such vile sinners as we should
be interested in blessings so great; therefore, the Lord condescends
to give us his oath; yet, such poor wretches are we, that there are
times of darkness, when unbelief and carnal reason appear to prevail so much that we cannot believe, for ourselves, either the promise or the oath of the Lord. Who beside the Lord would bear
with such wretches? But such is his matchless grace that, though
we believe not, yet God abideth faithful; he will not deny himself,
but accomplish his word, his promise, and oath, and bring his children to enjoy immortal blessedness in eternal life.

Let us look at some few things couched in "eternal life." Eternal
life is ineffable holiness, not a life of sin, but a life of immortal holiness. Here God has promised his people life in the world to come,

to be holy as Christ is holy. That is a sweet text, and it has, at times, refreshed and comforted my poor conscience when labouring in bondage, distress, and death: "Beloved, now are we the sons of God; and it doth not yet appear what we shall be; but we know that when he shall appear we shall be like him, for we shall see him as he is." It is against reason to believe that such poor, weak, helpless, sinful, polluted, despicable creatures shall be like the Son of God; yet the Lord says it shall be so, and that when he appears we shall be like him, and see him as he is. This is couched in eternal life; this is what is promised; even this mortal body is to be changed, and fashioned like unto his glorious body.

If you want to have a glimpse of the glorious body of Christ, you will not see it in his walk upon earth, when he went about doing good, when in the Garden sweating blood, or on the cross on Calvary's mount. O, no. It did not appear there; it was eclipsed by the awful sins of the church; therefore he appeared stricken, smitten, and afflicted; as a root out of a dry ground, there appeared no form or comeliness in him; and well there might not, when all the sins of the church were laid upon him: "The Lord laid upon him the iniquity of us all." If you have a feeling sense of only your own sins, they will make you stagger and tremble. Then look at the millions of sins of those whom the Lord saves, all being placed to the account of and laid on the Lord Jesus Christ, and you will never wonder at his appearing stricken and smitten; you will never be astonished at it. Therefore, when bearing this weight, we do not see him in his glory. But if we want to see his glorious body, we must have a spiritual view of him upon the mount with Moses and Elias. As it is written: "And after six days Jesus taketh Peter, James, and John his brother, and bringeth them up into a high mountain apart, and was transfigured before them; and his face did shine as the sun, and his raiment was white as the light." (Matt. xvii. 1, 2.) Well, beloved, ye that are brought from necessity to trust in the Lord, remember that the church of the living God are to have a body like unto his glorious body, shining as the sun, and appearing as glorious as Christ appeared on the mount of transfiguration. This is the blessed promise that God has made to us before the world was.

When our immortal spirits are quickened and made alive, God forms his image in our souls. This is done while here below. As it is written: "Seeing that you have put off the old man with his deeds, and have put on the new man, which is renewed in knowledge after the image of him that created him." (Col. iii. 9, 10.) And again: "For we are his workmanship, created in Christ Jesus unto good works, which God hath before ordained that we should walk in them." (Eph. ii. 10.) And when the Lord is pleased to shine upon his own glorious work, we, in vital faith and feeling, can trace a measure of the beauty of the Lord upon and in us. As it is written: "For God, who commanded the light to shine out of darkness, hath shined into our hearts, to give the light of the knowledge of the glory of God in the face of Jesus Christ." (2 Cor. iv. 6.) And again: "Arise, shine; for thy light is come, and the glory of the Lord is risen upon thee." (Isa. lx. 1.) But at the glorious resurrection, our body shall be made like unto the body of the Lord Jesus: "Who shall change our vile body, that it may be fashioned like unto his glorious body, according to the working whereby he is able even to subdue all things unto himself." (Phil. iii. 21.) Then soul and body will be perfect in Christ. In a word, the church, every believer, will be entirely swallowed up in God's Christ, and will have a view in glory of the rich displays of God's Christ; all shall be like him, and be entirely swallowed up in the bliss and blessedness of their Lord and Redeemer.

I observe, further, another branch of the promise is uninterrupted intercourse with God the Father, God the Son, and God the Holy Ghost. How it will be I cannot tell; but I believe in my soul that I shall see and converse with the Trinity in the Godhead, in the Person of the Redeemer, who is the mighty God. Say you, "So *you* believe?" I do. "But," say you, "have you anything in Scripture to confirm and prove this?" Yes. Let us glance at one or two passages. When poor Stephen was stoned to death for the truth of the gospel of the blessed God, whilst they were stoning him, he, being full of the Holy Ghost, saw the heavens opened, and beheld the glory of God, and Jesus standing on the right hand of God. "But he, being full of the Holy Ghost, looked up steadfastly into heaven, and saw the glory of God, and Jesus standing on the right hand of God, and said, Behold, I see the heavens opened, and the Son of Man standing on the right hand of God." (Acts vii. 55, 56.) When he was thus filled with the Holy Ghost, he saw distinctly the Father and the Son, and he appears to have had a solemn feeling and glorious view of a Three-One covenant God. Suppose, also, we look at what John saw. He says he saw one sitting on a throne, with a book in his hand, "written within, and on the backside, sealed with seven seals;" and the proclamation went forth, "Who is worthy to open the book, and loose the seals thereof? And no man in heaven nor on earth, neither under the earth, was able to open the book, neither to look thereon." No man—now mind; if there be anyone here who denies the Godhead of Christ—*no man* under heaven or in heaven was found worthy to open the book. John wept when he saw this was the case; and "one of the elders said unto him, Weep not; behold the Lion of the tribe of Judah, the Root of David, hath prevailed to open the book, and to loose the seven seals thereof. And he beheld, and, lo, in the midst of the throne and of the four beasts, and in the midst of the elders, stood a Lamb as it had been slain, having seven horns and seven eyes, which are the seven Spirits

of God sent forth into all the earth. And he came and took the book
out of the right hand of him that sat upon the throne." (Rev. v. 1,
10.)   Jesus took the book out of the right hand of Him that sat upon
the throne.   Stephen was full of the Holy Ghost, and saw the Father
and the Son, and John saw the Father and the Lamb, which is the
Son, the great Redeemer of the church, and he saw him with all the
fulness of the glorious Spirit (Rev. vi.); and at the baptism of Christ,
when the Son, in our nature, was baptized, the heavens were opened,
and the Spirit of God descended like a dove, and lighted upon Christ;
and the Father was heard to say, "This is my beloved Son, in whom
I am well pleased." (Matt. iii. 16, 17.)   And again: "That which
we have seen and heard declare we unto you, that ye also may have
fellowship with us; and truly our fellowship is with the Father, and
with his Son Jesus Christ." (1 John i. 3.)   These and such like portions of God's Word confirm in my mind the blessed truth that the
church of Christ will have a sight of the rich displays that God will
make of himself through Christ the Redeemer; and that I, being
interested in this promise of eternal life, shall have personal intercourse with the Three-One Jehovah; that I shall hold uninterrupted
converse with the Father, Son, and blessed Spirit for ever and ever.
This is the promise of bliss and blessedness which the Lord has given
to the church.

This eternal life will be free from all the power of sin and Satan.
Poor child of God, you will feel no more pride, no more wretchedness, no more carnal reason, no unbelief nor tempting devil, no
grumbling through want; there will be an end to that, and to all
your murmuring, fretting, and repining; all will be divine holiness,
bliss, and blessedness, and God will be all in all.   This is the life
God secured in his Son—eternal life promised to us, promised before
the world began.   It was not a conditional promise, but an absolute,
unconditional promise.   Paul, when speaking of this state, says,
"Not by works of righteousness which we have done."   "No," say
some; "we admit it is not *for* our works, but *according to* our works."
If it be as you declare, the Lord would (I speak it with reverence)
tell an untruth; which is a thing impossible.   "Why," say you, "this
is bold language."   It is, and I like to speak boldly, because, if I
mince the matter, there, perhaps, will be no more attention paid to
it; but if I bring it honestly and roughly forth, you will, perhaps,
begin to think about it.   "Then," say you, "how do you prove
it?"   By the following text: "Who hath saved us, and called us with
a holy calling, *not according to our works.*"   This is God's own word.
"Not according to our works," say you?   "What is it then?"   "But
according to his own purpose and grace, which was given us in Christ
Jesus before the world began." (2 Tim. i. 9.)   This is the life given
us in Christ Jesus.   Christ is the glory of this life.   This is the promise, "eternal life," and this promise was made to us before the

world began. "For ye have need of patience, that after ye have done the will of God, ye might receive the promise."

A few more storms, poor child of God, a few more temptations, a few more suggestions of Satan, a few more upsettings, inside and outside, a few more crosses and tosses respecting outward and inward circumstances, a few more unbelieving fits, a few more heart-rending groans and soul-tormenting pangs, and the storm will be over. But while in this dismal world, the child of God, at times, has such unbelieving fits, and such tremendous struggles under them, that all the men in the world cannot restrain them so as to make them still and quiet. But a few more of these, and eternal life will open in majesty and glory to our view, and we shall be blessedly baptized into the glory of Christ, and enter into that bliss and blessedness where all is light, life, love, and glory, and God is all and in all, and never, never more go out. This is the promise God has given to us in Christ, and it is secured to all the family of God by Christ, and by all that is dear to a Three-One God and safe to us.

II. I shall now endeavour to enter a little into the solemn business of *doing the will of God.*

1. What it is to do the will of God *solemnly and secretly* betwixt God and the conscience.

2. What it is to do the will of God *practically,* as becometh the saints of the Most High.

3. What it is to do the will of God *sufferingly,* by enduring what God is pleased to permit to come upon us.

1. What it is to do the will of God *secretly* betwixt God and the conscience. All vital religion begins here. Vital godliness has not its beginning in external parade, in great pomp, bustle, or show. No. Vital godliness springs from the secret manifestation of God to the conscience and of the conscience to God, brought about by the invincible energy of the Holy Spirit between God and conscience. Only those who have been there know anything about it. You may have a deal of external rounds, go on very zealously for weeks, months, and years, and be lost at last, if you have not vital godliness—that godliness which stands in the life which God reveals in the soul. This is doing the will of God betwixt God and conscience. God says, "If we confess our sins, he is faithful and just to forgive our sins, and to cleanse us from all unrighteousness." (1 Jno. i. 9.)

One of the first things God does manifestively is to quicken our souls, and then reveal to the soul the purity of his law, and by it the evil nature of sin. Not as some say, "Let us see; we are but sinners." It is a common thing for people to say, "You are but a sinner, and Jesus came to save sinners." But when God brings a man feelingly and experimentally, between God and his conscience, to know what he is, he cannot find a place in his conscience for the term "but a sinner." He finds himself so wretched, such a guilty creature before a heart-searching God, that he is obliged to confess, "We are all as an unclean thing;" and "We all do fade as a leaf; and our iniquities, like the wind, have taken us away." (Isa. lxiv. 6.) Yea, here he is, groaning, sighing, and moaning before God, confessing his vileness, pollution, and emptiness of all good, and he is ready to think the Lord will condemn him from his own mouth. When he tells God what a vile abominable wretch he is, sometimes the enemy tells him he is condemned, and by his own confession he proves it, and says, "You know you are obliged to confess that you are vile, polluted, and wretched, and God's holy law is against you in all its bearings; and you have sinned both against holiness, justice, goodness, and mercy. You are one of the vilest sinners living, and there is no hope for you." This staggers and confounds him; but he feels that it is true, and is obliged to confess it before the Lord. This confessing of sin, under a feeling sense of his vileness, is one branch of doing the will of God. Though the poor child of God is ready to conclude that there is no hope, no mercy for him, yet he feels the need of the mercy of God, but fears that it will never be bestowed upon him. Why, poor sinner, this is the very character God has mercy for; the very character to whom God will manifest himself and bring to know that mercy is fit for him, and he fit for mercy. Nothing under heaven suits so well; nothing fits so well as God's Christ and a guilty sinner. When the blessed Spirit brings Christ to the conscience of a guilty sinner, heaven cannot make a better match; he is just what the sinner wants; he just suits the sinner's condition. Herein God is glorified, and the sinner justly and blessedly saved; and all the honours of God are herein secured in the poor sinner's salvation, bliss, and blessedness. And thus to be brought by the power of God the Spirit to a feeling, spiritual acknowledgment of this blessed truth, is one branch of doing the will of God.

But another branch of doing the will of God, in connection with confessing our sin, is to feel and confess that we cannot help ourselves; that we feel so completely ruined that we are without might or power; so that if we perish we must perish, for there is no help in us. Perhaps some one will say, "That will never do; for I think any man may help himself, if he will but set about it." Have you, under a deep feeling of your guilty condition, ever in reality tried? If you have not, you are not a competent judge. The Lord says, "They that are in the flesh cannot please God." (Rom. viii. 8.) And again: "Without me ye can do nothing." (Jno. xv. 5.) And when the Lord quickens his people to feel their lost condition, they will feelingly know a measure of what Paul says, "For I was alive without the law once; but when the commandment came, sin revived, and I died. And the commandment, which was ordained to life, I found to be unto death; for sin, taking occasion by the commandment, deceived me, and by it slew me." (Rom. vii. 9–11.) And when a sinner is slaughtered by the law, all his fleshly props give way, and he feels the force of that solemn truth, "Thou hast destroyed thyself;" nor dare he at present say, "My help is in the Lord." Indeed, if he could obtain all the holiness there is now or ever was in the world since Adam's fall, separate from Christ, it would not save him. "What!" say you; "not if he could get all sin out of his heart, and get holiness in, will not that save him?" No; if he has not a better religion than that, he must perish, with all his supposed holiness; for, separate from Christ, there is not holiness enough in the world to save one sinner. "Why," say you, "that is quite outrageous; you are rather worse than I expected. I thought that half the holiness in the world would have been enough to save me." Have you not sinned already? What is to become of your old sins? There is the old score against you, and "he that offends in one point is guilty of all." And again: "Cursed is every one that continueth not in all things which are written in the book of the law to do them." (Gal. iii. 10.) If you think you could get holiness to do away with the old score, you had better set off to Italy. You would be a fit subject for that quarter, where they sell and purchase holiness. But if you go on that ground you will find yourself mistaken.

Then, doing the will of God is to acknowledge that what God says is true, that there is no health nor help in us, that we are not sufficient of ourselves to do anything of ourselves, but that our sufficiency is of God. It is doing the will of God to know we are not sufficient to pray as we ought; as says the Word of God: "Likewise the Spirit also helpeth our infirmities; for we know not what we should pray for as we ought." "For what man knoweth the things of a man, save the spirit of man which is in him? Even so the things of God knoweth no man, but the Spirit of God." "The Spirit of God maketh intercession for the saints, according to the will of God." How does he do this? Even sometimes "with groanings that cannot be uttered." In those very groanings that cannot be uttered the Spirit helps the child of God, according to the will of God. Therefore, poor soul, thou who art spiritually groaning and sighing, thou art doing the will of God. Between God and thy own conscience, the Spirit of the living God helpeth thy infirmities with those groanings that cannot be uttered. The poor child of God is so straitened, at times, that he cannot pray straight forward in prayer, as he has heard some. He has heard them pray at a wonderful rate; but he is such a poor, tried, cast-down creature, he thinks he cannot pray at all, and his attempts to make a prayer often manifest his foolishness and put him to shame, though sometimes a tempting devil and the evil of his heart will prompt him to try. When I lived in this village, many years ago, I used on the Lord's day to go to Coventry, to the meeting. I used to go to the prayer-meeting at seven o'clock in the morning. They very frequently asked me to pray. I felt myself so wretched, such a poor shut-up creature, that I dared not to venture. One morning I set off pretty early to Coventry, and as soon as I left the village I began to make a prayer. O the cursed pride of my fleshly mind! I thought what a pretty prayer I had made; that if they called upon me I should be ready; and when I got there they did call upon me. I attempted; but, alas! All my prayer was gone; all went to ruin. I can compare myself to nothing else than a man attempting to rob an orchard,—jump, jump; but the boughs were too high for him. All went to ruin, and there was I left alone; the Lord would not allow me to come in this way.* Here was I, then, sighing and groaning for mercy; crying to the Lord to be made humble before him. I was entreating his gracious Majesty to appear, and he did in his own time; but not in my way. The only acceptable prayer to God is what the Spirit pours into the soul, with which he prompts the soul; so that the soul, under his blessed influence, pours it out to God. Such prayers are acceptable to God. They are presented in brokenness of spirit and deep humility. This is doing the will of God.

Do you know anything what it is to groan for mercy, to sigh under a sense of your sinfulness, your inability to help your own soul, and feel a spiritual thirsting for God? If you do, you know what it is to do the will of God. If you do not know this, the Lord has not yet taught you to see and feel your own ruin; and whatever external "piety" you imagine you have, it is but self-deception, if you in any measure trust in it.

Another branch of doing the will of God *is to have a hope*—a hope that goes out as an anchor into Christ. You find yourself so helpless that you cannot manage your own affairs. You cannot bring yourself to the Lord. You can do nothing to help yourself. But at last God is pleased to say to you, "Hope thou in God;" and then you feel a secret going out of your soul, and a hanging on Christ. You are afraid the Lord will not hear your cry, and yet you cannot help leaning on him, and hoping in his mercy. This is hope going out as an anchor. Though you do not know whether it will grasp the rock or not, still hope goes out and brings a little tenderness in feeling and a little melting down in conscience before a heart-searching God. This, poor soul, is doing the will of God. "Why," says some poor sinner, "I think I can go with you here, though I am afraid I never have been doing the will of God in all my life." Come, poor soul, if you can feelingly say this, if God the Spirit has brought you here, depend upon it you will never perish.

Another branch of doing the will of God is *internally believing on the Lord Jesus Christ*. On the subject of faith I differ very materially from some men. I believe a child of God may have the full

* Mr. G. had 7 miles to walk, and used to say his prayer was 7 miles long.

assurance of faith in some branches of divine truth, and yet, at the
same time, believe he has not one grain of faith.   Say you, "Please
to explain yourself, for that appears to be a knotty point?"   The
Word of God shall give the explanation.   It says, "Faith is the substance of things hoped for, the evidence of things not seen."   We
will take the last clause, "the evidence of things not seen," things
which reason and common sense, with all their boasted powers, can
neither see nor comprehend.   Faith is God's evidence in the heart
of the reality of them.   How is it with a poor sinner when the Word
of God is brought home to his conscience?   It declares what a vile
wretch he is; he feels it, and that there is not such another wretch
in all the world.   There is not a man in all the world, with all the
powers of common sense, who can ever enter into the heinous evils,
the dreadful plague of sin in his heart. He may go a little outside; but
he cannot come to the core; he may believe God's law is holy, just,
and good, and try to keep it; but there is not a man in the world
can come into the real purity of God's holy law in its own intrinsic
holiness, with all the powers of reason, with all the faculties of his
carnal mind.   When God gives faith in our own impurity, impiety,
guilt, filth, and pollution, and the holiness of his law, we have
an evidence in our hearts of these things, and all the men in the
world cannot put it out.   We have then the testimony that God is
just, and righteous, and holy, and good; and were any man to say
that we were not so vile, he could not make us believe it.   You feel
that God is holy, and that you are "carnal, sold under sin;" that
"the law is spiritual;" that "the commandment is exceeding broad."
The sinner has the full assurance of faith in these things; but it is
not that branch of truth which brings peace to the conscience.   As
far as you go, you believe and feel assured of these things; and thus
you may be in real possession of the full assurance of faith in some
branches of divine truth, yet not have faith enough to believe that you
have a grain of faith.

By and by the Lord brings you to have *faith in Christ;* and this
is another branch of the work.   Faith is God's gift and favour.
You may believe in the Lord Jesus as a Saviour, a holy Saviour, a
complete Saviour, and as a Saviour suited to your need; this may be
sweet to you and bring a little hope in your conscience that, perhaps,
he may save you.   Many a child of God acknowledges that Christ
Jesus is a perfect Saviour, and they look on some of God's people
and say, "He is *your* Saviour;" "He is *their* Saviour;" but still they
are behind as to one word; that is, "*my* Saviour."   They cannot
get at *that;* and there the poor creature is; he cannot get to say,
"He is *my* Saviour."   This is what he wants to feel.   But he is
doing the will of God, by vital faith, when he is honouring the Saviour according to God's Word, being led to to see that "he is able
to save to the uttermost," that he is a complete Saviour, and that

there is neither salvation nor redemption in any other.   This is what the poor sinner believes; but he cannot say, "He is *my* Saviour." He splutters, and stammers, and longs to say, "My Lord and my God," but cannot, dare not.   But, perhaps, some of you will ask, "Why can he not do so?"   He is like a child that longs to speak plainly, but cannot.   He needs the blessed power of the Spirit to reveal salvation to his own conscience, give him faith in it for himself, and bless him with the enjoyment of the following portions of God's Word: "And the eyes of them that see shall not be dim, and the ears of them that hear shall hearken.   The heart also of the rash shall understand knowledge, and the tongue of the stammerers shall be ready to speak plainly." (Isa. xxxii. 3, 4.)   And again: "Strengthen ye the weak hands, and confirm the feeble knees.   Say to them that are of a fearful heart, Be strong, fear not; behold, your God will come with vengeance, even God with a recompense; he will come and save you.   Then the eyes of the blind shall be opened, and the ears of the deaf shall be unstopped.   Then shall the lame man leap as a hart, and the tongue of the dumb sing; for in the wilderness shall waters break out, and streams in the desert." (Isa. xxxv. 3–6.)   It is as much the power of God to bring a soul to have an appropriating faith, to say, "The Lord is my God," as to create a world.   As the apostle says, when speaking of faith, "And what is the exceeding greatness of his power to usward who believe, *according to the working of his mighty power.*"

But by and by the Lord will bring the poor soul to experience the reality of this truth: "I will bring the third part through the fire." Here you see the Lord divides the world into three parts: Two parts he cuts off—the merely professing part and the profane part, and the third part God means to save.   But by what road does he take them?   He brings them through the fire; and however they may shrink back, through the fire they must go.   The high-road to heaven is through the fire.   God has determined to try every man's work by fire.   Hear what he says.   Faith is to be tried by fire.   Their wood, hay, and stubble shall be burned, yet the man himself shall be saved as by fire: "I will bring the third part through the fire; and the Lord will say, It is my people, and they shall say, The Lord is my God."

What a solemn thing is doing the will of God, when the Lord brings faith into spiritual exercise, so that the soul can appropriate the Lord to himself.   If you are brought here, poor soul, to have God enjoyed in your conscience, whether in a dungeon, at the stake, or shut up in a room, be where you may or be doing whatever you may, your soul will burst forth in sweet breathings after him, saying, "My Jesus, thy love surpasseth knowledge; it is beyond all comprehension. He loved me; redeemed me; he saved me. O that he ever should have brought such blessings of salvation to me, to worthless *me!* That he should have redeemed me! That he should glorify me! O call on all the powers of my soul to bless and praise his name! O that I could adore him for ths sweet wonders of his salvation, which he has so blessedly and powerfully wrought in my soul!" This is doing the will of God. "Whoso offereth praise glorifieth me; and to him that ordereth his conversation aright will I show the salvation of God." Blessed is the soul that is in such a state.

Do you know anything of doing the will of God? Perhaps some one may answer, "I am as dutiful as most people." I am not saying that you are not; but this I tell you, vital religion begins betwixt God and conscience. "The kingdom of God is within" his called people. This kingdom is set up by God himself, by whose power Satan is dethroned in your conscience. When the Lord sets up his kingdom in your heart, he maintains it. If this has not been done to you, your religion is worth nothing; it will never stand the test when the Lord winds up the business. When God the Spirit, in the riches of his grace, takes a sinner in hand, he brings him spiritually to know what it is to have the kingdom of heaven set up in the soul. This is a secret work betwixt God and conscience. "For ye have need of patience, that, after ye have done the will of God ye might receive the promise."

2. There is a doing the will of God *practically*, as becometh the saints of the Most High. Some men tell us the doctrines of the gospel lead to licentiousness. We do know some professing the doctrines of the gospel who lead licentious lives; but how many do you know who oppose the doctrines of the gospel who lead licentious lives? Search the world through, and you will find fifty to one. I recollect, some time ago, when on this subject, a minister accused me of preaching licentious doctrines, because a man in London had acted a very licentious part. I did not know the man, though he professed the same doctrines as I did. "That shows," said the person who accused me, "what sort of doctrines yours are." I replied, "Sir, do you know Doctor — ? He, you are aware, has a D.D., and he is exactly a man of your kidney. Now, the very crime you have been charging on the other, of which he was only suspected, your man *was* guilty of. What led *him* into the commission of it? You know the doctor was obliged to leave the country." He replied that it was not his doctrine which led him to such things. This, my friends, is the blindness of their understanding, and shows the enmity of their hearts against God's discriminating truth. In reality, it wants no doctrine to lead a man to licentiousness; we are so by nature. So far from the truths of the gospel of the Lord Jesus Christ leading to licentiousness, whenever God, by his Divine power, convinces a man of his sinful state by nature, of the *secret* doing the will of God betwixt God and his own soul, it will bring forth the *practical* doing of the will of God.

There is no real proof of vital godliness where there is not, in some good measure, a life and conversation becoming the gospel! I have been a witness of a few hints from the pulpit, when carried by the Lord to the conscience, producing practical effects, even where the preacher had not the most distant thought of the matter; one of which I will state. When my children were small, and my income not quite so much as it is now, we were likely to have to pay £20 for one of the boys' schooling, and my wife said to me, "What are we to do for the money? Where is it to come from?" I said the Lord would appear, no doubt. "There it is," said she. "You have all the faith, while I have all the work." The next Tuesday night I preached from these words: "Lead us not into temptation." I was led to make the following remark: "Perhaps there may be some of you who have been tempted to do things for your own private emolument, or that which appears to be connected with it, thinking that by doing such things you would save so much money, and nobody would know. It was of such a secret nature that no mortal living knew anything of the transaction; so that there could be no discovery, nor could it bring any scandal upon the cause of God and truth, because no one could know. But, said I, the Lord knows, and he can bring the rod upon you." Part of my congregation fell under it, and confessed their sin before God, and that brought forth a practical doing the will of God. One of them came to me the next morning, and said, "Sir, when my wife's father was dying, he wished my wife's mother to give £5 to the poor; and that is not all, he also desired her to give you £20." I felt surprised; and he continued, "Sir, do you remember preaching last night from the words, 'Lead us not into temptation,' and what you said respecting what might be done in secret when there was profit connected with it?" I said, Yes. "Well," he said, "that has brought the £20." When God brings us to fall before his word, and to do the will of God in secret between God and conscience, that brings also the practical doing of it. That gave these persons the will to part with the £20. "Ah!" say you, "that pleased you." Yes, it did, my friends, because I greatly needed it at the time.

I have found the word of the ever-blessed Lord the Spirit graciously blessed to my soul; and have had a feeling sense of his mercy, kindness, love, and grace wrought in my heart. When this has been the case, not only with me but every child of God, it makes us practice holiness, and fear the Lord: "For the grace of God that bringeth salvation hath appeared to all men, teaching us" (and the Lord knows we all need it) "that, denying ungodliness and worldly lusts, we should live soberly, righteously, and godly in this present world." (Tit. ii. 11, 12.) Wherever the grace of God comes with divine power, there the poor soul is brought feelingly to do the will of God; and this will lead him to do it practically. Where there is a vital union to Christ, and Christ dwells in the heart the hope of glory, there will be a bringing forth of fruit. As it is written: "I am the Vine, ye are the branches. He that abideth in me, and I in him, the same bringeth forth much fruit; for without me ye can do nothing." (Jno. xv. 5.) The spiritual mind is led feelingly to say, "Lord, what wilt thou have me to do?" A real living child of God, in his right mind, does not want to shun practical obedience; no, nor to shun the cross. He wishes to live and act as a debtor to sovereign grace and show forth the praises of the Lord: "But ye are a chosen generation, a royal priesthood, a holy nation, a peculiar people, that ye should show forth the praises of him who hath called you out of darkness into his marvellous light."

We will just notice a few things which the grace of God will lead a man to do. According to the station he fills in life, he will be concerned to act as becometh that station. Is he a husband? He will love his wife and be concerned to nourish and cherish her. Can a man who professes religion hate his wife, forsake and condemn his wife, or abandon his wife? That is not the religion of Jesus Christ, but of the devil. The religion of Christ teaches a man to love his wife: "Husbands, love your wives, as Christ loved the church and gave himself for it." He goes on to say, "No man ever yet hated his own flesh, but nourisheth and cherisheth it, even as the Lord the church." This is doing the will of God. Also to the wife: "Wives, submit yourselves unto your own husbands as unto the Lord;" not gadding about, going up and down your neighbourhood, so that when the husband comes from his labour he finds nothing prepared for his meal. The wife who does the will of God will be concerned to make her husband comfortable, as far as lies in her power. Those gossiping women who gad about the country, canting about religion instead of minding their domestic concerns, give no proof of vital godliness. I would hurl their religion to Tophet; I would have nothing to do with it; it is not the religion of the Son of God. Wherever that religion comes with power to the heart, it regulates the conscience first, and the conduct afterwards. Whether they are wives or husbands, they will, in some measure, act in conformity to the will of God. Thus they do the will of God practically. If a parent, he will be concerned for his children's welfare. If a child, he will honour his parents. If a master, he will act with kindness towards his servant, giving unto him that which is just and right. If a servant, he will serve his master faithfully, in the fear of God.

If a minister, he will not set himself up in pride, and make himself a little pope, causing the people to bow at his feet; but he will let it be seen and known, by his conduct, that he is concerned for the welfare of the people and the honour of God. He will feed the flock of God, which he hath purchased with his own blood. If he be faithful, let him speak the word faithfully. If really a minister of the Lord Jesus Christ, he will be concerned to deal out God's truth, though he may offend some rich folks. If a minister says, "I know it won't do to preach such truths as those, or I shall offend that 'pious' lady, or such a 'pious' gentleman, and they give a large sum to the cause." If this is the case, such a minister acts a base part, and gives proof that he would rather offend God than these "pious" people, as he calls them. But what says the Lord? "I charge thee, therefore, before God, and the Lord Jesus Christ, who shall judge the quick and the dead at his appearing and his kingdom; preach the word; be instant in season, out of season; reprove, rebuke, exhort with all long-suffering and doctrine. For the time will come when they will not endure sound doctrine; but after their own lusts shall they heap to themselves teachers, having itching ears; and they shall turn away their ears from the truth, and shall be turned unto fables." (2 Tim. iv. 1–4.) This is a solemn charge, and it becomes God's ministers to attend to it in the fear of the Lord, looking to him for wisdom, and grace, and strength to enable them to act according to it. And again it is written: "The prophet that hath a dream, let him tell a dream; and he that hath my word, let him speak my word faithfully. What is the chaff to the wheat? saith the Lord." (Jer. xxiii. 28.) Such as know the fear of God will be concerned to do the will of God. As faithful ministers of the Lord Jesus, they will preach the Word, both in season and out of season. The hearers, if they are really doing the will of God secretly and feelingly before God, they will, when the minister stands forth, at times and seasons, lay their hearts open to the rebuke of the minister, and thank God for the rebuke.

Others there are who fill different offices. Whether deacons or private members they ought not to set themselves up in pride, but to act in their station that they shall be concerned to practise in the fear of the Lord what he hath enjoined upon them. "Blessed are they that hear the word of God, and keep it." (Lu. xi. 28.) Yes, the adorable Redeemer says, "If ye love me, keep my commandments." (Jno. xiv. 15.) And again: "Ye are my friends, if ye do whatsoever I command you." (Jno. xv. 14.) It is a poor look out when those who profess to love the Lord Jesus Christ endeavour to excuse themselves from obeying the Lord, because this or the other command is not essential to salvation. It is the spirit of presumptuous free-will and Antinomianism with a witness: "For this is the love of God, that we keep his commandments." (1 Jno. v. 3.)

3. There is a doing the will of God *sufferingly*. God's people have to endure hardness, as good soldiers of Jesus Christ. (2 Tim. ii. 3.) They must not expect a life of ease here; for they are strangers and pilgrims; but they must expect the dogs to bark at them, and sometimes to worry them; but they cannot devour them. It may be that they will, for conscience towards God, have to endure

grief, suffering wrongfully (1 Pet. ii. 19); and it becomes them patiently to endure; for "that is acceptable with God." (Ver. 20.) Therefore, to be patient in tribulation is doing the will of God. It is through much tribulation we are to enter into the kingdom of God; and whatever our fleshly feelings may say, Infinite Wisdom sees there is, at times, a needs-be that we should be in heaviness through manifold temptations. (1 Pet. i. 6.) Temptations, trials, and distresses of various sorts, from various quarters, must be the lot of the people of God; but the manifold wisdom of God will overrule them all for his own glory and their good. (Eph. iii. 10–16; Rom. viii. 28.) We may and do, at times, stagger at our trials, and think it strange that we should have to bear such things, forgetting that unto us it is given in the behalf of Christ, not only to believe on him, but also to suffer for his sake. (Phil. i. 29.) But the Lord, by Peter, says, "Beloved, think it not strange concerning the fiery trial which is to try you, as though some strange thing happened unto you; but rejoice, inasmuch as ye are partakers of Christ's sufferings, that, when his glory shall be revealed, ye may be glad also with exceeding joy. If ye be reproached for the name of Christ, happy are ye; for the spirit of glory and of God resteth upon you; on their part he is evil spoken of, but on your part he is glorified." (1 Pet. iv. 12, 14.) So that trials of various sorts we must expect. And sometimes our trials will evidently appear to come from the Lord himself; for the Lord trieth the righteous, to withdraw man from his purpose, and hide pride from man. His gracious Majesty knows well what we need, and when and which way will be the best to lay his rod upon us. But his chastenings are all in mercy, and we are doing the will of God when, under the teachings of the blessed Spirit, we patiently endure them. And in the end they will prove blessings: "For whom the Lord loveth he chasteneth, and he scourgeth every son whom he receiveth. If ye endure chastening, God dealeth with you as with sons; for what son is he whom the father chasteneth not? But if ye be without chastisement, whereof all are partakers, then are ye bastards, and not sons. Furthermore we have had fathers of our flesh which corrected us, and we gave them reverence; shall we not much rather be in subjection unto the Father of spirits, and live? For they verily for a few days chastened us after their own pleasure; but he for our profit, that we might be partakers of his holiness. Now no chastening for the present seemeth to be joyous, but grievous; nevertheless afterward it yieldeth the peaceable fruit of righteousness unto them which are exercised thereby." (Heb. xii. 6–11.) Many of the precious promises of the gospel suppose troubles and conflicts. As it is written: "When thou passest through the waters, I will be with thee; and through the rivers, they shall not overflow thee; when thou walkest through the fire, thou shalt not be burned; neither shall the flame kindle upon thee. For I am the Lord thy God, the Holy One of Israel, thy Saviour. I gave Egypt for thy ransom, Ethiopia and Seba for thee." (Isa. xliii. 2, 3.) We must have both watery trials and fiery trials, and both go into and through them, in order to enjoy the presence of the Lord therein, and to enter feelingly and spiritually into the blessedness of this promise. And thus we shall find many of the exceeding great and precious promises of God connected with great troubles, and sometimes exceedingly great troubles; but when, like Moses, we are enabled to choose rather to suffer affliction with the people of God than to enjoy the pleasures of sin for a season, we are doing the will of God; for this is one branch of the work of faith. (Heb. xi. 24–26.)

In connection with our text the apostle speaks of the believing Hebrews enduring a great fight of afflictions. Paul experienced fightings without and fears within (2 Cor. vii. 5); and David was no stranger to them. As it is written: "Be merciful unto me, O God! for man would swallow me up. He, fighting daily, oppresseth me. Mine enemies would daily swallow me up; for they be many that fight against me, O thou Most High! What time I am afraid, I will trust in thee. In God I will praise his Word; in God I have put my trust; I will not fear what flesh can do unto me. Every day they wrest my words; all their thoughts are against me for evil." (Ps. lvi. 1–5.) Both Paul and David found the Lord to be their comfort in their affliction.

But we now proceed,

III. To notice, that, in doing the will of God, we have *need of patience;* and if, under the teachings of the blessed Spirit, we are enabled to act faithfully, there will be abundance of trying circumstances which will call for patience. We shall have trials from the world, from Satan, from our own hearts, and from the direct hand of the Lord himself; yet it becomes the people of God to be daily concerned to do the will of God. Some of the people of God have been called upon by the Lord himself to do things very trying to nature and staggering to reason. The Lord promised Abraham a son by Sarah his wife; but before the promised son was born, reason seemed entirely out of patience, and free-will began to work very powerfully both in Sarah and Abraham. This led them to act very wrong, and they both smarted for it. Their free-will and impatience led them to try to hasten God's promise; and a pretty job they made of it. They brought misery and confusion into the family. Sarah must give Abraham her servant Hagar, and she brought forth a son, which caused much confusion. This was not doing the will of God, but doing their own will; they had not patience to wait the Lord's will. But, notwithstanding their impatience and folly, the Lord was graciously pleased to renew his promise, and bring forth the beloved Isaac. I dare say both Abraham and Sarah were very fond of the lad, and watched his growth with all the fond affection of parents, thinking, no doubt, what a comfort he would be to them in their old age. But the Lord came and called Abraham; and Abraham said, "Behold, here I am. And he said, Take now thy son, thine only son Isaac, whom thou lovest, and get thee into the land of Moriah; and offer him there for a burnt offering upon one of the mountains which I will tell thee of." What would nature say to this, think you? "O that can never be, Lord, What! Offer Isaac, after having had so much trouble about him, both before and since his birth! Isaac, who came in such a manifestive way of mercy! What! Cut his throat! Light a fire under *him!* Offer *him* to God for a burnt-offering! O no, Lord; not so. It is contrary to nature; it is contrary to thy law, which says, 'Thou shalt do no murder.' I can never attempt any such thing." Here nature would shrink! But the Lord brought patience into exercise, and said, "Abraham, go." He went, and believed in his soul that God would raise Isaac again from the dead. So Abraham went to offer up his son, and he did it intentionally. I have often thought how blessedly the Lord wrought with Isaac; for when they got near the hill, the lad said, "Father, here is the wood and the fire, but where is the lamb for a burnt-offering?" Perhaps he had some forebodings in his mind that he was to be offered up. Now he was a strong, lusty lad, and if the Lord had not made him willing, when his father bound him to the altar, he would have resisted, and endeavoured to make his escape. But the Lord so ordered it, in the riches of his grace and mercy, that Isaac should be willing. His father had taken the knife, and was just about giving the fatal stroke, when the Lord called to him, and told him to withhold his hand. Don't you think he had need of patience in doing that part of the will of God? If we search the Word of God, we shall find, in a variety of instances, God calls on his people to do his will in such a way and under such circumstances that it tries all the powers and faculties of nature; they have to give up all to the will of God. The Lord has promised to help them in trouble, and they will find him faithful to his promise.

In doing the will of God *sufferingly*, do not we need patience? We do the will of God sufferingly when we endure the contradiction of sinners against ourselves. If you read the next chapter to the one out of which the text is taken, you will see what a long list of God's saints there is, and what they had to endure and bear. They wandered about in sheepskins and goatskins; they were sawn asunder and put to cruel deaths; they were destitute of homes, and had no place in which they could lay their heads. They, being followers of Christ, endured affliction. I have often heard it said, "Such a minister is respectable; he has a respectable congregation." What does that savour of but human merit and pride? If you want to see a list of God's respectables, read Hebrews xi., and there you will see a wonderful list: "They were stoned, they were sawn asunder, were tempted, were slain with the sword; they wandered about in sheepskins and goatskins; being destitute, afflicted, tormented.'' What should we say to them in our day, if they called at the door of some of the good folks clothed in their sheepskins? They would shut the door upon them. These very characters were doing the will of God sufferingly: ''Of whom the world was not worthy. They wandered in deserts, and in mountains, and in dens and in caves of the earth.'' Mind what God says in his Word: ''If any man will live godly (mind!) in Christ Jesus, he *shall* suffer persecution.'' A man may live what he calls a godly life; he may go on with external religion, with an outward show of godliness, and so pass for a very good man; but let a man be brought to live godly in Christ, to trace all his religion up to Christ, to say and feel none but Christ, to have no religion but what comes from Christ, to maintain that that religion only is right which is between Christ and conscience, and that all other godliness is nothing worth; let a man come here, and he will suffer persecution; he will be sure to suffer if he will live godly in Christ Jesus. When this is the case, we are doing the will of God sufferingly, enduring the contradiction of sinners.

If we are made willing to submit to the will of God, we shall, in a variety of instances, see that there is need of patience. I have heard it said that Martin Luther made the following remark: ''At times I have need of patience with myself; I have need of patience with my church; I have need of patience with my wife Kate; and I have need of patience with my God. My conflicts, troubles, and sorrows are such that I need to have patience with God.'' ''Why,'' say you, ''that is outrageous. Surely we can be patient with God.'' When God's hand has gone out, and takes away a right eye—something that is very near and dear to us, as dear as a right eye, which we have been idolizing, and God says, ''Cut it off, pluck it out,''— I say, when this is the case, we are like Lot: ''O Lord, is it not a little one? Spare it.'' But God takes our right eyes, and cuts off our right hands; so that our trials make us ready to cry out with one of old, ''The hand of God has gone out against me;'' and it is at these seasons that we have need of patience to endure the will of God. Say you, ''Can you find any of the Lord's people in the Word of God who ever exhibited peevishness against God?'' Yes. One told God that he did well to be angry, even unto death; and another said, ''O that he would let loose his hand and cut me off!'' I will venture to say that some of the trials you have had in your families, some of your right eyes and right arms, some of the conflicts and trials which you have had within and without, in which you have experienced great darkness, have caused you to say, ''Surely the Lord hath hedged up my way with thorns; he hath broken my teeth with gravel stones; he hath covered me with ashes. Surely against me is he turned; he turneth his hand against me all

the day. Yea, all seems completely against me." But when the
Lord the Spirit comes into your conscience and shows you what you
are and where you are, you cry out, "Lord, I have need of patience.
Lord, give me patience." So you find that you need patience with
God in his dispensations. It is very blessed when we are enabled
to act and say with David, "I waited patiently for the Lord, and he
inclined unto me, and heard my cry. He brought me up also out
of a horrible pit, out of the miry clay, and set my feet upon a rock,
and established my goings. And he hath put a new song in my
mouth, even praise unto our God. Many shall see it, and fear, and
shall trust in the Lord." (Ps. xl, 1–3.) "For ye have need of patience, that, after ye have done the will of God, ye might receive
the promise."

I have often admired a hymn of good John Berridge's, the following words from which have been frequently applicable to me:

> "For patience when I raised a cry,
> Fresh burdens made me roar;
> My foolish heart would then reply,
> 'For patience pray no more.'"

But at length the Lord brings us forth from this tribulation, and
this tribulation worketh patience. I tell my people that this is the
Lord's grand piece of machinery, and it fits vastly well. The apostle
says, "Being justified, by faith we have peace with God, through
our Lord Jesus Christ. By whom also we have access by faith into
this grace wherein we stand, and rejoice in hope of the glory of God;
and not only so, but we glory in tribulations also, knowing that tribulation worketh patience, and patience experience, and experience
hope, and hope maketh not ashamed." Here tribulation drops into
patience, turns that round, and patience drops into experience, and
experience produces hope, and hope, being exercised, makes us not
ashamed. Here is the grand piece of machinery, well put together
by the God of heaven. First tribulation, then patience, after patience experience, and then hope; all these things work confidence.
Now in all this the machine wants some power to turn it. It will
not move, never do any execution without power. "True," say
you; "but what power does it want to make this grand machine,
tribulation, patience, experience, and hope all to work together?"
The Word of God shall tell you: "And hope maketh not ashamed,
because the love of God is shed abroad in our hearts by the Holy
Ghost which is given unto us." Here is the *power*,—the love of
God. When this is shed abroad in the heart by the Holy Ghost,
the machine runs well, works well, and brings glory to God. Even
in tribulation the Lord blesses us with patience. We have need of
patience in all these things. Tribulation worketh patience in a two-
fold way; for if the Lord sends patience he always finds patience
something to do.

Some men are of a naturally quiet, calm, easy temper, and they may talk about possessing patience; but the men who know anything about the need of patience, in a spiritual sense, are those who find everything within go wrong, who find all their schemes upset and crossed, and almost upset themselves. We meet with so much from men and devils that we always find patience something to do. But sometimes we seem to roar like a bear, and we act in such a manner that we are ready to conclude we have not a particle of patience left, and we are obliged to cry out for help, saying, "O Lord, help me! My patience is all gone." By and by the Lord is pleased to produce patience, and we are led to see that God has delivered, that he does deliver, and we trust also that he will deliver. Thus, he works patience, and patience is brought forth into sweet act and exercise: "For ye have need of patience, that, after ye have done the will of God, ye might receive the promise." The Lord comes and cuts off our right arms, and takes away our right eyes, in order to keep us from some horrible crime, some mischief into which we should fall that we are not aware of. There is a needs-be for all that the Lord brings upon us: "In all their affliction he was afflicted, and the angel of his presence saved them. In his love and in his pity he redeemed them; and he bare them and carried them all the days of old." You never were in one trouble, cross, trial, or perplexity *alone*, since the Son of God revealed himself to you, and you never will be. Whether you see him or not, he is there. When we pass through the waters he is with us, and he has promised in his Word, "When thou walkest through the fire, thou shalt not be burned; neither shall the flame kindle upon thee." His blessed Majesty has promised to hold you up with the right hand of his righteousness. See what patience Moses needed. He was raised up of God to be very useful, to be the deliverer of Israel. He believed it many a long year before the Lord called him to the work. I have often admired the dispensation of God to Moses. He believed God had raised him up to deliver Israel. He was a very strong man, and, when he saw the Egyptian smiting the Israelite, he thought the time was come for him to deliver Israel, for both the time and place seemed favourable; but the time had not come. Moses must have a little more patience. The Lord sent him forty years to college in the desert, to qualify him for bringing the people from Egypt. The Lord was teaching him to be humble and meek; and after he had been forty years in the wilderness he did not run so zealously; for he said, "O Lord, send by whom thou wilt send. I am not eloquent. I am slow of speech." There was not a word about this forty years before. Now that the Lord had been qualifying him for the work, he shrinks back, and does not like to go; but the Lord had determined to bring him forth. Moses had need of patience before the Lord made known his truth to him and brought him forth to lead his people through the desert. So we find in every instance that we need patience in doing the will of God.

Moses esteemed the reproach of Christ greater riches than all the treasures of Egypt. If the Lord has blessed your soul, you will esteem the reproach of Christ greater riches than all the treasures of Egypt. What an honour, what a glory is the very reproach of Christ! It is greater than all the treasures of the world. You see how God exercises the patience of his people. Sometimes he works in such a blessed way that we are made willing to suffer reproach, to be set at nought, to be contemned, to be held up to ridicule, to be anything, to suffer all things, and to bear the cross; and thus the Lord blesses us with patience, and we are enabled to say, "The will of the Lord be done." But the family of God will need daily supplies from the Fountain-head. Moses, with all his faith and the wonderful dealings of the Lord with him found that he needed patience in doing the will of God in leading Israel through the wilderness. He found it hard work to endure the murmurings, insults, and contradictions of the people, and he cried unto the Lord, saying, "What shall I do unto this people? They be almost ready to stone me" (Exod. xvii. 4); and though the Lord appeared so blessedly conspicuous, and brought forth water out of the rock,—a sweet and blessed type of the water of life that flows through a once-smitten Christ to poor parched-up sinners; I say, although this was the case, when they wanted water again, and the people chode with Moses, and the Lord said to Moses, "Take the rod, and gather thou the assembly together, thou, and Aaron thy brother, and speak ye unto the rock before their eyes; and it shall give forth his water, and thou shalt bring forth to them water out of the rock; so thou shalt give the congregation and their beasts drink" (Num. xx. 8); Moses does not appear to be over-burdened either with faith or patience; for when he had gathered the congregation together before the rock, instead of speaking to the rock, as the Lord commanded him, he spoke to the people, and that not in a very patient way either, and said, "Hear now, ye rebels; must we fetch you water out of this rock? And with his rod he smote the rock twice." (xx. 10, 11.) Had faith and patience been in sweet exercise, this swelling free-will "*we*" would never have fallen from his lips. This *we* and its connections kept him out of the land of Canaan." (Num. xx. 12; Deut. xxxii. 51, 52.) Indeed, Moses needed patience, and he smarted for his peevishness and unbelief. God's ways are sometimes very mysterious; and we need both faith and patience to wait upon him, and act according to his revealed will.

It was a strange way that the Lord took to raise Joseph next to the throne of Egypt, for the purpose of preserving Israel in time of famine, and to keep them in Egypt till the time appointed for their deliverance. And do you not think that poor Joseph needed patience in all the sharp trials he had to endure?

In a word, if we are led to examine the dealings of God with his people, as revealed in his Word, we shall find that in every age they have been a tried people, and have needed patience to endure and do the will of God with solemn submission. David, Daniel, Shadrach, Meshach, and Abednego, the various prophets and apostles, and the thousands who have suffered in and for the cause of the Lord Jesus Christ, all had need of patience.

God grant that we may be enabled to let patience have its perfect work, and in all things act as becometh the gospel of Christ. But mind, the promise is sure. What a mercy is that! Though we have unbelieving fits, the promise is fixed on the verity of God, and secured in the life of Christ. Thou shalt find, poor tried, tempted child of God, whatever trouble thou art in, that God's promise is sure, that eternal life is sure.

May God Almighty bless you and me with a feeling sense of his faithfulness, and enable us to cleave close to himself; for his name and mercy's sake. Amen.

SANCTIFICATION IN CHRIST.

Preached in Gower Street Chapel, London, on Lord's Day Morning, May 9th, 1841.

"Sanctified in Christ Jesus."—1 Cor. i. 2.

I HAVE no doubt that in this assembly, in some corner or other, there are some poor, hobbling souls who are terrified almost to death about the doctrine of sanctification. They read, in the book of God's Word, of the Spirit as a Sanctifier; but *they* are necessarily obliged to exclaim, "Lord, I am vile!" Sometimes we say respecting people's credit, "Why, it is wrought quite threadbare." Bless you, in some poor souls there is not a thread left to be made bare. If God the Spirit has brought you there, you will have indeed to exclaim, "Lord, I am vile!" But when God opens to them the mystery of divine sanctification, he will make them know that they are "sanctified in Christ Jesus." Who? The poor, the vile, the loathsome, and the base.

Perhaps there may be in this assembly a poor, helpless soul, who has come mourning, sighing, groaning, and has not power to trust in the Lord, has not power to believe. "O!" say some; "the Word says, 'All things are possible to him that believeth.' It is only the simple act of belief; and if a man has power to believe, 'All things are possible to him that believeth.'" But man has no power to believe. God has brought me to feel so much as this,— that if my salvation depended upon my doing this, that, or the other,

I should be damned as sure as the devil is; and I have been brought to feel that if faith believes, it must be God's work, for he must act it and he must do it.

In my late affliction there is one portion in God's Word which struck me. Afflictions always yield the "peaceable fruits of right-eousness to those that are exercised thereby;" and I believe the Lord opened the marrow of it to my soul in these words: "*To those that are exercised thereby.*" Some have affliction, and they are not exercised in it. They are like a man who puts on a soldier's dress, and just merely swings his sword a little, and marches but a few steps, and then lays it aside; but this will not make him a soldier, for a man before he is a soldier needs to be exercised again and again, and again. So it is with those who are in affliction and are not exercised. Does the affliction exercise? No; nor does the putting on of the dress make the man a soldier, but the exercising of him. And so it is with the soul in the affliction. As the Lord exercises them in the affliction, so will it yield the peaceable fruits of righteousness. If the Lord the Spirit does not exercise them at all, all they know is a little prating religion; but when the Lord the Spirit brings the word of truth home to the conscience, they will then know a little of being sanctified in Christ Jesus.

There are a few branches here which we will look into, as the Lord shall enable us; and if Christ is not the whole and sole of your religion, you know not much of sanctification. All the movements flow from Christ: "For it is the Spirit that worketh in us both to will and to do;" we have not so much as a will. Hence it is said, "Work out your own salvation with fear and trembling; for it is God which worketh in you both to will and to do of his good plea-sure." All real sanctification comes from Christ. He is the Spring-Head; he is the Treasury. "Of his fulness all we receive." And when the Lord the Spirit leads a man to receive out of Christ, he will have something worth having; but if it be of self, it will work confusion. What a matchless purity there is in Christ!

In my late affliction a person said to me, "Why do you not pray to the Lord?" And the Lord was pleased to open this text to my mind: "No man can come to me, except the Father which hath sent me draw him."

When God is about to sanctify a poor sinner, he unbinds every-thing of man's goodness; he breaks down every prop. Sometimes he will let them build up again; but he will unbind it again and again. I compare him to a man who is living in a poor tumble-down building, whose foundation has long been tottering, and which is ready to fall about his ears; and yet the poor man clings to it, till at length it gets so bad that he is compelled to leave it; and, as Berridge says,

> "Out I ran naked,
> And crept to the Rock."

Then God appears for us, and brings us to know something of being saved in the Lord with an everlasting salvation.

We will notice three things:

I. We are sanctified by God the Father, in *perfect council*, from before the foundation of the world.

II. Sanctified by the *bloodshedding of the Redeemer*. I know not what term to give it, but I will call it *meritorious* sanctification, by the blood of Christ.

III. *Manifestive* sanctification, by the communication and operation of God the Holy Ghost.

I. We are sanctified in *perfect council*, by God the Father, before the foundation of the world. Hence Jude says, "Sanctified by God the Father, preserved in Christ Jesus, and called." And upon this ground the Holy Ghost says, "Who hath saved us and called us with a holy calling." How? "Not according to our works." How then? "But according to his own purpose and grace, given us in Christ Jesus before the world began."

Perhaps I shall differ from some of you when I say innocent Adam had not the new covenant blessings.* In his primeval state he was created in the pure image of God. But he had nothing to do with the new covenant blessings; for the new covenant blessings were wrapped up and locked up in the heart of Christ Jesus. Hence, says the apostle, "Blessed be the God and Father of our Lord Jesus Christ, who hath blessed us with all spiritual blessings in heavenly places in Christ Jesus." So these new covenant blessings were wrapped up in the heart of Christ Jesus. And as the Immortal Treasury, they were locked up in him before the foundation of the world.

I know one thing which I have proved, that God builds up his church with some of the worst of materials, some of the vilest of the vile. No man can manage them, for they are fit for nothing but rubbish. And yet they are "sanctified in Christ Jesus." And I will tell you another thing. In Peter's vision, he saw a great sheet, "knit at the four corners, and let down to the earth, wherein were all manner of four-footed beasts of the earth, and wild beasts, and creeping things, and fowls of the air; and there came a voice to him, Rise, Peter; kill and eat! But Peter said, Not so, Lord; for I have never eaten anything that is common or unclean. And the voice spake unto him again the second time. What God hath cleansed that call not thou common." This was done thrice; and the vessel was received up again into heaven. There was no manifestive cleansing at that time, or else Peter would have seen it. What Peter was led to see in that vision was—in that vessel were wrapped up Jew and Gentile; for this vessel was a type of Christ

---

* As the new covenant blessings were for sinners, Adam could not experience them while he was innocent.

Jesus. The blessed Redeemer came to finish the work of redemption; as it is said, "He that sanctifieth, and they who are sanctified, are all of one;" one in family, having one Father; and, blessed be God, they can never be made two; for "what God hath joined together let no man put asunder." "He that sanctifieth, and they who are sanctified, are all of one." Hence, says the Redeemer, "For their sakes I sanctify myself, that they may be sanctified through the truth. Sanctify them through thy truth; thy Word is truth." He sanctified them through suffering.

II. He sanctified them *meritoriously*. He magnified the law and made it honourable. Some talk about a chance of being saved. In this day there is a great deal of talk about Jesus Christ, and giving all a chance. But our blessed Lord Christ, in his finished work, only bore the church's sins in his own body on the tree. He was made sin for them, not practically, but by solemn transfer. When he stood as our Surety at the bar of Pilate, and when upon the cross, all the sins of the church were laid upon him. All the sins of all whom God would save were transferred to Christ. They were brought before him as a debt, and he has discharged that debt, and has a receipt in full, that justice is satisfied, the law magnified and made honourable, God well pleased, and the whole elect saved in himself with an everlasting salvation. I tell you what; a conditional salvation will not do for me. That Christ has done his part and I must do mine will not do; for in everything I do I find sin working in some corner or other. Suppose you have the most solemn breathings with God in prayer, and you feel it blessed, you will not be above a minute or two before something of this arises in the mind: "This is something like religion—this will do;" and you are filled with pride; but, mark! Nothing can satisfy God but the pure work of Christ. That they might be sanctified, he suffered without the gate. "Sanctified in Christ Jesus."

III. They are *manifestively sanctified* by the communication and operations of God the Holy Ghost. Hence, our Lord says, "He shall take of mine and show them unto you. When he is come he shall reprove the world of sin, of righteousness, and of judgment. Of sin, because they believe not in me." Now it appears to me that this will never be discharged till the people of God are taken home. Suppose we look at one thing: "My God shall supply all my need according to his riches in glory by Christ Jesus." Do you believe this? Do you believe Christ here, that he will supply all your needs? If you believe, why all this murmuring that you have at times? You murmur at the Lord, and say, "O that he would supply my needs! O that he would let me know that I was a child of God!" And all the time God is working in his way, and fitting in one thing after another.

Now the Lord says, "All things shall work together for good to them that love God, to them who are the called according to his purpose;" and yet we are such unbelieving creatures that we cannot believe that all things shall work together for our good. There is one, perhaps, here this morning who, with all his toiling, seems as if he is going to ruin. He has some "ifs," and "buts," and "hows," disputing the promise that "all things shall work together for good." "O," say some; "why don't you see? Why don't you believe?" But it is difficult to see through a dark cloud; and we never shall believe all the time there is so much murmuring. But when the Lord the Spirit enables us, then we shall believe that "all things shall work together for good," and all the way through the wilderness. He convinces us of sin, because we believe not in Christ. Before I met with my "accident," I got into what some people call a melancholy fit; I got into such a state of wretchedness. I was thinking that I was getting old, that I should be a burden to my children who were about me, that my children would forsake me, and the church stand aloof from me. While I was filling my mind with this lumber, it pleased the Lord that my leg should be broken, and he laid me on a sick bed; but all my foes were put to the flight; for all my children came around me, and my friends came to sympathize with me so often that I was obliged to tell them I could not see them so often. The best of all was, the Lord appeared to me in this text: "I will never leave thee nor forsake thee;" and, as we say in Lancashire sometimes, I was struck all of a heap, and was filled as full of mercy as I was of lumber before.

God says he will put us in the furnace; and when the Lord the Spirit begins to burn up the hay and stubble, we think we are going to ruin. But, while it will burn the rubbish, it will leave Christ and the conscience; and then we shall know something of manifestive sanctification,—manifestively united to Christ, our living Head.

When the Lord gives life, we begin to feel; when he gives light, we begin to see; and as soon as we feel and see we feel our pollution, our wretchedness, our misery; and we conclude, instead of being a sanctified vessel, we feel we are truly wretched. But I tell you that you are a child of God. I know you won't believe me, nor do I wish you to do without a better evidence than mine; but God will make you by and by, and you will bless him for having been made so wretched.

Some of God's children have starved their body almost to death to cure the corruption of the heart; but the devil will never be starved to death. I remember reading of one,—I think it was good John Berridge, who stripped himself naked and flogged himself; but it was to no purpose. So

"Out he ran naked and fled to a Rock."

And I tell you what, there never will be, there never can be, a particle of creature work or merit in sanctification. Nothing will do but the finished work of Christ.   The hope must go of any betterness in self before we have any manifestive hope in Christ.   When the Lord is pleased to bring manifestive sanctification into your conscience, you will know something of being drawn by the cords of a man, and with the bands of love.   When your vows fail, when your promises fail, and all seems to fail, then you will know something of being sanctified in Christ Jesus and that there is no holiness but in and from him.

"Well," says some poor soul, "I can go with you as far as you have gone."   Well; by and by God will appear and give you divine faith to realize this; for "faith is the substance of things hoped for, the evidence of things not seen."   You may look at the command and you may look at sin externally, but you will not be enabled to look at the core till faith is given; and by and by the blessed Spirit will give you a faith's view of the atonement of Christ, a hope in God.   "Ah," says some poor soul.   "I should like a hope in God; for I can find nothing in man worth hoping for."   Here is the blessing of communicative sanctification; till by and by, it may be a long time, the Lord, in the riches of his grace, will communicate more of manifestive sanctification, perhaps from such a text as this: "For God, who commanded the light to shine out of darkness, hath shined into our hearts, to give the light of the knowledge of the glory of God in the face of Jesus Christ."   Paul says, "He loved me and gave himself for me."   Faith believes it; for every particle of spiritual life, every particle of spiritual feeling, every particle of spiritual love, every particle of spiritual faith, which purifies the heart, every particle of intercourse we have with the Three-One Jehovah; every lifting up that we have by the way, all comes from Christ, and endears us to him. "Sanctified in Christ Jesus."   Here is a cup of blessedness for all who are brought to feel that their sanctification is in Christ Jesus.

May the Lord guide us, preserve us, direct us, and bless us.   Amen.

FRAGMENTS OF SERMONS.

BY MR. W. GADSBY.

"GATHER UP THE FRAGMENTS THAT REMAIN, THAT NOTHING BE LOST."—JNO. VI. 12.

THE WHEELS IN EZEKIEL.

Preached in Manchester, March 22nd, 1840.

The following is from MS. *It is evidently, like all the following, fragmentary.*

"Now, as I beheld the living creatures, behold one wheel upon the earth by the living creatures, with his four faces. The appearance of the wheels and their work was like unto the colour of a beryl; and they four had one likeness; and their appearance and their work was, as it were, a wheel in the middle of a wheel; when they went, they went upon their four sides; and they turned not when they went. As for their rings, they were so high that they were dreadful; and their rings were full of eyes round about them four. And when the living creatures went, the wheels went by them; and when the living creatures were lifted up from the earth, the wheels were lifted up. Whithersover the Spirit was to go, they went; thither was their Spirit to go; and the wheels were lifted up over against them, for the Spirit of the living creature was in the wheels."—EZEK. I. 15-20.

You may, perhaps, say I am about to go beyond my depth. No man can truly preach God's Word unless the Spirit of God reveal it to him. I have long struggled with this passage, which now, I trust, God has been pleased to cast a ray of light upon; and as the Spirit of God shall enable me, I will boldly speak of the mystery therein. The solemn and divine mystery of the Holy Ghost is couched in these figures, which are confirmed in Ezekiel x. 10: "And as for their appearances, they four had one likeness, as if a wheel had been in the midst of a wheel." Some fleshly mind will reply, "Why then does not God reveal himself in more intelligible terms?" Such a question is insulting to God. When Christ was asked why he spake in parables, he answered, "Unto you it is given to know the mysteries of the kingdom of heaven, but unto them it is not given." He spake in parables, that in seeing they might not see, and hearing they might not understand. Yes, that the blindness of God's people might be made light, and that it might be hidden from the rest, as Christ most solemnly declares: "I thank thee, O Father, Lord of heaven and earth, that thou hast hid these things from the wise and prudent, and hast revealed them unto babes. Even so, Father; for so it seemed good in thy sight." This will, nay, does confound reason, and the wise understand it not. They go blindly on; they hear with their ears but understand not. The lame, the maimed, and the blind are led to put confidence in the Lord, and no one else.

My mind has been engaged with these wheels many times. They have proved too hard for me, and have, by their workings, many times made me giddy. But I will speak a few thoughts, as God is pleased to throw a light upon the subject in my soul.

I. What is meant by the *living creatures*.

II. What is understood by the *wheels*, and the *wheels within wheels*.

III. The living creatures *turned not;* for the Spirit of God appears to lead them within the wheels.

IV. That the *Spirit of God is the Leader* of the whole. The Spirit led the van, as we are told in verse 20: "Whithersoever the Spirit was to go, they went; thither was their spirit to go."

V. What is intended by the *rings being full of eyes*, and being *lifted up* so high that they were dreadful.

I. Then what are the *living creatures?* They are the ministers of the Son of God. They are also called cherubim in chapter x. Observe, they are living creatures. There are many learned and talented preachers who have not this living principle within. A minister of God has divine life and light in his soul. He walks in this divine light, through the invincible power of the Spirit operating within him. He knows the Spirit's movements, from himself being quickened by the Spirit. This humbles him in the dust before God, as in verse 3, concerning Ezekiel, the man of God. The hand of the Lord was then upon him. Immanuel is intended to lead the van. The church of God has many hurricanes; but she has never been in any, neither pain nor grief, but the Lord Jesus has been there too, and he will bring her safely through. There is not a temptation a child of God has endured but the Son of God has also waded through it. He was tempted in all points like unto us, yet without sin. Say you, "It was not great or hard to endure, because he was without sin; because, therefore, he had no inclination." Though he had no inclination, this makes the temptation no less. Nay, but it would make it the more horrifying. Do you not recollect the time when you could make your boast in sin? You were glad that you could sin so easily, so well; but now it is horrifying to your soul. What makes it so? The divine Spirit of purity in your soul. How much more piercing, then, were the darts which were hurled at Infinite Purity! How painful would they be to Christ! They never took fire in his bosom. He stood, and we stand through him, and shall finally gain the victory. Talk of creature goodness, creature strength, and creature ability to stand such a conquest! Hurl it from you, and cast it into oblivion.

What is meant by the living creatures coming out of the whirlwind, as in verse 4? That if you have no tribulation, no whirlwinds of temptation, as Christ had, your doctrines, your opinions, yea, even your troubles are merely superficial; you must be made to go through the fire. It is by this process alone God fits his ministers for his work. He furnishes them with wings, the wings of faith and love, that they may soar whithersoever the Spirit leads them, with hands under their wings, that they should handle the Word of Life. The creatures had four faces. You do not like what is called a two-faced person; but all the ministers of God have four Faces: 1. The face of a man, that they may discover and point out what man is—the temptations he is subject to, and his natural corruptions; 2. The face of a lion, that they may be courageous, majestic, and not shrink at trials or conflicts. The lion has great power, or man would trample on him to death. But the weak saint and the courageous lion are all one in Christ. 3. The face of an ox; for their work must be laborious, like that of an ox. "Thou shalt not muzzle the ox that treadeth out the corn." Some professors, who are rich in themselves, are like the muzzled ox; they cannot bite. But God's ministers must have liberty that they may eat the corn. Every one of them must be a partaker of it himself; and the people should encourage him, and deal out to him what nature requires, that he may work as an ox. 4. The face of an eagle. He must be eagle-eyed, as well as swift, that he may detect and point out hypocrites, and send his darts at them, and penetrate into the mysteries of the gospel which he preaches. And he should be swift in seeing after the people's welfare; visiting the poor and the sick, and attending to their necessities, as far as his flock, in the providence of God, enable him; so not swift to visit only.

II. What are we to understand by *the wheels?* There are four particulars that unite these great wheels; and these are high, so that they are dreadful. What does it take to form them? 1. The glorious gospel of God's grace; 2. The visible church united in one glorious body. 3. Outward ordinances, appointed by God for the comfort and fellowship of his church. 4. The solemn and awful dispensations of God, executed in a way of judgment and mercy. All these wheels form but one wheel; or rather, they are wheels within the wheel.

1. The glorious gospel of the grace of God. Ah! What a wheel this is! How it whirls round to catch poor sinners! Though they, like sheep, may run as far as sheep can run from the fold, it will catch them. It whirls round so fast that it is like a whirlwind in the sinner's conscience, and makes sad havoc of his self-righteousness, blowing it about in every direction. Then it comforts them in the Holy Ghost with power and with much assurance. It is moved by the Spirit. Men may study the letter of God's Word; they may judgmentally know and preach it; but if they are without the Spirit of the living creature within the wheels, there is no life. When there is, the wheels run well, and all are safe. The great apostle of the Gentiles went with this wheel. Did he go with a studied sermon, having previously considered how long it would

take him to deliver it? Had he so measured it that he knew to a minute what time he should have it concluded? Did he go with a fine oration and a fleshly task? No. You hear no word of this. He went in the fulness of the blessings of the gospel of grace. There was the Spirit of the living creature within the wheels. He had the immortal unction of the Holy One in his soul.

Some one may ask, "What is the gospel?" The gospel is good news, glad tidings, to poor cast-down, broken-hearted sinners; the teeming out of the love of Christ to a poor worm, made known to him by grace, and grace alone. The gospel of Christ is not made up of offers, and proffers, or overtures. It is not left to chance, or uncertainty, whether the creature can or will accept of it or not. It is the glory and majesty of Christ administered to the church in love. It is part of the wheels. The promise, love, blood, doctrine, pardon, and reconciliation, all united with this one wheel, and always going round with it. This cannot be learnt from books or men. The minister of Christ must feel the power; he must himself handle and taste the word of life. If none but living men stood up in our day as preachers, there would be very few; for the Spirit of life is not within their wheels. But whithersoever the Spirit goes the true ministers go. Then, when the church of God meet together, they enjoy each other's company; for the Spirit of the living creatures is in the wheels.

There are places in this nation the Spirit will visit, and then move to other places, as God shall direct. We read that the apostle, in traversing the earth, wanted to stop at one place; but God forbade him; at another he was unwilling to stop and preach; but God said he must, for he had much people in that place; and he was blessedly made the object of God's love, to declare his message and proclaim the promise of grace,—peace and pardon to the believing soul. Though you were and are a weak, sinful creature, not able to stand in yourself, he raised you up to the enjoyment of himself. The gospel came not to you in word only, but in power; not by me or you, delivered with fine compliments, or smooth speeches; it came with *power*, laid you low, sank you to hopeless despondency; then gave you faith and much assurance, and revealed pardon to your soul, through the powerful influence of the Holy Ghost. The door of your conscience was battered round, and artful fiends of hell tried to stir up carnal reason, but were not able. Through God the Spirit, you were enabled to wheel them all round, and say, "I am not ashamed of the gospel of Christ; it is the power of God unto salvation." Has it not thus wheeled round with you? Did not the first manifestation of love move you a little above your earthly sphere, like a worm peeping out of its hole, and then going in? By and bye, the Spirit of the blessed gospel comes with a sweet and comforting intimation of mercy, and, by an immutable life and power, you are again brought out of the hole and led to a sweet and joyful hope in Christ.

2. The visible church of God united in one glorious body is another branch of the wheel. And what does this mean? Do we understand the united sects and denominations of professing Christians, as the Presbyterian, Methodist, Calvinist, or Baptist, as one glorious church united in one body? No. This is an invention of the devil, to deceive souls. In what sect, then, does it consist? None, whatever sect they belong to, are of this glorious body, unless the Spirit of the living creature is within the wheels. Unless this is the case, none can truly believe. The great difference is, that one is the shadow, the other the substance; the Spirit of the living creatures is within the wheels; God is in them and they in him. This is what constitutes and cements this glorious church in one. Every individual soul forms a part, and in it must work, as a wheel has work to do when it moves round; which it is continually doing; one side up, the other down; and which continually whirling round is appointed by God to the praise and glory of his grace. As a wheel would be imperfect if one spoke was short or wanting, so would Christ's glorious body be imperfect if one child of God were missing; as every child of God constitutes a part of this wheel.

3. The outward means and ordinances God has appointed for the glory of his name and the blessing of his people. The rings were full of eyes; then they were not blind rings. In preaching the gospel, ministers must have eyes. In administering the ordinance of baptism and the Lord's supper, they should have eyes of faith. Thus, when it is done by faith, God, as it were, manifestively wheels himself into the hearts and consciences of his people.

Prayer is another branch; not prating; thousands prate who never pray, while many pray who do not prate. They stammer, and sigh, groan, and moan in prayer; but God hears such prayers; they are a part of these wheels. I have often admired a line of Hart's:

"Pray if thou canst, or canst not speak."

Words are but wind, and words cannot express the whole heartfelt prayer. Moses was a man of few words; yet while his arms were held up, the children of Israel conquered. Sigh, and cry; lay you down at mercy's door; if he trample upon you, yea, if you perish, perish there. God will appear, and however feeble you may be, he will support you:

"Prayer's a weapon for the feeble;
Weakest souls can wield it best."

Nothing but the Spirit of the living creatures within the wheels will enable you to go forward.

Watchfulness is another part. Christ tells us " to watch and pray, that we enter not into temptation." Paul tells us to " take the helmet of salvation and the sword of the Spirit, which is the Word of

God; praying always with all prayer and supplication of the Spirit, and watching thereunto with all perseverance and supplication for all saints." He who prays aright in the Spirit, will watch also, or the wheels will not move well. Many pray vehemently, but do not watch. It is right to watch the movements of the dispensations of providence, to warn, comfort, and caution the church. To illustrate my meaning, suppose a house to be on fire; if the watchmen, when they saw it, instead of sounding the alarm, stood and watched the blaze in its various movements, the consequence would be the premises would soon be burnt down. They must give an alarm. The child of God will be made to watch, lest the enemy should come and sow tares, raising the workings of old nature within, and sinking him into a sad labyrinth. He will, therefore, watch; and as soon as he perceives the breaking forth of this destructive fire within, I had nearly said he must cry "*Murder!*" but he will cry to God.

The rings were full of eyes, to see the designs of the enemy and the designs of God, that you may go on right. Frequently, in reading the Word of God, you read and think upon it, but cannot understand. It appears all a mystery; you cry out to the Lord, "Open thou mine eyes, that I may behold wondrous things out of thy law." He hears your prayer; and as you whirl round on this Bible wheel, you see therein eternal realities, and the grace of God shines in every page.

4. The solemn and awful dispensations of God executed in a way of judgment and mercy. Our Lord tells us, "If thy right eye offend thee, pluck it out and cast it from thee; for it is profitable for thee that one of thy members should perish, and not thy whole body should be cast into hell." By which I understand that those things which are dear to us, if they offend, must be moved from us. The Lord, in the dispensation of his providence, will whirl them from us, that we may, like Job, "come forth as gold, which is purified in the fire," and sing of judgment and mercy. When right arms and eyes are taken, and he has mowed us down as a thistle, we can say, "He has done all things well."

The rings were so high that they were dreadful. It is dreadful to solemnly sing of God's judgments, executed upon ungodly men; yet such a solemn song did the psalmist sing: "He drowned the Egyptians in the Red Sea; for his mercy endureth for ever." The wrath of men shall praise him. Men shall praise him for judgments, and for the honour of his name. Thus is there a perfect union maintained in the glory and honour of this majestic wheel. The Spirit of God moved in all its workings, and we are enabled to trace his wonder-working hand, because the Spirit of the living creature is within the wheels. Many of the dispensations of God are trying to flesh and blood; but they must come to lead you right. God works them out for your good, and you are brought sometimes to this blessed position,—resigned to the will of God, and to confess to the Lord, saying, "Thou hast done what is right. Go on, Lord; thy will be done!" Thus are these judgments sent for the honour of God and the blessing of our souls. But when they come, if you are left to rebel, depend upon this, you will have something worse; for all God's ways are right, and he is too wise to err, and too good to be unkind.

III. The creatures had two wings, which covered their bodies; demonstrating that they have nothing to boast of in themselves; God alone is all their glory, and they abide under his wings. "They went straightforward, and *turned not when they went.*" They were moved and guided *by the Spirit.* They followed only the Lord Jesus, or those who were led and taught by the Spirit. He who is led by the Spirit of God is led aright. "For as many as are led by the Spirit of God, they are the sons of God." In matters of religion, the minister of God should never advance any doctrine which God has not manifested in his own heart; and then he will come forward and bear a faithful testimony to the truth, the Holy Ghost bearing him witness in his conscience. As a living subject, he has then the vital power of God within him, is not one of those who are ever learning and never able to come to the knowledge of the truth.

"They turned not." A minister who can turn to accommodate his hearers is not worthy the name of a minister. Offend or not offend, if they have been rightly taught, they will go "straightforward." No qualifying of God's truth lest he should be called an Antinomian, or drive away a few respectables.

"As for the likeness of the living creatures, their appearance was like burning coals of fire, and like the appearance of lamps. It went up and down among the living creatures, and the fire was bright, and out of the fire went forth lightning;" showing the majesty and glory of God in the midst. Thus when God touches a minister's tongue with a live coal from the divine altar, light comes into the conscience. I would solemnly ask one question: Has God ever made the word as a flash of lightning in your conscience? Do you feel it, fall down under it, bowed down, humbled and crumbled at the feet of Jesus? And do you not enjoy his immortal love in your soul? If so, to God be all the praise.

The living creatures are said to be four, as typical of the four quarters of the earth,—east, west, north, and south. They having four faces but only one likeness, they could look to these four quarters at the same time; just as the Lord is represented as sitting on the circle of the earth, seeing all round at the same moment, and beholding the inhabitants as grasshoppers. (Isa. xl. 22.) But whatever work the creatures did, they were only instruments, merely creatures. The apostle Paul, under the teaching of the Holy Spirit, says, "We have this treasure in earthen vessels;" proving to a demonstration it is of God, and not of man. Therefore give him all the glory.

IV. The *Spirit of God is the Leader* of the whole, as in verses 19 and 20: "Whithersoever the Spirit was to go, they went; thither was their spirit to go." God's ministers are at the sole command of God the Spirit. The Spirit of God gives them to know where and what to preach. For instance, witness the apostles. The Spirit led them about from place to place, and taught them what to say. "Whithersoever the Spirit was to go, they went." But in our day it is as though money alone made the wheels to go. If they can only get plenty of money they can do work. How must we know God's ministers? The Spirit of God influences them to preach, and brings them through many an intricate circumstance. Sometimes they seem set fast, that they know not what to do. Still they have heart to preach. Though all avenues appear shut up, so that the poor soul shrinks at the sight, yet it is enabled to cry to God for his blessed Spirit to make known unto him the right way. He desires not fleshly honours, but wants to feel the solemn movement of God the Spirit within him, which will show him where he is. All ministers who have not the Spirit of God within them are strangers to the way of the Spirit. You go to hear the word of God; the minister is led to describe your case; the blessed Spirit moves in your conscience; and when that is the case, you look beyond the man to the Spirit which moveth him, because it is manifest he is led by the Spirit.

V. When the living creatures were *lifted up* from the earth, the wheels were lifted up. God's ministers are sometimes lifted up in the gospel and the chosen of God are lifted up with them; lifted up in their souls, rejoicing in God, because of his words. But the ministers of God are sometimes in a low place; they cannot feel the blessed unction of the Spirit in their souls; all seems a dead letter. They want this lifting up. They fret, murmur, and rebel, instead of crying to God for his aid and help. The command is, "Stand still;" for the strength of every saint is to sit still. Moses commanded the people, and said, "Fear ye not; stand still and see the salvation of the Lord, which he will show you to-day. The Lord shall fight for you, and you shall hold your peace." This was not a careless standing still; but a solemn waiting for God. O how sweet then to submit to his will as he is pleased to guide you, and may you pray that his presence may go with you. Moses said, "If thy presence go not with us, carry us not up hence." God promised, and said, "My presence shall go with thee." This has couched in it the presence of a Three-One God,—God the Father, God the Son, and God the Holy Ghost. Thus, when God's presence was there, they were lifted up. The rings were so high that they were dreadful; showing the solemn majesty and glory of God and the discriminating doctrines of his grace. And saints, by being lifted up, make hell tremble, and devils flee before them. The disciples of Christ appeared to rejoice at thus being lifted up, and they said unto him, "Devils are subject to us." But hear his reply: "Rejoice not that devils are subject to you; but rejoice that your names are written in heaven." You may rejoice one day that devils are subject to you, and at another time you may mourn that you seem to be subject to them; but rejoice that your names are written in heaven; for no sin, no devils, no power on earth or hell, can erase them. "Who is this that looketh forth as the morning, fair as the moon, clear as the sun, and terrible as an army with banners?"

The Queen of Scotland, it is said, dreaded the prayers of John Knox more than an army of Frenchmen. And, indeed, well she might; for God has stamped a majesty and efficacy on prayer, of his own inditing, that is mighty to the pulling down of strongholds. It is "terrible as an army with banners." In the days of the apostles there were certain vagabond Jews, who attempted to cast out devils by using the name of Christ; but they had not the power and Spirit of Jesus with them; therefore they were not obeyed. The evil spirit answered and said, "Jesus I know, and Paul I know; but who are ye? And the man in whom the evil spirit was leaped on them, and overcame them, and prevailed against them, so that they fled out of that house, naked and wounded." Had it been Paul, they would have obeyed him. His God-taught prayer would have been terrible as an army with banners. When raised or offered up it would have been dreadful.

The wheels were *full of eyes*, as in the 10th chapter; and their whole body, and their backs, and their hands, and their rings, and the wheels were full of eyes round about, even the wheels that the four had. Thus are the ministers of God exhibited to view, as being full of eyes. Their whole body, their backs, their hands, their wings,—they are all eyes; and why? They need to be full of eyes to see the purity and spirituality of God's law and gospel; they need to be full of eyes to see the dreadful distance the sinner is from God; to discern, between man and God, and to see his justice in damning sinners. They need to be full of eyes to see the deceitfulness of the heart. King Solomon prayed that "at what time prayers and supplications be made by any man, or by all thy people Israel, which shall know the plague of their own heart, and spread forth their hands towards this house, then hear thou in heaven, thy dwelling-place, and forgive." They should have eyes to see this plague. They should have eyes to pry into the mysteries of God's Word and not, as some do, purchase another man's words to read in the pulpit. They should see the mystery of Christ as suited to lost sinners; to see the Person of Christ, as making himself a Substitute for his people, in perfect obedience to God's law, in his death, in his burial, in his resurrection, in his ascension, in his glorification. They need to be full of eyes to see for God's people, to find out where they are and what they are about; to search into the nature of their troubles and conflicts; to comfort them, and to strike awe into the hearts of sinners. They are full of eyes—their hands, their looks, their wings, that they may look all around them; hands to handle: "Those things that we have handled," says Paul, "declare we unto you, that we may comfort you with the same comfort wherewith we ourselves are comforted of God." Wings,—the wings of faith and love, that they may soar above, and see their way in Christ. Behind him must be full of eyes; for God's people sometimes backslide. The minister must be able to find them out; for there are very few of God's people but do backslide, though not outwardly, in mean detestable crimes; yet they do backslide in heart and sometimes feet too.

Is it not the church that is here addressed? Have you eyes to see you are one of this church? But you perhaps dare not say you belong to this church. There is something gloomy hangs over your mind. You acknowledge your blindness, you feel you are a frail creature, and confess your weakness. You could not see this if you had no eyes. God, who commanded the light to shine out of darkness, hath shined into your soul. You see your own vileness, and a beauty in Christ which you never saw before. You could not see this if you were dead,—dead in sin; nor could you mourn over your vileness, as in the sight of God. This, then, is a proof that you have life and light within, the work of the Holy Ghost. We need eyes to see God's judgments as well as his mercy; for, in the dispensations of providence, how are our foolish hearts ready to say, "Let him let his hand go, and cut me off." What a mercy he does not take us at our word. It is because of the precious Stone God hath laid in Zion. Whosoever believeth on him shall never be confounded, shall never be put to shame. It is like the precious stones in the breastplate of the high priest, which had engraven on them the names of the twelve tribes of Israel, and which he wore upon his heart, and bore the judgment of the children of Israel before the Lord continually. So has Christ, our great High Priest. All his people are precious to him, and all are moved on, and lifted up as he directs; for the Spirit of the living creatures was in the wheels.

May God the Spirit apply his own truth to your hearts and mine; for his mercy's sake. Amen and Amen.

GOD'S PEOPLE DWELLING ALONE.
Preached in Manchester, Jan. 26th, 1840.

" And my people shall dwell in a peaceable habitation, and in sure dwellings, and in quiet resting places."—ISA. XXXII. 18.

WHERE are we at this present period of our existence? Are we amongst this blessed number, " My people?" Are we of those who are dwelling in peaceable habitations, sure dwellings, and in quiet resting places? What proof have we that we are in this state? Do some of you ask within yourselves, "How can I dwell in this peaceable habitation, when all is war and tumult within and without?" Or, "How can I dwell in these sure dwellings, and quiet resting places, amidst this busy, bustling, commercial town,—this deceitful world,—which tosses my poor fickle heart to and fro like the troubled sea?" Why, poor soul, this is the very time you shall dwell there; as you may perceive by reading the next verse: "When it shall hail, coming down on the forest; and the city shall be low in a low place;" or, as it is in the margin, "when it is utterly abased." Thus it is, when troubles come upon you like hail, so strong, so heavy,—then it is, when you are in the midst of confusion, that the Lord saith, "Call upon me in the day of trouble; I will hear thee, and deliver thee." And you have here a further declaration of mercy: "Ye shall dwell in peaceable habitations."

Some say the promise refers to the time when anti-Christ shall be destroyed, and the Millennium commences. But, no. We have all in this a personal interest, and it is my desire not to carry your minds to those speculative ideas, such as the Millennium; but so far as God shall make me the means, to impart unto you such blessed truths, by unfolding the mysteries of God's Word, you shall live in the enjoyment of from day to day; mysteries they are, inasmuch as they are hidden from the eyes of the world; but they are revealed unto babes."

Sometimes we are afar off, and we think this habitation is not for us; but you will not despair, for God has promised, and therefore will perform, "that you shall dwell there."

I. God *has a people:* "*My* people."

II. They *shall dwell in peaceable habitations, sure dwellings,* and *quiet resting-places.* And let us notice that we *shall,* not that we *do,* dwell in this peaceable habitation; we cannot, while on earth, always be in this blessed habitation.

I. God *has a people.* "Yes," say some; "all are the people of God." They are, as his creatures, as all are created by him; but not as his chosen people. All are not the chosen people of God. He has a *chosen* people, as he says, "But ye are a chosen generation, a royal priesthood, a holy nation, a peculiar people, that ye should show forth the praises of him who hath called you out of darkness into his marvellous light."

How very frequently is that parable of our Lord concerning the tares and the wheat misconstrued. Some say the field is the church and the tares are the hypocrites in the church; and they contend from this that hypocrites should not be turned out of the church, lest some of the good seed should go with them. But we are told by the Lord himself, "The field is the world. He that soweth the good seed is the Son of Man, and the good seed are the children of the kingdom; but the tares are the children of the wicked one; the enemy that soweth them is the devil; the harvest is the end of the world, and the reapers are the angels." (Matt. xiii.)   We are not to take away the lives of any in the world; for we know not how many of the good seed may be in their loins. All are to be left to the end of the world. (Matt. xiii. 40–43.)   What could be more explicit? The world is divided into two classes, compared to tares and wheat, sheep and goats.   Is it, then, not dishonourable to Christ to say it is his church, when his church is but one body, even as Christ is one?   For they are one in Christ their Head.

It has pleased God that, through the foolishness of preaching, men should be saved.   We are commanded to preach the truth; and when we have done so, to leave it to the blessing of God; and God says, "My people shall dwell in peaceable habitations."   What proof does it want to show that you are one of this number?   First, you must be absolutely unmanned by the blessed Spirit and become as helpless and dependant as a babe; for "of such, saith the Lord, is the kingdom of heaven;" yea, all our strength must be done away with, and all our goodness, and we must be made to view ourselves as fit subjects only for black despair.   Without all this, we are not fit subjects for Christ.   We may compare our hearts to an inn, crowded with fine inmates, as it were; so that there is no room for Christ, as there was none at his birth.   But when we have been emptied of all our self props, we shall seek elsewhere for a sure dwelling, and, like the dove, which found no place of rest for the sole of her foot, so returned to the ark.   You hope in Christ, you desire to lay fast hold of his garment, and live in him as your "peaceful habitation."   You cannot give up a hope that this will be your happy lot.   You look not so much at what may come to pass with all God's children, and that at one or some future period all shall enjoy these quiet resting-places; but you want to enjoy them yourself; for you feel so tossed about with sin and Satan that, unless you can get here, you must be for ever miserable, for ever lost. To you, then, is this promise given: "You shall dwell in sure dwellings, and in quiet resting-places."

"My people," not all people.   It is one of the greatest errors a man can fall into to deny the discrimination of God's grace in selecting a people for himself, and crying, "Peace, peace," where God hath not made peace, and saying, "If you live in peace with God, you will have no trials."   What!   If you have no trials, what need of humility?   What then can humble you?   What!   Those healed whose hearts have never been broken?   God causes repentance for sin, and a broken heart for your iniquities; but he has promised that he will not despise a broken and a contrite heart.

God draws a line of discrimination between his people and those who are not his people, which is decisive in itself. I would ask you, "Has God made this discrimination in your conscience?" If not, if you think you can still bring something to him to merit his favour, all is a dream. This little something must go; it must be cut off. You must be entirely stripped of all hope but in Christ. You must be made entirely dependent on him, and him alone; and not until then can you be brought to dwell in this "peaceable habitation."

II. Now, in the second place, let us consider what is meant by this *dwelling in a peaceable habitation*, &c. I would notice, that if all men are the people of God, all men will be saved and dwell here. But are all men as David was,—after God's own heart, God's own people? David says, "Behold, I am poor and needy." Such and these alone, "the poor and the needy," shall dwell there.

What is this dwelling? Christ is emphatically called "the Peace," "the Prince of Peace." How can we get into this peace? By the works of the law? No. If you seek this dwelling by your own good works, you will, like Israel of old, "stumble at that stumbling stone." The power of the killing letter must be removed out of your conscience; and until this is done, you will have no real peace. This is set forth by Hagar and Sarah. As saith the Scripture: "Cast out the bond-woman and her son; for the son of the bond-woman shall not be heir with the son of the free." Now I durst not have said this was typical of the law, had not Paul, the inspired penman of God, said so: "Which things are an allegory. This Hagar is Mount Sinai in Arabia, and answereth to Jerusalem which now is, and is in bondage with her children." Therefore must be cast out of your consciences this killing letter, which is the law; for in it no man shall live; and so long as Hagar remains in the house there will always be a quarrel. As also saith the apostle: "As then he that was born after the flesh persecuted him that was born after the Spirit, even so it is now." This is not setting aside good works, but the trusting in your own good works; for you cannot live by the law, neither can the law save you. Nay, the law will curse you for your best works. You cannot please Moses, do what you will; neither will you find this peaceable habitation in the law. Therefore may the Spirit lead you to Christ, the end of the law for righteousness to every one that believeth. May you have faith in him, and rest in the atonement he has made for his people. He has magnified the law and made it honourable for all his own. He has not merely *kept* the law. Honours crown his brow, he has also *magnified* it; as it has not merely had the obedience of man, but of God, even God in our nature. He is a peaceable habitation, and on this ground would I rest. "Who shall lay anything to the charge of God's elect?" Who? "Why," says the world, "any one may have plenty to lay to their charge. As they are always bemoaning themselves on account of their sins, they must be a vile, guilty people." But, no! What they most mourn about, the world would not call sins. "It is God that justifieth; who is he that condemneth? It is Christ that died; yea, rather, that is risen again, who is even at the right hand of God, who also maketh intercession for us." If God justifieth, what matters it who condemns? If Christ died in our room and stead, how can we be left to die? And if he make intercession for us, how can we be found guilty before God, unless his intercession be unavailing? No, beloved; he has gone to heaven with a receipt in full for all his blood-bought family. Has he, then, by this dishonoured the law? Nay, he has indeed magnified it and made it honourable. Some of these "pious" folks, as they think themselves, would rob the law of its awful and divine authority, and then make it a rule of life. But, now are we delivered from the law, that being dead wherein we were held, that we should live in newness of spirit, and not in the oldness of the letter. The law has gained honour in Christ. There is no peace but in Christ; but a sinner who is wrapt up in the beauty of Christ shall dwell in this peaceable habitation. It will be as a new world to him; it sweetens conscience and temper, and all seems quite new. If you read the Word of God, you see a beauty in it you never saw before. This is dwelling in a peaceable habitation. But without Christ, all is only a delusive peace. Therefore cease from your own works as any ground of peace. What good works can spring from an unregenerate heart, when the heart of man "is deceitful above all things and desperately wicked?" The apostle Paul said, "I know that in me, that is in my flesh, dwelleth no good thing." But where you have been brought to Christ, watchfulness looks out, patience waits, and God waters his vineyard, even your souls. You find a residence in him. You see your right and title to it, and are thus dwelling secure in God's heart. You dwell in him and he dwells in you. Thus there is a mysterious oneness between you and him; your hearts triumph; you feel it and rejoice.

This, then, is a peaceable habitation. But you are not always so. Sometimes you wander from this peaceable habitation, like a youth who has rambled from his home, thinking he can have more liberty away from home and enjoy himself; but he finds himself among strangers, who draw him aside from the path of rectitude. He squanders his money in riotous living, and thus brings upon himself want, and starvation. All is misery within and without. This is our case spiritually. These things afford us no comfort. God makes them prove thorns in our flesh and goads in our sides. All is confusion and disorder; nothing but misery within. Like the prodigal, guilt keeps us back, until we find we are destitute of even the common evidences of life; and then we are made to arise; but ere we get home, God comes and meets us, and welcomes us. Yea, he did not wait for his son to get home (he was his son all the time, even when among the swine), but ran out, met him, fell on his neck and kissed him.

"Come needy, come guilty, come loathesome and bare;
You can't come too filthy; come just as you are."

May the Lord enable you and me to rest in this peaceable habitation, for his mercy's sake. Amen.

THE BREAKER PASSED BEFORE THEM.
Preached April 13th, 1843.

"The breaker is come up before them; they have broken up, and have passed through the gate, and are gone out by it; and their king shall pass before them, and the Lord on the head of them."—MIC. II. 13.

IN all God's dealings and dispensations with the Jews, he kept a constant eye on the well-being of his elect people. You find frequently, when God is giving, by the prophets, solemn admonitions, warnings, and threatenings to the Jews as a nation, or teeming forth awful denunciations and curses against them, they suddenly break off to drop a word of comfort and encouragement to God's spiritual family. I believe that the world was created for the elect's sake; that the Bible is given for the elect's sake; and that if God had not had an elect people, there would never have been a Bible; for when God is speaking concerning it he says, "All Scripture is given by inspiration of God, and is profitable for doctrine, for reproof, for correction, for instruction in righteousness;" and it is that "*the man of God* may be perfect, thoroughly furnished unto all good works." And again: "Whatsoever was written aforetime was written for *our* learning, that *we*, through patience and comfort of the Scriptures, might have hope." Perhaps some one may say, "Well, then, if I am not one of the elect, it is of no use praying, no use reading, no use repenting." There never was a man in the world that ever did pray spiritually, there never was a man in the world that ever did repent evangelically, but God's elect, nor ever will be. Therefore, if you are brought really and spiritually to cry, to pray, and to repent before God, that is a proof that you are one of his elect; and the Lord says, "Shall not God avenge his own elect, which cry day and night unto him, though he bear long with them? I tell you that he will avenge them speedily." Some of God's dear family, after long waiting and crying before him, begin sometimes to be cast down, and even think that God will not hear them; but shall he not avenge his own elect?

I believe that the idea of a kind of universal salvation, universally offered to all men, is one of Satan's engines, in order to eclipse the glory of God's salvation, and is something like a lottery, to give to all what is called *a chance* of being saved. I believe that the salvation of God is a certain salvation; and that the redeemed of the Lord shall have a *chance* of being saved is a parcel of lumber. "The redeemed of the Lord *shall come*" (not have a chance), "they *shall come* to Zion with songs and everlasting joy upon their heads, and sorrow and sighing shall flee away;" and this shall be the result and the effect of the Breaker having come up before them.

Perhaps you will say, "Who are the men intended in the text?" Well, now; let us just look. "I will surely assemble Jacob; I will surely gather the remnant of Israel," &c. Well, then, it is this remnant before whom the Breaker is gone up. And do not you know what the Lord says in one place? "Though the number of the children of Israel be as the sand of the sea, a remnant shall be saved;" and in another place he says, "Except the Lord of hosts had left us a very small remnant, we should have been as Sodom, and we should have been like unto Gomorrah." Nothing is more common among men than to take it for granted that they are among the Lord's people, because they are so numerous and so respectable. If the Bible is a lie, they are right; but if the Bible is true, they are not; because God says it is a "small remnant." And again: "Ye see your calling, brethren, how that not many wise men after the flesh, not many mighty, not many noble, are called." And again: "Broad is the road that leads to destruction, and many there be that go in thereat; and strait is the gate, and narrow is the way, that leadeth unto life, and few there be that find it." Say you, "How strait is it?" I will tell thee, poor creature. It never did, nor ever will, let one sinner enter with one rag of his own. It tears every rag off the bones, and the sinner is obliged to go as a poor, naked, destitute creature; and if you are never made to go that way, you will never go, as sure as there is a God in heaven. It is common for a mercer to cut off from a piece of cloth fragments of it, which are thrown aside; and when it is a fag-end, he throws it under his feet. And God's people, in all ages of the world, have been a kind of fag-end people, considered as useless and worthless, and fit only to be trodden under foot by the men of this world.

"The Breaker is come up before them." Now I consider that the Lord Jesus Christ, who is their King, that is gone before them, is the character here intended; and I shall just attempt to glance at the movements of this Breaker in the two following senses:

I.* In his going up before his people in his *meritorious work*.

II. In his going up, and *breaking down* all before him in their hearts and consciences.

I. Let us, then, first, dwell upon the movements of this Breaker in his going up before his people in his *meritorious work*. From everlasting his delights were with the sons of men. His solemn Majesty saw what sin would do for us; he saw it would ruin us, he saw it would bring us into everlasting misery and render it as im-

---

* We do not know who reported this sermon, but it is clear from the insertion of so many asterisks that the reporter could not keep pace with the preacher.

possible for any sinner in himself to be just before God as it would be for God himself to cease to exist. He saw that sin was against his law, his justice, and his goodness; and yet he breaks forth, in solemn covenant bonds, to espouse his people's cause. "And do you think that he did?" Nay, I am beyond a think, for I am sure he did; I know he did. And so we are told that in the appointed time "he was made sin for us who knew no sin, that we might be made the righteousness of God in him." He was made, poor child of God, all thy pride, all thy unbelief, and all the abominable workings of thy heart. All was charged to him, placed to his account; and I believe he drank into his holy soul the whole of the hell we had merited; and when he had done, he had put out hell's flames with his own blood, that his people might be saved with an everlasting salvation. He entered into covenant for his people. Hence, long before his appearance in our nature, it is said, "Sacrifice and offering thou wouldst not; then said I, Lo! I come (in the volume of the book it is written of me) to do thy will, O God." And Paul tells us roundly that the will he came to do was the will by which we are sanctified. So that, in the book of God, Christ's eternal purpose was to come to do the will of God, and to bring about an eternal salvation. He came and "was made flesh, and dwelt among us, and we beheld his glory, the glory as of the only begotten of the Father, full of grace and truth."

"O," say you, "we don't believe Christ to be God." Then, if you die in that state, you will be cast into hell, as sure as there is a God in heaven. This blessed Person is Immanuel, God with us, God in our nature; and he came forth in this blessed and solemn capacity to break down every mountain that should stand between God and the sinner. And thus, in his solemn breaking, he has broken down the power of sin. He has honoured the law, magnified it, satisfied justice, and brought in an everlasting righteousness for his people.

* * * *

To enter upon particulars would serve us as long as we live, and what rejoices me is, I shall not have done with it when I die; for then it will be, "To Him that loved us, and washed us from our sins in his own blood, and hath made us kings and priests unto God and his Father, to him be glory and dominion, for ever and ever. Amen."

II. We shall pass on to notice the movements of this Breaker in his going up and *breaking down* all before him in the hearts and consciences of his people. We have a whole host of professors in our day who talk about having been pious ever since they were born. They had a pious education, went to a pious school, entered into a pious society, were piously instructed from an infant, and when they got to years of maturity they became decidedly pious; and their minister tells them they have no need to experience any particular convictions, or to experience any particular alarm, like notorious sinners. If that minister had made up his mind to carry you to black despair comfortably, he could not have set about doing it in a better way. "Except a man be born again, he cannot see the kingdom of God." All this beginning to be pious, and becoming decidedly pious, is the devil's holiday dress, to deceive men's souls and to blind their minds as to their real state and condition before a just and holy God; for when God is pleased to take a sinner in hand there will be a solemn breaking up of that sinner's hard heart, a solemn breaking in of light and life. * * * Look at the poor sinner when this great Breaker breaks into his conscience. I remember when the Lord began to break into my heart. I was a youth between 17 and 18. I had been up to nine years what many in our day call pious; but I lost all my piety in a moment, and have never recovered it since. Up to 17 I became dreadfully profane, and was notorious for nearly all kinds of wickedness. There was one sin which I was preserved from, into which many young persons fall, that of uncleanness. I was never suffered to fall into that; but in others I went to an awful degree. By and by God solemnly broke into my conscience, and although I had awful convictions before, they were not like those. * * *

Here I would notice the difference there is between natural convictions and spiritual convictions, when the great Breaker breaks into the hearts and consciences of his children. I believe men may have natural convictions till they are almost distracted, and may even put an end to their existence by committing suicide; but there is nothing like this in it,—a solemn feeling of the awful disparity there is betwixt a sinful worm of the earth and a holy, just, and good God. * * * When the great Breaker breaks in, he reads aloud in the sinner's conscience God's holiness, goodness, and justice; so that, instead of quarrelling with God and saying he cannot be just without giving him a chance of being saved, he is at a loss to know how God can be just without damning him. Now, have you ever been there? If you have, there is ground for hope that the Breaker has broken with divine light into your soul.

The poor sinner, finding himself in this dreadful predicament, attempts to do something to please God. O how he charges his eyes from seeing, his ears from hearing, yea, and his heart from thinking! He makes up his mind that, if it is possible, he will do something to appease the wrath of God. And he is permitted to try, for many days and sometimes for many months, to go on in this straightforward course, until he begins to hope that he is really getting on in the divine life, and to gain a little self-importance. And then the poor soul falls into some sin which he thought he had gotten complete victory over. But yet he does not despair. And so to work he goes again, until he becomes weary and begins to grow faint; but he will try all means till the Breaker comes, and leads him, as a guilty, ruined sinner, to the feet of Jesus, and, as a condemned criminal, leads him to acknowledge what a ruined, helpless, undone sinner he is. "Ah," says some poor soul, "I don't know what will become of me." He hears others say how they can repent, and love God, and do their duty; but, as for himself, he is led to feel that he can do nothing; and he finds that all his attempts to do anything only throw him in the background, like the woman with the issue of blood, who, after she had spent all that she had, was nothing better, but worse. Is there a poor sinner of this description here to-night? If there is, I bless God for thee, poor soul. "Why, man," say you, "you terrify me. I am ready to wish I had never been born." Well, if thou art really broken up, I thank God for thee again. Thou shalt find that whatever a poor sinner attempts to do, or to be, this Divine Breaker will break it all to pieces like a potter's vessel, and he must be brought at last to be entirely saved by the matchless, unmerited grace of God. All other things must be entirely put out of sight; so that there may be nothing but a precious Christ and a guilty sinner. And this will make the sinner rejoice and put no confidence in the flesh.

Now do you know anything of this? Has God ever broken into your heart? Sometimes this Immortal Breaker breaks in with a little melting down of the soul, and you experience it to be sweet to draw near to God. At other times you feel so dark and dead, you are nearly at your wits' end; you think it would be an insult offered to God to bow your knees before him, and you are ready to come to the conclusion never to attempt to pray again. But, somehow or other, you are obliged to bow your knees; somehow or other, you are obliged to go to the Lord, and to sigh, and groan, and cry before him. By and by you feel a little breaking down of unbelief, a little break-ing in of light, love, and liberty, and a little breaking out of freedom before a holy God. But again all is shut up, and you think it is all a delusion. When you are meditating upon your woeful state, a little divine light will break in, accompanied with a text of Scripture, some-thing like this: "Jesus Christ," the Saviour of sinners, "saves to the uttermost all that come unto God by him." This gives you a little hope; but again you are cast down, because you say you cannot come, you do not know how to come. But again the Lord breaks in with such a passage as this: "I drew them with the cords of love, and with the bands of a man;" and the soul breathes out, "Draw me; I will run after thee." And by and by he pauses, and wonders what has been going on, that he has had such holy familiarity with the Lord, and has been asking the Lord that he would draw him that he might run after him. All this is the blessed effect of the Breaker's breaking into the hearts of his dear children. In his own blessed time, he will break in with a full and free manifestation of pardon. O the blessedness when he breaks in with divine life, and says, "Son, be of good cheer; thy sins are all forgiven thee;" and to con-firm it, breaks in with such a text as this: "The blood of Jesus Christ, his Son, cleanseth from all sin." "What! *All* sin?" Aye, the whole of it. You are led to bless his name, and to say, "How? Is it all?" And he tells you that "the Lord hath laid on him the iniquity of us all," and he bore it all; and having broken down all before him, he now breaks into your heart, and brings the blessedness of his salvation to your conscience, and makes you know you have redemption through his blood. And by faith the man receives Christ, and, believing in him, rejoices, and has no confidence in the flesh.   *   *   *

Our blessed Lord, speaking of his people, says, "When he putteth forth his own sheep, he goeth before them and the sheep follow him, for they know his voice." But very often the sheep is so nimble-footed that he sets on and runs before him, and gets into some laby-rinth or other, till he does not know where he is. And in this state of backsliding he will wander on, like the man who went down from Jerusalem to Jericho, till he falls among thieves, and the poor crea-ture is in a sad plight. They stripped him and wounded him, and they would have taken away his life, if it had not been "hid with Christ in God."

There are some people in this country who say that a child of God never does backslide. It is the very spawn of the devil; it is insult-ing to God, and insulting to the feelings of one who knows what it is for God to restore him from such a condition. And as such a doc-trine is beginning to gain ground, and especially in Manchester, I wish with my whole soul to proclaim against it as the devil's own doctrine, and that it will produce nothing but disasters in the pro-fessed church of the Lord. But I know that the great Head of the church will break down this infernal doctrine, and if any of his peo-ple drink into it he will break it down, and make a way to restore them from such a delusion, and lead them sweetly on in the mysteries of his blessed truth.

Again, the Lord breaks into the hearts of his people when they are brought in straits and difficulties, when their way seems to be hedged up, and every avenue shut.   *   *   *

[The close of the above sermon—or, rather, portion of a sermon—is not given; but it appears the preacher was suffering from indisposition.]

AT THAT TIME YE WERE WITHOUT CHRIST.
Preached November, 17th, 1842.

"That at that time ye were without Christ, being aliens from the com-monwealth of Israel, and strangers from the covenants of promise, having no hope, and without God in the world."—EPH. II. 12.

A VERY trifling alteration of the words of our text would make it applicable, I greatly fear, to many before me to-night. If we were to read, "At *this* time ye *are* without Christ, being aliens from the commonwealth of Israel, and strangers from the covenants of promise, having no hope, and without God in the world." What an awful state you are in, if such be your case! And of others we may adopt the language of God's Word in another place, and say, "And such were some of you." There was a period when we were without Christ, without hope, and without God in the world.

The apostle is here, in the first place, addressing the church at Ephesus as being Gentiles, and not having even the common mercies that Israel, in a religious sense, possessed; for they, as a nation, had mercies that other nations never had. God was a God to Israel in an especial manner, as the God of nations. He says, "Thee only have I known of all the families of the earth; therefore will I punish thee for all thine iniquities." Now, some people lay it down as a rule that, as God has a special people whom he loves above all the rest, they have no cause to fear sinning; their God loved them from all eternity; therefore they have no cause to fear; sin can do them no hurt. I believe that doctrine which leads men to talk in such a way comes from hell and leads to hell; for God's people, above all other people, are visited most for their sins in this world. "If ye be without chastisement, whereof all are partakers, then are ye bastards, and not sons." God loves his people too well to let them live in the love and practice of sin, after he has made it manifest that they are his children; and if you see a professor who can boast of high attainments, and say, "I know my election, I know the Lord has called me by grace, therefore I fear no sin, sin can do me no harm; I'm not concerned about such trifles as sin;" sooner believe the devil to be a child of God than such a man as that. The child of God has a tender conscience, a tender regard for God's honour; and nothing is such a grief to him as sinning against his Lord. Nothing wounds his mind more than being left to practise sin against the loving-kindness and mercy of that God who has done so much for him. I believe such hardened professors as these ought to be shunned more than you would shun a common infidel.

But the text will be applicable to us all: "At that time we were without Christ." At what time? In our unregenerated state. Then we were without Christ. At that time we were "aliens from the commonwealth of Israel, and strangers from the covenants of promise;" and at that time were "without hope, and without God in the world."

Now, we shall make a few remarks upon the passage as it lies before us. And let us inquire whether or not it can be said of us, "At this time we are without Christ."

It may be that, in our state of unregeneracy, we did not all make the same public appearance in the world. One man lived in the love and practice of drunkenness; another lived in the love and practice of uncleanness; another lived in the love and practice of open profanity; another lived in the love and practice of covetousness,—and a covetous man is as far from God as the devil can make him, because his heart is wrapped up in the world, and the world is wrapped up in his heart; another lives in the love and practice of his free-will pride—of what he can do, does, and means to do, to please God, and looks upon his fellow mortals as the Pharisee looked upon the poor publican. He pays tithes of mint and cummin, says his prayers, does his duty, and goes to his church or chapel; and some of his friends extol him for his piety; but if you come to ask him about the divine law of God, about his own state as a lost and ruined sinner, and how he was brought to know and feel it, about the salvation of the sinner by Jesus Christ, and how he was brought to know his interest in it, you set him fast at once.

What the apostle here has in view is, what we were manifestively. What we were in the purpose of God, what we were as viewed by him in Christ before the foundation of the world, is another thing altogether; he is not talking about that, but of what we were manifestively: "At that time ye were without Christ." Now, do not some of you feel it was the case with you? I, for my own part, have felt a little solemnity about the matter. At one time I thought I had a great many things I could boast of. Sometimes I thought I had a little more knowledge in religious matters than others. But when God the Spirit brought me to a true knowledge of myself and my real state and condition, I felt before God that I was as destitute of Christ as are the dammed in hell, as regards the manifestation and sensible enjoyment of him; and I could no more get at Christ than I could pull God from his throne. Some of you may think it is not so difficult a matter as that. You think you can repent to-night, believe to-night, get pardon to-night, and bring Christ into your souls to-night. I believe the devil to be the author of such a faith and repentance as that; and the devil sets men about it to deceive their souls and to wrap them up in self-delusion. Faith and repentance are Christ's gifts; for God has exalted him "to give repentance to Israel, and remission of sins."

God tells us that his people are accepted in Christ. If we are without Christ, then we have nothing that God will accept; because his people are accepted in Christ. God has said that no man can come unto the Father but by Christ; therefore if we are without Christ we have no ground upon which we can approach unto God. Christ says, "I am the Way, the Truth, and the Life;" and if he is *the* Way, there is no other way; if he is *the* Truth, everything else is a lie; and if he is *the* Life, everything apart from him is death. Therefore, if we are without Christ, we are out of the way, we are ignorant of the truth, and we are dead in trespasses and sins.

Is this your case? Are you without Christ? If you are, whatever you possess besides, it will not do to bring it to God.

> "Sinners can say, and only they,
> How precious is a Saviour."

If there be any poor, rooted-up, broken-hearted sinner here to-night, who feels he is ruined, and guilty, and filthy, and is ready to cry out that he is too vile, too base, and that God will not receive such a vile sinner as he is, I tell thee what; a sinner never was received since the world stood, but on the ground of Christ; and thy felt sinfulness, vileness, and wretchedness, are rather a plea than anything else, that thou shouldst fall flat upon Christ as thine all-sufficient Saviour.

If we are without Christ, we are without holiness; for God says, "He is made unto us sanctification." But the child of God has got a holiness that Satan cannot sully, and which will stand the test amid all the confusion and noise around him. Without Christ, all the rest will leave us when we come to die; but, having Christ, we shall stand when the world is in a blaze, and we shall be able to say,

"Bold shall I stand in that great day,
For who aught to my charge shall lay,
While through thy blood absolved I am
From sin's tremendous curse and shame?"

Again, if we have Christ, we have his blood for pardon, his righteousness for justification, his fulness to supply all our needs, his promises to cheer us, his strength to support us, his wisdom to guide us in all our ways. We have him in all the offices he sustains,—as Prophet to teach and instruct us, as Priest to atone and plead for us, and as King to rule over us and in us. We have him in all the blessed characters he bears,—as our Shepherd, our Captain, our Bread of Life, Water of Life, and the Wine of God to cheer us. We have him in the endearing relationship he sustains as our Elder Brother. And, which is more endearing than all, we have him as our Husband; and he does not take his bride as we are in the habit of taking ours,—for better or for worse. O no! He knew she would have no better about her; it would be all worse: therefore he took her with all her sin and guilt, and stood answerable for all her debts.

Cannot some of you recollect a time when you were without Christ? Up to the time that I was nearly eighteen years of age, I was without Christ; but before I was eighteen, Christ, in distinguishing love, revealed himself to me. I am now within a few weeks of 70; and I feel up to this moment as much necessity of Christ as ever. I have not gained a bit of ground here. Since that time I have preached many thousands of sermons about Christ, I have travelled many thousands of miles to preach about him; and in this respect I think I may say I have laboured more abundantly than many. But, if you would take away Christ, I would as soon trust the devil as all my doings; and the devil would have as good a hope as I should have; for all my hope comes from, and is centered in, a precious Christ. If we are without Christ, we have nothing but sin and wretchedness; nothing but what will lead us to ruin.

"Having no hope." That is, having no real, good hope. All people have a hope of some sort. What sort of a hope have *you?* "O," says one, "I have a hope of getting to heaven." And what do you ground it upon? "Why, I think God is too merciful to send anybody to hell." If that be true, you think God is too merciful to tell the truth, for he says, "The wicked *shall* be turned into hell."

Another says, "I have some hope that I shall be saved, for I am as good as my neighbours and better than many of them; and though I am a sinner, I am but a little sinner after all; and so I hope I shall go to heaven." Now, I will tell you this; if you ever committed one sin, and God were to take you to heaven, he would not be true; for God says, "He that offendeth in one point is guilty of all;" "Cursed is every one who continueth not in all things written in the book of the law to do them;" "He that believeth not shall be dammed." So that being what you call a little sinner is only a delusion.

Another says, "I have a hope, because I really am decidedly pious; I lay by a certain sum every week for Tract Societies and Missionary Societies; and I have heard men say, on public occasions, that God would reward these pious deeds, and that he would be sure not to forget such acts of charity and love." Well, it is all very well to lay by part of our substance for the Lord; but I tell you what, poor sinner, if you rest here, if you make a Saviour of it, you insult God, and do as much as you can to damn your own soul; you do indeed.

"Without God in the world." If we are without God, we have no God to go to in trouble, in storms, and in tempests; no God to carry our grievances to. We may have our tens of thousands of riches; our knowledge may be wonderful; we may cultivate our intellects, store up a great treasure of useful knowledge; but to be without God; O what an awful thing! By and by we shall have to stretch ourselves upon a dying bed and to drop into eternity. What will become of us then, if we are without God as our God? Without God. This is the state we are all in by nature. Sinner, are you without Christ? *Where art thou?* * O may the Lord God omnipotent send a dart into your conscience, if it be his blessed will, and lead you to a sight and sense of your condition before him, as being without God in the world!

A REST FOR THE PEOPLE OF GOD.
Preached in a village near Ely.

"There remaineth therefore a rest to the people of God."—HEB. IV. 9.

THE whole human race is comprised in two descriptions of people, viz., the people of God's election, and the people of God's curse, against whom he hath indignation for ever. A solemn line of demarcation is made between these two classes by God himself, and

---

* We imagine we are near the preacher, as we have heard him exclaiming, like thunder, "Where art thou?"

it is as impossible for a soul to pass this line as it is for God to cease to exist.

The first thing which the child of God is brought to feel is as contrary to "rest" as hell is to heaven. But the hypocrite may and does walk and live in error and sin, until he sinks into a horrible black despair. The poor child of God may be toiling, tugging, and roaring under horrors and terrors, fears and sorrows of mind and of heart, yet God will preserve him through all these toils of affliction, losses, crosses, and sorrows, until he brings him to feel and believe he has not had one affliction too long, one burden too heavy, one conflict too sharp. His God will overrule them to his eternal rest, and he shall be forced to cry out, "Surely goodness and mercy shall follow me all the days of my life, and I will dwell in the house of the Lord for ever." (Ps. xxiii. 6.) Thus is sin destroyed, the law of God honoured, justice satisfied, and God glorified in their everlasting salvation, and they are brought to see there remaineth a rest for the people of God.

If there is a self-sufficient hypocrite here to-night, may God the Holy Ghost send him home as damned in his feelings as a soul can feel; and if God the Spirit shall heal up the breach of a poor child of God, I shall be gratified.

I. I shall endeavour to show, *that God has a special property in his people;* they are formed for himself, and they shall show forth his praise.

II. *What is intended by this rest;* and that whatever changes or vicissitudes they pass through, whatever losses they are called to sustain, whatever projects they form and God blasts, whatever prospects are cut up, nevertheless, *there remaineth a rest for God's people.*

I. God's people are not claimed or chosen for any excellence in them. O no! For when God speaks of them, he compares them to beasts of the field, dragons of the wilderness, and owls of the desert, saying, "The beast of the field shall honour me, the dragons and the owls, because I give waters in the wilderness, and rivers in the desert, to give drink to my people, my chosen." (Isa. xliii. 20.) What a wonder it is God did not choose better characters to people heaven with! We all know that a common workman, with good materials, can make a job; but if he has rough materials he cannot get on at all. But our God picks some of the most knotty, crabbed, and rough pieces of timber to make him a house; and yet what a beautiful house it is, as seen by the beloved disciple John in Patmos! If Jehovah compares the church to inanimate creation, then he speaks of her as a desert, or a wilderness, wherein we behold nothing that is comely, beautiful, or entertaining; yet God loves her. If we look into the New Testament, also, the Holy Ghost by Paul hath set forth the fallen state of man's soul when writing to the Corinthian church: "Know ye not that the unrigh-

teous **shall** not inherit the kingdom of God? Be **not deceived;**
neither fornicators, nor idolaters, nor adulterers, nor **effeminate,**
nor **abusers** of themselves with mankind, nor thieves, nor **covetous,**
nor drunkards, nor revilers, nor extortioners, shall inherit the **king-**
dom of God. And such were some of you; but ye are washed, **but**
ye **are** sanctified, but ye are justified in the name of the Lord **Jesus,**
and by the Spirit of our God." (1 Cor. vi. 9–11.) The apostle **fur-**
ther, to **set** aside all boasting, when speaking of some "whose **end**
is **destruction,** whose God is their belly, and who mind **earthly**
things," says, "Are we better than they? No, in no wise; for **God**
hath **concluded** all under sin." I do believe God never takes **grown-**
up persons but he will make them feel that they deserve **to be**
damned as much and as deep as devils and damned spirits who **are**
now **in** hell. It is now nearly fifty years since God first **began to**
cut **at** me, and he has not done yet; and I can heartily say, **Amen,**
to the blazing of the chips he thus cuts off me, for,

> "Bastards may escape the rod,
>   Sunk in earthly, vain delight;
>   But the true-born child of God
>   Must not, would not, if he might."

We **shrink** from the rod; but our heavenly Father keeps on **cutting**
still, and will, until we are led to thank him for it.

I shall now notice that each divine Person in the Godhead **has**
an interest in the church.

God the Father has a special property in them, for they engaged
his eternal mind before time. To make an everlasting **settlement**
for the church with and in Christ, and to confirm this **settlement,**
he gave her grace in Christ, who betrothed her: "Blessed be **the**
God and Father of our Lord Jesus Christ, who hath blessed **us** with
all spiritual blessings in heavenly places in Christ, according as **he**
hath chosen us in him before the foundation of the world, that **we**
should be holy and without blame before him in love." (Eph. i. **3,**
4.) Therefore she cannot perish, God the Father having made **pro-**
vision for her eternal safety and security before the fall. He **fore-**
saw the fall of man; and by this covenant determined that **millions**
should be redeemed to eternal life.

Therefore, when God begins a work upon the heart of a **sinner,**
he sends a dart into his soul, and brings him to Christ, in **whom**
having made ample provision, Jesus the Son of God manifests **that**
he too has a special property in him. He betrothed her unto **him-**
self,—as we take our wives, for better, for worse? O no! He **took**
her all for the worse. He knew she would have no better about **her.**
But he presents her unblameable and unreprovable in love.

Now, have you not often wondered how Jesus Christ should **fall**
in love with you, when you can see so many prettier than you **that**
he might have chosen? But Jehovah looked not at you in the **Adam**

fall, but as Paul writes: "Husbands, love your wives, even as Christ also loved the church, and gave himself for it, that he might sanctify and cleanse it with the washing of water and the word." (Eph. v. 25, 26.) Having thus betrothed her unto himself, Jesus Christ took our nature into union with Deity, in order to follow her into and through all the vile places she got into, and to bring her out, and present her before his Father without spot or wrinkle; thereby surrounding her with everlasting arms and walls of flame.

Now there is a great outcry of, "The Church is in danger." *Not so with this church,* for she is built upon the Rock of Ages, and is in no danger, for the gates of hell shall not prevail against her. Likewise she is both perfect and pure in Christ her Husband. Which church our dear Lord represented in a figure to his servant Peter, who "fell into a trance, and saw heaven opened, and a certain vessel descending unto him, as it had been a great sheet knit at the four corners and let down to the earth; wherein were all manner of four-footed beasts of the earth, and wild beasts, and creeping things, and fowls of the air. And there came a voice to him, Rise, Peter; kill and eat. But Peter said, Not so, Lord; for I have never eaten anything that is common or unclean. And the voice spake unto him again the second time, What God hath cleansed, that call not thou common. This was done thrice; and the vessel was received up again into heaven." (Acts x. 10–16.) Therefore, this church (or *wife*) is sanctified by God the Father, and preserved in Christ Jesus—there is her *eternal safety;* and called in time by God the Holy Ghost—there is her *cleansing.* Now mind. This vessel was let down from heaven *three times* (to show the equal love of God the Father, Son, and Holy Ghost), with all these creatures in it; yet none flew out, none crept out, none ran out, none jumped out, and none got in; all to give the greatest proof of God's eternal election in the choice, love, preservation, and glorification of his bride; for they were wrapt up in it as the special property of Jesus Christ her Husband.

God the Holy Ghost has an equally peculiar property in this church, which is sweetly set forth in the hymn just now sung; that the sheep ran

"As far from God as sheep can run;"

but they never shall rove

"Beyond the limits of his love;
Fenced with eternal shalls and wills,
Firm as the everlasting hills."

How solemn and awful it is to think they could not and had no will to turn to God, although hell flamed in their faces, and they could see the horrors of the damned, and hear the bellowing of lost souls! Yet some ministers have declared that if the damned in hell could hear the glad tidings of the gospel and were permitted, how gladly would they embrace it! How awful such declarations are! Why, if even they could hear of a Saviour, but had no spiritual hunger or thirst for Christ and his salvation, they could not love God; and if even they could come out of hell upon earth, it would only be to be damned again.

We have many meetings in Manchester. There was one held some time since by a party of infidels. Two persons hearing thereof agreed to go and hear the speeches; when a man got up, and said, "Who is the greatest man—Jesus Christ or Robert Owen?" He paused, and then replied, "Why, Jesus Christ is dead and buried, and we know not what has become of him; but Robert Owen is here; therefore Robert Owen must be the greatest and best man." This, under God, was the means of conviction to the two strangers. Soon after, they came to sit under my ministry; when God, having thoughts of love to them, led me to speak pointedly on the subject of infidelity; and, pointing undesignedly towards the place where the men were sitting, I said, "That's the man, and that's the man;" when both the men nearly swooned away. After a while they visited my chapel again, and God the Holy Ghost led me to speak again to their hearts; and they fainted quite away, and were carried into the vestry. Afterwards they came and related the whole of the matter to me in the vestry.

Moreover, the Holy Ghost manifested his special property in and towards the thief on the cross, by giving him new life and a spirit of prayer. Also by sending Paul and Silas to preach at Philippi, where they were called before the magistrates, who sentenced them to be put into prison. And when led there, the gaoler said he had no notion of the justices sending these fanatics to him, for he was troubled enough with common offenders. "Well," said he, "I will add to their sorrows;" and he fulfilled it, too, by scourging their backs, and then thrusting them into the inner prison, and making their feet fast in the stocks. But God sent an earthquake, both in the prison and into the heart of the gaoler. Also by sending the law of God home with divine power into his conscience, so that he would fain have stabbed himself to the heart, but God kept him back, and brought his soul to cry, "Sirs, what must I do to be saved?" When Paul said, "Believe on the Lord Jesus Christ, and thou shalt be saved."

But some in our day say we need no law-work on the conscience now. Then Paul was wrong when he said, "I was alive without the law once, but when the commandment came, sin revived, and I died."

Further, the Holy Ghost manifested his special love to, and property in Mary Magdalene. She was a wretch indeed; but not too vile for Jesus Christ to visit her and cast out of her seven devils.

Perhaps there may be some here to-night, saying, "It is not so bad with me; for I had pious parents, and received a pious education too, and I do not feel so vile; yes; and I can pray in public as often as I am called upon." And so you may, and be the greatest hypocrite upon earth too. Do not think you are the character intended by God the Holy Ghost in this text. But it is the soul who is under the teaching of God the Holy Spirit; when he lifts up that poor worm, when the burden of guilt and sin is removed, under which he groans, being burdened, he blesses him with the application of the precious blood of Christ. And O! What special pains he takes to draw these souls, and to anoint their eyes with eye-salve too! Then after a while he plunges them into fires, to burn up all their plans. Then again, he leaves them for a while, like farmers, to dress up and trim their stacks so neat and pretty, and then soon the Holy Ghost burns them down. Many here present know there is generally a deal of vermin in corn; and O! What a cracking and groaning there is heard within, while the fire rages. For our God declares his fire is in Zion and his furnace in Jerusalem. Gold must be refined. Afterwards, when the ashes are blown off, then the fine gold appears; then the soul feels his interest in God, and God shows and owns his interest in him. But there are two characters I must notice.

Some here may say, I believe in election, but live in all manner of uncleanness. I tell you that you are almost like devils; for they have knowledge and arrogance; and, like them, you are fitting for eternal damnation.

The other class, not so bold or manifest, had a fine conversion, though not very deep. "I went to hear a minister who offered Christ, and I accepted him." Poor sinner! The devil has been drugging you with his infernal opium. You may pretend to know God, and at the last die an ignorant fool.

But, there may be some poor child of God here to-night, saying, "There is no hope for me, then; for I can no more believe than I can make a world. I would read the Word and would pray to God, but cannot, for I am like a distracted man." Why, if you could believe when you please, how would the Bible be true, that faith is the gift of God? Nevertheless, he will bring that soul again amidst it all to believe in Jesus Christ.

II. *Rest, what is it?* "We that believe do enter into rest." There is a sweet calmness imparted, distinct from false peace, even a rest in that soul, yes, a believing in that heart. What from? By faith, from the damning consequences of sin, and the torturings of sin too, and the springing up of old sins. "For if the blood of bulls and of goats, and the ashes of an heifer sprinkling the unclean, sanctifieth to the purifying of the flesh, how much more shall the blood of Christ, who through the eternal Spirit offered himself without spot to God, purge your conscience from dead works to serve the living God?" (Heb. ix. 13, 14.)

Further.   It is a solemn rest from law curses and law claims too; for Christ, thy Surety, hath magnified the law and made it honourable.   I will endeavour to illustrate this by a simile.   Now, suppose a man was greatly in debt; and hearing and fearing there is a warrant out and the bailiffs are after him, he, poor man, will not and dare not go out of his house, but keeps all the doors locked, and peeps out of the keyhole and corners of the windows, and sees the men watching at every corner.   Poor man, he goes to bed, but fears to go to sleep, fearing they will get in and take him; but, through weariness, he falls asleep, and dreams he is in prison, and awakes and finds it is not so.   While thus harassed, day and night, some friend, altogether unknown to him, goes to the officer and pays the debt and all the law expenses too, and somehow sends the poor man the receipt, wherein he finds the debt and law costs are all satisfied.   Whereupon the next morning he unlocks his door, and, seeing the bailiff go by, says, "Good morning to you, Mr. Bailiff. Good morning to you, Gentlemen."   He is not afraid of the officers now.

Again.   The seventh day was a type of this rest, wherein they were to enjoy the rest of the Sabbath when they arrived in Canaan. The year of Jubilee also was a type of rest, inasmuch as all those who had sold or mortgaged their inheritance had it restored to them again freely when that year arrived.

Canaan, likewise, may be said to be a type of that rest; for after the Lord had destroyed their enemies, the land (that is, the church) had rest.   "There remaineth, therefore, a rest (or keeping of the Sabbath) to the people of God."

There is also a rest by faith in Christ.   But the true rest shall be and end in glory, where there shall be no more hankering after sin, no more infernal workings, no more dismal foreboding thoughts, causing you to feel like a walking plague.   There we shall have no more asthmatic lungs; then no more afflictions for ever.   "There remaineth therefore a rest to the people of God."

Now, the child of God has no promise of rest here.   But I laboured hard to prove God not true; for the Word of God tells me that it is through much tribulation I must enter the kingdom, while I laboured to get through without tribulation and without crosses. But God's Word is true; therefore these troubles will come on. But though foes increase and trials follow hard upon me, nevertheless, there remaineth a rest to the people of God.   When that day arrives, then farewell to all that would hinder!

[We are obliged to the kind friend who has sent us the above Notes, which bear every mark of being authentic.   Still, we feel they are but "notes"—mere loose, disjointed scraps, and give a very inadequate representation of what the sermon doubtless was as preached by Mr. Gadsby.—*J. C. Philpot, in "G. S.," Dec.*, 1847.]

CHRIST'S INVITATION TO HIS SPOUSE.

"Come with me from Lebanon, my spouse, with me from Lebanon; look from the top of Amana, from the top of Shenir and Hermon, from the lions' dens, and the mountains of the leopards."—SONG IV. 8.

IT is not my design to give a minute statement of the meaning of this portion of the Word of God, but only to drop a few hints that may be useful to some of God's dear tried family, if the Good Spirit of life and grace is pleased to make them so.

If by Lebanon we understand the pleasures of the world, so odoriferous to the fleshly mind; and if by Amana, Shenir, and Hermon, the lions' dens, and mountains of leopards, we understand the horrible haunts and roarings of the powers of hell, the lions of the bottomless pit, the dreadful various-coloured workings of the corrupt heart, we shall find that there is a great needs-be for this precious invitation of the dear Lord, not only to be spoken, but to be applied to the conscience of his dear spouse. There are times and seasons when the dear spouse of Christ is too much captivated with the pleasures of the world, till deadness and darkness of mind render her wretched, and as a scourge for her movements from Jerusalem towards Jericho, the Lord sometimes suffers the lions of hell to roar out the most horrible blasphemies into her already gloomy mind, and suffers her detestable filthy nature to rise up in a thousand forms, enough to horrify an infidel, were it possible that an infidel could see and feel it. And here the poor soul is sinking in a horrible pit and the miry clay, till all the powers of the mind seem swallowed up in awful dismay, and every struggle she makes to deliver herself only sinks her deeper till, in the greatest horror of mind, she roars out, "Let not the waterflood overflow me, neither let the deep swallow me up. Let not the pit shut her mouth upon me." (Ps. lxix. 15.) In very deed, the poor soul can then say to corruption, "Thou art my father," and to the worm, hatched and bred in filth and putrefaction, "Thou art my mother and my sister." (Job xiii. 14.)

Well, here the poor soul is, till the dear Lord is pleased to come and speak with power to the mind, and give her a sweet lift. And how amazing is the love of the dear Lord, as displayed in the blessed portion of his Word we have chosen for our text. He owns her as his spouse, and speaks to her with all the tenderness of a loving husband. Notwithstanding the deplorable state into which she has plunged herself, still he says, "My spouse." Nay, in the preceding verse he calls her his love, and says she is all fair, and there is no spot in her. And in verses 9 and 10, he says, "Thou hast ravished my heart, my sister, my spouse. Thou hast ravished my heart with one of thine eyes and with one chain of thy neck." This is love, tenderly expressed; matchless, free, undeserved love,— love that many waters cannot quench and that the floods cannot drown! Here creature-strength, creature-beauty, creature-goodness, and even creature-vileness too, with all the roarings of hell, must all give place together, and Christ alone must be exalted. Matchless grace has made this poor filthy wretch comely in the Lord's comeliness and beautiful in his beauty. (Ezek. xvi. 14.) Though black in herself, she is comely in Christ (Song i. 5; vi. 4); and the dear Lord speaks to her with all the love and tenderness of his loving and lovely heart: "Come with me from Lebanon." As though he had said, "Come, poor soul. In thy own sight and feelings thou art sunk into indescribable filth and ruin, and art ready to say, 'There is no hope for me;' as all thy efforts to deliver thyself only sink thee lower, and produce more horror of mind. But remember, 'my grace is sufficient for thee, and my strength shall be made perfect in weakness;' therefore, lean upon my arm; bear all thy weight on the arm of my blood, love, and righteousness; for here thou shalt find sufficient virtue and strength to raise thee up out of all thy horror, and to defend thee against all dangers. It is by the blood of my covenant that poor prisoners are brought out of the pit wherein is no water. (Zech. ix. 11.) Neither the allurements of the world, the lions of hell, nor the corruptions of thy own heart, shall destroy thee. Be of good cheer; I have overcome the world, defeated Satan, and made an end of sin, and am in very deed thy great salvation. Cast all thy cares upon me; lean wholly upon my atoning blood for pardon, my righteousness for justification, and my all-conquering arm for thy defence. I have waded through all the floods of thy woes, fought thy battles for thee, and defeated all thy enemies; therefore drop into my embrace, and come up with me, my spouse, with me. Thy complete conquest is secured in the victories I have gained, and it is thy high privilege to rest in my love, blood, and obedience. Thou art my spouse, and thou art one in and with me. My life is thy life, my righteousness is thy righteousness, my strength is thy strength, my holiness is thy holiness; for I am made of God unto thee, wisdom, and righteousness, and sanctification, and redemption, and I will bring thee safely through all thy trials, and present thee to myself 'all glorious.' Thy own heart will deceive thee; but my salvation-arm is Almighty, and will never deceive thee nor fail thee; therefore come up with me, out of all thy foes, and fears, and faintings, and filth, and wretchedness. Again, I say, poor, tried, tempted, distracted soul, come up with me, and lean wholly upon my arm. I will never leave thee, nor forsake thee, but will be a very present help in all thy troubles, and thou shalt prove me a God and Friend near at hand. No weapon formed against thee shall prosper, and every tongue that riseth against thee in judgment thou shalt condemn. Therefore, come up with me from all thy miseries to the sweet enjoyment of my glorious conquest; and by faith in my love, blood, and obedience, sing the wonders of my grace. Come, lovely spouse, and hold a few moments' sweet communion with me. I freely give thee my heart and take thine, to realize a little of the blessedness arising from and connected with thy eternal election, thy special and absolute redemption, and thy spiritual and vital vocation. All the glories arising from the everlasting love of thy Three-One-God are made over to thee, as thou standest in union to me; I in thee, and thou in me, and thou art complete in me. Come up with me, for thy God will converse with thee, and smile upon thee. Thou art chosen in me, redeemed by me, and hast redemption through my blood, the forgiveness of all thy sins. Thou art made holy in me, thou art accepted in me, and in me thou hast obtained an inheritance; and all to the praise of God's glory. Therefore thou mayest safely sing, 'Rejoice not against me, O mine enemy; when I fall I shall arise; when I sit in darkness the Lord shall be a light unto me. I will bear the indignation of the Lord, because I have sinned against him, until he plead my cause, and execute judgment for me. He will bring me forth to the light, and I shall behold his righteousness; then she that is mine enemy shall see it, and shame shall cover her which said unto me, 'Where is the Lord thy God? Mine eyes shall behold her; now shall she be trodden down as the mire of the streets.'" (Mic. xii. 8–10.)

May the dear tried family of God be enabled to look unto, rest upon, and trust wholly in the Lord Jesus Christ, and come up with him from all their filth and enemies into the solemn enjoyment of the mysteries of God, and of the Father, and of Christ; that so they may feelingly say, "My Beloved is mine, and I am his."

GOD IN OUR NATURE.
"God with us."—Matt. i. 23.

There will be such a mystery unfolded, in "God in our nature," as will fill the church of God with immortal wonder for ever and ever. When Christ speaks of it, he says, "Father, I pray for them; I pray not for the world, but for them which thou has given me; for they are thine," and "that they may be one in us." This blessed Redeemer, this Person of the Son, takes our nature, and is "God with us." I believe that our blessed Christ really took soul and body, the whole of humanity. He was "God with us" in his weakness; "God with us" in his conflicts; "God with us" in his victories; "God with us" in his exaltation; "God with us" to strengthen us, to watch over us, to direct us, and to deliver us; completely to save us; to rule over us and in us; to defeat all our foes; to give us exalted views and feelings of God; to raise us to ineffable felicity and glory. "God with us!" And there are thousands more that I cannot name! He has promised to be "our God and our Guide, even unto death."

I have been struck with that hymn of Hart's:

> " Behold from what beginnings small
> Our great salvation rose;
> The strength of God is owned by all,
> But who his weakness knows?"

Devils tremble at this moment to hear this. What weakness was this! And let me tell thee, poor child of God, he was made like his people in all their weakness and in all their littleness, that he may come to the help of the weakest child of God in existence.

Observe, further, he was "God with us" in all his solemn concerns. Born in Bethlehem, he was hunted into Egypt that he might find his hunted people, to seek them "out of every nation." And now, poor child of God, your Jesus has been here before you. The Lord help you to go to this blessed Jesus!

He was "God with us" in his temptations. O what solemn seasons! He was "God with us" in the solemn field of temptation; he was driven into the wilderness of temptation! What a solemn conflict! Here what a battle had to be fought! If Christ had been beaten, the whole world would have been damned. "Do your duty, and God will love you," is one of the devil's cradles, in which to rock a hypocrite to sleep. God will bring all his people into such a state that nothing but "God with us" can bring them out. And when they have been brought sweetly to feel this, they sweetly sing, "God with us." The more we are brought to feel sick of self, and in a famishing condition, the fitter we are for a precious salvation.

Christ was "God with us" in Gethsemane and on the cross. We were there, poor sinners, to spit in his face, to kill him, to despise him and set him at nought. He was a solemn Day's Man, to stand up between God and us.

He was "God with us" in the solemn mystery of his love. He suffered the vengeance of hell and the vengeance of insulted Justice. The sun went into mourning, the dead were alarmed, earth and hell were all in arms. Poor child of God, poor broken-hearted sinner, it was all for thee. And yet, O how grievous! There are times when we in truth can say:

> "I can read each moving line,
> And nothing move this heart of mine!"

We can read of the sufferings of Christ, the Son of God, and feel as hardened as a devil; and after our hardness of heart and backsliding, the Lord hides his face: "Ephraim is joined to idols; let him alone." He goes "like a bullock to the yoke;" and there he is as fast as a thief. He can neither go backward nor forward; and if he goes to the Lord, Satan says, "You must go back again; he will have nothing to do with you; not he, indeed!" What! Has the Lord given him up? If he were to give one up, all heaven would go in mourning and all hell would be illuminated.　But it cannot be.

He was "God with us" in his finished work.　He gave up the ghost.　Bless his holy name, he is "God with us" in applying all these blessings to the soul.　Nothing but this will remove guilt from the conscience; nothing but this will do for the poor burdened child of God.

He was "God with us" in his resurrection and ascension.　"He died unto sin once; but in that he liveth, he liveth unto God."　The Holy Ghost, when further speaking by Paul, stamps a higher glory on his resurrection and ascension: "Who is he that condemneth? It is Christ that died; yea, *rather*, that is risen again; who is even at the right hand of God, who also maketh intercession for us."　He died for thy offences, he died for thy sins.　Could death have kept him in his cold jaws, there would have been no proof that he was "God with us,"— "God with us" in his glorious resurrection and ascension on his throne : "For Christ is not entered into the holy place made with hands, but into heaven itself, now to appear in the presence of God for us."

Now do not you see this, poor child of God?　"Blessed are the people that know the joyful sound."　What a shout will that be, when "the trumpet shall sound, and the dead shall be raised incorruptible, and we shall be changed.　For this corruptible must put on incorruption, and this mortal must put on immortality;" when millions "God with us" shall bring, to give one immortal shout of harvest home, and proclaim his honour for ever and ever.

A BRAND PLUCKED OUT OF THE FIRE.

"Is not this a brand plucked out of the fire?"—Zech. iii. 2.

1. What is meant by *a brand;* 2. *The fire* and being *plucked out;* 3. *For what purpose* are they plucked out of the fire?

1. *A brand* is a dry stick, destitute of sap, so that it may easily be lighted.　All sinners are as a brand, dry and sapless, without any spirituality of mind or soul.　They are full of sinful self until God takes them in hand and strips them, and bestows upon them his Holy Spirit, and thus plucks them as a brand from the fire. To be preserved in morality, strictly enjoined, is very good; but it must not be considered as a ground-work for salvation.　I would warn youth to refrain from all common vices and evil company, which will be much to their credit as creatures of God; and may they be led to pray to God to pluck them as brands from the fire, or keep them from such evils.

2. *The fire.*　What fire can there be in this world worse than the burning flame, or cursed propensities of the heart,—the lust of the world, the riches of the world, the pleasures of the world, "the lust

of the eye, the pride of life," with other sinful propensities? The
fire, too, is the torturing flame of a guilty conscience; the flame of
Satan, standing by and rebuking the conscious sinner,—the consciousness of a broken law. And is it not a wonder God did not condemn *you*? For where did he find you in the days of your youth?
But now he finds you saying, "What will become of the sins I have
formerly committed?" And in your soul you have felt the fiery darts
of the law, and viewed the terrors of God's just vengeance; the condemnation of the law, and the wrath to come. These things are
kindling in your hearts a burning flame, which seems ready to utterly consume you. But the Lord appears, and brings repentance
into your souls, makes you cry to him in prayer; he hears, and gives
you faith to believe in him, and thus sends a cordial to your soul, and
brings you to know that you stand guilty before God. Thus he
plucks you as a brand from the fire.

3. For *what purpose* are they plucked out of the fire? Some say
the gospel is an offer of mercy; but if men make an effort to save
themselves it only tends to increase the flame, misery, &c. The death
of Christ alone can save us. The moment the fountain of his blood
is opened manifestively to sinners, it puts out the flame, quenches
lusts, their pride, &c., and brings salvation to the soul, and all to
show the power of his grace, which shall reign and conquer. The
sovereignty of God shall pluck sinners out of the fire for the saving
of his elect and the glory of God.—*Manchester, March,* 1839.

GOING FROM JERUSALEM TO JERICHO.

"A certain man went down from Jerusalem to Jericho, and fell among
thieves," &c.—LU. x. 30-35.

THE circumstance which led to this parable was, a certain lawyer
going to Christ, and asking him what he must do to inherit eternal
life. A principle of having something to merit life is in our very
nature. Thousands ask what they are to do, and promise but never
fairly start. The Jews were constantly found to promise what they
would do. When God was delivering them from the hands of their
enemies and supplying them with food from heaven, "O," said they,
"all that the Lord hath commanded will we do;" but they never
fulfilled their promise. Perhaps some of you in this congregation, when there has been some affliction in your own person or
in the family, have been so alarmed that you have said, "O how
good you would be in the future." But instead of this, when
the affliction was removed, you have lived more in sin than you did
before.

Well; the Lord set this lawyer a job,—to keep the commandments; and, amongst the rest, told him to love his neighbour as
himself. I believe if my salvation depended on my always loving

my neighbour as myself I should be damned; and so would you too, by the same rule; for no mere man ever did it. "Why, then," say you, "how can we expect to go to heaven?" You never can on *that* ground. But the Lord Jesus Christ did love his neighbour as himself, and this he did for his people. The poor Papist may think he will get to heaven by telling his beads and paying his priest to give him absolution; but, so dying, his will be an awful end. The Arminian may think he can get to heaven by self-mortifications, giving of his goods to the poor, and praying night and day, and striving perpetually to keep the law; but, so dying, his end will be no better than that of the Papist. Take away Christ, and there is not holiness enough in all the world to save one sinner. But give me Christ, let my soul enjoy Christ, let the love, blood, and righteousness of Christ, be graciously given to me, and there is not a law that ever God promulgated from his throne but I can solemnly face it; because Christ has magnified it and made it honourable for me. Thus I am led to know a little about the life of Christ and the death of Christ. As for human virtue, or perfection in the flesh, it is an awful delusion. As a good man once said, "Human virtue was once in the world, and the world crucified it." "Ah, well," perhaps some may say, "I know I am not perfect; but I have a good heart at the bottom." Well, now; just try your heart by this touchstone: Do you love your neighbour as yourself? Or by this: "Every evil thought is sin." Suppose the thoughts of your good heart for even a single day were printed in large letters and put on your forehead, how many streets in Manchester would you like to walk through? Would not people say, "If that man's heart is a good heart, what must a bad heart be?"

But the lawyer wanted to know who *was* his neighbour, and the Lord pointed out the parable before us.

Jericho was a city cursed of the Lord by Joshua, and is an emblem of an ungodly world. Jerusalem is a blessed type of the church of God, and the peace of God in that church. A believer, by the power of the Spirit, is brought to know what it is to have his peace in this heavenly Jerusalem. There are solemn moments when the child of God can go to his bed and say,

> " I lay me down and sweetly sleep,
> For I have peace with God;
> And when I wake he shall me keep,
> Through faith in Jesu's blood."

I had rather have this feeling, thus spiritually enjoyed, than be emperor of the whole world. To be here, is to be at Jerusalem.

Now Jerusalem, literally, is said to stand on an eminence, and some parts of it are higher than others; therefore, it is said, " A certain man went *down* from Jerusalem to Jericho; and you know it is an easy path down hill; flesh and blood like it well. But the way from Jericho to Jerusalem is up hill; and going up is hard work, especially for poor weaklings or asthmatics, like me.

The passage we have read sets forth a poor child of God, left to turn his back upon Jerusalem, and is going *towards* Jericho. What a mercy God would not let him get *quite* there! Perhaps he started off at a good pace, as is sometimes the case. He might be *running*; and it is hazardous to *run* down hill, and especially such a hill as that from Jerusalem to Jericho; so no wonder that he fell. And when he fell, he found himself among thieves. Perhaps he fell from fright, when he saw the thieves.

[The person who took the notes of the above exposition here makes a remark in pencil: "Some of the above, and especially this part, is very meagre, as Willey is very tiresome."]

Well, at any rate, he fell among thieves. What else could he expect? If a man leaves his house, and goes into the very spot where thieves are, how can he expect other than that he shall fall amongst them? It is arrogant to expect safety, if we travel in the high road of thieves.

Well; this man fell among thieves; and they stripped him. What did they strip him of? All his peace, all his sweet enjoyment of God, and almost, but not quite, all his hope. Bless the Lord that, though, perhaps, he bled much from his wounds, *all* his hope did not bleed out of him. He was not *quite* dead.

Now what where the thieves, think you? I do not know any thief that pesters, and plagues, and tortures a child of God more than pride and self-importance, It is a thief near at hand. "O," say you; "I must maintain my dignity. I must have my own way. I am determined not to be mastered." O, thou cursed thief! Thou hast distressed many a child of God, and brought them into bondage.

Another thief that a child of God meets with, on his way to Jericho, is stubbornness of temper. He seems determined, though conscience speaks to him, not to give way. I have seen many instances of this kind; and more than once have we had to exclude members because of this hateful thief.

[Another remark in pencil says, "An illustrative dialogue was given here." But it is not recorded.]

How often does the child of God find this to be the case. He stifles conscience, because he is determined not to give way.

Another thief is worldly-mindedness, an over-anxious care after the world; a thirsting for worldly honour, worldly greatness, &c. This thief comes to a child of God with such plausibility that he would almost make a man a rogue to get a little of this world's good. Self is close at heel, and a thousand things will be presented to the mind, to lead it from the simplicity that is in Christ The great things of God appear to become secondary matters only, and they must give way to worldly circumstances. And O what deadness of soul does this lead to! I have known cases where persons have become possessed of thousands who have declared they were far happier when they had only a few shillings a week than they were in the midst of their wealth.

[The above is all that is given, as the said Willey seems to have become increasingly tiresome.]

ON CHRISTIAN LIBERTY.
Preached in 1842.

"If the Son make you free, ye shall be free indeed."—JNO. VIII. 36.

MUCH we talk of freedom in our day; much is our mind perplexed about it; but how little is said, and how little we think of the freedom in the text. Freedom in this life concerning temporal matters will benefit us little compared with the freedom which the Son of God gives to his children. The former endureth only a little while, but the latter endureth for ever. O may this freedom be made manifest unto us, through God's dear Son.

We understand, in consideration of this subject,

1. Freedom signifies a prior bondage. 2. What is this freedom? 3. God's Son makes us free.

1. All men, by nature, are in bondage. Hence, whosoever sinneth is the servant of sin. We groan under this bondage every day, except when in the enjoyment of the freedom in our text. And such a deplorable state of slavery was never known, nor ever would have been known;—we should never have known of vice, famine, and distress, but for sin. Youth would not have been in danger of falling into the temptations which continually await them, but for sin; the child would not have cause to weep over a dying parent but for sin; or a mother anxiously watching over the pains and struggles of her suffering babe, but for sin.

Sin is a baneful curse, and has spread its awful contagion over all the world; and so alluring is its nature to ours, and so fond are we of it, by nature, we would not let it go, were it not for the mercy of God in sending his invincible power into our souls. We are under bondage *to Satan.* He is the first transgressor, the father of lies, indeed of all wickedness. God is not, nor can he be, the author of sin. When made free, then do we find that the devils are subject to us; but rejoice not in this, but rather that your names are written in heaven.

By nature, we are in bondage to *the world.* Its charms, its pleasures, its wickedness, and deceit, carry us like a flood from the ways of God, and truth. We are in bondage *to the law.* The law, when given to Adam, was in perfect accordance with his nature. It was holy, just, and good; and so was Adam. But Adam, having the management of it himself, broke its commands. But the law remained the same; God determined it should not be sullied; it must be fulfilled in every point. And here are we, the sons of Adam, bound to produce a perfect obedience to a perfect law. The child of God is made to feel all this and groan under it.

2. What is this freedom? Sometimes God is pleased to grant a manifestation of pardon at once, but oftener gradually. The first token of freedom is, to feel that we are in bondage, that we are sinners; for though all men are alike sinners in the sight of God, all are not blessed with freedom to know it, and to cry out for mercy in consequence thereof. We never cry for mercy, feelingly so, till we enjoy a little of this freedom. Then we pant for the water of life, and at last we are enabled to rejoice in a precious Redeemer.

3. The Son makes us free, and not ourselves. Suppose we were in debt and had nought to pay the debt, and a kind friend were to come and pay it for us, we should justly be free. And so it is with Christ. He paid our enormous debt and set us free. "He is the end of the law for righteousness to every one that believeth." And thus is the law magnified more than if Adam had fully obeyed its commands, inasmuch as it has the obedience of God and man. By faith we realize this great truth, and are made free. God grant us the enjoyment of this freedom, and we shall then be free indeed.

THE BODY SOWN AND THE BODY RAISED.

[I have two MSs., one by Mr. Player, of the following. They differ somewhat, one being a little fuller than the other. See also the " G. S.," for 1862 and 1872.—J. G.]

"It is sown in dishonour, it is raised in glory; it is sown a natural body, it is raised a spiritual body."—1 Cor. xv. 43, 44.

This chapter clearly shows the resurrection of the dead, and arguments are brought forward to prove it which are of the greatest force. Paul brings forward the objections that an unbelieving mind would make against it; such, for instance as, "How are the dead raised up, and with what body do they come?" His answer is, "Thou fool, that which thou sowest is not quickened except it die." All the ear is not sown, but merely a bare grain. That dies, and then it is quickened, and brings forth fruit according to its nature. There are some who assert that in heaven the saints of God will differ from each other in glory as the stars; but there is no passage in Scripture to prove such a statement. Our bodies are sown in corruption, they shall be raised in incorruption; and thus the body raised in incorruption will differ in glory from what it was when sown in corruption. As the dimmest star differs from the brightest planet, God shall change it and fashion it like unto his glorious body. The brightest minister will not shine one whit brighter than the humblest hearer. Hence we read, "They that be wise shall shine as the brightness of the firmament, and they that turn many to righteousness, as the stars for ever and ever." Thus it does not appear that the ministers of the gospel, who have been the means of turning many to righteousness will outshine those that be wise, or those whom they may have been the means, in the hand of God, of turning to righteousness; for these shall shine as the *brightness* of the firmament, not as the *dark* firmament, which needs the stars to light it; but as when the sun is up in his meridian splendour, emitting its beams of light on the firmament, and causing it to shine with a glorious brightness.

Again. "It does not yet appear what we shall be; but we know that when he shall appear we shall be like him; for we shall see him as he is." And if all who die in Christ, all who are raised in incorruption, raised to glory, will be like Christ, there will be no difference; for Christ hath not many likenesses. Some people say there are large souls and small souls. Now just notice a babe. It grows and gradually increases in knowledge. Its intellectual faculties become enlarged, but its soul is no greater; otherwise, when it gets old it droops with the body, and becomes as the soul of a little child once more. I believe that the soul of every child which dies in its infancy will shine as bright and be as great as that of Paul or any of the apostles; and I believe also that William Gadsby, vile as he is, will shine as bright as Paul too.

All men are in nature, of nature, and by nature, corrupt. "Their throat is an open sepulchre." Now, a sepulchre is a place in which to deposit the dead, and is generally filled with a stench, proceeding from the corrupt bodies; and when it is opened it emits that horrid stench. So are we all by nature. O what wickedness proceeds from our bodies! Our tongues, what evil have they spoken! Our eyes, what lustful, proud, and sinful acts have they committed! Let the glass tell what they have done! Our hands, how have they been laid on that which is unholy, unclean! Our feet, how have they run in the way of evil! And after all, your bodies must moulder away in the earth, be food for worms, and become a stench, a nuisance to the living.

But now let us look at the new man, which is Christ in us; and at the old man, which is sin in us. Both live in us. There is a difference between you living in sin, and sin living in you. Sin lives in a child of God, and plagues and harasses him continually; but he does not live in it. He hates it and abhors it. This body, which is by nature corrupt, is actually the seat of all the inventions of Satan. And O how many there are who spend their whole time in washing, dressing, and adorning it. They little think that at one time it will be raised, not in glory, but to their shame and confusion. The wrath of God shall come upon them, and they shall burn with unquenchable fire.

Again. "It is sown in dishonour." Our bodies are sown in sin. They are vile and polluted; but if changed by the regenerating grace of God, through Christ Jesus, we shall be raised in glory.

And that glory who can describe? We cannot describe the glory which the disciples beheld on the Mount of Transfiguration; which glory was so great that the disciples fell at Christ's feet, as dead; how can we then describe the glory which shall hereafter be when our bodies are raised, when God himself will be our glory? "Thy God thy glory."

THE POOR AND THE NEEDY SEEKING WATER.

Preached in Gower Street Chapel, London, on Lord's Day Morning, Aug. 3rd, 1823.

"When the poor and needy seek water, and there is none, and their tongue faileth for thirst, I the Lord will hear them, I the God of Israel will not forsake them."—Isa. xli. 17.

A PERSON who is a stranger to his own depravity and does not know his own heart, wonders, when he reads of Israel of old, to find that, after the Lord had done such great things for them, they should so revolt as to make a calf of gold, worship it, sacrifice thereunto, and say, "These be thy gods, O Israel, which brought thee up out of the land of Egypt." (Exod. xxxii. 8.) But one who is acquainted with his own depravity and knows and feels the plague of his own heart wonders at nothing. except it is that mankind at large do not carry things to a greater pitch than they do and that this world is not a very Bedlam. And indeed, if God did not lay a restraint upon mankind, this world would be as bad as hell itself.

In speaking upon the passage I have taken as a text, I will, as God shall enable me,

I. Describe the *poor and needy.*

II. Their *seeking water,* their *not finding it,* and the *effect* it has upon them.

III. The Lord's promise, to *hear them and not forsake them.*

I. We are to describe a *poor and needy man.* If we saw a man destitute of food and raiment, house, home, and credit, and so in debt as to be forced to hide himself, knowing that a warrant was out to arrest him, we should say he was indeed a poor wretch. Well, what such a man would be temporally, God's people are spiritually. A quickened sinner feels, in some measure, the weight of his sins and the wrath of God due to him on their account; yet his experience is not so keen as is the experience of one who has known pardon and is now brought to mourn the absence of God. Satan suggests that he has committed the unpardonable sin, and this aggravates his misery; but the Lord has left on record a very encouraging word to such: "Fear thou not, for I am with thee; be not dismayed, for I am thy God. I will help thee; yea, I will uphold thee with the right hand of my righteousness." The soul says, "Lord, I am a worm, and so weak I am afraid." "Well," the Lord adds, "Fear not, thou worm Jacob, and ye men of Israel. I will help thee, saith the Lord, and thy Redeemer the Holy One of Israel. Behold, I will make thee a new sharp threshing instrument, having teeth, and thou shalt thresh the mountains and beat them small, and shalt make the hills as chaff." You may wish to know what this instrument is. It is *faith;* and with it the worm, who thought he should be crushed to atoms, is enabled to beat down unbelief, devils, hell, and sin.

But to speak more particularly of the soul that is under conviction of sin. Much is said in our day about treason against the king; and very justly. Treason is a great crime; but a soul which the Holy Ghost has taken in hand is convicted of treason and of many other crimes against the King of kings; and he needs the application of pardon to his heart; for Jehovah pardons sinners. Our king can grant a pardon by a single stroke of his pen. It costs him nothing; it is called an act of grace. But, before the King of kings could pardon a sinner, he must die for him. Justice must be satisfied and honoured; wherefore the King, to pardon the traitor, poured out his heart's blood.

It is common for persons under conviction of sin not to know what is the matter with them. I knew a youth who told his feelings to a medical man, and he prescribed for him; but he found it of no use. He required a better Physician to heal his wound. If such a one talks to nominal professors, they think he is going mad. I knew a young woman who was under convictions of sin, and her mother (a professing woman) put her into a madhouse, and was caressed by her connections for so doing. Some time afterwards, she went to see her, when the daughter told her how graciously the Lord had appeared for her, and visited her soul with his love, and filled her with happy enjoyment. When her mother returned home, she told her connections that, alas! her daughter was quite as bad, only the disorder had taken a *turn.* This was all she knew about it. But blessed be God for such *turns.* I believe there are more of God's elect in St. Luke's and other lunatic asylums than in all the noblemen's families in this kingdom; for I know that when a soul convicted of sin is observed by the ungodly, they often call it melancholy, and think the madhouse the fittest place for him. Some will say such a one is nervous, and such a one is a poor nervous creature; but I believe all God's people are so, more or less, that conviction often shakes every nerve, and is sometimes so powerful as to impair the reason.

There was a member of our church who, when under conviction, could not bear to hear the tolling of a bell, for he thought it said, "Damn him! Damn him! Damn him!" and that all nature seemed to curse him; and he said, as David said of Shimei, "Let him curse, for the Lord hath bidden him." This is a trying experience. Such a man reads his Bible, weeps, mourns, and is disconsolate. In the hours of common repose he cannot rest, but perhaps often has to rise and go to prayer while his partner is asleep. She will say to her neighbours, "I cannot think what is come to my John. He goes moping about, and seems not fit for his employment; and when he comes home he does not joke nor tell me any curious tales to cheer me up, as he used to do." And so, if conviction take hold of a wife, "O," says the husband, "she is not fit to manage for the family, nor to assist in the business. If I had known this before, I would not have married her." And if the person is in the single state, it is in a manner the same. He can neither satisfy himself nor those about him.

A man who is poor literally might be relieved with a little, for at most we want but little here; but not so the poor in my text. Nothing will satisfy him but everlasting life, and God says, by the apostle Paul, "My God shall supply all your need, according to his riches in glory by Christ Jesus."

II. This poor man is said to *seek water*, &c. He has a burning fever in his heart, and desires that it may be satiated. If he is in a country where the gospel is preached, he will be found under the Word, perhaps running from one place to another; but can get nothing. A few duties will not satisfy his conscience, like that of a mere professor. He fears he is mocking God. Some advise him to frequent places of amusement, and play at cards, it may be; others to be up and doing, and to double his diligence, and to get holiness; and others to receive the sacrament, &c. So he goes, perhaps, to the parish church and receives it; but now he feels worse than before, fearing he has taken it unworthily, and has eaten and drunk damnation to himself, and thinks he is not a whit behind Judas, who received the devil in the sop. Glad would he be to sink into nonentity and remain in non-existence, or at last to be damned only with the *common* sinner; but he fears his punishment will be greater than any one's, as he feels he is an *uncommon* sinner. Jeremiah thus speaks of the distress of his soul: "He has brought me into darkness, and not into light. Surely against me is he turned. He turneth his hand against me all the day. My flesh and my skin hath he made old. He hath broken my bones; he hath set me in dark places, as they that be dead of old; he hath made my chain heavy. Also when I cry and shout, he shutteth out my prayer. He hath also broken my teeth with gravel stones; he hath covered me with ashes." Nor did he rise till he saw that his affliction was for his good, and looked upon his Saviour's sufferings: "Remembering mine affliction and my misery, the wormwood and the gall. My soul hath them still in remembrance, and is humbled within me."

The great bulk of professors are utter strangers to these things. Our Lord thus describes the two classes, the self-righteous Pharisee and the convicted sinner: "Two men went up in the temple to pray; the one a Pharisee, and the other a publican. The Pharisee stood and prayed thus with himself: God, I thank thee that I am not as other men are—extortioners, unjust, adulterers, or even as this publican. I fast twice in the week, I give tithes of all that I possess." Here you see he tells God how *good* he is, and even thanks God he is so. But "the publican, standing afar off, would not lift up so much as his eyes to heaven, but smote upon his breast, saying, God be merciful to me, a sinner. I tell you, this man went down to his house justified rather than the other; for every one that exalteth himself shall be abased; and he that humbleth himself shall be exalted."

When you go from the house of God and converse together, take care to let it be on the things which are of the greatest importance; for the poor and needy, who cannot speak of his feelings to God's people, yet will listen to their talk to find if their path is like his; but if you talk only of this world, you will greatly distress him. I knew a man who, on one Lord's day, was, in the course of providence, led to a distant place, where he went with his relations to their chapel. When service was over, he was desirous of conversing with some of the hearers, and as he saw several parties talking together, he listened; but could hear no talk but of war and trade. He then inquired of them if they could direct him to any place where the gospel was preached. "O yes," said they, "here," pointing to their chapel. "O no," said he, "that it is not; at least if it is, it has had no good effect upon you, for I have not heard one word from any of you about the gospel, or anything except war and trade." Beware, brethren, that you do not bring a similar reproach upon yourselves, for you do not know how you may wound the feelings of the poor and needy.

Again. If this poor soul seeks for comfort amongst God's own people, why, in some frames of mind, if they saw him coming in at the front door, they would rather run out at the back than stay to speak with him, for they have so much trouble going on within that they are unwilling to be burdened by him, forgetting that souls in trouble are often the means of comforting each other.

The effect of the poor soul's not finding the water he is seeking, is said to be that his tongue faileth for thirst. Job desired time to swallow down his spittle, being pressed, and pursued, and driven, as it were, to his wits' end. I should not be surprised if there is one here to-day, come to seek the Lord, determined, if the Lord does not show him mercy, to come no more, nor read the Bible any more, nor pray any more; but to go and destroy himself. You will, perhaps, say such a one is a lunatic; and I will tell you that such a lunatic you may be if ever God brings you into very close quarters. "I went," says a poor soul, perhaps, "the other day to our minister and told him my pitiful condition. 'Ah!' said he. 'You have committed some great sin; you must remove the cause, and the effect will cease; you must watch and strive, and repent!' 'True,' said I, 'I have committed many great sins, by which I have brought fresh guilt upon my conscience; and not only so, but I sin with every breath I draw; and as to the cause you bid me remove, it is in my breast, and *I* cannot remove it.'" But the poor parson, who is in reality much more poor than the poor soul himself, knows nothing about it. He is like Jonathan's lad, entirely out of the secret. But we will now leave such legal parsons and their legal preaching, and speak,

III. Of the Lord's promise to the poor and needy, to *hear them and not forsake them*. He hears them with attention, compassion, and delight: "The Lord hearkened and heard; and a book of remembrance was written before him, for those that feared the Lord and that thought upon his name;" "I have seen, I have seen the affliction of my people, and have heard their groanings, by reason of their taskmasters, and am come down to deliver them." God is pleased to see the soul seeking him, because it is the work of his own blessed Spirit, who has brought him to feel his wretched condition; and he has promised that "whosoever calleth on the name of the Lord shall be delivered." "Call upon me in the day of trouble; I will deliver thee, and thou shall glorify me." If a man literally poor came to our door for relief, we might, for decency's sake, stay and hear his tale, but perhaps pay but little attention to it, and at last say, "We can do nothing for you." But God could as soon cease to be God as to deny mercy to his redeemed, the poor and needy: "I said not to the seed of Jacob, Seek ye my face in vain."

Again. In one place we read of the heavens dropping down and of the mountains flowing down at the presence of the Lord. The Holy Ghost descends, and discovers to the soul how Christ became his ransom, and, by his sufferings and death, payed his infinite debt and reconciled him to God. But though his pardon is thus proclaimed, it is the soul's union to Jesus that brings him to heaven. Being so related, as being a joint heir with him, he has a right and title to heaven. Christ is bone of his bone and flesh of his flesh: "Father, I will that they also, whom thou hast given me, be with me where I am, that they may behold my glory." Such a soul now enjoys a treasure not to be pent up; and though the Lord may exercise him in this world, for the trial of his faith, it is that he may know more of his faithfulness and goodness.

In conclusion, I would ask you if you know these things for yourselves; for they are personal matters, which we must know for ourselves, if ever we are saved.

That those who do may enjoy the happiness of them, more and more, and that those who do not may be brought to do so in God's time, is my desire and prayer.

NOT WILLING THAT ANY SHOULD PERISH.

Preached in Manchester, Feb. 9th, 1840.

"The Lord is not slack concerning his promise, as some men count slackness; but is long-suffering to us-ward; not willing that any should perish, but that all should come to repentance."—2 PET. III. 9.

To add to, or diminish from, the Word of God is a crime, though much employed in the frivolities of the world; and the office of a minister is a very responsible one. He is God's steward, and he must one day give up his stewardship; and if he seeks to please men, he is not a true servant of God; nay, it is insulting God. Some say God is not willing that any creature should perish, but every one should come to repentance; but in our text we are told it is this "*us-ward*" for whom he is long-suffering, not willing that any should perish, but that all should come to repentance. "Then," say you, "if it is only to this us-ward, why preach the gospel?" Because God has ordained the preaching of the gospel for the gathering in of his people. If it were to all men, would he not send his Word into all men? When God designs to save his people, he sends his gospel into them; as he did into the Philippian jailor. He sent ministers unto him in the prison. Zaccheus, who must climb a tree; and God brought him down and abode with him. And where were some of you when God met with you? You had no inclination to hear his Word, but he brought you forth out of nature's darkness into his marvellous light. And what is the sense of the text? God's long-suffering with, and promise to, his people, the us-ward, not willing that any of his people should perish, but that all should come to repentance. In the last days scoffers shall come, and shall say, "Where is the promise of Christ's coming, without sin in the world? One generation passeth away, and another, and there is no appearance of his coming; how is it?" It is his long-suffering to us-ward; therefore, beloved, account his long-suffering salvation. When he shall fold up the skies as in a scroll, and wind up the business, all his people shall be brought in; and I would ask if God is not willing that any man should perish, is he not able to give him repentance? For repentance is the gift of God; and is he incapacitated to do what he wished? Or will his designs be frustrated by such frail creatures as you and I? He says, "O Jerusalem, Jerusalem, which killest the prophets and stonest them that are sent unto thee, how often would I have gathered thy children together, as a hen gathereth her chickens together, and ye would not." Here we find that Christ refers to the Scribes, and Pharisees, and heads of the people, the Sanhedrim. He worked many miracles before them, but they did not believe on him; he would have gathered thy children, "but ye would not;" not "they would not." And, again: "When the righteous turneth from his righteousness, and committeth iniquity, he shall die," "but if the wicked turneth from his wickedness, and doeth that which is lawful and right, he shall live." This is according to the Jewish nation; not the preaching of the gospel, but the law. For what saith the law? Do and live; leave undone and die. Therefore there is no salvation by the law, "that every mouth may be stopped, and all the world become guilty before God." That it might be by grace, not of works, lest any man should boast. Salvation is entirely of free, unmerited, discriminating grace. But this it could not be if it depended on any thing the creature does.

What is intended by the promise, "The Lord is not slack?" &c. And why this apparent delay and long-suffering? God declared in the beginning concerning the temple, that it should be destroyed, and that one stone should not be left upon another. But the Jews laughed it to scorn; they could not believe it; but it came to pass at last. His long-suffering bore with their manners until its accomplishment, and the execution thereof was awful in the extreme. Never was known such an appalling devastation. There was a great famine; and so great was their distress that men butchered each other for food to support their dying frames, and women tore their own children from their bosoms for the same purpose. Never was known in the history of time such a day of misery. And what made the scene more appalling, the destruction happened on a festival day, wherein all that were met together in the temple perished; but all the children of God escaped, out of the way; not one of them perished.

What an awful sight to them; that the departed spirits should in a moment's warning quit this world and enter into hell, and then in agonizing torments behold the just God whom they had despised and mocked. May God enable you to confide in his promise, and trust him for his grace, that when the time comes for its accomplishment you may be found ready. We have the promise of Christ's second coming. The apostle Paul had a blessed view of this, as recorded in Heb. ix. 27: "And as it is appointed unto men once to die; but after this the judgment; so Christ was once offered to bear the sins of many, and to them that look for him shall he appear the second time, without sin, unto salvation." He shall come the second time without sin; he will be holy, harmless, undefiled, and separate from sinners. At his first coming, his visage was marred, and there was neither form nor comeliness in him, that we should desire him; but he bore the sins of many; he hath appeared once to put away sin by the sacrifice of himself. God hath laid upon him the iniquity of his usward. If God had not done it, we never should; for our sins are so numerous we should have forgotten many; and there are many that we should not have thought were sins; they are so amiable and pleasing to our nature that we should not look upon them as sins; and from our first breath in infancy, to our last, though it be to old age, there is not a moment of our existence that we live without sin, except when we are bathing in the blood of the Lamb.

> "Thy garden is the place,
> Where pride cannot intrude ;
> For should it dare to enter there
> 'Twould soon be drown'd in blood."

Yes, Gethsemane is the place where our sins were put away; our sins of omission and sins of commission were all gathered together and put upon Christ. He bore them, and hath nailed them to his cross.

He finished the work which his Father gave him to do; "he ascended to his God and our God;" "to his Father and our Father, and ever liveth to make intercession for us." He is not slack concerning his promise, but will come at the appointed time. Before him shall be gathered all nations, and every man shall be judged according to the deeds done in the body. His apparent delays do not prove that he is slack concerning his promise, but rather his long-suffering; for if it were not for his long-suffering, would you not all be damned? For unless ye repent, ye shall all likewise perish; and, therefore, is it not of his long-suffering that he brings us to repent, and cleanseth us from dead works, by washing us in the washing of regeneration, that we may have pardon through his blood? Did not God promise Abraham that he should possess the land of Canaan, and that in his seed should all the nations be blessed? And was not the promise apparently delayed? But it was his long-suffering. And though Abraham and Sarah his wife became old, yet did not God perform his promise at the appointed time? And though Abraham took a bond-woman to his bosom, yet it did not in any wise further the execution of God's promise, but rather was the very means of causing discord in the family. And so with us; for anything that we may do will not hasten the promise of God. "And Abraham, by faith, sojourned in the land of promise, not knowing whither he went."

"But the Lord was not slack concerning his promise; but is long-suffering to us-ward." Did he not promise that Joseph should be above his brethren? And though he experienced many changes on his way for this purpose to bring him to become lord of Egypt, and apparently all things went against him, yet all things worked together for its accomplishment. The Lord was not slack concerning his promise; but his long suffering bore with their manners.

He bore with the manners of the children of Israel forty years; but at length brought them to the land of promise. All things shall work together for good to them that love God and are the called according to his eternal purpose. Honours crown his brow! "He is not slack concerning his promise, as some men count slackness," but will perform his promises in his own time and in his own way.

May the Lord bless you and me with patience to wait his time; for his mercy's sake. Amen.

THRESHING THE MOUNTAINS.

"Behold, I will make thee a new sharp threshing instrument, having teeth. Thou shalt thresh the mountains, and beat them small, and shalt make the hills as chaff. Thou shalt fan them, and the wind shall carry them away, and the whirlwind shall scatter them; and thou shalt rejoice in the Lord, and shalt glory in the Holy One of Israel."—ISA. XLI. 15, 16.

1. We will consider *to whom* these words are addressed.
2. The *mountains*.
3. The *threshing instrument*.
4. He shall *fan* them, and the wind shall *carry them away*.
5. The *end* to be answered.

1. To *whom* spoken. The character is a worm, called in the preceding verse, "worm Jacob." It refers, in the first instance, to the Lord Jesus Christ; secondly to his ministers, and thirdly to his people. Christ in his humble state is called a worm; yes, the Lord of life and glory became a worm of the earth. He was in this state the meek and lowly Jesus. "The foxes had holes, the birds of the air had nests, but the Son of man had not where to lay his head." O what a state of humiliation was that! "He became flesh and dwelt among us." And why? That we might have fellowship with him and that he might be able to call us brethren, and know how to come to our low estate as the compassionate High Priest of God. Indeed, if it were not so, what should we do? For many of God's little ones cannot soar so high in their faith as to rejoice in him in his glorification; but happy are they who have fellowship with him in his humility; they shall have fellowship with him in his glorification. "For if we suffer with him we shall also reign with him."

But where in his Word is the Lord Jesus called a worm? In Ps. xxii. 6: "But I am a worm and no man, a reproach of men and despised of the people." These are his own words, which he spake in the distress of his soul. O who can describe his humiliation, or who can fully enter into his sufferings? See "him, without form or comeliness, without beauty, that he should be desired." He became a reproach to the scorner, and hid not his face from shame and spitting. See him at Gethsemane. And all this he endured for his poor suffering people. Ah! Where shall we hide our faces? Shame belongeth unto us; for we are proud, we are vile sinners; we have need to lament our sins; but Jesus stooped lower than we can in the horrible pit and miry clay of human degradation and suffering, and at last bore our sins in his own body on the tree.

Secondly. The ministers of God are worms,—poor crawling worms of the earth; so that if it was not for the power of God they could not breathe, or lift up their voices to him. I have often wondered at sovereign mercy making such a poor crawling worm as I into one of his ambassadors, to thresh mountains. But so it is; to him be all the praise; for God hath chosen the foolish things of this world to confound the wise, and weak things of the world to confound the things which are mighty; and base things of the world, and things which are despised, hath God chosen, yea, and things which are not, to bring to nought things that are; that no flesh should glory in his presence. Here I can come in; for I have often thought and felt if there was one sinner more base than another, it was I.

Thirdly. The people of God are worms. And indeed if you are never brought to feel this truth in this life you may depend upon it hell will be your portion. However moral you may have been, however high you may have stood in the esteem of others, you must be brought to feel that, in spiritual things, you are a poor crawling worm of the earth. Look at Job. What a poor worm he considered himself to be, when he cried out, "My flesh is clothed with worms and clods of dust, my skin is broken and become loathsome." May the Lord bring you to feel it, that you may glory in him, and in him alone.

These poor worms are longing for and pursuing after a manifestation of God's grace. Hence it is written in the next verse: "When the poor and needy seek water and there is none, and their tongue faileth for thirst, I the Lord will hear them, I the God of Jacob will not forsake them." They are seeking the water of life, that water that flowed from Jesus' side,

"To quench the fiery law
And blood to purge their sin."

They are blessed indeed, when, under a consciousness of their guilt, they have this longing desire; for blessed are they who hunger and thirst after righteousness, for they shall be filled. The desire of their heart shall be granted.

2. The *mountains*. A conscious child of God cannot do without a religion that comes home to his conscience. There is no vitality in religion without sweet access to God. It is not *talking*, but *feeling*. What then are we to understand by some of these mountains? Fresh contracted guilt in the conscience is one mountain. Some think lightly of sin; but it is a solemn matter. What! "Shall we sin that grace may abound? God forbid." Was it a light thing to Christ when he groaned under it and sweat, as it were, great drops of blood on account of it? O then is it nothing to you, all ye that pass by? Is it nothing to *you?* Sin is a curse to us; yea, to the whole human race, and without the blood of the Lamb we could never be delivered from it.

Another mountain is the temptations of the wicked one. The sinner has sometimes a greater regard for his character than for the honour of God in abstaining from sin; and so, lest he should be called narrow-minded, or a fanatic, he will join in unbecoming conversation; but God takes notice of this and causes it to become a mountain between God and his soul. And sometimes a poor soul, though not exactly joining in, secretly listens to it. And then such a passage as this is sent home to him, and seems like a mountain: "If I regard iniquity in my heart, the Lord will not hear me." The poor soul knows that he regards iniquity in his heart, and therefore he feels condemned. Some of the "decidedly pious" folks will say, "Remove the cause, and the effect will cease." That is an insult both to God and conscience. How can a drowning man save himself? What a mockery it would be to tell him he must remove the cause, and the effect would cease. It would be like telling him he must not tumble into the water, and then he would not be drowned. But the man is in already; so how *can* he remove the cause?

Another mountain is inbred corruption. If it does not come out it is there, and is a sore burden to the poor man. He feels it to be a mountain between God and his soul.

Another is worldly cares. If he is poor, he sometimes envies the rich, and asks himself how it is that they have so much while he has so little; and he thinks if he had plenty, as they have, he should be happy. But no! Rich men are not always happy. Indeed, on the contrary, riches often prove a great mountain. For how often do you see well-to-do men consider religion only a secondary matter, and neglect the means of grace, especially on a week-day, lest they should, if tradesmen, miss sixpence by a sale. And if they have retired, they are often constantly fearing that that bank will break or that that man who owes them money will fail. Riches do not open a way to communion with God, but often raise a mountain against it.

Again. How often has a child of God a mountain of horrible temptation between God and his own soul. He sometimes has hard views of God the Father, God the Son, and God the Holy Ghost; and the enemy will accuse him of sinning against the Holy Ghost. And O what a mountain this is! The poor man will run to his minister, and first to one friend and then to another, almost in despair. Has he *indeed* committed the unpardonable sin? That is his anxious inquiry. But no man, who is really afraid he has committed the sin and is sorely distressed on account thereof, ever did or ever can commit it. He has the life of God in his soul, or he would not trouble about it.

Then there are mountains of legality. The poor soul does want to do something to secure God's favour; but his favour is not to be obtained *that* way. It is the humble and contrite heart that the Lord will not despise. And sometimes he feels the chastisements of his Father; for whom the Lord loveth he chasteneth, and scourgeth every son whom he receiveth; but not with the anger or passion of a man. When he chastises us, he makes us feel that we deserve it;

so that we tremble before him, until he applies his precious promise unto us, "Fear not."

3. I will make thee a new sharp *threshing instrument*. This instrument may refer, in the natural sense, to such a one as is described in Isa. xxviii., beginning at the 25th verse. But let us see what the Holy Ghost means. He means vital faith in the love and blood of the Son of God. But first the man is brought to have faith in his own weakness,—to feel his own weakness; for out of weakness hath Christ ordained strength; and then he is brought to have faith in Christ's strength. This last will overcome all difficulties; for the battle is not to the strong, nor the race to the swift, but the Son of God is made perfect in our weakness; and as God, in his mercy, leads us into this mystery, we shall indeed be enabled to thresh down mountains. When Christ was in the flesh, he said to his disciples, "If ye had faith as a grain of mustard seed, ye shall say unto this mountain, Remove hence to yonder place, and it shall remove, and nothing shall be impossible unto you." (Matt. xvii. 20.) It is supposed by some that when Christ spoke this, he pointed to a mountain called Mount Corruption. I know nothing about this; but doubtless the mountain was figurative of corruption, and the sea, referred to in another place, was the atoning blood of Christ. Into this your mountain is cast; and, while you feel free from the burden of that mountain, you find freedom of access to Christ, and can praise and adore his precious name.

Moses threshed mountains. He had faith given him to believe that God had called him to deliver the Israelites out of Egyptian bondage. He went and slew an Egyptian, who was quarrelling with a Hebrew; but he went too soon. He proved himself to be only a man, and, therefore, met with a rebuke; for the next time he went the Hebrew said unto him, "Who made thee a prince and a judge over us? Intendest thou to kill me as thou killedst the Egyptian?" At this Moses feared, as well he might, and said, "Surely this thing is known." And he fled into the land of Midian. This place became a sort of college to Moses; for here he was taught a little humility by his God; here he was taught manifestively that he was only a worm; and yet he was a fit subject to thresh the mountains. Hence, when God called him to go up to Egypt on that business, he felt his own weakness and worm-like condition, and begged to excuse himself, saying, "I am no orator," &c. But God told him to say, "I AM hath sent me unto you." And this I AM is the mystery of his Word. All hell is moved before him; for if it were not for this I AM, we might for ever preach in vain. Even Moses, if he had not been sent in the strength of this I AM, would have gone in vain.

When the people passed through the Red Sea, this I AM divided the waters. And when they met with the Amalekites, what did

Moses do? Why, while Joshua engaged the Amalekites, Moses went to the top of a hill and held up his arms, emblematical of his faith in God. Some would have laughed at him, and have said, "What is the old fool doing up there? Why does he not come down and help us to fight?" But Moses believed in God as their deliverer; and as long as his arms were up, the Israelites prevailed; but when his arms, through weakness, dropped, the Amalekites overcame. But the great I AM was the Thresher. Aaron and Hur went up to the top of the hill, and they took a stone and put it under Moses, and he sat thereon; and Aaron and Hur stayed up his hands; emblematical of the Lord holding up his people in prayer and in their conflicts. Moses's arms having to be supported was also to show that, though God will be inquired of by his people, prayer is not at their own command. When the Lord designs to give them a blessing, he causes them to pray for that blessing, and the answer is certain. However great your guilt, beloved, faith in Christ makes you feel free. May the Lord the Spirit impart unto us more of this faith, that we may overcome all our enemies, through the blood of the Lamb; and to his name be all the praise.

4. These worms, after thus threshing the mountains, shall *fan* them away. By which the Holy Ghost is figured forth; as we find John the Baptist saying of Christ, "Whose fan is in his hand." The whirlwind sets forth God's vengeance and judgment against our inventions; but it spares our persons. As it is written: "When the Lord shall have washed away the filth of the daughters of Zion, and shall have purged the blood of Jerusalem from the midst thereof, by the spirit of judgment and the spirit of burning," &c. That is, separating between flesh and spirit; burning up our hay, wood, and stubble. The whirlwind shall scatter them.

5. The *end*. There are three ways in which a sinner's self-righteousness is manifested: First, he feels his sinfulness and mourns under its weight. The enemy comes in and says, "God's people are a holy people; but what are you?" He feels condemned, knowing his own sinfulness; and his self-righteous principle desires to have some holiness of its own. But when the Holy Spirit comes into the soul, the man can turn round to the enemy, and say, "I know it; I feel it; but the Lord Christ is my Surety; he is my holiness." Thus, by faith, he fans it away.

The second is, he now experiences a sweet frame of mind, a full reliance upon God, and can pour out his soul unto him in a familiar manner. The enemy, Self-righteousness, says, "Now that *is* religion! How amiable you are!" If a young man, he is for being a parson; if a young woman, she almost wishes she was a Quakeress, so that she could stand up in the chapel and speak what she feels. This is not Christ; it is not a ground of humility. Christ and Christ alone is the ground of our joy and salvation. If it is not so, when a whirlwind attacks us, all goes; it sweeps away all our self-confidence, makes our hearts tremble, till the Spirit of the Lord comes and blows upon us, and fans away all our fears.

The third is, when the Lord works this deliverance for you and makes you rejoice in the Lord and glory in the Holy One of Israel, you are ready, after a time, to overlook whence it comes, and to put it in the place of Christ.   Thus self creeps in and

" Makes even grace a snare."

But, ere long, you have to prove that even your sweet frames cannot recommend you to God.   The *end* desired and to which the Lord will bring the poor soul is that he shall rejoice in Him alone.   However dark and mysterious your path, you shall find the Lord to be your portion for ever, your holiness, your beauty, your strength, your all and in all; and then you will indeed glory in the Holy One of Israel.   Amen and Amen.

THE LORD LEADING AND INSTRUCTING HIS PEOPLE.

Preached in the Chapel, Artillery Street, Bishopsgate, London, on Behalf of the Aged Pilgrims' Friend Society.

"He found him in a desert land, and in the waste howling wilderness; he led him about, he instructed him, he kept him as the apple of his eye."— DEUT. XXXII. 10.

FROM this portion of God's Word, I shall endeavour, as the Lord may enable me this evening, to speak a little, in the first place, of where God finds all his people; namely, in a desert land.   Secondly, shall speak a little of his leading his people about, and of the seemingly strange methods the Lord sometimes takes to instruct his people.   And lastly, of the care with which his people are kept; he keeps them as the apple of his eye.

In the first place, where the Lord finds his people.   I am certain it is where none but himself would ever think of looking for them : "In a desert land, and waste howling wilderness."   Now from this portion of God's Word, you may in some measure be able to judge whether your religion is of the right kind ; I mean whether the Lord found you, and where he found you, or whether you found the Lord; whether God began with you, or you began with God—for much depends upon a right beginning.

Now all the account that some people can give of their religion is that they had the privilege, they say, of being born of pious parents, and were brought up under the means of grace ; but they cannot tell when the work began, or how.   But they were brought up to attend the Sunday School, and in time they became teachers themselves, and as they grew up to years of maturity, they became decidedly pious.   And if this is all the account you can give of the matter, there is no account of the Lord's finding you in a desert land ; you seem to me never to have known you were lost.

Now I will tell you where the Lord found me, and then I will endeavour, if the Lord will, to find out some of you. I remember, when quite a boy, I was so convinced of my wickedness that I resolved to reform my life, and go to church. This lasted for a few days, and I was greatly pleased with myself and my good resolutions; and as I went to the church, I thought all around me appeared so holy; the people appeared holy, and the very ground I walked upon seemed holy, and the bells of the church appeared holy also. But I was tempted to rob a turnip field, that I had to pass through; and here I fell, and lost all my holiness and religion together. But when the Lord began the work upon my soul in reality, he made me to feel I was indeed in a desert land, a waste howling wilderness. But the Lord did not find me that agreeable pliant creature that some people represent; for I resisted as long as I could.

I remember hearing a man preach once from the words, "Behold, I stand at the door and knock," &c. And he represented the Lord Jesus as standing at the door of the heart, and knocking and beseeching for us to let him in. But it was not the way the Lord came to me; for he knocked door and all down, or he might have knocked long enough before I should have let him in. But this poor thing represented the Lord as quite disappointed, and not able to accomplish his own work. But, honours crown his blessed brow! he is, and he makes his people willing in the day of his power. And although some say he gently opened the heart of Lydia to receive him, God does not open hearts with feathers; so he shook the jailer by an earthquake when he took possession of his heart, and soon made the lion like a lamb.

Again. When the Lord comes to seek out his people, he makes no mistake in the matter. When he sent Ananias to seek Saul of Tarsus, Ananias thought it must be a mistake, and told the Lord, "he had heard by many of this man," &c. But he was silenced with, "Go thy way, for he is a chosen vessel unto me, to bear my name among the Gentiles." We sometimes look upon one and another that we think are saints of God, and are very much mistaken in the matter.

I remember, many years ago, at my own place, some young men, what the world calls respectable, came to my chapel for some time; and I was mightily interested in them, and I thought if the Lord would but convert these young men, they would be quite an honour to my church; and my mind was kept upon the subject some time.

Well, one Saturday evening, a poor man came to invite me to go and see his dying child; but as it was a name I knew nothing of, I was unwilling to go. And I said, "Surely Monday morning will do." But the man said, "No; my lad will not be alive then, and he so wishes to see you." So I went with the man, and found he had been to nearly all the parsons in Manchester before he found out who the boy meant.   And when I got there, I found an Arminian parson with him, praying that he might work out his salvation with fear and trembling; and the boy said that that had been done eighteen hundred years ago.   And then he prayed that the Lord would increase his faith.   "Yes, that he will," the boy said.   " Where the Lord has given faith, he will be sure to increase it."   The man did not seem to know what to make of the boy's comment upon his prayer; so he soon said, " Amen," and finished up the business.

When he was gone, I said, "My lad, where did you hear of these things?"   And he said, " O Sir, I am so glad to see you; I seemed as if I could not die until I had seen you."   And he gave me a sweet account of the Lord's dealings with him, and of the terrors of the law that he had passed under; and I said, " My lad, I never saw you before that I know of."   "No, Sir, I dare say not; I belonged to Paul's church Sunday school, and there I felt distress enough; for we said, " Lord, have mercy upon us, and incline our hearts to keep this law," and our parson preached nothing but law, until I really thought we should all be damned together.   But under this distress I was one day passing your chapel, and seeing the people go in, I thought I would go in too; but I am a poor cripple.   So I waited until all were gone in, and then creeped in, and sat on the gallery stairs, where I could get out again before the people, so that they should not tread upon me ; and your text was, ' Christ is the end of the law for righteousness to every one that believeth;' and the Lord enabled me to believe it to my own comfort and consolation."   So the poor lad, you see, sweetly slid to the far end at once.   He was led to the believing end of the law, and found that Christ had fulfilled it all for him.   And O, how my soul was humbled under this discovery; but it was rather mortifying to the pride of my evil heart.   I had been fishing after these young men, but never caught one; and I remembered I had them on my mind when I preached this very sermon. But the Lord, you see, at the same time was at work upon the heart of a poor cripple upon the gallery stairs, that none of the people seem ever to have noticed or known; but he was one that the Lord found in the waste howling wilderness.

Secondly, " He instructed him, and led him about," and he will lead you about, and into some strange places too, if you are his children and live long.   For instance; look at Job, that wondrous character whom the Lord declared to be a perfect, upright man, and that there was not such another upon the face of the earth; and yet he let the devil loose upon him; and who was ever tried like Job? Indeed so wonderful appears the whole history and character of this eminent child of God, that were it not confirmed by other parts of God's Word, we should perhaps almost doubt whether there ever was, in reality, such a person.   The fear of God in his heart and tenderness of conscience were such as made him the very butt of

Satan's envy and malice; and being rich in the blessings of God's providence, he was a blessing to all around.

I fear such characters are quite as scarce now as they were in his days.   There are plenty of hardhearted, covetous wretches, even under a profession of the gospel.   But where are the characters that can say, "The blessing of him that was ready to perish came upon me; and I caused the widow's heart to sing for joy," &c.? And the poor child of God said he should die in his nest, as the kind providence of God had made it very comfortable.   But the Lord pulled the bottom out, and let Job slip through into such trials that would puzzle all the Arminians in the world to make it lie straight with their views of God's truth.

The Lord said to Satan, "Hast thou considered my servant Job, that there is none like him in all the earth, a perfect, upright man, one that feareth God and escheweth evil?"   "O yes," said the devil. "I know all about him. I have considered" (and he might have said envied) "him long enough; but I cannot get at him. Hast thou not made a hedge about him on every side? He does not fear thee for nothing."   Now how did the devil know there was a hedge about Job, and about his substance, if he had not tried to break through it? I dare say the devil had had many a thrust at that hedge, but you see he could not touch poor Job without the Lord's permission. It may truly be said they are well kept whom God keeps, for we see the malice of that old infernal in the case of Job; for no sooner does he obtain permission of the Lord, than he kills all his children at a stroke, and sends his own children to steal most of the cattle; and, to make it still more terrible, burns up the rest, and altogether causes such destruction to all the comforts of the dear man of God that would have melted the heart of any one to witness, except the devil.   Here was indeed a mysterious way of the Lord's instructing his poor child, and leading him about, with a witness.

Well; having by his instruments done all this mischief, the impudent old wretch presents himself again before the Lord, and his blessed Majesty condescends to speak to him again: "Hast thou considered my servant Job," &c.? As much as if he had said: "Well, Satan, I see what thou hast done, and what dost thou think of my servant now?"   "Never saw such a selfish old wretch in my life," says the devil. "Job cares for nobody but himself; neither children, nor cattle, &c.; but let me just get at his person, and he will curse thee to thy face." But this was like himself, liar as he was; for Job was an affectionate, tender father, and deeply felt the loss of his children, &c.   But the Lord gives still further permission for the devil to do his worst, except to spare Job's life; and so hot and dreadful is the trial, that the poor man curses almost every thing but his God.   This was the devil in him.   The old wretch was filled with such malice that no doubt he said to himself, "O, he will do it presently—he will curse his God." And Job's poor wife took the devil's part against him, and urged him to do the same; but he did not, for the grace of God in the heart of Job was more than a match for the very devil.

We see, my friends, by this, what an enemy we are exposed to in this old restless, roaring lion, that goeth about seeking whom he may devour. When Job lived we know not—most probably thousands of years ago; but the devil was made to confess this before the Lord, that he was constantly going about; and it is evident his only object was to do mischief. And Peter, hundreds of years after, gives the same testimony concerning him; and if God's dear saints are thus instructed and harassed by the terrible temptations and cruel insults of Satan, depend upon it, you that know nothing of these things are under his powerful influence. The strong man armed keeps the palace, and his goods are·in peace.

But lastly, he kept him as the apple of his eye. You see, in the text, the children of God are spoken of in the singular, as if there was but one: "He found *him*, instructed *him*, and kept *him*." We see also by this the eternal security of the people of God. They are spoken of as one person—the body of Christ; different members, but making up one perfect body; so those that would thrust upon Christ more members than make a perfect body would make him a *monster*. But surely you would not have Christ a *monster* in heaven. And those who believe that some that Christ died for are in hell would make him a *cripple*, being without some of his members in heaven. But who these members are we are often mistaken about. Some of my people at home are such in-and-out sort of creatures that I really do not know, at times, what to make of them. I do hope sometimes that they make a part of this blessed complete body. If they form but part of the feet, they are equally safe with the Head; but the feet you know, are often in the dirt.

Again. They are spoken of as a complete building, of whom Christ is the Foundation; just as large as the building; also called a building fitly framed. Now, if you should employ a builder to build, say a building like this chapel, or a factory, and just as you expected it was nearly finished, some of the beams should fall out,—a piece of timber here and a stone there, why you would say, "This builder will craze me, will ruin me." But not so with our God, who is a Master Builder indeed, and looks up his materials, as I said at first, where no one else would look for them; and really these living stones are composed of such materials that no one else could do any thing with them; and they are hewed and squared exactly to fill up their place in this blessed building, and shall never fall out. No, bless his dear name! He does not come into the waste howling wilderness to search and seek out his poor scattered sheep to lose them at last. He instructs them, and leads them about, and keeps them as the apple of his eye. O what a text is that! What is the apple

of God's eye? It is his own glory, secured in the Person of the
Son of God; and such is the security of his dear people; for our
blessed Jesus says, "They shall never perish, neither shall any
pluck them out of my hand."

"The foregoing can only be called recollections of a sermon by the
late Mr. Gadsby, as the writer of these remarks has no notes of the
sermon, and is not certain when it was preached, but thinks in 1839.
It is only from the powerful impression on the memory, at the time
of its delivery, that has enabled him to lay these few fragments before the children of God; which he does not profess to do in the order
in which they were delivered.

"I had the privilege of hearing him several times in London, and
always felt there was a power attended his ministry that I hardly
ever felt under the ministry of any other man. The Lord certainly
honoured him much; for if he felt shut up, I could not discover it.
I remember hearing him at Gower Street, in 1836, when under great
temporal distress, and expectations of worse to come. He preached
from Isa. liv. 1. And although at that time I did not know the blessedness of pardon, yet so powerful was that discourse that all that
appeared to me as mountains of temporal trouble flowed down before
the presence of the Lord, and I was carried honourably through them
all. The mountain indeed became a plain. (Zech. iv. 7.)

"Many striking things I have heard from his lips, which I shall
never forget. I remember once hearing him speak of the efficacy of
the blood of Christ; and, speaking of some that abused the very grace
of God, he said, 'Some people seem to know like angels and yet can
sin like devils; and then fly to the Word of God, and say, "O! The
blood of Christ cleanseth from all sin." It never was shed for you,
you presumptuous wretch, let me tell you, whoever you are, if any
such are before me this night.' So thrilling seemed to be the effect
of this solemn appeal, that I trust it will never be forgotten by me.

"In 1840 the Lord honoured a few poor outcasts in Norwich, by a
visit from his dear servant, when he opened Jireh Chapel, and manifested such an affectionate interest in the welfare of the little cause
that will not soon be forgotten by the few who had the privilege of
his company on that occasion. This was the only time I ever heard
him beg for the cause of God, and he did it most successfully, for we
collected upwards of £20 under two sermons. He told the people God
had a nice pair of scales, very nicely adjusted indeed; and he weighed
what was left, as well as what was given, to see what proportion it
bore to each other; which he proved by the case of the widow's mite,
when the dear Redeemer sat over against the treasury. And then his
willingness in travelling about, and preaching the gospel wherever
doors were opened, was a pleasing trait in his character. Blessed be
God, there are a few young men raised up who preach the same doctrines; but I know of none so willing as William Gadsby was, even
in his old age, to run on errands of mercy, in preaching the unsearch-
able riches of Christ, and seeming always alive in his Master's cause.

"It was impossible not to smile, at times, at some of the witty remarks that seemed so natural to him; but in preaching this sermon,
he severely reproved the people, and said, 'Poor empty creatures, to

laugh at the solemnities of eternity! You will not laugh when the world is in flames.' Take him all in all, I never expect to see his like again. But after all that has been said about him, it may seem presumption in such a poor ignorant creature as the writer of these remarks in giving his opinion; but I only state a little of what I knew and have heard from his lips. It was not the man we admire, but the grace of God that shone so eminently in him.

"Norwich."   "ANDREW CHARLWOOD."

THE CLOUD OF WITNESSES.

"Wherefore, seeing we also are compassed about with so great a cloud of witnesses, let us lay aside every weight, and the sin which doth so easily beset us, and let us run with patience the race set before us."—HEB. XII. 1.

FIRST, Who are these witnesses? They are those who have witnessed to God's truth, as Abraham, Isaac, and others, as mentioned in the preceding chapter; also apostles, ministers, and people who have borne testimony to the truth as it is in Jesus.

Secondly, What did they witness to? Salvation being all of grace, through faith; not of works, lest proud men should boast.

Thirdly, Why called a cloud? Because, when gathered together, they are a number which no man can number, any more than he can tell how many drops of water there are in a cloud, or grains of sand on a sea shore. What a crowd, or cloud, will appear in glory, when all those who are gone, those who are going, and those yet to go, will all appear in one glorious body before the throne of God, praising redeeming grace!

Because as a cloud is a recipient of water, and drops down rain, so are the witnesses of God recipients of the Water of Life, Christ Jesus; and at times they drop down showers of blessings upon the earthen vessels around them, filling them instrumentally with heavenly treasure.

What is this race? In order to run in this race, you must have no legs of your own to stand upon. That is, you must be stripped of all dependence upon yourself, and stand alone upon the finished work of Christ; and then, when you are enabled to do this, you will run well.

What is it to lay aside every weight? For your mind to be divested of worldly care, sinful company, sinful propensities, which are heavy weights to the mind. The blood of the Lamb, when applied to your conscience by the Holy Ghost, will affect this; nothing else can.

What is the besetting sin? Not only any evil propensity of the heart, such as to drunkenness, lewdness, and other works of the flesh, with temptations to which some are beset and tortured; but legality and unbelief combined. This, more or less, besets us all.

What is it to run with patience? Those who go smoothly on have no work for patience to do; but those who run in this race have need of patience that, after they have done the will of God, they may inherit the promise. Tribulation worketh patience; therefore in patience may you possess your souls; the Lord help you so to do.—*Jan. 9th*, 1842.

TO KNOW CHRIST.

Preached in Manchester April 19th, 1840, prior to the preacher going his London journey.

" That I may know him and the power of his resurrection."—PHIL. iii. 10.

THESE are the words of the apostle who was caught up into the heavens, and there had revealed to him what was not lawful for him to utter; and yet he desired to know Christ, whom to know is life eternal. To know him here is like a bud of spring; and when we die, it will break forth into a flower, full blown, and beauteous to behold. Now we know him but in part; but then we shall know him perfectly, for we shall see him as he is.

1. Let us consider this Him;

2. What it is to *know* Him, not merely to talk about him;

3. What is the *knowledge of the power of his resurrection?*

1. There is a vital religion in this text, which, if you possess in your heart, you will live at last. When the world is in a blaze, all other religions will die, because they are false. Therefore let us consider this HIM. He is Christ, the Eternal Son of God, who is in union with the Father, and the Spirit,—Creator of all things; "immensely great, immensely small." Yes; the greatest things show his greatness and the smallest things show his greatness. This Him made them all, great and small; all are the work of his hands. He made mountains rise and valleys sink. This is amazing to angels, and confounding to devils. Then what an inestimable blessing it is to know Him who has power over devils. Why, they could not enter a herd of swine without his permission. The apostle Paul has a blessed view of Christ as related in the first chapter of Col. 16–17: "For by him were all things created, that are in heaven, and that are in the earth, visible and invisible, whether they be thrones, or dominions, or principalities, or powers; all things were created by him and for him; and he is before all things, and by him all things consist!"

Some say Christ was a mere man, though he made all things. Then, if that be true, he made only some things, *he himself being made*. But Paul knew Christ was *before* all things, and *created* all things; and therefore he had power to defend him amidst the hurricanes to which he was exposed.

This Him became flesh and dwelt amongst us. He was the Babe of Bethlehem. He it is of whom it is written: "The foxes have holes, and the birds of the air have nests, but the Son of man hath not where to lay his head." He it is who was tempted in the wilderness forty days and forty nights. He was immersed in Jordan's swelling flood, which figured forth our salvation. He it was who groaned in Gethsemane, till, by his agony, blood gushed through the pores of his body under the pressure of your sins and mine, poor child of God. "Yes, though he was rich, yet for our sakes he became poor, that we, through his poverty, might be made rich." He is our Mediator. He is the Head of the body, his church. He is the beginning of the first-born from the dead, that in all things he might have the pre-eminence.

2. To *know* Him. He is Head over all things to the church; therefore look not at yourself, nor into self; for you might as well look into Satan as your own heart for any real holiness; neither look at your moping, and groaning, and sighing, simply because you are moping; but look at your glorious Head. Ah! If he were to show you his face, and say, "Do you know me?" And if you once have known him, have you not left him, and are you not ashamed, and say, "We have forgotten the Lord?" O how little have we known of him! And now we are often sorely troubled on account of his absence! Afflictions of body distress us; but they are light compared with the one great trouble. Of them we can say, "These light afflictions are but for a moment, and shall work out for us a far more exceeding and eternal weight of glory."

"All shall come, and last, and end,
As shall please my heavenly Friend."

He is not only our Head, but in him all fulness dwells, all that we need. He is all our holiness, and to know him is to draw holiness out of his heart, who is the Fountain of holiness.

This Him was delivered up "by the determinate counsel and foreknowledge of God," for our sins. He was taken to Pilate, judged, or rather misjudged, crucified, and slain; yea, they slew the Lord of life and glory,—God-man, Christ Jesus, the Mediator of the new covenant, by the foreknowledge of God. Who slew Christ? Who put him to shame, scorned him, spat upon him, pierced him? Not the Jews only. They were only instruments in God's hands; they were not the real cause. You have pierced him by your sins, if you are of his family, and you it was who put him to shame. He was delivered up for you, to bring you to God, and is now exalted a Prince and a Saviour, to give repentance unto Israel and remission of sins. O what a pattern of patience is here! "Consider him that endured such contradictions of sinners against himself, lest ye be weary and faint in your mind." In your afflictions, crosses, and trials, consider Him. He is the mystery of godliness. But it is not the mystery of godliness if it is to be seen by common sense. For as Moses lifted up the serpent in the wilderness, even so must the Son of man be lifted up, that whosoever believeth in him should not perish but have eternal life. Many bitten by the serpent might say, "O! I am dying! I shall be sure to die; what efficacy can there be in looking up? Well, friends, it is God's way of saving sinners. He gives them faith to look to Him whom they have pierced, and by faith they experience his salvation. "But of him are ye in Christ Jesus, who of God is made unto us wisdom, and righteousness, and sanctification, and redemption." He is wisdom, we are foolish; He is righteous, we are unrighteous; He is holy; we are unholy. Then it is folly to present to God anything but his holiness. He is all, and in all. In Him rests the fulness of grace and precious promises. Has he promised his Holy Spirit unto you? Then may you look on Him whom you have pierced, and mourn.

This is the most solemn spot a child of God can be brought to on this side eternity,—to look by faith upon Him whom we have pierced, and to be bathed in the sea of Christ's blood. He will not then think God unjust, because he has not given all men a chance of being saved; but his wonder will be why God has not cut them all off long ago. But he will come in company with his mighty angels, taking vengeance on them that know not God. And before him shall be gathered all nations; and every eye shall see him, and they also which pierced him. Careless sinner, where are you? Profane sinner, Pharisee sinner, where are you? What will then become of you, when the pleasures of the world will have fled, and when the world is in a blaze? Can you think on this subject with pleasure? O may you, if it be consistent with the will of God, desire to know Him, and the power of his resurrection, and be ready at his coming.

3. What is the *knowledge* of the power of his resurrection? This we are permitted, now and then, to know a little of; but we cannot fully know it until we also are raised from the dead. But to know it now, in a small degree, is a blessing indeed. The doctrine of a universal atonement has now become quite universal; the design of which is to please the hypocrites of the present day, who profess godliness, but deny the power thereof. But if it were not for the power of his resurrection, not a soul would be saved. But because he is risen, ye shall rise also. This is, then, the most important doctrine of his revealed Word.

Some tell us that Christ came on earth, merely to set us a pattern which we must imitate. He is indeed our pattern and glorious example of the church, and may we imitate him; but if this is all, it will leave us to be lost. He became flesh and dwelt among us; he endured many contradictions against himself; he was tempted and resisted the devil. "Then," say you, "What must we bring to God as a ground of acceptance with him? Must we not bring our obedience?" No. What *is* your best obedience? Your righteousness is filthy; and by doing so, you wish to make God filthy likewise. Nothing less than a perfect obedience will do. And where will you find it? Not in yourself; it is in Christ, and in him alone.

What a deal of talk there is about co-working with God; you must do your part and then God will do his. This was the case some thousands of years before Christ; and as to his disciples, when the work came to be done, they all fled.

He took with him three disciples into the garden of Gethsemane —not to help him; he did not ask them to help him. When he looked there was none to help; therefore his own arm brought salvation. He merely asked them to watch for one hour, and he then retired to endure the wrath of God poured into his soul for the sins of his people; and when he came again they were asleep; and he wondered there was none to uphold. He might well wonder, seeing they had talked so much about it. But he gently awoke them, and said, "Could ye not watch with me one hour?" Still he did not ask them to help him. What a blessing! He only says, "Watch and pray, that ye enter not into temptation;" and then departed. But their eyes were heavy; they could not even watch. Then his own arm brought salvation. O that right arm! O may we trust only to his right arm! He bore the heavy load of guilt his people had contracted; he groaned under it; then he was nailed to the cross. He put it all away, and, with his last expiring breath said, "It is finished!" What was finished? The work his Father gave him to do. He has made an end of sin, and brought in an everlasting righteousness for his people; a crown of glory, which will never fade away. He has justified them before God

But what proof have we of this? He died: was that a proof? He was buried; was that a proof? No. If he had stopped here we should have been in doubt. But, says Paul, "He died; yea, rather, that is risen again." He says *rather*, for he knew his death was not a sufficient proof. "He was delivered for our offences and raised again for our justification." May we know the power of his resurrection; for none of us liveth to himself, and no man dieth to himself. "For whether we live, we live unto the Lord; and whether we die, we die unto the Lord. Whether we live, therefore, or die we are the Lord's. For to this end Christ both died and rose, and revived, that he might be Lord both of the dead and the living." "Therefore if ye be dead with Christ, ye shall also live with him, knowing that Christ, being raised from the dead, dieth no more; death hath no more dominion over him." Therefore, says Paul to the Colossians, "If ye be then risen with Christ, seek those things which are above, where Christ sitteth at the right hand of God. Set your affections on things above, not on things on the earth; for ye are dead, and your life is hid with Christ in God. When Christ, who is our life shall appear, then shall we also appear with him in glory."

I must now bid you farewell for the present. I do not know whether I shall ever see you again on this side the grave; but may the

God of peace be with you, and keep you in the bond of unity and love. And if it be his pleasure that I see you no more on earth, I hope to meet some of you in heaven on the right hand of God, to sing his praise for ever and ever. Amen and Amen.

NO GUILE IN THE SPIRIT, AND KEEPING SILENCE.

"Blessed is the man in whose spirit there is no guile."—Ps. xxxii. 2.

"O!" says some poor soul; "that is not me; for I feel that I am full of guile." Indeed! Can you then go to the Lord and tell him you have no sin, that you are as good as your neighbours, and that you have a claim upon his mercy? "No," say you. "I have to tell the Lord that I am full of sin and that I deserve nothing but his wrath." Then in your spirit there is no guile. God has made you honest, that you can neither attempt to deceive him nor yourself. There is no deceit in you nor about you in this respect. "When I kept silence," &c. (Ver. 3.) Kept silence! Why what does that mean? Is it possible for a child of God to keep silence? Yes, it is. I was going to say something that would have alarmed some of you; and if it did not alarm you, there are many congregations that it would.

"Well," say you, "it must be something very bad if you are afraid of it, for you are not amazingly nice." Well; I was going to say that there are times and seasons when, through the temptations of the devil, and the deceitfulness of their own hearts, the children of God turn sulky with God. "Turn sulky with God?" say you. Yes. Perhaps there has been something they have particularly desired, and thought they had prayed earnestly for, and even imagined they had some claim upon God for it; when, instead of giving it, God has sent them something directly opposite; and then they have turned sulky. Just like a child naturally sulking with his father and with his food; he will not have it, but knocks it away from him. This is keeping silence with a witness.

But, though God's people may be in this state, they cannot be comfortable in it. Hence, says the psalmist, "When I kept silence, my bones waxed old through my roaring all the day long." Not his natural bones, but his spiritual bones,—his comforts, and his enjoyments; for day and night God's hand was heavy upon him. The more he kicked the more God laid on, till at length he says, "My moisture is dried up like the drought of summer;" and he now begins to feel the wretchedness of his state. And what then? Why, he says, "I acknowledge my sin unto thee." This was what God brought him to. Instead of saying, "If he sulks, I will too," he brought him to confess his iniquity, as a poor guilty wretch.

HUNGERING AND THIRSTING AFTER RIGHTEOUSNESS.

" Blessed are they which do hunger and thirst after righteousness; for they shall be filled."—MATT. v. 6.

THE righteousness intended here is not creature-righteousness, worth, or worthiness; for that is as the morning cloud, and as the early dew it goeth away; nay, at best it is only filthy, and its fountain unclean. Eternal truth declares that all flesh is grass, and all the *goodliness* thereof is as the flower of the field, which withereth and fadeth away when the Spirit of the Lord bloweth upon it. But the righteousness the dear Lord has in view in this text is that blessed righteousness which is unto all and upon all them that believe, even the glorious Person and obedience of the Lord Jesus Christ; for "Christ is the end of the law for righteousness to every one that believeth." This is that righteousness which justifies the ungodly; and when this glorious righteousness is received into the heart, by faith, through the divine power of God the Holy Ghost, the soul will unite with the church of old, and say, "In the Lord have I righteousness and strength;" not merely *by* him, or *from* him, but *in* him; and the Lord the Spirit solemnly says that "in the Lord shall all the seed of Israel be justified, and shall glory." God is determined that no flesh shall glory in his presence, but *in the Lord* alone. Therefore "Christ is made of God unto his people wisdom, and righteousness, and sanctification, and redemption." Yea, "God hath made him to be sin for them, that they might be made the righteousness of God in him." Here it is the child of God stands acquit of all charge, and is viewed by the God of gods perfect and complete; for, by the blessed Lord Jesus Christ, all that believe are justified from all things, not partially, but fully and completely.

Now, this blessed justification is all of free grace: "Being justified freely by his grace, through the redemption that is in Christ Jesus." It is on this glorious ground the apostle sends forth his God-glorifying, soul-supporting challenge, "Who shall lay anything to the charge of God's elect? It is God that justifieth. Who is he that condemneth? It is Christ that died; yea rather, that is risen again, who is even at the right hand of God, who also maketh intercession for us." Here divine faith makes a solemn stand, and, with indescribable pleasure, makes its boast of the Lord, putting no confidence in the flesh. Let Christ be seen and received into the heart by faith, and the sinner may challenge earth and hell to bring him in guilty; for Christ is the Lord his righteousness.

Well, "blessed are they which do hunger and thirst after this righteousness, for they shall be filled." Now, no one will ever hunger and thirst after this righteousness till the Holy Ghost has quickened his soul, and brought him to feel that he is a sinner before the heart-searching God; that his sins have been committed against a righteous God; that he has no righteousness of his own, nor any

power to work one out; and yet, that without a righteousness perfectly adequate to the requirements of law and the demands of justice, he must for ever perish.   To describe the various workings of
mind and the feelings of such a soul, under the heart-rending tortures of the awful nature of sin and the holiness and inflexible justice of God, as revealed in the law, would fill a volume.   Suffice it,
therefore, to say, that night and day he hungers and thirsts for that
righteousness which justifies the ungodly.   A religion which consists of creature goodness, creature duties, and creature piety, will
not do for him.   He proves that both duty-works and duty-faith
fail him, and leave him a lost sinner, without help and without hope.
He therefore sighs, and groans, and cries for mercy, pardoning mercy,
justifying mercy, in the Person, blood, and obedience of Christ.   Nothing short of this will satisfy his hungry soul.   He can in very deed
enter into the feelings described in the first part of Isa. xli. 17:
"When the poor and needy seek water."   He feels that he is poor,
wretchedly poor, and very needy; for he needs all that is necessary
to make him righteous and holy in the sight of God; and though he
has sought this in a variety of ways, still he can neither see nor feel
anything in himself, nor of himself, but sin and loathsomeness.   With
deep concern, he has earnestly sought the water of life, but cannot
find it; so that his tongue faileth for thirst, and he appears, at times,
unable to speak the feelings of his heart to either God or man.   Hungry and thirsty, his soul fainteth within him.   Well, in this desert
land, in this waste, howling wilderness, the Lord, in his own blessed
time, is graciously pleased manifestively to find him, and to lead
him about, and to instruct him; yea, and he will keep him as the
apple of his eye.

Now, the Lord of the house says such souls are blessed.   And
indeed it is no small blessing for them to know their poverty, feel
their need, and be sensible of their own helplessness.   There are a
people who say that they are increased with goods, and have need
of nothing, and know not that they are wretched, and miserable,
and poor, and blind, and naked.   These are not spoken of very
favourably by the Lord of the house; but the poor and needy, who
seek water and can find none, *are* blessed of the Lord; yea, and *in*
the Lord, for in him they have all spiritual blessings; and the Lord
has promised them, saying, "I the Lord will hear them, I the God
of Israel will not forsake them.   I will open rivers in high places,
and fountains in the midst of the valleys; I will make the wilderness
a pool of water, and the dry land springs of water."

They shall be filled; not with self-righteousness, but with Christ
and his glorious righteousness.   The blessed Spirit shall reveal Christ
in their hearts the hope of glory; then their soul will enjoy a sweet
measure of the work and effect of the righteousness of Christ, which
are peace, quietness, and assurance for ever.   They shall find that

Christ is unto them a peaceable habitation, and here they have rest; and having thus tasted that the Lord is gracious, and feasted upon his blood, love, and obedience, they will joyfully unite with the psalmist, and say, "Because thy loving-kindness is better than life, my lips shall praise thee. Thus will I bless thee while I live; I will lift up my hands in thy name. My soul shall be satisfied as with marrow and fatness, and my mouth shall praise thee with joyful lips."

Thus they that hunger and thirst after righteousness shall be abundantly satisfied with the fulness of God's house, and shall drink of the river of his pleasure; for "with the Lord is the fountain of life." The time shall come when they shall say, "O magnify the Lord with me, and let us exalt his name together. I sought the Lord and he heard me, and delivered me from all my fears." Their mouth shall be filled with praise and with the honour of God. Blessed be the name of our adorable Three-One God, he filleth the hungry with good things, while the rich he sendeth empty away; and when body and soul are transformed into the image of Christ in glory, then in very deed they will be filled with all the fulness of God, and eternally enjoy the blessedness of being blessed in and with Christ, and filled with his righteousness.—*July* 13*th*, 1835.

GOD IS LOVE.
"God is love."—1 Jno. iv. 8, 16.

BELOVED of the Lord,—It is your blessedness to prove, by the divine teaching of God the Holy Ghost, that God is Love,—eternal, immutable love. This precious truth you will not deny; but then you may often struggle under very deep depression of spirit and heartrending groans, lest you should not be interested in this glorious Three-One God of love. It is not enough for you to hear that God is love, nor to believe it as a most blessed truth, nor to say he loved David, Isaiah, Jeremiah, Paul, &c., nor to look round you and say, concerning others, he loved *them*, or, he loved *you*, or, he loved *thee*. No; your heart thirsts to say, feelingly to say, he loved *me*. You feel that vital godliness is *personal*, and to you it matters but little, as it respects your own comfort, who he loved, or how greatly he loved them, if he do not love you. The vehement desire of your heart is that the blessed Jehovah, by the mighty power of the Holy Ghost, would speak this precious truth to your heart: "Yea, I have loved thee with an everlasting love; therefore with loving-kindness have I drawn thee." It will not do for you to be told that you must simply believe, do your duty, and be decidedly pious, and then God will love you. This ground you have proved to be boggy, and have been necessitated to flee from it, and cry, "Like a crane or a swallow, so did I chatter; I did mourn as a dove; mine eyes fail with looking upward. O Lord, I am oppressed; undertake for me." The Lord has given you faith to believe that they that are in the flesh cannot please God; and that however fair a show they may make in the flesh, it is but a show, leaving them destitute of vital godliness. Christ's kingdom is not of this world; for the kingdom of God is righteousness, and peace, and joy in the Holy Ghost; and this kingdom must be set up in the heart; not in word merely, but in *power*, and that power the power of God: "For our gospel came not unto you in word only, but also in power, and in the Holy Ghost, and in much assurance." Therefore, having eyes to see the emptiness of a mere duty religion, nothing short of an enjoyment of the power of Christ's religion in your heart can satisfy you. For this you hunger, thirst, and pant; and even when you dare not say, "The Lord is my God," still nothing but Christ and his blood and obedience brought home to your conscience, by the power of the Holy Ghost, can give you rest; but when Christ and his complete salvation is enjoyed, with solemn pleasure you can then say, "He loved *me*, and gave himself for *me*;" and, as the glorious effect of vital union to Christ, by a living faith in him, you can, in some measure, trace the almighty love of God the Father in your election, of God the Son in your redemption, and of God the Holy Ghost in his quickening, enlightening, teaching, sanctifying, anointing, and sealing power, and with solemn joy say, "This God is *my* God for ever and ever; he will be my guide even unto death." And as the blessed Spirit leads you on, you can enter a little into the nature of the undivided love of the glorious Three-One God and see that the love of each dear Person is of the same nature and extent; so that all that the Father loved and chose in Christ, the Son loved and redeemed from their sins: "Who gave himself for us, that he might redeem us from all iniquity, and purify unto himself a peculiar people, zealous of good works;" and all that the Son redeemed, the blessed Spirit loves, quickens, teaches, and sanctifies: "For such were some of you; but"—O the blessedness of this precious *but*, when brought home to the heart—"but ye are washed, but ye are sanctified, but ye are justified, in the name of the Lord Jesus, and by the Spirit of our God;" and the whole nor any part of this is neither by works of righteousness which ye have done, nor according *to* your works, "but according to Jehovah's own purpose and grace, which was given you in Christ before the world began." Therefore, your salvation, in all its bearings, is of rich, free, discriminating love. God grant that you may daily live as becomes creatures so highly favoured, showing forth the praises of him who hath called you out of darkness into his marvellous light. Trials you may have; yea, you *must* have; for it is the settled purpose of God that "through much tribulation ye must enter the kingdom." But this is all in love, and everlasting love is still sure; and this blessed God of love has engaged to succour, support, and defend you. Your light, as it respects the manifestation of it, may not always be as the morning when the sun riseth, even a morning without clouds, nor the blessed graces of the Spirit spring up in your souls like the tender grass springing out of the earth by clear shining after rain.   Clouds and darkness may surround the Lord, hiding his glory from your view, and in your feelings you may be very, very dark, and very, very barren.   But your dear God of love will not forsake you.   New covenant mercies are still sure, everlastingly sure; for "unto the upright there ariseth light in the darkness;" and "to this man will I look that is poor and of a contrite spirit, and trembleth at my word."

God Almighty enable you to trust in him at all times ; and that he may direct your hearts into his love, and into Himself as Love, and into the patient waiting for of Christ is my prayer.

———◆———

THE WILDERNESS AND THE HIGHWAY.

"The wilderness and the solitary place shall be glad," &c.—ISA. xxxv. 1-10.

THERE is no class of persons who disbelieve God's Word more than God's children, at times, do; and, strange as it may appear and criminal as it is, they frequently labour harder to make God a liar than they do to prove his Word true. They take their feeling sense of being such loathsome, hard-hearted, unbelieving sinners as a proof that God will have nothing to do with them; whereas, if it were not for such poor, groaning, mourning souls, we should not know what to do with one part of the Bible. Here (ver. 1) God says, "The wilderness and the solitary place shall be glad, and the desert shall rejoice and blossom as the rose." Now, if there were no deserts, no wildernesses, &c., what could we make of such a passage ? But, it is added, "It shall blossom abundantly, and rejoice even with joy and singing." Come, poor, barren desert; poor, waste wilderness; the promise is made, and it will assuredly be fulfilled. In the end, thou shalt rejoice, and see the glory of the Lord, and the excellency of our God. Your hands (of faith) may be so weak that you cannot lay hold of God's promises; your knees so feeble that you cannot bend them in sweet communion with God; your hearts so fearful that you are continually doubting and fearing God will have nothing to do with you, and cannot believe there is any blessing for you. But, by and by, waters shall break out in the wilderness and streams in the desert. Then shall your blind eyes be opened and your deaf ears unstopped; then shall you be healed of your lameness and shall leap as a hart and your dumb tongue sing. And the parched ground shall become a pool and the thirsty land springs of water. And a highway shall be there, and a way; and it shall be called The Way of Holiness. The unclean shall not pass over it, but it shall be for those. Now what does that mean—the unclean shall not pass over it, but it shall be for those? I will tell you. It does not say the unclean shall not *touch* it, but, shall not *pass over* it. So that, the moment a poor unclean sinner is brought by faith to put a single foot on this way, that moment he becomes clean. The way itself makes him clean; and, therefore, he passes over it, pure in the sight of God. And as this way makes clean all who come upon it, there shall be none of the lions of hell there, nor the ravenous beasts of the world; but the *redeemed* shall walk there; and they shall return, and come to Zion with songs and everlasting joy upon their heads; they shall obtain joy and gladness, and sorrow and sighing shall flee away.—*Dec.* 13, 1835.

COMFORT FOR SPIRITUAL MOURNERS.

"Blessed are they that mourn; for they shall be comforted."—MATT. v. 4.

NOT all kinds of mourners are here intended; for there is the sorrow of the world, which worketh death and produces nothing but sin, misery, and rebellion against God. Some mourn because they cannot increase in riches, honours, and pleasures; but there is no blessing promised to them. The mourners which God has pronounced blessed are such as mourn over themselves and after God. The Lord's spiritual mourners mourn over their sinfulness and wretchedness, as sinners against a holy, righteous, good, and kind God. The filth and corruption of their fallen nature give them real grief and pain of heart. Its daily bubblings and risings up are a real plague to them. They are no strangers to what Solomon means by the plague of the heart (1 Kings viii. 38); and daily experience, under the teachings of God the Holy Ghost, proves to them that this plague is deeply rooted, and breaks out in bubblings up in a thousand different ways; and when the Lord is pleased to hide the light of his countenance and make them feel his righteous displeasure against sin, with the psalmist they mourn and say, "There is no soundness in my flesh, because of thine anger; neither is there any rest in my bones, because of my sin." (Ps.xxxviii.3.)

The dear child of God sometimes mourns over hardness of heart and darkness of soul. Neither judgments nor mercies appear to move him, nor does he seem able to raise a tender thought up to God, if he must perish for the want of one. At times, the only feeling he appears to have is a secret mourning because he is so hard, and so dark, and so incapable of deeply mourning. Now and then a solemn sigh heaves up his breast, which speaks language like unto this: "O wretched man that I am. Who shall deliver me from the body of this death?" (Rom. vii. 24.) All the life he seems to have is to mournfully breathe out Job's confession, "Behold, I am vile." And as the Lord is pleased to give him a deeper feeling of his vileness, he is led sensibly to cry, "Wherefore I abhor myself, and repent in dust and ashes." (Job xlii. 6.)   Yea, "I am ashamed, and blush to lift up my face to thee, O God." (Ezra ix. 6.)   Such souls mourn because they have so little intercourse with God, and are so much entangled with the things of the world.

Now while the poor children of God mourn over themselves, they mourn after God.   They mourn after the liftings up of the light of his countenance and a sweet and solemn enjoyment of his pardoning mercy, through the precious blood of the Lamb; and with panting desires they cry, "Lord, lift thou up the light of thy countenance upon me" (Ps. iv. 6); "For thy name's sake, O Lord, pardon mine iniquity; for it is great.   Turn thee unto me, and have mercy upon me, for I am desolate and afflicted.   The troubles of my heart are enlarged.   O bring thou me out of my distresses.   Look upon mine affliction and my pain; and forgive all my sins." (Ps. xxv. 11, 16–18.)   Thus God's people will, at times, deeply pant for and mourn after God's rich manifestive mercy and pardoning love.   The believer has no real happiness when he has no sweet intercourse with the Lord.   He daily pants to feel more and more of the blessedness couched in this soul-refreshing, God-glorifying truth: "And truly our fellowship is with the Father, and with his Son Jesus Christ."   Like David, he can say, "As the hart panteth after the water-brooks, so panteth my soul after thee, O God.   My soul thirsteth for God, for the living God;" for a sweet and blessed enjoyment of interest in him, as my own covenant God,—Father, Son and Spirit.—"Yes," says the mourning soul; "I want to feel that Israel's One Triune God is my God, for ever and ever, and that he will be my guide even unto death.   My great fear is, lest I should be sitting down content with a dead, formal religion, without the life and power of vital godliness.   O that I could feel a greater conformity to Christ, and live more in the enjoyment of him, as my all in all!"

"More frequent let thy visits be,
    Or let them longer last;
I can do nothing without thee;
    Make haste, O God, make haste."

Such mourners are blessed.   The dear Lord of the house does not merely say they may, or shall be, blessed; but they absolutely *are* blessed; *now* blessed, though they may not be able to enjoy the blessings which belong to them: "Blessed be the God and Father of our Lord Jesus Christ, who hath blessed us with all spiritual blessings in heavenly places in Christ."   Thus they have secured in Christ all that can make them holy or happy, all that can give them a title to heaven and a meetness for it, and convey them safe there, and be their glory when they are there: "He that spared not his own Son, but delivered him up for us all, how shall he not with him also freely give us all things?"

Poor, sin-burdened, Satan-hunted, broken-hearted mourners! All things are yours; for ye are Christ's and Christ is God's. Your life is hid with Christ in God, and because he lives ye shall live also. The blessed Redeemer is anointed to comfort his mourners, "to appoint unto them that mourn in Zion, to give unto them beauty for ashes, the oil of joy for mourning, and the garment of praise for the spirit of heaviness." Yes, bless his precious and glorious name! In his own time he will, by the power of his Spirit, discover unto them the beauty of his own Person and righteousness; and then they shall see the King in his beauty (Isa. xxxiii. 17), as the Lord their righteousness and strength. Jesus, in his Person, blood, and obedience; in his glorious offices, characters, relationship, names, honours, fulness, love, and loveliness, shall be revealed unto them, by the glorious power and under the divine anointing of God the Holy Ghost; and this shall produce a solemn joy in their souls, a joy unspeakable and full of glory. Then shall their sorrow be turned into joy, and with holy pleasure and heavenly tranquillity, they shall blessedly sing, "I will greatly rejoice in the Lord; my soul shall be joyful in my God; for he hath clothed me with the garments of salvation, he hath covered me with the robe of righteousness."

Faith shall triumph in Christ, and sing "Victory," even with a prospect of great trouble before its eye: "Although the fig tree shall not blossom, neither shall fruit be in the vines; the labour of the olive shall fail, and the fields shall yield no meat; the flock shall be cut off from the fold, and there shall be no herd in the stalls; yet I will rejoice in the Lord, I will joy in the God of my salvation. The Lord God is my strength, and he will make my feet like hinds' feet, and he will make me to walk upon mine high places."(Hab. iii. 17–19.) Zion's mourners must and shall have their times of comfort, their feasts, as well as their fastings. The enemy may, at times, appear to triumph, and with sneering contempt say, "Where is now thy God?" and the soul appear to sink a thousand fathoms in a moment, and say, "My way is hid from the Lord, and my judgment is passed over of my God;" but the Lord will appear, and draw forth faith in divine exercise, into the Person, oath, and promise of a covenant God; and, with solemn confidence in God, faith shall say, "Rejoice not against me, O mine enemy; when I fall, I shall arise; when I sit in darkness, the Lord shall be a light unto me. I will bear the indignation of the Lord, because I have sinned against him, until he plead my cause, and execute judgment for me. He will bring me forth to the light, and I shall behold his righteousness. Then she that is mine enemy shall see it, and shame shall cover her which said unto me, Where is the Lord thy God? Mine eyes shall behold her; now shall she be trodden down as the mire of the streets." (Mic. vii. 8–10.) And O what heavenly comforts await the child of God in the world to come: "Beloved, now are we the sons of God, and it doth not yet appear what we shall be; but we know that, when he shall appear, we shall be like him; for we shall see him as he is." "Blessed are they that mourn; for they shall be comforted."—*May*, 1836.

————◆————

THE LOVE OF GOD.

"Because the love of God is shed abroad in our hearts by the Holy Ghost which is given unto us."—ROM. v. 5.

THE love of God! Whenever we venture on a subject of such importance, we venture on a profound deep.

There is a love which God, as the God of nature, bears to creation as the work of his own hands; for he saw that it was very good. But the love of God, as shed abroad in the heart of a believer, as far exceeds it as heaven exceeds earth. God's love, as a covenant God, the love of each glorious Person in the Trinity, was fixed on his people, without any reason assigned for it, only his own sovereign pleasure. Not because they were lovely more than others in themselves; for, considered as sinners, had Jehovah never loved us till we had turned our hearts to love him, till he had seen some beauty in us, he would never have loved us at all. But God loves us because he would, and this is the only reason he assigns for it. And this love is bounded by God's sovereignty; we cannot get an iota beyond it, nor can any who were not interested in it in eternity ever creep into a knowledge of its infinite excellence. When Paul is entering into this solemn mystery, he stands amazed, and prays that the church at Ephesus might be able to comprehend with all saints what is the height, and depth, and length, and breadth, thereof. Neither angels nor men can ever sound the depth, scan the height, or measure the length of this love. In its depth, it is deeper than all our miseries and all our woes; in its height, it is higher than all the rebellion of our hearts; in its length, it is from everlasting to everlasting; and in its breath, it reaches through all the dark avenues of time, and beyond all the wanderings of the affections of his people; and, therefore, it is underneath them, above them, behind them, and before them. In short, they are hemmed in on every hand with this love.

Now this love of God is shed abroad in the heart of the believer. Each glorious Person in the one undivided Jehovah has evidenced this in a wonderful degree. What induced the Father to give his only Son to be stricken, smitten, and afflicted? Love. What induced the Son to stoop to come to this lower world, and take our nature, and suffer, bleed, and die? Love. He had fixed his heart on his people; and though he saw that Zion would prostitute herself, yet he never took his heart away from her. He will never divorce his spouse nor for one moment forsake her. Love binds her to his heart, and as a proof that he loved her, he took her nature into union with his Godhead, that he might be able practically, fully, and efficaciously to follow her through all the dark avenues where sin might drive her; and he put away her transgressions by the sacrifice of himself, and will at last bring her to glory. "Though he was rich, yet for our sakes he became poor, that we, through his poverty, might be made rich." And he loves his people the same now he is in glory as he did when he appeared upon the earth the despised Nazarene, and he sympathizes with them in all their trials, temptations, and distresses; and when they come to him with their temptations, he knows what they mean, and what will relieve them; for he has undergone the same. There is not a temptation of any description that any of his people can have, but he has endured the same, that he might in his great love be able to succour them.

The love of the Spirit is seen in our text, shedding abroad this love of God in our hearts.

I know some of God's people are saying, "This love cannot be shed abroad in my heart. I am so wretched, so loathsome, so destitute of life, there can be no love of God in me." Well; what has put you out of conceit with your own pretty selves? There was a time when you thought so well of yourselves that you said, "If I am not saved, God help such a one;" but now you begin to look at yourselves and you think you are as far from God as the vilest of the vile. Well; how came this change about, that you now see your own unloveliness, and that you seem so filthy and polluted, and that you groan under a sense of the loathsomeness that sin raises up within you? It is a measure of the love of God shed by the Spirit in your heart; and its shining there has made such a manifest display that you see yourselves as vile as the devil can make you, and wonder that God will have anything to do with you, except it is to send you to hell. Through the love of God shining in a measure in your heart, you see yourselves just the very reverse of what you once thought you were.

"Well," says another child of God, "I once thought I had the love of God shed abroad in my heart, and thought I enjoyed it; and O, what sweet moments I had then! I could pray, and praise, and sing, and be joyful in God; but now my heart is quite out of tune, and I seem as if I could neither pray nor praise. If there be any passage suits me, it is that I have lost my first love." Indeed! There is no such passage. It says, "Thou hast *left* thy first love;" not *lost* it. God will take care we shall never lose it. "Well," say you, "I have left it. I cannot sing, I cannot rejoice; and, therefore, whatever may have been my case, there is no love of God in my heart now." You are a little mistaken, poor soul. It may be covered a little with lumber; but it is there. Perhaps you made more of your feelings of love than you did of the God from whence it came; and, therefore, God is now letting you know that you must not rest upon your feelings, but upon him. The people of God are prone to stumble here; and though a religion without feelings is not the religion of Christ, and though no quickened child of God can be satisfied without a feeling religion, yet when we are left to lean upon, and trust in, our feelings rather than the dear Lord from whence they come, the Lord, for wise ends, withholds them for a season, that we may know more sweetly and blessedly how to appreciate the glorious truths couched in the following texts: 2 Sam. xxiii. 5; Heb. vi. 17, 18; Micah vii. 8–10, 18, 19.

But when darkness envelopes the mind, and the heart feels almost as cold as ice, and as hard as a stone, it wants more than the efforts of nature to enable a poor sinner to realize an interest in the precious things of God, as couched in the just-named Scriptures.

Perhaps some poor trembling, tortured sinner is now saying, "I am both cold and dark and wretched, beyond the power of man to describe, and I dare not say that these passages of God's Word belong to me; but I can say that I do not feel at home, nor can I be satisfied with my present feelings." Well, poor child of God, here you are; groaning, and sighing, and mourning, because you cannot manifestively enjoy God, the God of all your hope, because you cannot sweetly trace your interest in him. Now, if there were no love at the bottom, there would be no uneasiness on account of this. You want to have sweet intercourse with God, to have your heart more in communion with him, and to worship him more sweetly and blessedly. Now, did you ever want to have intercourse with any character you hated and abhorred—that your heart is at enmity with? Then, if your grief is that you cannot enjoy God more, that you cannot have more sweet access unto him, that you cannot pour out your soul more freely to him, that you cannot tell him more your whole heart, that you cannot enter more deeply into his secrets, then God's love must be there; for nature never can rise above its own source; no stream can rise above its fountain. But though the quickened children of God have the love of God in their hearts, yet it may be there like moisture in a sponge, and needs the sweet and powerful hands of the Spirit, which first communicated it to the heart, to press it down, or draw it forth, into act and exercise, or there will be no flowing out. If you are brought, in real feeling before God, to say, "I abhor myself, and repent in dust and ashes;" "O wretched man that I am! Who shall deliver me from the body of this death?" There is the love of God at the bottom." Then," say you, "O when shall I come and appear before God? Search me, Lord, and try me, and see if there be any wicked way in me, and lead me in the way everlasting." I say again, if this be your case, there is the love of God at the bottom, and most assuredly, in the Lord's own time, this love will spring up, and you shall be brought to know that

God himself was underneath the whole. But we must wait his time; for no man can get at it of himself; it is God's special gift.

As far as God enables me, I like to pick up poor forlorn creatures in the hedges and highways. You know the commission of old was to compel such to come in. "For I will restore health unto thee, and I will heal thee of thy wounds, saith the Lord, because they called thee an outcast, saying, This is Zion, whom no man seeketh after." (Jer. xxx. 17.) Bless your souls, the Gospel is for them that none but God and poor sinners like themselves will have anything to do with; and God takes them in hand, and brings them to banquet upon his love, causing them to rejoice in his blessed name. We may, and some of us have, put to sea in a vessel of our own rigging. The sails of our zeal have, as we thought, been well arranged, and we have gone sweetly along, expecting to get to the end of our voyage, in eternal matters, without having even to tack about. But anon, a storm has arisen; our sails have been torn to shreds, and we have expected every moment to be dashed against the rocks and drowned. Just at this moment, the Captain of Everlasting Love life-boat has heaved in sight, and, with his immutable, "Thou shalt not be drowned," the Lord has grappled hold of us, put us manifestively in his own vessel, and made it known to us that his watchful eye has been over us, and that though we seemed ready to perish, love has been in it all.

There are solemn moments, when such a sweet measure of God's love is shed abroad in the heart as to deaden it to the world, driving out everything connected with the world, and the man can feelingly before God say,

"I love the Lord with mind and heart,
    His people and his ways;
Envy, and pride, and lust depart,
    And all his works I praise."

His language is, "Lord, what wilt thou have me to do?" Everything that honours God is esteemed by him, and he seems swallowed up in obedience, thanksgiving, and praise. How solemn this worship is! Could you follow him to his secret place, there might not be much noise; but he is in God's sanctuary, consecrated ground, secluded from the world; the heavens are opened, the Son of Man appears on the right hand of the Father, and there is a solemn going up to God and coming down from God, and the Person, blood, righteousness, and love of Christ are shed abroad by the Holy Spirit. There is a pleasure in it that no heart can describe, if God's love has not been shed abroad in it. No fear of parting with right hands or right eyes here; for the soul feels that he could part with every fleshly thing for God. Give up the truth for fear of persecution, or be alarmed at the idea of losing his popularity? No. God's love being thus shed abroad in the heart leads him to rest in the faithfulness of

God, and he feels persuaded that though the mountains may depart, and the hills be removed, yet God's kindness shall not be taken away. The brook may be dried up, but the Spring-head is the same; and God will see to it that nothing shall hurt him. Torturing fear cannot possibly enter the heart while there is this glorious shedding abroad of the love of God. The believer can view all circumstances chained to the throne of God, and with solemnity of heart can sing,

> " Life, death, and hell, and worlds unknown,
> Hang on his firm decree;
> He sits on no precarious throne,
> Nor borrows leave TO BE."

Not a sparrow can fly without his notice, nor can a hair of our head fall to the ground without his bidding. He marshals all creatures, circumstances, and events for the well-being of his family; and faith, working by love, grasps in a solemn, "This God is my God, for ever and ever; he will be my guide even unto death." And thus there is a sweet springing up into the Lord when his love is shed abroad in the heart by the blessed Spirit.

Well, brethren, how many of us are there here? Very few; and when we are there, we do not stop long; we soon get on the back ground again; but it is sweet work while we are there. We want nothing to be done but what will crown God's brow. Reason gives way to revelation; faith takes God's Word as a rule; and hope confidently looks forward to the fulfilment of the precious promises therein revealed. The believer feels as though he really had not soul enough to show forth the praises of God, and calls upon all his saints to unite, saying, " O love the Lord, all ye his saints, and let us exalt his name together." These are sweet and blessed expressions of a heart that has the love of God shed abroad in it. Stephen was full of this love, and of the Spirit and of power, when he saw the heavens opened, and the Son of Man standing on the right hand of God. They stoned him; but what did he say? "Lord, lay not this sin to their charge." He had too much to do with God's love to want to be revenged of his enemies. He greatly rejoiced in the Lord, and his soul was joyful in his God. O, brethren! When faith can say, "*My* God," and "*he* hath clothed me with the garment of salvation, and covered me with the robe of righteousness," it has well nigh grasped in all the blessedness that we can enjoy while travelling below; for if God has covered us with the robe of righteousness, he has wrapped us up in the righteousness of his Son, and heaven has no better to give; for it is perfect. When the love of God is powerfully shed abroad in the heart, faith sees everything, in measure, as God sees it. God says, "I see no spot in thee," and faith sees that there is no spot; and thus beholds a blessedness in the righteousness of the Son of God more prizable than all the kingdoms of the world.

This love is the spring-head of all prayer, praise, faith, peace, joy, hope, humility, patience, and every other grace. I stand in need myself of it for the reviving of every grace, and none more than patience; and yet I am almost afraid sometimes to pray for it, lest I should have more trouble; for God does not give patience to play with. It is by tribulation that we arrive at patience.

This love is what Paul had in view in 1 Cor. xiii., which he there calls charity: "Now abideth faith, hope, charity; these three; but the greatest of these is charity;" because it is the greatest teeming out of God's heart to the sinner, and the sinner's to God: "Whom have I in heaven but thee, and there is none upon earth I desire beside thee."

If this love is shed abroad powerfully in the heart, it is sure to lead to obedience: "If ye love me, ye will keep my commandments." Love makes us wishful continually to keep idols away from the heart. I have heard some professors say, "Ah, well. I know I did wrong at such a time and at such a time; the Lord delivered me then, and I believe he will again." It is tempting God, and insulting his blessed Majesty. If you are a child of God, you will be made to smart for it; and if you are not, you may go on till you open your eyes in black despair.

This love is shed abroad in the heart, as God's gift to us. God has given himself and his Son, and, to complete the blessedness, he has given the Holy Spirit. How highly honoured are God's people, to have the Trinity in Unity made manifest in their hearts as their God for ever.

This Spirit is the Spirit of life, to quicken our dead souls; he is the Spirit of power, to subdue our iniquities, and raise our hopes to God; of prayer, and praise, to draw out our hearts in supplication, thanksgiving, and adoration; of truth, to seal it on the heart; and indeed, of all blessedness; for he shall "take of the things of Christ, and show them unto us;" so that, strictly speaking, he is God's hand, to hand down the blessings of salvation to suit the wretched sinner's case.

With such a gift as this, what can we need? He is given us to protect us, to defend us, to guide us, and to do all in us, and for us, and by us, that we shall stand in need of through this wilderness; and thus we have secured to us all that is required to make us holy and happy.

Brethren, are we concerned about this gift? Is it your desire to nourish it, and to refuse everything in the way of it? May it be our happiness to know and feel the importance of being interested therein; for his name's sake. Amen.—*July 3rd*, 1836.

IS IT NOTHING TO YOU?

Preached in Manchester, Aug. 2nd, 1836.

"Is it nothing to you, all ye that pass by? Behold, and see if there be any sorrow like unto my sorrow, which is done unto me, wherewith the Lord hath afflicted me in the day of his fierce anger."—LAM. i. 12.

THE Prophet Jeremiah here speaks of himself. The Lord had been pleased to lay upon him heavy afflictions, grievous for him to bear; but he cried to the Lord in the agony of his soul; and the Lord enabled him to stand.

The language of the text perhaps refers also to the afflictions of the children of Israel in their Babylonish captivity. They had wandered from the way of God, and committed whoredoms against him; for they had joined themselves to idols. But the Lord had melted their hearts, and afflicted them in the day of his fierce anger; therefore did they cry out in the travail of their souls, "Was there ever sorrow like unto my sorrow?"

But mainly it is also prophetically the language of Christ, who agonized under the enormous weight of guilt which his people had contracted. He bore it all. And was there ever sorrow like unto his? Was there ever sorrow so great as his? Humanity was supported by the Godhead, or he would have sunk; for he bore, as the poet says, "A thousand hells." And that it was he, we may know from his own words, spoken in Psa. lxix: "Save me, O God, for the waters are come in unto my soul; I sink in deep mire where there is no standing. I am come into deep waters where the floods overflow me." There he compares his sufferings to deep waters, wherein he was immersed; for, saith he, "The waters are gone over my head; the floods overflow me."

Was there ever sorrow like unto his sorrow? And is it nothing to you, all ye that pass by? And they that passed by, spat upon him. Was it nothing to them? Ah! If they do not experience that it is something to such, they will everlastingly perish. There may be some who read this, who have been committing abominations against the Lord, and are hardening themselves in their crimes. If so, you may be sure God will make you smart for it. "Be sure your sins will find you out." And is it nothing to you? Is it a a trifling matter to sin against a holy God? Remember, trifling sinners, careless sinners, whoremongers, and adulterers, God will judge you.

There may be a covetous person present this morning, who will get riches, whether honestly or not. He may be doing his best to cheat another; and if he does cheat his fellow creatures, he will make merry in his heart to think how cleverly he has done it. Sinners! Remember that covetousness is idolatry; and whoremongers and idolaters have no inheritance in the kingdom of heaven. And is it nothing to you? There will come a time when you will not say it is nothing to you. For your covetousness and crimes, God will pour into your souls the burning liquid fire of his wrath. Then, O then, is it nothing to you?

There may be here a drunkard, or a profane person, who will delight in revelling, and drunkenness, and perhaps calling on God to curse them, and taking his holy name in vain. How awful is their case! Drunkard and swearer, is it nothing to you? Remember, that drunkenness is an abomination in the sight of God; and the Lord will not hold them guiltless who take his name in vain. And is this nothing to you?

There may be some who are wrapping themselves up in Pharisaical pride, and who consider they can do something towards saving themselves. They can look at the poor mourning, cast down, helpless child of God, who is crying to God for his salvation; and proudly they may say, "I thank God I am not as this man." Deluded creature! And can you thus set at nought the sufferings of Christ? Can you thus think lightly of the atonement? Is it nothing to you? You are insulting Christ, and, so living and dying, you will be cast into the bottomless pit.

"But," say you, "Christ made atonement for all, as well for the lost as the saved; and if men reject his atonement they will be lost." Then it follows that this atonement was not sufficient to save a single soul; for there are two questions that here present themselves: What is it that curses the lost? And, What is it that saves the saved? It is said that Christ put away all sin by the sacrifice of himself. He hath atoned for sin once, and once for ever. His people can never perish.

Brethren, you to whom Christ's sufferings are something, feeling you would be lost without him, I tell you, for the comfort and edification of your souls, that Christ Jesus hath cast all your sins into the depth of the sea,—the sea of his blood, never to be remembered any more. He has carried them into the land of forgetfulness, so that if they are sought for they cannot be found. He hath atoned for sin once, and once for ever.

> "And payment God cannot twice demand,
> First at my bleeding Surety's hand,
>   And then again at mine."

And if he atoned for your sins, then your sins are put away by that atonement. Therefore what will harm you? Not your sins; for they are put away. And is *that* nothing to you?

Christ's sorrow was like unto no man's sorrow ; and he bore all for his people in his own body. And is it nothing to you?

But, perhaps, there are some among this assembly of God's little ones, who have tasted the Lord is gracious, and enjoyed his presence and love in their hearts, who are now in a careless state. They have felt their security, but have become in a measure unconcerned, and are ready, at times, to deny their Lord before men. There was a time when it might have been said that in the congregation of the righteous there were little Benjamins and others. It might be now said, "Where is little Benjamin and Judah?" Where are you now? "Is it nothing to you, all ye that pass by?"

Remember, believer, every sin thou hast committed has sent a dagger into the heart of Christ, thy Lord. And is *that* nothing to you? The sins of the non-elect never touched the heart of Christ; but thy sins pierced him through and through, and made his heart to bleed. And is it nothing to you?

> " The powers of hell united press'd,
> And squeezed his heart and bruised his breast.
> What dreadful conflicts raged within,
> When sweat and blood forced through the skin."

Is *that* nothing to you? O! May the Lord soften your hard hearts, and make you feel that his sufferings were entirely on your account. And is *that* nothing to you? Behold, look at your dying Saviour, and say, "Was there ever sorrow like unto his sorrow?" And may you *feel* that he sorrowed for *you;* that the afflictions wherewith he was grievously afflicted were for *you;* that he agonized, and groaned, being burdened with your guilt and shame, for *you;* that he died for *you;* that he gave himself a ransom for *you;* that he rose again for *you;* and that now he ever liveth to make intercession for *you.* And is all this nothing to you? Can you look on and see this glorious scene unconcerned, unaffected?

May the Lord, in his infinite goodness and mercy, make us more and more deeply concerned to feel our interest in him; for his great name's sake. Amen.

THE FALL OF PETER.

Preached in Manchester, Aug. 9th, 1842.

" And Peter followed afar off." . . . Lᴜ. xxii. 54-62.

1. Let us look at the *weakness of man* and the *power of temptation.* 2. The *criminality* of Peter. 3. The *matchless display of God's grace.* 4. The *effect produced.* 5. *The lesson taught us.*

First. The *weakness of man* and the *power of temptation.*

The weakness of man is very great. Compared with the Almighty God, his Creator and Upholder, he is at his best estate altogether vanity; he is weakness itself. We are not sufficient of ourselves, so as to do anything of ourselves; we know not even what to pray to God for as we ought. May we in humility pray to him to direct us how to pray, and what to pray for; to hold us up in his righteous ways, to keep us weak in ourselves; for when we are thus weak, then are we strong in the Lord and in the power of his might; to keep our eyes from beholding vanity, and our feet from the very shadow of evil. For some most eminent men have been left to themselves, and, alas! have proved their weakness to be great indeed. Why should we so easily forget this and think ourselves strong? We think often that we can manage things better than they. This is our weakness, and if God were to let us try, we should feel it. Righteous Lot, though miraculously preserved from the wrath of God poured upon the city of Sodom and Gomorrah, awfully fell afterwards.

Sarah also, being past child-bearing, could not believe God, but laughed at his promise, which was that though she was old, she should have a son. David, a man after God's own heart, being in the way of temptation, awfully fell. And indeed the principle of freewill is the offspring of the bottomless pit, and has led many of God's children into awful labyrinths.

What a company of poor incautious creatures we all are! The best of men are but helpless worms, whose life is not their own; and yet how they trifle with God, who supports them even in nature. And if he did not keep his people, where would they be? Into what awful sins would they not fall? Abraham was remarkable for his faith, and his faith was accounted unto him for righteousness, yet he twice denied the wife of his bosom. Samson, though the strongest man that ever lived, except Christ, had not strength enough to keep himself from sinning, but was overcome by the deceitfulness of his tempter, or seducer, at last. David, though "a man after God's own heart," could not keep his own heart, but was infatuated by the beauty of a woman, and awfully fell! Solomon, though the wisest of mankind, became indifferent, and departed from the path of rectitude and wisdom, and sank into the depths of folly and criminality. And the apostle Peter, though he loved his Master, denied him, and swore he never knew him. And if our minds were now to be arraigned at the bar of God, and our hearts opened before him, who could stand? For who is clean? "We have all sinned; we have turned every one to his own way." (Isa. liii. 6.) There is no help in us; and if God has made it known unto us, and we have felt his life-giving power in our hearts, we have sinned even against that. Talk of creature doings! If the creature has no better salvation to depend upon than his own doings he will be condemned; he will sink for ever in black despair, to rise no more! He will then find that all he can do is insufficient.

2. The *criminality of Peter.*—Peter's crime, I consider, was far more outrageous than that of Judas; because we find that Peter held more converse with Christ his Lord, than did Judas. He went up into the mount of Transfiguration, and saw the glory of Christ; but Judas did not. Christ said unto Peter, when Peter confessed his belief in the Sonship of his Lord, "Flesh and blood hath not revealed this unto thee, but my Father which is in heaven." But Judas never had such a revelation. And Peter was before cautioned that

he would deny his Lord; but he said, "Though all men forsake thee, yet will not I." And Christ said to him, "Before the cock crow, thou shalt deny me thrice." And notwithstanding all this previous caution, and even seeing Christ before him, and in his hearing, he dared to deny him with oaths and curses. And if Peter could thus fall, what could you and I do? We are as weak and helpless as Peter. O that we may not, then, be left to trust our own hearts, or put confidence in the flesh; but pray the Lord to keep us, and preserve us in Christ Jesus, who is our only strength, and in him alone are we safe.

3. The *matchless grace of God*, displayed in the salvation of a sinner. What should you or I have done with Peter? If some one that we esteemed as a dear friend, or if a brother whom we loved, was to deny us before others, and in our presence, what should we do? We should doubtless, considering ourselves greatly insulted, order him to depart from us, or to be taken from our presence. But not so with Christ, our Friend, our Elder Brother. The wounds which Peter made in Christ's heart brought forth grace; he looked upon him. He looked upon him with an eye of pity, and had mercy upon him, and softened his hard heart by his grace; as though he would have said, "Ah! Ah! Peter! Hast thou forgotten the very many admonitions I have given thee, the glory which I revealed to thee, and that my enemies would thus deal with me, and still canst thou deny me?" And have you, my hearers, never denied your Lord? Have you not sometimes been ashamed of owning him in company? And have you not denied him in your heart? And are you still here? Why has he not cut you off long ago? "Ah!" Many of you can say, "By the grace of God I am what I am." You once could only look at chance as the ruler of all your actions; but now you can attribute good to the grace of God, from first to last. It is greater than the depths of your depravity and awful backslidings. Some say to the backslider, "You can make an atonement by your future good conduct." It is always with something you must do. Ah, confess and acknowledge your vileness before God, saying, "Behold, I am vile! What shall I answer thee! I have nothing to bring before thee, and would trust in thy atoning sacrifice alone!"

4. And what is the *effect produced?* Some say the grace of God leads to licentiousness. But did it lead Ephraim to licentiousness, when he cried out, "Thou hast chastised me, and I was chastised, as a bullock unaccustomed to the yoke. Turn thou me, and I shall be turned; for thou art the Lord my God?" And God said, "Since I have spoken against him I do earnestly remember him still; therefore my bowels are troubled for him. I will surely have mercy upon him, saith the Lord." And in Ezekiel xvi. the Lord says he will not deal with the sinner "according to thy covenant; but I will deal with thee according to my covenant;" which humbles the backslider,

who has committed whoredoms against the Lord; and it makes him to weep bitterly, and to sorrow with a godly sorrow, which worketh repentance not to be repented of. Though you may want to hide your faults from the world, you cannot hide them from God.

Did the grace of God lead Peter to sin? No; but his own deceitful heart. And see how the grace of God reigned! Was it Peter's own heart that made him weep? No; but the matchless grace of God, sent into his soul by his Saviour's look. In the Garden the floodgates of hell were opened upon Christ; and I believe a sight of this was sent into Peter's soul; as though Christ, by his look said, "I bore all this for *thee;* and though thou hast denied *me*, I will not deny *thee!*" O this wonderful, matchless, sovereign, free grace of God!

Peter wanted to conceal himself; he went out of the palace, and wept. No doubt he would ask himself, "Where shall I go to cover my head and to vent my feelings?" But he felt that the Lord had laid his hand upon him, and he could not leave him; and, therefore, he, as it were, in deep humility, said within himself, "Hast thou, Lord, taken advantage of my guilt to make me know more of myself and thee?"

Some talk of "Piety!" Piety! Piety! Piety! Were it not that it does once occur in the Word of God I should hate the very word; people make so much of it, as though piety were to save them. Their parents were pious, they were brought up pious, and they have continued pious. But even where the word does occur in the New Testament (1 Tim. v. 4), it simply means kindness, as the margin has it—let them show kindness at home. The word has nothing to do with salvation.* True religion humbles a sinner. Angels assemble together in the court of heaven and rejoice over broken-hearted sinners. O then, to rely upon Christ, to plead his love and blood, and to lean upon him and upon him alone and not upon your own repentance; this is the effect of grace. It is said of some kind of stones that they will not break until they have been steeped for a certain length of time in goat's blood; this may be so, but whether or not, it is so with your adamantine hearts; nothing will break them but being steeped in blood, the blood of the Scape-goat of the wildernesss.

5. What are the *lessons* taught us by these things? When you are reading your Bibles, and you find there this admonition and the other caution, do you not sometimes say, " I don't like this and that; I do not require such cautions?" Why do you say it? Because it touches your pride. But, instead of saying so, ought you not to fall down before God, and say, "Behold, Lord, I am vile! Make me humble

---

* An eminent Greek commentator says, "Piety is a general term, comprising all our relative duties; but particularly those which arise from relationship."

and wash me clean! I am estranged from thee by lies and vanity; lead me into all truth. I am in many dangers; be thou my guide, even unto death. I am weak and helpless; O Lord, hold thou me up that my footsteps slip not?" Thus the admonitions of God would be turned into a matter of prayer, and not trusting your own hearts. And if a brother sin, though you may have an utter hatred to that sin, yet you ought not to set your heart against him as a flint, but admonish him, and try to pray for him, remembering your own weakness; for if you should fall next, where then are you? O that you may pray to the Lord to search you, and try you, to make and keep you paupers, and purge you from dead works; for "he that trusteth his own heart is a fool;" and "cursed is the man that trusteth in man, and maketh flesh his aim." Do not even trust yourself alone; for, says the Scripture, "two are better than one." Do not trust yourself in improper company; for though the people of God cannot sin themselves into black despair, they may awfully fall, and bring guilt upon their consciences which will make their very breast-bones ache. May you, therefore, like Moses, say to the Lord, "If thy presence go not with us, carry us not up hence." It is dangerous to walk alone. O then cry to God to be always with you in your daily walks through life; and may you be enabled to put your trust in him; for he that trusteth in the Lord shall never be confounded, shall never be put to shame. Amen.

CHRIST AND HIS CHURCH, ONE.

" For as the body is one, and hath many members, and all the members of that one body being many, are one body; so also is Christ."—1 COR. XII. 12.

THE inseparable union which subsists between Christ and his church is a most glorious part of the dispensation of God's matchless grace. The blessed Lord Jesus Christ, as the Christ, and his church, are one, and always were one. They never were, never will be, two. In the eternal purpose of the glorious Trinity, Christ and his church sprang up together, as one glorious body, the Lamb and his wife, having all grace and glory secured in the Head, for the eternal blessedness of every member, and the declaration of the glory of all the perfections of Jehovah. Thus Christ and his spouse are one, and God is glorified in that one glorious body. "Blessed be the God and Father of our Lord Jesus Christ, who hath blessed us with all spiritual blessings in heavenly places in Christ; according as he hath chosen us in him before the foundation of the world, that we should be holy and without blame before him in love; having predestinated us unto the adoption of children by Jesus Christ to himself, according to the good pleasure of his will, to the praise of the glory of his grace, wherein he hath made us accepted in the beloved" (Eph. i. 3-6.)

The whole church, as one blessed body, with its various members, in one inseparable union to the glorious Head, are emphatically called Christ; and the whole context proves that each member is a part of this one glorious Christ mystical; and in this body there cannot be a schism: "Now ye are the body of Christ, and members in particular."

In this chapter, the apostle makes up a simile from the human body, to show that Christ the Head, and the church the members, are but one body; for as the human body hath many members, as the eyes, the nose, the ears, the feet, &c., yet it is but one body; so also, the body of Christ consists of many members, yet it is but one perfect body. One member cannot justly say to another, I have no need of thee; nor can one branch of the church be considered perfect, separate from the rest. (Heb. xi. 40.) Indeed, the church is declared to be "members of Christ's body, of his flesh, and of his bones" (Eph. v. 30), and "the fulness of him that filleth all in all." (i. 23.) As the glorious Head, Husband, and Surety of this one blessed body, Christ came, and came for the express purpose of redeeming her from all iniquity, and presenting her to himself a glorious church: "For the husband is the head of the wife, even as Christ is the head of the church; and he is the Saviour of the body. Therefore, as the church is subject unto Christ, so let the wives be to their own husbands in every thing. Husbands, love your wives, even as Christ also loved the church, and gave himself for it; that he might sanctify and cleanse it with the washing of water by the word, that he might present it to himself a glorious church, not having spot, or wrinkle, or any such thing; but that it should be holy and without blemish." And again: "Who gave himself for us"—not, who came to make an indefinite atonement, that might or might not save sinners; not for *sin* indefinitely; no, beloved; he came to redeem his church, and save his body, and "gave himself for *us* (*persons*) as I have said, that he might redeem us from all iniquity;" not merely to give us a chance of saving ourselves; no, no; but "that he might redeem us from all iniquity, and purify unto himself a peculiar people, zealous of good works." (Tit. ii. 14.) Of this one blessed church, as the glorious body of Christ, it is said, "Christ hath redeemed *us* from the curse of law, being made a curse for us." (Gal. iii. 13.) When, under the sweet unction of God the Holy Ghost, Paul enjoyed a measure of this blessing, as one of the members of this inseparable body, he solemnly exclaims, "Who loved *me*, and gave himself for *me*" (Gal. ii. 20); not merely for sin, indefinitely, but for me; for, through matchless grace, he has made it manifest that I am one of his blood-bought family; and, therefore, by the grace of God I am led to sing this glorious song, "He loved *me* and gave himself for *me*." And when God's dear people, in the present day, enjoy the same witness of the Spirit, under the same solemn unctuous power, they can sing with Paul, and say, "He loved *me*, and gave himself for *me*." "He was wounded for my transgressions, the chastisement of my peace was laid upon him, and with his stripes I am healed." (Isa. liii. 5.)

What highly-esteemed persons are those who are thus loved and redeemed, and who constitute the body of Christ! Where grace has made it manifest to the poor sinner that he is *one*, what manner of person ought he to be, in all holy conversation and godliness. O, my dear brethren, how ought we to walk in love, as Christ also hath loved us, and hath given himself for us, an offering and a sacrifice to God for a sweet-smelling savour. (Eph. v. 2.)

The great love of Christ to his blessed church runs through all his works. God the Father hath put all things under his feet, and given him to be "Head over all things to the church." (Eph. i. 19–22.) And his blessed Majesty overrules all circumstances and events for his own declarative glory and the good of his church; and it is one branch of the church's solemn employ to sing both of mercy and judgment. (Ps. ci. 1.) All the wrath of men, the rage of hell, no, nor the dreadful wanderings and sins of his own people, can ever divert him from this glorious purpose,—his and his Father's honour in the complete blessedness of his church. The awful sins of his people fell upon him in most dreadful torrents of horror, and, like piercing swords, they stabbed him to the heart. Yet such is his matchless love that the very blood which flowed from his broken and pierced heart, side, and hands, he by his Spirit applies to the hearts of his people, to heal the horrid malignancy of their crimes; so that, "with his stripes we are healed." Bless his holy name, he was made sin for us, and for us bore all the curse and wrath due to our vile transgressions, and, in the riches of his grace, he has made us the righteousness of God in himself. (2 Cor. v. 21.) He stood before the Father and divine Justice in our sins, and bore all the wrath due unto us; and, by a matchless, glorious transfer, we stand before God and Justice in his holiness and righteousness, and are "complete in him." (Col. ii. 10.)

This is God's blessed method of saving, completely saving, the one mystical body of Christ, that no flesh should glory in his presence. Their whole salvation, holiness, righteousness, and happiness is in, from, and by, the Lord; and he shall have all the glory. "But of him are ye in Christ Jesus, who of God is made unto us wisdom, and righteousness, and sanctification, and redemption; that according as it is written, He that glorieth, let him glory in the Lord."

The blessed body, the church, is of God, in Christ, chosen in him before the foundation of the world, and shall abide in him for ever. In him she is free from condemnation: "Who shall lay anything to the charge of God's elect? It is God that justifieth. Who is he that condemneth? It is Christ that died; yea, rather, that is risen again; who is even at the right hand of God, who also maketh intercession for us." (Rom. viii. 32, &c.) Now all the blessedness contained in these notable verses flow from everlasting, electing, redeeming love, and are freely and graciously bestowed on the members of Christ's body; and so dear is this body to the Three-One God that the Father "spared not his own Son, but delivered him up for *us* all, and with him also freely gives *us* all things." And mind, it is the same blessed *us* for whom Christ hath died, and rose again, and for whom he makes intercession at the right hand of God. Yea, it is the same blessed *us* in whom the Spirit "maketh intercession, with groanings which cannot be uttered." It is the same *us* which can "never be separated from the love of God, which is in Christ Jesus."

Matchless, unparalleled love! And blessed, thrice blessed, are the people that are in such a case!

Such is the love of Christ, the Head, to his glorious body, that when he was personally upon earth, wading through deep waters and drinking full draughts of the wrath of incensed Justice, the just due to his church, all he felt, and all he viewed that he had to undergo, for her, could not move his heart from her, nor cause him for one moment to forget her. Read Jno. xvii. There you will perceive that when the dreadful hour drew near that death and hell must be let loose upon him, his loving heart and busy thoughts were all engaged in the solemn business of God's glory and the blessedness of his spouse.

Poor, desponding, broken-hearted child of God, what hast thou to fear? The life of Christ and thy life are but *one* life; for he is thy Life, and "because he lives thou shalt live also." Hear his holy prayer to his Father in thy behalf, thou poor, weak worm, poor, worthless, mourning, sin-sick soul: "I pray for them. I pray not for the world, but for them which thou hast given me; for they are thine; and all mine are thine, and thine are mine, and I am glorified in them." See the blessed ground upon which he goes, as if he were determined to remind the Father of the relationship which subsisted between the Father, and himself, and the church: "And they are *mine* and *thine*; and I *pray* for them, and for them *only*. Thou gavest them me, and I give them eternal life, and that life is in myself. This is my body, and my flesh, and my bones; my glorious church (Eph. v. 27), and thy glorious house, which thou hast determined to glorify. (Isa. lx. 7.) Yea, thou hast said thou wilt be unto her an everlasting light, and her glory. This is thy chosen Zion; thy rest for ever. Here thou wilt dwell, for thou hast desired it. Therefore, they are thine and mine; and what they are in thy love and purpose of grace, as chosen in me, and as they stand in me, I pray that they may be brought to a sweet view and feeling of in their own souls, and live and act accordingly; that they all may be one, as thou, Father, art in me, and I in thee, that they also may be one in us; that the world may believe that thou hast sent me. And the glory which thou gavest me I have given them; that they may be one, even as we are one; I in them, and thou in me, that they may be made perfect in one.''

The Lord enable each believing soul to realize a little of the blessedness of this glorious union,—''That they may be one, even as we are one; I in them, and thou in me, that they may be made perfect in one.'' Poor sinners taken up into union with God, by virtue of their union to Christ, their Head; one with Christ, as he is one with the Father! Bless his holy name, he has taken their nature into union with his Godhead, that he might come down and suit himself to their cases and circumstances, and, by power divine, vitally make manifest what they are by virtue of an eternal union to him, in the ancient settlements of heaven; and he makes them partakers of his Spirit, life, and holiness, to raise them vitally up to God (Eph. i. 17, 18; Rom. viii. 11; John vii. 38, 39; xiv. 17–19; Heb. xii. 10; 2 Pet. i. 4); that by faith in Christ, under the divine unction and teachings of God the Holy Ghost, they may hold converse with the Father, as their own covenant God and Father, in the openings of his love in eternal election and sovereign choice of them in Christ before the world was; and in the gift of Christ to them, and them to Christ, and all the blessings secured in him for them, both for time and eternity, and to hold solemn converse with Christ, as their glorious Head, in his incarnation, holy life, and dreadful sufferings for them, and in all the endearing offices he fills, characters he sustains, names he bears, and relationship in which he stands to them; together with the fulness that in him dwells; and to hold converse with the Holy Ghost, in his soul-quickening, enlightening, convincing, reproving, teaching, anointing, sealing, comforting, sanctifying operations. And thus, by virtue of their union to Christ, are they raised above the world to have fellowship with God, and, at some blessed moments, are brought to enjoy the grace of the Lord Jesus Christ, and the love of God, and the communion of the Holy Ghost, and are looking for that blessed hope, and the glorious appearing of the great God and our Saviour, Jesus Christ. (Tit. ii. 13.) And when the world is in a blaze, this glorious church shall share in all the beauties of Christ, their glorious Head, and receive the kingdom prepared for them of the Father, before the world was; and so shall be for ever with the Lord.— *Feb.*, 1835.

ANOTHER.

" For by one Spirit are we all baptized into one body, whether we be Jews
or Gentiles, whether we be bond or free, and have been all made to drink into one Spirit."—1 COR. XII. 13.

MAY I entreat you to ask your consciences this important question. As you have read from the Word of God, that Christ is the
Head of the church, and that his people are the members of his
mystical body, " Am I really one of these members?"

Some deny the baptism of the Spirit, yet admit the baptism of
water. Others believe the baptism of the Spirit to be all that is needful,
and deny the baptism of water. But I am not, this morning, going
to speak of baptism, but of the union existing between Christ and
his church. O Lord, baptize me by thy Spirit in speaking thy Word,
without which I cannot speak aright; I cannot get into it, I may,
indeed, skip around it, but not enter into its fulness, its glory and
beauty.

1. Let us consider the blessed and inseparable *union* between
Christ and his church.   2. The glorious *Person* engaged in behalf of
this union.   3. As a *confirmation* of this union, he baptizes the whole
church into this glorious body.   4. How God *pours out his Spirit* into
their souls and causes them to drink into one Spirit.

1. The blessed and inseparable *union* between Christ and his
church.

The church of God is safe.   First, because this union was decreed
before all worlds; and secondly, because this union of the elect with
Christ is preserved in Christ by the life and power of the Spirit.

Blessed be the Lord, who hath chosen us *in* him, and not *out* of him.
As Jude says, "Sanctified by God the Father, preserved *in* Christ
Jesus, and called."   So that our calling is a proof we are preserved.

In what sense are we preserved?   "According as he hath chosen
us in him before the foundation of the world."   Did Christ lose any
of his people?   No; they were preserved in him from all eternity.
In old Adam they all fell; but in Christ they never fell.   There were
none of them lost.   See how the sheet, let down to Peter, gloriously exhibits the mystical body of Christ!   What a blessed knitting together is this union!   This glorious union does away with all
confusion.   What confusion and uncertainty there would be if what
some say were true,—that if they improve grace they will be saved,
and if they neglect it they will be damned.   Do they remember that
the Head of the church is Christ, and that through and in him there
are many members; yet they are but one body?   If first one member were cut off and then another, all would be confusion, disorder,
and misery.   But God has cemented the whole body together by his
eternal decree, that his church should be one in him, " even as he
and the Father are one."   And at last he shall ascend and triumph
with all his blood-bought family in his bosom.

Then each one of you ask yourselves, "Do I belong to this glorious number, united in one body by the everlasting love of God?" O, sinners! Ask yourselves what proof you have that you belong to this body, which is Christ. Paul was one of this union, even when he held the witnesses' clothes while Stephen was being stoned, he consenting to his death. He was even then a vessel of mercy, chosen in Christ to minister unto the Gentiles. The Philippian jailor was one, and he in deep humility and concern for his soul, cried out, "What must I do to be saved?" Mary Magdalene was one, who, in deep penitence of soul, anointed the feet of her Lord. Who would have thought of a Paul, a jailor, or a Magdalene being of this number? But they were, though wrapped up in divine obscurity. So you may be thus wrapped up,—a member of this glorious body; and you may be fully persuaded that salvation is in Christ alone; and yet not clearly see your own interest in him. People tell you, "You are only a sinner, and Christ died for sinners; so be one with Christ, and all will be well with you." But you feel your helplessness; you want something more than knowing you are only a sinner, and that Christ died for sinners. You feel all hope in self and of self is gone, and that you cannot find any place to abide in, except in Christ. Then you feel a knitting of your soul to him, and hear him sweetly saying, "Behold the Lamb of God, that taketh away the sin of the world." God shines into your soul with divine light and love, and draws you nearer to himself by his Spirit. You know it, and feel it, and realize a divine oneness between Christ and your own soul.

2. And now, let us briefly notice the glorious *Person* engaged in behalf of this union, which is the Holy Spirit. He had not come when Christ was upon the earth; but the Lord Jesus said he would send him when risen from the dead: "Even the Spirit of truth, which proceedeth from the Father, the Comforter; he shall testify of me, and *shall dwell with you and be in you.*" He shall testify of me as your glorious Head, and shall testify to you that you are members of my body. And,

3. "As a *confirmation* of this union, he shall baptize you manifestively into this glorious body." The first glorious manifestation of this was on the day of Pentecost, when the disciples were all met together with one accord, to worship God in one place.

So Christ, when he was about to leave his disciples, in his prayer for them, said, "Neither pray I for these alone, but for them which shall believe on me through their word." They were all of one body.

4. O that I could express in words how richly God pours out his blessed Spirit into the souls of his people! It is a river to swim in, —a river to bathe in; a river of pardoning love; a river that no man can fathom; a river without bottom or shore,—from everlasting to

everlasting; "the blood of Jesus Christ that cleanseth from all sin." And when the blessed Spirit powerfully applies that precious blood to our hearts, he baptizes us in love; so that away goes all the world; Jesus is our all in all; and our souls shout aloud for joy, while our hearts are melted and our tongues are let loose. O, believer, have you ever experienced this? God grant that you may, again and again, as you journey through this wilderness.

> "Hail, sacred union, firm and strong;
> How great the grace; how sweet the song,—
> That worms of earth should ever be,
> One with incarnate Deity."

May the Lord bless his truth to your hearts and mine; for his Name's sake. Amen.

THE LORD'S PEOPLE RIGHTEOUS.

" Perfect and upright."—Job i. 1.

You have read the history of Job, how that Satan desired to sift him as wheat is sifted, affirming that he would make him curse God to his face, and that God granted his request, so far as to suffer his infernal majesty to do his utmost to make Job curse God. But was this to satisfy Satan, or torture Job? No; though no doubt it did both; but to show that wherever God has put his life, it is out of the power of the devil to remove it; and though Beelzebub, with all the soldiers under his command, blew into Job all their infernal venom, yet God held him up, and would not let him curse him; and though Job cursed a variety of things, the Lord preserved him from cursing his God. Job, at that time, appears to have been in a dreadfully hot fire, and Satan blew it into a horrible blaze, yet he could not make him curse God. By and by, we find Job with his hand upon his mouth, crying out, "Behold, I am vile!" And I believe Job had never more holiness in him than he had then.

The Lord's eyes are continually upon us, to watch over and keep us, notwithstanding our unbelief. The great point, therefore, is, *are* we righteous? A man may have a great zeal for what he may call his holy Church, and even fight and bleed for it, and yet not be righteous; he may have a kind of humility and repentance, and yet not be righteous. Judas repented, and threw down the money, saying, "I have betrayed innocent blood;" but we know the place he went to. He may give his assent and consent to all the doctrines of the Bible, even to regeneration being the special work of God the Holy Ghost, to sanctification being the absolute act of a Triune God, to the resurrection of the dead, &c. &c., and yet have no vitality. He may, from constant hearing or reading, patch up an experience and be able to state it very clearly, and yet never feel it. Numbers have by this means crept into the church below, deceiving them, and ultimately causing them agony, by turning out despicable characters. Nay, they may be thought so highly of as to have great trust placed in them by the church. Judas deceived the apostles, even to that degree that they intrusted him with the purse; but he never deceived Christ. He knew who would betray him. Further. He may stand up to preach, preach the truth, and preach it in a masterly manner, and expose error in its various branches, and yet never experience the power of it in his conscience by the blessed Spirit.

Then what does constitute a man righteous? Why, say you, I suppose, *real* grace in the heart, *real* obedience, &c. No, they do not. This is only like sending down, as it were, a *copy* of the title-deed, not the *deed* itself. They are *proofs* that he is righteous; but the fact of his *being* righteous is another thing. He is constituted righteous by being interested in the precious blood and righteousness of Christ, having his obedience, &c., placed to his account; and here he stood justified before all worlds.

Perhaps some poor trembling sinner says he wants the manifestation of it. I know he does. Well, if ever he obtains it, most likely he will soon after have to feel many things very trying to his flesh. Says the poor soul, " What will they be ? " Why, the blessed Spirit, by his quickening power, will put him out of conceit with himself, with his holiness, his duties, his sins, and everything else he has, and thus take all his strength from him. God help you to have no strength; then his strength will be made perfect in your weakness. Professors may gallop; but God's children have often to go upon crutches; and sometimes, poor things, down they come, crutches and all. Good works and bad works of their own are all alike to them, in this respect.—*Manchester*, 1838.

WHO HATH BELIEVED OUR REPORT?

"Who hath believed our report? And to whom is the arm of the Lord revealed?"—Isa. liii. 1.

This solemn question might have been put to God himself; for no human being in existence is capable of answering it; for though, in the dispensations of the Lord's providence, God's ministers are now and then encouraged by hearing of one and another having been brought under their ministry to believe their report, yet there may be hundreds of others of whom they may never hear.* And then again, they may be so distressed, through unbelief, as to cry out, " Unto whom is the arm of the Lord revealed? Who hath believed our report?" But, though we do not see the works of the arm of

---

* This is a very striking observation; and certainly to no minister of recent times will the remark apply more than to the preacher himself; as witness the numerous instances recorded, from time to time, in letters and obituaries in the "Gospel Standard."

the Lord, our blindness shall not in any wise hinder God's work. He is ever faithful, and cannot deny himself.

If believing in and coming unto the Lord depended upon my management, I should fall far short. Some, indeed, speak about short comings; but if God were not to reveal himself to me, I should never come at all. I should not take one step towards him. Nay, I should go farther off still; therefore, whatever comings to God I have, they are not mine, but God's, who comes unto me, reveals himself to me, and thus draws me nearer to him.

Then 1. Let us consider what is this *report*.

2. What is the *design* of the arm of the Lord being revealed?

1. Who hath believed our *report?* None of themselves have savingly done so. This is couched in the 6th verse: "All we, like sheep, have gone astray; we have turned every one to his own way." There is here no exception—*all*, both God's elect and the rest; all have gone into sin, and the paths of destruction. All have, by nature, made a league with Satan. Not a soul, by nature, can truly believe this report; for the carnal mind is enmity against God. And if hell were to blaze before your eyes, it would not make you spiritually believe. "Then," say you, "we are excused." But, no; for, suppose a man, by dissipation, had so marred his constitution that he was not fit for work, would not this be the effect of his vileness? Has he not aggravated his crimes and driven himself from all hope of recovery by so doing? Then we are just in this awful state. We stand on the brink of an awful precipice; and, if God does not reveal his arm unto us, sink we must, and none can help.

God gave his Son; but even his own people abhorred him, scorned him, and trampled upon him: "We hid, as it were, our faces from him. He was despised, and we esteemed him not." And why? Because, as we are told in the 2nd verse, "He hath no form nor comeliness; and when we shall see him, there is no beauty in him that we should desire him." He had nothing attractive to our fleshly views. He did not come in pomp and splendour, as a popular character; for though the Jews were looking for his coming at the time, yet, because of his humility, they rejected him. They said, "As for this man, we know him; he is the son of Joseph, the carpenter." But they were deceived; for they neither knew him nor his Father.

There is, in our day, a great anticipation of Christ's Second Coming, when he shall sit upon a throne, as King, and all his subjects be princes; but what I look for is that Christ may come and dwell in my heart, and let me enjoy his presence, and that I may not be deceived by vain imaginations. "Who hath believed our report?"

There are, according to what is generally preached, few in this so-called Christian country who do not believe this report; for they are taught in their infancy to say, "I believe in God the Father Almighty, Maker of heaven and earth," &c., and also to repeat the

Lord's Prayer; and then are they said to be Christians and to believe this report. But until God burns up these prayers in your heart, and makes you feel that from merely learning these prayers by rote you cannot address God as your Father. Until he strips you of all power in self and of self, and blesses you with vital faith in him, you cannot truly believe this report. But when God thus sends his Spirit into your heart, you then do believe his report.

God has laid the iniquity of his church upon Christ. He hath borne our griefs and carried our sorrows. He was, as it were, pounded in a mortar, until his soul was mangled with the heavy load of our guilt, until he cried out, "My soul is exceeding sorrowful, even unto death." Yes, "he poured out his soul unto death, and he was numbered with the transgressors." Yea, he suffered the billows of Divine wrath to be poured upon him, that we might be saved. But who hath believed our report?

He hath justified his people: "He shall see of the travail of his soul and be satisfied." But could he be satisfied if part of his purchase were taken from him and lost? "He shall bear their iniquities." There are none charged upon the sinner; he is irreprovable and without rebuke, through the atonement of Christ. There is more glory in justification than even in pardon. For instance, at this present time, there are petitioners to her majesty to pardon three men who have been condemned to death; and suppose the queen were to pardon them, that would not justify them. No. They might escape the gallows, but they would still be guilty. But this is one branch of the report,—that in Christ's righteousness shall his people be justified and exalted. Here is the difference,—though the queen can pardon a man, she cannot justify him; she cannot make a guilty man innocent. But the sinner, to whom the righteousness of Christ is imputed, is, in the sight of God, as free from sin as if he had never sinned. There is not even a blemish upon him. (Eph. v. 27.) This is a wonderful mystery,—one which even angels cannot understand. Strictly speaking, pardon, abstractedly considered, would not give a sinner a title for heaven. He must be made holy; for "without holiness no man can see God," and this can only be by Christ's holiness being made the sinner's; for the best of human holiness is sin. This was Christ's design in coming to dwell with us; not only that he might satisfy law claims, so that our salvation might not be by works of righteousness which we could do, but according to his sovereign mercy; but also that by his perfect obedience we might be holy in his holiness. It is on this ground that the apostle said, "There is, therefore, now no condemnation to them who are in Christ Jesus." "Yes," say you; "we have it in that passage. It is not to them who walk after the flesh, but to them who walk after the Spirit." It is so. But which way does the Spirit go? He has promised to convince of sin, to blast our false hopes, and to convince of righteousness and of judgment. He shall take of the things of Christ and show them unto us. He shall strip us of self; and cause us to walk after Christ. This is walking after the Spirit.

There is a certainty of all God's people entering into this salvation. It is not a chance salvation. If we have no better hope than chance we had much better have no hope at all. How encouraging it is when we can trace this report for ourselves, and therein find our security. "My sheep hear my voice and follow me." Christ does not say they shall not experience any hurricanes or troubles. He himself experienced them, and so must they, as followers of him. "Who hath believed our report?"

2. The *design* of the arm of the Lord being revealed. The Lord makes bare his own arm, as also does a warrior when he is about to enter into battle, that he may go unshackled, and have freedom of his limbs, not being encumbered with unnecessary appendages of dress; and the Lord hath done gloriously—and his own right arm hath gotten him the victory. Christ is the ground of our victory; by his blood are we cleansed, by his righteousness are we justified. I am not ashamed of the gospel of Christ; it is the power of God unto salvation, to every one that believeth. Christ has wrought out a complete salvation. In his Person, in his character, in his obedience, in his agonizing death, he hath made us perfect. He who was without sin took upon him our nature, and became sin for us, who knew no sin, that we might be made the righteousness of God in him. And all this to satisfy justice. Without Christ there is no salvation. There is none other name given under heaven whereby we can be saved. Take away Christ and God could not save a soul. His holy law forbids it; holiness forbids it; justice forbids it. Christ is the all and in all of a sinner's salvation. Talk about cleansing your own heart and saving yourself! Why, as I often say, if you had all the holiness in the world, separate from Christ, it would not save you. God demands a perfect obedience; and in Christ alone is there that perfect obedience found. He is our Surety; and, though a debtor were not able to pay one mite of his just debt, yet if his surety pays it he would be free. Therefore Christ's people are free.

Who reveals the arm of the Lord? Christ himself by the Holy Spirit. He is revealed in the conscience of every heaven-born soul. He revealed himself to Saul of Tarsus, as he was journeying to Damascus. He spoke with power to his conscience, saying, "Saul, Saul, why persecutest thou me?" And with this revelation Saul was pricked in the heart, and, in humble submission to his will, cried out, "Who art thou, Lord?" And he said, "I am Jesus, whom thou persecutest." Did Paul then set about patching up his own righteousness? No; yet, according to the letter of the law, he was blameless. The Lord said to Ananias, "Behold, he prayeth!" Behold! Why did he never pray before? He was one of those who loved praying,—standing at the corners of the streets, and in the highest places in the synagogue; but he never prayed until now. The Lord had revealed himself unto him; and now, behold, he prayeth! But Ananias seemed not to believe the report, though the Lord himself spoke to him. It was as though he said to the Lord, "Ah, Lord! I have heard of this man. I believe he has said tons of prayers; but thou knowest he has come here to put us all to death." "Aye," answered the Lord; "but go thy way; he is a chosen vessel unto me." I can imagine how quickly Ananias started up after this, and went to Saul, and called him his brother,—"Brother Saul!" (Acts ix.) Ah, brethren! You and I stand as much in need of this revelation as Paul did; for, "we are gone out of the way; we are altogether become filthy; there is none that doeth good, no not one." And without this divine revelation in the conscience, we cannot enter into the spirit of this report.

"It is not in word only, but in power." Has your mouth been stopped? Have you been in hopeless despondency? For nature cannot produce this divine revelation in your hearts. Have you heard a voice behind you, saying, "Behold the Lamb of God, that taketh away the sin of the world." Have you then been in great straits, not knowing which way to turn, to know if he had taken away your sins? Have you been in those trials and difficulties, and could not make a way? Have you not felt as though you sank a thousand fathoms in a moment? And then has Christ spoken to your conscience, and said, "I am the way." This, then, is the divine revelation; and there is no faith in Christ without it, as God tells us in Eph. i. 17–23: "The eyes of your understanding being enlightened, that ye may know what is the hope of his calling, and what the riches of the glory of his inheritance in the saints," &c. And, if you are brought to believe, it is the exceeding greatness of his mighty power, his arm being revealed, that you are in such a state. You will feel and acknowledge that without him you can do nothing. Do you believe this report?

May God the Spirit reveal Christ to your souls, the hope of glory. Amen.—*Manchester, Feb. 2nd,* 1840.

THE FOUNDATION OF GOD STANDETH SURE.

"The foundation of God standeth sure; having this seal, The Lord knoweth them that are his."—2 TIM. ii. 19.

A FOUNDATION is the basis of an edifice. Hence, when you build, you must have a foundation; and if you intend your building to stand, it must be a sure, a safe, and a sound foundation,—immovable. Then will your building be strong. The man's house built upon a rock stood secure against storm and tempest; but the man who built his house upon the sand, when the floods came, and the winds blew, the house fell; and great was the fall thereof. How many in our day build upon an unsound foundation, that will not stand the blast of poverty, the power of temptation, or the floods of error. But where is the Christian's foundation? It is in God, and the foundation of God is in Jehovah's purpose and eternal counsel, made sure in the Lord Jesus Christ before the world was. Why is it in Christ? First, because God the Father laid it there; and secondly, he built his church thereon. He laid it in his covenant of grace: "Behold, I make a covenant with you, even the sure mercies of David." It is in Christ: "Behold, I lay in Zion for a foundation, a stone, elect, precious; and he that believeth in him shall not be confounded." Christ is the Stone, the Rock of Ages. His people are built upon him. The apostles and prophets were not the foundation. They preached Christ, and Christ was their only sure foundation. It is laid in the heart of his people; and, in order to lay a foundation, there must be some digging work to remove the rubbish. So the imaginary goodness of man must be dug up and removed; and then a sure foundation will be laid. Thus his people are built on Christ, a habitation of God, through the Spirit, and will remain so when the world is in a blaze and through all eternity, because they are well founded, well built. "He brought me up out of a horrible pit, and out of the miry clay, and set my feet upon a Rock, and established my goings."

What do you know of this? Are you upon the Rock? O that you may fall upon God in Christ, and wait for his salvation, that, when death comes, you may say, "Now, Lord, lettest thou thy servant depart in peace, for mine eyes have seen thy salvation." It is a sealed foundation, and no man can break this seal, and tell the extent of it, or even the size of the building, but Christ. "The Lion of the tribe of Judah hath prevailed, and he alone can open the seal." Man may be deceived in the knowledge of God's people; but Christ cannot be deceived. "The Lord knoweth them that are his."—*Manchester.*

COME, AND LET US REASON TOGETHER.

"Come now, and let us reason together, saith the Lord."—Isa. i.18.

HERE is a special people addressed, "a small remnant." They tremble and fear under a feeling sense of their guilt and utter unworthiness; but God mercifully calls unto them, saying, "Come, let us reason together."

Some people think they are as good as any of their neighbours, and a deal better than most; and they try to thus comfort themselves. But unless God brings them to repentance and teaches them to place entire dependence upon Christ, they will sink into black despair. The Lord does not say, "Come pious, come virtuous;" but "though your sins be as scarlet they shall be as white as snow; though they be red like crimson they shall be as wool."

The Pharisees have a zeal for God, but not according to knowledge; they, being ignorant of God's righteousness, go about to establish their own righteousness, not submitting themselves to the righteousness of God; and thus they delude their own souls. But the characters alluded to in our text feel themselves to be double-dyed sinners,—outcasts from society and from God; justice seems to cast them off; law and mercy, all seem against them, to cast them off as sinners. Do *you* really feel it? Do you confess it before God? If so, you are precious in his sight.

> "A sinner is a sacred thing;
> The Holy Ghost hath made him so."

God will appear and save such as feel their need of him; he came to seek and to save such, even them that were lost. The seeds of iniquity are sown in your heart. Saul of Tarsus walked according to the law, blameless; but when God opened his heart, sin revived, and he died; and sin, taking occasion by the commandment, wrought in him all manner of concupiscence. He felt more deeply lost; his heart was circumcised, and he lay, before a heart-searching and rein-trying God, vile, polluted, and miserable.

Listen to the nature of the call: "Come unto me." How endearing is this word, "Come." What soul-subduing language! To think that the great Eternal Three-in-One should thus affectionately invite poor sinners to come and reason with him! We should think it an act of condescension if the queen were to reason with her plebeian subjects, or if a dignified person were to say to a poor sick and famishing creature, "Come to me, and I will be your friend. I will relieve your distress, and comfort you." The poor thing's heart would gladly listen and leap for joy. But here you see Infinite Purity standing at the door of mercy, and saying to such as feel their desolate state, "Come unto me." Then think not to place any hope in what you have done, or what you can do; but come, poor sinner, just as you are, with your burden of sin and guilt; for Jesus says, "Come unto me, all ye that are weary and heavy laden, and I will give you rest." You stand between love and mercy on the one hand, and law and justice on the other. Of old, the leper had to be taken to the priest before he could be pronounced clean. You have the leprosy in your heart, and the blessed Spirit must lead you to Christ, who is our High Priest, to be cleansed. Some might ask, "How are we to be led?" You must be blest with that faith which is of the operation of God the Spirit. Faith in him will lead you to holiness and purity. "The Spirit and the bride say, Come; let him that heareth say, Come; let him that is athirst come; and whosoever will, let him come, and take of the water of life freely."

Here is the Eternal Spirit saying, "Come;" and the bride, the Lamb's wife, saying, "Come;" and John, who heard, and all Christ's ministers say, "Come." To whom do they speak? Are you a sensibly-lost sinner? Have you been led to believe that Christ is a Saviour for the lost? Are you thirsting, panting, and groaning for mercy? You are the characters addressed. Are you willing to be saved in God's own way,—by grace, and that God shall be glorified in your salvation? The Lord never says "Come" to any before he has made them feel their need of Him; and he makes them not only willing but glad to come. "Thy people shall be willing in the day of thy power."

So that there is a lawful coming. It is to come as a beggar, poor and helpless, maimed, halt, blind; feeling that you have no legs to stand upon, all your earthly props being gone. You then come breathing after mercy, sighing like the prisoner for liberty to believe. "But," say some, "I cannot believe." Why, you cannot disbelieve; for if some one attacked you and attempted to make you believe there is no God, he could not. What *is* believing? First, to believe that God is, that he is a rein-trying God, who will by no means clear the guilty, and not such a careless Judge as some imagine. Next, that Christ is a mighty Saviour,—one who can save the guilty. And, next, that *you* are guilty and need such a Saviour. In these things you have the full assurance of faith; and by and by you shall have faith to believe that that Saviour is yours. The Lord draw you. Ask yourselves, can you seek refuge anywhere else? Then cry mightily to God for pardon; for Christ, the God of your salvation, will hear you. Why, poor dear soul, if it were possible for such a one as you to be sent to hell, they would not know what to do with you there. What! A poor sinner, groaning on account of his sins and panting after Christ as his Saviour, be sent to hell? Impossible! The very thought gives the lie to the gospel of God's grace.

"Come and let us reason together." "What are we to reason about?" "About your unbelief." As though Christ had said, "Did I not come to save the lost? And yet, because you feel *you* are lost, you think I did not come to save *you*. You believe I came to deliver the captives and to set the prisoners free. *You* are bound, *you* are in prison, yet you think I will not set *you* free. Well; this is your carnal unbelief; but by my Spirit you shall be made free. You say your sins are so great and so many. Did I not save a David, a Manasseh, a Magdalene, a Saul of Tarsus, a Peter, though he swore he never knew me, even after it had been revealed to him by my Spirit that I am the Christ? Is anything too hard for me? I came to save sinners, not the righteous. And has it not been revealed to thee that I am just such a Saviour as thou needest? Come, now, and let us reason about these matters."

This reason is not of a carnal nature. We cannot rightly go before

God in our own strength, but in his strength; namely, in Christ, who is our strength and our shield. If we truly confess our wretchedness, vileness, and total inability, God will enable us to reason, as expressed in Hosea xiv. 2: "Take with you words, and turn to the Lord, and say, Take away all iniquity and receive us graciously; so will we render the calves of our lips." Jacob wrestled with God and prevailed; but not in his own strength but in the strength of Christ he had power with God and prevailed. Moses pleaded with God for the children of Israel; and what were his arguments? He prayed, "For the glory of thy great Name, save this people." As though he had said, "The glory of thy great Name is at stake." And where is God's great Name? It is in Christ. But some in our day say, "Christ has done all he can to save sinners; and it only remains for sinners to do their part, and then they will be saved;" and yet they are so foolish as to pray to God to help them. Thus does human reason contradict itself. But this is not the reason God intends. A poor sinner will be like Job, confessing his vileness, and saying, "What shall I answer thee?" God will answer thee, "I am thy salvation." You will say, "I am unworthy;" but God will say, "In me thou shalt have peace." Thus he will glorify his Name in the hearts of the people.—*Manchester.*

THE FAITHFUL GOD.
"The faithful God."—DEUT. VII. 9.

WITH what inexpressible satisfaction can the people of God sit at the feet of Jehovah, who is all holiness and purity and greatness; for what a ground of contentment it is to them to have this God as their faithful God; not merely believing it in their judgment, but feeling the truth in their hearts, that he is the faithful God. This couches in it many particulars, a few of which we will notice · the promises expected from him—his power, his covenant engagements. God is faithful in the relationship he bears to his church.

In what *relation*, let us ask ourselves, do we stand to this faithful God? He is our Creator and Preserver. Nothing is left by him in a precarious state. The ravens fed the prophet at the brook. See the lilies of the field. They toil not, neither do they spin; yet Solomon, in all his glory, was not arrayed like one of these. Not a sparrow falls to the ground without his notice; even the very hairs of your head are all numbered.

> "Life, death, and hell, and worlds unknown,
> Hang on his firm decree;
> He sits on no precarious throne,
> Nor borrows leave to be."

In what does he prove this faithful relationship? He has declared that the wicked shall be cast into hell. He will be found faithful and true. If you live and die without matchless grace, without repentance towards God and faith in the Lord Jesus Christ, his infinite wrath will be poured upon you; his threatenings will be executed.

Let me, then, urge upon youth to look at this solemn warning: "Rejoice, O young man, in thy youth, and let thy heart cheer thee in the days of thy youth; but know thou that for all these things God will bring thee to judgment." How many of you set at defiance the faithfulness of God! Your carnal inclinations, wantonness, and dissipation are all your cares, and you say, "How does God know?" The Spirit of God is everywhere. He sees your every action; you cannot hide yourselves from him; and without repentance "ye shall all likewise perish." Out of Jesus Christ there is no salvation. Young men and young women! Think of this. Ask yourselves, are you in possession of the precious promises which are treasured up in Christ for those who love him? Are you prepared to meet him at his coming? Ah! My dear young friends! Trifle not with eternity! Think upon these solemn truths; ponder them over in your hearts; and may you be made sincere and honest, forsaking the follies of youth, and live entirely to his glory. God will not be mocked; he knows your hearts, and will not be deceived. He is faithful; the faithful God in his threatenings.

[O what solemn words he would sometimes address to ungodly young men and young women at the close of a "funeral sermon" for their godly parents! "Young man, you have lost a praying father; he will pray for you no more. You, who have laughed at his prayers and scoffed at his tears, and wished the old fool would be quiet, or that he was far enough away, so that you might have your fling in sin; young woman, you who have seen your mother's tears and heard your mother's prayers, but have turned your hardened hearts and backs away; if grace prevent not, you will sink into black despair.]

Aged men and women, remember that he who has seen your every action is faithful; and how many of you aged have lived in sin from your youth, careless about your own salvation and the ordinances of God, and breaking his commandments. And now are even more hardened in your crimes than ever. How often have you been the means of destroying even the principles of virtue in youth. You have not so much as restrained them from attending those haunts of vice which are destructive even to their temporal welfare. This is neglect. But how many amongst you have done more? Have you not led your sons and daughters thither? O, let me beseech you to stay your mad career; for there is a time coming when God will prove faithful. If you have thus violated his laws and neglected his ordinances, you will find he is for ever the faithful God.

The people of God have God for their Husband and Father. And do some of you say, "Can I be so intimately connected with Christ,—with Him who is infinitely holy, infinitely pure; and I so unholy, so base, so vile?" Hear, poor soul, who art ready to faint under the pressure of thy guilt, he has declared, "Thy Maker is thy Husband." It is realized to thee in Christ; thou art redeemed by his blood; thou wast created out of the dust of the earth; and art, in mercy and faithfulness, preserved unto this moment. And art thou still repining, and he so good and true? Pause a moment and reflect upon the faithfulness of God. How merciful! how kind! how good! and how great! how faithful is our God! And we still remain ungrateful for all these mercies, and forget the gracious Giver? Bring the matter home to yourself, as between God and conscience. Ask, "What evidence have I that he has betrothed me to himself? Where are my affections? Are they toward the faithful God? What can God find in me that is worthy of his notice; nay, more, that I should be married to him in love? Alas! I am abashed and confounded." Ah! You may indeed wonder. Did you not promise him you would return his love, and have you not broken your vows? Frail creature! You have indeed proved unfaithful; but have you not found Him to be ever faithful? Can you not say, in faith and feeling, "The faithful God?" How much, then, the reverence due to him! Stand in awe at his word; for you have need to cry out, "I am for ever lost if God is not faithful!" And may you be enabled to trust in God and his promises. He has further declared for your consolation, he will never leave nor forsake you. He will not deal with you according to your deserts. And in this have you not proved him faithful? Are you not deserving of his righteous indignation? And has he not had compassion upon you, and pardoned your offences? Keep this blessed truth in view: "Ye are the body of Christ;" and if it were possible for one member of his mystical body to perish, you think you would be that one. But no. If even *you* were lost, there would be a blank in heaven. But, honours crown his brow! He is the faithful God. He is your Husband; and will he be content to be in heaven and see his bride in hell?

O, ye husbands, love your wives, even as Christ also loved his bride—the church. And ye wives, love your husbands. Are you fretful and peevish with each other? You thus plunge yourselves into deeper misery. This is because, by nature, there is no soundness in you. But Christ promises to present you a glorious church,—more glorious than the angels in heaven. May the sweet savour of his precious promises be never lost to you. Christ is ever the same immortal and faithful God. He is thy God and thy glory for ever. Then is it not amazing we should be so fretful and repine at our few trials and difficulties? It is. But it is the mystery of godliness that, though we are so far unfaithful to each other, and more so to him, yet he abideth faithful.

We have now entered on another year. Let us take a retrospect of the past, and ask ourselves what has been our conduct during the past year. We have sinned against God, and have greatly failed in the performance of our various duties. Ah! Could we meet God on the ground of our own works? Alas! If this must be the covenant, we must perish. But he has safely brought us through, and we are here now, living testimonies of his love and faithfulness. O, then, may we sink before his footstool, adore his goodness, trust him for the future, and glorify him with our bodies and spirits, which are his. He has promised to supply all our needs. He does not say he will supply all our *wants*, but our *needs;* and he is wise in not supplying all our wants; for our wants are often foolish; so in wisdom he withholds them. You say, "If I had an abundance of food and raiment, I should be content." If you had this, then you would want a comfortable house to dwell in; if you had that, you would want a larger one and a servant or two; and by-and-bye you would want a carriage to ride in, as walking would feel too fatiguing for you. And thus your wants would never end. Our needs are very little, as it respects these temporary matters; our greatest needs in this respect are a grateful heart and contented mind. This would make us so far happy. Moreover, then, may we put our trust in God, who is ever faithful in supplying our needs. He is the faithful God.

The Lord stands in relation to his church as a father to his son; and as a father chasteneth his son, in whom he delighteth, so doth the Lord them who fear him. And how often do you deserve the divine chastisement? He says, "If ye forsake my ways, I will visit your iniquities with a rod, and your transgressions with stripes." O, see what follows: "But my loving-kindness will I not take away from him." He fails not in so many tokens of his affection to his children. A professor without chastisement, one who lives at ease, is of that character who are styled "bastards." For "whom the Lord loveth he chasteneth, and scourgeth every son whom he receiveth." And thus are they made partakers of his holiness, and are brought to live nearer to him. He is faithful in all this.

David was enabled to view the matter clearly, when he cried out, "I know that in very faithfulness thou has afflicted me." And can you and I say anything to the contrary? If we do, we murmur against him, and bring upon ourselves a sharper correction. And for what purpose? To hide pride from our eyes.

Sometimes the Lord is pleased to leave us for awhile to ourselves; but if he were to leave us entirely to ourselves we should be ruined. It is to humble us, and to bring us to know our own weakness, and to teach us to confide in him. Wherever we may be, we have to do with a faithful God; and in whatever situation we are placed, it is only to prove God's faithfulness. Who would have dreamed of God sending ravens to feed the prophet, increasing the widow's oil, and sending bread from heaven to feed the children of Israel for forty years? All our poverty and distress are ordered by him to show his faithfulness, and for our good, that we may cry out, in the real exercise of faith, "My faithful God! Mine Holy One! All is well!"—*Manchester, Jan. 5th,* 1840.

THE NATURE AND GROUND OF FAITH.

"O Lord, my God, mine Holy One! We shall not die. O Lord, thou hast ordained them for judgment; and O, mighty God, thou hast established them for correction."—HAB. I. 12.

This is truly the language of faith. To say, in faith and feeling, "O Lord my God," is a blessed thing, and also to feel assured that you will not die. Christ says, "Because I live, ye shall live also." And it was on this ground that Habakkuk's faith was built: "Art thou not from everlasting?" Some speak about faith as though it were a mere trifle, a bauble, or a toy, and that they could use it as their fleshly nature felt disposed; as if they could take it up and lay it down at their pleasure. But this is an awful delusion. Such men are entirely ignorant of vital faith. They cannot, with such fleshly ideas, rightly say, "O God, thou art my God." But the language of our text truly bespeaks the convincing power of precious faith living in the heart: "My God."

1. Let us consider the *nature and ground* of this faith.

2. The *claim* faith makes: "My God."

3. The *conclusion faith comes to*: "We shall not die," though "we are ordained for judgment, and established for correction," and though faith seems sometimes at a distance from us, and we are ready to say, "Ah! Why all this judgment, and why all this correction? Why are we thus taken through the furnace of affliction? But faith anon comes with power, and we see our everlasting security in Christ, and are enabled to draw the blessed conclusion, '"We shall not die."

1. The *nature and ground* of faith. The Pharisee of old thought he had great faith, and talked largely of his goodness; but he was deceiving his own soul; he was unacquainted with the operations of divine faith. While he was thus boasting of his goodness, the poor publican could not say anything; he was, as it were, struck dumb; and, perhaps, while thus trembling with fear, he was wishing he was half as good as his friend opposite. But no. He felt that he had no righteousness of his own that he could bring to God; he felt himself destitute of faith and all that was good, and durst not even so much as lift up his eyes to heaven, but smote upon his breast, and groaned out, "God be merciful to me, a sinner." Thus we see that vital faith is of such a *nature* that it stops the mouth from speaking

such high-flown language as the self-righteous, who think they can
pray and believe, and can command all good gifts and graces; all
are at their control; they can take them, and make use of them, or
reject them at their pleasure. They are too proud to receive these
as gifts. Their faith being presumption, not vital faith, can act with
self-control in these matters. But ah! Vital faith cannot swell itself
thus big with importance. The mouth of the sinner is stopped, under
feelings of his own sinfulness and helplessness; but the heart is enlarged, and is led to taste of the rich bounty, which God has provided for his people; and the application of Christ's blood completes
the cure of his malady. A dreadful sore in the flesh may probably
receive probing before it can heal, on account of the foulness that may
be in it; and though it is a painful operation it must first be probed,
or it will not heal. So it is with the Christian. His false hopes must
first be rooted up, his fleshly pride brought down, and he must be
humbled in the dust under a sense of his lost condition and his awful malady as a sinner; then the blood of the Lamb cures his malady: "The blood of Jesus Christ cleanseth him from all sin." Not
a tittle is left for us to manufacture, or work out a part of the cure
by good deeds, &c. "What!" some will say. "Will not piety in us,
charity to all mankind, and love to our neighbours, make us pure in
his sight, and blot out those stains of sin and guilt?" No; for the
core is impure, and nothing less than divine unction will effect the
cure. This then is the *nature* of faith.

And now notice the *ground* of faith. God hath taken a solemn
oath, in making the covenant for his people, that all the seed of Abraham should be saved: "And because he could swear by no greater,
he swore by himself;" thus confirming his engagement with an oath.
And faith rests there, feeling that Christ is the only Saviour by covenant love; and though sin assail the believer, and sometimes he doubts
and fears, yet, eventually, he is brought to see that Christ is for him,
and such as he only; his atoning blood is the only basis whereon he
can rest his soul; and is his only ground of faith.

2. The *claim* faith makes. We have noticed the language of faith;
and now, that we may better illustrate our meaning on this head,
let us compare it to the husband and wife. While the husband is at
home with his wife she can converse with him, and his soothing
language will cheer her spirits, and console her in her trying moments
by his unremitting kind attentions. Thus they sweetly commune together and enjoy each other's company. She needs not then the exercise of faith to believe that she has a kind and affectionate husband;
for he is with her. But suppose he is away, at a distance, where troubled seas roll between them, and that during his absence there should
rise storms and tempests; this may cause the anxious loving wife
much trouble, and she is ready to believe her husband may be lost,
she a widow and destitute. This apparent transition of her circum-

stances and situation requires the exercise of faith to believe that he is yet alive,—a tender and loving husband. But, though billows roll between them, his mind is fixed on her, and he loves her still; and she still claims him as her husband. This seems to have been the case with Jerusalem. God had for a while hid his face, and they were desolate of comfort. All was wretchedness and misery. But amidst these trying circumstances, the prophet is enabled, by faith, to look to God, believing that he is from everlasting his Lord and his God, his Holy One. Therefore he should not die. He not only desires to know God as the God of nature, the God of providence, and the God of grace, but as his own God.

3. The *conclusion faith comes to:* "We shall not die." "Thou hast ordained them for judgment, and established them for correction." This may refer, first, to the designs of God in providence; secondly, to the wicked; thirdly, to the people of God.

First. The designs of God in providence. How prone is human nature to repine at the dispensations of God's providence. If they are poor, they wish to be rich. If they are rich, they are tormented by the poor, and fear of losing their property. If one is bereaved of a member of his family, he repines at his loss. If he is sick, he frets and desires to be soon well. If he experiences hardships, he is impatient and murmurs. How few consider that sin has brought all these troubles into the world; that even the ground is cursed for man's sake, and that man is born to trouble, and must live by the sweat of his brow. O could men but look to the Lord, whose ever watchful eye surveys all our actions, and who does not willingly afflict the children of men, then would they cease their murmurings. See the rebellious children of Israel. Although the Lord led them by the pillar of the cloud by day, and a pillar of fire by night, and conducted them dry shod through the Red Sea, and sent them bread to eat and water to drink; yet, notwithstanding, they murmured, and remembered the flesh-pots of Egypt. And the Lord bore with their manners in the wilderness forty years. Thus are the dispensations of the Lord's providence ordained for judgment and established for correction.

Secondly, it may refer to the wicked. God is all wise, and just, and good, and all things are ordained by him, in the counsels of his providence, for a wise purpose. "He knoweth the end from the beginning;" "He hath made all things for himself; even the wicked for the day of evil." It is wise, just, and good that all things are all ordered after the council of his own will. The wicked condemn the righteous, or their malicious projects would not exist. But they will one day have to stand before the awful tribunal of a just and holy God, the Judge of all. Their actions will be weighed in a balance, and, being found wanting, the awful sentence, "Depart from me, ye workers of iniquity; I never knew you," will be pronounced against them, and they will be hurled from the presence of Jehovah, to spend eternity in everlasting punishment. They are thus ordained for judgment and established for correction.

Thirdly, it refers to the people of God. The people of God are a peculiar people. Their ways and their experience, their language and their opinions, are peculiarly different to those of other men. They are the third part which shall be brought through the fire,—the fiery trial of affliction. "Through much tribulation they must enter the kingdom." The other two parts—the nominal professor and the profane, are both estranged from God. A life of ease, a calm undisturbed mind is all they desire. "The wicked have no bands in their death; they are not plagued like other men." They get into a profession of religion and the full assurance of faith without any bands, any strugglings, any feeling of the plague of sin or of their own hearts. The profane delight in sin. "The fear of God is not before their eyes." But the people of God have troubles on every side, from without and from within. They are often in perplexity and doubt, and feel the plague of sin and of their evil hearts. They loathe the pleasures of this world and the evils thereof. They die daily; and how can they who are dead to sin live any longer therein? They wade through judgments and corrections; and thus become cleansed from the dross and tin of their corrupt nature, and purified by the blood of Jesus, even as he is pure.—*Manchester*.

AN EXPOSITION.

"The Spirit of the Lord God is upon me, because the Lord hath anointed me to preach good tidings unto the meek."—Isa. LXI. 1-3.

WHAT a divine cluster of immortal blessings rests in the Man Christ Jesus; and how blessed it is for poor sinners that he is appointed to give them these blessings and is filled with the Spirit without measure, that he might give them in measure to such poor vile sinners, loathsome sinners, God dishonouring sinners as we; and his blessed Majesty has to deal out these blessings to these poor sinners. However men may despise these poor hobbling creatures, the Lord will find them out, in some corner or another. God's method is to deal out his pity to these poor, forlorn creatures.

Now, if the Lord has given you to feel something of the blessedness of these three verses, when you come on a death bed you will outshout angels and triumph in the mysteries of the cross.

Who shall be redeemed priests? Why, these poor hobbling creatures, these poor captives, these sin-sick souls—they shall be named Priests; and God the Spirit shall so direct them that he will show them the mysteries of the cross. God's method is to take these poor creatures from the dust and the beggars from the dunghill; he lifts them up and he rejoices over them.

"For your shame ye shall have double." "Ah!" says some poor soul. "I am afraid I shall have double confusion and condemnation; for I feel so much boiling-up of my inward sins that I am almost distracted." Notwithstanding all this, and all the shame and confusion that it produces, still the Lord says, "Ye shall have double." Double of what? A double knowledge of God's method of salvation; first, that all the human race were ruined and that he came into the world to save sinners; and, next, that he came to save *you*. You shall have this double in your land here, and instead of confusion you shall rejoice in your portion, and everlasting joy shall be your portion hereafter. *Dear forlorn child of God*, can you have a better double than this? And are you not often ashamed, when you think of God's goodness and your sinfulness? Well. Some commentators say this should read, "For your double shame you shall have a double inheritance." The greater your shame, the greater will be your rejoicing when the blessing comes.

"And their seed shall be known among the Gentiles," &c. These poor broken-hearted sinners, men despised,—this obscure family, is the seed which the Lord hath blessed. Yes, and their enemies shall see it and acknowledge it too. And when God makes this manifest you will be enabled to say with Isaiah, "I will greatly rejoice in the Lord; my soul shall be joyful in my God; for he hath clothed me with the garments of salvation, he hath covered me with the robe of righteousness."

Has the Lord the Spirit brought this feeling into your hearts and consciences? Since I saw you last, I have been laid on a bed of affliction. But while there, I was brought to feel that he had wrapped me up in his righteousness; and he passed the sentence of death so on self and all connected with self, that I felt no solid pleasure out of Christ. I want nothing else. Let others have what they may, I want to be wrapped up in Christ's righteousness and to feel the mysteries of redeeming love.

[There are some similar remarks to the above in the "Gospel Standard" for 1849; but the above was taken from a MS. by a Mr. Hudson, who was a member with Mr. G.]

------◆------

A HOLY CALLING.

"Who hath saved us, and called *us* with a holy calling, not according to our works, but according to his own purpose and grace, which was given us in Christ Jesus before the world began."—2 Tim. i. 9.

HERE we find salvation stated before calling by grace; and, indeed, if we take a proper view of the subject, it was so in the mind and purpose of God. God the Father saved, or secured, the elect in Christ before the foundation of the world. Hence Jude says, "Sanctified by God the Father;" that is, set apart by God the Father, as the people of his holy choice, and so made the special care and charge of Christ. "According as he hath chosen us in him before the foundation of the world, that we should be holy and without blame before him in love; having predestinated us unto the adoption of children by Jesus Christ to himself, according to the good pleasure of his will, to the praise of the glory of his grace, wherein he hath made us accepted in the Beloved." And though the elect fell, with the rest of mankind, in Adam the first, they never fell as considered in Christ; but, as the Holy Ghost says by Jude, they were "preserved in Christ Jesus;" and in God's own time they are called.

It is the believer's blessedness that each glorious Person in the Godhead has a glorious hand in his salvation. God the Father saved, chose, sanctified, or set him apart, in Christ, before the world was; God the Son took humanity into union to his personal Godhead, and thus became incarnate, lived a holy life, suffered, bled, died a solemn death, rose again from the dead, ascended up on high, having led captivity captive, and is now exalted at the right hand of the Father, ever living to make intercession for him. Thus Christ has meritoriously saved the elect by his life, obedience, death, resurrection, exaltation, and intercession. As it is written: "He that spared not his own Son, but delivered him up for us all, how shall he not with him also freely give us all things? Who shall lay anything to the charge of God's elect?" God? No. "It is God that justifieth. Who is he that condemneth?" Christ? No. "It is Christ that died; yea rather, that is risen again, who is even at the right hand of God, who also maketh intercession for us." Thus the blessed Redeemer "was delivered for our offences and raised again for our justification;" and, bless his precious name, he has been the destruction of death, hell, and sin. The gloriously-blessed God-man Mediator "gave himself for us, that he might redeem us from all iniquity, and purify unto himself a peculiar people, zealous of good works." So that, before the world was, the church was saved purposedly by God the Father; in time, meritoriously by the God-man Mediator, who now lives above to make intercession for them; and, in the day of God's power, they are saved manifestively and vitally, by the "washing of regeneration, and the renewing of the Holy Ghost."

Now, not a particle of this is either for, or according to, our works; for it is "not by works of righteousness which we have done, but according to his mercy he saved us;" or, as our text has it, "Who hath saved us, and called us with a holy calling, *not according to* our works."

What an indescribable mercy it is that salvation is of the Lord; yea, that God himself, as the God of Zion, is our salvation. Blessed, triumphant faith, under the sweet power and unction of God the Holy Ghost, can, at times, sweetly sing, "Behold, God is my salvation! I will trust and not be afraid; for the Lord Jehovah is my strength and my song; he also is become my salvation." This salvation contains a complete deliverance from every foe and soul-damning danger, and it is a complete salvation to every real good. We have all spiritual blessings in Christ, all bliss and blessedness secured in him; for it pleased the Father that in him should all fulness dwell. He is full of grace and truth; and of his fulness we receive, and grace for grace. All things are the real believer's; for he is Christ's, and Christ is God's; and, as I said before, this glorious salvation is all of grace, not of works, lest any man should boast.

Now, my text says, "Who hath saved us, and called us with a holy calling." This call is the solemn, soul-quickening, heart-rending call of a holy God; not a mere call to hear the Word preached, nor to attend upon public means; many are called to these things whom God never chose in Christ; but this is a holy calling from death to life, from darkness to light, from the power of sin and Satan to the living God. This call makes the sinner feel his own guilty and ruined condition as a sinner against a holy God. He is called to see sin in the light of God's countenance, to feel its awful plague, and to tremble before God on the account of it; and he is called to feel that his case is too desperate for him to help his own soul. The more he tries and toils, the deeper he sinks in a feeling sense of his own ruin and misery. *Help himself!* He finds he can as soon create a world as do it. Therefore, with heartrending groans, he is called to cry, "God be merciful to me, a sinner!" But he is effectually called to feel and see the emptiness of creature goodness, and to thirst for the living God; nor will anything short of Christ, and a full and free salvation by and in him, satisfy his quickened soul. Hope deferred often makes his heart sick; but still the divine power by which he is called keeps him to the point; and the issue shall prove that he is called to have fellowship with the Lord Jesus Christ, with his love, blood, sufferings, and obedience, to hold sweet converse with him, as his own Lord and Redeemer, and to sweetly say, "My Beloved is mine, and I am his." For "God is faithful, by whom ye were called unto the fellowship of his Son, Jesus Christ our Lord." All the blessings couched in this glorious, endearing charactor, God has called the real believer to the fellowship of; and, in the Lord's own time, he shall share in the sweet enjoyment of them.

O the wonders of God's love to his people! Come, poor sin-oppressed, guilt-smitten, law-wrecked, world-despised, Satan-hunted, self-condemned, heart-tortured, self-loathing sinner, hope thou in the Lord; for, with all thy fears and faintings, misgivings, staggerings, stumblings, sighings, and groanings, by and bye thy dear Lord will manifestively put his arms of everlasting love under thee, and say, "Come with me from Lebanon, my spouse, with me from Lebanon; look from the top of Amana, from the top of Shenir and Hermon, from the lion's dens, from the mountains of the leopards. Thou hast ravished my heart, my sister, my spouse; thou hast ravished my heart with one of thine eyes, with one chain of thy neck. How fair is thy love, my sister, my spouse! How much better is thy love than wine, and the smell of thine ointments than all spices!" Thus the real Christian is called to be made partaker of Christ's holiness, and to hope in him as the God of hope; yea, to believe in him as the glorious Resurrection and the Life; and in the end feelingly to say, "O Lord, thou art my God, and I will praise thee." He is called to receive a full and free pardon through the blood of the Lamb, and to feel the soul-cleansing efficacy of that blessed fountain. In a word, he is called to hope in Christ, believe in Christ, trust in Christ, glory in Christ, teem out all his complaints unto Christ, confess with abhorrence his vileness to Christ, and supplicate his throne for daily grace and mercy; to live for Christ, and to live to Christ, and to be daily concerned to honour and glorify him in this world. Christ dwells in him, and he dwells in Christ, and they are manifestively one. Holiness is his delight, and sin is his burden. His sweetest and most heavenly moments are when he can hold intercourse with God the Father, God the Son, and God the Holy Ghost, when the world drops its charms and God is all and in all. He is, in the Lord's own time, called to feel that Christ has made him free, and he is free indeed; and with holy solemnity he exclaims, "What, then! Shall I sin that grace may abound? God forbid! Shall I sin because I am not under the law, but under grace? God forbid!" Thus, he is called with a holy calling, by a holy God, to holy things; and at last he shall be called to heaven, when it shall be fully made manifest that he is called to a holy end.

A few more struggles, poor burdened believer, and thou shalt see all is well. Expect no good from corrupt nature. God has called thee to feel that in thy flesh dwells no good thing. Why look for the living in such a dead, corrupt mass? God help thee to flee to, rest upon, and live in Christ. Thou art called to be partaker of his holiness, not thy fleshly works, but to flee from them, and daily to twine round and hang upon Christ. There may thy soul be stayed, for in him thou art complete, and nowhere else.

Well; this salvation and this holy calling are not according to our works, but according to God's purpose and grace, which was given us in Christ Jesus before the world began. Salvation, in all its bearings, is according to God's own purpose and grace, secured in Christ before time. Thanks be to God for that. All we feel and fear, all our sins and woes, all our darkness and deadness, loathsomeness and vileness, cannot alter God's purpose and grace, which is secured in Christ. Remember, poor, tried, tempted, tossed-about sinner, it is of God's grace; yea, God's purposed grace. Thy miseries tend to prove that this glorious salvation, this holy calling, are just what thou needest—just suited to thee; and it is God's own purpose to call thee to the sweet participation of them. They are thine by the solemn purpose and free-grace grant of a covenant God; and each glorious Person in the one undivided Jehovah takes pleasure in putting thee in possession of it. The time will come when thy Lord will say to thee, "Thou shalt no more be termed Forsaken; neither shall thy land any more be termed Desolate; but thou shalt be called Hephzibah, and thy land Beulah; for the Lord delighteth in thee; and thy land shall be married. For as a young man marrieth a virgin, so shall thy sons marry thee; and as the bridegroom rejoiceth over the bride, so shall thy God rejoice over thee;" "The Lord thy God in the midst of thee is mighty. He will save, he will rejoice over thee with joy; he will rest in his love; he will joy over thee with singing." The glorious marriage of the Lamb and his wife will very soon be consummated in everlasting bliss and blessedness; and "blessed are they which are called to the marriage supper of the Lamb."

That the Lord may, from day to day, be graciously pleased to grant to his saved, called children much of his presence and love, is my prayer.—1835.

PAUL AND JAMES.
GAL. II. 16; JAS. II. 24.

PAUL and James appear to clash with each other; for Paul says we are justified without works and James says we are justified by our works. But the fact is, the one was speaking of what justified us in the sight of God and the other of what justified us in the sight of men; for in the sight of God we are justified freely by grace, but in the sight of men only by our works. We cannot insult God more than by endeavouring to bring something of our own to recommend us to his notice. The very blaze of his transcendently excellent glory is to give us Christ's righteousness. Christ was made sin for us— really made sin. What! Every vile thought, every abominable act that I feel within? Yes; make it as black as you will, and let Satan help you, and yet he was made *that;* not by actual transgression, but by transfer; just the same as a tradesman is made a debtor by merely putting his name on a piece of paper for another; and he becoming insolvent, the tradesman is made to pay, while the insolvent is set at liberty. And we are made righteous in God's sight through Christ's righteousness, as Christ himself is; not partially, but fully. What can be more blessed than this—the sinner's crimes all transferred to Christ and Christ's righteousness and holiness being imputed to the sinner, and the sinner realizing it in his heart by faith?

There is a deal of talk amongst some people that they fear antichrist will reign. But, bless you, what is antichrist? Creature merit; it is the very soul of it. Take away creature-merit, and the devil himself could not make a pope. A body, you know, without a soul,

cannot do much harm. Ye believe in God, says Christ, believe also
in me. As though he had said, "Ye believe in a just and holy God,
believe also in me, as being all your holiness, righteousness," &c.
For whatever beauty, or glory, there is in Christ, believer, God places
it all to thy account. One evidence in the heart of a sinner of his
being righteous is, when he is brought to loathe himself because of
his vileness and wretchedness, and to cry out to be delivered. Some
will say, "I have no righteousness of my own to bring before God,
and yet I can't believe Christ died for me!" Why can't you? "Because I am such a sinner." There, now; that's it; you want to bring
something to God, and that's the very spawn of self-righteousness.

Another evidence is, and this is one that a poor child of God can
well understand sometimes, "Now to him that worketh not, but believeth on him that justifieth the ungodly, his faith is counted for
righteousness." That is, to be solemnly persuaded that there *is* redemption through his blood, the forgiveness of sins, and that you
really and truly, in the sight of God, have no power to work; and,
therefore, if you are justified, it must be by him that justifieth the
ungodly. A hypocrite never felt this, nor ever will, while the world
stands. If you could work, you would have no need of Christ's finished
work. If you were not dead, you would not need Christ's life. If you
were not vile, you would not need his sanctification. If you were
not unholy, you would not need his holiness. If you were not blind,
you would not need his light. If you were not weak, you would not
need his strength. If you were not a fool, you would not need his
wisdom. But you being all these things, only shows you are the
character fit for believing. "Ah," says one, "I once could say,
as I thought, I do believe, and I told the Lord I would never disbelieve again." I dare say you did; just like a little child when its
father has been giving it some little present. "O," it will say, "father,
I'll always love you now; I'll always do as you tell me." "Ah,"
says the father, "You don't know what you're talking about." So
says the child of God, when his heavenly Father gives him a glimpse
of hope, "I'll always praise thee now." But, like Gideon with his
fleece, he keeps wanting another and another proof; for unbelief
gives him a pull-back, and he is once more poor. As the poet says,

"Now they believe his word, While rocks with rivers flow."

I am not talking about those who have faith at their command, and
who say it is our duty to believe, and we ought to believe now, and
so forth; but about a poor child of God, who has been made to feel
what a conflict he has within. Sometimes you feel a little anticipa-
tory faith; that is, you cannot help thinking the time will come when
you can call God, Father; as though something within you said,
"Who can tell but the time may come?" You can't account for this
feeling; but, amidst all your unbelief, it is there. If God has put

these things into your heart, he has done more for you than he has for all the kings and emperors in the earth, who have never known him. For what are kingdoms and empires? Ah, bless you; they all vanish away like smoke. You have all God can give. There is not an angel in heaven so highly honoured as you; for God will make you shine in the light of Immanuel. You don't half believe in Christ; for if you did you would know that you had in him all a holy God can require, or a just God demand. Christ says, "I go to prepare a place for you;" as if created heavens were not enough for his dear people. Therefore, he is gone to prepare a place for them, and bespangle it with his blood, and spread a glory through it that never could have been there only through the God-man Mediator. Angels, bless you, if I may so speak, are only the horses that will draw you there; the chariot is the heart of the Son of God, and they and you shall resound it to the glory of God. The Lord's eyes are upon you; his eye of love, and his eye of mercy. Thousands of unhallowed steps we should fall into, did not his eye watch over us. Ofttimes do we lay our plans; but, watching over us, he upsets them, and when he gives us to see a little as he sees, we perceive his eye was upon us. He will guide us with his eye; and O, how blessed it is to have the eye of Almighty God to guide us. It is a thousand times better than if he had sent all the holy angels in heaven to guide us. It is the eye of the great I AM THAT I AM, as he said unto Moses. Do we need omnipotence, do we need omniscience, do we need omnipresence—I am *that*, I am. And this eye he will never withdraw from them. All their unbelieving fits, all their rebellion, will never make him turn against them. He *will* use the rod; but this is only a proof that they are children; for if you are without chastisement of which all [children] are partakers, then are ye bastards and not sons.—*Manchester*, 1837.

BROUGHT THROUGH THE FIRE.

" I will bring the third part through the fire."—ZECH. XIII. 9.

OUR God is a God who loves us as well when he hides the light of his countenance as when he shines upon us; as well when he suffers us to grope within as when he raises our hopes and expectations to himself; as well when he chastens us as when he smiles upon us; as well when he afflicts us as when he comforts us; as well when in the fire as when on the mount. It is easier to talk about God's love than always to believe in it. The third part will be brought *through* the fire; not merely made to look at it, but be brought through it; the other two-thirds—the carnal profane and the dead professor, will be *left*.

God's word is called a fire: " Is not my word a fire, saith the Lord?"

And I believe no man was ever yet sent to preach whose ministry was not a fire; for wherever the word is faithfully dispensed, there is sure to be a burning up of our hay, wood, and stubble,—all our false hopes, false zeal, &c.; but the true gold sustains no loss. Christ is compared to a fire, and it is said he shall sit as a refiner, &c.

Many of God's children have a deal of fleshly love, fleshly charity, &c.; but Christ will purge them, and refine them. Nothing shall stand in his sight but what comes from him, stands in him, and leads to him. He will burn it up; and it must be Christ alone for salvation and every thing connected with it. Right eyes, right arms, right hands, dearest friends, must all go, that wish to stand in his way. When God brings Christ and the sinner together, there is an alarming blaze of the whole of the sinner's lumber.

I have heard it said that as soon as a refiner can see his own image distinctly in the silver, he considers it pure. So God removes every thing from the sinner but his own image; that is, he views him in Christ. We never prayed spiritually till we were put into the fire. Saul of Tarsus thought he had prayed many a time; but when God put him into the fire he found he had never prayed before; and even God himself then said to Ananias, "Behold! He prayeth." Bless you, it is more wonderful for a sinner to be made to pray than it is for a king to be made a beggar; because natural circumstances may bring and have brought that to pass; but God the Spirit must take possession of the man and bring him into the fire before he can pray. We cannot even rightly *think* of prayer without; for the Spirit helpeth our infirmities with groanings. When God was blessedly pleased first to put me into this fire, one of the first things he did was to burn up my prayers. I formerly was so regular in them that I durst not go to sleep till I had said what is called the Lord's Prayer; and very often I went off in a doze before I had done; just like the poor Papist counting his beads. But now I could not even begin it. I dared not to call God, Father. What right had I to say, *Our* Father? I felt there was something more in prayer than I was possessed of. Pretty words would not do now. I felt I stood before God as a law-breaker.

You know it is very often the case, when you are called upon to go to prayer before a few friends, that you study more how to place your words prettily than to express the feelings of your heart; and sometimes God puts you in the fire in the midst of it, and conscience says, "You don't feel that, nor you don't feel that," till you are obliged to groan out, "O Lord, I am vile! Lord, teach me to pray! Come down, dear Lord, and support me, wretched man that I am!" There is more prayer in a few broken, unconnected sentences, sighs, or groans, from a poor soul in the fire, than in all the fine words that can be used by the greatest orators in the world; for theirs is only like a knife with two backs, as it were, and no edge; there is nothing to cut. Now, God will bring his people *through* this fire—not leave them in; and they shall be brought out as monuments of his discriminating mercy and shall show forth his praise to all eternity, that ever he separated them from the world, and put them into the fire.—*Manchester, Oct.*, 1837.

<hr>

NOW ARE WE THE SONS OF GOD.
PREACHED AT EBENEZER CHAPEL, DEPTFORD, SEPTEMBER 19TH, 1827.

"Beloved, now are we the sons of God; and it doth not yet appear what we shall be; but we know that when he shall appear we shall be like him; for we shall see him as he is."—1 JOHN III. 2.

MOST of you are strangers to me, and I suppose I am as great a stranger to you, in the flesh; but, if we can meet in our text, and set to our seal that God is true, we are blessed with the greatest blessings that God can possibly bestow. And can we wonder at meeting so few friends here? While we are in an enemy's country, can we wonder that we are hated! Depend upon it, God has made up his mind, and you may as well make up yours, that "through much tribulation we must enter the kingdom." Besides, as Paul says, "Our light affliction, which is but for a moment, worketh for us a far more exceeding and eternal weight of glory." Now, seeing that this is the case, how highly ought we to esteem afflictions! If we had servants who wrought for us exceedingly well, we should esteem them, and take from them many pert replies which we would not take from those who worked with "eye service" only; and so ought we to do with afflictions, which are God's servants, and are made to work for our good; but how often do we think they are hard taskmasters rather than servants!

I shall, as the Spirit of God shall enable me,

1. Speak of the *Persons* by whom the sons of God are loved.

2. The *objects* of that love.

3. Refer to some states in which it may be said, "*Now*" are we the sons of God.

4. Mention some things in which it may be said, "*It doth not yet appear what we shall be;*" and speak of *the knowledge* we have of it.

1. *By whom* are these sons of God loved? First, They are beloved of *God*. Secondly, They are beloved of *one another*.

First. They are beloved of God,—Father, Son, and Holy Ghost. I know this is not a very fashionable way of preaching in the present day; but I am one of the old-fashioned sort. People do not like to speak of distinct Personalities in the Godhead; but I must have Father, Son, and Holy Ghost brought home to my heart, or I shall be damned. God the Father's love is seen in his eternal election of us in Christ before time began, and blessing us with all spiritual blessings in him. He "spared not his own Son, but freely gave him up for us all;" and heaven is a spiritual blessing given us in Christ. God the Son's love is seen in his laying down his life for us: "Herein is love, that, when we were yet enemies, Christ died for us." God the Holy Ghost's love is seen in his quickening us when dead in sin: "God, who is rich in mercy, for the great love wherewith he loved us, even when we were dead in sins, hath quickened us together with Christ;" and also in his "convincing of sin, of righteousness, and of judgment," and "taking of the things of Christ and showing them unto us." He watches over the dust of the saints, and will raise them again at the last day. But neither prophet nor apostle ever spake of God's love to the full. John says, "God *so* loved us;" "Behold *what manner* of love," &c.; and, "Jesus, having loved his own which were in the world, loved them to the end." Not, as Arminians tell us, that we may be God's children to-day, and yet be lost for ever, and that Christ died for the damned in hell. I hate Arminianism as I hate Satan himself. The great apostle Paul says, "His love passeth knowledge;" yet he *knew* it was higher than all his rebellion, deeper than all his filth, wider than all his wanderings, and as long as from eternity to eternity. It is a vast ocean, without bank, brim, bottom, or shore.

Sons of God! The nearest relations God has. Angels are not so near. Yea, this love has puzzled angels and confounded devils. He chose elect angels, but he never died for them. It is said, "Which things the angels desire to look into!"

God loves his people, his sons, not their sins, like a parent. The heart of Christ bled for their crimes; yet he prays to God for them; they are yet his loved ones.

Secondly. They are loved by *one another*. John says, "If any man say that he loveth God and hateth his brother, he is a liar; for if he loveth not his brother whom he hath seen, how can he love God whom he hath not seen?" That text, "We know that we have passed from death unto life because we love the brethren," is, I think, much abused by some. They suppose it to consist of a universal love to all mankind; whereas, that has nothing to do with it. It is a child of God loving God's image in his children that is intended. You may love your wife, husband, children, or parents, and it is your duty to do so; but, if you do not see the image of God in them, you cannot love them with the same love as you do the greatest stranger, whom you believe to be a child of God. You love your relations with a natural love, and it is your duty to provide for them before others; but the love of the brethren is very different. Don't you sometimes feel taken up in love to David, or Job, or some other saint who is gone to glory, as though you were with them? And sometimes, when strife is stirred up among brethren, and especially when Satan can persuade you that such a one is not a child of God who you thought was, then you think you may lay on pretty savagely; but what cuts of conscience you begin to feel when you begin to think again that he is a child of God, and how harshly you have spoken of him!

2. The *objects* of this love. It is said, "I will have mercy on whom I will have mercy;" and "whom he will he hardeneth." He loves his people, as Moses says, not because they were the greatest of all people, or most in number, but because he would, for his own glory; and I believe there never would have been a being or creature created but for the glory of Christ; for "by him and for him" they were created; and he will have his own, let the devil, hell, and sin drive them where they may. He loved thee, poor child of God, when thou wast as vile as Satan and as hell itself. Thou canst not say, "I was better than those who are left." If thou dost, I well know there is a fall at thy heels; but thou well knowest thou art the chief of sinners; and perhaps thou art, except William Gadsby.

I suppose I may venture to suppose there are some here like a poor man I was with the other day. I was going to preach, and I said, "I am very dark and confused, and have no text; what text shall I speak from, John?" He replied, "I don't care what text you speak from, if you can but scripturally prove me to be a child of God."

Sometimes a child of God is tempted to think he is deceived; and others, if he does not walk exactly in their shoes, tell him he is quite out of the secret; but I wish always to condescend to men of low estate. None but a child of God can point out the various holes we get into.

I remember the time when I was afraid to open my mouth to any child of God; for I thought if I did, he would see in a moment what a vile creature I was, and tell everybody of it, and that nobody would have anything to do with me. I had about three miles to walk on a Lord's day, where part of the truth was preached; I say part of the truth, for the feelings of God's children were not mentioned; and I was so afraid of falling into talk with any of the people that, if I saw one on the road before me, I durst not overtake him. There was one man on crutches; but I would walk slower than even he, rather than he should speak to me; but if one was coming behind me, I would run fast enough. Then you will say, "How did you act when you were between two, coming and going?" I used to make a gap, and get over the hedge till they were past. Thus was I scared about for many months; till once, as I was going to Coventry, passing a house where a good man dwelt, the woman called after me, and asked me to stay; for her husband was going there. At this I trembled, and said, "I cannot stay; I am in a hurry." "He is ready," said she; so that I could not get away; but I determined to say nothing about religion; so I began to speak of the war, and trade; but he dropped that, and said, "Come, let us talk of soul feelings." At this I thought I should have fainted; but at length I began telling him some of my feelings. He smiled. "Now," thought I, "it is as I thought; he sees through me." But, to my surprise, he began to bring forward text after text, and showed me their meaning so sweetly that, by the Spirit of God, I was delivered from the temptation I had laboured under so long.

And now I will tell you a story, by way of introducing what I intend to bring forward. I was travelling in a stage-coach soon after I became a preacher, and there was an Arminian parson also in the coach, and he spoke a great deal of holiness and piety. As I was in clothes of various colours, I knew he could not know I was a parson; so I thought I would ask him a question or two. I said, "You are a minister, I suppose?" "O yes;" he replied. "Now," said I, "suppose I were a professor of religion, I should like to ask some of you preachers what is the lowest evidence of a person being a child of God?" "O!" he said, "I should say, 'Go on.'" "But," I said, "would you not tell them first they were in the right road, before you told them to go on?" "O no," said he; "I should tell them to go on." "Well," I said, "this looks very strange, to tell people to go on without telling them anything whether they are in the way or not." But this, my hearers, is the general way of the professors of the present day.

Now, I shall mention two evidences of a person being one of the objects of this love, which are, I think, as low as the Scriptures will warrant. One is: "Blessed are the poor in spirit, for theirs is the kingdom of heaven," and "hungering and thirsting after righteousness" is joined with it. Now, had the Redeemer said, "Blessed are the *rich* in spirit," you could not have come in; but, poor dear soul, he says the *poor* in spirit; and here you *can* come in; for sometimes you are so broken down under a sense of your own vileness that you know, if ever you find mercy, it must be a free gift. You are too poor to pay for it. If your salvation depended upon a single good thought of your own, you could not produce it; you must be lost. The other is: "Then they that feared the Lord spake often one to another." "Ah," say you, "I am quite shut out now, for I cannot speak!" Stop; you should have let me go on with my text: "And the Lord hearkened, and heard." Their voice was so low that, speaking after the manner of men, the Almighty had to *lean his ear down* to hear what they said. They were afraid to speak at all, except in a whisper, and hardly that. "And a book of remembrance was written before him for them that feared the Lord, and that thought upon his name." Poor child of God, if thou canst not speak, canst thou think? All God's family are not talkers; there are thinkers amongst them; and a book of remembrance is written for *them*. These poor trembling thinkers are amongst the objects of this love. Yes; those solemn thoughts they have and those hungerings and thirstings after him are of his own doing, and never arose from sin, Satan, nor thine own heart. "And they shall be mine in that day when I make up my jewels." Mind that; "*shall be* mine." There is nothing doubtful about it.

3. When may it be said, "*Now* are we the sons of God?" At all times and under all circumstances; in trials, in difficulties, in disappointments, in losses, in crosses, in adversities, in temptations, in persecutions, "*now* are we the sons of God." Yes, and in prosperity too; though sometimes it is not so manifest then as it is in adversity; for there is often a deal of dust about prosperity, which obscures everything but pride. But nothing can alter this love. "Though we believe not, he abideth faithful." "He cannot deny himself." But were he to deny the objects of his love, he would deny himself; for they are one with him, "bone of his bone and flesh of his flesh." "*Now* are we the sons of God." It was *now* when the apostle wrote his epistle, it was *now* in eternity past, and it will be *now* in eternity to come. "For I am persuaded that neither death, nor life, nor angels, nor principalities, nor powers, nor things present, nor things to come, nor height, nor depth, nor any other creature, shall be able to separate us from the love of God, which is in Christ Jesus our Lord."

4. "*It doth not yet appear what we shall be.*" Not even in our greatest manifestations; they are far short of what we shall be. Even the three on the Mount of Transfiguration must have owned that it did not then appear what they shall be. Nor Paul, when caught up to the third heavens, though he heard things he could not utter, and he knew not whether in the body or not; it did not then appear what he shall be. But we *shall* know, for body and soul will be filled with immortal glory. "We *shall be like him,* for we shall see him as he is;" and not one more happy than another, not one near and another a thousand miles off, as some would suppose.* When Christ shall appear, the whole church will be like him; and how can they all be like him if they differ in glory? All shall come to the full stature of a man in Christ; one Bridegroom and one bride; one Lamb and one Lamb's wife. And not only shall all who are there be like their Head, but all the members shall be there; for, as the poet says,

"He'll not live in glory, and leave her behind!"

"Because I live," says he, "ye *shall* live also." O what a blessed *shall!* "Father, I will that they also whom thou gavest me be with me where I am." And will the Father frustrate his Son's *will?* O no!

"Whom once he loves he never leaves,
But loves them to the end."

Now, these are great truths; but what good can they do us if we have them only in our heads? We must have the Spirit to bear wit-

---

* See pages 286, 287.

ness to our spirits that we are interested in them before they can bring any consolation to us; and when this is the case, Satan himself cannot argue us out of them.

May God command his blessing.

[The above " Notes " with a few alterations, were written by a friend from memory a day or two after the sermon was preached. They are necessarily condensed; but the preacher's original language is discernible throughout.— *J. C. Philpot, in " Gospel Standard."*]

GOD'S GLORY CONNECTED WITH HIS PEOPLE'S GOOD.

" A new heart will I give you, and a right spirit will I put within you. I will take away the stony heart out of your flesh and will give you a heart of flesh."—EZEK. XXXVI. 26.

WHAT a precious cluster of solemn declarations of undeserved mercy and free grace are here! Blessed, thrice blessed, art thou, O Israel! Thy God,—O the wonders of his love! Thy God has connected his own glory and thy well-being together; so that, though thy froward heart has led thee to profane his Name among the heathen, and though there be nothing in thee, nor of thee, considered in thyself, but what is awfully depraved, the regard the glorious God has to the honour of his own Name, and by inseparable connection with his honour, binds his blessed Majesty, by all the ties of infinite love to thee and by all that is dear to himself, to do thee good.

Brethren, beloved of the Lord, read the account, pause as you read, and stand astonished at the matchless methods the Lord takes of making known his love and loveliness to you, and with deep humility say, "Dear and blessed Lord! Shall I still insult such matchless love as this? Shall I still mix with the men of the world and make them my chief companions? And shall the things of the world be the principal objects of my pursuits, and thus profane thy great and glorious Name among the heathen? God forbid! Let the honour of thy Name and the greatness of thy love lead me to love, worship, and adore thee; and may it be my great concern from henceforth to seek first the kingdom of God and his righteousness, being assured that all other needful things shall be added unto me. O thou Fountain of blessedness! Make me more watchful, prayerful, and thankful, and enable me to stand fast in the glorious liberty of the Lord Jesus Christ."

Beloved, it is the church's blessedness that Jehovah has inseparably connected his glory with her real good; so that, while his blessed Majesty regards his own honour, he cannot, he will not, forsake or neglect his dear people. This is a blessing big with infinite importance. O that we were able at all times, under the blessed teaching of God the Holy Ghost, to fix a right estimate upon this glorious truth! Then we should find that in the greatest straits and difficulties, and even when our own worthlessness and sinfulness appear in their deepest hue, we have every encouragement to come boldly to the throne of grace. Mark that!—"the throne of grace, that we may obtain mercy and find grace to help us in time of need."

The church of Christ is called the City of our Solemnities; and it is one of the solemn acts of faith to plead with God for his Name's sake. David, the man after God's own heart, put in his plea upon that sacred ground: "For thy Name's sake, O Lord, pardon my iniquity, for it is great." (Ps. xxv. 11.) But he not only pleaded for himself but also for the whole church upon this blessed ground : "Help us, O God of our salvation, for the glory of thy Name, and deliver us and purge away our sins, for thy Name's sake." And under the glorious teachings of the blessed Spirit, Jeremiah goes upon the same sure ground: " O Lord, though our iniquities testify against us, do thou it for thy Name's sake ; for our backslidings are many. We have sinned against thee." (Jer. xvi. 7.) But, beloved, though the Lord has in infinite love determined to bestow the greatest blessings of his heart upon his people, he has made it their great privilege, as his children, to ask these blessings at his hands. Hence he says, in connection with that matchless cluster of blessings promised in Ezek. xxxvi., "Thus saith the Lord God, I will yet for this be inquired of by the house of Israel, to do it for them."

Do I hear some poor sensible sinner say, " Alas for me ! I am such a poor sinful, wretched creature that I fear Jehovah would consider his solemn Majesty insulted were I to crave a single blessing at his hands. I have awfully backslidden from him and have given the professed enemies of God cause to blaspheme his holy Name ; and what can I expect but the doom of those who trample underfoot the Son of God, and who do despite to the Spirit of grace ? Wretch that I am! I am more brutish than any man ! " Come, come, poor desponding soul ! Sink not into despair! Thy base proceedings cannot make the Lord cease to regard his own glory. That is as dear to him as ever; and this should encourage thee to plead with the Lord, not for *your* sakes, but for his great Name's sake. God puts within his people a new heart and a right spirit, and cleanses them from all their idols and filthiness.

A GODLY MAN.

" For this shall every one that is godly pray unto thee at a time when thou mayest be found."—Ps. xxxii. 6.

LET us inquire what constitutes a godly man; and, in order to clear the way for this, we will first notice a few things that men may possess, and yet not be godly. We live in a day when we are to have charity for every body and every thing but God and truth, and when we are to have none for them. Men are to be allowed to reject truth, and set up something or anything to oppose it, and we must have charity for them, but none for the truth itself ; but this is not the charity of the gospel, for that rejoiceth in the truth.

I will, then, be as charitable as I can—as I dare ; but I firmly believe that by far the greatest part of professors are ungodly men. They may profess free will, or boast of free grace ; they may strenuously maintain the truths of the gospel, in doctrine, and practise what the world calls piety, and yet have no vital religion—be ungodly men. A nominal knowledge of doctrines, however great that knowledge may be, will never constitute the possessor a godly person, nor prove that he is so. They are like the foolish virgins, who had lamps, and had trimmed them; but having no oil they soon went out. Arminians say they must have had oil, else they could not have gone out. Indeed! Well; the Word of God says, " they took no oil with them " (Matt. xxv. 3); and I had rather believe that than all the men in the world. But let us look at it. Is it not possible to take a lamp, trim it, put in the wick, &c., and make it look very nice, and yet have no oil; so that when the wick is lighted, it just makes a bit of a flash, and then goes out for want of oil ? So it is with professors in general. They never had any oil; no divine life or unction of the Spirit; a mere external profession; not a particle of the grace of God. Their character is described in 2 Tim. iii. 1–8: A form of godliness, both in doctrine and practice, men may have, and at the same time deny the power thereof. I need not tell you who they are that " creep into houses," &c. Some of you are well aware of some of that description, who are ever learning, and never able to come to a knowledge of the truth." And nothing short of the same almighty power that built the world can accomplish it. God communicates to the soul what it never had before. The great Head of the church began his ministry with this solemn statement : " Ye must be born again." This new birth is a heavenly one. Hence they are said to be born of God. With divine life and light he quickens the dead soul, and causeth it to feel and see what it never felt or saw before. He stamps his image on the heart, shines on it, and in God's light it discovers to us the hideous image we wore before. We sicken at it, groan under it, and are led to cry vehemently for mercy. We are made partakers of the divine nature, of the communicable holiness of God ; and when this change takes place, the man becomes a new creature. All hell can never make him what he was before; nor could all the angels in heaven have accomplished the change.

This change, that constitutes us godly, is made more blessedly manifest to us as God is pleased to shine on it and to bring this passage home to the heart: "Now to him that worketh not, but believeth on him that justifieth the ungodly, his faith is counted for righteousness." Real godliness discovers to us our ungodliness; and we sink, and are a stench in our own nostrils, and feelingly cry out, "Unclean! Unclean!" And when we are favoured with faith to view God's loveliness, in the face of Jesus Christ, and, under the divine unction of the Spirit, feel our own interest in it and enjoy its soul-transforming power (2 Cor. iii. 17, 18, iv. 6), it wraps up our souls, and we are wrapped up in him. Whenever this takes place, the sinner becomes an envied man. The devil knows it, and will soon be up in arms against him. Perhaps some of you will say, I don't see how the devil can know. Well; I'll tell you. We read of the unclean spirit going out of a man, but, finding no rest, he goes back again, finds the house "empty, swept, and garnished." It had no furniture in—no grace, no spiritual life, no vital faith, no love, nothing but an empty profession. But when God takes a sinner in hand, he does not give the devil an opportunity of *going* out, but he *turns* him out, delivereth the soul from the consumer, and sets up his own kingdom in the heart. Satan well knows the difference between going out and God turning him out. When he goes out, he can go in again when he pleases; but when he is turned out by a stronger than he, he is *barred* out; and when thus barred out, he will do all he can to plague and horrify the poor soul, but he cannot reign; he may tear and worry him, but he cannot devour him; for he cannot undo what God has done. The Spring-head of all vital godliness is the Lord Jesus Christ, all centres in, comes from, and leads to him. The godly man is made partaker of his communicable nature, and clothed in his righteousness, and thus stands complete in him.—1838.

GOD A FATHER.

"If I, therefore, be a father, where is mine honour?"—MAL. I. 6.

WE might notice that the Speaker is the God of nature, that he is the Father of all in a natural sense, that he is the Father of the Jews nationally, but that principally he is the Father of all his heaven-born children, and deserving of all honour. And what proof do you give that you honour him?

Let us first consider him as being the Father of all heaven-born souls. What a field is open here for our work. Can we honour him in it? He is their Father in his eternal council and love, in his personal election, in his choice of his children in Christ their Head,—the mystical body, the church; and these are bound together in one eternal union; for which reason Christ says, "I go to my Father and your Father, to my God and your God." They are his children in a manifestive way. They are safe in Christ, though not in themselves; for "the carnal mind is enmity against God." But when the Holy Ghost quickens their souls, he works in them a divine change, whereby they eventually cry, "Abba, Father!" thus manifesting that God is their Father.

The word "Abba" is one which, spelt backwards or forwards, is the same, and denotes our relation to him. It teaches us, look which way we will. If we look backward to eternity, he is our Father; and if we look forward to eternity, he is still our Father. If we examine the mysterious providences we have passed through, he has been to us a Father; and if we look to his promises, he is our Father. Not that we must therefore be indifferent as to our conduct as children. Christ has taught us better things. The love of Christ constraineth us, and we love him because he first loved us. God has provided blessings for us in Christ; we have our eternal glory in him, and he will bring all his children unto his Father. Like as Judah said concerning Benjamin, "I will be surety for him; of my hand shalt thou require him. If I bring him not to thee, and set him before thee, then let me bear the blame for ever."

And for this reason it is said Christ will present his church a glorious church. Not that men might present it a glorious church, but that Christ should so present it. Some ministers think that the passage in Isa. viii. 18 : "Behold, I and the children whom the Lord hath given me are for signs and wonders," belongs to them, and that they will present before the Lord those who have been called under their ministry; but this is a piece of fleshly pride and lumber. It applies to Christ, with his children. The Lord, in his good providence, has provided blessings for the rest of mankind. He has given them this earth to live upon, with many of its riches and honours. But with the children of God it is often the reverse. They are very often tried and tempted; and if they happen to possess a little of this world's goods, it is very often taken from them; but he has reserved for them an inheritance, incorruptible, and that fadeth not away. And thus do they outshine angels in glory; for, as a father, doth the Lord watch over them and keep them. Ah! If he had left you to yourselves, where would you have been? You would all have gone the downward road to destruction. You would have been cast away long ago, if it had not been for your Father's care. But he checked you in your course of sin; he stopped your mad steps and put his fear in your hearts, and then propped up your hope and visited you with a manifestation of mercy, even though you had insulted him over and over again. And thus death is yours. "Ah!" some may say, "I wish it was not." Do you know what you mean? There is a difference between death being yours and you being death's. If you are death's, then will you never have the victory over it; but if death is yours, it is your servant, and will carry you safely home. It will, strictly speaking, be subordinate to you. O, brethren, may your Father give you a lift by the way, that you may triumph over death!

There is honour due to God, as your Father. When you experience a settled solid belief in his Word, you give him honour. If, when your natural father spoke to you, you were to tell him he did not speak the truth, you would dishonour him; you could not have any regard for him as your father. Well, then; is not the Bible God's Word? It is the testimony of him, and of his Son Jesus Christ; and sometimes, when you look at the Bible, and read about troubles or persecution, you say, "I don't like that," and turn over the leaf and read something else. Is that honouring your Father? No. It is like a father sending his son a letter, and the son does not like some portion of it; so he puts it into his pocket. Would that be honouring his father? It is so by many in our day, who have a great zeal for God, but only so far as it pleases their carnal mind. It is not the zeal of the Holy Ghost, or they would reverence his Word.

To honour your Father is to be concerned to give him glory in all things, to obey his precepts, to watch for his coming, to pray unto him, and to be cautious of your steps, to attend to his rebukes, to live righteously, soberly, and godly, and to exhibit Christ to view, as your all and in all.

Be concerned, then, brethren, to honour him, to walk in the foot-steps of Jesus, to obey his commands; for he says, "If ye love me, keep my commandments;" and a son who honours his father will strive to keep his commands. O that he may give you a heart to keep his commandments, to yield obedience to his ordinances, the preaching of the Word, Baptism, and the Lord's Supper. He commissioned his disciples to go into all the world, discipling and baptizing in the name of the Father, of the Son, and of the Holy Ghost; as an emblem of their being immersed in the love of God the Father, God the Son, and God the Holy Ghost; and that in so doing they should honour him. Some will ask the question, "Is it essential to salvation?" and others may say, "Ah, well! I know that such and such things are revealed in the Bible; but they are not essential to salvation; I can go to heaven without them." It is an insult to God, and is telling Christ you know better than he, and that he has instituted ordinances which are useless and unnecessary! You give no proof that the love of God is shed abroad in your heart. You say you believe your salvation is secure in Christ, and, therefore, you need not yield obedience to his Word. Shame upon you! Shame! Blush, if you can, blush for shame, that you can bring forth such an unholy argument. Suppose a father secured an inheritance for his son for life, would that justify the son in not being obedient to his father and treating him with respect? True, that obedience and respect would not be essential to the inheritance, as that is irrevocably secured for him. His father has secured the inheritance for him, therefore he should honour him. And you should honour your heavenly Father by obeying his commands, by being baptized in the name of the Father, of the Son, and of the Holy Ghost. "If I be a Father, where is mine honour?" Would not such a son as the above grieve his father's very heart? Surely, then, we should be concerned to honour our heavenly Father, by obeying his commands and following his example! You may say you have been baptized in the Holy Ghost, and, therefore, no other baptism is needed. But, if you *have been* thus baptized, or have even received (or realized) the Holy Ghost, you are the very characters who ought to be baptized in water. As saith Peter: "Can any man forbid water, that these should not be baptized who have received the Holy Ghost as well as we?"

Some, there may be, who do not see the beauty of the ordinance of believers' baptism. O that the Lord would open their eyes! "If I be a Father, where is mine honour?"

We read in Matt. iii. 13 of Jesus being baptized and the Father and the Holy Spirit signalizing the act. Therefore, as the Father and the Holy Spirit crowned the deed with approbation,

> "Shall my pride disdain the deed
> That's worthy of my God?"

On the day of Pentecost, God baptized the believers in the Holy Ghost; for the Holy Ghost filled all the house where they were sitting; so that all in the house must have been immersed. It is a solemn immersion when God fills his people with the Holy Ghost, or a manifestation of his love in their consciences. But how can any one experience the Baptism of the Holy Spirit if he does not believe in the Personality and Godhead of that blessed Being? There is no hope of salvation for such, dying as they are.

I remember reading of an aged minister who died, and a young man came in his place. Some of God's family began to grumble and mourn, as their souls were not fed. Amongst the rest, one poor old woman seemed to make more stir than others of them. The minister got to hear of it, and went to her, and said, "I understand you find fault with my ministry." She said, "I do; for I don't profit under it." "Well," said the young man, "I don't think you understand the first principles of religion, and, therefore, I am come to try you. How many Persons are there in the Trinity?" "Two," emphatically answered the old lady. "I thought," said the young man, "you did not know; for there are Three." "I know," said the good woman, "the Bible tells us there are Three, and our minister used to preach Three; but you only preach Two." Now, did that minister know anything of the *baptism* of the Spirit? No; he had not even experimentally *received* him; much less been bathed by him in the love and blood of Immanuel.

John baptized in Enon, because there was much water there. Some say he only went ankle deep. How ridiculous! If sprinkling would have done, he might have had enough water in a bowl to serve a thousand. A minister once told me that the word rendered "much" in the passage signified in the Greek "many." I told him if it did mean many, that did not mend it; for why should many waters be required for sprinkling ?*

True, we read of households, and some argue that there must necessarily have been children amongst them. Why, I can count more than twenty families before me this morning without a young person in them. So there was the household of the jailor. The jailor believed in God "with all his house." They were all believers. There was the household of Lydia. Whether Lydia was married or not we are not told, but those in her house were " brethren," and Paul and Silas "*comforted*" them. There was the household of Stephanas, and these had addicted themselves to the ministry; so there could have been no children there. They that gladly received the Word were baptized ; so there could have been no infants there. Cornelius and others were baptized, as they had received the Holy Ghost. Cornelius was one of God's covenant people; he "feared God with all his house," and the time of his deliverance was come.

As for baptism having come in the room and stead of circumcision, the very nature of the ceremony of circumcision utterly excludes so absurd an idea.

Some say the children only of believers ought to be baptized; others that it is sufficient if one of the parents be a believer; and others that *all* children ought to be baptized. But neither the one nor the other has a "Thus saith the Lord" for what they do. I

---

* Lieut. Conder, employed by the Palestine Exploration Committee, discovered Enon where John baptized. He writes as follows :

" John the Baptist is said to have been baptizing in Ænon, near to Salim, because there was much water there.

"Now, due east of Nablus is found the village of Salim, the Salem mentioned more then once in the Old Testament, and even thought by some to be the city of Melchisedec ; and north of this, as Dr. Robinson pointed out, are copious springs in a broad open valley. Curiously enough, this also, like the Jerusalem site, bears the name of Far'ah, though spelt rather differently in the Arabic. The most satisfactory confirmation of the theory is found in the preservation of the name Ænon in the modern village of Aynun, which is marked on Vandervelde's map, at a distance north of the springs (three or four miles), about equal to that of Salim on the south. Thus the requisites of two names and an abundant supply of water are satisfied, although the existence of Aynun appears hitherto to have escaped notice.

"The Nablus site seems naturally to suggest itself for such a purpose—an open valley, a plentiful supply of water, and a station on one of the main lines through the country from Jerusalem to Nazareth. * * *

"This important valley, which forms a great geological feature in the country, rises near Salim, and separates Mount Ebal from the chain of Nebi Balan. It becomes a deep and narrow ravine, with steep hill sides burrowed with caverns, and runs north under the name of Wady Beidan, until it forms a junction with another branch near the small ruin called Burj Far'ah. Here the first springs are found, and a stream, which, even late in the summer, is copious, runs between bushes of oleander eastwards towards the Jordan. The whole course of the valley presents here a succession of springs, and the flat slopes on either side allow the approach of an *unlimited crowd to the banks of the stream*." . . . (*See J. Gadsby's* "*Baptism*," pp. 54, 55.)

once heard of two persons who were discussing this matter, when
a third person who was present observed that they had forgotten the
sign of the cross on the forehead. Upon which he was sharply asked
where it was enjoined in the Word of God. To which he replied
that it was the very next text to the one in which infant sprinkling
was commanded.

Ah! To what shifts do men resort when they have not a "Thus
saith the Lord" for what they do, or when they don't like what the
Lord has commanded, either as to his ordinances or his Gospel precepts!" "If I be a Father, where is mine honour?"

I once went into the collegiate church [now the cathedral] when
a confirmation was going on. I heard a person say, "What a flock
of lambs!" I looked at those scores of tittering girls, all dressed in
white, and I said to myself, "What a flock of giddy creatures!" Yet
all these were said to have been baptized! And what were they
to be confirmed in? In awful delusion! The bishop, addressing
God, said, "Almighty and everlasting God, who hast vouchsafed
to regenerate these, thy servants, by water and the Holy Ghost, and
hast given unto them forgiveness of all their sins," &c. The bishop
then laid his hands on them respectively, and said, "Defend, O
Lord, this thy child," &c. O, brethren, the hands of only one
Bishop will do us any good, even those of the Shepherd and Bishop
of our souls.—*Manchester.*

THE LORD'S SUPPER.

THE following meagre scraps are all I have been able to meet with as
to my father's observance of the Lord's Supper. If there were any one
part of the services of God's house in which he was more solemn and
impressive than another, it was at this ordinance, and every time, month
after month and year after year, he was always favoured with something
new to lay before the people.

On leaving the vestry and reaching the table, he first gave out a suitable hymn, which was sung. He then, if any persons were to be received
into the church, they having previously taken their seats in the table-
pew, he requested them to stand up ; and he then frequently addressed
them collectively after the following manner:

"My dear Friends (or Brethren), you have to-day professedly put
on the Lord Jesus Christ. God help you to be circumspect in your
walk and conversation! Angels will watch you; the church of God
will watch you; the world will watch you; your friends, who are now
in the galleries, some of whom, perhaps, do not approve of the step
you have taken, will watch you; enemies to the truth will watch you;
and devils will watch you. God help you to watch yourselves, and to
look up to him to keep you, to support you, and to succour you. In
the name of this church, I give you the right hand of fellowship.
May the Lord make you a blessing to the church and the church a
blessing to you, for his Name's sake."

He then quoted from 1 Cor. xi. 23, 24: "'In the same night in which the Lord was betrayed he took bread; and when he had given thanks he brake it, and said, Take, eat; this is my body which is broken for you; this do in remembrance of me.' Let us call upon the Name of the Lord.'' He then engaged in prayer.

A friend, an old member of the church, has favoured me with the following recollections of part of an introductory prayer on one occasion, which was so impressed upon her mind that she has it still in her memory and in her heart:

"Precious Jesus! Look down, in mercy, upon a few poor sinners. We are out of hell, Lord; and some of us now and then have the assurance that we never shall be there; while some who are there deserve it less than we, as we are in and of ourselves; for we have sinned against light; we have slighted thy mercies; we have gone after idols; our eyes have gazed on forbidden objects; we have cherished and nourished in our hearts the vile affections of our carnal natures. O presence thyself with us this afternoon, and help us to praise and magnify thy glorious name, that thou hast not dealt with us after our sins; that we are here to celebrate thy dying love! Put us in mind of it. Let us discern thy body as broken for us, and thy blood as shed for us, that we may not partake of these symbols unworthily; but O do enable us to eat thy flesh and drink thy blood by precious faith; for thy great Name's sake. Amen.''

He then began to break the bread, and addressed the members while he was doing so. This occupied some time; not only because the number of members was large, but also because he often paused while he enlarged upon some particular point. He then gave the plates to the deacons, repeating the words, "This do in remembrance of Him whose body was broken for you.'' He then sat down, and perfect silence prevailed while the deacons were handing round the bread.

This surely is the right course; for how can any secretly meditate while another is addressing them?

Next he quoted from 1 Cor. xi. 25, 26: "After the same manner also, when he had given thanks (Mark xiv. 22), he took the cup, when he had supped, saying, This cup is the new testament in my blood; this do ye, as oft as ye drink it, in remembrance of me. For as often as ye eat this bread and drink this cup ye do show the Lord's death till he come. Let us try to give thanks.'' He then, after prayer, gave the cups to the deacons, saying, "Drink ye all of it. This do ye, as oft as ye do it, in remembrance of Him whose blood was shed for you.''

There was again perfect silence, while the cup was being taken round.

Before concluding, he generally suitably addressed the persons in the galleries, as none but members sat below. And then said,

"After supper they sang a hymn." Another hymn was sung, which was followed by a short prayer, or the Benediction.

The ordinance was always administered in the afternoon, as an independent service. The chalice was never used; it is a Romanist innovation. The cups had (and have) two handles, for passing from member to member.

The following are a few scraps from his addresses:

Through the kind providence of God, we are assembled together this afternoon, to commemorate his love in sending his Son to redeem such vile wretches as we are, and in Christ's suffering and dying on our behalf. We are invited, my brethren, to drink freely, for his blood was freely shed for us. O for faith freely to enjoy this! Will this lead us to sin—to licentiousness? O no; but it will humble us in the dust before God, and fill us with wonder and gratitude that ever he should stoop to pick up such hell-deserving sinners.

God mostly manifests his love to us when we least expect it, and at those times, and under those circumstances, that prove to demonstration that it is all free, matchless, and unmerited. If we take a solemn survey of the way God has brought us, we shall find that he has often appeared unto us, and shed upon us the light of his countenance, when we have been filled with rebellion against him, murmuring and fighting against his will. When was it that he showed himself most conspicuous on behalf of the Israelites? Why, when they were fit to stone Moses for bringing them out of Egypt, and wishing they were at their flesh-pots again. Then God came down, as it were, and delivered them, working miracles on their behalf. But he took care to let them know that it was not for their sakes, but for his own name's sake, and that his glory he would not give to another. O how great was his mercy towards such rebellious undeserving worms!

I copy the following from a MS. by Mr. Hudson, already named:

I recollect the time when I first went to see what I then called a dipping. I went with as much levity of mind and purpose as any one. The chapel was a great distance from our house. I went in, and soon found out the baptistery. I placed myself as near to it as possible, that I might have a full view of the scene; for my only object was to satisfy my fleshly mind. The minister preached upon the subject; but I remember not a word he said, for I paid no attention, but longed for him to have done that I might see how he managed the dipping. At length he concluded the sermon and approached the baptistery; and then, O what a solemn change took place in my mind! The minister spoke of the death, burial, and resurrection of our Lord and Saviour Jesus Christ, of which that ceremony was emblematical. And it pleased the Lord then and there to melt my hard and stubborn heart; and from that moment I have been a Baptist, and, if God keeps me in my right mind, I believe I ever shall be. For in that ordinance I saw figuratively the death, burial, and resurrection of Christ; his death in delivering the soul from the power of the law, his burial in baptizing it in his blood, and his resurrection in raising it to newness of life.

Then O! What a banquet of love is here! To you who have tasted that the Lord is gracious, what a feast of fat things you have here!

ON SANCTIFICATION.

" For by One offering he hath perfected for ever them that are sanctified." —HEB. x. 14.

ON page 241 there is the first of a Sermon on the above subject, from 1 Cor. i. 2. Had the following come under my notice at the time, I would have inserted it next the above. I feel, however, I should do wrong if I omitted it. It is in the " Gospel Standard " for 1835–1836.

The doctrine of Sanctification is clearly revealed in the Word of God; and when the mind of the saint is led into it by the blessed Spirit, the doctrine of a Triune Jehovah shines forth; for we are sanctified by the Three that bear record in heaven,—the Father, the Word, and the Holy Ghost; as will evidently appear if we take into consideration the different acceptations the term bears in the Bible.

1. By the term Sanctification, or sanctify, we are sometimes to understand the setting apart of a thing or person to a certain use or office. As for instance; God sanctified, or set apart, the seventh day as a Sabbath of rest. Before the Lord formed Jeremiah in the womb of his mother, he sanctified, or ordained, him, a prophet unto the nations. (Jer. i. 5.) In this sense, Christ, the Father's first Elect, was sanctified, or set apart (John x. 36), as the Mediator of the better covenant, before all worlds. In like manner, the election of grace were sanctified, or set apart, by God the Father, as his chosen people, in Christ, from everlasting. Hence Jude, the servant of Christ, dedicates his epistle to them that are "sanctified by God the Father, and preserved in Christ Jesus, and called" by God's grace. And Paul, writing to the church at Corinth, uses a similar mode of expression: "Unto the church of God which is at Corinth, to them that are sanctified in Christ Jesus, called to be saints;" and in his solemn address to the elders of the church at Ephesus, we have the same principle maintained : "And now, brethren, I commend you to God, and to the word of his grace, which is able to build you up, and give you an inheritance among all them which are sanctified." Also in Heb. x., where he says, that Christ "hath, by one offering, for ever perfected them that are sanctified."

From the above passages, how evident it is that God's predestinated people were eternally sanctified by God the Father, in Christ Jesus, and that election and sanctification are of the same eternal date; and, as it is said in the Articles of the Church of England: "The godly consideration of it is full of sweet, pleasant, and unspeakable comfort to godly persons, and such as feel in themselves the working of the Spirit of Christ, mortifying the works of the flesh and their earthly members, and training up their mind to high and heavenly things; as well because it doth greatly establish and confirm their faith of eternal salvation to be enjoyed through Christ, as because it doth fervently kindle their love towards God."

2. By Sanctification we are sometimes to understand a cleansing from that which in itself is unclean or impure, as we all are, both by nature and practice. This sanctification, or cleansing, is by the precious blood of Christ, which cleanseth from all sin. Of this, Paul speaks: "Wherefore, Jesus also, that he might sanctify the people with his own blood, suffered without the gate" (Heb. xiii. 13); "Husbands, love your wives, even as Christ also loved the church, and gave himself for it, that he might sanctify and cleanse it with the washing of water by the word, that he might present it to himself a glorious church, not having spot, or wrinkle, or any such thing; but that it should be holy and without blemish." Again, in Heb. ix. 13, 14, Paul, contrasting the blood of the Levitical priesthood with the blood of Christ, says, "If the blood of bulls and of goats, and the ashes of an heifer, sprinkling the unclean, sanctifyeth to the purifying of the flesh, how much more shall the blood of Christ, who, through the eternal Spirit, offered himself without spot to God, purge your conscience from dead works to serve the living God?" And, in 1 Cor. vi. 11, having reckoned up the black catalogue of crimes to which the unrighteous are given up, adds: "And such were some of you; but ye are washed, but ye are sanctified, [by Christ,] who of God is made unto us sanctification and redemption; for (Heb. ii. 11), he that sanctifieth, and they who are sanctified, are all of one."

"This sanctification we greatly need, for we were born in sin and conceived in iniquity; we are men of unclean lips and dwell amongst a people of unclean lips; and if we know the plague of our own hearts, we feel, at times, such swarms of vain and sinful thoughts working within, even when on our knees in our closets, that we have to cry out from our very souls, "O Lord, I am vile!" "Unclean, unclean!" "Wretched man that I am, who shall deliver me from this body of sin and death?" And were it not for the fountain of Jesus's sanctifying blood, which is open for sin and uncleanness, such black, polluted, guilty sinners as we are must sink in despair. But we rejoice to hear our gracious Lord say unto us, "Come now, and let us reason together; though your sins be as scarlet, they shall be as white as snow, and though they be red like crimson, they shall be as wool." Such is the power and efficacy of the blood of atonement, that when it is applied to the conscience, by the power of the Spirit, it removes the burden of guilt, softens the hard heart, and brings that joy, peace, and rest that the world can neither give nor take away; for it speaks better things than the blood of Abel.

Abel's blood called for vengeance to burst on Cain's guilty head; but the blood of Christ is crying for peace and pardon to rest on all the ransomed of the Lord. The church triumphant in glory, having proved the power and efficacy of the sanctifying, cleansing, purifying blood of the Lamb, make it the glory of their song: "Unto him that loved us, and washed us from our sins in his own blood, and hath made us kings and priests unto God and his Father, to him be glory and dominion for ever and ever. Amen."

> " Happy songsters,
> When shall I your chorus join?"

3. The work of Sanctification is also ascribed to the Holy Ghost: "But we are bound to give thanks always to God for you, brethren, beloved of the Lord, because God hath from the beginning chosen you to salvation, through sanctification of the Spirit, and belief of the truth" (2 Thess. ii. 13); "Elect, according to the foreknowledge of God the Father, through sanctification of the Spirit, unto obedience, and sprinkling of the blood of Jesus Christ."

In treating upon the sanctification of the Spirit, as it is laid down in the Word of God, it must be observed,

First, As God the Father hath eternally sanctified his people in Christ, so for them Christ hath obtained eternal redemption; yet who these people are is only made known by the sanctification of the Spirit; for before the Holy Ghost takes possession of their hearts in regeneration, they are dead in trespasses and sins and enemies to God by wicked works, both body and soul being given up to work wickedness with greediness. But when he takes them in hand, he sanctifies them, or sets them apart, for the service of God; according to that exhortation: "As ye have yielded your members servants to uncleanness and to iniquity unto iniquity, even so now yield your members servants to righteousness unto holiness." (Rom. vi. 19.) They are a people the Lord hath formed for himself, and, under the sanctifying influence of his Spirit, they shall show forth his praise, making it manifest that they are a peculiar people, zealous of good works, which God hath before ordained that they shall walk in them. Lighted up by the Holy Ghost, they are as a candle put in a proper place to give light to all around; or as a city set upon a hill which cannot be hid. By their fruits, they are known to be the Lord's sanctified ones: "For this is the will of God, even our sanctification, that we should abstain from fornication, &c.; for God hath not called us unto uncleanness, but unto holiness." "If a man (by the Spirit's influence) purge himself from these, he shall be a vessel unto honour, sanctified and meet for the Master's use, and prepared unto every good work." (2 Tim. ii. 21.) This can only be the case with us as the Lord works in us to will and do of his own good pleasure; for from him is our fruit found. In 1 Thess. v. 23, Paul says, "And the very God of peace sanctity you wholly; and I pray God, your whole spirit, and soul, and body, be preserved blameless unto the coming of our Lord Jesus Christ. Faithful is he that calleth you, who also will do it." Thus the Lord makes it manifest that his people are not of the world, but that he hath chosen them out of the world, as a seed to serve him, and a generation to call him blessed.

Secondly, In considering the sanctification of the Spirit, as an internal work of grace in the heart of the believer, we shall find that it is a growing work: "Grow in grace, and in the knowledge of our Lord Jesus Christ." (2 Pet. iii. 18.)

Here a question arises, Does the old man of sin, which is corrupt, according to the deceitful lusts, grow better and better? The answer to this question is, No; for the old man, which is the flesh, is always the same, lusting against the Spirit, which causes the spiritual warfare in the Christian's breast; for "what shall we see in the Shulamite? As it were, the company of two armies." This contest between the old man of sin and the new man of grace will never cease while we are in the body. The doctrine of the old man of sin growing better and better, the Christian, by daily experience, proves to be the doctrine of fools, and he will have to say with Paul, even down to the Jordan of death, "I know that in me, that is, in my flesh, there dwelleth no good thing; for to will is present with me, but how to perform that which is good, I find not."

"If any man be in Christ Jesus, he is a new creature; old things are passed away, behold, all things are become new." This new creature, or new man, which, after God, is created in righteousness and true holiness, grows, or is renewed, in knowledge after him that created it. The outward man, the body, perishes; but the inward man is renewed day by day. Hence we are said to be strengthened with might, by the Spirit, in the inner man.

It is light that discovers darkness; so, as we are sanctified by the Holy Ghost, we have a growing knowledge and feeling sense of the depravity of our nature, and of our lost, helpless state and condition, as guilty sinners. This has a tendency to humble us before God, and to make us say with Job, "I abhor myself, and repent in dust and ashes." Thus we grow out of love with ourselves and our own worth and worthiness, placing no confidence in the flesh, and renouncing every thing but Christ and him crucified. Proud flesh must fall, that Christ may rise. The blessed Spirit, in his work, has two things in view, namely, the laying low of the sinner, and the setting up of Jesus on high; and to this end he leads us out of ourselves into Christ, daily to feel that we are lost in ourselves, to look to Christ, by faith, for complete salvation. By nature we are black and polluted with sin, and the Spirit leads us to the fountain of Christ to be cleansed; naked, and he enables us, by faith, to put on the garment of salvation; guilty and condemned, he makes us sue for pardon at Jesus's feet, like the poor publican, and seals pardon and peace in the conscience; weak and helpless, he leads us to trust in the Lord Jehovah, in whom there is everlasting strength; foolish, he leads us to Christ, the wonderful Counsellor, for wisdom. He creates within us a hungering and thirsting for the bread of heaven and the wine of the kingdom and enables us to feed, by faith, upon Christ, the feast of fat things.

In a word. To be sanctified by the Holy Spirit is to be made to feel that we are nothing in ourselves, and less than nothing, and vanity, that Christ may be our all and in all. The highest height of sanctification that we can attain unto in this life is to have our mind and will resigned unto the mind and will of God,—to say from our very hearts, "Thy will be done." As we are thus led by the Spirit out of ourselves into Christ, we love him for the great things he has done for us, whereof we are glad. The Holy Ghost sheds abroad a Saviour's love in our hearts, and it constrains us to love Christ, who first loved us, and gave himself for us, an offering and a sweet smelling savour. The love of Christ inclines our hearts after him, and our feet run in the way of his commandments. The precepts and exhortations of the gospel are our delight, and it is as our meat and drink to do the will of God. It is our desire that the mind that was in Christ Jesus may be in us, and that we may live under the influence of the Spirit, making it manifest that we are predestinated to be conformed to the image of Christ, taking his yoke upon us, that we may learn of him who is meek and lowly in heart, and find rest unto our souls. Our happiest moments are when we can sit at the feet of Jesus, and hear his precious words, which are sweeter than honey to our taste.

How different this view of the doctrine of sanctification to that of the old man of sin, or the flesh, growing better and better every day of our lives, until sin is completely eradicated out of our nature. If the man gets better and better in himself, he must become more and more independent of Christ, the great Physician; for as a diseased person applies to a doctor, and receives from him medicines, which prove effectual in removing the disease, and then tells him he can do without him, being cured; so in the case before us. If the sinner gets better and better, till the plague of sin is gone, he has no more need of the balm of Gilead, nor of the great Physician. Thus it makes the sinner independent of Christ and his efficacious blood; and, therefore, cannot be of God.

There is one thing connected with this subject, at which I have often wondered. Some of the ministers who vindicate the above doctrine, when asked how much better they are in themselves than at the first, cannot tell us anything about it. But ask others, who are made alive to God and who daily feel the plague of their own hearts, and they speak out freely, and say, that the longer they live, the greater sinners they feel themselves to be; and they experience a

growing need of the finished salvation of Christ, his efficacious blood
and justifying righteousness, and of the influences of his Holy Spirit
upon their hearts, to enable them to use the weapons of warfare,
which are not carnal but mighty, through God, to the pulling down
of strong holds, casting down imaginations and every high thing that
exalteth itself against the knowledge of God, and bringing into captivity every thought to the obedience of Christ. (2 Cor. x. 4, 5.) It
is only as the grace of God reigns in our hearts, through righteousness, that we are enabled to tread upon the necks of our internal
enemies, and to rejoice in Christ Jesus; for when the Lord leaves off
communing with us by his Spirit and grace, we, like Abraham, return to our own place—hardness of heart, coldness, deadness, barrenness of mind, vain, worldly thoughts, evil murmurings against
the Lord and against one another, and, like Paul, we cannot forbear
crying out, "O wretched man that I am! Who shall deliver me from
the body of this death?"

Some time since I went to see an old Christian woman who was one
of the unmarried women that Paul speaks of, who " care for the things
of the Lord." She had been bending her steps Zionward for more
than half a century. I found her in great distress of mind. She
said she felt she was on the very brink of death and eternity, and
that she had sat under a Baptist minister more than thirty years, who
had taught her to believe that before she was ready to die she must
be fully sanctified; by which she understood she was to be holy in
herself, and without sin. She had been expecting to attain to this
all the way she had travelled, and especially when she came to be
on a deathbed. But instead of this, she said she saw herself to be
a greater sinner than ever she was, and that she began with the
prayer of the publican, "God be merciful to me, a sinner!" And it
had been her prayer all the way through; and she never could get
above it, for it was her prayer then, on a dying bed. If she looked
at her past life, she had to say with Jacob, "Few and evil have been
the days of my pilgrimage;" and if she looked into her heart, it was
a cage of unclean birds, in which were swarms of evil thoughts; so
that there was nothing in her, or done by her, that she could look
to, or trust in, for eternity. She was much distressed that she had
not experienced progressive sanctification, and that she was not now
"fully sanctified;" inasmuch as that she had not attained to it, she
feared that, after all her profession, she should be a castaway. After
I had heard all her tale of woe, I laboured to direct her attention to
the glorious Person of Immanuel, his ability to save the very chief
of sinners, and to the sanctifying blood of the Lamb, that taketh
away all iniquity, and to the robe of righteousness, wrought out by
Christ, which is the wedding garment, in which we must appear with
acceptance at the marriage supper of the Lamb; and I endeavoured
to encourage her, by saying, if she were enabled to put all her trust

in the Person, blood, and righteousness of Christ, she would never be lost. As I was speaking of the safety of those who shelter by faith in the wounded side of Christ, she rose up in bed, and said, "O, my dear friend! I like him; he is precious to my soul! I feel a view of him by faith does my soul good. He will never suffer my soul to be lost or put to shame." In this happy strain she continued speaking for some time; and, after reading to her a portion of God's Word, and going to prayer with her, I left her; and the next day I heard she was dead.

Paul tells us the just shall live by faith. While this old pilgrim was looking to herself, it brought darkness and death into her soul; but when she was enabled to look by faith to Christ, she experienced life, light, joy, and peace; and I doubt not there are many of the Lord's people in a state of bondage, who sit under a ministry in which they are directed to look for perfection in themselves, instead of having set before them the glorious finished work of Immanuel.

But I fear I am swelling these remarks to too great a length; and, therefore, must conclude.

The Lord sanctify us to his service, that we may live to the honour and glory of his great name; that if we be buffeted, it may be for the truth's sake and not for any untoward step; for "Blessed are ye when men shall revile you, and persecute you, and shall say all manner of evil against you falsely, for my sake. Rejoice and be exceeding glad; for great is your reward in heaven, for so persecuted they the prophets which were before you."—*November*, 1835.

HAPPY ISRAEL.

"Happy art thou, O Israel, who is like unto thee, O people saved by the Lord."—Deut. xxxiii. 29.

You all know the circumstances which gave rise to the name Israel, when Jacob wrestled, really and truly, with a man, and prevailed; so much so, that when break of day came, the man said, "Let me go;" and Jacob said, "I will not let thee go, except thou bless me." It would have been much more likely for Jacob to have let him go in the gloomy and dark night, than at break of day. What! A child of God let Christ go when he has begun to shine into his heart? O no! All the powers of hell cannot make him let him go then. His whole soul is with him, and he will not let him go—he will obtain the blessing.—There is a solemn blaze of vitality in real religion, which all the rounds of forms and duties can never supply. You can no more get at the virtue of it by this means than you can get virtue out of an orange by turning it round in your hand. God must break into it, and put it into our mouths; aye, and squeeze it too, else we never can get at it.

Though all Jacob's posterity were called Israel, that was only the shell, for "they are not all Israel which are of Israel;" the kernel is God's spiritual family; and it is in this light that I shall consider the subject.

Israel signifies a prince with God, and couches in it power and dignity. Hence it is said, "Thy name shall be called no more Jacob, but Israel, for as a prince hast thou power with God, and hast prevailed." And again: "We are made kings and priests unto God." This power contains a living, never-dying faith, not a speculative faith, not a nominal faith, not a faith that is the duty of all men to have, for in such a faith there is no vitality. Real faith, princely faith, powerful faith, makes a solemn stand, and all the powers of hell cannot move it from its object. One of the first objects that God fixes this mighty faith upon is God in his law and the man as a sinner against that law; and if all the orators in the world were to try to make that man believe he is not so bad as he feels himself to be, and that if he would but simply believe and do his duty all would be well, they would make him believe anything as soon as that. I appeal to the consciences of those of you who know something of the power of it, whether anything could totally divert you from such an object, till God broke into your souls. You might, and perhaps did, read pretty books, preparations, &c., but each turn made you feel worse, till you found that you could not do even what you called your duties but in such a way that you really must be damned for them, they were done so badly. Well, bless you, this is faith, mighty faith; and a sinner never really felt this till God gave him faith; and this is the reason why it *is* there, and why it *keeps* there, notwithstanding all the forces and artillery of hell that are brought to move it. You tried to do your duties better; but you found nothing but pricking thorns in your path, till you imagined if there were one sinner more vile and abominable in the sight of God than another, it was you. You have envied the brute creation, nay, the very croaking of a toad; and have said, though it was not so pleasant to the eye, yet it had no immortal soul, to suffer eternally in the horrors of the damned. Well; even this is faith; and I'll tell you why. Faith never persuades the soul to acts of presumption, therefore never leads him to say he is one of God's elect, till God seals it upon his heart. Perhaps some poor soul says, "Well, I believe God has an elect family; thousands have been benefited by it, but I fear it is not for me. If I am damned I deserve it; therefore, I must leave myself with him, cast myself at his feet, and, damned or saved, there I must lie; for I have proved I cannot help my own soul." May God the Spirit help thee to keep there, and, as sure as God is God, in his own blessed time, he will give thee a dead lift, and thou shalt find that, notwithstanding all thy fears, thou art indeed one of this Israel.

By and by, this faith is led to behold Christ, as the poor soul's

Redeemer. When we feel him as our fulness, life, righteousness, holiness, &c., it brings peace, pardon, and solemn composure into our souls. We can then say, "Bless the Lord, O my soul, and all that is within me, bless his holy name. I was brought low, and he helped me, and brought me up out of a horrible pit, and the miry clay."

You may perhaps say that, when faith has got here, it has reached its summit; but when God the Spirit reads a little before our text in your heart, you will find it different. For though it is now riding on high horses, and leaping over the mountains, it has some strange work to do. We will read a few verses: "Thy shoes shall be iron and brass;" then you will have some rough paths, some thorns and briars, and gravel stones; but you shall tread them all down with your shoes of iron and brass; for, "as thy days thy strength shall be." Mind that; whatever thou mayest have to pass over, thy strength shall surmount it. "There is none like unto the God of Jeshurun." Then thou hast nothing to fear. Thy misgivings, thy workings within and without, only open a way for thee to cast thyself upon this blessed God of Jeshurun; who rideth upon the heaven in thy help, and in his excellence on the sky." That's too high for us always to see him, you know; but, bless his precious name, he *is* there whether we can see him or not, and he is there for our help, too. "The eternal God is thy refuge." Then, after all, you will stand in need of a refuge. The work of the devil is to make you seek shelter in your duties; so that after perhaps approaching God in prayer, you will say, "I have done that well; how humble I have been; how fervent I have been!" It is the devil. You must have God, and the God of Jeshurun alone, in his Trinity of Persons, as your Refuge.

But, perhaps you will say, "I sometimes sink very low, under a sense of my loathsomeness, my vileness, and perplexing disappointments. Bless you, "underneath are the everlasting arms;" so that, sink as low as you may, still it stands the same,—"underneath are the everlasting arms;" and though thy enemies may perplex thee, and thou canst not get rid of them, God "shall thrust them out before thee, and shall destroy them." "Israel shall then dwell in safety alone;" yes, you shall dwell alone then, when you are blessed with faith to lean upon God as your refuge, and have all your enemies destroyed; for nobody can keep you company, except those who are there, and you will not find many. The world will pity you as a poor fanatic; but you shall banquet with God alone. Your "fountain shall be upon a land of corn and wine; also his heavens shall drop down dew." There is a solemn bedewing of the soul which we can never describe; but it may well be added, "Happy art thou, O Israel; who is like unto thee, O people, saved by the Lord?"—*Manchester, Jan.* 10*th*, 1836.

THE STARVING BEGGAR RELIEVED.

"Call upon me in the day of trouble; I will deliver thee."—Ps. L. 15.

Here is a poor ragged starving wretch, seeking for some one to relieve him; but he can find no helper. He sees nothing but starvation and death before him. He must lie down and die. Why, his very seeking for help is praying for it and a proof that he is alive. But a passer-by, seeing him, goes up to him and tells him if he can only go to such a house he will be sure to be relieved; for the owner and occupier of the house never turns any one away, if he is in real distress. "But," the poor man says, "no one so ragged and dirty as I am ever went." " O yes, yes," says the visitor. "Many quite as bad as you are, or worse, have been taken in, and fed and clothed. So come. You are very weak and don't know the way; I'll support you and lead you." So off they go, the poor man dragging heavily along. At last they reach the house. The poor man goes to the door; but he says, "I dare not knock. What! Such a beggar as I knock at the door of such a grand house as that?" The very thought makes him feel faint, and he has to lay hold of the knocker to keep him from falling. He trembles all over. "I dare not knock," he says; but his hand shakes so violently that he is knocking all the time, though he does not know he is knocking—knock, knock, knock! And his wants are speedily relieved.

"The poorer the wretch, the welcomer here."

[It is impossible to give the slightest idea of the impressive manner in which the above was spoken, especially as the preacher, at the same time that he was speaking of the poor trembling man knocking, he himself loudly, yet tremblingly, knocked with his knuckles on the side of the pulpit.]